MW01515401

Present complicated, expert evidence in a way judges will accept and juries will understand.

The Reference Manual on Scientific Evidence

by the Federal Judicial Center

The Reference Manual on Scientific Evidence is the one-of-a-kind book <u>judges rely on</u> when deciding issues involving scientific and technical evidence. It can help you, as an attorney:

▶ Select more persuasive evidence and experts

▶ Avoid admissibility problems

▶ Anticipate questions from the bench

▶ Save time to prepare the rest of your case

Use the manual for quick, authoritative information for a broad range of federal and state litigation, including:

▶ Economic loss in personal injury, contract, wrongful termination and business injury cases

▶ Products liability

▶ Toxic torts (including lead paint cases)

▶ Job discrimination, where statistics are at issue

▶ DNA and other criminal evidence, such as in trademark and antitrust cases

Seven reference "guides" cover **epidemiology, toxicology, forensic analysis of DNA, survey research, statistical inference, multiple regression analysis** and **economic loss estimates**. Each provides a primer on methods and reasoning for scientific evidence, issues commonly disputed, case citations and recommended references.

The Federal Judicial Center developed this new manual to help judges manage expert testimony under the amended Rules of Civil Procedure, Rules of Evidence, and the recent Supreme Court *Daubert* decision. It can help you, too! *Published 1995, one softcover volume, 637 pages.*

Order now:
1-800-328-9352

For information about other West Publishing products and services, visit us on the Internet at the URL:
http://www.westpub.com

West Publishing

*Price subject to change without notice.

© 1995 West Publishing   *West. An American company serving the legal world.*   5-9687-7/6-95   568429

Handy, concise, economical!

Stay up-to-date on federal civil and criminal law with these convenient references!

Why chance missing a new development?

Stay current with these thorough compilations of the federal statutes and rules that govern civil and criminal law:

Federal Civil Judicial Procedure and Rules, 1995 Edition

Convenient access to rules and statutes that govern procedure before federal courts at every level. You'll find the complete text of:

- ▶ Rules of Civil Procedure
- ▶ Rules of Evidence
- ▶ Rules of Appellate Procedure
- ▶ Rules of the Supreme Court
- ▶ Rules of Judicial Panel on Multi-district Litigation
- ▶ Habeas Corpus Rules
- ▶ Motion Attacking Sentence Rules
- ▶ U.S. Code Title 28, Judiciary and Judicial Procedure

Federal Criminal Code and Rules, 1995 Edition

The most current statutes and procedural rules relating to criminal practice before the federal courts incorporate the Violent Crime Control and Law Enforcement Act of 1994 and the Freedom of Access to Clinic Entrances Act of 1994. Included is the complete text of the following:

- ▶ Rules of Criminal Procedure
- ▶ Habeas Corpus Rules
- ▶ Motion Attacking Sentence Rules
- ▶ Rules of Evidence
- ▶ Rules of Appellate Procedure
- ▶ Rules of the Supreme Court
- ▶ U.S. Code Title 18, Crimes and Criminal Procedure
- ▶ Other selected federal criminal statutes

Both of these important, comprehensive resources are softbound, single-volume publications that are published annually, with mid-year supplements of Supreme Court amendments to court rules. Quantity discounts are available.

Extremely CONVENIENT PAPERBACK FORMAT **Affordable!**

Call now to order your copies or to obtain more information.

1-800-328-9352

West Publishing

© 1995 West Publishing   West. An American company serving the legal world.   5-9687-7/6-95   568429

Manual for Complex Litigation, Third

Federal Judicial Center
1995

This Federal Judicial Center publication was undertaken in furtherance of the Center's statutory mission to develop and conduct education programs for judicial branch employees. The views expressed are those of the authors and not necessarily those of the Federal Judicial Center.

Contents

Contents

Contents

Preface

It has been nearly thirty-five years since the publication of this manual's progenitor, the *Handbook of Recommended Procedures for the Trial of Protracted Cases,*[*] the first effort to distill judicial experience in case management. The *Handbook* was followed by the original *Manual for Complex Litigation,* published in 1969. It largely reflected the experience of judges who managed the electrical equipment antitrust litigation in the 1960s and focused on judicial control and scheduling of discovery and pretrial preparation. In 1985, the *Manual for Complex Litigation, Second* appeared, broadening the scope of litigation management to include issue definition and narrowing.

Publication of the *Manual Second* was a recognition of the rapid and dramatic changes taking place in the nature of federal litigation and the courts' need to respond with appropriate management techniques and practices. Those changes have continued apace, marked by the emergence of new kinds of claims and processes for litigating them, expansion of the federal courts' jurisdiction, and increases in their workload. New legislation, case law, and rules have altered the framework in which litigation is conducted. The editors of the *Manual Second* foresaw these trends when they said that it would "not represent the final word on proper management of complex litigation" and urged that it be "periodically revised on the basis of new developments and experiences."[†] The magnitude of new developments and the variety of experiences in complex litigation over the last ten years warrants publication of this *Manual for Complex Litigation, Third.*

The *Handbook* and the original *Manual* broke new ground in advocating judicial case management. By 1985, however, the role of the judge as a case manager had become widely accepted—in the Federal Rules of Civil Procedure, in local rules and standing orders, in the literature, and in the prevailing practices in the federal courts. And by 1994, that role had evolved from an option to an acknowledged judicial responsibility.[‡] Given the federal courts' growing dockets and the increasing complexity, cost, and time demands of litigation, judicial control through effective management techniques and practices is now considered imperative.

These changes in the environment of complex litigation also lead to a change in the role of the *Manual:* The procedures it describes and suggests have now

---

[*] 25 F.R.D. 351 (1960).

[†] Manual for Complex Litigation, Second, at 2 (1985).

[‡] See, e.g., Fed. R. Civ. P. 26(b)(1): "The frequency or extent of use of the discovery methods . . . *shall be* limited by the court . . ." (emphasis added). *See also* Rule 16(c), listing subjects for consideration and action by the court at a pretrial conference, and generally the Civil Justice Reform Act of 1990, 28 U.S.C. §§ 471–482.

moved from the cutting edge into the mainstream of litigation. What this manual offers is less novelty than update and refinement—collection and analysis of experience in the management of litigation, translation of generalized concepts into specific techniques and practices, and application of case management to newly emerging problems in complex litigation. At the same time, the *Manual Third* also speaks to the continuing need for innovation and creativity.

The *Manual Third* builds on the earlier editions and, indeed, retains the organization and most of the substance of the *Manual Second*. The work of the Board of Editors of the *Manual Second*, headed by Chief Judge Sam C. Pointer, Jr., remains a foundation for this manual. The innovative and constructive work of the many judges and practitioners who contributed to the earlier works continues to enrich the *Manual*. It also benefits from the contributions of numerous judges, academics, and practicing attorneys who provided new material, assisted in drafting revisions, and critically reviewed and commented on drafts.

This project was carried out by staff of the Federal Judicial Center pursuant to the Center's statutory mission "to further the development and adoption of improved judicial administration in the courts of the United States." Significant contributions were made by Jon Heller, Esq., of the New York Bar, law clerk to the director during this project, and by Thomas E. Willging, senior research associate, and Laural L. Hooper, research associate. The views expressed are not necessarily those of the Center or its Board. As always, the Center welcomes comments and suggestions from readers.

William W Schwarzer, Director
Federal Judicial Center
December 1994

Note: As this edition goes to press, bills are pending in Congress that could impact, in ways not now predictable, various aspects of complex litigation—in particular securities, product liability, and certain types of civil rights litigation.

Part I:
Introduction

10. Purpose and Use of the Manual

10.1 Purpose of the Manual

The purpose of this manual is to assist in the management of complex litigation. Although the roles of judges and lawyers differ, they share the responsibility for managing complex litigation in which they are involved. Judges must look to lawyers to conduct the litigation in a professional manner and to assist them, not only by advising them on the facts and the law of the case, but also by submitting fair, practical, and effective proposals for the management of the litigation and by making management succeed. At a time when the demands on the time of judges weigh heavily, judges are more dependent on lawyers than ever in striving to achieve the purpose of Rule 1 of the Federal Rules of Civil Procedure. Lawyers in turn must look to judges for clear directions, timely decisions, and firm control when needed to effectuate case management. This manual is therefore directed at both groups.

What is complex litigation? The original manual defined complex litigation as including "one or more related cases which present unusual problems and . . . require extraordinary treatment, including but not limited to the cases designated as 'protracted' and 'big.'" The *Manual for Complex Litigation, Second* dropped this elusive description but made no effort to arrive at a substitute. Yet a definition is important to understanding the objective of this manual, for there is always a risk that complexity may be *introduced* simply by calling litigation "complex."

A functional definition of complex litigation recognizes that the need for management in the sense used here—judicial management with the participation of counsel—does not simply arise from complexity, but is its defining characteristic: The greater the need for management, the more "complex" is the litigation. Clearly, litigation involving many parties in numerous related cases—especially if pending in different jurisdictions—requires management and is complex, as is litigation involving large numbers of witnesses and documents and extensive discovery. On the other hand, litigation raising difficult and novel questions of law, though challenging to the court, may require little or no management, and therefore may not be complex as that term is used here.

How does the manual aid management? Management is not an end in itself. It must be conducted to serve its purpose of bringing about "the just, speedy, and inexpensive determination" of the litigation, avoiding unnecessary and unproductive activity. The manual provides an arsenal of litigation management techniques or, perhaps more accurately, a kit of management tools that have proved effective in the past, from which the participants should select those useful for the particular circumstances. Some of what this manual contains will be appropriate in only a few cases, while other material will have much wider application. This reflects the fact that it is neither practical nor helpful to attempt to draw a bright line between complex litigation and other litigation. Different cases will have different management needs. Even the most widely accepted and effective management techniques have little utility if in the particular litigation they are not needed—and suitable—to help control cost and delay fairly.

In offering an array of litigation management techniques and procedures, the manual does not recommend that every litigation necessarily use any of them or follow a standard pattern. The techniques and procedures suitable for one litigation will not necessarily be suitable for another. Choices will depend on the needs of the litigation and many other considerations. What the manual does urge is that choices *be* made, and that they be made starting early in the litigation, lest it drift for lack of decisions about its management. While those decisions are largely the responsibility of the judge, their purpose is not to take the case from the lawyers but to provide guidance and direction, setting limits and applying controls as needed.

Although much of what this manual contains is transubstantive, complex litigation should not be viewed as monolithic. Substantive law in the different areas in which complex litigation is pursued shapes procedure and management as well. In some areas of law, such as antitrust and securities litigation, substantive and procedural rules are relatively well settled, as are management techniques. In others, such as environmental, civil rights, and mass tort litigation, they are still emerging or undergoing change. While all complex litigation challenges courts, the latter areas present the greatest challenges, requiring courts to adapt procedures designed for the adjudication of one-on-one disputes in a discrete forum to litigation with many parties on both sides and related cases pending in different courts, often including state courts.

Much complex litigation, therefore, will take the judge and counsel into sparsely charted terrain with little guidance on how to respond to pressing needs for management. Practices and principles that served in the past may not be adequate, their adaptation may be difficult and controversial, and novel and innovative ways may have to be found.[1] While this manual should be helpful within the limits of its mission, it should be viewed as open ended, and judges are encouraged to be innovative and creative to meet the needs of their cases, though remaining mindful of the bounds of existing law.

---

1. *See, e.g.,* American Law Institute, Complex Litigation Project (1993); American Bar Association, Revised Final Report and Recommendations of the Commission on Mass Torts (1989).

This manual retains, in substantially expanded form, a chapter on complex criminal litigation. It does so because the manual is a convenient vehicle to provide material thought to be helpful to judges and lawyers concerned with criminal litigation, at least until a separate criminal manual is published. Although it is indisputable that complex criminal litigation has been increasing, there is, as in civil litigation, no bright line dividing complex cases from the rest. Some of the material, though relevant to complex litigation, may also be considered useful for criminal case management generally. For the most part, the problems of criminal litigation are unique and the generic portions of this manual have only limited application; where they do apply, cross-references have been supplied.

10.2 Use of the Manual

While this edition contains much new and revised material, it follows the format and retains the numbering system of the *Manual for Complex Litigation, Second*. This manual is divided into four parts. Part I contains a brief description of the purpose and use of the manual. Part II, "Management of Complex Litigation," discusses basic principles of effective management of complex litigation and then describes various procedures for their implementation as the litigation moves through the pretrial phase—issue definition, discovery, motion practice, and preparation for trial—and to summary disposition, settlement, or trial. Part III discusses the application of management techniques and procedures to particular types of complex civil and criminal litigation. The reader interested in a particular kind of action may wish to begin by reviewing the applicable sections in this part before consulting the generic material in Part II. Part IV contains litigation checklists and sample orders and forms.

The organization of this manual belies the fact that its subject matter is not neatly divisible into distinct topics. A topic, such as settlement or class actions, will be relevant to the discussion at different points in the manual. To minimize repetition, the manual generally discusses a topic at a single logical location, but provides extensive cross-references throughout the text. The reader is urged to make liberal use of these, as well as the checklists in section 40, to ensure that all relevant matter is accessed.

The manual is offered as an aid to management, not as a treatise on matters of substantive or procedural law. Footnotes have been expanded to provide the reader with a convenient starting point for research where needed, but the text cannot be assumed to remain a current and comprehensive statement of the law. Nor is the manual intended for citation as authority on points of law or as a statement of official policy.

Finally, although the manual is textually directed at the federal courts, the techniques and procedures may be useful in state courts as well, particularly in view of the convergence that is occurring in related litigation pending in both state and federal court systems. Reference to the manual may assist in the coordination of such litigation.

10.3 Other Publications on Litigation Management

This manual contains references to other publications of the Federal Judicial Center bearing on aspects of management of complex litigation. Those publications and their availability are listed below:

- *Manual for Litigation Management and Cost and Delay Reduction* (1992)—a concise generic manual on civil case management with forms (and a comprehensive bibliography on case management), available to federal judges from the Federal Judicial Center and to others on Westlaw.

- *The Elements of Case Management* (1991)—a brief analytical essay on civil case management, available to federal judges from the Federal Judicial Center and to others on Westlaw.

- *Reference Manual on Scientific Evidence* (1994)—a manual providing guidance on the application of the Federal Rules of Evidence to scientific evidence and on the management of cases involving issues of scientific evidence, including the use of court-appointed experts and special masters, and an analysis of pivotal issues in certain forensic sciences (DNA, epidemiology, toxicology, statistics and multiple regression, surveys, and economic loss), available to federal judges from the Federal Judicial Center, to state judges from various state judicial education agencies, and to others from various legal publishers.

- *Manual on Recurring Problems in Criminal Trials* (3d ed. 1990)—a compendium of citations to appellate decisions on issues commonly encountered in the trial of criminal cases, available to federal judges from the Federal Judicial Center and to others on Westlaw.

- *Benchbook for United States District Judges* (1993 ed.)—available to federal judges from the Federal Judicial Center.

Part II:
Management of
Complex Litigation

20. General Principles

Fair and efficient resolution of complex litigation requires that the court exercise early and effective supervision (and, where necessary, control), that counsel act cooperatively and professionally, and that the judge and counsel collaborate to develop and carry out a comprehensive plan for the conduct of pretrial and trial proceedings. The generic principles of pretrial and trial management are covered in *infra* sections 21 and 22, and are applied to specified types of litigation in *infra* section 33. Section 20 discusses matters that cut across all phases of complex litigation.

20.1 Judicial Supervision

Although not without limits, the court's express and inherent powers enable the judge to exercise extensive supervision and control of litigation. The Federal Rules of Civil Procedure, particularly Rules 16, 26, 37, 42, and 83, contain numerous grants of authority that supplement the court's inherent power[2] to manage litigation. Fed. R. Civ. P. 16(c)(12) specifically addresses complex litigation, authorizing the judge to adopt "special procedures for managing potentially difficult or protracted actions that may involve complex issues, multiple parties, difficult legal questions, or unusual proof problems."

In planning and implementing case management, its purpose must be kept in mind. Case management is not an end in itself; rather it is intended to bring about a just resolution as speedily and inexpensively as possible. It should be tailored to the needs of the particular litigation and to the resources available; make-work activity should be avoided. Those resources include not only those of the parties but also those of the judicial system. Judicial time is the scarcest of these, and an important part of case management is for judges to use their time wisely and efficiently and to make use of all available help. Time pressures may lead some judges to think that they cannot afford to devote time to civil case management. It is true that the extra attention given by the judge to a complex case can encroach upon the time immediately available to attend to other matters. But judges have found that an investment of time in case management in the early stages of the litigation will lead to earlier dispositions, less wasteful activity, shorter trials, and, in the long run, to economies of judicial time and a lessening of judicial burdens.

---

2. *See, e.g.*, Chambers v. NASCO, Inc., 111 S. Ct. 2123, 2132–37 (1991).

20.11 Early Identification and Control

Judicial supervision is most needed and productive early in the litigation. To this end, an initial pretrial conference under Rule 16[3] should be held as soon as practical (many judges hold the conference within 30 to 60 days of filing), even if some parties have not yet appeared or even been served. Rule 16(b) requires that the judge, usually after holding a scheduling conference, issue a scheduling order[4] "as soon as practicable but in any event within 90 days after the appearance of a defendant and within 120 days after the complaint has been served on a defendant" (local rules may establish different deadlines). The initial pretrial conference may be used for this purpose unless a separate scheduling conference is thought to be needed. Many judges use standing case orders—sometimes tailored to specific types of litigation—to elicit specific information prior to the conference and inform counsel of the matters they must be prepared to discuss.[5]

The assigned judge should therefore be alerted as soon as possible to the filing of a potentially complex case. Some courts require the clerk's office to notify the judge immediately of the filing of certain types of cases—such as class actions and mass tort, antitrust, and securities fraud cases—that typically merit special judicial attention. Courts often require that a civil cover sheet be filed with the complaint indicating, among other things, whether a case should be considered "complex." Whether a case will require increased judicial supervision, however, may not be apparent from the docket sheet or the complaint itself. Counsel should be directed to notify the court of the filing of a potentially complex case and identify by name and court all pending cases (state and federal) that may be related; many courts require this by local rule.

20.12 Assignment to Single Judge

Each multijudge court should determine for itself whether complex litigation should be assigned according to the court's regular plan for case assignment, under a special rotation for complex cases, or perhaps to one or more judges particularly qualified by reason of experience. In courts in which actions are not as-

---

3. For discussion of the matters that should or may be covered in this and subsequent conferences, see *infra* § 21.2 (pretrial conferences). Special procedures may be needed even before the initial conference; for example, it may be necessary to take immediate action to preserve evidence. See *infra* § 21.442 (documents; preservation).

4. For a sample scheduling order, see *infra* § 41.33.

5. For a sample order, see *infra* § 41.54; *see also* Manual for Litigation Management and Cost and Delay Reduction (Federal Judicial Center 1992) [hereinafter Litigation Manual], form 12, at 193–95.

signed automatically to a specific judge upon filing, an individual assignment nevertheless should be specially made as soon as a case is identified as complex or a part of complex litigation. In unusual situations, the demands of complex litigation may be so great that the assigned judge should be relieved from some or all other case assignments for a period of time or be given assistance on aspects of the litigation from other judges.

20.121 Recusal/Disqualification

The judge to whom a complex case is assigned (or has been reassigned) should promptly review the pleadings and other papers in the case, the identities of parties and attorneys, and the nature of interests affected by the litigation for possible conflicts that may require recusal or disqualification.[6] To assist the judge, counsel should submit a list of all entities affiliated with the parties and all attorneys and firms associated in the litigation. This review must be conducted at the outset, but the court needs to consider both present and potential conflicts that may arise as a result of the joinder of additional parties, the identification of class members, or the assignment of other related cases, with the accompanying involvement of additional litigants and counsel.[7] As the case progresses, the court should remain alert to conflicts that may arise as additional persons and interests enter the litigation or as the judge's staff changes.[8]

A judicial officer is required to recuse (1) in any proceeding in which the officer's "impartiality might reasonably be questioned"[9] or (2) if any of the conflicts of interest enumerated in 28 U.S.C. § 455(b) exist. Where the ground for disqualification arises under the former provision only, the parties may waive it after full disclosure on the record; the conflicts of interest enumerated in § 455(b) may *not* be waived.[10] Where the officer has devoted "substantial judicial time" to a matter, however, disqualification based on a financial interest in a party (other

6. Judges are required by federal law to inform themselves about their personal and fiduciary financial interests, and to make a "reasonable effort" to inform themselves about the personal financial interests of their spouse and minor children residing in their household. 28 U.S.C. § 455(c).

7. *See, e.g., In re* Cement Antitrust Litigation, 688 F.2d 1297 (9th Cir. 1982), *aff'd under 28 U.S.C. § 2109 sub nom.* Arizona v. United States Dist. Court, 459 U.S. 1191 (1983) (disqualification of judge, five years after suit instituted, upon discovery that spouse owned stock in a few of the more than 200,000 class members).

8. In particular, law clerks should avoid having a relationship (including a pending offer) with any party or counsel. *See, e.g.,* Linda S. Mullenix, *Beyond Consolidation*, 32 Wm. & Mary L. Rev. 475, 539–40 (1991) (discussing complex case in which magistrate judge recused when law clerk was offered employment with firm of counsel representing party).

9. 28 U.S.C. § 455(a); Code of Judicial Conduct for United States Judges, Canon C3(c)(1), *reprinted in* 69 F.R.D. 273, 277.

10. 28 U.S.C. § 455(e).

Manual for Complex Litigation, Third

than an interest that might be "substantially affected by the outcome") may be avoided by divestment.[11]

Reassignment, when warranted, should be accomplished as promptly as possible, and the judge to whom the litigation is to be reassigned should make a similar inquiry into potential grounds for recusal before accepting the reassignment and giving notice to the parties.

20.122 Other Judges

Although one judge should supervise the litigation, other judges may be requested to perform special duties, such as conducting settlement discussions (see *infra* section 23.11). Moreover, in the course of consolidated or coordinated pretrial proceedings, severable claims or cases may appear that could be assigned to other judges.

20.123 Related Litigation

Complex litigation frequently involves two or more separate but related cases. All related cases pending or which may later be filed in the same court, whether or not in the same division, should be assigned at least initially to the same judge (local rules often provide for the assignment of related cases to a single judge, typically the judge receiving assignment of the earliest-filed case). Pretrial proceedings in these cases should be coordinated or consolidated under Fed. R. Civ. P. 42(a), even if filed in more than one division of the court.[12] It may be necessary to transfer to the district judge related adversary proceedings in bankruptcy, including proceedings to determine the dischargeability of debts.[13] Counsel should be directed to inform the assigned judge of any pending related cases (as many local rules require); related cases may be identified on the face of the complaint. The judge to whom complex litigation has been assigned should also attempt to ascertain whether related cases are pending in the judge's court.

Assignment of related criminal and civil cases to a single judge will improve efficiency and coordination, especially when the cases are pending at the same time. Other factors, however, such as the possibility that extensive judicial supervision of pretrial proceedings in the civil litigation may be needed during the time the criminal trial is being conducted, may suggest that the cases be handled by different judges. See generally *infra* section 31.2.

Consolidation may be possible even when related cases are filed in different courts. Cases in other districts may be capable of being transferred under 28

---

11. *Id.* § 455(f).

12. Under 28 U.S.C. § 1404(b) the court may, upon motion, transfer cases pending in the same district, or motions or hearings therein, to a single division.

13. *See, e.g., In re* Flight Trans. Corp. Sec. Litig., 730 F.2d 1128 (8th Cir. 1984).

U.S.C. § 1404(a) or 1406[14] to the consolidation court by the court in which they are pending. Pretrial proceedings in related cases may also be consolidated in a single district by the judicial panel on multidistrict litigation under 28 U.S.C. § 1407. See *infra* section 31.13. Cases brought in state court may be removed to federal court[15] and transferred, or refiled in the consolidating district court following voluntary dismissal or dismissal based on *forum non conveniens*.

When transfer of all cases to a single court for centralized management is not possible, the affected courts should attempt to coordinate proceedings through informal means to the extent practicable in order to minimize conflicts, inconsistent rulings, and duplication of effort. Coordination can be accomplished by arrangements made by counsel, appropriate communications between judges, joint pretrial conferences and hearings at which both judges preside, and the issuance of parallel orders. It may be facilitated by designation of a "lead" case in the litigation; rulings in the lead case would presumptively apply to the other coordinated cases, and pretrial proceedings in those cases may be stayed pending its resolution. Coordination of related litigation is discussed more fully in *infra* section 31.14 (cases in different federal courts) and *infra* section 31.31 (cases in federal and state courts).

20.13 Effective Management

Effective judicial management generally has the following characteristics:

- **It is active.** The judge attempts to anticipate problems before they arise rather than waiting passively for matters to be presented by counsel. Because the attorneys may become immersed in the details of the case, innovation and creativity in formulating a litigation plan may frequently depend on the court.

- **It is substantive.** The judge's involvement is not limited to procedural matters. Rather, the judge becomes familiar at an early stage with the substantive issues in order to make informed rulings on issue definition and narrowing, and on related matters, such as scheduling, bifurcation and consolidation, and discovery control.

- **It is timely.** The judge decides disputes promptly, particularly those that may substantially affect the course or scope of further proceedings. Delayed rulings may be costly and burdensome for litigants and will often

---

14. These statutes authorize such transfer only if personal jurisdiction and venue lie in the transferee court. *See, e.g.,* Shutte v. Armco Steel Corp., 431 F.2d 22, 24 (3d Cir. 1970) (§ 1404(a)); Dubin v. United States, 380 F.2d 813 (5th Cir. 1967) (§ 1406). If they do not, transfer is improper even if plaintiffs consent. Hoffman v. Blaski, 363 U.S. 335 (1960).

15. *See* 28 U.S.C. §§ 1441–1452.

delay other litigation events. Sometimes the parties may prefer that a ruling be timely rather than perfect.

- **It is continuing.** The judge periodically monitors the progress of the litigation to see that schedules are being followed and to consider necessary modifications of the litigation plan. The judge may call for interim reports between scheduled conferences.

- **It is firm, but fair.** Time limits and other controls and requirements are not imposed arbitrarily or without considering the views of counsel, and they are subject to revision when warranted by the circumstances. Once having established a program, however, the judge expects schedules to be met and, when necessary, imposes appropriate sanctions (see *infra* section 20.15) for derelictions and dilatory tactics.

- **It is carefully prepared.** Heavy-handed case management by an unprepared judge may often be counterproductive, while an early display of careful preparation sets the proper tone and can enhance the judge's credibility and effectiveness with counsel.

The judge's role in developing and monitoring an effective plan for the orderly conduct of pretrial and trial proceedings is crucial. Although the elements and details of the plan will vary with the circumstances of the particular case, each plan must include an appropriate schedule under which the case is to proceed to resolution. Ordinarily, the plan should prescribe a series of procedural steps with firm dates giving direction and order to the case as it progresses through pretrial proceedings to summary disposition or trial. In some cases, the court may be able to establish an overall plan for the conduct of the litigation at the outset; in others, the plan must be developed and refined in successive stages. The more prudent course is to err on the side of over-inclusiveness in the plan rather than risk omission of critical elements; components of the plan that prove impractical may always be modified. Time limits and deadlines will often be necessary for effective case management, though a firm but realistic trial date, coupled with immediate access to the court in the event a dispute cannot be resolved by agreement among counsel, may suffice in litigation involving experienced attorneys working cooperatively.

The attorneys—who will be more familiar than the judge with the facts and issues in the case—should play a significant part in developing the litigation plan and are primarily responsible for its execution. The judge should provide supervision and maintain control in a manner that recognizes the burdens placed on counsel by complex litigation, and he or she should foster mutual respect and cooperation not only between the court and the attorneys but also among the attorneys.

20.14 Supervisory Referrals to Magistrate Judges and Special Masters

The judge should decide early in the litigation whether to refer all or any part of pretrial supervision and control to a magistrate judge. In making that decision, the judge needs to consider a number of factors, including the experience and qualifications of the available magistrate judge, the relationship and attitude of the attorneys, the extent to which a district judge's authority may be required, the time the judge has to devote to the litigation, the novelty of the issues presented and the need for innovation, and the judge's personal preferences. Some judges believe that judicial supervision of complex litigation should ordinarily be exercised directly by them rather than by a magistrate judge, even in courts that routinely make such referrals for discovery or other pretrial purposes. They believe that referrals in complex cases may cause additional costs and delays when the parties seek review by the judge, weaken the impact of directions given to counsel during pretrial proceedings, diminish supervisory consistency and coherence as the case proceeds to trial, create greater reluctance to try innovative procedures that might aid in resolution of the case, and cause the judge to be unfamiliar with the case at the time of trial. Other judges have found that magistrate judges have the competence, experience, and authority to be able to provide effective case management during the pretrial stage, enabling the judge to devote time to more urgent matters.

Even if no general referral is made to a magistrate judge, referral of particular matters may be helpful. The judge may refer supervision of all discovery matters, or supervision of particular discovery issues or disputes, particularly those that may be time consuming or require an immediate ruling; examples include resolving deposition disputes by telephone, ruling on claims of privilege and motions for protective orders, and conducting hearings on procedural matters, such as personal jurisdiction. Magistrate judges may also be called on to assist counsel with formulation of stipulations and statements of contentions, and to facilitate settlement discussions. The law of the circuit should be consulted with respect to the limits on referrals to magistrate judges. See generally *infra* section 21.53.

Referral of pretrial management to a special master (not a magistrate judge) is not advisable. Rule 53 permits referrals only in "exceptional cases," and because pretrial management calls for the exercise of judicial authority, its exercise by someone other than a judicial officer is particularly inappropriate.[16] Moreover the additional expense imposed on parties as a result militates strongly against such

---

16. *See* LaBuy v. Howes Leather Co., 352 U.S. 249 (1957) (the length and complexity of a case and the congestion of the court's docket do not alone justify a comprehensive reference to a special master). See *infra* § 21.52.

appointment.[17] Appointment of a special master (or of an expert under Fed. R. Evid. 706) for limited purposes requiring special expertise may sometimes be appropriate (e.g., when a complex program for settlement needs to be devised).[18] See *infra* sections 21.51–21.52.

Any referral should be covered by an order that specifically describes what is being referred, the authority being delegated to the magistrate judge or master, and the procedure for review by the judge. The court should call for regular progress reports from the magistrate judge or master.

20.15 Sanctions

20.151 General Principles

The rules and principles governing the imposition of sanctions are the same in complex as in other litigation, but the potential of sanctions requires careful attention in complex litigation because misconduct may have more severe consequences. Because the litigation will generally be conducted under close judicial oversight and control, there should be fewer opportunities for sanctionable conduct to occur. If the court's management program is clear, specific, and reasonable—having been developed with the participation of counsel—the parties will know what is expected of them and should have little difficulty complying. The occasions for sanctionable conduct will therefore be reduced. Indeed, the need to resort to sanctions may reflect a breakdown of case management. On the other hand, the stakes involved in and the pressures generated by complex litigation may lead some parties to violate the rules. Although as a general matter sanctions should not be a means of management, the court needs to make clear its willingness to resort to sanctions, *sua sponte* if necessary, to assure compliance with the management program.[19]

The design of the case management program should anticipate compliance problems and include prophylactic procedures, such as requiring parties to meet

---

17. Prudential Ins. Co. of Am. v. United States Gypsum Co., 991 F.2d 1080 (3d Cir. 1993) (writ of mandamus issued overturning appointment of master to hear merits of a claim for cost of testing, monitoring, and removing asbestos-containing products at thirty-nine sites).

18. *See* Wayne Brazil et al., Managing Complex Litigation: A Practical Guide to the Use of Special Masters (1983).

19. *See* Fed. R. Civ. P. 11(c)(1)(B); Chambers v. NASCO, Inc., 111 S. Ct. 2123, 2131 n.8 (1991).

and confer promptly in the event of disputes and providing ready access to the court if they cannot resolve them. In addition, the court should inform counsel at the outset of the litigation of the court's expectations about cooperation and professionalism. Perceptions of the limits of legitimate advocacy differ; advance guidance from the court can reduce the need for sanctions later.

Though at times unavoidable, sanctions should be considered a last resort. The court should exercise its discretion with care and explain on the record or in an order the basis for its action and the purpose to be achieved. Sanctions may be imposed for general or specific deterrence, to punish, or to remedy the consequences of misconduct.

Sanctions proceedings can be disruptive, costly, and may create personal antagonism inimical to an atmosphere of cooperation. Counsel should therefore avoid moving for sanctions unless all reasonable alternatives have been exhausted.

20.152 Sources of Authority

The primary codified sources of authority to impose sanctions in civil litigation are 28 U.S.C. § 1927 and Fed. R. Civ. P. 11, 16, 41, and 56(g).[20] Sanctions relating to discovery are authorized by Fed. R. Civ. P. 26, 30, 32(d), 33(b)(3)–(4), 34(b), 35(b)(1), 36(a), and, most prominently, Rule 37.[21] Under limited circumstances sanctions may also be imposed under local rules.[22]

Sanctions may also be imposed through the exercise of the court's inherent powers.[23] The court may resort to this power even where the conduct at issue could be sanctioned under a statute or rule; the court should, however, avoid resort to its inherent power if the statute or rule is directly applicable and adequate to support the intended sanction.[24] The court may assess attorneys' fees pursuant to its inherent power, but when sitting in diversity should avoid doing so in

---

20. A number of federal statutes allow the court, in its discretion, to award prevailing parties costs, including attorneys' and sometimes experts' fees. *See, e.g.,* 42 U.S.C.A. §§ 1988, 2000e-5(k) (West Supp. 1993); 15 U.S.C. §§ 78i(e), 78r(a). Such statutes may expressly predicate such an award on a finding that the action (or defense) was meritless, *see, e.g.,* 15 U.S.C. § 77k(e), and common law may impose the same requirement when awards under such statutes are sought by defendants. *See* Christansburg Garment Co. v. EEOC, 434 U.S. 412, 416 (1978). *But see* Fogerty v. Fantasy Inc., 62 U.S.L.W. 4153 & 4155 n.12 (U.S. March 1, 1994) (same standard applies to plaintiffs and defendants seeking fees in copyright, patent, and trademark cases). Such awards may therefore be considered a sanction for meritless litigation.

21. Note that Rule 11 is expressly made inapplicable to discovery. Fed. R. Civ. P. 11(d).

22. *See, e.g.,* Rule 11.1 of the Local Rules for Civil Cases, E.D. Mich.; Miranda v. Southern Pacific Transp. Co., 710 F.2d 516 (9th Cir. 1983).

23. See *Chambers,* 111 S. Ct. at 2132–33, and cases cited therein.

24. *Id.* at 2135–36 & n.14 (*distinguishing* Societe Internationale v. Rogers, 357 U.S. 197 (1958) (Rule 37)); United States v. One 1987 BMW 325, 982 F.2d 655, 661 (1st Cir. 1993) (where civil rule limits sanction that may be imposed, court may not circumvent by resort to inherent power).

contravention of applicable state law embodying a substantive policy, such as a statute permitting prevailing parties to recover fees in certain classes of litigation.[25]

Because the applicable standards and procedures and the available sanctions will vary depending on the authority under which the court proceeds, it needs to decide on the choice of the authority on which it will rely and make that choice clear in its order. For example, 28 U.S.C. § 1927 authorizes the assessment of costs and fees against an attorney only—it therefore cannot provide authority to impose sanctions on a party.

20.153 Considerations in Imposing

In considering the imposition of sanctions, the judge should take these factors into account:

- the nature and consequences of the dereliction or misconduct;
- the person(s) responsible;
- the court's discretion under the applicable source of authority to impose sanctions and to choose which sanctions to impose;
- the purposes to be served by imposing sanctions, and what is the least severe sanction that will achieve the intended purpose; and
- the appropriate time for conducting sanctions proceedings.

With respect to the consideration of the nature and consequences of the dereliction or misconduct, the court should take these factors into account:

- whether the act or omission was willful or negligent;
- whether it directly violated a court order or a federal or local rule;
- its effect on the litigation and the trial participants;
- whether it was isolated or part of a course of misconduct or dereliction;[26] and
- the existence of any extenuating circumstances.

Rule 11 substantially limits the authority of the court to impose monetary sanctions, but they may still be available in unusual cases or under other rules or powers. If monetary sanctions are warranted, they should generally be imposed only on the person(s) responsible for the misconduct; if assessed against counsel, they should be accompanied by a direction not to pass the cost on to the client. It may be appropriate to sanction the client or the client and attorney jointly. If the proper allocation of responsibility between counsel and client is unclear, its de-

---

25. *Chambers*, 111 S. Ct. at 2136–37.
26. *See* Fed. R. Civ. P. 11(b), (c) advisory committee's note (listing these and other considerations).

termination may raise problems; by pitting the attorney against the attorney's client, it can create a conflict of interest.[27] In addition, it may require inquiry into potentially privileged communications.[28] The court should seek the least disruptive alternative, which may be to impose joint and several liability on both counsel and client,[29] or to defer the matter of sanctions until the end of the litigation.[30]

Some types of nonmonetary sanction, such as dismissal, default, or preclusion of a claim or evidence, will or may affect the outcome. They should be imposed only in egregious circumstances and only after consideration of the following factors:

- the policy favoring trial on the merits;
- whether the sanction will further the just, speedy, and inexpensive determination of the action;
- the degree to which the sanctioned party acted deliberately and knew or should have known of the possible consequences;
- the degree of responsibility of the affected client;
- the merits and importance of the claim(s) affected;
- the impact on other parties or the public interest; and
- the availability of less severe sanctions to accomplish the intended purpose.

20.154 Types

In imposing the least severe sanction adequate to accomplish the intended purpose, the court can select from a broad range of options.[31] These include the following:

- **Reprimand.** For most minor violations, particularly a first infraction, an oral reprimand will suffice. In more serious cases, a written reprimand may be appropriate.

---

27. *See* Healy v. Chelsea Resources, Ltd., 947 F.2d 611, 623 (2d Cir. 1991); White v. General Motors Corp., 908 F.2d 675, 685 (10th Cir. 1991).

28. Though it may be ethically permissible for an attorney to reveal client confidences to the extent necessary in this context, *see* Model Rules of Professional Conduct 1.6(b)(2); Model Code of Professional Responsibility DR 4-101(c), this does not resolve the privilege issue.

29. *See* Martin v. American Kennel Club, 1989 U.S. Dist. LEXIS 201, at *22–23 (N.D. Ill. 1989) ("Absent a clear indication of sole responsibility" liability should be joint and several).

30. *See, e.g.,* O'Neal v. Retirement Plan for Salaried Employees of RKO Gen. Inc., 1992 U.S. Dist. LEXIS 237, at *12–13 (S.D.N.Y. 1992); Fed. R. Civ. P. 11 advisory committee's note.

31. *See* Chambers v. NASCO, Inc., 111 S. Ct. 2123, 2132–33 (1991) ("a primary aspect" of court's discretion to invoke inherent sanction power "is the ability to fashion an appropriate sanction" for abuse of judicial process).

- **Cost shifting.** The purpose of Rule 11 sanctions is deterrence rather than compensation; the rule therefore permits cost shifting only in "unusual circumstances."[32] In contrast, many of the discovery rules (primarily Rules 26(g) and 37) and Rule 16(f) (dealing with pretrial conferences) require or permit cost shifting in specified situations. See generally *infra* section 21.433. Under 28 U.S.C. § 1927, Fed. R. Civ. P. 56(g) (depositions), and its inherent power, the court may order cost-shifting sanctions for actions taken in bad faith.

- **Denial of fees or expenses.** The court may decline to award otherwise recoverable attorneys' fees and expenses, or order counsel not to charge them to their client, when incurred through dilatory or otherwise improper conduct, or in proceedings brought on by such conduct.

- **Remedial action.** Counsel and parties may be required to remedy a negligent or wrongful act at their own expense, as by reconstructing materials improperly destroyed or erased.

- **Grant/denial of time.** Improper delay may justify awarding opposing parties additional time for discovery or other matters,[33] or denying otherwise proper requests for extension of time.

More serious sanctions, reserved for egregious circumstances, include the following:

- **Demotion/removal of counsel.** An attorney may be removed from a position as lead, liaison, or class counsel, or (in an extreme case) from further participation in the case entirely. Such a sanction, however, is likely to disrupt the litigation, may cause significant harm to the client's case and the reputation of the attorney or law firm, and can conflict with a party's right to counsel of its choosing.

- **Removal of party as class representative.** Before imposing this sanction, the court should consider ordering that notice be given to the class under Rule 23(d)(2) to enable them to express their views concerning their representation or intervene in the action.[34]

- **Enjoining party from commencing other litigation.** While there is a strong policy against denying access to the courts, a party may be enjoined from commencing other actions until it has complied with all orders in the current action, or from bringing, without court approval, other actions involving the same or similar facts or claims.

---

32. *See* Fed. R. Civ. P. 11 advisory committee's note (monetary sanctions ordinarily paid into court, but may be directed to those injured if deterrence would otherwise be ineffective).

33. *See, e.g.*, Fed. R. Civ. P. 30(d)(2).

34. *See* Fed. R. Civ. P. 23(d)(2) & advisory committee's note.

- **Preclusion/waiver/striking.** Failure to timely make required disclosures or production, raise objections, or file motions may be grounds to preclude the introduction of related evidence, deem certain facts admitted and objections waived, strike claims or defenses, or deny the motions, including those seeking to amend pleadings or join parties.[35]
- **Dismissal.** This severe sanction should generally not be imposed until the affected party has been warned and given a chance to take remedial action, and then only when lesser sanctions, such as dismissal without prejudice and assessment of costs, would be ineffective.
- **Vacation of judgment.** The court may vacate a judgment it has rendered if procured by fraud.[36]
- **Suspension/disbarment.** The court may initiate proceedings to suspend an attorney from practice in the court for a period of time or for disbarment.[37]
- **Fine.** The court may assess monetary sanctions apart from or in addition to cost shifting, even without a finding of contempt. The amount should be the minimum necessary to achieve the deterrent or punitive goal, considering the resources of the person or entity fined.[38]
- **Contempt.** The court may issue a contempt order under its inherent authority,[39] statute,[40] or rule.[41] The order should indicate clearly whether the contempt is civil or criminal. The procedure and possible penalties will depend on that determination and the nature and timing of the contemptuous act.[42]

---

35. *See, e.g.,* Fed. R. Civ. P. 37(b)(2), (c)(1).

36. *Chambers,* 111 S. Ct. at 2132 (inherent power); Fed. R. Civ. P. 60(b).

37. The court has inherent power to suspend or disbar attorneys, but should follow applicable local rules. *See In re* Snyder, 472 U.S. 634, 643 & n.4 (1985). For discussion of the standard for taking such action, see *id.* at 643–47 (refusal to supplement fee petition or accept CJA assignment coupled with single instance of discourtesy insufficient to support suspension).

38. *See, e.g.,* Fed. R. Civ. P. 11(c)(2).

39. *See Chambers,* 111 S. Ct. at 2132; Roadway Express, Inc. v. Piper, 447 U.S. 752, 764 (1980).

40. See, e.g., 18 U.S.C. §§ 401–403, 28 U.S.C. § 1784, and statutes cited in Fed. R. Crim. P. 42 advisory committee's note.

41. *See, e.g.,* Fed. R. Civ. P. 37(b)(2)(D), 45(e), Fed. R. Crim. P. 17(g).

42. *See* Bench Book for United States District Judges §§ 2.08 (civil contempt), 1.24 (criminal contempt) (Federal Judicial Center 1986) [hereinafter Bench Book]; 18 U.S.C. § 3691 (jury trial of criminal contempts), § 3692 (jury trial for contempt in labor dispute cases), § 3693 (summary disposition or jury trial; notice); Fed. R. Crim. P. 42 (criminal contempt). Since there is no federal rule establishing a procedure for civil contempt, the court should follow the procedures of Fed. R. Crim. P. 42 to the extent applicable.

- **Referral for possible criminal prosecution.** Where the misconduct rises to the level of a criminal offense,[43] the matter may be referred to the U.S. Attorney's Office.

20.155 Procedure

The appropriate timing for the imposition of sanctions depends on the basis for their imposition. Generally sanctions are most effective when imposed promptly after the improper conduct has occurred.[44] This maximizes their deterrent effect in the litigation. Prompt imposition also allows the court to try to deal with the problem by imposing less severe sanctions before resorting to more severe measures should they become necessary.

Some sanctions, however, depend for their predicate on further proceedings. The frivolous nature of a paper may not be established until further action by the court. Some misconduct or the extent of its consequences may not become apparent until the litigation has developed further; some sanctions are expressly conditioned on later developments.[45] Certain facts may have to be established before the court can decide the sanctions issue, a process which may delay the litigation unless deferred until its conclusion. Similarly, as discussed above, deferral is advisable where the decision may require inquiry into potentially privileged communications and create a conflict of interest between counsel and client. Delaying rulings on sanctions may allow the court to consider the issue more dispassionately; the court must be careful, however, not to apply the wisdom of hindsight.

Sanctions should not be assessed without notice and an opportunity to be heard.[46] The extent of the process afforded, however, depends on the circumstances, primarily the type and severity of sanction under consideration.[47] An oral or evidentiary hearing may not be necessary for relatively minor sanctions; the issue may be decided on papers.[48] To provide notice when acting *sua sponte*, the court should issue an order to show cause why sanctions should not be imposed,

---

43. In particular, see 18 U.S.C. §§ 1501–1517 (obstruction of justice).

44. *See* Thomas v. Capital Sec. Servs., Inc., 836 F.2d 866, 881 (5th Cir. 1988).

45. *See, e.g.,* Fed. R. Civ. P. 37(c)(2) (recovery of expenses for failure to admit depends on later proof of matter not admitted); Fed. R. Civ. P. 68 (assessment of costs incurred after settlement offer refused depends on failure to obtain more favorable judgment).

46. Roadway Express, Inc. v. Piper, 447 U.S. 752, 767 (1980). Some rules expressly require this. *See, e.g.,* Fed. R. Civ. P. 11(c).

47. *See, e.g.,* Media Duplication Servs. v. HDG Software, 928 F.2d 122, 1238 (1st Cir. 1991) (*citing* Roadway, 447 U.S. at 767 n.14 (due process concerns raised by dismissal are greater than those presented by assessment of attorneys' fees)); G.J.B. Assoc., Inc. v. Singleton, 913 F.2d 824, 830 (10th Cir. 1990) (same); Fed. R. Civ. P. 11 advisory committee's note.

48. *See, e.g., In re* Edmond, 934 F.2d 1304, 1313 (4th Cir. 1991); Hudson v. Moore Bus. Forms, Inc., 898 F.2d 684, 686 (9th Cir. 1990); Fed. R. Civ. P. 11 advisory committee's note.

specifying the alleged misconduct.[49] To avoid disrupting a settlement, monetary sanctions should generally not be assessed *sua sponte* once the parties have reached agreement.[50]

Unless the sanction is minor and the misconduct obvious, the court should memorialize its findings and reasons on the record or by written order.[51] The findings should identify the objectionable conduct clearly, state the factual and legal reasons for the court's action, including the need for the particular sanction imposed and the inadequacy of less severe measures, and the authority relied on. Making such a record will facilitate appellate review and help the appellate court understand the basis for the court's exercise of its discretion.[52] Normally the court need not explain its denial of sanctions.[53]

20.2 Role of Counsel

20.21 Responsibilities in Complex Litigation

Judicial involvement in the management of complex litigation does not lessen the duties and responsibilities of the attorneys. To the contrary, such litigation places greater demands on counsel in their dual roles as advocates and officers of the court. Because of the complexity of legal and factual issues, judges will be more dependent than ever on the assistance of counsel, without which no case-management plan can be effective. Greater demands on counsel arise for other reasons as well: the amounts of money or importance of the interests at stake; the length

---

49. El Paso v. Socorro, 917 F.2d. 7 (5th Cir. 1990); Maisonville v. F2 Am., Inc., 902 F.2d 746 (9th Cir. 1990); Fed. R. Civ. P. 11(c)(1)(B) & advisory committee's note.

50. *See* Fed. R. Civ. P. 11(c)(2)(B) & advisory committee's note.

51. *See* Fed. R. Civ. P. 11(c)(3).

52. The standard of review is abuse of discretion. Chambers v. NASCO, Inc., 111 S. Ct. 2123, 2138 (1991) (inherent power); Cooter & Gel v. Hartmax Corp., 496 U.S. 384, 405 (1990) (Rule 11); Blue v. United States Dep't of the Army, 914 F.2d 525, 539 (4th Cir. 1990) (28 U.S.C. § 1927).

53. Fed. R. Civ. P. 11 advisory committee's note. Only the First Circuit has held to the contrary. *See* Metrocorps, Inc. v. Eastern Mass. Junior Drum & Bugel Corps Ass'n, 912 F.2d 1, 3 (1st Cir. 1990); Morgan v. Massachusetts Gen. Hosp., 901 F.2d 186, 195 (1st Cir. 1990).

and complexity of the proceedings; the difficulties of having to communicate and establish effective working relationships with numerous attorneys (many of whom may be strangers to each other); the need to accommodate professional and personal schedules; the problems of having to appear in courts with which counsel are unfamiliar; the burdens of extensive travel often required; and the complexities of having to act as designated representative of parties who are not their clients (see *infra* section 20.22).

The added demands and burdens of complex litigation place a premium on professionalism.[54] An attitude by counsel of cooperation, professional courtesy, and acceptance of the obligations owed as officers of the court is critical to successful management of the litigation. Counsel need to perform their obligations as advocates in a manner that will foster and sustain good working relations among themselves and with the court. They need to communicate constructively and civilly with one another and attempt to resolve disputes informally as much as possible. Even where the stakes are high, counsel should avoid unnecessary contentiousness and limit the controversy to material issues genuinely in dispute.[55]

The certification requirements of Fed. R. Civ. P. 11 and 26(g) reflect some of the attorneys' obligations as officers of the court. By presenting a paper to the court, an attorney certifies that "to the best of the person's knowledge, information, and belief, formed after an inquiry reasonable under the circumstances . . . it is not being presented for any improper purpose, such as to harass or to cause unnecessary delay or needless increase in the cost of litigation."[56] An attorney's signature on discovery requests, responses, and objections certifies that they are not "unreasonable or unduly burdensome or expensive, given the needs of the case, the discovery already had in the case, the amount in controversy, and the importance of the issues at stake in the litigation."[57] These provisions implement a policy of having attorneys "stop and think" before taking action.

---

54. It is professional misconduct for a lawyer to engage in any conduct that is "prejudicial to the administration of justice." Model Rules of Professional Conduct 8.4(d); Model Code of Professional Responsibility DR 1-102(A)(5).

55. Model Rule of Professional Conduct 3.2 requires lawyers to make "reasonable efforts to expedite litigation consistent with the interests of the client." *See also* Model Rules of Professional Conduct 3.1 (meritorious claims and contentions); Model Code of Professional Responsibility DR 7-102(A)(1) (action taken merely to harass).

56. Fed. R. Civ. P. 11(b)(1). Fed. R. Civ. P. 26(g) contains substantially similar language. Case law in the circuit interpreting these provisions should be considered.

57. Fed. R. Civ. P. 26(g)(C).

20.22 Coordination in Multiparty Litigation—Lead/Liaison Counsel and Committees

Complex litigation often involves numerous parties with common or similar interests but separate counsel. Traditional procedures in which all papers and documents are served on all attorneys, and each attorney files motions, presents arguments, and conducts witness examinations, may result in waste of time and money, in confusion and indirection, and in unnecessary burden on the court. Special procedures for coordination of counsel are therefore needed and should be instituted early in the litigation to avoid unnecessary costs and duplicative activity.

In some cases the attorneys coordinate their activities without the court's assistance to eliminate duplication of effort, and they should be encouraged to do so. More often, however, the court will need to institute procedures under which one or more attorneys are selected and authorized to act on behalf of other counsel and their clients with respect to specified aspects of the litigation. To do so, the court should invite submissions and suggestions from all counsel and conduct an independent review (usually a hearing is advisable) to ensure that counsel appointed to leading roles are qualified and responsible, that they will fairly and adequately represent all of the parties on their side, and that their charges will be reasonable.[58] Counsel designated by the court should be reminded of their responsibility to the court and their obligation to act fairly, efficiently, and economically in the interests of all parties and their counsel.

20.221 Organizational Structures

Attorneys designated by the court to act in the litigation on behalf of other counsel and parties in addition to their own clients (referred to collectively as "designated counsel") generally fall into one of the following categories:

---

58. In cases where the court may award or approve fees, or where court-designated counsel are entitled to compensation, the court should be aware of the importance of controlling attorneys' fees from the outset and the need to adopt appropriate procedures to that end. See *infra* § 24.2. Some courts have developed innovative approaches—for example, competitive bidding has been used in securities fraud actions to select lead class counsel and determine the basis for their compensation. *See In re* Wells Fargo Sec. Litig., 156 F.R.D. 223, 157 F.R.D. 467 (N.D. Cal. 1994); *In re* Oracle Sec. Litig., 131 F.R.D. 688, 132 F.R.D. 538 (N.D. Cal. 1990).

- **Liaison counsel**: charged with essentially administrative matters, such as communications between the court and other counsel (including receiving and distributing notices, orders, motions, and briefs on behalf of the group), convening meetings of counsel, advising parties of developments in the case, and otherwise assisting in the coordination of activities and positions. Such counsel may act for the group in managing document depositories and in resolving scheduling conflicts. Liaison counsel will usually have offices in the same locality as the court.[59]

- **Lead counsel**: charged with major responsibility for formulating (after consultation with other counsel) and presenting positions on substantive and procedural issues during the litigation. Typically they act for the group—either personally or by coordinating the efforts of others—in presenting written and oral arguments and suggestions to the court, working with opposing counsel in developing and implementing a litigation plan, initiating and organizing discovery requests and responses, conducting the principal examination of deponents, employing experts, arranging for support services, and seeing that schedules are met.

- **Trial counsel**: serves as principal attorney for the group at trial in presenting arguments, making objections, conducting examination of witnesses, and generally organizing and coordinating the work of the other attorneys on the trial team.

- **Committees of counsel**: often called steering committees, coordinating committees, management committees, executive committees, discovery committees, or trial teams—may be formed to serve a wide range of functions. Because the appointment of committees of counsel can lead to substantially increased costs, they should not be made unless needed; a need is most likely to exist in cases in which the interests and positions of group members are sufficiently dissimilar to justify giving them representation in decision making. Committees may be assigned tasks by the court or lead counsel, such as preparing briefs or conducting portions of the discovery program, but should not be formed to accomplish tasks that one lawyer can perform adequately. Great care must be taken, however, to avoid unnecessary duplication of efforts and to control fees and expenses. See *infra* section 24.21 on controlling attorneys' fees.

The types of appointments and assignments of responsibilities will depend on many factors, the most important of which is achieving efficiency and economy

---

59. The court may appoint (or the parties may select) a liaison for each side, and, if their functions are strictly limited to administrative matters, they need not be attorneys. *See In re* San Juan Dupont Plaza Hotel Fire Litig., 1989 WL 168401, at *19–20 (defining duties of "liaison persons" for plaintiffs and defendants).

without jeopardizing fairness to parties in the litigation. Depending on the number and complexity of different interests represented, both lead and liaison counsel may be appointed for one side, with only liaison counsel appointed for the other. The roles of liaison, lead, and trial counsel may be filled by one attorney or by several. The functions of lead counsel may be divided among several attorneys, but the number should not be so large as to defeat the purpose of making such appointments.

20.222 Powers and Responsibilities

The functions of lead, liaison, and trial counsel, and of each committee, should be stated in either a court order or a separate document drafted by counsel and reviewed and approved by the court.[60] This writing will inform other counsel and parties of the scope of authority conferred on designated counsel and define responsibilities within the group. It will usually be impractical and unwise, however, to spell out in detail the functions assigned or to specify the particular decisions that may be made unilaterally by designated counsel and those that may be made only with the concurrence of an affected party. To avoid controversy over the interpretation of the terms of the court's appointment order, designated counsel should seek consensus among the attorneys (and any unrepresented parties) when making decisions that may have a critical impact on the litigation.

Counsel selected for a position of leadership have an obligation to keep the other attorneys in the group advised of the progress of the litigation and consult them about decisions significantly affecting their clients. Counsel must use their judgment about this communication: too much may defeat the objectives of efficiency and economy, while too little may prejudice the interests of the parties. Communication among the various counsel on one side and their respective clients should not be treated as waiving work-product protection or the attorney–client privilege, and a specific court order on the point may be helpful.[61]

Judgment should also be exercised in dealing with disputes within the group, or indeed within a committee of counsel. An effort should first be made to achieve consensus, but if such an effort fails, members of the group may have to proceed on the matter individually or by subgroups. Individual action in particular may be necessary in connection with the examination of witnesses—examination in depositions or at trial by lead counsel should not preclude nonduplicative examination by another attorney with respect to matters peculiar to that attorney's client.

Designated counsel may be in an advantageous position to initiate, conduct, and evaluate settlement discussions for the group, since the designated counsel

---

60. See Sample Order *infra* § 41.31.
61. See Sample Order *infra* § 41.31, ¶ 5.

will communicate regularly with opposing counsel and be more familiar with developments in the case. Here they must be aware, however, of the limits of their authority to act on behalf of the group and of the potential for conflict between the interests of their clients and those of others in the group. Designated counsel should not bind the group without specific authority; nor should they, without court authorization, allow settlement discussions to interfere with their responsibility to move the litigation to trial on schedule. Because a serious problem can be created by offers of partial settlement made to clients of designated attorneys playing key roles in the conduct of the litigation, those attorneys must understand that their responsibilities in the litigation extend beyond the resolution of their own clients' involvement.

20.223 Compensation

Expenses incurred and fees earned by designated counsel acting in that capacity should not be borne solely by their clients, but rather shared equitably by all benefiting from their services. If possible, the terms and procedures for payment should be established by agreement among counsel, but subject to judicial approval and control (see *infra* section 24.214, compensation for designated counsel). Whether or not agreement is reached, the judge has the authority to order reimbursement and compensation and the obligation to ensure that the amounts are reasonable.[62] Terms and procedures should be established before substantial services are rendered and should provide for, among other things, the following: periodic billings during the litigation or creation of a fund through advance or ongoing assessments of members of the group; appropriate contributions from parties making partial settlements with respect to services already rendered by designated counsel; and contributions from parties in later filed or assigned cases who benefit from the earlier work of designated counsel.

Designated counsel should render services as economically as possible under the circumstances, avoiding unnecessary activity and limiting the number of persons attending conferences and depositions and working on briefs and other tasks. The court should make clear at the first pretrial conference that compensation will not be approved for unnecessary or duplicative activities or services. The court should also inform counsel what records should be kept and when they should be submitted to the court to support applications to recover fees and ex-

---

62. *See, e.g.*, Walitalo v. Iacocca, 968 F.2d 741 (8th Cir. 1992); Smiley v. Sincoff, 958 F.2d 498 (2d Cir. 1992); *In re* FTC Line of Business Report Litig., 626 F.2d 1022, 1027 (D.C. Cir. 1980); *In re* Air Crash Disaster at Fla. Everglades, 549 F.2d 1006, 1016 (5th Cir. 1977).

penses from coparties.[63] See *infra* section 24.21, which discusses ground rules and record keeping where attorneys' fees are awarded by the court.

20.224 Court's Responsibilities

Few decisions by the court in complex litigation are as difficult and sensitive as the appointment of designated counsel. Because of the stakes involved, competition for appointment is often intense, and judges need to be prepared to manage it appropriately. Appointment by the court will often be prized for the promise of large fees and a prominent role in the litigation. Negotiations and arrangements among attorneys of which the judge is not made aware may have a significant effect on positions taken in the proceedings. At the same time, because appointment of designated counsel will alter the usual dynamics of client representation in important ways, attorneys will have legitimate concerns that their clients' interests be adequately represented.

For these reasons, the judge needs to take an active part in making the decision on the appointment of counsel. Deferring to proposals by counsel without independent examination by the court, even those that seem to have the concurrence of a "majority" of those affected, invites problems down the road when designated counsel may turn out to be unwilling or unable to discharge their responsibilities in a manner satisfactory to the court or when excessive costs are incurred. The court should take the time necessary to make an assessment of the qualifications, functions, organization, and compensation of designated counsel. The court should satisfy itself that full disclosure has been made of all agreements and understandings among counsel, that the attorneys to be designated are competent for their assignments, that clear and satisfactory guidelines have been established for compensation and reimbursement, and that the arrangements for coordination among counsel are fair, reasonable, and efficient. The court should also ensure that designated counsel fairly represent the various interests in the litigation; where diverse interests exist among the parties, the court may designate a committee of counsel representing different interests.

Attorneys should not be appointed or approved by the court to serve as designated counsel unless they have the resources, the commitment, and the qualifications to accomplish the assigned tasks. They should be able to command the respect of their colleagues and work cooperatively with opposing counsel and the court. Prior experience in similar roles in other litigation may be useful, but past performance may also demonstrate that an attorney may have generated personal antagonisms that will undermine effectiveness in the present case or is oth-

---

63. See Sample Order *infra* § 41.32. Though these records may be filed under seal, the court should monitor them to determine that they are within the range of appropriate expenditure of time and expense.

erwise ill-suited for the contemplated assignment. Although the court should move expeditiously and avoid unnecessary delay, an evidentiary hearing may be needed to bring all relevant facts to light, or to allow counsel to state their case for appointment and answer questions from the court about their qualifications (the court may call for the submission of résumés and other relevant information). Such a hearing is particularly appropriate when the court is unfamiliar with the attorneys seeking appointment. The court should inquire as to normal or antici-pated billing rates, define record-keeping requirements, and establish guidelines, methods, or limitations to govern the award of fees.[64] While it may be appro-priate and possibly even beneficial for several firms to divide work among them-selves,[65] the court should satisfy itself that such an appointment is necessary and not simply the result of a bargain among the attorneys.[66]

The court's responsibilities are heightened in class action litigation, where the judge must approve counsel for the class (see *infra* section 30.16). In litigation in-volving both class and individual claims, class and individual counsel will need to coordinate.

20.225 Related Litigation

If related litigation is pending in other federal or state courts, the judges should consider the feasibility of coordination among counsel in the various cases. See *infra* sections 31.14 and 31.31. It may be possible through consultation with other judges to bring about the designation of common committees or of counsel and to enter joint or parallel orders governing their function and compensation.[67] Where that is not feasible, the judge may direct counsel to coordinate with the attorneys involved in the other cases to reduce duplication and potential conflicts and to further efficiency and economy through coordination and sharing of re-sources. In any event, it is desirable for the judges involved to exchange informa-tion and copies of orders that might affect proceedings in their courts. See gen-erally *infra* section 31, multiple litigation.

In approaching these matters, the court will want to consider the status of the respective actions (some may be close to trial while others are in their early stages), as well as the possibility that some later filed actions may have been filed in other courts by counsel seeking to gain a more prominent and lucrative role.

---

64. *See* Litigation Manual, *supra* note 5, at 19; see also *infra* § 24.21.

65. *In re* Fine Paper Antitrust Litig., 751 F.2d 562, 584 (3d Cir. 1984).

66. *See, e.g., Smiley,* 958 F.2d 498; *In re* Fine Paper Antitrust Litig., 98 F.R.D. 48 (E.D. Pa. 1983), *aff'd in part and rev'd in part,* 751 F.2d 562 (3d Cir. 1984).

67. See Sample Order *infra* § 41.51.

20.23 Withdrawal and Disqualification

In view of the number and dispersion of parties and interests in complex litigation, counsel should be particularly alert to the existence of present or potential conflicts of interest.[68] All attorneys and their firms should make an early and thorough conflict check—preferably before accepting representation—to determine whether the firm or any of its lawyers are presently representing or have in the past represented any other party in any matter substantially related to the present litigation. This check should take into account not only persons and companies formally aligned as adverse parties, but also companies and organizations affiliated with such parties, coparties whose posture might change as the litigation progresses, and persons or companies that might later be added as parties. Firms should also guard against disqualifying conflicts arising during the course of the litigation as a result of acceptance of new clients or taking on of new partners or associates. These checks and safeguards are particularly important for attorneys representing a class or seeking to act as lead counsel in multiparty litigation.[69]

Questions about possible disqualification of an attorney should be addressed as soon as they become known and promptly resolved. If a conflict arises or is discovered after representation has been taken on, the attorney may be required to withdraw, unless otherwise ordered by the court.[70] In case of a withdrawal, the attorney must take steps to avoid disrupting the litigation while protecting the former client's interests; this involves giving reasonable notice, allowing time for employment of a new attorney, and surrendering any papers or property to which the client is entitled.[71]

A conflict of interest may be ground for a motion to disqualify counsel. While motions for disqualification should be carefully reviewed to ensure that they are not being used merely to harass,[72] the court should order disqualification when a

---

68. *See* Model Rules of Professional Conduct 1.7–1.9; Model Code of Professional Responsibility DR 5-101(A), 5-105(A), 5-104(A); *see also* Model Rules of Professional Conduct 3.7; Model Code of Professional Responsibility 5-102 (lawyer as witness).

69. It is unsettled whether individual class members who are not named plaintiffs are considered "parties" for the purpose of disqualification; one case suggesting that they are is *In re* Cement Antitrust Litig., 688 F.2d 1297, 1308–13 (9th Cir. 1982) (upholding judge's recusal based on spouse's ownership of stock in class members), *aff'd under 28 U.S.C. § 2109, sub nom.* Arizona v. District Court, 459 U.S. 1191 (1983).

70. *See* Model Rules of Professional Conduct 1.16.

71. Model Rules of Professional Conduct Rule 1.6; *see also* Model Code of Professional Responsibility DR2-110(B), (C).

72. Panduit Corp. v. All States Plastic Mfg. Co., Inc., 744 F.2d 1564, 1577–80 (Fed. Cir. 1984); Optyl Eyewear Fashion Int'l Corp. v. Style Companies, Ltd., 760 F.2d 1045, 1050–51 (9th Cir. 1985).

reasonable likelihood of a prohibited conflict is demonstrated.[73] Where disqualification is sought on the ground that an attorney may be called as a witness, the court may deny the motion if the testimony is unlikely to be necessary and the prejudice to the client is likely to be minor.[74]

Motions for disqualification often raise ancillary legal issues requiring research into applicable circuit law; because uncertainty as to the status of counsel hampers the progress of the litigation, they should be addressed immediately and resolved promptly. Additional delays may result if appellate review is sought[75] or if replacement counsel are precluded from using the work product of the disqualified firm.[76] Issues raised by disqualification motions include whether disqualification of counsel extends to the entire firm,[77] whether cocounsel will also be disqualified,[78] and whether counsel may avoid disqualification based on con-

73. Though often premised on violations of state disciplinary rules, disqualification in federal court is a question of federal law. *In re* American Airlines, Inc., 972 F.2d 605, 615 (5th Cir. 1992); *In re* Dresser Indus., Inc., 972 F.2d 540, 543 (5th Cir. 1992).

74. *See, e.g.,* Cresswell v. Sullivan & Cromwell, 922 F.2d 60, 72–73 (2d Cir. 1990); Telectronics Proprietary, Ltd. v. Medtronic, Inc., 836 F.2d 1332, 1337 (Fed. Cir. 1988).

75. The denial of a motion to disqualify counsel in a civil case is not immediately appealable as a matter of right, Firestone Tire and Rubber Co. v. Risjord, 449 U.S. 368 (1981), nor is an order granting such a motion in a criminal case, Flanagan v. United States, 465 U.S. 259 (1984), or in a civil case, Richardson–Merrell, Inc. v. Koller, 105 S. Ct. 2757 (1985). A petition for a writ of mandamus may be filed even if there is no right of appeal; see Fed. R. App. P. 21, but the standard of review may be more stringent. *See In re Dresser*, 972 F.2d at 542–43.

76. While disqualified counsel usually must turn over his or her work product to new counsel upon request, *see* First Wisc. Mortg. Trust v. First Wisc. Corp., 584 F.2d 201, 207–11 (7th Cir. 1978) (en banc) *and* International Business Machs. Corp. v. Levin, 579 F.2d 271, 283 (3d Cir. 1978), the request may be denied when there is a danger that confidential information will be disclosed. EZ Paintr Corp. v. Padco, Inc., 746 F.2d 1459, 1463–64 (Fed. Cir. 1984).

77. *See* Model Rules of Professional Conduct Rule 1.10 (imputed disqualification); Model Rules of Professional Conduct DR5-105(D). *Compare Panduit*, 744 F.2d at 1577–80 *with* United States v. Moscony, 927 F.2d 742, 747–48 (3d Cir. 1991) *and* Atasi Corp. v. Seagate Technology, 847 F.2d 826, 830–32 (Fed. Cir. 1988). Timely erection of a "Chinese wall" to screen other firm members from the attorney(s) possessing confidential information may avoid imputed disqualification. *See, e.g.,* Blair v. Armontrout, 916 F.2d 1310, 133 (8th Cir. 1990); Kennecott Corp. v. Kyocera Int. Inc., *affirmance at* 899 F.2d 1228 (Fed. Cir. 1990) (unpublished opinion); United States v. Goot, 894 F.2d 231, 235 (7th Cir. 1990); Manning v. Waring, James, Sklar & Allen, 849 F.2d 222 (6th Cir. 1988); *Atasi,* 847 F.2d at 831 & n.5; *Panduit,* 744 F.2d at 1580–82; LaSalle Nat'l Bank v. County of Lake, 703 F.2d 252, 257–59 (7th Cir. 1983) (screening not timely). Disqualification of an attorney on the ground that he or she will be called as a witness generally does not require disqualification of the attorney's firm. *See Optyl Eyewear,* 760 F.2d at 1048–50; Bottaro v. Hatton Assoc., 680 F.2d 895, 898 (2d Cir. 1982).

78. Disqualification of counsel generally does not extend to cocounsel; *see, e.g.,* Brennan's, Inc. v. Brennan's Restaurants, Inc., 590 F.2d 168, 174 (5th Cir. 1979); Fred Weber, Inc. v. Shell Oil Co., 566 F.2d 602, 607–10 (8th Cir. 1977); Akerly v. Red Barn Sys., Inc., 551 F.2d 539, 543–44 (3d Cir. 1977); American Can Co. v. Citrus Feed Co., 436 F.2d 1125, 1129 (5th Cir. 1971), but disqualification is proper when information has been disclosed to cocounsel with an expectation of confidentiality. *See*

sent,[79] substantial hardship,[80] or express or implied waiver.[81] If the court determines that the motion has been improperly filed in order to harass, delay, or deprive a party of chosen counsel, it should consider appropriate sanctions under 28 U.S.C. § 1927 or Fed. R. Civ. P. 11 (see *supra* section 20.15).

Fund of Funds, Ltd. v. Arthur Andersen & Co., 567 F.2d 225, 235 (2d Cir. 1977); *cf.* State of Ark. v. Dean Food Prods. Co., 605 F.2d 380, 387–88 (8th Cir. 1979); *Brennan's*, 590 F.2d at 174.

79. *See, e.g.*, Unified Sewerage Agency v. Jelco, Inc., 646 F.2d 1339, 1345–46 (9th Cir. 1981); Interstate Properties v. Pyramid Co., 547 F. Supp. 178 (S.D.N.Y. 1982); *cf.* Westinghouse Elec. Corp. v. Gulf Oil Corp., 588 F.2d 221 (7th Cir. 1978).

80. Disqualification on the ground that an attorney is also a witness may be denied where it would cause "substantial hardship" to the client. Model Rules of Professional Conduct 3.7(a)(3); Model Code of Professional Responsibility DR 5-101(B)(4). This exception is generally invoked when disqualification is sought late in the litigation, and it requires the court to balance the interests of the client and the opposing party. Model Rule 3.7 comment at ¶ 3. It may be rejected when the likelihood that the attorney would have to testify should have been anticipated earlier in the case. *See* General Mill Supply Co. v. SCA Servs., Inc., 697 F.2d 704 (6th Cir. 1982).

81. *See, e.g.*, United States v. Wheat, 486 U.S. 153, 162–64 (1988) (court in criminal case may decline waiver of conflict); Melamed v. ITT Continental Baking Co., 592 F.2d 290, 292–94 (6th Cir. 1979) (waiver found); City of Cleveland v. Cleveland Elec. Illuminating Co., 440 F. Supp. 193, 205 (N.D. Ohio), *aff'd*, 573 F.2d 1310 (6th Cir. 1977) (same); *cf. In re* Yarn Processing Patent Validity Litig., 530 F.2d 83, 88–90 (5th Cir. 1976) (waiver and consent).

21. Pretrial Procedures

21.1 Preliminary Matters

21.11 Scheduling the Initial Conference

The first step in establishing control of the litigation is the scheduling of the initial conference with counsel. It should be scheduled promptly, generally within 30 to 60 days of filing, but sufficient time should be allowed for counsel to become familiar with the litigation and adequately prepare for the conference. The conference should occur before any adversary activity begins, such as filing of motions or discovery requests, and the order setting the conference may order that all such activity be deferred. Although Fed. R. Civ. P. 4(m) allows 120 days from filing to effect service, earlier service or appearance should be encouraged.[82] Notice of the conference and of any interim administrative measures may then be given even before responsive pleadings are filed. If the primary parties have been given notice, the court need not wait for service to be made on every party.

In preparing the order scheduling the conference,[83] reference should be made to Fed. R. Civ. P. 16(c), which lists subjects for consideration at such a conference. In addition, the court should consider the following matters:

- requiring counsel to meet and confer in advance to discuss claims and defenses, a plan for disclosure and discovery, and possible settlement;[84]

- identifying specific topics that the court expects to address at the conference;

- inviting suggestions from counsel for additional topics to address;

---

82. Instead of making formal service, plaintiff may request waiver of service under Fed. R. Civ. P. 4(d), but this will extend the time for filing a responsive pleading; see Fed. R. Civ. P. 4(d)(3), or, if defendant refuses to waive, postpone the making of effective service; see Fed. R. Civ. P. 4(d)(2)(F)—note that a refusal to waive service may create a statute of limitations problem since limitations are generally not tolled until formal service is effected. See Fed. R. Civ. P. 4 advisory committee's note. The waiver procedure may be most useful where the defendant is located in a foreign country (even though such a defendant may not be assessed costs of service if it fails to waive service), since otherwise such service must be made in accordance with the Hague Convention on the Service Abroad of Judicial and Extrajudicial Documents, Feb. 10, 1969, 20 U.S.T. 361, T.I.A.S. 6638, 658 U.N.T.S. 163, *reprinted* following Rule 4, if it applies. Volkswagenwerk Aktiengesellschaft v. Schlunk, 486 U.S. 694, 705 (1988). For more on this convention, see Bruno A. Ristau, International Judicial Assistance Part IV (1990).

83. See Sample Order *infra* § 41.2.

84. Such a conference of counsel prior to discovery and the Rule 16 conference is required by Fed. R. Civ. P. 26(f).

- directing counsel to submit a tentative statement, joint if possible, identifying disputed issues as specifically as possible;
- directing counsel to submit a proposed schedule for the conduct of the litigation, including a discovery plan (see *infra* section 21.421);
- calling on counsel to submit brief factual statements to assist the court in understanding the background, setting, and likely dimensions of the litigation;
- ordering the suspension of all discovery and motion activity pending further order of the court;
- specifying that statements provided in response to the order shall not be treated as admissions or be otherwise binding upon the parties; and
- directing counsel to provide information about all related litigation pending in other courts.

See also *infra* section 33.22 (mass torts, case-management orders).

21.12 Interim Measures

The court may also *sua sponte* initiate special procedures at the outset of the case, pending the initial conference, such as the following:[85]

- suspend temporarily some local rules, such as those requiring the appearance or association of local counsel or limiting the time for joining new parties;[86]
- create a single master file for the litigation, eliminating the need for multiple filings of similar documents when related cases have common parties;
- extend the time for filing responses to the complaint until after the initial conference, making unnecessary individual requests for extensions;
- reduce under Fed. R. Civ. P. 5 the number of parties upon whom service of documents must be made;[87]
- modify the timing of the initial disclosures required by Fed. R. Civ. P. 26(a)(1);[88]

---

85. See *infra* § 33.22 (case-management orders in mass tort litigation), Sample Order *infra* § 41.2.

86. Rule 6 of the Rules of Procedure of the Judicial Panel on Multidistrict Litigation provides that parties in actions transferred under 28 U.S.C. § 1407 may continue to be represented in the transferee district by existing counsel, without being required to obtain local counsel.

87. Liaison counsel may be appointed to receive service of all papers and distribute copies to cocounsel. See *supra* § 20.221.

88. See *infra* § 21.13.

- preclude or suspend discovery requests and responses until after the initial conference, except as permitted by order of the court in exceptional circumstances;
- provide for joint briefs and limit the length of briefs and appendices;
- order that records, files, and documents and other potential evidence not be destroyed without leave of court;[89] and
- appoint interim liaison counsel or committees of plaintiffs' or defense counsel.

21.13 Prediscovery Disclosure

Fed. R. Civ. P. 26(a)(1) requires parties to exchange certain core information within ten days of their initial discovery planning conference[90] without awaiting a discovery request.[91] The purpose of prediscovery disclosure is to avoid the cost of unnecessary formal discovery and to accelerate the exchange of basic information useful to the planning and conduct of discovery and to settlement negotiations. The rule should be administered to serve those purposes; disclosure should not place unreasonable or unnecessary burdens on the parties (it does not require disclosure of any information that would not have to be disclosed in response to discovery requests). In complex litigation, the application of this rule may therefore have to be modified or suspended entirely.

The scope of disputed issues and relevant facts may not be sufficiently clear from the pleadings to enable parties without further clarification to make the requisite disclosure. One purpose of the meeting of counsel required by Rule 26(f) is to identify issues and reach agreement on the content and timing of the initial disclosures. To the extent agreement cannot be reached by the parties at the conference, disclosure should be deferred until after the Rule 16 conference, at which the court can fashion an appropriate order defining and narrowing the factual and legal issues in dispute and, on the basis of that order, establish the scope of disclosure. This will require suspending, by stipulation or order, the rule's presumptive ten-day deadline for making disclosure.

Although the rule defines certain information that must be disclosed, it should not be seen as limiting the scope of prediscovery disclosure and exchange of information. Whether by agreement of counsel or court order, prediscovery

---

89. Because preservation orders may impose undue burdens on parties and be difficult to implement, the court should hold an early conference or hearing to work out appropriate terms for such orders. See *infra* § 21.442.

90. For discussion of the discovery planning conference see *infra* § 21.421. *See* Fed. R. Civ. P. 26(f). Rule 26(g) and Rule 37 provide for the imposition of sanctions for violation of Rule 26(a)(1).

91. Some districts have opted out of Rule 26(a)(1) or have adopted different disclosure requirements.

disclosure and exchange of substantial—though carefully defined—relevant information and materials can substantially reduce the need for discovery, facilitate issue definition and narrowing, speed and simplify the remaining discovery, and accelerate settlement. While the rule does not require actual production (except for damage computations and insurance agreements) but only identification of relevant information and materials, the court may call on the parties to produce and exchange materials in advance of discovery, subject to appropriate objections. Although the court needs to guard against imposing excessive and unnecessary burdens on the parties, effective use of this device can streamline the litigation.

Rule 26(e)(1) requires parties at appropriate intervals to correct or supplement disclosures if they learn that the information (even if correct when supplied) is materially incomplete or incorrect, unless the corrective or additional information has already been made known to the other parties during discovery or in writing. The parties or the court should set a schedule for such supplementation and may wish to qualify or clarify the scope of the obligation to supplement in order to fit the particular litigation.

21.2 Conferences

Fed. R. Civ. P. 16 authorizes the court to hold pretrial conferences in civil cases as it deems advisable. These conferences serve as the principal means of implementing judicial management of litigation. Although Rules 16(a) and (c) suggest, respectively, appropriate purposes for these conferences and subjects to discuss, these provisions are not intended to be exhaustive. This section discusses the use of conferences in complex litigation, with reference both to matters found in the rule and to others in aid of effective management.

21.21 Initial Conference and Orders

The initial conference launches the process of managing the litigation. It provides the first opportunity for the judge to meet counsel, hear their views of the factual and legal issues in the litigation, and begin to structure the litigation and establish a management plan for later proceedings. It is therefore crucial that the judge, as well as the attorneys, be prepared to address the range of topics that the conference should cover. The principal topics (discussed in detail in the following section) include:

- the nature and potential dimensions of the litigation;
- the major procedural and substantive problems likely to be encountered; and
- the procedures for efficient management.

The judge should make clear that the conference is not a perfunctory exercise. The tone needs to be set to make it productive, with counsel being adequately prepared, avoiding contentiousness, and acting with professional courtesy. The judge, for his or her part, needs to promptly make the necessary rulings. The success of the conference depends on the establishment and subsequent maintenance of effective communication and coordination between counsel and among counsel and the court (see *supra* section 20.22).

21.211 Case-Management Plan

The primary objective of the conference is to develop (subject to later revision and refinement) a plan for the "just, speedy, and inexpensive determination" of the litigation. This plan should include procedures for identifying and resolving disputed issues of law, identifying and narrowing disputed issues of fact, carrying out disclosure and conducting discovery in an efficient and economical manner, and preparing for trial if the case is not resolved by settlement or summary disposition. The agenda for the conference needs to be tailored to the needs of the particular litigation. Following is a checklist of topics relevant to the development of case-management plans (see also *infra* section 33.22 and checklist at *infra* section 40.1):

- identification and narrowing of issues of fact and law (see *infra* section 21.33);
- deadlines and limits on joinder of parties and amended or additional pleadings (see *infra* section 21.32);

- coordination with related litigation (both in federal and state courts), including later filings, removals, or transfers (see *infra* section 31);
- early resolution of jurisdictional issues;
- severance of issues for trial (see *infra* section 21.632);
- consolidation of trials (see *infra* section 21.631);
- the possibility of referring some matters to magistrate judges, special masters, or other judges (see *supra* sections 20.122, 20.14, and *infra* section 21.5);
- appointment of liaison/lead/trial counsel and special committees, and maintenance of time and expense records by counsel (see *supra* sections 20.22, 24.211);
- reduction in filing and service requirements through use of a master file and orders under Fed. R. Civ. P. 5 (see *supra* section 21.12 and *infra* section 31);
- exemption from or modification of local rules, standing orders, or provisions of the court's Civil Justice Reform Act plan (see *supra* section 21.12);
- applicability and enforceability of arbitration clauses;[92]
- plans for prompt determination of class action questions, including a schedule for discovery and briefing on class issues (see *infra* sections 21.213, 30.11);
- management of disclosure and discovery, including such matters as:

    –preservation of evidence (see *infra* section 21.442);

    –use of document depositories and computerized storage (see *infra* section 21.444);

    –adoption of a uniform numbering system for documents (see *infra* section 21.441);

    –informal discovery and other cost-reduction measures (see *supra* section 21.13 (prediscovery disclosure) and *infra* section 21.423);

    –procedures for resolving discovery disputes (see *infra* sections 21.424, 21.456);

---

92. *See, e.g.,* Volt Info. Sciences, Inc. v. Board of Trustees, 489 U.S. 468 (1989); Shearson/American Express, Inc. v. McMahon, 482 U.S. 220 (1987); Perry v. Thomas, 482 U.S. 483 (1987); Mitsubishi Motors Corp. v. Soler Chrysler–Plymouth, Inc., 473 U.S. 614 (1985); Dean Witter Reynolds Inc. v. Byrd, 470 U.S. 213 (1985); Moses H. Cone Memorial Hosp. v. Mercury Const. Corp., 460 U.S. 1 (1983).

−protective orders and procedures for handling claims of confidentiality and privilege (see *infra* section 21.43); and

−sequencing and limitations, including specific scheduling and deadlines (see *infra* sections 21.212, 21.421–21.422, 21.451, 21.462);

- procedures for management of expert testimony (see *infra* sections 21.48, 21.51 (court-appointed experts));
- schedules and deadlines for completion of various pretrial phases of the case and the setting of a tentative or firm trial date (see *infra* section 21.212);
- consideration of any unresolved issues of recusal or disqualification (see *supra* section 20.121);
- prospects for settlement (see *infra* section 23.1) or possible referral to mediation or other dispute resolution procedures (see *infra* section 23.15); and
- any other special procedures that may facilitate management of the litigation.

Rule 16(e) requires that following the conference the court enter an order reciting any action taken. The order should address the various matters on the agenda and other matters conducive to the effective management of the litigation.[93] It should memorialize all rulings, agreements, or other actions taken, and it should set a date for the next conference or other event in the litigation. Counsel may be directed to promptly submit a proposed order.

21.212 Scheduling Order

Scheduling orders are a critical element of case management. They help ensure that counsel will complete the work called for by the management plan in timely fashion and prevent the litigation from languishing on the court's docket. Rule 16(b) requires that a scheduling order issue early in every case, setting deadlines for joinder of parties, amendment of pleadings, filing of motions, and completion of discovery. Scheduling orders in complex litigation should also cover other important steps in the process of the litigation, in particular discovery activities and motion practice; scheduling orders should be informed by the parties' discovery plan submitted pursuant to Rule 26(f) (see *infra* section 21.421).[94] An order may also:

- modify the time set by Rule 26(a)(1) for initial disclosure and set dates for its supplementation under Rule 26(e)(1) (see *supra* section 21.13);[95]

---

93. For an illustrative list of items, see *infra* § 33.22.
94. Fed. R. Civ. P. 16(d).
95. Fed. R. Civ. P. 16(b)(4).

- establish a schedule for amendment of discovery responses as required by Rule 26(e)(2);[96]
- set dates for future conferences (see *infra* section 21.22), the final pretrial conference (see *infra* section 21.6), and trial; and
- provide for any other matters appropriate in the circumstances of the case.[97]

Some courts defer the scheduling conference to a time following the initial conference when additional information may have been gathered. It should, however, be held soon after the initial conference, both to maintain momentum and to comply with the rule requiring the scheduling order to issue "as soon as practicable" and within 90 days of a defendant's appearance and 120 days of service. In any event, the scheduling order should be based on information and recommendations from the parties, rather than on a standard form. Developments in the litigation may call for subsequent modification of a scheduling order entered early in the litigation.

21.213 Class Actions

When actions include claims by or against a class, the court should consider the appropriate procedure for dealing with the certification issues. In most cases, a schedule should be set at the initial conference for an early ruling on class certification. Class certification or the denial thereof will usually have a substantial impact on further proceedings in the litigation, including the scope of discovery, the definition of issues, the length and complexity of trial, and the opportunities for settlement. Indeed, denial of class certification may put a practical end to the litigation. The court should ascertain what discovery on class questions is needed before a ruling on certification and how such discovery can be conducted efficiently and economically. Other discovery may be stayed if the court believes that resolution of the certification issue may obviate some or all further proceedings, but if bifurcating class discovery from merits discovery would result in significant duplication of effort and expense to the parties, discovery may proceed concurrently.

For a detailed discussion of the principles and procedures involved in the management of class actions, see *infra* section 30—for discovery in class actions, see *infra* section 30.12.

---

96. The rule requires parties to amend most discovery responses "seasonably" if they learn that the response is materially "incomplete or incorrect and if the additional or corrective information has not otherwise been made known to the other parties during the discovery process or in writing." To maintain order and clarify counsel's responsibilities, the scheduling order may specify a series of dates on which the parties must provide any amendment required.

97. Fed. R. Civ. P. 16(b)(6).

21.214 Settlement

At each conference, the judge should explore the settlement posture of the parties and the techniques, methods, and mechanisms that may lead to a resolution of the litigation short of trial. While settlement is most advantageous early in the litigation (before much time and money have been expended), meaningful negotiations may not be possible until specific critical discovery has been conducted and the parties have acquired a fuller understanding of the strengths and weaknesses of their respective cases. Discovery may be targeted for this purpose, but settlement discussions should not be permitted to delay or sidetrack the pretrial process. See the discussion at *infra* section 23.11. Counsel should advise the court promptly when an agreement has been reached or is imminent.

21.22 Subsequent Conferences

Conferences following the initial conference are a useful device to monitor the progress of the case and to address problems as they arise in the litigation. Conferences should be scheduled well in advance to ensure maximum attendance. While some judges schedule conferences only as the need arises, others have found it effective to schedule conferences at regular and frequent intervals, with agendas composed of items suggested by the parties or designated by the court. Perfunctory appearances by counsel should be avoided, however. Parties may be directed to confer and submit written reports in advance of each conference so that it may be canceled if it appears unnecessary.

Conferences may also be held in conjunction with motion hearings. No conference should be adjourned without setting the date for the next conference or report from counsel; maintaining firm return dates will ensure that the litigation moves ahead. Between conferences, the court may remain advised of the progress of the case through written status reports or by conference telephone calls. When the court has scheduled a conference, it should distribute to counsel an agenda of items to be addressed, perhaps after calling for suggestions from counsel.

Although "off-the-record" discussions may promote greater candor, on-the-record conferences will avoid later disagreements—particularly important if the judge anticipates issuing oral directions or rulings. Many judges find it preferable to hold all conferences on the record[98] and, particularly where there are numerous attorneys, in the courtroom. Nevertheless, depending on the specific circumstances and the personalities of the judge and the attorneys, an informal conference held off the record in chambers or by telephone can be more productive; a reporter can later be brought in to record the results of the conference. As stated above, Rule 16 requires (and sound practice dictates) that all matters decided at

---

98. For the requirements for recording various proceedings, see 28 U.S.C. § 753(b).

pretrial conferences be memorialized on the record or in a written order. Counsel may be directed to submit proposed orders incorporating the court's oral rulings.

When discovery and other pretrial matters have been substantially completed, the court should hold a final pretrial conference.[99] This conference should be held once a firm trial date has been set, usually about thirty to sixty days before that date. More than one such conference may be needed, particularly if more than one trial is to be held. See *infra* section 21.6.

21.23 Attendance

All attorneys and unrepresented parties should attend the initial pretrial conference. Requirements for attendance at subsequent conferences should be determined based on the purposes of each conference. Costs can be reduced by relieving counsel from the obligation to attend when their clients have no substantial interest in the matters to be discussed or when their interests will be fully represented by designated counsel. While the court should not bar any attorney's attendance, it can advise that attorneys who appear unnecessarily will not be entitled to claim court-awarded fees for that time. Similarly, the court may minimize attorneys' fees by authorizing compensation only for more junior attorneys at routine conferences. On the other hand, as Rule 16(c) requires, each party participating in a conference should be represented by an attorney with authority to enter into stipulations and make admissions as to all matters the participants may reasonably anticipate will be discussed at that conference. Lead trial counsel should always attend the final pretrial conference. Rule 16(f) allows the court to impose sanctions for unexcused nonattendance at any conference. See *infra* section 41.2 ¶ 2.

Rule 16 also authorizes the court to require persons with authority to settle to attend or make themselves available by telephone. This includes insurance carriers or their representatives when their interests are implicated and their presence will facilitate settlement. On the other hand, the presence of parties, while it may facilitate settlement or stipulations, can inhibit counsel and reduce cooperation. If parties do attend, they can periodically be excused from discussions with counsel, but this in turn may undermine the parties' confidence in their attorneys and in the fairness of the proceedings.

The court may also invite a magistrate judge or special master to whom matters to be discussed at the conference have been or may be referred, as well as counsel involved in related litigation.

---

99. *See* Fed. R. Civ. P. 16(d).

21.3 Management of Issues

21.31 Relationship to Discovery

The *sine qua non* of management of complex litigation rests on the definition of the issues in the litigation (see *infra* section 21.33). Unless the controverted issues have been identified and defined, the materiality of facts and the scope of discovery (and later of the trial) cannot be determined. The pleadings, however, will often fail to define the issues with clarity, and the parties may lack sufficient information at the outset of the case to enable them to arrive at definitions with certainty. Probably the most important function the judge performs in the early stages of litigation management is to press the parties toward identification, definition, and narrowing of issues. The initial conference should be used to start this process.

Efforts to clarify and narrow the issues may be met by resistance from the plaintiffs, the defendants, or both—plaintiffs asserting that substantial discovery must first be conducted, and defendants contending that plaintiffs must first refine their claims. Nonetheless, the judge must start the process of defining and structuring the issues, albeit tentatively, to establish the appropriate sequence and limits for discovery.

Although some issues may surface only after discovery is underway, the controlling factual and legal issues can almost always be identified by a thorough and candid discussion with counsel at the initial conference. The court should use the pleadings and the positions of the parties developed at the initial conference as a starting point for identifying the issues on the basis of which to construct the discovery plan. Discovery may then provide information for the further defining and narrowing of issues, which may in turn lead to revision and refinement of the initial discovery plan.

21.32 Pleading and Motion Practice

The process of defining and narrowing issues will be advanced if pleadings are finalized and emerging legal issues are promptly resolved by appropriate motions.

The court should first establish a schedule for the filing of all pleadings in the case, including counterclaims, cross claims, third-party complaints, and amendments to existing pleadings adding parties, claims, or defenses, to avoid later enlargement of issues and expansion or duplication of discovery. The court may also suspend filing of certain pleadings if statutes of limitations present no problems and make orders providing that specified pleadings, motions, and orders, unless specifically disavowed by a party, are "deemed" filed in cases later brought, transferred, or removed, without actually filing the document (see Sample Order *infra* section 41.52).

The pleadings may disclose issues of law that can be resolved by motion to dismiss, to strike, or for judgment on the pleadings. Challenges to the court's personal or subject matter jurisdiction should generally be given priority, since they are dispositive. The legal insufficiency of a claim or defense may be raised by motion for failure to state a claim or for partial judgment on the pleadings. If the court considers evidence in connection with such a motion, the motion must be treated as one for summary judgment.[100] Insufficient defenses and irrelevant or duplicative matter may be stricken under Rule 12(f). If a motion concerns a pivotal issue which may materially advance the termination of the litigation, the court may certify its ruling for interlocutory appeal under 28 U.S.C. § 1292(b) if, in the court's judgment, there is "substantial ground for difference of opinion." The court may also provide for appellate review by entering final judgment as to a particular claim or party under Fed. R. Civ. P. 54(b). See *infra* section 25.1.

Motion practice can be a source of substantial cost and delay unless appropriately managed. Following are some points to consider:

- Because a motion under Rule 12 can result in unnecessary expense if the asserted defect can be cured by amendment, it is generally advisable for a party to notify the opposing party and the court of its intention to file such a motion to ascertain whether it will serve to narrow the issues in the case.

- Some courts have found prefiling conferences useful in avoiding useless or unnecessary motions.

- Some motions can be decided on the basis of oral presentations and reference to controlling authority, without the filing of briefs.

- The court may limit the length of briefs and of appendices, affidavits, declarations, and other supporting materials, and require joint briefs whenever feasible.

- The court may limit the filing of reply or supplemental briefs, or motions for reconsideration, requiring leave of court for good cause shown.

- Prompt rulings by the court will expedite the litigation and result in savings by avoiding unnecessary litigation activity by the parties; whenever possible, judges should rule from the bench, avoiding the delay caused by the preparation of a written disposition.

---

100. Fed. R. Civ. P. 12(b), (c). For discussion of summary judgment, see *infra* § 21.34.

- Some courts issue tentative rulings on motions in advance of the motion hearing. If the parties accept the rulings, no hearing is necessary. If there is a hearing, the parties can direct their arguments to the issues that concern the court.

- In multiparty litigation, particular attention needs to be given to scheduling. Counsel should be directed to inform the court as soon as possible of any motion to be filed, with sufficient time allowed for opposing counsel to respond and the court to review the parties' submissions in advance. Expedited motions should be avoided unless they concern matters that will delay further proceedings if not resolved. Motion hearings should be specially set rather than be part of a regular motion docket or calendar call of the court, but they may be combined with other conferences in the litigation.

21.33 Identifying, Narrowing, and Resolving Issues

As noted, the process of identifying, defining, and narrowing issues begins at the initial conference. The attorneys may be directed to confer and submit a tentative statement of disputed issues in advance, agreed on to the extent possible (see *supra* section 21.11). The court should treat the conference as an opportunity to learn about the material facts and legal issues, and counsel should treat it as an opportunity to educate the judge. At the same time, counsel will learn about the opponent's case and gain a better perspective on their own, helping them to evaluate their case more realistically. For the process to be productive, the judge must be willing to admit ignorance and ask even basic questions. The court's questions should probe into the parties' claims and defenses and seek *specific* information. The judge, instead of being satisfied, for example, with a statement that defendant "was negligent" or "breached the contract," should insist that the attorneys describe the material facts they intend to prove and the manner in which they intend to prove them.

The judge should inquire not only into the amount of damages claimed but also into the proposed proof and manner of computation, including the evidence of causation, and the specific nature of any other relief sought (data which may also be subject to mandatory prediscovery disclosure, see *supra* section 21.13). Similar inquiry should be made of the defense: what specific allegations and claims it disputes, the specific defenses it intends to raise, and the proof it intends to offer. This process should lead to identification of the genuine disputes and may facilitate admissions and stipulations between the parties, eliminating the need to litigate undisputed issues and narrowing the scope of the remaining issues. The parties may be able to stipulate to the authenticity of documents or the accuracy of underlying statistical or technical data while reserving the right to dispute assumptions, interpretations, or inferences drawn from the evidence.

Facts may be shown to be subject to judicial notice, after the opposing party has had an opportunity to proffer contradictory evidence.[101]

A variety of techniques have been used to facilitate the identification, defining, and narrowing of issues in complex litigation, including the following:

- nonbinding statements of counsel, such as those that may be required at the initial conference (see *supra* section 21.11)—these may be updated periodically by written reports or oral statements at later conferences;

- voluntary abandonment of tenuous claims or defenses by the parties, often after probing by the court into the likelihood of success and the potential disadvantages of pursuing them;

- requiring counsel to list the essential elements of the cause of action— this exercise, designed to clarify the claims, may assist in identifying elements in dispute and can result in abandonment of essentially duplicative theories of recovery;

- formal amendments to the pleadings, including those resulting from an order under Fed. R. Civ. P. 12 striking allegations or requiring a more definite statement;

- use of the court's powers under Fed. R. Civ. P. 16(c)(1) to eliminate insubstantial claims or defenses;[102]

- contention interrogatories (see *infra* section 21.461) and requests for admission (see *infra* section 21.47), especially when served after adequate opportunity for relevant discovery;

- rulings on motions for full or partial summary judgment (see *infra* section 21.34);

- sanctions for violations of Fed. R. Civ. P. 16, 26, and 37 in the form of orders precluding certain contentions or proof (see *supra* section 20.15);

- requiring, with respect to one or more issues, that the parties present a detailed statement of their contentions, with supporting facts and evidence (see *infra* section 21.641)—the statements may be exchanged, with each party marking those parts it disputes; the order directing this proce-

---

101. *See* Fed. R. Evid. 201; Tampa Elec. Co. v. Nashville Coal Co., 365 U.S. 320, 332 (1949); William J. Flittie, *Judicial Notice in the Trial of Complex Cases,* 31 Sw. L.J. 819, 829–39 (1978).

102. *See, e.g.,* Diaz v. Schwerman Trucking Co., 709 F.2d 1371, 1375 n.6 (11th Cir. 1983) (noting trial court's power under Rule 16 to summarily decide matters where no issue of fact exists); Holcomb v. Aetna Life Ins. Co., 255 F.2d 577, 580–81 (10th Cir. 1958) (trial court may enter judgment at Rule 16 pretrial conference if no issue of fact); Fed. R. Civ. P. 16(c) advisory committee's note; *cf.* Fox v. Taylor Diving & Salvage Co., 694 F.2d 1349, 1356–57 (5th Cir. 1983) (judge may summarily dispose of unsupportable claim after Rule 16 conference held during recess in trial).

dure will provide that other issues or contentions are then precluded and no additional evidence may be offered absent good cause;

- requiring the parties to present in advance of trial proposed instructions in jury cases (see *infra* sections 21.65, 22.43), or proposed findings of fact and conclusions of law in nonjury cases (see *infra* section 22.52);
- conducting preliminary hearings under Fed. R. Evid. 104 on objections to evidence (see *infra* section 21.642); and
- conducting a separate trial under Fed. R. Civ. P. 42(b) of issues that may render unnecessary or substantially alter the scope of further discovery or trial (see *infra* section 21.632); special verdicts and interrogatories (see *infra* section 21.633) may be helpful, and on some issues the parties may waive jury trial (see *infra* section 21.62).

21.34 Summary Judgment

Summary judgment motions can help define, narrow, and resolve issues. As the Supreme Court has stated, summary judgment is "not . . . a disfavored procedural shortcut, but rather . . . an integral part of the Federal Rules."[103] If granted, summary judgment may eliminate the need for further proceedings or at least reduce the scope of discovery or trial. Even if denied, in whole or in part, the parties' formulations of their positions may help clarify and define issues and the scope of further discovery. In addition, the court may, under Fed. R. Civ. P. 56(d), issue an order specifying those facts which "appear without substantial controversy" and shall be "deemed established" for trial purposes.

Summary judgment proceedings can, however, be costly and time consuming. To avoid the filing of unproductive motions, the court may require a prefiling conference at which it can ascertain whether issues are appropriate for summary judgment, whether there are disputed issues of fact, and whether the motion, even if granted, is likely to expedite the termination of the litigation. In some circumstances, a separate trial of an issue bifurcated under Rule 42(b) may be a preferable alternative.

Although summary judgment is as appropriate in complex litigation as in routine cases[104]—indeed it offers the potential of substantial savings of money and time—and, as a general proposition, the standard for deciding a summary judgment motion is the same in all cases,[105] the court needs to be concerned with

---

103. Celotex v. Catrett, 477 U.S. 317, 329 (1986).

104. *See* Matsushita Elec. Indus. Co. v. Zenith Radio Corp., 475 U.S. 574 (1986) (approving grant of summary judgment in complex antitrust case).

105. *See* William W Schwarzer et al., The Analysis and Decision of Summary Judgment Motions (Federal Judicial Center 1991), *reprinted in* 139 F.R.D. 441 (1992) [hereinafter Summary Judgment]. For U.S. Supreme Court cases discussing the standard and the parties' respective burdens, see

whether the record is adequately developed to support summary judgment. Complex litigation may present complicated issues not as readily susceptible to resolution as issues in more familiar settings. More extensive discovery may be necessary to ensure an adequate record for decision.[106] The party opposing summary judgment should, however, be required to make the necessary showing under Rule 56(f) in support of its request for additional discovery.[107]

To avoid expenditure of effort on pretrial activities that may be rendered unnecessary if the motion is granted, the schedule should call for filing of the motion as early as possible to maximize the potential benefits that may be realized from its disposition while affording the parties an adequate opportunity to conduct discovery relevant to the issues raised by the motion, obtain needed evidence, and develop a sufficient record for decision.[108] Allowing adequate time for preparation before the motion is filed should reduce the need for granting the opposing party a continuance under Rule 56(f) to obtain affidavits or conduct further discovery to oppose the motion. In support of its request for a continuance, the party must specify (1) the discovery it proposes to take, (2) the evidence likely to be uncovered, and (3) the material fact issues that evidence will support.

Under Rule 56(c), the court is to rule on the motion on the basis of "the pleadings, depositions, answers to interrogatories, and admissions on file, together with the affidavits."[109] The affidavits "shall be made on personal knowledge, shall set forth such facts as would be admissible in evidence, and shall show affirmatively that the affiant is competent to testify to the matters stated therein."[110] Because of the volume of discovery materials in complex litigation, and the potential for disputes over admissibility, these provisions can be a par-

---

Eastman Kodak v. Image Technical Servs., 112 S. Ct. 2072 (1992); *Celotex,* 477 U.S. 317; Anderson v. Liberty Lobby, Inc., 477 U.S. 242 (1986); *Matsushita,* 475 U.S. 574.

106. *See* William W Schwarzer and Alan Hirsch, *Summary Judgment After Eastman Kodak,* 45 Hastings L.J. 1 (1993).

107. *See, e.g.,* Keebler Co. v. Murray Bakery Prods., 866 F.2d 1386, 1388–90 (Fed. Cir. 1989); Dowling v. Philadelphia, 855 F.2d 136, 139–40 (3d Cir. 1988); VISA v. Bankcard Holders, 784 F.2d 1472, 1475 (9th Cir. 1986).

108. *See Celotex,* 477 U.S. at 327 (court must allow "adequate time" for discovery); *Anderson,* 477 U.S. at 2525 n.5 (nonmoving party must have opportunity to discover information "essential to [its] opposition"). The court must use its discretion to determine what constitutes "adequate time" and what information is "essential" in opposition; requiring all discovery to be completed before entertaining the motion defeats the purpose of summary judgment.

109. Fed. R. Civ. P. 56(c). The court may also hold an evidentiary hearing under Fed. R. Civ. P. 43(e), but when the motion cannot be decided because the parties' submissions are unclear, the court may instead simply require additional, clarifying submissions.

110. Fed. R. Civ. P. 56(e). The requirements of personal knowledge and admissibility in evidence presumably apply also to the use of depositions and interrogatory answers. *See* 10A Charles A. Wright et al., Federal Practice and Procedure § 2722 (2d ed. 1983).

ticular source of problems for the court. The court should direct the moving party to specify the material facts claimed to be undisputed; it should direct the opposing party to specify the evidence upon which a claimed factual dispute is based.[111] Objections to evidence may be resolved by a hearing under Fed. R. Evid. 104, if necessary.[112] Each party should also be required to submit a clear and unambiguous statement of the theories of its case. Such statements in the motion and the opposition will minimize the risk of error, as will the issuance of a tentative ruling by the court before hearing the motion. The court should fix a schedule for the filing of moving and opposition papers (and replies, if needed).

The ruling on the motion should be in writing or be read into the record, and it should lay out the court's reasoning. The court should try to decide such motions promptly; deferring rulings on summary judgment motions until the final pretrial conference tends to defeat their purpose of expediting the disposition of issues.

21.4 Discovery

---

111. For example, the parties should identify relevant deposition evidence by deponent, date, place of deposition, and page numbers; similarly detailed information should be provided for all other evidence submitted. Copies of relevant materials should be included with the moving and opposing papers. *See* Summary Judgment, *supra* note 105, at 480–81 & n.221; Schneider v. TRW, Inc., 938 F.2d 986, 990 n.2 (9th Cir. 1991).

112. *See In re* Japanese Elec. Prods. Antitrust Litig., 723 F.2d 238, 260 (3d Cir. 1983).

Discovery in complex litigation, characterized by multiple parties, difficult issues, voluminous evidence, and large numbers of witnesses, tends to proliferate and become excessively costly, time consuming, and burdensome. Early and ongoing judicial control is therefore imperative for effective management. The Federal Rules of Civil Procedure, along with the court's inherent power to manage the litigation before it, provide ample authority.[113]

For a checklist for discovery and prediscovery disclosure, see *infra* section 40.2.

21.41 Relationship to Issues[114]

Fundamental to control is that discovery be directed at the material issues in controversy. The general principle governing the scope of discovery stated in Rule 26(b)(1) permits discovery of matters "relevant to the subject matter . . . [of] the action" if "[t]he information sought . . . appears reasonably calculated to lead to the discovery of admissible evidence." But Rule 26(b)(2) directs the court to limit the frequency and extent of use of the discovery methods permitted by the rules, to prevent "unreasonably cumulative or duplicative" discovery and discovery for which "the burden or expense . . . outweighs its likely benefit, taking into account

---

113. *See* Oppenheimer Fund, Inc. v. Sanders, 437 U.S. 340, 350–54 (1978); Herbert v. Lando, 441 U.S. 153, 177 (1979).

114. See also *supra* § 21.31 (management of issues; relationship to discovery).

the needs of the case . . . the importance of the issues at stake . . . and the importance of the proposed discovery in resolving the issues." Application of this underlying principle of proportionality means that even in complex litigation, conducting discovery does not call for leaving no stone unturned.

Early identification and clarification of issues (see *supra* section 21.3) is therefore essential to meaningful and fair discovery control. It enables the court to assess the materiality and relevance of proposed discovery and provides the basis for formulating a fair and effective discovery plan. A plan established early in the litigation needs to take into account the possibility of revisions based on information gained through discovery, while seeking to avoid duplicative discovery. The costs and benefits of alternative approaches to the sequencing of discovery should be considered. For example, deferring discovery on damages until liability has been decided may result in savings, but may also lead to duplication should discovery have to be resumed. Conversely, conducting discovery on damages before discovery on liability will sometimes facilitate early settlement by informing the parties of their potential exposure, but may prove to have been unnecessary if the defendant is found not liable.

21.42 Planning and Control

A discovery plan should be designed to facilitate the orderly and cost-effective acquisition of relevant information and materials and the prompt resolution of discovery disputes. No single format is appropriate for all cases; the discovery plan should be tailored to the circumstances of the litigation. While the court needs to take responsibility for the adoption of a discovery plan, its development and implementation must necessarily be a collaborative effort with counsel. Because the lawyers will be more familiar with the case, the court should call on them initially to propose a plan. Agreement among counsel is, of course, desirable, and joint recommendations should be given considerable weight. Nevertheless the judge should not accept them uncritically and may need to place limits on discovery even if agreed on by counsel. The judge's role is to oversee the plan and provide guidance and control, always recognizing that the litigation is conducted by the lawyers and not the court. In performing that role, the judge, while recognizing his or her limited familiarity with the case, should not as a result abdicate the responsibility for control. Judges should not hesitate to ask counsel why particular discovery is needed and whether needed information can be obtained more efficiently and economically by other means. Regular contact with counsel through periodic conferences will enable the court to monitor the progress of the plan, ensure that it is operating fairly and effectively, and from time to time adjust it as needed.

21.421 Discovery Plan/Scheduling Conference

Adoption of a discovery plan is one of the principal purposes of the initial conference.[115] That conference should be preceded by a meeting of counsel for the purpose of developing a discovery plan for submission to the court.[116] Rule 26(f) requires such a meeting,[117] and Rule 26(d) bars discovery, absent stipulation or court order,[118] before that meeting.[119] Within ten days after the meeting the parties must submit to the court a written report outlining the plan.[120] The plan is to address:

- the form and timing of disclosure;
- the subjects of and completion date for discovery; and
- the possibility of phasing, limiting, or focusing discovery in light of the issues.

The parties' submission will be the starting point for the development of the plan. The court should hold the parties to their responsibility under Rule 26(f) and, if necessary, direct them to resume discussion to prepare a useful proposed plan.[121] Orderly management of the litigation will ordinarily be served by deferring commencement of discovery until after adoption of a plan.

Subjects for consideration at the conference bearing on the discovery plan may include the following:

---

115. *See* Fed. R. Civ. P. 16(c)(6). See also *supra* §§ 21.11, 21.33.

116. For a discussion of the factors to be considered in formulating a discovery plan, see William W Schwarzer et al., Civil Discovery and Mandatory Disclosure (1994).

117. The rule places joint responsibility on the attorneys of record and all unrepresented parties to arrange, attend (or be represented at), and participate in good faith in the conference.

118. The one exception is found in Rule 30(a)(2)(C), which allows a deposition to be taken before the discovery conference if the notice contains a certification, with supporting facts, that the deponent is expected to leave the United States and be unavailable for examination in this country unless deposed before that time. Such a deposition may not be used against a party who demonstrates that it was unable through diligence to obtain counsel to represent it at the deposition. Fed. R. Civ. P. 32(a)(3).

119. Some courts have local rules that allow preconference discovery; Rule 26(d) expressly provides that such rules supersede its general prohibition on such discovery. It may be appropriate for the court to enter a specific order on the matter in the particular litigation.

120. For a sample report, see form 35 of the *Fed. R. Civ. P. Appendix of Forms*.

121. Rule 37(g) allows the court, after opportunity for hearing, to assess reasonable costs, including attorneys' fees, against a party or attorney failing to participate in good faith in the development and submission of a proposed discovery plan as required by Rule 26(f).

- detailed examination of the specifics of proposed discovery in light of the provisions of Rule 26(b)(2) calling for

    –limiting discovery that is cumulative, duplicative, more convenient or less burdensome or expensive to obtain from another source, or seeks information the party has had ample opportunity to obtain; and

    –balancing the burden and expense of any discovery sought against its benefit, considering the need for the discovery, the importance of the amount or issues at stake, and the parties' resources;

    (These provisions confront the parties with the need to make choices; some documents may remain undiscovered and some discovery forgone. Parties need also to avoid early, unproductive discovery lest later discovery, though needed, be barred as creating an undue aggregate burden under Rule 26(b)(2).)

- directing disclosure of core information where appropriate to avoid the cost and delay of formal discovery (see *supra* section 21.13);

- reminding counsel of their professional obligations in conducting discovery and the implications of the certification under Rule 26(g) that all disclosures and discovery responses are complete and correct when made, and that requests, objections, and responses conform to the requirements of the Federal Rules;

- providing for compliance with the supplementation requirements of Rule 26(e)(1) and (2),[122] by setting periodic dates for reports;

- providing for periodic status reports to monitor the progress of discovery (which can be informal, by letter or telephone); and

- issuing an order, which may be a part of the scheduling order required by Rule 16(b) (see *supra* section 21.212), incorporating the schedule, limitations, and procedures constituting the discovery plan. For a sample order, see *infra* section 41.33.

21.422 Limitations

Limitations to control discovery in complex litigation may take a variety of forms, including time limits, restrictions on scope and quantity, and sequencing. As noted above, the Federal Rules and the court's inherent power provide broad authority. Among other provisions, Rule 16(b) directs the court to limit the time

---

122. Rule 26(e)(2) does not apply to deposition testimony, but when the deposition of an expert from whom a report was required under Rule 26(a)(2)(B) reveals changes in the expert's opinion, it triggers the duty of supplementation imposed by Rule 26(e)(1). *See* Fed. R. Civ. P. 26 advisory committee's note; Fed. R. Civ. P. 26(a)(2)(C).

for discovery, and Rule 26(b) directs the court to limit the "frequency or extent of use of the discovery methods" under the rules, including the length of depositions. Rule 30(a) imposes a presumptive limit of ten depositions per side, and Rule 33 establishes a presumptive limit of twenty-five interrogatories per party (see *infra* sections 21.451, 21.462). Rule 26(f)(3) requires the parties to address discovery limits in their proposed discovery plan.

Limits (which may be made merely presumptive) should be set early in the litigation, before discovery has begun. Because information about the litigation will be limited at that time, limits may need to be revised in the light of later developments. But they should be imposed on the basis of the best information available at the time, after full consultation with counsel, and on the understanding that they will remain binding until further order. In determining appropriate limits, the court will need to confront difficult questions of balancing efficiency and economy against the parties' need to develop an adequate record for summary judgment or trial. The difficulty of this task should not deter the judge from undertaking it, but it underlines the importance of clarifying and understanding the issues in the case before imposing limits.[123]

- **Time limits and schedules.** The discovery plan should include a schedule for the completion of specified discovery, affording a basis for judicial monitoring of progress. Setting a discovery cutoff date[124] at the initial conference, however, may not be feasible in complex litigation, though the setting of such a date at the appropriate time should remain an objective. When a discovery cutoff date is set, it should not be set so far in advance of the anticipated trial date that the product of discovery becomes stale and the parties' preparation outdated. Time limits impose a valuable discipline on attorneys, forcing them to be selective and helping to move the case expeditiously, but standing alone may be insufficient to control discovery costs. Unless complemented by other limitations, attorneys may simply conduct multitrack discovery, increasing expense and prejudicing parties with limited resources. To prevent time limits from being frustrated, the court should rule promptly on disputes so that further discovery is not delayed or hampered while a ruling is pending.

- **Limits on quantity.** Time limits may be complemented by limits on the number and length of depositions, on the number of interrogatories, and on the volume of requests for production. Such limitations should be imposed only after the court has heard from the attorneys and is able to make a reasonably informed judgment about the needs of the case. They are best applied sequentially to particular phases of the litigation, rather

---

123. *See* Schwarzer and Hirsch, *supra* note 106.
124. *See In re* Fine Paper Antitrust Litig., 685 F.2d 810 (3d Cir. 1982).

than as aggregate limitations. When limits are placed on discovery of voluminous transactions or other events, statistical sampling techniques may be used to measure whether the results of the discovery fairly represent what unrestricted discovery would have been expected to produce (for a general discussion of statistical sampling, see *infra* section 21.493).

- **Phased, sequenced, or targeted discovery.** It will rarely be possible for counsel and the court to determine conclusively early in the litigation what discovery will be necessary; some discovery of potential relevance at the outset may be rendered irrelevant as the litigation proceeds and the need for other discovery may become known only through later developments. For effective discovery control, therefore, the court should direct initial discovery at matters—witnesses, documents, information—that appear pivotal. As the litigation proceeds, this initial discovery may render other discovery unnecessary or provide leads for further necessary discovery. Initial discovery may also be targeted at information that may facilitate settlement negotiations or provide the foundation for a dispositive motion; a discovery plan may call for limited discovery to lay the foundation for early settlement discussions. Targeted discovery may be nonexhaustive, conducted to rapidly produce critical information on one or more specific issues. In permitting this kind of discovery, the court must balance the potential savings against the risk of later duplicative discovery should the deposition of a witness or the production of documents have to be resumed. Targeted discovery may in some cases be appropriate in connection with a motion for class certification; matters relevant to such a motion may, however, be so intertwined with the merits that targeting discovery would be inefficient. See *supra* section 21.41 and *infra* section 30.12.

- **Subject matter priorities.** Where the scope of the litigation—as, for example, in the case of antitrust litigation—is in doubt at the outset, discovery may be limited to particular time periods or geographical areas, until the relevance of expanded discovery has been established. See *supra* section 21.41.

- **Sequencing by parties.** Although discovery by all parties ordinarily proceeds concurrently, sometimes one or more parties should be allowed to proceed first. For example, if a party needs discovery to respond to an early summary judgment motion, that party may be given priority. The court may establish periods in which particular parties will be given exclusive or preferential rights to take depositions, and in multiple litigation the court may direct that discovery be conducted in some cases before others. Sometimes "common" discovery is ordered to proceed in a specified sequence, without similarly limiting "individual" discovery in the various cases.

- **Forms of discovery.** The court may prescribe a sequence for particular types of discovery—for example, interrogatories may be used to identify needed discovery and documents, followed by requests for production of documents, depositions, and finally requests for admission.

If the court directs that discovery be conducted in a specified sequence, leave should be granted to vary the order for good cause, as when emergency depositions are needed for witnesses in ill health or about to leave the country.

21.423 Other Practices to Save Time and Expense

Various other practices can help minimize the cost, delay, and burden associated with discovery. They include the following:

- **Stipulations under Fed. R. Civ. P. 29.** The rule gives parties authority to alter procedures, limitations, and time limits on discovery so long as they do not interfere with times set by court order. Thus the parties can facilitate discovery by stipulating with respect to notice and manner of taking depositions and adopting various informal procedures. The court may, however, require that it be kept advised to ensure compliance with the discovery plan and may by order preclude stipulations on particular matters.

- **Informal discovery.** Counsel should be encouraged to exchange information, particularly relevant documents, without resort to formal discovery (see *supra* section 21.13). Early exchanges can make later depositions more efficient. Informal interviews with potential witnesses can help determine whether a deposition is needed, inform later discovery, and provide the basis for requests for admission through which the results of informal discovery are made admissible at trial.

- **Automatic disclosure.** Rule 26(a)(1) and many local rules and standing orders require the parties to identify relevant witnesses and categories of documents early in the litigation, without waiting for discovery requests. By stipulation or court order, the timing and content of this disclosure may be tailored to the needs of the particular case. See *supra* section 21.13.

- **Reducing deposition costs.** Savings may be realized if depositions are taken, when feasible, by telephone, by electronic recording devices, or by having deponents come to central locations. Likewise, parties may forego attending a deposition in which they have only a minor interest if a procedure is established for supplemental questions—as by telephone, written questions, or resumption of examination in person—in the event that, after a review of the transcript, they find further inquiry necessary. See *infra* section 21.45 for additional discussion of deposition practices.

- **Information from other litigation and sources.** When information is available from public records (such as government studies or reports), from other litigation,[125] or from discovery conducted by others in the same litigation, the parties may be required to review those materials before additional discovery is undertaken. If those materials will be usable as evidence in the present litigation,[126] the parties may be limited to supplemental discovery. Cost savings may also be realized through coordination of "common" discovery in related litigation, even if pending in other courts. If related cases are pending in more than one court, common discovery should be coordinated to avoid duplication and conflicts, as by formulating a joint discovery plan for all cases, agreeing that one of the cases will be treated as the lead case (with its discovery plan serving as the starting point for development of supplemental plans in the other courts), or using joint deposition notices. See *infra* section 31. Counsel may also agree that discovery taken in one proceeding can be used in related proceedings as though taken there.

- **Joint discovery requests and responses.** In multiparty cases in which no lead counsel has been designated, parties with similar positions may be required to submit a combined set of interrogatories, requests for production, or requests for admission. If voluminous materials are to be produced in response, the responding party may be relieved of the requirement of furnishing copies to each discovering party. For further discussion of document discovery, including use of document depositories, see *infra* section 21.44.

- **Modified discovery responses.** When a response to a discovery request can be provided in a form somewhat different from that requested, but with substantially the same information and at a saving in time and expense, the responding party should make that fact known and seek agreement from the requesting party. For example, information sought on a calendar year basis may be readily and inexpensively available on a fiscal year basis. Similarly, if some requested information can be pro-

---

125. Access to materials and testimony given in other cases may be impeded because of confidentiality orders, restrictions on release of grand jury materials, and other limitations. See *supra* § 21.43 and *infra* § 31.

126. Interrogatory answers, depositions, and testimony given in another action ordinarily are admissible if made by and offered against a party in the current action. *See* Fed. R. Evid. 801(d)(2). Similarly, they may be admissible for certain purposes if made by a witness in the current action. *See* Fed. R. Evid. 801(d)(1). The parties may stipulate to the admissibility of other information.

duced promptly but additional time will be needed for other items, the responding party should produce the information presently available and indicate when the remainder will be produced. Preferably, formal discovery requests should be prepared only after counsel have informally discussed what information is needed and how it can be produced most efficiently.

- **Combined discovery requests.** Several forms of discovery may be combined into a single request. For example, a party may be asked to admit a particular fact under Fed. R. Civ. P. 36; if not so admitted, the party is asked to respond under Rule 33 by stating its position as to that fact and indicating whether it has any evidence to support it. If so, the party is asked to identify and produce under Rule 34 any such documentary evidence and to identify the persons having knowledge of the matter for possible deposition under Rule 30 or 31. This technique eliminates the need for documentary or deposition evidence on matters that the opposing party admits or is unable to refute. Ordinarily, more time should be allowed for responding to a combined discovery request; even so, less time may be consumed overall than if traditional separate discovery requests were made. Because the rules impose no limits on requests for admission as they do on interrogatories, an order enlarging the number of permissible interrogatories may be necessary.

- **Conference depositions.** If knowledge of a subject is divided among several people and credibility is not an issue, a "conference deposition" may be feasible. Each witness is sworn, and the questions are then directed to the group or those having the information sought. Persons in other locations who may also be needed to provide information may be scheduled to be "on call" during the conference deposition. This procedure may be useful in obtaining background information, identifying and explaining documents, and examining reports compiled by several persons.

- **Subpoenas.** Under Fed. R. Civ. P. 45, an attorney may subpoena documents or other tangibles from nonparties, avoiding unnecessary depositions. The rule also provides for subpoenas to permit inspection of premises in the possession of nonparties, rendering unnecessary the commencement of an independent proceeding. See *infra* section 21.447.

21.424 Resolution of Discovery Disputes

Discovery disputes, with their potential of breeding satellite litigation, are a major source of cost and delay. Few aspects of litigation management are more important than bringing about the prompt and inexpensive resolution of such disputes. The mere availability of such a procedure—and the court's insistence that it be adhered to—will deter counsel from the kind of conduct that often obstructs discovery, since no advantage can be gained from it. Many district judges have found that use of procedures such as those described here take little of their time but result in substantial improvement in the conduct of discovery. Such procedures are equally effective where discovery management is referred to a magistrate judge.

A discovery plan should therefore include specific provisions, such as the following, for the fair and efficient resolution of discovery disputes.

Presubmission conference of counsel. No dispute or request for relief should be submitted to the court until after the parties have met and attempted to resolve it. Rules 37(a) and 26(c) condition the right to make a motion to compel or for a protective order upon certification that the movant has in good faith conferred or attempted to confer with the opponent to resolve the matter without court action. Most local rules require such a conference before any discovery dispute is brought to the court (some judges require the participation of local counsel in this conference).[127] It is advisable, however, for the discovery plan or scheduling order to specify the ground rules for such conferences, such as requiring that the party requesting the conference send the opponent a clear and concise statement of the asserted deficiencies or objections and the requested action; having to narrow and define the dispute and the requested relief will cause counsel to prepare for the conference, consult with clients, and seek a resolution that will avoid the need for judicial intervention. Any resulting resolution should be reduced to writing.

Submission to the court. Although opinions differ, many judges believe that by making themselves available to resolve such disputes informally, disputes are in fact discouraged and those that are submitted can be resolved quickly. Many judges direct counsel to present disputes by conference telephone call. Others direct submission by letter. In many courts, magistrate judges use such procedures. A brief excerpt of the transcript containing relevant proceedings, either in writing or read by the reporter over the phone, will be helpful to the decision maker. The availability of a speedy resolution process, particularly in the course of a deposition, tends to deter unreasonable and obstructive conduct; when the attorneys know that the judge (or magistrate judge) is readily available by telephone and the opponent can obtain prompt relief, the incentive for unreasonable behavior is reduced. Judges who use such procedures have found that they in fact hear few disputes (see *infra* section 21.456).

Avoiding formal motions in discovery disputes has the additional merit of forcing attorneys to narrow and simplify the dispute rather than to elaborate on it as they would in a brief. Questions from the judge will further narrow and clarify

---

127. *See, e.g.,* Standing Orders of the Court on Effective Discovery in Civil Cases (E.D.N.Y. 1984) *and* Guidelines for Discovery, Motion Practice and Trial (N.D. Cal. 1987), *reprinted in* Litigation Manual, *supra* note 5, forms 27 and 16, respectively.

the dispute. Often, the resolution of the dispute becomes self-evident during the course of the conference. Even if informal presentation does not resolve a dispute, it can help to define and narrow it for further proceedings.

If informal procedures fail or are rejected, the court should adopt procedures to minimize the activity needed to resolve the dispute. Motions, memoranda, and supporting materials should be restricted in length, replies normally barred, and time limits for submission set. At times, of course, discovery disputes involving issues having a significant impact on the litigation, such as rulings on privilege, may require substantial proceedings. Discovery with respect to the dispute itself should be avoided except in extraordinary circumstances.

Special masters have been successfully used to oversee discovery, particularly where there are numerous issues, such as claims of privilege to resolve. Because appointments of special masters can increase substantially the cost of litigation (though the resulting efficiencies could result in offsetting savings), they should not be made except in cases where the parties can afford the cost, and preferably not over the parties' objections.[128]

Submission of certain discovery disputes may be made to a judge outside of the district. A motion to compel or to terminate a deposition held outside the district where the action is pending, or for a protective order, may be presented either to the judge before whom it is pending or to a judge in the district where the deposition is being held.[129] In complex litigation, particularly if procedures have already been established for expedited consideration, it may be well to require all such matters to be presented to the assigned judge. Fed. R. Civ. P. 37(a)(1) requires that motions to compel be presented to the court where the action is pending if directed at a party; only if directed at a nonparty must it be presented to a court in the district where the discovery is taken. When a dispute is presented to a deposition-district court, however, the assigned judge may have or be able to obtain authority to act also as deposition judge in that district, and indeed may be able to exercise those powers by telephone.[130] In multidistrict litigation under 28 U.S.C. § 1407(b), "the judge or judges to whom such actions are assigned, the members of the judicial panel on multidistrict litigation, and other circuit and district judges designated when needed by the panel may exercise the powers of a district judge in any district for the purpose of conducting pretrial depositions." In other cases, arrangements may sometimes be made for an interdistrict or

---

128. See *infra* § 21.52; Wayne Brazil et al., *supra* note 18 (based on experience in United States v. American Tel. & Tel. Co., 461 F. Supp. 1314 (D.D.C. 1978), 552 F. Supp. 131 (D.D.C. 1982), *aff'd mem. sub nom.* Maryland v. United States, 460 U.S. 1001 (1983)).

129. Fed. R. Civ. P. 26(c), 30(d).

130. *See In re* Corrugated Container Antitrust Litig., 662 F.2d 875, 877, 879 (D.C. Cir. 1981); *In re* Corrugated Container Antitrust Litig., 620 F.2d 1086, 1089 (5th Cir. 1980); *In re* Corrugated Container Antitrust Litig., 644 F.2d 70 (2d Cir. 1981) (tacitly assuming power).

intercircuit assignment, enabling the judge to whom the case is assigned to act as deposition judge in another district. In any event, the deposition-district judge may always confer with the forum-district judge by telephone and thereby expedite a ruling.

Rulings. Whatever procedure is adopted, the court should expedite the resolution of discovery disputes. While such disputes remain pending, they tend to disrupt the discovery program and result in additional cost and delay. It is generally more important to the parties that the dispute be decided promptly than that it be decided perfectly. The resolution should be memorialized on the record or by written order; prevailing counsel may be asked to prepare a proposed order and submit it to the opponent for review and then to the court. If the order is made at a conference during a deposition, the conference and order can be transcribed as part of the deposition transcript.

21.43 Privilege Claims and Protective Orders

Attention should be given at an early conference, preferably before discovery begins, to the possible need for procedures to accommodate claims of privilege or for protection of materials from discovery as trial preparation materials,[131] as trade secrets, or on privacy grounds.[132] If not addressed early, these matters may later disrupt the discovery schedule. Consideration will need to be given not only to the rights and needs of the parties but also to the existing or potential interests of those not involved in the litigation.[133]

21.431 Claims of Privilege/Full Protection

Certain materials may qualify for full protection against disclosure or discovery as privileged,[134] as trial preparation material,[135] or as incriminating under the Fifth

---

131. "Trial preparation materials" include, but are not limited to, traditional "work product." *See* Fed. R. Civ. P. 26(b)(3) & advisory committee's note.

132. Although there is no privacy privilege, maintenance of privacy can be the ground for a protective order. *See* Seattle Times Co. v. Rhinehart, 467 U.S. 20, 30, 35 n.21 (1984).

133. For a thorough discussion of the issues raised by protective orders, see Zenith Radio Corp. v. Matsushita Elec. Indus. Co., 529 F. Supp. 866 (E.D. Pa. 1981) (Becker, J.). *See also Seattle Times,* 467 U.S. 20; Richard L. Marcus, *The Discovery Confidentiality Controversy,* 1991 U. Ill. L. Rev. 457 (1991).

134. Rulings on claims of privilege in diversity cases are governed by Fed. R. Evid. 501, which provides that privilege is determined by state law where state law supplies the rule of decision.

135. See Fed. R. Civ. P. 26(b)(3), which extends qualified protection to such materials.

Amendment.[136] To minimize their potentially disruptive effects on discovery, the possibility of such claims should be addressed at an early conference and a procedure established for their resolution or for avoidance through appropriate sequencing of discovery.[137] A claim for protection against disclosure on the ground of privilege or protection of trial preparation materials must be made "expressly" and describe the nature of the allegedly protected information sufficiently to enable opposing parties to assess the merits of the claim.[138] This is usually accomplished by submission of a log[139] identifying documents or other communications by date and by the names of the author(s) and recipient(s), and describing their general subject matter (without revealing the privileged or protected material).[140] Unresolved claims of privilege should be presented directly to the judge for a ruling; if necessary, the judge can review the information in dispute *in camera*.

The party seeking protection may, however, request that the trial judge not see the document, especially in a nonjury case. In such circumstances, the court may, in its discretion, refer the matter to another judge, a magistrate judge, or a special master. Since judges are accustomed to reviewing matters that may not be admissible, counsel should restrict such requests to the most sensitive, potentially prejudicial materials and be prepared to indicate, at least in general terms, the basis for the request.

In complex litigation involving voluminous documents, privileged documents are occasionally produced inadvertently. The parties may stipulate, or an order may provide, that such production shall not be considered a waiver of privilege and that the party receiving such a document shall return it promptly without making a copy.

---

136. Potential Fifth Amendment claims are one reason why discovery in civil litigation may be stayed, in whole or in part, until termination of related criminal proceedings. See *infra* § 31.2. Conclusion of the criminal case, however, will not necessarily avoid further assertions of the privilege against self-incrimination.

137. The parties may facilitate discovery by agreeing that the disclosure of a privileged document will not be deemed a waiver with respect to that document or other documents involving the same subject matter. Some courts, however, have refused to enforce such agreements. See *In re* Chrysler Motors Corp. Overnight Evaluation Program Litig., 860 F.2d 844, 846–47 (8th Cir. 1988); Khandji v. Keystone Resorts Management, Inc., 140 F.R.D. 697, 700 (D. Colo. 1992); Chubb Integrated Sys. v. National Bank, 103 F.R.D. 52, 67–68 (D.D.C. 1984).

138. Fed. R. Civ. P. 26(b)(5), 45(d)(2). Withholding materials otherwise subject to disclosure without such notice may subject a party to Rule 37 sanctions and waive the privilege or protection. *See* Fed. R. Civ. P. 26 advisory committee's note.

139. A frequently used term for this log is a "*Vaughn* Index." *See* Vaughn v. Rosen, 484 F.2d 820 (D.C. Cir. 1973).

140. Rule 26(b)(5) does not specify the information that must be provided, which may depend on the nature and amount of material withheld. *See* Fed. R. Civ. P. 26 advisory committee's note.

21.432 Limited Disclosure/Protective Orders

Complex litigation will frequently involve information or documents a party may consider sensitive. Two alternative approaches are available for seeking protection for such material: one or more parties may seek "umbrella" protective orders, usually by stipulation, or the claim to protection may be litigated document by document.

Umbrella orders. When the volume of potentially protected materials is large, an umbrella order will expedite production, reduce costs, and avoid the burden on the court of document-by-document adjudication. Umbrella orders provide that all assertedly confidential material disclosed (and appropriately identified, usually by stamp) is presumptively protected unless challenged. The orders are made without a particularized showing to support the claim for protection, but such a showing must be made whenever a claim under an order is challenged. Some courts have therefore found that umbrella orders simply postpone, rather than eliminate, the need for the court to closely scrutinize discovery material to determine whether protection is justified, thereby delaying rather than expediting the litigation.[141]

Applications for umbrella orders, usually presented to the court by stipulation of the parties, should specify the following matters:[142]

- the categories of information subject to the order;[143]

- the procedure for determining which particular documents are within protected categories;[144]

---

141. *See* John Does I–VI v. Yogi, 110 F.R.D. 629, 632 (D.D.C. 1986). The problems of preserving protection for documents produced under umbrella orders are aggravated by the understandable tendency of counsel to err on the side of caution by designating any possibly sensitive documents as confidential under the order. The time saved by excessive designations, however, may be more than offset by the difficulties of later opposing some request for access or disclosure. Although the judge, in the interest of reducing the time and expense of the discovery process, should be somewhat tolerant of this practice, counsel should not mark documents as protected under the order without a good faith belief that they are entitled to protection. Counsel should also be cautioned against objecting to document requests without first ascertaining that the requested documents exist. The designation of a document as confidential should be viewed as equivalent to a motion for a protective order and subject to the sanctions of Fed. R. Civ. P. 37(a)(4), as provided by Fed. R. Civ. P. 26(c).

142. See Sample Orders *infra* § 41.36, forms (A) and (B).

143. Umbrella orders should specify the classes or categories of documents that may be designated as confidential. A standardless stipulation or order violates Rule 26(c) and can be counterproductive by inviting disputes.

144. Umbrella orders do not eliminate the burden on the person seeking protection of justifying the relief sought as to every item, but simply facilitate rulings on disputed claims of confidentiality. *See* Cipollone v. Liggett Group, Inc., 785 F.2d 1108, 1122 (3d Cir. 1986).

- the procedure for designating and identifying material subject to the confidentiality order;[145]
- the persons who may have access to protected materials;[146]
- the extent to which protected materials may be used in related litigation;[147]
- the procedures for maintaining security;[148]
- the procedures for challenging particular claims of confidentiality;[149]
- the exceptions, if any, to the general prohibitions on disclosure;[150]
- the termination of the order after the litigation or at another time;
- the return or destruction of materials received; and

---

145. Items produced under a claim of confidentiality should be identified with some special marking at the time of production to ensure that all persons know exactly what materials have been designated as confidential throughout the litigation. Specific portions of deposition transcripts may be marked as confidential through a written designation procedure; see Sample Order *infra* § 41.36, ¶ 5. If numerous documents are involved, a log may be maintained describing the documents and identifying the persons having access to them.

146. For example, counsel are ordinarily permitted to disclose such information to assistants in their offices and potential expert witnesses. On the other hand, disclosure to clients may be prohibited where, for example, the information has commercial value and the parties are competitors; alternatively, the order may (1) limit disclosure to named individuals not involved in the relevant corporate activity, (2) create a special class of highly confidential documents that only attorneys and nonclient experts may view, (3) require particularized record keeping of disclosures to client personnel, and (4) require individual undertakings by those receiving such information not to misuse it. An attorney (not a paralegal or employee) should review the list of persons to whom disclosure may be made and all related provisions of the order.

147. Restrictions on use in other litigation may not provide complete protection. *See, e.g., In re Dual-Deck Video Cassette Recorder Antitrust Litig.*, 10 F.3d 693 (9th Cir. 1993) (reversing contempt order where party used confidential information but did not reveal trade secrets).

148. For example, information may be sealed or exempted from filing with the court under Fed. R. Civ. P. 5(d) or 26(a)(4). Copying or computerization of particularly sensitive documents may be prohibited or tightly controlled. See Sample Order *infra* § 41.36, ¶ 9. The order may require that each person shown a document designated as confidential also be shown the order and advised of the obligation to honor the confidentiality designation. To ensure binding effect, all persons to whom disclosure is made should be required to sign a copy of the order.

149. A common procedure is for the producing party to mark all assertedly protected material "confidential"; the opposing party then has a specified period, usually about two weeks, within which to contest the designation. *See Poliquin v. Garden Way, Inc.*, 989 F.2d 527, 529 (1st Cir. 1993). The burden remains on the party seeking protection; the opposing party need not offer affidavits to support a challenge. *See id.* at 531.

150. For example, the order may allow otherwise protected information to be shown to a witness at or in preparation for a deposition. The order usually provides that if a party desires to make a disclosure not clearly permitted, advance notice will be given to the other parties and the dispute, if not resolved by agreement, may be presented to the court for a ruling before disclosure.

- the court's authority to modify the order, both during and after conclusion of the litigation.

Particularized protective orders. A person from whom discovery is sought may move under Fed. R. Civ. P. 26(c) for a protective order limiting disclosure or providing for the confidentiality of information produced. As with other discovery motions, the movant must first make a good faith attempt to resolve the dispute without court action;[151] the parties should address the subject of protective orders in their proposed discovery plan.[152] Rule 26(c) allows the court to "make any order which justice requires to protect a party or person from annoyance, embarrassment, oppression, or undue burden or expense." A protective order should be entered only when the movant makes a particularized showing of "good cause," by affidavit or testimony of a witness with personal knowledge, of the specific harm that would result from disclosure or loss of confidentiality; generalities and unsupported contentions do not suffice.[153] When directed solely at discovery materials, protective orders are not subject to the high level of scrutiny required by the Constitution to justify prior restraints; rather, courts have broad discretion at the discovery stage to decide when a protective order is appropriate and what degree of protection is required.[154]

In fashioning the order, the court should balance the movants' legitimate concerns about confidentiality against the needs of the litigation, protecting individual privacy, or the commercial value of information while making it available for legitimate litigation use.[155] The objective should be to protect only material for which a clear and significant need for confidentiality has been shown;[156] this will reduce the burdensomeness of the order and render it less vulnerable to later challenge.

Modification and release. A protective order is always subject to modification or termination for good cause.[157] Even where the parties have consented to entry of a protective order, they may later seek its modification to allow dissemination

151. Fed. R. Civ. P. 26(c).

152. Fed. R. Civ. P. 26(f)(4).

153. *See* Cipollone v. Liggett Group Inc., 785 F.2d 1108, 1121 (3d Cir. 1986), and cases cited therein; *see also* Smith v. BIC Corp., 869 F.2d 194 (3d Cir. 1989).

154. Seattle Times Co. v. Rhinehart, 467 U.S. 20, 36–37 (1984).

155. *See* Arthur R. Miller, *Confidentiality, Protective Orders, and Public Access to the Courts*, 105 Harv. L. Rev. 428, 476 (1991).

156. *See* Poliquin v. Garden Way, Inc., 989 F.2d 527, 532 (1st Cir. 1993) (citing Francis H. Hare, Jr. et al., Confidentiality Orders § 4.10 (1988)).

157. *See* Public Citizen v. Liggett Group, Inc., 858 F.2d 775, 782–83 (1st Cir. 1988) and cases cited therein; *In re* "Agent Orange" Prod. Liab. Litig., 821 F.2d 139, 145 (2d Cir. 1987). Even without modification, a protective order may fail to prevent disclosure of information as required by law. *See, e.g.*, 15 U.S.C. § 1321(c)(2) (requiring access to discovery materials pursuant to a civil investigative demand despite protective order).

of information received; nonparties, including the media, government investigators, public interest groups, and parties in other litigation, may seek modification to allow access to protected information.[158] In assessing such requests, courts balance the potential harm to the party seeking protection against the requesting party's need for the information and the public interest served by its release.[159] Circuits apply different standards in balancing the continuing need for protection against the gains in efficiency and judicial economy that may result from release.[160] If the court finds that the latter factors support release of otherwise confidential material, it may redact the material, allowing access only to that information necessary to serve the purpose for which release was granted. In addition, the court should define the terms of the release, including precisely who may have access to the information and for what purpose.

A common basis for nonparty requests for release is the need for the information in related litigation.[161] Even where the protective order contains a provision prohibiting such use, the court that entered the order may require such disclosure, subject to appropriate restrictions on further use and disclosure.[162] In making this determination, the court must balance the continuing need for protection against the efficiency and judicial economy that may result from release. Questions to consider include the following:

---

158. *See Public Citizen*, 858 F.2d at 781–82. Some states have passed legislation limiting courts' ability to prevent public access to litigation materials that relate to public safety; there have been proposals for similar reform in many states and in Congress. *See* Miller, *supra* note 155, at 441–45.

159. The court may also want to consider the disclosing party's degree of reliance on the protective order when disclosure was made. If a party freely disclosed information without contest based on the premise that it would remain confidential, subsequent dissemination may be unfair and may, in the long run, reduce other litigants' confidence in protective orders, rendering them less useful as a tool for preventing discovery abuse and encouraging more strenuous objections to discovery requests. *See* Miller, *supra* note 155, at 499–500; *cf.* Meyer Goldberg, Inc. v. Fisher Foods, Inc., 823 F.2d 159, 163 (6th Cir. 1987); Palmieri v. New York, 779 F.2d 861, 863 (2d Cir. 1985).

160. *See* United Nuclear Corp. v. Cranford Ins. Co., 905 F.2d 1424, 1428 (10th Cir. 1990) (citing cases). If the party seeking information would be entitled to obtain it in the other litigation, there is little need to require redundant discovery proceedings. *See id.* at 1428 (*citing* Wilk v. American Medical Ass'n, 635 F.2d 1295, 1299 (7th Cir. 1980)).

161. Conversely, the parties before the court may seek discovery of information subject to a protective order in other litigation. Generally, the party seeking discovery should first establish its right to it in the court in which the discovery will be used. If that court permits discovery, the effect given the earlier protective order should normally be determined by the court that issued it. For discussion of the use of documents from other litigation, see *supra* § 21.423.

162. *See United Nuclear Corp.*, 905 F.2d 1424; *Wilk*, 635 F.2d 1295 (protective orders should ordinarily be modified on request from other litigants, subject to appropriate conditions as to further use and cost); AT&T v. Grady, 594 F.2d 594 (7th Cir. 1978) (confidentiality order modified to permit nonparty U.S. government to obtain discovery); *but see Palmieri*, 779 F.2d 861 (denying modification to allow state to gain access to settlement agreement).

- Was the disclosing party unqualifiedly obligated to produce the material sought?
- Would the material be discoverable in subsequent litigation involving other parties?
- Does the other litigation appear to have merit?[163]
- Would granting release save significant time and expense?
- Can the material be released in redacted form so as to aid legitimate discovery while minimizing the loss of confidentiality?
- Will modification of the protective order disrupt settlement of the case in which it was entered?
- Did the person providing discovery do so in reliance on the protective order?
- Would informal communication between the two judges be productive in arriving at an accommodation that gives appropriate consideration to the interests of all involved?[164]

Even if designated as confidential under a protective order, discovery materials will lose confidential status (absent a showing of "most compelling" reasons) if introduced at trial or filed in connection with a motion for summary judgment.[165] Confidential materials filed solely in connection with pretrial discovery, however, remain protected as long as the "good cause" requirement of Rule 26(c) is satisfied.[166] The general rule, enunciated by the Supreme Court, is that a public right of access to material produced in connection with a particular pretrial or trial proceeding arises when (1) the proceeding has historically been open, and (2) public access plays a significant role in the proper functioning of the pro-

---

163. The court should be alert to the possibility that the information is sought merely for a "fishing expedition," nuisance value, harassment, or other improper purpose. *See* Miller, *supra* note 155, at 473. These possibilities are greater, and the case for disclosure therefore weaker, when the related litigation for which the information is sought is merely anticipated rather than pending. *See id.* at 499.

164. The role of the two courts is similar to when access to grand jury materials is sought for use in proceedings in another court.

165. *See, e.g., Poliquin,* 989 F.2d at 532–33; Littlejohn v. BIC Corp., 851 F.2d 673, 677– 78, 684 (3d Cir. 1988); FTC v. Standard Man. Corp., 830 F.2d 404, 410 (1st Cir. 1987); *Meyer Goldberg,* 823 F.2d at 163; *In re* Knoxville News-Sentinel Co., 723 F.2d 470, 476 (6th Cir. 1983); Joy v. North, 692 F.2d 880, 893 (2d Cir. 1982). *See also* Leucadia Inc. v. Applied Extrusion Tech., Inc., 998 F.2d 157, 161–65 (3d Cir. 1993) (protection lost if filed with any nondiscovery motion).

166. *See Seattle Times,* 467 U.S. 20; *Leucadia,* 998 F.2d at 161–65; Anderson v. Cryovac, Inc., 805 F.2d 1, 5–7, 10–13 (1st Cir. 1986).

cess.[167] To ensure continued protection, counsel should consider stipulating to material nonconfidential facts to avoid the need to introduce confidential material into evidence. Counsel may also move to have confidential material excluded from evidence as prejudicial and of low probative value under Fed. R. Evid. 403.[168]

Administration of protective orders does not necessarily end with the disposition of the case. While it is common for protective orders to include provisions for posttrial protection, an order is still subject to modification after judgment or settlement, even if the order was entered on consent of the parties.[169]

21.433 Allocation of Costs

The cost of seeking and responding to discovery is a part of the cost of litigation each party normally must bear, subject only to specific provisions for shifting contained in statutes or rules. But the cost of particular discovery is a matter the judge is directed to take into account in exercising the authority to control discovery under Rule 26(b)(2). Among other things, that rule directs the judge to consider whether the information sought "is obtainable from some other source that is more convenient, less burdensome, or less expensive," and to limit discovery if, in the circumstances of the case, its "expense . . . outweighs its likely benefits." Protective orders are a means of implementing the proportionality principle underlying the discovery rules. Rule 26(c) permits the court to issue an order "to protect a party or person from . . . undue burden or expense," including orders "that the discovery . . . may be had only on specified terms or conditions . . . [or] only by a method of discovery other than that selected by the party seeking discovery."

Taken together, these provisions give the court broad authority to control the cost of discovery. They permit the court to impose not only limits but also conditions. The court can implement the cost/benefit rationale of the rule by conditioning particular discovery on payment of its costs by the party seeking it. Short of barring a party from conducting certain costly or marginally necessary discovery, the court may require that party to pay all or part of its cost as a condition to permitting it to proceed. Similarly, where a party insists on certain discovery to elicit information that may be available through less expensive methods, that discovery may be conditioned on the payment of the costs incurred by other parties. Such a protective order shifting certain costs may require payment at the time, or

---

167. Press-Enterprise Co. v. Superior Ct., 478 U.S. 1, 8 (1986); Globe Newspaper Co. v. Superior Ct., 457 U.S. 596, 605–06 (1982).

168. *See Poliquin,* 989 F.2d at 535.

169. *See id.; United Nuclear Corp.,* 905 F.2d at 1427; *Public Citizen,* 858 F.2d at 781–82; *Meyer Goldberg,* 823 F.2d 159.

may simply designate certain costs as taxable costs to be awarded after final judgment.[170]

Reference to the court's authority to shift costs will tend to give the parties an incentive to use cost-effective means of obtaining information and a disincentive to engage in wasteful and costly discovery activity. For example, where production is to be made of data maintained on computers, and the producing party is better able to search for and produce the data efficiently and economically than the discovering party, they may agree to use the former's capability subject to appropriate reimbursement for costs. Where it is less expensive for a witness to travel to a deposition site than for several attorneys to travel to the witness's residence, the party seeking discovery may agree to pay the witness's travel expenses.

Cost allocation may also be an appropriate means to limit discovery that is unduly burdensome or expensive. Although it is not the purpose of Rule 26 to equalize the burdens on the parties, Rule 26(b)(2)(iii) expressly requires the court to take the parties' resources into account in balancing the burden or expense of particular discovery against its benefit. Thus, where the parties' resources are grossly disproportionate, the court may condition discovery that would be unduly burdensome on one of them upon a fair allocation of costs.

Some of the factors relevant to cost allocation are:

- What is the most efficient and economical way of obtaining the information?

- Is the information of sufficient importance to warrant the expense of obtaining it?

- Can one party obtain the information with less time and expense than another?

- Should some or all of the costs be shifted between the parties, either absolutely or by an order conditional upon future events,[171] considering efficiency, economy, the significance of the information, and the relative resources of the parties?

---

170. *See* Fed. R. Civ. P. 54(d); 28 U.S.C. § 1920.

171. For example, the order might make cost shifting dependent on whether the information discovered proves relevant and material at trial.

21.44 Documents

Complex litigation usually involves the production and handling of voluminous documents. Efficient management during discovery and trial requires careful planning and ongoing attention to the documentary phase of the litigation by the attorneys and the judge from the beginning of the litigation.

21.441 Identification System

Document production under the Federal Rules may occur in a variety of ways. Production may be voluntary and informal. It may occur under Rule 34 (see *infra* section 21.443) or under Rule 33(d) by making documents available for inspection.[172] Deponents may be required to produce documents by a subpoena *duces tecum*,[173] and nonparties may be commanded to produce documents by a subpoena issued under Fed. R. Civ. P. 45.[174] At the outset of the case, before any documents are produced or used in depositions, the court should direct counsel to establish a single system for identifying all documents produced (by any procedure) or used in the litigation. To reduce the risk of confusion, each document should be assigned a single identifying designation that will be used by all parties for all purposes throughout the case, including depositions and trial.

Usually consecutive numbering is the most practicable; blocks of numbers are assigned to each party in advance to make the source of each document immediately apparent. Every page of every document is Bates-stamped consecutively. The numbers of each document may be later used to designate it; if identified differently in the course of a deposition or on an exhibit list, the stamped number should be included as a cross-reference. If other means of designation are used, no designation should be assigned to more than one document, and the same

---

172. Under Rule 33(d) the party may "specify the records from which the answer may be derived or ascertained . . . in sufficient detail to permit the interrogating party to locate and identify, as readily as can the party served, the records from which the answer may be ascertained." If the information sought exists in the form of compilations, abstracts, or summaries, these should be made available to the interrogating party. Fed. R. Civ. P. 33 advisory committee's note.

173. *See* Fed. R. Civ. P. 30(b)(1).

174. Fed. R. Civ. P. 34(c).

document should not receive more than one designation unless counsel have reason to refer to different copies of the same document. In multitrack depositions, a block of numbers should be assigned to each deposition in advance. To avoid later disputes, a log should be kept recording each document produced and indicating by, to whom, and on what date production was made. A record of the documents produced by a party and copied by an opposing party may also be useful.

Courts have traditionally given new designations to documents marked as exhibits for trial, often by assigning sequential numbers to one side and sequential letters to the other. The existence of duplicate designations of documents, however, can be a source of confusion; exhibits can readily be marked for trial by their discovery designations. If desired, a supplemental designation can be used to identify the offering party.

21.442 Preservation

Before the commencement of discovery—and perhaps before the initial conference—the court should consider whether to enter an order requiring the parties to preserve and retain documents, files, and records that may be relevant to the litigation.[175] Because such an order may interfere with the normal operations of the parties and impose perhaps unforeseen burdens, the judge should discuss with counsel at the first opportunity the need for a preservation order and, if one is needed, what terms will best serve the purposes of preserving relevant matter without imposing undue burdens. A preservation order may be difficult to implement perfectly and cause hardship when records are stored in data-processing systems that automatically control the period of retention. Revision of existing computer programs to provide for longer retention, even if possible, may be prohibitively expensive (though print-out and retention of hard copies, or duplication of databases at periodic intervals before deletions occur, may be feasible). Such an order should ordinarily permit destruction after reasonable notice to opposing counsel; if opposing counsel objects, the party seeking destruction should be required to show good cause before destruction is permitted. The order may also exclude specified categories of documents whose cost of preservation is shown to outweigh substantially their relevance in the litigation, particularly if copies of the documents are filed in a document depository (see *infra* section 21.444) or if there are alternative sources for the information. If relevance cannot be fairly evaluated until the litigation progresses, destruction should be deferred. As issues in the case are narrowed, the court may reduce the scope of the order. The same considerations apply to the alteration or destruction of physical evidence.

---

175. See Sample Order *infra* § 41.34.

21.443 Rule 34 Requests/Procedures for Responding

In litigation with voluminous documents, requests for production and responses can become mired in confusion unless carefully administered. Requests can be overlooked, responses can be lost in the shuffle, failures to respond can be obscured, and uncertainty can arise over what was requested and what was produced. The process must therefore be handled with care, and the discovery plan should set in place procedures to that end.

The starting point is strict observance of the requirements of Rule 34, under which requests to produce documents for inspection and copying must specify the items sought individually or by category and describe each with "reasonable particularity."[176] Each request must specify a reasonable time, place, and manner for inspection and copying.[177] A party served with a request must respond in writing within thirty days, stating for each item or category either that inspection and copying will be permitted as requested or that the party objects to the request; in the latter case, the reasons for the objection must be stated. If the responding party objects to only part of an item or category, inspection of the remaining parts must be permitted. Documents must be produced for inspection "as they are kept in the usual course of business" or organized and labeled "to correspond with the categories in the request."

The discovery plan should establish a schedule for submitting requests and responses, and for subsequent supplementation of responses under Rule 26(e). In developing the plan, the court should consider counsel's proposals for document discovery and the possible imposition of limits based on Rule 26(b)(2). The court may initially limit production to the most relevant files or may require a preliminary exchange of lists identifying files and documents from which the requesting party may then make selections. The court may also require, even if lead counsel or committees of counsel have not been appointed, that similarly situated parties confer and present joint Rule 34 requests and conduct their examinations at the same time and place; if extensive copying will be involved, counsel should consider whether economies may be achieved by sharing copies.

In overseeing document production, the court should:

- ensure that the burdens are fairly allocated between the parties;
- prevent indiscriminate, overly broad, or unduly burdensome demands (the court should generally not permit sweeping requests, such as those for "all documents relating or referring to" an issue, party, or claim—requests should instead be framed to call for production of the fewest documents possible; this may be facilitated by the use of prediscovery confer-

---

176. Fed. R. Civ. P. 34(b).
177. *Id.*

ences or discovery devices to identify relevant files before the request is made);

- avoid overwhelming or confusing responses; and
- guard against tampering with files and other abusive practices.

21.444 Document Depositories

Central document depositories can help meet the need for efficient and economical management of voluminous documents in multiparty litigation. Requiring that all discovery materials be produced to and stored at one or more convenient locations, where they may be inspected and copied by parties seeking discovery, may reduce substantially the expense and burden of document production and inspection. Use of a depository also facilitates determination of which documents have been produced and what information is in them, minimizing the risk of later disputes.

On the other hand, the cost of establishing and maintaining a central document depository may be substantial; before ordering or approving one, the court should satisfy itself that the cost is justified by the anticipated savings and other benefits. The court, in consultation with counsel, will need to allocate costs fairly among the parties,[178] considering their resources, extent of use of the depository, and benefit derived from it. One way of allocating costs is to charge parties for each use of the depository. The charge should be set no higher than necessary to cover costs; a depository should not be a profit-making enterprise. Special arrangements for less affluent parties may be needed to ensure fair access.

It may be necessary to appoint an administrator to operate the depository, with the cost allocated among the parties.[179] If document depositories have been established in related cases in other courts, counsel may be able to arrange for their joint use, sharing the expense; likewise, consideration should be given to the requests of litigants in other cases, wherever pending, to use a depository established in the case before the court. Where significant costs are involved, the court should consider periodic assessments to fund operations, usually beginning with the order establishing the depository.

To establish a depository, counsel and the court must first select a suitable location. If sufficient space is available in the courthouse, planning should be co-

---

178. The cost of establishing and maintaining a central document depository is not a "taxable cost" under 28 U.S.C. § 1920 and Fed. R. Civ. P. 54(d). *In re* San Juan, 964 F.2d 956, 964 (1st Cir. 1993). Counsel should also be aware that expenses incurred during discovery which would ordinarily be taxable costs may not be recoverable if the party could have avoided them by using the depository. *See In re* San Juan, 142 F.R.D. 41, 46–47 (D. P.R. 1992).

179. For a list of possible duties for the administrator, see section VI. D. of the amended case-management order in *In re* San Juan Dupont Plaza Hotel Fire Litigation, *reprinted in* 1989 WL 168401 (D. P.R.) [hereinafter San Juan Order].

ordinated with the clerk of court. More often space will need to be acquired in another adequately sized and conveniently located building.[180] Counsel and the court should collaborate in establishing a regime for the operation of the depository, including procedures for acquisition, numbering, indexing, and storing of discovery materials and rules governing when and by whom documents may be examined and copied.[181] If a party objects to depositing documents in a central depository, the court may enter an order under Rule 26(c)(2) directing production at the depository (or the place designated by the requesting parties) or permit the producing party at its expense to furnish copies to all parties.

The availability of technology such as CD-ROM and other optical discs on which discovery materials can be recorded in computer-accessible form can result in substantial savings. The court may direct that some or all discovery materials be "imaged" on discs, which then may be distributed to parties seeking discovery[182] (special provision for the retention of originals may be necessary). Because a single disc can store a large amount of information, voluminous discovery materials can thus be distributed much more conveniently and inexpensively.[183] Computerized search and retrieval of information on a disc can facilitate review of voluminous discovery materials, particularly if adequately indexed.[184] Computerization of discovery documents may be either an alternative or a supplement to the use of a central document depository. For more on this technology, see *infra* sections 34.33–34.34, 34.37.

21.445 Evidentiary Foundation for Documents

The production of documents, either in the traditional manner or by filing in a document depository, will not necessarily provide the foundation for admission of those documents into evidence at trial or for use on motion for summary judgment. Management of documents should therefore also take into account the need for effective and efficient procedures to establish the foundation—by stipu-

---

180. *See, e.g., In re* Shell Oil Refinery, 125 F.R.D. 122 (E.D. La. 1989) (over 600,000 documents maintained in depository on defendant's business property, near original files); section VI.B. of the San Juan Order, *supra* note 179 (document depository located on five floors leased in conveniently located building).

181. *See* section VI. of the San Juan Order, *supra* note 179. Special procedures may be necessary to safeguard material designated as confidential. *Id.* at section IX.J.4; *In re* San Juan, 121 F.R.D. 147, 150 (D. P.R. 1988).

182. See *In re* Silicone Gel Breast Implant Prods. Liab. Litig., MDL 926, where the court ordered imaging of defendants' discovery documents, but not deposition transcripts or plaintiffs' discovery documents.

183. In MDL 926, each disc held approximately 15,000 pages and could be obtained for $25.

184. For example, the software utilized in MDL 926 allowed documents to be located according to such things as key words, names, dates, document types, or any combination thereof.

lation, requests for admission,[185] interrogatories, or depositions (particularly Rule 31 depositions on written questions).

21.446 Discovery of Computerized Data

Computerized data have become commonplace in litigation. Such data include not only conventional information but also such things as operating systems (programs that control a computer's basic functions), applications (programs used directly by the operator, such as word processing or spreadsheet programs), computer-generated models, and other sets of instructions residing in computer memory. Any discovery plan must address the relevant issues, such as the search for, location, retrieval, form of production and inspection, preservation, and use at trial of information stored in mainframe or personal computers or accessible "online." For the most part, such data will reflect information generated and maintained in the ordinary course of business. Some computerized data, however, may have been compiled in anticipation of or for use in the litigation (and may therefore be entitled to protection as trial preparation materials). Discovery requests may themselves be transmitted in computer-accessible form; interrogatories served on computer disks, for example, could then be answered using the same disk, avoiding the need to retype them. Finally, computerized data may form the contents for a common document depository (see *supra* section 21.444).

Some of the relevant issues to be considered follow:

Form of production. Rule 34 provides for the production, inspection, and copying of computerized data (i.e., "data compilations from which information can be obtained, translated, if necessary, by the respondent through detection devices into reasonably usable form"); Rule 33(d) permits parties to answer interrogatories by making available for inspection and copying business records, including "compilations," where "the burden of deriving or ascertaining the answer is substantially the same for the party serving the interrogatory as for the party served." The court will need to consider, among other things, whether production and inspection should be in computer-readable form (such as by translation onto CD-ROM disks) or of printouts (hard copies); what information the producing party must be required to provide (such as manuals and similar materials) to facilitate the requesting party's access to and inspection of the producing party's data; whether to require the parties to agree on a standard format for production

---

185. *See* Fed. R. Civ. P. 36. While admissions are only binding on the party making them, authenticity (as opposed to admissibility) may be established by the admission of any person having personal knowledge that the proffered item is what the proponent claims it to be, see Fed. R. Evid. 901(a), (b)(1), subject to the right of nonadmitting parties to challenge that persons' basis of knowledge. *See In re* Japanese Elec. Prods. Antitrust Case, 723 F.2d 238, 285 (3d Cir. 1983).

of computerized data;[186] and how to minimize and allocate the costs of production (such as the cost of computer runs or of special programming to facilitate production) and equalize the burdens on the parties.[187] The cost of production may be an issue, for example, where production is to be made of E-mail (electronic mail) or voice-mail messages erased from hard disks but capable of being retrieved.

Search and retrieval. Computer-stored data and other information responsive to a request will not necessarily be found in an appropriately labeled file. Broad database searches may be necessary, and this may expose confidential or irrelevant data to the opponent's scrutiny unless appropriate safeguards are installed. Similarly, some data may be maintained in the form of compilations that may themselves be entitled to trade secret protection or that reflect attorney work product, having been prepared by attorneys in contemplation of litigation. Data may have been compiled, for example, to produce studies and tabulations for use at trial or as a basis for expert opinions.[188]

Use at trial. In general, the Federal Rules of Evidence apply to computerized data as they do to other types of evidence.[189] Computerized data may, however, raise unique issues concerning the accuracy and authenticity of the database. Accuracy may be impaired as a result of incorrect or incomplete entry of data, mistakes in output instructions, programming errors, damage and contamination of storage media, power outages, and equipment malfunctions. The proponent of computerized evidence has the burden of laying a proper foundation by establish-

186. For example, the parties may agree on a particular computer program or language and the method of data storage. *See* Martha A. Mills, Discovery of Computerized Information, Legal Times Seminar, June 22, 1993, at tab 6.

187. See *infra* § 21.433 re protective orders allocating costs. *See also* National Union Elec. Corp. v. Matsushita Elec. Indus. Co., Ltd., 494 F. Supp. 1257 (E.D. Pa. 1980) (Becker, J.).

188. Rule 26(a)(2)(B) requires that, unless otherwise stipulated or ordered, a party must disclose in advance of trial (among other things) "the data or other information considered by" an expert witness in forming the opinions to be expressed. However, records computerized for "litigation support" purposes, not considered by an expert or intended for use at trial, may be protected trial preparation materials under Rule 26(b)(3) to the extent that they reveal counsel's decisions as to which records to computerize and how to organize them.

189. For an analysis and checklists, see Gregory P. Joseph, *A Simplified Approach to Computer-Generated Evidence and Animations,* 156 F.R.D. 327 (1994); see also Daniel A. Bronstein, *Leading Federal Cases on Computer Stored or Generated Data,* Scientific Evidence Review, Monograph No. 1 at 92 (ABA 1993). For example, the "business records" exception to the hearsay rule applies to a "data compilation, in any form." Fed. R. Evid. 803(6). A printout or other output of such data readable by sight is an "original" and is required to prove the contents of the data. Fed. R. Evid. 1001(3), 1002. Noncomputerized materials may be computerized during pretrial proceedings and presented in lieu of the individual records as a chart, summary, or calculation. Fed. R. Evid. 1006.

ing its accuracy.[190] Issues concerning accuracy and reliability of computerized evidence, including any necessary discovery, should be addressed during pretrial proceedings and not raised for the first time at trial.[191]

When the data are voluminous, verification and correction of all items may not be feasible. In such cases, verification may be made of a sample of the data. Instead of correcting the errors detected in the sample—which might lead to the erroneous representation that the compilation is free from error—evidence may be offered (or stipulations made) by way of extrapolation from the sample of the effect of the observed errors on the entire compilation. Alternatively, it may be feasible to use statistical methods to determine the probability and range of error.

The complexity, general unfamiliarity, and rapidly changing character of the technology involved in the management of computerized materials may at times make it appropriate for the court to seek the assistance of a special master or neutral expert. Alternatively, the parties may be called on to provide the court with expert assistance, in the form of briefings on the relevant technological issues.

21.447 Discovery from Nonparties

Under Fed. R. Civ. P. 34(c), a nonparty may be compelled to produce and allow copying of documents and other tangibles or submit to an inspection by service of a subpoena under Rule 45; the producing person need not be deposed or even appear personally.[192] A party seeking such production has a duty to take reasonable steps to avoid imposing undue burden or expense on the person subpoenaed.[193] Objections to production must be made in writing by the subpoenaed person; the requesting party must then move for an order to compel produc-

---

190. The proponent is not required, however, to prove that the tabulation is free from all possible error. Authentication may be provided by "[e]vidence describing a process or system used to produce a result and showing that the process or system produces an accurate result." Fed. R. Evid. 901(b)(9). The standard for authenticity "is satisfied by evidence sufficient to support a finding that the matter in question is what its proponent claims." Fed. R. Evid. 901(a). In the case of summaries, accuracy is an issue "for the trier of fact to determine as in the case of other issues of fact." Fed. R. Evid. 1008. Accordingly, the existence or possibility of errors usually affects only the weight, not the admissibility, of the evidence, except when the problems are so significant as to call for exclusion under Rule 403. Of course, if computerized data provided by a party are offered against that party, inquiry into the accuracy of the data may be unnecessary.

191. The court may order that any objections to the foundation, accuracy, or reliability of data are deemed waived unless raised during pretrial (or good cause is shown for the failure to object). See Fed. R. Civ. P. 26(a)(3); Shu-Tao Lin v. McDonnell Douglas Transport, Inc., 742 F.2d 45, 48 & n.3 (2d Cir. 1984).

192. Fed. R. Civ. P. 45(c)(2)(A). Despite the absence of a deposition, notice must be given to other parties. Fed. R. Civ. P. 45(b)(1).

193. Fed. R. Civ. P. 45(c)(1).

tion.[194] If the motion to compel is granted, the order must protect the nonparty from significant expense resulting from the inspection or copying,[195] and may also protect against disclosure of privileged, confidential, or otherwise protected material and undue burden.[196] Before resort to subpoenas, consideration should be given to the possibility of acquiring the needed information through informal means or from other sources, such as materials produced in other litigation in which the nonparty was involved or public records, or, if the nonparty is a government agency, using requests under the Freedom of Information Act.[197]

21.45 Depositions

Depositions are an effective and necessary means of discovery and trial preparation. They are, however, often over-used and conducted inefficiently. As a result, depositions tend to be the most costly and time-consuming activity in complex litigation. Management of litigation should therefore be directed at avoiding unnecessary depositions, limiting the number and length of those that are taken, and ensuring that the process of taking depositions is conducted as fairly and efficiently as possible.

21.451 Limitations and Controls

Depositions should be limited to those that are necessary. In determining necessity, counsel should consider the purpose for which any particular deposition is to be taken. Depositions can serve three purposes:

- to obtain relevant information from knowledgeable witnesses;
- to perpetuate the testimony of witnesses who may be unavailable at trial; and
- to commit adverse witnesses to their testimony.

While the latter two purposes are uniquely served by depositions, the first, obtaining information, can often be accomplished more quickly and less expensively by a variety of formal and informal discovery devices (see *infra*

194. Fed. R. Civ. P. 45(c)(2)(B).
195. *Id.*
196. Fed. R. Civ. P. 45(c)(3).
197. 5 U.S.C. § 552.

section 21.452). In developing the discovery plan, counsel should determine that each proposed deposition will serve a useful and necessary purpose and that it will be relevant to material issues in dispute and not cumulative.

The court, of course, has broad authority to limit depositions. Fed. R. Civ. P. 30(a)(2)(A) and 31(a)(2)(A) impose a presumptive limit of ten depositions each for plaintiffs, defendants, and third-party defendants (local rules may also restrict the number of depositions). While the parties may stipulate around the presumptive limit, the court has final authority under Rule 26(b)(2) to limit the number and length of depositions. Rule 30(d)(2) provides additional authority to control the length of depositions (as do some local rules). Limits on depositions may also be imposed indirectly by the setting of the trial date or a discovery cutoff date. In large-stake cases, such limits can be evaded by multitrack discovery (concurrent depositions) in the absence of a further order by the court.[198]

The court's authority should be exercised on the basis of the information provided by the parties bearing on the need for the proposed depositions, the subject matter to be covered, and the available alternatives. The extent to which the judge considers each particular deposition, categories of depositions, or only the deposition program as a whole will depend on the circumstances of each litigation; the court may, for example, condition the taking of certain depositions, such as those of putative class members, on prior court approval. The judge's involvement in the development of this phase of the discovery plan should, however, be sufficient to establish meaningful control over the time and resources to be expended. Aside from setting appropriate limits, the judge should also be concerned with the time and place of taking the depositions, including proposed travel, and the methods to be used for recording.[199]

To ensure that the limits placed on depositions in the discovery plan are not frustrated by abusive practices, the court should insist on observance of rules for the fair and efficient conduct of depositions. Rule 30(d)(1) requires that objections be stated "concisely and in a non-argumentative and non-suggestive manner"; local rules or standing orders may also establish guidelines for objections.[200] Rule 30(d)(1) allows counsel to instruct a deponent not to answer only for the purpose of preserving a privilege[201] or enforcing a court-imposed limitation on evidence, or in preparation for a motion under Rule 30(d)(3) to limit or terminate the examination for bad faith or harassment; more stringent limitations

---

198. Despite their cost and the potential for unfairness, such "multiple track" depositions may be a practical necessity to expedite cases in which time is of the essence. See *infra* § 21.454.

199. See Sample Order *infra* § 41.38 (deposition guidelines).

200. *See, e.g.,* Rule 12, Standing Orders of the Court on Effective Discovery in Civil Cases (E.D.N.Y. 1984).

201. To the extent possible, disputed claims of privilege should be resolved in advance of the deposition.

may be imposed by local rule or by court order when necessary.[202] In addition, some courts issue guidelines covering matters including the following:

- who may attend depositions;
- where the depositions are to be taken;
- who may question the witness;
- how the parties are to allocate the costs; and
- how the attorneys are to conduct themselves.[203]

Rule 30(d)(2) expressly authorizes sanctions for persons responsible for "impediment, delay or other conduct that has frustrated the fair examination of the deponent."

Inefficient management of documents at deposition can interfere with its proper conduct. The discovery plan should establish procedures for marking deposition exhibits, handling copies and originals, and exchanging in advance all papers about which the examining party intends to question the witness (except those to be used for genuine impeachment).[204]

21.452 Cost-Saving Measures

In addition to the general discovery practices discussed in *supra* section 21.42, techniques which may be helpful in streamlining deposition discovery include the following:

- **Informal interviews.** Informal interviews of potential witnesses may be arranged with the agreement of counsel.[205] This procedure may be useful for persons who have only limited knowledge or involvement and who are unlikely to be called as witnesses at trial. If counsel desire, the witness may be sworn and the interview recorded electronically for possible use

---

202. *See, e.g.,* Article VI(6) of the Civil Justice Expense and Delay Reduction Plan for the Eastern District of Texas (complete prohibition on instructions not to answer except to assert privilege). The court may prohibit counsel from even conferring with the deponent during interrogation for any purpose but deciding whether to assert a privilege. *See* Hall v. Clifton Precision, 150 F.R.D. 525 (E.D. Pa. 1993); Rule 13, Standing Orders of the Court on Effective Discovery in Civil Cases (E.D.N.Y. 1984).

203. See Sample Order *infra* § 41.38.

204. *See, e.g.,* section IX.H(12) of the San Juan Order, *supra* note 179 (five days advance notice).

205. An attorney may not communicate with a represented party without the consent of that party's counsel. ABA Model Rule of Professional Conduct 4.2. If the represented party is an organization, the prohibition extends to persons with managerial responsibility and any other person whose act or omission may be imputed to the organization or whose statement may constitute an admission on the part of the organization. *See id.* comment. The prohibition does not extend to former corporate employees. ABA Comm. on Ethics and Professional Responsibility, Formal Op. 91-359 (1991). The law of the circuit should be consulted for recent developments in this area of the law.

later in the case;[206] the interview may also be converted by agreement or court order into a nonstenographic deposition.

- **Nonstenographic depositions.** Unless otherwise ordered by the court, the party taking a deposition may record it on audio or videotape instead of stenographically without having it transcribed.[207] Any other party may make its own tape recording of the deposition.[208] Videotaped depositions offer a number of advantages: they help deter misconduct by counsel at the deposition; they can preserve the testimony of witnesses who may be unavailable to testify at trial (such as experts having scheduling conflicts preventing their appearance at trial or persons suffering from an infirmity) and in dispersed litigation can avoid multiple live appearances by the same witness; they tend to hold a jury's attention better than the reading of a deposition transcript and help the jury assess the witness's demeanor and credibility; and they are more effective in helping clients considering settlement to evaluate the quality of the opposition's case. On the other hand, editing tape for showing in court to eliminate objectionable and irrelevant material may be difficult and time-consuming.[209] Safeguards may be necessary, such as having (1) the videotape operator sworn and certify the correctness and completeness of the recording; (2) the deponent sworn on tape; (3) the recording device run continuously throughout the deposition; and (4) counsel agree to (or having the court order) standard technical procedures to avoid distortion.[210] Both sides may record a deposition, each bearing its own expense.

---

206. Although the use of such a statement at trial is more limited than that of a deposition, it may be useful for impeachment.

207. Fed. R. Civ. P. 30(b)(2). With the concurrence of the deponent, a written transcript often may be deferred until need for it arises, and, even then, only parts of the deposition may need to be transcribed. Counsel can save additional time by entering into a stipulation (with the deponent's consent) waiving presentation to the deponent.

208. Fed. R. Civ. P. 30(b)(3).

209. *See* Spangler v. Sears Roebuck and Co., 138 F.R.D. 122, 126 n.3 (S.D. Ind. 1992) (setting out guidelines for use of videotaped depositions at trial). To facilitate this process, and for ease of reference at trial, the court may require the creation of a log index identifying the location on the tape of each stage of the examination and every objection, as well as other information. *See* Michael J. Henke, *The Taking and Use of Videotaped Depositions*, 16 Am. J. Trial Advoc. 151, 160 n.45 (1992); *In re* "Agent Orange" Prod. Liab. Litig., 28 F. R. Serv. 2d 993, 996 (1980).

210. These procedures might cover such matters as the use of zoom lens, lighting, background, and camera angle. *See* Henke, *supra* note 209, at 158. Fed. R. Civ. P. 30(b)(4) requires that "[t]he appearance or demeanor of deponents or attorneys shall not be distorted through camera or sound-recording techniques."

- **Telephonic depositions.** The use of telephonic depositions can reduce travel costs.[211] Supplemental examination by parties not present when a person was first deposed may be conducted effectively by telephone. Through use of speaker phones, conference calls, or video teleconferencing, distant witnesses (such as a willing witness located abroad) may be examined by counsel from counsel's offices, with the court reporter located with the witness or, by stipulation, at one of the attorneys' offices (see *infra* section 21.494, extraterritorial discovery). A telephonic deposition may also be recorded nonstenographically. Telephonic depositions are most often used for examinations that are expected to be relatively brief and do not involve numerous documents, but may also be used to avoid last-minute continuances or trial interruptions when deposition testimony becomes unexpectedly necessary. To ensure that deponents are not coached, ground rules should specify who may be present with the deponent during the examination.

- **Conference depositions.** In special situations, such as a Rule 30(b)(6) deposition of an organization, several persons may be deposed simultaneously (in person or by telephone) in a conference setting.[212]

- **Representative depositions.** Where there are many potential nonparty witnesses, typically in the case of eyewitnesses, counsel may agree on a few representative depositions and stipulate that the testimony of other named witnesses would be the same.

- **Written questions.** In some circumstances, the rarely used procedures of Fed. R. Civ. P. 31 for depositions on written questions may be a cost-effective means of obtaining trial evidence. For example, Rule 31 deposition questions—unlike interrogatories—may be directed to nonparties and the answers used at trial to provide evidentiary foundation for documents. Rule 31 questions may also be useful in follow-up examinations by absent or later-added parties of persons whose depositions have been taken earlier.

- **Reduction in copies.** Costs can be controlled by limiting the number of copies of deposition transcripts ordered, particularly if a document depository is established; waiving filing of the original with the court; and not having transcripts prepared of depositions that turn out to be of no value.

---

211. Under Fed. R. Civ. P. 30(b)(7), the court may order or the parties may stipulate to taking of a deposition by telephonic "or other remote electronic means."

212. See *supra* § 21.423.

- **Limited attendance.** Limits may be set on the number of attorneys for each party or each side who may attend depositions, particularly in cases in which fees may be awarded or approved by the court. Restraint can also be encouraged by the use of deferred supplemental depositions (see *infra* section 21.453). Nonattending counsel may, of course, suggest topics for examination to colleagues who will be attending, and Fed. R. Civ. P. 30(c) allows parties to serve sealed written questions, which the presiding officer will propound to the deponent. Nonattending counsel may also listen to key depositions by telephone and suggest additional questions to their representatives at recesses. In the exceptional case where the expense is justified, counsel may arrange for computer-assisted stenographic reporting, allowing the court reporter's stenographic notes to be telephonically transmitted to terminals located in attorneys' offices in other cities.

21.453 Deferred Supplemental Depositions

In multiparty cases the court should consider an order relieving parties of the risk of nonattendance at depositions in which they have only a peripheral interest.[213] Such an order may provide that a copy of the deposition transcript will promptly be made available to nonattending parties, who within a specified period thereafter may conduct supplemental examination of the deponent,[214] either by appearing in person at a designated time and place for resumption of the deposition or by presenting questions in written form under Rule 31 or in a telephonic deposition under Rule 30(b)(7). The order should specify whether the absent party has the right to require resumption of the adjourned deposition or—as is usually preferable—must show cause why resumption is necessary. The order should also state whether the initial examination is admissible at trial if the deponent later becomes unavailable for supplemental examination.

These procedures are designed to relieve parties, particularly those with limited financial resources, from incurring the expense of attending depositions in which their interest is minimal or will likely be adequately protected by others in attendance. They should not be used as a tactical device to harass witnesses or to inconvenience other parties. Counsel for litigants with a substantial interest in a deposition should attend or be represented by other counsel.

The court should also provide for the use of depositions against persons who may become parties to the litigation by later amendment of the pleadings or the filing, removal, or transfer of related cases. The order may state that all previously

---

213. See Sample Order *infra* § 41.38.

214. A stipulation or court order will be required to depose a person who has already been deposed in the case. Fed. R. Civ. P. 30(a)(2)(B).

taken depositions will be deemed binding on new parties unless, within a specified period after their appearance in the litigation, they show cause to the contrary. Even in the absence of such an order, resumption of earlier depositions should be controlled and limited to questioning relevant to the new parties. Like other parties who have not attended a deposition, the new parties are typically given a specified period of time to conduct supplemental examination of the deponents, although the court may require that some need for additional questioning be shown. Repetition of earlier examination can be avoided by having deponents adopt their earlier testimony.

21.454 Scheduling

The scheduling of depositions involves the sequencing of depositions in relation to other discovery,[215] the order in which witnesses are to be deposed, and the setting of times and places to which all of the attorneys and witnesses can be committed.

General considerations concerning the sequencing of discovery have been discussed at *supra* section 21.422. How depositions should be sequenced with respect to other discovery in the litigation calls for careful consideration. Often, discovery intended to identify persons knowledgeable on specific matters and secure production of documents relevant to their examination should precede the taking of depositions. In some cases, however, the early deposition of a central witness can provide information critical to further proceedings, including settlement negotiations. Similarly, the order of depositions depends on the circumstances. The discovery plan should not assume that all potentially relevant depositions will invariably be taken; other things being equal, it is preferable to begin with witnesses crucial to the case before embarking on depositions of peripheral persons. Depositions relevant to a prospective motion for summary judgment or the early trial of a severed issue should precede those that might be obviated by a ruling on the motion or trial.

Ordinarily, discovery by all parties proceeds concurrently. One purpose of a discovery plan is to establish an orderly procedure and avoid indiscriminate noticing of depositions, which may result in inconvenience, harassment, and inefficiency. Dates and witnesses for depositions should be scheduled to accomplish the objectives of the discovery plan, minimize travel and other expense, and make reasonable accommodation of parties, counsel, and witnesses. A plan might set specific dates for specific witness or set aside specified time periods during which designated parties are given either exclusive or preferential rights to

---

215. Absent stipulation or court order, depositions may not be taken before the Rule 26(f) discovery conference unless the notice is accompanied by a certification, with supporting facts, that the person to be examined is expected to leave the country and be unavailable for examination in this country unless deposed before that time. Fed. R. Civ. P. 30(a)(2)(C), 26(d).

Manual for Complex Litigation, Third

schedule depositions, subject to exceptions for emergencies. Arrangements should be sought with deponents to take their depositions at a convenient central location, such as the place where a document depository and perhaps counsel are located; the parties may find it economical to share such witnesses' travel expenses to avoid the expense of having counsel travel to distant depositions. Parties should be expected to work out these arrangements with little involvement by the court other than to lend assistance when needed.

When depositions cannot be scheduled at times or places convenient to all counsel, attorneys should try to arrange for participation by others from their offices or counsel representing litigants with similar interests. Moreover, to meet discovery deadlines, it may be necessary to conduct depositions on a "multiple track" basis, with depositions of several different witnesses being taken at the same time in one or more locations.

21.455 Coordination with Related Litigation

Discovery plans in related cases pending before the same judge should be coordinated to avoid conflicts and duplication. If the cases are pending before different judges, counsel should nevertheless attempt to coordinate the depositions of common witnesses and other common discovery. Examination regarding subjects of interest only to particular cases may be deferred until the conclusion of direct and cross-examination on matters of common interest. Parties may also stipulate to the use in related cases of depositions taken in one particular case.

Economies may also be achieved when parties in the present litigation have access to depositions previously taken in other litigation (see also *supra* section 21.423). Depositions of opposing parties and their employees are generally admissible against such parties under Fed. R. Evid. 801(d)(2). Depositions of other witnesses may be usable for impeachment under Fed. R. Evid. 801(d)(1)(A). In other situations, such as those involving nonparties or a party's own witnesses, a new deposition may be necessary, but (with advance notice) the answers given at the earlier deposition may be adopted as the current testimony of the witness, subject to supplementation; telephonic nonstenographic depositions may be used for this purpose at little cost to either side.

See *infra* section 31 on coordination with related litigation.

21.456 Control of Abusive Conduct

As noted above, to prevent frustration of the discovery plan the court needs to insist on counsel's observance of the rules for the fair and efficient conduct of depositions. See *supra* section 21.451. Those rules include Rules 30(d)(1) and (3), local rules, and the judge's standing orders; some judges have also issued written guidelines that advise attorneys how the judge expects discovery to be conducted. The likelihood of problematic conduct will be greatly reduced if the court informs counsel at the outset of the litigation of its expectations with respect to the conduct of depositions, including speaking and argumentative objections, instructions not to answer, coaching of witnesses (including restrictions during recesses in the deposition),[216] and evasive or obstructive conduct by witnesses. (See *supra* section 21.451, Sample Order *infra* section 41.38.) A speedy and efficient procedure to resolve discovery disputes also helps (see *supra* section 21.424).

In cases where abuses are rampant, the court may require that depositions be videotaped for judicial review or may require counsel to expeditiously deliver a copy of the transcript of each deposition for review by the court. Alternatively, the court may direct that one or more depositions be supervised in person by a judge, magistrate judge, or special master. The judicial officer or special master may need to be present only briefly, setting the tone and making a few early rulings, and then remain on call. Even where a special master is appointed to exercise continuous oversight, the resulting savings in avoiding disputes and satellite litigation may justify the cost. Some judges have required that depositions be taken in court to allow periodic monitoring.

In rare cases, sanctions may need to be imposed. Although sanctions may have a prophylactic effect for later depositions, they will do little to cure the damage that has already occurred and may further poison relations between counsel. They should therefore be a last resort. See *supra* section 20.15.

21.46 Interrogatories

Used with care and restraint, interrogatories can be a useful device to supplement other discovery methods, mainly to obtain specific factual information. Because interrogatories are often poorly drafted, misused, or employed to burden and harass an opponent, courts generally restrict the number permitted. Counsel will therefore have to make the best use of the limited number of interrogatories likely to be allowed through skillful and thoughtful drafting designed to accomplish a legitimate purpose.

21.461 Purposes

Interrogatories primarily serve the purpose of determining the existence, identity, and location of witnesses, documents, and other tangible evidence as a prerequisite to planning of further discovery. Much of this type of information is subject to prediscovery disclosure under the Federal Rules or local rules and, even if not,

---

216. *See* Hall v. Clifton Precision, 150 F.R.D. 525 (E.D. Pa. 1993).

can be required to be exchanged by the court under a discovery order. See *supra* sections 21.13, 21.423. Interrogatories may be useful in filling gaps and ensuring full compliance with informal requests, obtaining information dispersed among a number of persons under the opponent's control, and gathering technical information when the requesting party may need assistance from an expert in formulating precise questions and the answering party may need time and special assistance to respond (e.g., when discovery is sought concerning systems and programs for the storage and retrieval of computerized data).

Contention interrogatories may sometimes be useful in defining issues, though the procedures discussed in *supra* section 21.33 are usually more productive in clarifying and narrowing issues and the contentions of the parties. Rule 33(c) permits interrogatories calling for "an opinion or contention that relates to fact or the application of law to fact," but permits the court to defer an answer "until after designated discovery has been completed or until a pretrial conference or other later time." Before contention interrogatories are filed, the court should consider whether they are likely to be useful at that stage of the proceeding and should ensure that they will not be argumentative.

Interrogatories may also be used, either alone or in conjunction with requests for admission under Fed. R. Civ. P. 36 (see *infra* section 21.47), to provide the foundation for a summary judgment motion. Whether certain facts are genuinely in dispute may be difficult to ascertain from depositions and affidavits, and even in response to Rule 36 requests the opposing party may state that, although reasonable inquiry has been made, it can neither admit nor deny the truth of particular matters that depend on the credibility of third persons. Interrogatories are a means to require a party to disclose any facts asserted to raise a triable issue with respect to particular elements of a claim or defense.

Interrogatories should never be used for cross-examination or to elicit argumentative answers. Except in certain specialized areas of practice, form or pattern interrogatories are generally regarded as unacceptable.

21.462 Limitations

Rule 33(a) imposes a presumptive limit of twenty-five interrogatories, including subparts, per party, and many local rules also restrict the number of interrogatories that may be propounded without stipulation or a court order. In complex litigation, where the range of potentially relevant facts is great and much largely noncontroversial background information must be gathered, adhering to such limits may be counterproductive, although some control of the use of interrogatories should be retained by the court. In granting leave to file additional interrogatories, the court should be guided by the principles of Rule 26(b)(2) and satisfy itself that the resulting benefits will outweigh the burdens.[217] Whatever the permitted number of interrogatories, lengthy and elaborate definitions and instructions in the interrogatories and verbose and evasive responses should be avoided.

21.463 Responses

Responses to interrogatories should be served in a timely manner.[218] Rule 33(b) requires that interrogatories be answered "fully" and under oath; if an objection is made, the responding party must not only state the grounds for the objection "with specificity," but also must answer to the extent the interrogatory is not objectionable.[219] Answers should be provided to the extent information is available at the time (even if incomplete), subject to supplementation as new information is acquired. Rule 26(e)(2) requires parties to seasonably amend interrogatory responses if, as new information comes to light, the responding party learns that a response—even if complete and correct when made—is now incomplete or incorrect (unless this information has otherwise been made known to opposing parties during discovery or in writing). The discovery plan should schedule periodic dates for review and amendment of interrogatory responses (see *supra* section 21.421). If an answer is withheld on privilege grounds, the claim must be accompanied by a description of the information withheld sufficient to enable other parties to assess the applicability of the privilege.[220] Answers must be signed by the person making them, and objections by attorneys, subject to the certification required by Rule 26(g) when propounding and responding to interrogatories.[221] Some courts require that responses to contention interrogatories be signed by counsel; others permit a party to sign, stating in substance, "I have been advised by my attorneys that . . . "—but such a statement may waive the attorney–client privilege.

21.464 Other Practices to Save Time and Expense

Use of the following techniques may increase the effectiveness and efficiency of interrogatories:

- **Master interrogatories; precluding duplicate requests.** Similarly situated parties may be required to confer and develop a single or master set of

---

217. *See* Fed. R. Civ. P. 33(a).

218. Fed. R. Civ. P. 33(b)(3) requires answers and objections to be served within thirty days of service unless the parties stipulate otherwise. The court may establish a different period by order and should consider doing so after determining, in consultation with counsel, how much time is truly needed to respond to specific interrogatories.

219. Fed. R. Civ. P. 33(b)(1), (4). Any ground not stated in a timely objection will be deemed waived in the absence of good cause. Fed. R. Civ. P. 33(b)(4).

220. Fed. R. Civ. P. 26(b)(5). *See supra* § 21.431.

221. The requirements of Rule 26(g) are described in *supra* § 21.421.

interrogatories to be served on an opposing party. If interrogatories have already been served by one party, other parties should be barred from asking the same questions since any party may use the answers to interrogatories served by another regardless of who propounded the interrogatory.[222]

- **Use of interrogatories from other litigation.** Parties may also be barred from propounding interrogatories that an adversary has already answered in other litigation, when such answers are available or may be made available by the adversary.[223]

- **Successive responses.** If some questions will require substantially more investigation than others, counsel may stipulate that the responding party will provide answers in stages as the information is obtained, rather than seek additional time for the first response. Fed. R. Civ. P. 29(2) requires court approval of stipulations extending the time to respond to interrogatories only if they would interfere with court-ordered time limits (see *supra* section 21.423).

- **Modified responses.** When interrogatories seek information that the responding party lacks or can obtain only with significant expenditure of time and money, and the information can be provided in a different form, that party should not object but rather advise the opponent and attempt to reach agreement on an acceptable form of response. For example, information requested on a calendar year basis may be readily available on a fiscal year basis, or information on overtime hours may be derived from records of compensation rates and overtime paid.

- **Early resolution of disputes.** The parties may be required to object to interrogatories before expiration of the time for filing answers, particularly in cases where more than the standard thirty-day period is allowed for filing answers. The parties should promptly attempt to resolve the objections by modifying or clarifying the troublesome interrogatories. If negotiations are unsuccessful, the parties should present their dispute to the court in a clear and concise manner, avoiding lengthy motions and briefs, and the court should rule promptly to avoid disruption of the progress of the litigation (see *supra* section 21.424).

---

222. *See* Fed. R. Evid. 801(d)(2).
223. *See id.*

- **Informal discovery.** Counsel should attempt to informally exchange information that would otherwise be elicited by interrogatories. Interrogatories may then be used to create a record admissible at trial.[224]
- **Rule 30(b)(6) depositions.** When a party seeks discovery from an organization but does not know the identity of individuals with relevant knowledge, the party may name the organization as the deponent, requiring it to designate persons to testify in response. This avoids the need for the two-step process of using an interrogatory to discover the identity of knowledgeable individuals and then deposing them individually.

21.47 Stipulations of Fact/Requests for Admission

Stipulations of fact. Stipulations of fact can reduce the time and expense both of pretrial proceedings and the trial itself. Rule 16(c)(1) provides that at any pretrial conference, the court "may take appropriate action, with respect to . . . the possibility of obtaining admissions of fact . . . which will avoid unnecessary proof . . . ." Although premature efforts to obtain stipulations may be counterproductive,[225] the judge should encourage stipulations of facts that, after an appropriate opportunity for discovery has been afforded, should no longer be genuinely in doubt. Admission should be expected not only of facts of which each party has personal knowledge, but also of those that can be established by evidence from others. If the parties insist, facts of the latter type may be shown as "uncontested," "uncontroverted," or "conceded" rather than as "admitted," but with the same effect in the litigation. Stipulations may be sought with respect both to the facts of the case and to matters that affect the admissibility of other evidence, such as the authenticity of records and the foundation requirements for exceptions to the hearsay rule under Fed. R. Evid. 803(6) and similar provisions. Parties may be more willing to enter into stipulations for specified limited purposes, such as an injunction proceeding, motion for summary judgment, or bifurcated trial of an issue. They may be willing to enter early stipulations if provision is made, analogous to that in Fed. R. Civ. P. 36(b), for timely withdrawal from an incorrect stipulation on the basis of newly discovered evidence when no substantial prejudice to other parties would result.

The court can assist the stipulation process by stressing the distinction between conceding the truth of some fact or agreeing not to contest it, and conceding its admissibility or weight. Counsel's admission of the truth of an uncontroverted fact does not affect the right to object to its admissibility or to contest its

---

224. Interrogatory answers are admissible to the extent permitted by the rules of evidence. Fed. R. Civ. P. 33(c).

225. Consideration should be given, however, to the early use of the combined discovery request described in *supra* § 21.423, in which a party may admit that particular facts are true in lieu of proceeding with other discovery regarding those matters.

probative value. Indeed, if a party contends that some fact is irrelevant or otherwise inadmissible, there is less reason not to admit to its truth without the exhaustive investigation and discovery that might be warranted for an obviously critical fact. A party may stipulate to the accuracy of tabulations and compilations whose significance it intends to dispute.[226]

The parties may also be reminded of the tactical disadvantages of contesting at trial some matter on which their opponents will certainly prevail or, indeed, of being confronted at trial with an earlier denial of some matter that could not have been fairly disputed. Since an angry client, rather than the attorney, is often the person responsible for an "admit nothing" posture in the litigation, the court may direct that the clients themselves attend a conference at which the desirability of early stipulations is discussed. Appointment of a special master may at times assist the parties in arriving at stipulations.

Requests for admission. When voluntary means to narrow factual disputes have been exhausted, admissions may be obtained under Fed. R. Civ. P. 36. The rule's advantage is that it prescribes procedures, responsibilities, and consequences respecting admissions. It has its limitations, however. As discussed in *supra* section 21.463, complementary or supplementary interrogatories may be needed if a party in apparent good faith declines to admit the truth of some fact that depends on the credibility of other witnesses. In addition, like interrogatories, Rule 36 admissions are usable only against the party who made them and only in the action in which they were made. In multiparty litigation, requests may therefore have to be directed to each party in each related action.[227] Because parties often deny a requested admission on the basis of a trivial disagreement with a statement or without indicating the portions of the stated fact that are true, the court should urge the parties to observe their obligation under the rule to respond in good faith, and point out the availability of sanctions for failure to do so.[228]

Statements of contentions and proof. The limitations of Rule 36 and the difficulties often encountered when attorneys attempt, even in good faith, to negotiate stipulations of fact have led to the use of a third method for arriving at

226. Caution should be exercised in requiring a party to admit the accuracy of voluminous data or summaries of the same. As discussed in *supra* § 21.446, a response based on some limited study may be more appropriate even though this results in a summary with known errors.

227. Rule 36 requests answered by a party in prior or related litigation should be renewed; a simple new request that asks the party to admit each matter previously admitted should suffice.

228. "[W]hen good faith requires that a party qualify his answer or deny only a part of the matter of which an admission is requested, he shall specify so much of it as is true and qualify or deny the remainder." Fed. R. Civ. P. 36(a). Sanctions are available under Rule 37(c)(2). Marchaud v. Mercy Medical Ctr., 22 F.3d 933 (9th Cir. 1994) (affirming award of attorney fees incurred at trial based on failure to admit).

stipulations and admissions. Counsel for one side, typically the plaintiff's, are ordered by the court to draft a series of numbered, narrative statements of objective facts which they believe can be established, avoiding argumentative language, labels, and legal conclusions.[229] Opposing counsel must then indicate which of the proposed facts are admitted (or will not be contested) and which are disputed, specifying the nature of the disagreement by appropriate interlineation or deletion, as well as drafting narrative statements of additional facts that they believe can be established. The newly added statements are then returned to the first party for admission (or nondenial) or for specific disagreement. A consolidated statement reflecting what is agreed and what remains in dispute is then filed with the court as a stipulation of the parties. The court may incorporate the stipulation in a pretrial order, specifically providing that all (or only specified) objections to admissibility at trial are reserved.

This procedure for narrowing factual issues may be employed as one of the final steps before trial, coupled with a provision precluding a party from offering at trial evidence of any fact not included in the narrative listing, except for good cause shown. It may also be used earlier in the litigation (after adequate opportunity for discovery) with respect to specified proceedings, such as a class certification hearing or a Rule 56 motion. Whether all facts that the party proposes to prove must be listed—or only those that may possibly be admitted and, if admitted, would reduce the scope of evidence presented—will depend on the circumstances of the case. The more extensive the required listing, the greater the opportunity to narrow the facts that remain for proof at trial; the judge should, however, weigh the potential for reduction in the length and cost of trial against the time and expense expended in identifying facts that will probably remain in dispute.

The degree to which stipulations can be obtained may depend not so much on the procedures used as on the attitude of the parties. Attorneys are sometimes reluctant to make concessions that will ease their opponents' burden. The judge may be able to persuade counsel that, in addition to fulfilling their responsibilities as officers of the court, they will serve their clients' interests by streamlining the litigation through appropriate concessions and admissions. The refusal to stipulate provable facts almost never results in an advantage through a failure of proof and usually imposes additional costs on both sides in discovery, at trial, or both.

Requests for judicial notice. The judicial notice procedure provided by Fed. R. Evid. 201 may also be used to eliminate the need for some fact finding at trial. With respect to matters "capable of accurate and ready determination by resort to sources whose accuracy cannot reasonably be questioned," an appropriate request

---

229. See Sample Order *infra* § 41.61.

may be filed with the court under Fed. R. Evid. 201, requiring opposing counsel to justify their refusal to stipulate.

21.48 Disclosure and Discovery of Expert Opinions[230]

Expert witnesses are being used in complex litigation with increasing frequency and in growing numbers[231]—effective litigation management will therefore often require the exercise of reasonable judicial control over their use. Some judges have found it useful to confer with counsel before experts are retained to testify, to determine whether the proposed testimony will be necessary and appropriate, and to establish limits on the number of expert witnesses and the subjects they will cover.

Management of the disclosure and discovery of expert opinions is also essential to ensure adequate preparation by the parties, avoid surprise at trial, and facilitate rulings on the admissibility of expert evidence.

Trial experts. Rule 26(a)(2) requires the prediscovery disclosure by the parties of the identity of expert witnesses[232] to be called at trial and extensive additional information:

- a signed written report stating all opinions to which the expert will testify;
- the bases for those opinions;
- the data or information *considered* in forming the opinions;[233]
- exhibits to be introduced as a summary or in support of the opinions;
- the expert's qualifications (including a list of all publications authored in the last ten years);
- the compensation the expert is to receive; and
- a list of other cases in which the expert has testified within the last four years.[234]

---

230. For more detailed discussion of the management of expert testimony, see Reference Manual on Scientific Evidence (Federal Judicial Center 1994).

231. See *infra* §§ 33.22, 33.27–33.28, 33.35, 33.65, 33.73.

232. The rule applies only to experts "retained or specially employed" to give expert testimony or "whose duties as an employee of the party regularly involve giving expert testimony," but the court may extend the rule to other experts, such as treating physicians (or, conversely, waive it as to certain experts). Fed. R. Civ. P. 26 advisory committee's note.

233. The effect of this requirement is to substantially eliminate work product protection from communications between counsel and the expert. Fed. R. Civ. P. 26 advisory committee's note. The court may conduct an *in camera* inspection if necessary to redact irrelevant material. *See* Bogosian v. Gulf Oil Corp., 738 F.2d 587, 595–96 (3d Cir. 1984).

234. Fed. R. Civ. P. 26(a)(2)(A), (B).

Similar requirements may be contained in local rules or standing orders, and the court may itself enter an order adapting these requirements to meet the needs of the litigation.

At the initial conference, the court should establish a timetable for expert disclosure[235] and such other procedures as may be needed to implement it. Scheduling should take into account that the parties may lack sufficient information to select expert witnesses until the issues have been further defined and certain discovery completed; a party's decision may also await the disclosure of the opinions of experts selected by other parties.[236] Disclosure must, however, be made sufficiently in advance of trial for the parties to take depositions if necessary,[237] and for the court to conduct appropriate pretrial proceedings, such as hearing motions under Fed. R. Evid. 104(a) directed at expert evidence and motions for summary judgment.[238]

Experts may wish to modify or refine their disclosed opinions in the light of further studies, opinions expressed by other experts, or other developments in the litigation. Although Rule 26(e)(1) requires that opposing counsel be advised of these changes, a final cutoff date should be set by which all additions and revisions must be disclosed to be admissible at trial.[239]

Early and full disclosure of expert evidence can have an impact on efforts to define and narrow issues. Although experts often seem hopelessly at odds, when the assumptions and underlying data on which they have relied in reaching their opinions are revealed, the bases for their differences may become clearer and substantial simplification of the issues may be possible. In addition, disclosure can facilitate rulings well in advance of trial on objections to the qualifications of an expert, the relevance and reliability of opinions to be offered, or the reasonableness of reliance on particular data.[240] Courts use various procedures to identify and narrow the grounds for disagreement between opposing experts; the

---

235. *See* Fed. R. Civ. P. 26(a)(2)(C). Absent stipulation or a court order, these disclosures must be made at least ninety days before trial or, if the evidence is intended solely for rebuttal, thirty days from the opposing party's disclosure; supplementation under Rule 26(e) is also required. *Id.*

236. Normally the party with the burden of proof on an issue should be required to disclose its expert testimony on that issue before the other parties. Fed. R. Civ. P. 26 advisory committee's note.

237. Expert depositions are authorized by Rule 26(b)(4)(A); the discovering party must pay the expert's reasonable fees for responding. Rule 26(b)(4)(C). Disclosure may reduce the need for expert discovery, however, and warrant substantial limitations on it. *See* Fed. R. Civ. P. 26 advisory committee's note.

238. The court at that time may also want to consider appointment of an expert under Fed. R. Evid. 706. See *infra* § 21.51.

239. *See* Fed. R. Civ. P. 37(c)(1) (failure to make Rule 26(a) disclosures "without substantial justification" precludes introduction of nondisclosed witnesses or information at trial).

240. *See generally* Daubert v. Merrell Dow Pharmaceuticals, 113 S. Ct. 2786, 2796 (1993) (rejecting "general acceptance" test of Frye v. United States, 293 F. 1013 (D.C. Cir. 1923)).

experts may, for example, each be asked to explain the reasons for their disagreement.

Consulting experts. Discovery with respect to experts who will not testify at trial is much more limited. Such experts are not covered by Rule 26(a)(2), and may be deposed only upon a showing of "exceptional circumstances under which it is impractical . . . to obtain facts or opinions on the same subject by other means."[241] If such a deposition is allowed, the court should consider imposing time limits and must require the party seeking discovery to pay an appropriate share of the cost reasonably incurred in obtaining facts and opinions from the expert.[242]

The stringent disclosure requirements applicable to testifying experts may lead parties to rely on consulting experts, deferring a decision whether to designate them as trial experts. This matter should be addressed at the initial conference and a cutoff date established for designation of trial experts and compliance with disclosure requirements.

Court-appointed experts.[243] Although Rule 706 provides that an expert appointed by the court may be deposed, the court should establish the terms on which an expert serves and the nature of the functions the expert is to perform. When such an appointment is made, the extent of discovery permitted should be determined at the outset. This may depend on whether the expert is to testify or only to consult, and on the issue(s) the expert is to address.[244]

21.49 Special Problems

21.491 Government Investigations/Grand Jury Materials

Early in the litigation, the court should inquire about the existence of relevant government reports and other materials. Access to such materials can reduce the need for discovery and assist in defining and narrowing issues. If not a matter of public record, they may sometimes be obtained by agreement with the agency, by subpoena, or by requests under the Freedom of Information Act.[245]

---

241. Fed. R. Civ. P. 26(b)(4)(B). When a physical or mental examination is made under Fed. R. Civ. P. 35, a party may obtain the examiner's report even if the examiner is not testifying.

242. Cost shifting under Rule 26(b)(4)(C) is mandatory "unless manifest injustice would result."

243. See *infra* § 21.51.

244. *See generally* Reference Manual on Scientific Evidence (Federal Judicial Center 1994).

245. 5 U.S.C.A. § 552 (West 1977 and Supp. 1994).

Factual findings of a government agency may be admissible under Fed. R. Evid. 803(8)(C), but some discovery may be needed to determine whether the information meets the rule's "trustworthiness" standard.[246] Objections to the admissibility of the findings may be addressed in a pretrial hearing under Fed. R. Evid. 104, if necessary.[247]

Grand jury materials may also be used to reduce discovery in related civil litigation. Fed. R. Crim. P. 6(e)(3)(D) and (E) set out the procedures that must be followed when seeking disclosure of grand jury materials. Grand jury proceedings are presumptively secret, but the court may order disclosure upon a showing of a particularized need.[248] Disclosure may be ordered of testimony given before the grand jury and of documents subpoenaed or otherwise obtained for its use,[249] but a person may invoke the Fifth Amendment privilege against self-incrimination and refuse to answer questions about such testimony even if it was given under a grant of immunity.[250] The production to a grand jury of otherwise discoverable material does not, however, entitle it to Rule 6 protection.[251] Copies made by a person of material produced to a grand jury are subject to discovery.

Requests for disclosure of grand jury materials are generally addressed to the court that supervised the grand jury proceedings.[252] Nevertheless, because that court may not be able to assess the "particularized need" for the materials in the litigation for which they are sought, it should consult with the judge assigned to that litigation.[253] If disclosure is ordered, the court may include in the order protective limitations on the use of the material.[254]

---

246. The rule provides a hearsay exception, in civil cases and against the government in criminal cases, for "[r]ecords, reports, statements, or data compilations . . . of public offices and agencies, setting forth . . . factual findings resulting from an investigation conducted pursuant to authority granted by law, unless the sources of information or other circumstances indicate lack of trustworthiness."

247. See In re Japanese Elec. Prods. Antitrust Litig., 723 F.2d 238, 260 (3d Cir. 1983), rev'd on other grounds sub. nom. Matsushita Elec. Indus. Co. v. Zenith Radio Corp., 475 U.S. 574 (1986).

248. See Fed. R. Crim. P. 6(e)(2), (3)(C)(i). The "particularized need" requirement derives from case law and is described in detail in Douglas Oil Co. of Cal. v. Petrol Stops Northwest, 441 U.S. 211, 222–23 (1979); see also United States v. Sells Eng'g, Inc., 463 U.S. 418, 443 (1983); Illinois v. Abbott & Assocs., Inc., 460 U.S. 557, 567 & n.14 (1983).

249. Some courts give greater protection to transcripts of testimony than to documentary evidence. See, e.g., In re Grand Jury Proceedings (Miller Brewing Co.), 717 F.2d 1136 (7th Cir. 1983). Production under Fed. R. Civ. P. 33(d) or 34 of documents previously subpoenaed by a grand jury may be facilitated if the producing party has retained copies.

250. Pillsbury Co. v. Conboy, 459 U.S. 248 (1983).

251. See Blalock v. United States, 844 F.2d 1546, 1551 (11th Cir. 1988).

252. Douglas Oil, 441 U.S. at 226.

253. Id. at 226–31.

254. Id. at 223.

21.492 Summaries

Voluminous or complicated data should be presented at trial, whenever possible, through summaries, including compilations, tabulations, charts, graphs, and extracts.[255] While counsel in jury cases usually recognize the need for summaries, they may overlook their utility in nonjury cases; the trial judge, however, should not be expected to "wad[e] through a sea of uninterpreted raw evidence."[256]

Summaries may be offered under Fed. R. Evid. 611(a) solely as an aid to understanding, with the underlying evidence separately admitted into the record. Whenever possible, however, summaries should be received as substantive evidence under Rule 1006, in lieu of the underlying data. When summaries are so used, opposing parties must be given an adequate opportunity to examine the underlying data in advance of trial and raise objections in time to enable the proponent of the summary to make necessary corrections. As noted in *supra* section 21.446, the use of sampling techniques to verify summaries and quantify possible errors may be adequate and preferable to an item-by-item examination of the underlying data. When the summary is received as substantive evidence of the data it contains, the underlying data will not become part of the record, although receipt of a few examples of the source materials may be helpful in illustrating the nature of the underlying data summarized.

21.493 Sampling/Opinion Surveys[257]

Statistical methods may often be useful to estimate, to specified levels of accuracy, the characteristics of a "population" or "universe" of events, transactions, attitudes, or opinions by observing those characteristics in a relatively small segment or "sample" of the population. The use of acceptable sampling techniques, in lieu of discovery and presentation of voluminous data from the entire population, may produce substantial savings in time and expense. In some cases, sampling techniques may provide the only practicable means to collect and present relevant data.[258]

The choice of appropriate methods will depend on the purpose to be accomplished. A distinction must be drawn between sampling for the purpose of

---

255. Fed. R. Evid. 1006 creates an exception to the "best evidence" rule, allowing writings, recordings, or photographs which cannot conveniently be examined in court to be presented in the form of "charts, summaries or calculations." The rule does not affect the requirement that the originals be admissible.

256. Crawford v. Western Elec. Co., 614 F.2d 1300, 1319 (5th Cir. 1980).

257. For a more detailed discussion of the use of surveys, see Reference Manual on Scientific Evidence (Federal Judicial Center 1994).

258. For example, in *In re* Shell Oil Refinery, 136 F.R.D. 588 (E.D. La. 1991), a statistical expert profiled the compensatory damage claims of the class members to assist the jury in fixing the amount of punitive damages.

generating data about a population to be offered for its truth, and sampling in the nature of polling to measure opinions, attitudes, and actions by a population.

In the case of the former, the reliability and validity of estimates about the population derived from sampling are critical. The methods used must conform to generally recognized statistical standards. Relevant factors include whether:

- the population was properly chosen and defined;
- the sample chosen was representative of that population;
- the data gathered were accurately reported; and
- the data were analyzed in accordance with accepted statistical principles.

Laying the foundation for such evidence will ordinarily involve expert testimony and, along with disclosure of the underlying data and documentation, should be taken up by the court well in advance of trial. Even if the court finds deficiencies in the proponent's showing, the court may receive the evidence subject to argument going to its weight and probative value.[259]

Sampling for the purpose of establishing the characteristics of a population must be distinguished from sampling (e.g., opinion polls or surveys) for the purpose of questioning individuals about such matters as their observations, actions, attitudes, beliefs, or motivations. Such sampling is not intended to establish the truth of an objective fact, but rather to provide evidence of public perceptions. The four factors listed above are relevant to assessing the admissibility of a survey, but need to be applied in light of the particular purpose for which the survey is offered. In addition, assessment of the validity of a survey should take into account whether:

- the questions asked were clear and not leading;
- the survey was conducted by qualified persons following proper interview procedures; and
- the process was conducted so as to ensure objectivity (e.g., was the survey conducted in anticipation of litigation and by persons connected with the parties or counsel or aware of its purpose in the litigation?).

When sampling or survey evidence is proposed to be offered, parties may want to consider whether details of the proposed sampling or survey methods should not be disclosed to the opposing parties before the work is done (including the specific questions that will be asked, the introductory statements or instructions that will be given, and other controls to be used in the interrogation process). Objections can then be raised promptly and corrective measures

---

259. *See* E. & J. Gallo Winery v. Gallo Cattle Co., 967 F.2d 1280, 1292 (9th Cir. 1992); McNeilab, Inc. v. American Home Prods. Corp., 848 F.2d 34, 38 (2d Cir. 1988).

taken before the survey is completed. A meeting of the parties' experts can expedite the resolution of problems affecting admissibility.

Objection is sometimes raised that an opinion survey, although conducted according to generally accepted statistical methods, involves impermissible hearsay. When the purpose of a survey is to show what people believe—but not the truth of what they believe—the results are not hearsay.[260] In the rare situation where an opinion survey involves inadmissible hearsay, experts may nevertheless be allowed to express opinions based on the results of the survey.[261]

21.494 Extraterritorial Discovery

Discovery directed at witnesses, documents, or other evidence located outside the United States will often create problems, since many countries view American pretrial discovery as inconsistent with or contrary to their laws, customs, and national interests.[262] The need for evidence located outside the United States should be explored early in the proceedings to allow for the extra time that may be required to obtain it and consider ways to minimize cost and delay, or to develop alternate methods of proof when the evidence cannot be obtained. For example, the parties may achieve substantial savings by paying a willing deponent to come the United States or, if permitted by the laws of the host country, conducting short depositions telephonically.

The following factors may affect whether, to what extent, and in what manner foreign discovery is conducted:

- **Laws of the United States.** The procedures for obtaining evidence from other countries are prescribed by (1) the Federal Rules of Civil Procedure, particularly Rule 28(b) (depositions in a foreign country);[263] (2) statutes, particularly 28 U.S.C. § 1781 (transmittal of letter rogatory or request), § 1783 (subpoena of person in a foreign country), and § 1784 (contempt); and (3) international agreements, particularly the Hague Convention on the Taking of Evidence Abroad in Civil or Commercial

---

260. *See* Fed. R. Evid. 801(c), 803(3).

261. *See* Fed. R. Evid. 703.

262. In civil law jurisdictions in which the gathering and presentation of evidence is under the control of the courts and not the litigants, taking a deposition may be considered the performance of a judicial act by another sovereign. In addition, many common law jurisdictions disfavor discovery requests directed at obtaining material other than evidence to be presented at trial. *See, e.g.,* Rio Tinto Zinc Corp. v. Westinghouse Elec. Corp., [1978] 1 All E.R. 434 (H.L. 1977); Extraterritorial Discovery in International Litigation 24 (PLI 1984).

263. *See also* Fed. R. Civ. P. 44(a)(2) (authentication of foreign official record). This rule must be read in conjunction with the 1981 Hague Convention Abolishing the Requirements of Legalization for Foreign Public Documents, October 5, 1981 (entered in force for the United States on October 15, 1981), 527 U.N.T.S. 189, T.I.A.S. No. 10072, *reprinted* following the rule; *see also* 28 U.S.C. §§ 1740, 1741, 1745.

Matters (the "Hague Convention").[264] Attention must also be given to applicable decisional law[265] and the Federal Rules of Evidence.[266]

- **Laws and attitude of the foreign country.** The extent and form of pretrial discovery that will be compelled or even permitted by other sovereigns vary widely. Even within a particular country, the rules may differ depending on the nature and identity of the person or body from which the discovery is sought and on the type of information sought. For example, the breadth of discovery may depend on whether the evidence is testimonial or documentary.[267] Some countries not only refuse to compel a witness to provide evidence, but also prohibit the voluntary production in any manner of some items of evidence. The attitude of the other country may also be affected by the current state of its diplomatic relations with the United States and by the nature of the litigation. This latter factor is particularly important if the American litigation involves claims (such as antitrust) that conflict with the law or policies of the foreign country.

- **Position of the person or body from which discovery is sought.** Foreign discovery rules may vary depending on whether discovery is sought from (1) a national of the United States, of the country in which the discovery is to be conducted, or of another country; (2) a person or entity party to the American litigation or otherwise subject to the jurisdiction of the American courts;[268] (3) an instrumentality or arm of a foreign country; or (4) a person or entity willing to provide the information.

- **Posture of the litigant.** Extraterritorial discovery will be expedited if the parties to the litigation cooperate by entering into stipulations under Fed.

264. March 18, 1970 (entered into force for the United States on October 7, 1972), 23 U.S.T. 2555, T.I.A.S. No. 7444, *reprinted at* 28 U.S.C.A. § 1781 (West. Supp. 1993). As its title implies, the convention does not apply to criminal cases. *See* Obtaining Discovery Abroad 9 (ABA 1990).

265. *See, e.g.,* Societe Nationale Industrielle Aerospatiale v. District Court, 482 U.S. 522 (1987); Insurance Corp. of Ireland v. Compagnie des Bauxites de Guinea, 456 U.S. 694 (1982); Societe Internationale v. Rogers, 357 U.S. 197 (1958); *In re* Westinghouse Elec. Corp. Uranium Contracts Litig., 563 F.2d 992 (10th Cir. 1977).

266. *See, e.g.,* Fed. R. Evid. 902(3) (self-authentication of foreign public documents).

267. For example, most countries party to the Hague Convention will not execute letters of request for the purpose of obtaining pretrial disclosure of documents. *See* Hague Convention, art. 23, *supra* note 264.

268. Where the entity or person from whom discovery is sought is subject to the court's jurisdiction, it will often be faster and less costly to utilize the standard discovery methods of the Federal Rules of Civil Procedure. *See* Obtaining Discovery Abroad 2 (ABA 1990). In considering whether to use the Federal Rules or the Hague Convention, the court should consider the particular facts of the case, the sovereign interests of the two countries, and the likelihood that resort to the procedures of the Hague Convention will be effective. *Societe Nationale,* 482 U.S. at 549.

R. Civ. P. 29 as to the manner and location of discovery.[269] The refusal of a party with foreign connections or interests to enter into stipulations may not, however, reflect an uncooperative attitude but may be compelled by the laws or customs of the foreign country.

Because procedures for obtaining foreign discovery vary from country to country and are often complex, it is generally advisable for the attorneys to associate local counsel. The Department of State and the appropriate American Embassy or Consulate can also provide assistance in planning discovery in foreign countries.[270] The Department of State's Office of Citizens Consular Services can provide lists of local counsel and current information regarding such matters as reservations and declarations under the Hague Convention, practices in nonsignatory countries, the procedures to be followed in particular countries, and actual results of discovery efforts in specific countries.[271]

Depositions. Fed. R. Civ. P. 28(b) establishes four alternate procedures for taking depositions in other countries.[272] Under Rule 28(b)(1), when the country where discovery is sought is a signatory to the Hague Convention,[273] depositions may be taken in accordance with the convention, as described below, though resort to the convention is not mandatory.[274] When the country is not a signatory, resort must be had to one of the procedures in Rule 28(b)(2)–(4). Under Rule 28(b)(2), the American court may issue a "letter of request"[275] seeking the voluntary assistance of the court or other agency of the foreign country to compel

---

269. Stipulations for nonstenographic and telephonic depositions under Fed. R. Civ. P. 30(b)(2), (7) also may be valuable (the court may also order the use of these procedures, see *supra* § 21.452), but such procedures may violate foreign law. Stipulations as to admissibility are particularly important because the discovery may not be in the question-and-answer form traditional in American litigation. In this regard, the court should note that under Rule 28(b), "[e]vidence obtained in response to a letter of request need not be excluded merely because it is not a verbatim transcript, because the testimony was not taken under oath, or because of any similar departure from the requirements for depositions taken within the United States under these rules." For discussion of this issue in a criminal case, see United States v. Salim, 855 F.2d 944 (2d Cir. 1988).

270. For the State Department's regulations on foreign discovery, see 22 C.F.R. § 92 (1993).

271. Inquiries should be directed to the Office of Citizens Consular Services, Room 4817, Dept. of State, 2201 C Street, N.W., Washington, DC 20520.

272. *See also* Restatement (Third) of the Foreign Relations Law of the United States § 474(2) (1987).

273. The rule refers to "any applicable treaty or convention," but the intended reference is to the Hague Convention. *See* Fed. R. Civ. P. 28 advisory committee's note.

274. *See Societe Nationale,* 482 U.S. at 529–40; *see also* Restatement (Third) of the Foreign Relations Law of the United States § 473 (1987).

275. The more commonly used term for this device had been "letter rogatory," but the federal rules and the Hague Convention, and therefore this manual, now use the more accurate "letter of request."

the deponent to provide evidence.[276] The foreign country ultimately decides whether to honor and execute the letter of request.[277] When the deponent is willing to give evidence, the parties may utilize the "notice" or "commission" methods of Rule 28(b)(3) and (4), respectively, if not prohibited by foreign law.[278] The "notice" method is essentially the same used for a typical domestic deposition. Under the "commission" method, the American court appoints a person—typically an American consular officer[279]—to administer the oath and preside over the deposition.

Much foreign discovery will occur in countries that are signatories to the Hague Convention.[280] The convention generally allows evidence to be taken compulsorily pursuant to a letter of request[281] or voluntarily before a diplomatic officer or consular agent or any person "commissioned" for the purpose.[282] The convention must, however, be read in light of the numerous reservations and declarations made by the signatories, through which they have modified or

276. For a thorough discussion of the issues and procedures involved in obtaining judicial assistance from a foreign country, see Ristau, *supra* note 82. For the form and substance of a letter of request, see the Model for Letters of Request located after 28 U.S.C.A. § 1781 at 141–43 (West Supp. 1993). There may be a long delay, perhaps as much as two years, between the issuance of a letter of request and receipt of the evidence. The Department of State's Office of Citizens Consular Services often can provide information about recent experiences in particular countries.

277. Many countries not parties to the Convention, such as Switzerland and Canada, routinely execute letters of request from United States courts.

278. For example, in Japan and Turkey a deposition on notice is permissible only of an American citizen, while Swiss law makes it a crime to take any deposition in that country without governmental authorization.

279. *See* 22 C.F.R. § 92.4(a).

280. Currently, twenty-one countries are signatories; for a list, see 28 U.S.C.A. § 1781 at 125–26 (West Supp. 1993). Ireland is the twenty-first and most recent signatory. Fed. R. Civ. P. 4 editorial notes (West Supp. 1994).

281. Although the judicial authority executing the request will apply its own procedures, the convention states that special requests—for example, for a verbatim transcript or for answers in writing and under oath—are to be honored unless incompatible with the law of the executing state or otherwise impossible or impracticable. Hague Convention, art. 9. In practice, though, such requests are commonly not complied with. Under the convention, letters of request must be sent to a "Central Authority" designated by the receiving country; the identities of the authorities designated are given in notifications appended to the treaty. *See* 28 U.S.C.A. § 1781 at 125–41 (West Supp. 1993). For discussion of the procedures and problems associated with letters of request, see Spencer W. Waller, International Trade and U.S. Antitrust Law § 7.08 (1992).

282. Hague Convention, arts. 16, 17. Issuance of both a commission and a letter of request, as authorized by Rule 28(b), may be a useful measure to guard against the risk that a deponent may not remain willing to testify voluntarily.

declined to adopt various provisions.[283] These create variances among the discovery rules applicable in the signatory countries, and may be complex.

When "necessary in the interest of justice," a United States national or resident in a foreign country may be subpoenaed to testify or produce documents.[284] Failure to comply may subject the person to punishment for contempt.[285]

Blocking laws. Efforts to obtain or compel production of documents located outside the United States may be impeded by one of the increasing number of foreign nondisclosure (or "blocking") laws.[286] These laws take the form of general commercial and bank secrecy laws, as well as more specific and discretionary blocking statutes aimed at combating perceived excesses in American discovery.[287] The fact that certain discovery is prohibited under foreign law, however, does not prevent the court from requiring a party to comply with a demand for it,[288] though it may be relevant in determining the sanctions to be imposed for noncompliance.[289] Where a party fails to comply with a discovery order because of a blocking statute, the court may impose any of the sanctions set out in Fed. R. Civ. P. 37(b), though it may also consider factors such as the party's good faith efforts to comply in declining to do so.[290]

Judicial control. The Supreme Court has cautioned that United States courts should exercise special vigilance to protect foreign litigants from unnecessary or unduly burdensome discovery and should supervise pretrial proceedings particularly closely to prevent discovery abuses.[291] The additional cost may increase the danger that foreign discovery will be used for an improper purpose, such as to burden or harass; objections to abusive discovery advanced by foreign litigants should therefore receive "the most careful consideration."[292] In deciding whether to issue an order directing production of information abroad, and in framing such an order, the court should consider the following:

- the importance to the litigation of the discovery requested;
- the degree of specificity of the request;

---

283. Many countries, for example, require that a judicial officer conduct depositions, and a majority will not execute letters of request issued for the purpose of obtaining documents related solely to pretrial discovery. Each country's declarations and reservations are listed in the notifications at the end of the convention. *See* 28 U.S.C.A. § 1781 at 125–41 (West Supp. 1993).

284. 28 U.S.C. § 1783.

285. 28 U.S.C. § 1784.

286. *See* Obtaining Discovery Abroad *passim* (ABA 1990).

287. *See* Waller, *supra* note 281, § 7.09.

288. Societe Nationale Industrielle Aerospatiale v. District Court, 482 U.S. 522, 544 n.29 (1987).

289. Societe Nationale v. Rogers, 357 U.S. 197, 204–06 (1958).

290. *See* Obtaining Discovery Abroad 18–22 (ABA 1990).

291. *Societe Nationale,* 482 U.S. at 546.

292. *Id.*

- whether the information sought originated in the United States;
- the availability of alternate means to secure the information; and
- the extent to which noncompliance with the request would undermine important United States interests or compliance would undermine important interests of the country in which the information is located.[293]

Comity also dictates that American courts take into account special problems confronted by the foreign litigant because of its nationality or location, and any sovereign interests expressed by a foreign state.[294] A court order requiring that *all* extraterritorial discovery be conducted using the procedures in the Hague Convention when available may serve this purpose.

The risk that a foreign country will refuse to execute a letter of request can be minimized by careful drafting. In most cases the request should be directed at evidence for use at trial. Requests for documents should be as specific as possible; Hague Convention countries that have executed a reservation under Article 23[295] will ordinarily not execute general requests for broad categories of documents for use in discovery.[296] The language of the letter should be simple and nontechnical, and no unnecessary information should be included.[297] The court should incorporate findings as to the extent of discovery to be permitted and the need therefor in a separate order that can be presented to foreign authorities, even if letters of request are not being issued.

Federal judges are not authorized to travel abroad to control the conduct of depositions, at least in the absence of specific approval by the Judicial Conference of the United States.[298] For this reason, the court should adopt in advance appropriate guidelines to govern such depositions consistent with the laws of the other country.[299] Moreover, if permissible under the laws and customs of that country, the judge may be available by telephone to resolve disputes or may appoint a special master to supervise the deposition personally.[300] Before either of these procedures are employed, advice should be sought from the Department of State's Office of Citizens Consular Services.

---

293. Restatement (Third) of the Foreign Relations Law of the United States § 442(1)(c) (1987), *earlier draft cited in Societe Nationale*, 482 U.S. at 544 n.28.

294. *Societe Nationale*, 482 U.S. at 546.

295. *See supra* note 268.

296. *See* Waller, *supra* note 281, § 7.08[3].

297. U.S. Dept. of State Circular, Preparation of Letters Rogatory (March 1992).

298. Report of the Proceedings of the Judicial Conference of the United States 4 (1980).

299. For suggested deposition guidelines, see *supra* § 21.45.

300. *See supra* §§ 21.424, 21.456.

21.5 Special Referrals[301]

Complex litigation often involves the need for complex fact finding during pretrial, in preparation for trial, or in aid of settlement. Referrals to a neutral may at times be helpful, either by relieving the judge of time-consuming proceedings or by bringing to bear special expertise. The authority to make such referrals is, however, circumscribed and conditioned, and the resulting costs and benefits must be balanced.

21.51 Court-Appointed Experts

As complex litigation increasingly involves issues calling for scientific, technical, or other specialized knowledge, and judges and juries are confronted with contradictory opinions from opposing experts, interest in court-appointed experts has grown. Such experts may serve a number of purposes: to advise the court on technical issues, to provide the jury with background information to aid comprehension, or to offer a neutral opinion on disputed technical issues.[302] The court has broad discretion to appoint such an expert, *sua sponte* or on request of the parties, but should consider the problems and implications of making an appointment; it is advisable to consider whether there are adequate alternatives to such an appointment, such as directing the experts to clarify, simplify, and narrow the differences between them.[303] These problems include:

- **Cost.** Because the parties have to bear the expense, court appointment of an expert increases the already high cost of complex litigation.[304]

---

301. This section of the manual is primarily concerned with referrals of factual disputes that will be subject to proof at trial. Use of special masters and magistrate judges to exercise judicial supervision over all or specified portions of the pretrial proceedings or to perform administrative functions is discussed in other sections. See *supra* §§ 20.14, 21.424.

302. For an extensive discussion of the various aspects of using court-appointed experts, see Joe S. Cecil & Thomas E. Willging, Court-Appointed Experts: Defining the Role of Experts Appointed Under Federal Rule of Evidence 706 (Federal Judicial Center 1993); Reference Manual on Scientific Evidence (Federal Judicial Center 1994).

303. See *supra* § 21.48; Cecil & Willging, *supra* note 302, at ch. 6.

304. Under Rule 706(b), except in the rare cases where such funding is provided by statute the parties must pay the expert's compensation; the judge allocates this expense among the parties and determines the time of payment (usually periodic deposit in court during the litigation, subject to reapportionment at the outcome). Courts often decline to appoint an expert when one party is indigent, to avoid the unfairness of requiring the other side to pay all of the expert's compensation. The court has the authority, however, to order the nonindigent party to pay this expense in com-

- **Neutrality of the expert.** Truly neutral experts are difficult, if not impossible, to find; though they will have no commitment to any party, they do not come to the case free of experience and opinions that will predispose (even if only subconsciously), or may be perceived to predispose, them in some fashion on disputed issues relevant to the case.
- **Neutrality of the court.** Testimony from a court-appointed expert may be seen as the court taking sides.[305]
- **Delay.** The testimony of a court-appointed expert may lengthen the trial, although there may be offsetting savings by the narrowing of issues, reducing of the scope of the controversy, and perhaps promoting settlement.
- **Timing of the appointment.** The need for an appointment will not always be clear early in the litigation; by the time it becomes clear, the case may be at or about to go to trial, and introduction of a court-appointed expert at that point would cause delay.

Nevertheless, in appropriate cases, appointment of a neutral expert can be beneficial:

- Court-appointed experts can have "a great tranquilizing effect" on the parties' experts, reducing adversariness and potentially clarifying and narrowing disputed issues.[306]
- They may facilitate settlement or at least stipulations.
- They can help the court and jury comprehend the issues and the evidence.

If an appointment is made, the order should clearly specify the duties, functions, compensation, and authority of the expert.[307] A court-appointed expert is not limited when forming opinions to information presented by the parties at a hearing, and, at least if the expert is to serve as a witness, is subject to discovery with respect to his or her opinions; the order should specify the ground rules for depositions and other discovery directed at the expert, including the extent to which materials used or considered by the expert will be subject to discovery. The order should specify whether the expert is to provide a written report to the par-

pelling circumstances when the indigent party's claim has merit. *See* McKinney v. Anderson, 924 F.2d 1500, 1510–11 (9th Cir. 1991); United States Marshals Service v. Means, 741 F.2d 1053, 1057–59 (8th Cir. 1984) (en banc); Cecil & Willging, *supra* note 302, at 62–65. Provision for payment must be made at the time of appointment to ensure that the expert will be compensated.

305. Disclosure to the jury of the fact of court-appointment is discretionary. Fed. R. Evid. 706(c).

306. E. Barrett Prettyman, Proceedings of the Seminar on Protracted Cases for United States Circuit and District Judges, 21 F.R.D. 395, 469 (1957).

307. *See* Cecil & Willging, *supra* note 302, at ch. 7.

ties before trial, and whether ex parte communications with the judge will be permitted. The order may also state how the jury should be instructed; generally it would be told that the opinions of a court-appointed expert should be treated the same as those of other expert witnesses—the opinions are entitled to only such weight as is warranted by the witness's knowledge, expertise, and preparation.

If the expert serves only as a technical advisor to the judge,[308] ex parte communications may be necessary but may be subjected to procedural safeguards. Such safeguards might include (1) giving the parties notice of the expert's identity and precise function; (2) providing written instructions detailing the expert's duties; and (3) requiring the expert to submit a written report or otherwise advising the parties of the substance of the advice given.[309]

In selecting an expert witness for appointment, the court should seek a person whose fairness and expertise in the field cannot reasonably be questioned and who can communicate effectively as a witness. Although the appointment is made by the court, every effort should be made to select a person acceptable to the litigants; the parties should first be asked to submit a list of proposed experts and may be able, with the assistance of their own experts, to agree on one or more candidates. The court may also call on professional organizations and academic groups to provide a list of qualified and available persons (though not delegating the selection to any such organization), giving the parties an opportunity to comment. In making appointments, judges must avoid even the appearance of patronage or favoritism.[310]

21.52 Special Masters

Fed. R. Civ. P. 53 authorizes the appointment of special masters in actions to be tried to a jury, when the issues are "complicated," and in nonjury actions, for "matters of account and difficult computation of damages"[311] or upon a showing that an "exceptional condition" so requires.[312] But the rule provides that reference to a special master "shall be the exception and not the rule."[313] Courts have generally limited the appointment of special masters on matters involving the merits to exceptional cases in light of the limitations imposed by Rule 53, Article

---

308. The court may appoint an expert to render assistance other than testifying at trial, such as analysis and evaluation of the reports prepared by the parties' experts or attorneys. *See, e.g.,* Webster v. Sowders, 846 F.2d 1032, 1035, 1039 (6th Cir. 1988) (asbestos).

309. *See* Reilly v. United States, 863 F.2d 149, 158–59 (1st Cir. 1988); Cecil & Willging, *supra* note 302, at 39–45; Reference Manual on Scientific Evidence (Federal Judicial Center 1994).

310. *See* 28 U.S.C. § 458.

311. This may also include settlement negotiations and awards of attorneys' fees.

312. Fed. R. Civ. P. 53(b).

313. *Id.*

III of the Constitution,[314] and the Supreme Court's decision in *Labuy v. Howes Leather Co.*,[315] holding that the general complexity of the litigation, the projected length of trial, and the congestion of the court's calendar did not constitute exceptional circumstances. These considerations, however, would not preclude more limited references, such as those regarding resolution of pretrial or nondispositive matters,[316] mediation of settlement negotiations (see *infra* section 23.13), or post-trial implementation of a decree.[317] Further, they do not preclude designation of a magistrate judge to perform duties of a special master; party consent is required, however, if the appointment is to be without regard to the provisions of Rule 53(b).[318]

The decision whether to appoint a special master involves largely the same considerations discussed in *supra* section 21.51 with respect to court-appointed experts,[319] in particular the imposition on parties of extra expense[320] and the

314. *See, e.g.*, Stauble v. Warrob, Inc., 977 F.2d 690 (1st Cir. 1992) (Article III prohibits reference to master of "fundamental" issue of liability).

315. 352 U.S. 249 (1957).

316. *See In re* Bituminous Coal Operators Ass'n, Inc., 949 F.2d 1165, 1168–69 (D.C. Cir. 1991) (improper to refer dispositive matters, but proper to refer pretrial preparation or calculation of damages); *In re* United States, 816 F.2d 1083, 1091 (6th Cir. 1987) (improper to refer dispositive matters, proper to refer nondispositive matters); *In re* Armco, 770 F.2d 103 (8th Cir. 1985) (*per curiam*) (improper to refer trial on merits, though proper to refer all pretrial matters, including dispositive motions). The court in *Stauble*, while making a similar distinction, noted that the reference would not have violated Article III if the judge had afforded de novo review of the special master's determination. 977 F.2d at 698 n.13.

317. *See, e.g.*, Ruiz v. Estelle, 679 F.2d 1115, 1159–63 (5th Cir. 1982); Gary W. v. Louisiana, 601 F.2d 240 (5th Cir. 1979).

318. 28 U.S.C. § 636(b)(2); Fed R. Civ. P. 53(b). There is also statutory authorization for comprehensive reference to a special master of employment discrimination cases not scheduled for trial within 120 days after issue has been joined. 42 U.S.C. § 2000e-5(f)(5).

319. It may be particularly difficult to appoint a completely disinterested master with no prior relationship to any of the parties, since special masters are often practicing attorneys and tend to have substantial experience with similar disputes. Although courts disagree on whether the standard applicable to special masters is as strict as that for judicial officers, they should be disqualified if they have an interest or relationship that poses a substantial risk of the appearance of bias. *See* Rios v. Enterprise Assoc. Steamfitters Local Union, 860 F.2d 1168, 1173–75 (2d Cir. 1988); Jenkins v. Sterlacci, 849 F.2d 627 (D.C. Cir. 1988); Lister v. Commissioner's Court, 566 F.2d 490, 493 (5th Cir. 1978); Morgan v. Kerrigan, 530 F.2d 401, 426–27 (1st Cir. 1976); *In re* Joint E. & S. Dists. Asbestos Litig., 737 F. Supp. 735, 739–42 (E. and S.D.N.Y. 1990). *See also* the Code of Conduct for United States Judges, in II Guide to Judiciary Policies and Procedures I-45 (AO November 1993) (any "judicial officer of the federal judicial system performing judicial functions" is subject to the Code). As with experts, the court may not appoint as special master anyone related to any justice or judge of the court. 28 U.S.C. § 458.

320. *See* Fed. R. Civ. P. 53(a); Prudential Ins. Co. of America v. United States Gypsum Co., 991 F.2d 1080, 1085, 1087 (3d Cir. 1993) (disqualifying master, in part because of availability of magistrate judges).

question of neutrality, both inapplicable if appointment is of a magistrate judge. Appointment of a magistrate judge may be appropriate where the purpose is to collect, assemble, and distill voluminous data presented by the parties, and the primary qualifications are objectivity and familiarity with evidentiary hearings rather than expertise in some technical field. Appointment of a special master to supervise discovery may be appropriate where the financial stakes justify imposing the expense on the parties and where the amount of activity required would impose undue burdens on a judge. It is generally preferable to appoint special masters with the parties' consent, and either to permit the parties to agree on the selection or to make the appointment from a list submitted by the parties. The clerk and deputy clerks of court may not be appointed as special masters "unless there are special reasons requiring such appointment which are recited in the order of appointment."[321]

Special masters have increasingly been appointed for their expertise in particular fields, such as accounting and finance or the science or technology involved in the litigation.[322] Hence the distinction between special masters under Rule 53 and court-appointed experts under Fed. R. Evid. 706 has become blurred. The court may make an appointment under the latter rule without the restrictions imposed under Rule 53. Although Rule 706 by its terms speaks of a "witness," it also specifically permits the appointed expert to make "findings." Thus, when the court is calling on a neutral for that person's "scientific, technical, or other specialized knowledge," as contemplated by Rule 702, it may consider making the appointment under Rule 706 even though no testimony is contemplated. Presumptively, however, a person appointed under Rule 706 would be subject to discovery; Rule 53 makes no provision for discovery of special masters but the parties have access to the special master's report.[323]

An order of reference to a special master should define with specificity the scope of the reference, the issues to be investigated, the time when the report is to be delivered, and the special master's powers.[324] Subject to the terms of that order, a special master may require production of tangible evidence, examine witnesses under oath,[325] and "do all acts and take all measures necessary or proper" to

---

321. 28 U.S.C. § 957.

322. For discussion of the roles played by special masters and magistrate judges, see Linda Silberman, *Judicial Adjuncts Revisited—The Proliferation of Ad Hoc Procedure*, 137 U. Pa. L. Rev. 2131 (1989).

323. The special master may, however, prepare a draft report and submit it to counsel for their suggestions before filing a final report. Fed. R. Civ. P. 53(e)(5).

324. *See* Fed. R. Civ. P. 53(c).

325. The special master may call parties to testify (see *id.*), and other witnesses may be subpoenaed by the parties. Fed. R. Civ. P. 53(d)(2).

perform the special master's duties.[326] A special master may be asked to make findings of fact, but due process requires that these be based upon evidence presented at an adversarial hearing.[327] The order should also provide for appropriate arrangements to ensure that the special master's fees will be paid.

When appointed to resolve disputed issues, the special master must produce a report on the matters submitted by the order of reference, including in it any findings of fact or conclusions of law.[328] In nonjury actions, the court may accept the findings of fact unless "clearly erroneous." The findings are also admissible in jury trials,[329] but the court should be mindful that they may carry undue weight with the jury. The parties may stipulate that the special master's findings of fact are to be accepted as final, leaving only questions of law for review.[330]

21.53 Magistrate Judges Under 28 U.S.C. § 636(b)(1)[331]

Referrals, apart from referrals of supervision of pretrial proceedings as discussed at *supra* section 20.14, may also be made to magistrate judges, pursuant to 28 U.S.C. § 636(b)(1), Fed. R. Civ. P. 53(f), 72, and local rules.[332] Like a special master, a magistrate judge acting under these provisions makes factual determinations based on evidence presented at an adversarial hearing and submits a disposition or recommendation for a disposition, along with proposed findings of fact when appropriate, by written report filed with the court and served on the parties.[333] The parties have no right to engage in discovery from, or to cross-examine, the magistrate judge. Under Rule 72, the magistrate judge's ruling on nondispositive matters may, if objected to within ten days of service, be modified or set aside only if "clearly erroneous or contrary to law."[334] On matters dispositive of a claim or defense, the magistrate judge's recommended disposition is, on timely, specific, written objection by a party,[335] subject to de novo determination by the judge, who may, but need not, take further evidence.[336] This dis-

---

326. Fed. R. Civ. P. 53(c).

327. Unless otherwise directed by the order of reference, the special master may rule on the admissibility of evidence. *Id.* Although, unlike a court-appointed expert, a special master is not authorized to conduct a private investigation into the matter referred, special masters are expected to utilize their individual expertise and knowledge in evaluating the evidence.

328. Fed. R. Civ. P. 53(e)(1).

329. *See* Fed. R. Civ. P. 53 (e)(2), (3).

330. Fed. R. Civ. P. 53(e)(4).

331. This section does not address magistrate judges exercising the powers of a district judge under 28 U.S.C. § 636(c); see Fed. R. Civ. P. 73–76.

332. *See also* A Constitutional Analysis of Magistrate Judge Authority, 150 F.R.D. 247 (1993).

333. 28 U.S.C. § 636(b)(1)(C).

334. Fed. R. Civ. P. 72(a).

335. Even in the absence of an objection, the judge should review the report for "clear error." Fed. R. Civ. P. 72 advisory committee's note.

336. Fed. R. Civ. P. 72(b) and advisory committee's note.

tinction is clarified by 28 U.S.C. § 636(b)(1), which allows the designation of a magistrate judge only to provide proposed (i.e., subject to de novo review) findings of fact and recommendations for disposition of motions for injunctive relief, judgment on the pleadings, summary judgment, dismissal of indictment, suppression of evidence in a criminal case, class certification, dismissal for failure to state a claim, or involuntary dismissal,[337] while allowing determination of any other pretrial matter subject to reconsideration only if "clearly erroneous or contrary to law."[338] There is no explicit authority (as there is in Rule 53(e)(4)) for the parties' stipulating to be bound by the magistrate judge's findings.[339]

In considering whether to make a referral to a magistrate judge, the court needs to balance the advantages from obtaining the magistrate judge's assistance against the risk of delay resulting from requests for review of the magistrate judge's order, proposed findings, or recommendations.

21.54 Other Referrals

Use of other resources, such as referral to a private or public technical agency, use of an advisory jury of experts in a nonjury case, or consultation with a confidential adviser to the court[340] may be considered in complex litigation. Unless specifically authorized by statute or agreed to by the parties, however, the court should be cautious in experimenting with such procedures in cases in which, if the judge is held to be in error, a lengthy and costly retrial might be required. The referrals to court-appointed experts, special masters, and magistrate judges authorized by statute or rule should be adequate in most cases to provide the needed assistance. These comments are not intended to inhibit innovative uses of recognized procedures, such as appointing a team of experts to serve under Fed. R. Evid. 706. These procedures should, however, be used not to displace the parties' right to a resolution of disputes through the adversary process, but rather to make that process more fair and efficient when complicated issues are involved.[341]

---

337. 28 U.S.C. § 636(b)(1)(B).

338. 28 U.S.C. § 636(b)(1)(A).

339. This situation must be distinguished from that in which a magistrate judge is authorized, by the parties' consent, to act as a district judge under 28 U.S.C. § 636(c).

340. See Cecil & Willging, supra note 302, at 40–41.

341. For a discussion of the use of outside neutral persons in facilitating settlement, see infra § 23.13.

21.6 Final Pretrial Conference/Preparation for Trial

While the final pretrial conference may sometimes be considered superfluous or treated as little more than a perfunctory exercise, it is in fact of critical importance to the management of complex litigation expected to go to trial. Its purposes explicated in Rule 16(a), to "improv[e] the quality of the trial through more thorough preparation" and to "facilitat[e] the settlement of the case," take on special importance in complex litigation. Thus the provisions of Rule 16(d) should be observed, requiring that:

- the final pretrial conference be held as close to the time of trial as is reasonable under the circumstances;

- the parties formulate a plan for trial, including a program for facilitating the admission of evidence; and

- the conference be attended by the attorneys who will conduct the trial.

The court should issue an order setting the conference and specifying the items to be taken up. To maximize the utility of the conference, summary judgment motions and (to the extent feasible) motions *in limine* should be decided well in advance (see *supra* section 21.34, summary judgment). Preparation for the final pretrial conference, rather than generating massive unnecessary paper work, should be tailored to accomplish the purposes of Rule 16. Essential agenda items include exchange and submission of the following:[342]

- a final list identifying the witnesses to be called and the subject of their testimony, including a designation of deposition excerpts to be read;

---

342. For a comprehensive list of potential agenda items, see Litigation Manual, *supra* note 5, at 30–33. For a checklist of items that often merit attention at this conference, see *infra* § 40.3.

- copies of all proposed exhibits and visual aids;
- proposed questions for voir dire;
- concise memoranda on important unresolved legal issues;
- nonargumentative statements of facts believed to be undisputed;
- proposed jury instructions (see *infra* section 21.65);
- proposed verdict forms, including special verdicts or interrogatories;[343] and
- in nonjury cases, proposed findings of fact and conclusions of law.[344]

The following sections address special problems to be considered in connection with the final pretrial conference in complex litigation.

21.61 Date and Place of Trial

Although the setting of civil trial dates is problematic in many courts because of their criminal dockets, a trial date set for complex litigation should be firm, given the number of people involved and the expense incurred in preparation. The trial date needs to take into account the commitments of the court and counsel and should permit an uninterrupted trial. Counsel should be advised in advance that once the date is set, the court will not grant continuances; the court may set a deadline after which it will not permit partial settlements that might necessitate a continuance of the trial (see *infra* section 23.21).

Where litigation includes cases originally filed in other districts and transferred to the court for coordinated or consolidated pretrial proceedings under 28 U.S.C. § 1407, the court needs to consider whether those cases should be referred to the multidistrict panel for remand to the districts from which they were transferred[345] or whether consolidation with the cases pending in the district is feasible, depending on whether the cases transferred for pretrial are eligible for a change of venue to the district, permitting them to be tried there.[346] Venue motions may have been deferred, but should now be promptly decided. In referring cases back to the panel, the judge may indicate the nature and expected duration of remaining discovery, the estimated time before the case will be ready for trial, and the major rulings that, if not revised, will affect further proceedings, and may make appropriate recommendations for further proceedings. In most cases transferred under 28 U.S.C. § 1407, substantially all discovery will be completed before remand. In some cases, however, such as mass tort litigation, discovery re-

---

343. *See* Fed. R. Civ. P. 49. See also *infra* §§ 21.633, 22.451.

344. *See* Litigation Manual, *supra* note 5, Form 34.

345. 28 U.S.C. § 1407(a).

346. The court may be able to order transfer to the district under 28 U.S.C. § 1404 or 1406. *See supra* note 14.

garding individual damages may have been deferred and must be conducted in the transferor district after remand. For a fuller discussion of remand, see *infra* section 31.133.

21.62 Reevaluation of Jury Demands

Although a general demand for a jury trial may have been made early in the litigation,[347] the court may, at the final pretrial conference, consider whether the parties are entitled to a jury trial on particular issues and, if not, whether those issues should be decided by the court in a separate trial (which may be concurrent with the jury trial), by motion,[348] or submitted to an advisory jury.[349] If both jury and nonjury issues are to be tried, the court should determine whether *Beacon Theatres, Inc. v. Westover*[350] requires that the jury issues be decided first. Even if so, the judge may hear evidence during the jury trial on related nonjury issues, later affording the parties the opportunity to supplement the record with evidence relevant only to the nonjury issues and deferring a decision on the nonjury issues until after the verdict has been returned. In mass tort cases, the court may ask the parties to consider whether to try liability and lump sum damage issues to the jury, leaving the resolution of individual damage claims to special agreed procedures (see *infra* section 33.28, mass tort litigation, trial).

21.63 Structure of Trial

.631 Consolidation   119
.632 Separate Trials   119
.633 Special Verdicts and Interrogatories   120

Because complex cases often involve numerous parties and issues, a fair and efficient trial structure is needed. Suggestions should be sought from counsel for approaches to structuring that will improve the trial process. They may include, in addition to the devices discussed in the following paragraphs, the trial of one or more test cases, with appropriate provision being made concerning the estoppel effect of a judgment. The interplay of these various devices can have a significant effect on the fair and efficient resolution of complex litigation.[351] Consideration of any of these devices must take into account their potentially disparate impact on the parties, given their respective trial burdens and possibly unequal resources, their effect on the right to trial by jury, the possibilities of settlement, and the interests of the court and the public.

---

347. *See* Fed. R. Civ. P. 38.
348. *See* Fed. R. Civ. P. 39(a).
349. Fed. R. Civ. P. 39(c).
350. 359 U.S. 500 (1959).
351. For an illustration, see *In re* Plywood Antitrust Litig., 655 F.2d 627 (5th Cir. 1981).

21.631 Consolidation[352]

Actions pending in the same court involving common questions of law or fact may be consolidated under Fed. R. Civ. P. 42(a) for trial or pretrial if it will avoid unnecessary cost or delay. Consolidation may be for trial of the entire case or of only separable common issues. It may be appropriate even if some issues or cases are to be tried before a jury and others before the court; the same evidence needs to be presented only once even though the judge may consider it in some of the cases and the jury in others. Class actions may be consolidated with cases brought by opt-outs or other individual plaintiffs. Care should be taken in such situations to ensure that counsel for parties in the nonclass actions are given a fair opportunity to participate in the presentation of evidence and arguments at trial, particularly when their clients are primarily affected.

Whether consolidation is permissible or desirable will depend in large part on the extent to which the evidence in the cases is common. Unless common evidence predominates, consolidated trials may lead to jury confusion while failing to improve efficiency. To avoid this problem, the court may sever for a joint trial those issues on which common evidence predominates, reserving noncommon issues for subsequent individual trials. For example, in mass tort litigation, liability issues may be consolidated for joint trial, reserving damage issues for later individual trials. If most of the proof will be common but some evidence admissible in one case should not be heard in others, a multiple-jury format may be considered. Cases in which major conflicts exist between the basic trial positions of parties should not be consolidated, at least without ensuring that no prejudice results. Consolidation is also inappropriate where its principal effect will be unnecessarily to magnify the dimensions of the litigation.[353]

In massive litigation, innovative procedures have been used to bring about the resolution of large numbers of cases in a consolidated trial without a separate trial of each individual case.[354] Such procedures should be designed so as to protect the essentials of the parties' right to jury trial.

21.632 Separate Trials

Whether the litigation involves a single case or many cases, severance of certain issues for separate trial under Fed. R. Civ. P. 42(b) can be advantageous. Severance can reduce the length of trial, particularly if the severed issue is dispositive of the case, and can also improve comprehension of the issues and evidence. Severance may permit trial of an issue early in the litigation, which can impact settlement negotiations as well as the scope of discovery. The advantages

---

352. See also *supra* § 20.123 and *infra* § 33.21.
353. *See In re* Repetitive Stress Injury Litig., 11 F.3d 368 (2d Cir. 1993).
354. *See, e.g.,* Cimino v. Raymark Indus., Inc., 751 F. Supp. 649 (E.D. Tex. 1990).

of separate trials should, however, be balanced against the potential for increased cost, delay (including delay in reaching settlement) and inconvenience, particularly if the same witnesses may be needed to testify at both trials, and of unfairness if the result is to prevent a litigant from presenting a coherent picture to the trier of fact.[355]

Care must be taken in deciding which issues may and should be severed for separate trial and the order in which to try them. Under *Beacon Theatres*, the right to trial by jury on legal claims may not (except under "the most imperative circumstances") be lost by a prior determination of equitable claims; this may require trial of legal claims before the court decides related claims in equity, or that they be tried concurrently.[356] In addition, issues should not be severed for trial if they are so intertwined that they cannot fairly be adjudicated in isolation,[357] or when severance would create a risk of inconsistent adjudication.

Generally when issues are severed for separate trials, they should be tried before the same jury unless they are entirely unrelated. Severance may take the form of having evidence on discrete issues presented sequentially, with the jury returning a verdict on an issue before the trial moves on to the next issue (see *infra* section 22.34).

21.633 Special Verdicts and Interrogatories

Special verdicts or interrogatories accompanying a general verdict may help the jury focus on the issues, reduce the length and complexity of the instructions, and minimize the need for, or scope of, retrial in the event of reversible error.[358] They can provide guidance in conducting discovery, ruling on nonjury issues (possibly with some issues presented to the jury while others are reserved for decision by the court) or motions for summary judgment,[359] trying remaining issues, or negotiating settlement. Having counsel draft (and submit at the pretrial conference) proposed verdict forms along with jury instructions will help focus counsel's attention on the specific issues in dispute and inform the court.

Special verdicts and interrogatories should be drafted so as to help the jury understand and decide the issues while minimizing the risk of inconsistent verdicts. The questions should be arranged on the form in a logical and comprehensible manner; for example, questions common to several causes of action or de-

---

355. *See In re* Bendectin Litig., 857 F.2d 290 (6th Cir. 1988) (severed trial creates risk of "sterile or laboratory atmosphere").

356. *See* 359 U.S. at 510–11.

357. *See* Gasoline Prods. Co. v. Champlin Ref. Co., 283 U.S. 494, 500 (1931) (antitrust).

358. Fed. R. Civ. P. 49. *See infra* § 22.451.

359. *See In re* Plywood Antitrust Litig., 655 F.2d 627 (5th Cir. 1981) (special verdicts following a joint trial of all cases (including "opt-out" cases) on all issues except individual amounts of damages provided foundation for summary judgment motions regarding damages).

fenses should be asked only once, and related questions should be grouped together. Where the legal standards applicable to similar claims or defenses differ (for example, where different law may apply to different parties), careful drafting of questions on a special verdict form can ease problems that consolidation could otherwise cause. Issues not in dispute should be excluded from the verdict form.

Special verdicts may also be used in connection with a procedure by which issues are submitted to the jury sequentially. The jury may be asked to consider a threshold or dispositive issue and return its verdict before submission of other issues, which may be rendered moot by the verdict.

Some judges and attorneys are reluctant to use these devices out of fear of inconsistent verdicts and jury confusion. These problems can be avoided by careful draftsmanship. Parties' views on the desirability of special verdicts or interrogatories will differ, however, if they are seen as more advantageous to one side than the other; the court will have to evaluate the arguments for and against them in the particular case.

The court may also wish to suggest that the parties stipulate to accept a majority verdict if the jury is not unanimous[360] or to waive a verdict and accept a decision by the judge based on the trial evidence. Although such stipulations may be obtained after the case has gone to trial, the parties may be more amenable before trial begins.

21.64 Procedures to Expedite Presentation of Evidence

The principal purpose of the final pretrial conference is the "formulat[ion of] a plan for trial, including a program for facilitating the admission of evidence."[361] The plan should eliminate, to the extent possible, irrelevant, immaterial, cumulative, and redundant evidence, and further the clear and efficient presentation of evidence. Essential to the accomplishment of this purpose is a final definition of the issues to be tried, after elimination of undisputed and peripheral matters. The process begun at the initial conference of defining and narrowing issues, discussed in *supra* section 21.3, should reach completion at the final pretrial conference. Attention may then be directed to the proof the parties expect to offer at trial.

Review of that proof should be accompanied by consideration of fair, effective, and perhaps innovative ways of presenting it. This may include, in addition

360. *See* Fed. R. Civ. P. 48.
361. Fed. R. Civ. P. 16(d).

to the procedures considered in the following paragraphs, the presentation of voluminous data through the use of summaries or sampling (see *supra* sections 21.492–21.493); the use of summaries of deposition testimony; the use of computer-based evidence to present data or background information (see generally *infra* section 34.3); and the presentation of expert testimony in the form of reports or on videotape. Other techniques to expedite the presentation of evidence are discussed in *infra* section 22.3.

21.641 Statements of Facts and Evidence

One of the methods sometimes used to ensure adequate preparation, streamline the evidence, and prevent unfair surprise is statements of facts and evidence, or contentions and proof. Each party prepares and submits a statement listing the facts it intends to establish at trial and the supporting evidence. The statement should be sufficiently detailed to be informative and complete, but free of argument and conclusions. No evidence not included in the statement would be permitted at trial. The exchange of such statements may be useful in narrowing factual disputes and expediting the trial (see also *supra* section 21.47). The substantial amount of work required for their preparation, however, may outweigh the benefits, and such statements should not be required routinely without prior consideration.

21.642 Pretrial Rulings on Objections

Objections to evidence should be resolved and technical defects (such as lack of foundation) cured before trial whenever possible. Where the admissibility of evidence turns on other facts, the facts should be established where possible before trial, by stipulation if there is no basis for serious dispute (see *supra* section 21.445). Parties should therefore be required, to the extent feasible, to raise their objections to admissibility in advance of trial (usually by motions *in limine*),[362] with all other objections, except those based on relevance or prejudice, deemed waived. Pretrial rulings on admissibility save time at trial and may enable parties to overcome technical objections by eliminating inadmissible material, obtaining alternative sources of proof, or presenting necessary foundation evidence. In addition, they may narrow the issues and enable counsel to plan more effectively for trial. Time may also be saved by receiving exhibits into the record at pretrial, avoiding the need for formal offers at trial.

Objections to documentary evidence may be indicated in a response to the pretrial listing of such evidence by opposing counsel. Objections to deposition

---

362. Objections (other than under Fed. R. Evid. 402 or 403) to the admissibility of proposed exhibits disclosed as required by Rule 26(a)(3)(C) or the use of depositions designated as required by Rule 26(a)(3)(B) may be deemed waived unless made within fourteen days of disclosure. Fed. R. Civ. P. 26(a)(3).

testimony may be noted in the margin of the deposition where the objectionable matter appears, and the court's ruling may be indicated in the same place. Objections to other types of evidence may be made by means of a separate motion or other written request, describing the nature of the proposed evidence and the grounds of the objection.

The court should try to rule on objections without argument, but may call for written or oral argument or even a pretrial evidentiary hearing under Fed. R. Evid. 104. In such a hearing the court is not bound by the rules of evidence, except those respecting privileges.[363] Evidentiary rulings that cannot be made with confidence except in the light of developments at trial may be made on a tentative basis, subject to later revision, rather than be entirely deferred for consideration at trial.

The benefits of advance rulings on objections should be weighed against the potential for wasteful pretrial efforts by the court and counsel. For example, ruling on objections within a deposition may require the judge to read it before trial, despite the fact that the deposition or the objections to it may be partially or entirely mooted or withdrawn because of developments during trial. The court may therefore prefer to make pretrial rulings only on those objections that are considered sufficiently important by counsel to merit an advance ruling, either because of their significance to the outcome of the case or because of their effect on the scope or form of other evidence.

Pretrial rulings on evidence may be particularly important with respect to often expensive and elaborate demonstrative evidence, such as computer simulations (see *infra* section 34.32). It may be advisable to obtain at least a preliminary ruling or guidance concerning the admissibility of a proposed exhibit before substantial expense is incurred in its preparation (e.g., at the storyboard stage of a computer animation).

Computer-generated animations or simulations raise a number of issues that should be addressed at pretrial, including the treatment of any narration (possibly including hearsay statements), the need for limiting instructions (such as to clarify the specific purpose for which the evidence is offered), the authenticity and reliability of the underlying data, and the assumptions on which the exhibit is based. Opposing parties and the court should be given an early opportunity to view the evidence so that objections may be raised and ruled on in advance of trial.[364]

Pretrial rulings are also advisable with respect to proffered expert testimony that may be pivotal. The court may rule on the basis of written submissions, but

363. Fed. R. Evid. 104(a).
364. *See* Joseph, *supra* note 189, 156 F.R.D. at 335–37.

an evidentiary hearing under Fed. R. Evid. 104(a) may be necessary to determine whether the evidence is admissible under Rules 702 and 703.[365]

21.643 Limits on Evidence

Some attorneys understand the advantages of being selective in the presentation of evidence. Others prefer to leave no stone unturned, resulting in trials of excessive length unless limited by the judge. Where the parties' pretrial estimates suggest that trial will be excessively long, the judge should first discuss the possibility of voluntary, self-imposed limits with the lawyers, perhaps suggesting exhibits or testimony that could be eliminated and inviting further suggestions.

If this approach is not productive, the judge should consider imposing limits in some form, using the authority under Rule 16(c)(4) and Fed. R. Evid. 403 and 611. The mere announcement of the court's intention to impose such limits may suffice to motivate counsel to exercise the discipline necessary to expedite the case. Before imposing limits, the court, based on the pretrial submissions and consultation with counsel, should be sufficiently familiar with the litigation to form a reasonable judgment about the time necessary for trial and the scope of the necessary evidence.

Limits may be imposed in a variety of ways:

- on the number of witnesses or exhibits to be offered on a particular issue or in the aggregate;
- on the length of examination and cross-examination of particular witnesses;
- on the total time to be allowed each side for all direct and cross-examination; and
- by narrowing issues, by order or stipulation.

Judges who have imposed limits have found that they have not hampered the ability of counsel to present their case; indeed, they seem to have been welcomed by counsel. At the same time, limits must not be permitted to jeopardize the fairness of the trial. In designing limits, the respective evidentiary burdens of the parties need to be taken into account. Limits should generally be imposed before trial begins so that the parties can plan accordingly, but at times the need for limits may not become apparent until trial is underway. Limits must be firm so that one side cannot take advantage of the other; at the same time, however, the judge may have to extend the limits if good cause is shown. If a party requests, the jury may be advised of any limits imposed, in order to prevent unwarranted inferences from a party's failure to call all possible witnesses.

---

365. The subject is discussed at length in Reference Manual on Scientific Evidence (Federal Judicial Center 1994). See also *infra* §§ 33.2, 33.6, and 33.7.

21.65 Proposed Jury Instructions

The final pretrial conference should complete the pretrial process of identifying and narrowing issues. To that end, the parties should submit and exchange proposed substantive jury instructions (both preliminary and final) before the conference; some judges require counsel to confer and submit a single set of those instructions on which there is no disagreement.[366] This process compels counsel to analyze the elements of their claims and defenses and the supporting and opposing evidence. Working with the parties' submissions, many judges then prepare their own substantive instructions and have found that they are generally accepted by counsel with little argument. Proposed instructions can be submitted on disks in compatible word processing programs to enable the judge to make revisions on chambers computers. Many judges provide their own standard instructions to counsel for comment.

21.66 Briefs and Final Pretrial Motions

If legal issues remain to be resolved, briefs should be submitted in advance of the final pretrial conference. Early submission will assist the court and counsel in preparing for the conference and make it more productive.

With discovery complete and critical evidentiary rulings made, some additional issues may be ready for summary judgment. Motions for summary judgment should be presented and decided no later than the final conference, absent special circumstances. Deferring such motions and their resolution to the eve of trial may cause unnecessary expense and inconvenience to counsel, witnesses, jurors, and the court, and may interfere with planning for the conduct of the trial.

21.67 Final Pretrial Order[367]

At the conclusion of the final pretrial conference, an order should be entered reciting all actions taken and rulings made, whether at the conference or earlier. The order should provide that it will govern the conduct of the trial and will not be modified except "to prevent manifest injustice."[368]

The order should, among other things, state:

- the starting date of the trial and the schedule to be followed;
- the issues to be tried;
- if separate trials are to be held, the issues to be tried at the initial trial;
- the witnesses to be called and the exhibits to be offered by each side (other than for impeachment);

---

366. For more on jury instructions, see *infra* § 22.43.
367. See Sample Order *infra* § 41.63.
368. Fed. R. Civ. P. 16(e).

- whether additional undisclosed or other specified evidence is pre-cluded;[369]
- which objections are to be deemed waived;[370]
- procedures for consolidation or severance or transfer of cases;
- procedures for the presentation of testimony and exhibits; and
- other housekeeping matters to expedite the trial.

See also the checklist at *infra* section 40.3.

No single format can be prescribed for a final pretrial order that will be suitable for all complex litigation. Like that for pretrial proceedings, the plan and program for the trial must be tailored by the judge and attorneys according to the circumstances of the particular litigation.

---

369. Fed. R. Civ. P. 26(a)(3).
370. *Id.*

22. Trial

Excessively long and complex trials increase the cost of litigation, diminish jury comprehension, burden jurors, courts, and parties, and diminish public access to, and confidence in, the justice system. Management is needed to reduce complexity, cost, and trial time, and improve the quality of the trial. Its effectiveness depends on the design and implementation of flexible and creative plans that take into account the specific needs of particular litigation and permit the attorneys to try their case in an orderly fashion.

While judicial management is equally important in civil and criminal litigation, the two frequently pose different problems and considerations. This section deals primarily with civil trials; criminal trials are discussed in *infra* section 32.3. As noted below, however, some principles of civil trial management may be relevant to criminal trials as well.

22.1 Administration

22.11 Trial Schedule

A trial schedule is essential to the orderly conduct of a trial. The schedule may, but need not, limit the length of the trial itself or the time allotted to each side for examination and cross-examination of witnesses (see *infra* section 22.35). Whether or not it imposes time limits, the schedule should specify the days of the week and the hours each day that the trial will be held, and the holidays and other days when the trial will be in recess (such as for a weekly motions day). The trial schedule should be set only after consultation with counsel and, to be realistic, must take into account the court's, counsel's, and parties' other commitments. Once appropriate accommodations have been made for other demands on the time of the participants, the schedule should ordinarily be regarded as a commitment by all, to be modified only in cases of extreme urgency. An exception may be made in very lengthy trials, which may require review of the schedule from time to time.

Adherence to the schedule requires that all trial participants make appropriate arrangements for their other activities. The jurors should be informed of the schedule at the time of voir dire and, if unable to commit to it, should be excused if possible. They should be kept informed of any changes in the schedule during the trial and advised of the progress of the trial in order to make their own arrangements. Unforeseen events may, of course, arise during a trial affecting a juror's availability. Ordinarily, the court will need to accept minor delays in order not to lose a juror who may later be needed to enable the jury to return a verdict.

The judge should insist that all trial participants be punctual and prepared to proceed on schedule. To minimize interruptions while allowing the attorneys to function effectively, the court may permit attorneys to enter and leave the courtroom discretely during the proceedings. The jury should be informed of this, to avoid any perception of discourtesy.

To expedite the trial and avoid keeping the jury waiting, the trial day should be devoted to the uninterrupted presentation of evidence. Objections, motions, and other matters that may interrupt should as much as possible be raised at a time set aside for the purpose, before the jury arrives in the morning or after it leaves in the afternoon. Any matter that must be raised during the presentation of evidence should be stated briefly without argument and ruled on promptly. If an objection is too complex for an immediate ruling, the judge should consider deferring it until it can be resolved without taking the jury's time and proceeding with the presentation of evidence, possibly directing counsel to pursue a different line of questioning for the moment. In managing the trial, the court should not hesitate to use its authority under Fed. R. Evid. 611(a) to "exercise reasonable control over the mode and order of interrogating witnesses and presenting evidence."

Judges employ different approaches to the scheduling of trial:

- **Six-day week.** Some feel that an extended trial week is the best way to expedite a lengthy trial. Others believe that such a schedule takes too great a toll on trial participants and leaves insufficient time for other activities.
- **Four-and-a-half-day week.** With this commonly used schedule, one half day each week is reserved for administrative matters, hearings outside the presence of the jury, and matters other than the trial.
- **Morning schedule.** Holding trial in the morning only (for example, from 9 A.M. to noon for a short day, from 8 A.M. to 2 P.M. for a long day) permits jurors to continue working during the trial (which can in turn reduce requests to be excused) and allows the court and counsel substantial time to keep up with other work.

22.12 Courthouse Facilities

When a trial is expected to involve a large numbers of attorneys, parties, and witnesses, and numerous exhibits and documents, advance planning for appropriate accommodations is advisable. It may be necessary to make arrangements for:

- a larger courtroom, in the courthouse or elsewhere;
- physical modifications to the courtroom, such as additional space for counsel, parties, files, exhibits, or persons such as experts or consultants whose presence may be needed;
- jury accommodations, particularly in a lengthy trial;
- witness and attorney conference rooms; and
- courtroom security and access during nontrial hours.

These needs should be made known to those responsible for allocating space and maintaining the building as far in advance as possible. The parties should be allowed access before trial to the courtroom and other areas as necessary to prepare and to advise the court of potential problems. Advance preparation is particularly important (and may require more time and effort than usual) if special equipment, such as computers, video playback equipment and monitors, systems to aid interpreters or court reporters, or additional telephone lines, will be installed.[371] The judge should designate court personnel with whom the parties may coordinate these activities.

22.13 Managing Exhibits

To avoid trial delay and interruption, each document or other item to be offered in evidence or used at trial (other than for impeachment) should be:
- premarked with an identification number, preferably in advance of trial but at least one day before it is to be offered or referred to at trial (preferably a single identification designation should be used for pretrial discovery and trial (see *supra* section 21.441));
- listed on the form used by the court to record such evidence; counsel should obtain from the clerk's office in advance of trial copies of the form used by the court, or, subject to the judge's approval, create a form for use in the particular case;
- made available to opposing counsel and the court before trial begins;
- copied, enlarged, or imaged[372] as necessary for use at trial; and
- redacted, if lengthy, to eliminate irrelevant matter.

As discussed in *supra* section 21.64, the court should require pretrial disclosure of proposed exhibits and objections thereto, and make pretrial rulings on admissibility to the extent feasible. The trial may be expedited, and trial interruptions avoided, by use of the following procedures:

---

371. The use of technology at trial is discussed in *infra* § 22.3; for more detailed descriptions of available technology, see *infra* § 34.

372. Imaging of documents for computerized storage and retrieval is discussed in *supra* § 21.444.

- exhibits not objected to or to which pretrial objections were overruled may be admitted into evidence without formal offer and ruling;
- pretrial rulings on objections to evidence should preclude renewal of the offer or objection at trial in the absence of a substantial basis for reconsideration;[373]
- objections made at trial should be ruled on from the bench without argument; if the court wants to hear argument, it should be deferred to the next scheduled recess and counsel should proceed with other matters (see *infra* section 22.15);
- alternatively, attorneys not needed in the courtroom may present objections and arguments to a magistrate judge while the trial is proceeding—unresolved objections can later be presented to the judge if necessary, along with the magistrate judge's summary of the arguments, for resolution after the jury has been excused.[374]

22.14 Transcripts

Because expedited, daily, or hourly transcripts add substantially to the expense of the litigation, their cost must be balanced against their utility. Having access to the transcript in the course of trial aids counsel's preparation for cross and redirect examination, helps resolve disputes over testimony during trial, facilitates rulings on evidence, and can speed preparation of the record on appeal. The decision whether to incur the extra costs of such transcripts should be left to counsel.[375]

Having a transcript available can speed readbacks requested by the jury during deliberations, but the transcript should not ordinarily be given to the jury for fear that the text may overshadow the mental impression of witness demeanor and credibility. Jurors should be advised at the outset of the trial that they should expect to have to rely on their recollection and not assume that a transcript will be available to them.

In courts with access to computer-aided transcription (CAT), transcription may be virtually in real time, accessible on computer screens as well as in hard

---

373. Counsel should, however, consult local law to determine whether renewal of the objection is required to prevent waiver. *See* United States v. Rutkowski, 814 F.2d 594, 598 (11th Cir. 1987).

374. *See* Harry M. Reasoner and Betty R. Owens, *Innovative Judicial Techniques in Managing Complex Litigation*, 19 Fed. Litig. Guide 603, 605–06 (1989) (discussing ETSI v. Burlington N., Inc., B-84-979-CA (E.D. Tex.)).

375. Under 28 U.S.C. § 1920(2), the court may tax as costs "fees of the court reporter for all or any part of the stenographic transcript necessarily obtained for use in the case." Courts do not ordinarily include in taxable costs the additional fees for expedited or daily transcript. *See* 10 Charles A. Wright et al., Federal Practice and Procedure § 2677 (2d ed. 1983) and cases cited therein.

copy, and often at standard rates.[376] For further discussion of this technology, see *infra* section 34.38.

22.15 Conferences During Trial

The court should schedule a conference with counsel for the end of each trial day after the jury has been excused. The conference may be brief, but should generally be on the record to avoid later misunderstandings. Holding such a conference helps avoid or at least minimize bench conferences and other interruption of the trial. It should be used to plan the next day's proceedings and to fix the order of witnesses and exhibits, avoiding surprise and ensuring that the parties will not run out of witnesses. Counsel can raise anticipated problems with the court and the court may hear offers of proof and arguments. The court may, in light of other evidence previously presented, determine that further evidence on a point would be cumulative. In large litigation, attorneys working on the case but not directly engaged in the courtroom can prepare motions for consideration at the conference. The judge can provide guidance to attorneys without the stigma of courtroom admonitions, remind them when necessary of appropriate standards of conduct, and cool antagonism generated in the heat of trial. A short conference before the jury arrives in the morning may also be useful, to deal with last-minute changes in the order of witnesses or exhibits or to follow up on matters raised at the previous day's conference.

22.2 Conduct of Trial

22.21 Opening Statements

Opening statements, intended to help the jury understand the issues and the proof at trial, are of particular importance in complex litigation. To maximize their utility, the court should consider some of the following points:

- opening statements should outline the facts expected to be proved, not argue the case—their effectiveness will be enhanced if they are preceded by preliminary instructions from the court outlining the principal issues to be decided;

---

376. In Cimino v. Raymark Indus., Inc., 751 F. Supp. 649 (E.D. Tex. 1990), CAT typically allowed production of transcripts of the morning's testimony by 1:30 P.M. and the afternoon's testimony by the evening of the same day. See generally, with respect to organizing trials, Robert M. Parker, *Streamlining Complex Cases*, 10 Rev. Litig. 547, 556 (1991).

- opening statements should be brief—the court may want to set a reasonable time limit;
- ground rules should be set in advance for dealing with sensitive issues such as punitive damages and evidence that may yet be ruled inadmissible;
- in long trials, the court may allow time for each side to make supplementary opening statements at appropriate points during trial to help the jury understand evidence as it is presented;
- ground rules should be set for the use during opening statements of charts and other demonstrative aids not then in evidence—while the use of such aids at this stage can aid jury comprehension and should be encouraged, opposing counsel should have an opportunity to review and object to them in advance of trial;
- in multiparty cases, the court should consider whether it is necessary to permit each party to present an opening statement to establish its separate identity with the jury, and, if so, whether repetition can be minimized and time limited; and
- in nonjury cases, opening statements may be briefer but are still useful in informing the court of each party's contentions and proposed order of proof.

22.22 Special Procedures for Multiparty Cases

The proliferation of counsel in multiparty cases can lead to delay and confusion. The court should therefore consider appropriate procedures, including the following:

- assigning primary responsibility for the conduct of trial to a limited number of attorneys, either by formal designation of trial counsel (see *supra* section 20.22) or by informal arrangement among the attorneys, taking into account legitimate needs for individual representation of parties;
- in cases in which the court will be awarding or apportioning attorneys' fees, overseeing the arrangements for trial preparation, including clarifying the extent to which attorneys in subsidiary roles will be entitled to compensation and ensuring that attorneys will not claim compensation for unnecessary time spent at trial (see *infra* section 24.213);
- providing that objections made by one party will be deemed made by all similarly situated parties unless expressly disclaimed—other counsel should be permitted to add further grounds of objection, again on behalf of all similarly situated parties unless disclaimed;

- to minimize repeated objections, ordering that objections to a particular line of examination will be deemed "continuing" until its completion, without the need for further objection unless new grounds arise as the examination proceeds; and

- in cases where collusion or conspiracy is alleged, allowing counsel reasonable leeway to demonstrate their independence from one another, and, if requested, giving cautionary instructions.

22.23 Advance Notice of Evidence and Order of Proof/Preclusion Orders

Counsel should be directed to exchange lists of expected witnesses and exhibits for each trial day (with copies if not previously supplied), indicating the order in which they will be called or offered. If portions of depositions are to be read, the portions should be identified. The court should specify the amount of advance notice required, balancing opposing counsel's need for time to prepare against the possibility that intervening developments will require changes. Some courts require a tentative listing of the order of witnesses and exhibits a week or more in advance, with changes to be communicated as soon as known and a final list to be given at a conference held at the close of the preceding day.

Counsel should (absent unusual circumstances) indicate in advance when adverse parties or their employees will be called to testify, and endeavor to accommodate personal and business conflicts as well as avoid surprise and possible embarrassment by calling on the opponent to produce a person without warning. If numerous employees are called, counsel should order them so as to avoid disrupting the adversary's affairs unnecessarily. When plaintiffs call significant defense witnesses, defendants may be permitted to offer their case on redirect examination. Counsel for the adverse party should be encouraged, upon sufficient advance notice, to arrange for the presence of witnesses under its control at the agreed-upon time without the need for a subpoena (and even if not subject to subpoena). The court should ordinarily allow witnesses, whether or not subpoenaed, to agree to report on timely request rather than remain in continuous attendance.

A party may, however, be unwilling to make available employees who are beyond the court's subpoena power.[377] Though the court probably lacks authority to compel their appearance, it may encourage cooperation by precluding that party from later calling such witnesses itself. The court may similarly preclude witnesses who have earlier successfully resisted testifying for the opposing side on privilege or other grounds; an effective procedure is for the court to enter an or-

---

377. In such a case, any party may offer that witness's deposition for any purpose "unless it appears that the absence of the witness was procured by the party offering the deposition." Fed. R. Civ. P. 32(a)(3)(B).

Manual for Complex Litigation, Third

der requiring witnesses to elect between testifying or asserting a privilege at least forty-five days prior to trial.

22.24 The Judge's Role[378]

Although the lawyers are responsible for preparing and presenting the case, the judge must always be in control of the courtroom and the proceedings. This is not inconsistent with the adversary process or with being humane and considerate. The interests of parties, counsel, and jurors are best served by making prompt, firm, and fair rulings, keeping the trial moving in an orderly and expeditious fashion, barring cumulative and unnecessary evidence, and holding all participants to high professional standards (see *infra* section 22.35 for discussion of judicial control of time and proof). Adhering to these management principles will help reduce the stress and tension of a long trial.

The judge should be sensitive to the right of counsel in the adversarial process to employ legitimate strategies and tactics to serve the interests of their clients, consistent with fairness and efficiency. Counsel should have a clear understanding of the judge's courtroom procedure, such as the location from which witnesses are to be examined and the mechanics for submitting exhibits to witnesses, the clerk, or the jury. Some judges have found providing written guidelines helpful to attorneys, particularly those attorneys unfamiliar with local customs.

In jury trials judges should use restraint in questioning witnesses lest they appear, albeit unwittingly, to be taking sides or disrupting counsel's presentation. It is generally advisable to refrain from asking questions until counsel have finished their examination and even then to limit questions to matters requiring clarification. See *infra* section 22.35.

---

378. This section sets out general principles; for specific actions the judge may take to control the presentation of evidence at trial, see *infra* § 22.35.

22.3 Presentation of Evidence

Although the presentation of the evidence at trial is normally controlled by the strategies and tactics of counsel, in complex litigation other considerations also require attention, primarily jury comprehension and the length of the trial. These are not unrelated concepts, since a shorter trial promotes jury comprehension, and effective presentation of evidence saves time. Moreover, many jurors in today's society expect information to be presented succinctly, even where it deals with legal or other complex matters.

While recognizing counsel's prerogatives, the judge should nevertheless take responsibility for encouraging and directing the use of techniques that will facilitate comprehension and expedition, primarily simplification of facts and evidence, use of plain language, and use of visual and other aids. Some techniques are time-tested, others are more creative. While some are concerned that innovative practices risk error, their potential to improve the trial process justifies their consideration.

22.31 Glossaries/Indexes/Demonstrative Aids

Jury comprehension can be significantly enhanced by aids that organize massive evidence and familiarize jurors with relevant vocabulary. Such aids include glossaries of important terms, names, dates, and events, informative indexes of exhibits to assist in identification and retrieval, and time lines of important events in the case. To the extent feasible, the parties should develop glossaries, indexes, and time lines as joint exhibits. They may be prepared using the procedure suggested for developing statements of agreed and disputed facts (see *supra* section 21.47); if necessary, the court can refer disputes to a magistrate judge. Stipulated facts should be presented in the form of a logically organized statement.

Jurors understand better and remember more when information is presented visually rather than only verbally. Graphics, such as charts and diagrams, are commonly used demonstrative aids (see *supra* section 22.21 on the use of demonstrative aids during opening statements and *infra* section 34.32 on computer-generated graphics). This type of demonstrative evidence may be admitted whatever its source, when in the judge's discretion it will help the trier of fact understand other evidence.[379] Graphics can be deceptive, however. For example, the physical representation of data (i.e., the area occupied on the chart) may be disproportionate to the ratio of the numbers represented. The relationship of data may also be distorted by representation (e.g., representing one-dimensional data by three-dimensional bars), creating a misleading visual reaction. Graphs of amounts of money may not be shown in constant dollars. Graphs taking figures out of context or using different scales may create the appearance of disproportionately large or small differences in data.[380]

22.32 Use of Exhibits

Ordinarily exhibits are offered for the purpose of communicating to the jury some significant fact. Exhibits should be presented in a manner that will achieve that purpose (except when an exhibit is simply a link in a chain of proof). Thus, documentary proof should be redacted to eliminate irrelevant matter and its contents offered, whenever possible, by way of summary or other streamlined procedure that will help focus the jury's attention to the material portions. See *supra* section 21.492.

Circulating exhibits among the jurors is time consuming, disrupts the examination of witnesses, and should be avoided except where the physical qualities of an object are themselves relevant. Whenever possible, exhibits should be displayed so that the jurors and the judge can view them while hearing related testimony. Some options include:

- **Enlargements.** They may be posted, or projected on a screen located so as to be easily visible to the witness, judge, and jurors; counsel will then be able to direct attention to particular portions of an exhibit during examination.

- **Computerized imaging systems.** In document-intensive cases, such systems facilitate the storage, retrieval, and presentation of documents and graphics (see discussion of laser discs and CD-ROM in *supra* section 21.444 and *infra* sections 34.33–34.34). Devices such as bar code notebooks permit instantaneous retrieval for display of documents, videotaped and other depositions (see *infra* section 22.33), and computer-generated graphics (see *infra* section 34.32). Although the systems used may vary—the parties will usually want to develop their systems independently to maintain confidentiality and exclusive access and control—counsel may be able to agree on common courtroom hardware (such as

---

379. *See* 2 McCormack on Evidence § 212 at 9–10 (4th ed. 1992).

380. *See* Edward R. Tufte, The Visual Display of Quantitative Information (1983) *and* Envisioning Information (1990).

monitors, see *infra* section 34.31). If technologically advanced systems are to be used, counsel should familiarize themselves with their operation, and should test them before trial to avoid later problems that may disrupt the presentation of evidence. Such systems (and the preparation they require) may be costly, but can significantly assist jury comprehension and expedite trial. They may also, however, affect a jury's evaluation of the relative positions of the parties in unpredictable ways; some jurors may be swayed by high-tech evidence, while others are more impressed with a chart on a cardboard poster.

- **Copies and exhibit books.** In some cases it may be cost-effective for counsel simply to provide jurors with individual copies of selected exhibits central to the presentation at trial. These may then be organized, indexed (with updates as needed), and placed in individual binders either before or during trial when the jury is not sitting. Exhibits may be accompanied on separate pages by a summary of counsel's contentions concerning their significance; if juror note taking is allowed (see the discussion of juror notebooks in *infra* section 22.42), space may be left for juror notes relating to exhibits. Other less important exhibits may be distributed and collected by the courtroom clerk on a daily basis, with jurors instructed not to make notes on their copies.

Attention should also be given to the physical handling of exhibits during the trial in order to avoid cumbersome and time-consuming procedures. To the extent possible, exhibits should have been premarked and previously received into evidence. Copies of the exhibits to be used with a witness should be available to the witness on the stand and in the hands of counsel before the examination begins. If voluminous, they can be kept in tabbed notebooks stacked on a cart located within easy reach of the witness; counsel can then direct the witness to the volume and tab number of exhibits as needed.

22.33 Depositions

Because the reading of depositions at trial is boring for the jury and a poor way to communicate information,[381] it should be avoided whenever possible, and techniques such as those discussed below should be considered.

---

381. One judge has called the reading of depositions "[b]eyond a doubt, the single least effective method of communicating information to a jury." Parker, *supra* note 376, at 550.

22.331 Summaries

If the contents of a deposition is a necessary element of a party's proof, the preferred mode of presentation should be a succinct stipulated statement or summary of the material facts that can be read to the jury. The parties should be directed to attempt to reach agreement on a fair statement of the substance of the testimony, possibly with the assistance of a magistrate judge. The effectiveness of summaries may be increased when combined with video presentation, as discussed below.

22.332 Editing, Designations, and Extracts

A fair presentation of the contents of a deposition may, however, also require presenting to the jury a colloquy with the witness. The portions read should be limited to the essential testimony of the witness, but may include not only the deponent's "final" answer but also testimony that reflects demeanor, attitude, recollection, and other matters affecting credibility. Rather than going through a deposition to eliminate unnecessary portions, counsel should be directed to select for designation only the genuinely material parts that cannot be presented by way of summary. Background information, such as that bearing on the qualifications of an expert, may be covered by a brief stipulation read to the jury in advance. Most of the contents of pretrial depositions are irrelevant or at least unnecessary at trial; the material portions rarely exceed a few lines or pages.

Before trial, each party should be required to designate those portions of depositions it intends to read at trial. Using this information, other counsel can designate additional portions, if any, to be read.[382] The process is repeated until, after a series of exchanges, the parties have finished designating the portions to be offered. Those portions usually will be introduced at trial in the same sequence in which they appear in the deposition, although another sequence can be adopted if it would improve comprehension.

A common and convenient method for making designations is for the parties to enclose the portions to be offered in brackets on the pages of the deposition, each using a different color. Opposite the brackets other parties may indicate any objections in abbreviated language (e.g., "D obj. hearsay, not best evidence"). The court's rulings may be indicated in a similar fashion, enabling counsel to read only the admitted portions from the original deposition.

Developments during trial may cause changes in the parts of depositions that the parties want to offer. Ordinarily the court should permit parties to change their designations, as long as other parties are advised promptly of such changes

---

382. Under Fed. R. Civ. P. 32(a)(4), if only a part of a deposition is offered, "an adverse party may require the offeror to introduce any other part which ought in fairness to be considered with the part introduced, and any party may introduce any other part." *See also* Fed. R. Evid. 106.

and have sufficient notice to revise their counterdesignations. Alternatively, in a long trial the court may allow counsel to designate portions of depositions to be offered several days before their expected use.

22.333 Presentation/Videotaped Depositions

In nonjury cases, relevant excerpts of depositions or summaries can be prepared and offered as exhibits, usually without being read at trial and transcribed by the court reporter. The judge can later read these excerpts along with other exhibits in the record, but should instead hear the testimony if expecting to rule from the bench. The same procedure can be used in jury trials; it will reduce the volume of deposition evidence but increase the number of exhibits.

In jury cases, deposition testimony is usually read by attorneys or paralegals; the use of actors for this purpose has generally been discouraged. The judge needs to be concerned that the reader's pauses, inflection, and tone do not unfairly distort the witness's deposition testimony. If a tape recording (sometimes made by court reporters during depositions as a back-up to their notes) is available, it may be played for the jury at critical points. Under Fed. R. Civ. P. 32(c), deposition testimony may be offered at trial in nonstenographic form (indeed, in a jury trial, on a party's request it must be so presented if available unless the court for good cause orders otherwise) if the offering party provides a transcript of the pertinent portions to the court and (under Rule 26(a)(3)(B)) to other parties. Recordings may, however, be difficult to hear and understand.

Videotape is generally more effective for the presentation of deposition testimony, for impeachment and rebuttal, and for reference during argument.[383] Videotaped depositions may be used routinely or for key witnesses only; any party may videotape a deposition without court order.[384] As with all depositions, videotaped depositions should be purged of irrelevant and inadmissible matter. Although videotaped depositions may be more time consuming and difficult to edit, doing so allows the proponent to present testimony in a logical and comprehensible manner. Typically, testimony concerning various matters will be interspersed throughout the witness's testimony; editing by subject matter provides a more coherent presentation.[385] To aid comprehension, a witness's testimony from multiple depositions may be combined into a single presentation

---

383. For discussion of the use of videotaped depositions during argument, see Henke, *supra* note 209, 16 Am. J. Trial Advoc. at 165 (*citing* Gregory P. Joseph, Modern Visual Evidence § 3.03[2][f] (1984)).

384. Fed. R. Civ. P. 30(b)(2), (3). To avoid an unfair difference in emphasis, however, the court should not allow testimony to be presented by different means on direct and cross-examination. *See* Traylor v. Husqvarna Motor, 988 F.2d 729, 734 (7th Cir. 1993) (disapproving presentation of live direct testimony and videotaped cross).

385. *See* Parker, *supra* note 376, at 552.

(variations in setting or the witness's clothing should be explained to the jury). Extending this principle, the testimony of multiple witnesses relating to the same subject may be spliced together and played for the jury at the point when that subject is at issue. Videotaped depositions are also an efficient means for repeatedly presenting the same testimony of a witness—such as an expert or corporate official—in different trials involving the same issue.[386]

Split-screen techniques can be effective in depositions relating to, or in which the witness refers to, documents or other exhibits.[387] The witness may be presented on one side and the document or exhibit on the other, with portions referred to highlighted for emphasis and clarity. This allows the jury to observe the witness's testimony in context without the distraction of having to look away from the monitor.[388]

The use of deposition summaries, discussed in the preceding section, may be improved by combination with video presentation. A portion of a videotaped deposition may be shown to the jury and the remainder summarized. This combines the time savings of summaries with the opportunity to observe witnesses on video. If in counsel's judgment dispersed portions of a videotaped deposition are of particular importance, summaries may be interrupted by video presentation. The same end may be accomplished by uninterrupted presentation of a video portraying the witness's testimony interspersed with periodic summaries recorded by counsel in advance of trial.

As with written depositions, when edited versions of videotaped depositions are offered, other parties may request introduction of deleted parts.[389] Counsel should therefore provide other parties access to recordings in their entirety before trial, allow them to designate the portions they contend should be shown, and present unresolved disputes promptly to the court.

While video provides potentially attractive and effective alternatives to conventional presentation of deposition testimony, the persuasive power of visual presentation carries with it the potential for prejudice, a risk heightened by the opportunities for manipulation provided by technology, making rulings on objections critical. Unless the parties can reach substantial agreement on the form and content of the videotape to be shown to the jury, the process of passing on objections can be so burdensome and time consuming as to be impractical for the court. It is therefore advisable to address the process for determining the admissibility of videotape testimony early in the litigation, before the parties have made extensive investments.

---

386. *See id.*
387. Split-screen presentation may require large monitors for clarity. *See id.* at 551.
388. *See id.* at 551–52.
389. *See* Fed. R. Civ. P. 32(a)(4); Fed. R. Evid. 106.

22.334 Alternative Means of Presenting Testimony

New communication technology makes it possible to present the testimony of absent witnesses without incurring the cost and other disadvantages of depositions.[390] The cost and burden of obtaining the physical presence of a witness may be disproportionate to the importance of the expected testimony, particularly if a witness who has previously testified is recalled for only brief testimony. In such circumstances, the examination of witnesses has been conducted using satellite or other remote video transmission.[391] The procedure for examination is similar to that used in the courtroom—the witness is sworn and examined on direct and cross—though additional safeguards may be needed.[392] The cost should generally be borne by the party calling the witness, though a portion may be allocated to other parties who prolong examination by extensive cross-examination or objections.[393]

Fed. R. Civ. P. 43(a), however, requires that testimony be taken "orally in open court."[394] Nevertheless, although courts have disagreed on whether (in the absence of agreement) the rule permits testimony to be taken telephonically,[395] televised transmission has not been held to violate the rule. In criminal cases, remote transmission of testimony may violate Fed. R. Crim. P. 26 (whose text is identical to that of Fed. R. Civ. P. 43(a)) or the Confrontation Clause,[396] and

---

390. *See In re* San Juan Dupont Plaza Hotel Fire Litig., 129 F.R.D. 424, 425–26 (D. P.R. 1989).

391. This technique was used in the *San Juan* litigation, MDL 721, and *In re* Washington Public Power Supply Sys. Litig., MDL 551. In both cases, the court held that witnesses (at least if under a party's control) may be compelled to testify by such means despite being beyond the court's subpoena power, reasoning that the limits on that power are intended only to protect witnesses from undue inconvenience. *See San Juan*, 129 F.R.D. at 426 (approving Judge Browning's reasoning in *Washington Public*).

392. For a sample protocol, see *San Juan*, 129 F.R.D. at 427–30 (adapted from protocol used in *Washington Public*). For example, it is necessary to control the presence of other persons in the room in which the witness is being interrogated by remote means.

393. *See id.* at 428.

394. Despite its wording, the rule is not intended to prohibit those unable to communicate orally from testifying through writing, sign language, or technological means; a proposed amendment to the rule would make this explicit.

395. *Compare* Murphy v. Tivoli Ent., 953 F.2d 354, 358 (8th Cir. 1992) *with* Official Airline Guides, Inc. v. Churchfield Pubs., Inc., 756 F. Supp. 1393, 1398 n.2 (D. Or. 1990).

396. *See* Maryland v. Craig, 497 U.S. 836 (1990) (permissible for child sexual assault victim to testify over closed-circuit television given trial court's finding of necessity); Cumbie v. Singletary, 991 F.2d 715, 720 (11th Cir. 1993) (findings insufficient to permit same); *Murphy*, 953 F.2d at 358 n.2 (state courts do not allow telephonic transmission of substantive testimony in criminal case without defendant's consent). Conducting arraignment or pretrial conferences in criminal cases by remote video transmission is discussed in *infra* § 34.31.

therefore should normally be avoided. In any event, prior to resort to this technique, counsel and the court should consider all alternatives.[397]

22.34 Sequencing of Evidence and Arguments

Jury recollection and comprehension in lengthy and complex trials may be enhanced by altering the traditional order of trial. Techniques that have been used include the following:

- **Evidence presented by issues.** Rather than have evidence presented in the conventional order, the court may organize the trial in logical order, issue by issue, with both sides presenting their opening statements and evidence on a particular issue before moving to the next. See *supra* section 22.21. This procedure, roughly equivalent to severance of issues for trial under Fed. R. Civ. P. 42(b), can help the jury deal with complex issues and voluminous evidence, but may result in inefficiencies if witnesses must be recalled and evidence repeated.

- **Arguments presented by issues/sequential verdicts.** If it is impractical to arrange the entire trial in an issue-by-issue format, it may still be helpful to arrange closing arguments by issue, with both sides making their closings on an issue before moving to the next. The entire case may be submitted to the jury at the conclusion of all argument, or the issues may be submitted sequentially (see *infra* section 22.451 (special verdicts and general verdicts with interrogatories) and *infra* section 33.86 (civil RICO trials)). The latter procedure may be advantageous if a decision on one issue would render others moot or if the early resolution of pivotal issues will facilitate settlement; on the other hand, it can lengthen the total time for deliberations and requires recurrent recesses while the jury deliberates.

- **Interim statements and arguments.** Some judges have found that in a lengthy trial it can be helpful to the trier of fact for counsel from time to time to summarize the evidence that has been presented or outline forthcoming evidence. Such statements may be scheduled periodically (for example, at the start of each trial week), or counsel may be allowed to make one when they think appropriate, with each side allotted a fixed amount of time to use as it sees fit. Some judges, in patent and other scientifically complex cases, have permitted counsel to explain to the jury how the testimony of an expert will assist them in deciding an issue. Although such procedures are often described as "interim arguments," it may be more accurate to consider them "supplementary opening statements" since the

---

397. See *In re* Washington Pub. Power Supply Sys. Sec. Litig., 720 F. Supp. 1379, 1390 (D. Ariz. 1989) (court required plaintiffs to choose among (1) foregoing testimony, (2) offering videotaped or written depositions, or (3) taking testimony by live satellite transmission).

purpose is to aid the trier of fact in understanding and remembering the evidence and not to argue the case. The court should remind the jury of the difference between evidence and counsel's statements.[398] Interim jury instructions, discussed in *infra* section 22.433, may also be helpful.

22.35 Judicial Control/Time Limits

Ordinarily limits on time and on evidence will be set at the pretrial conference in order that counsel can plan accordingly before the trial begins. See *supra* section 21.643. But the course of the trial may make it appropriate for the court to assert its authority under Fed. R. Evid. 611(a) to "exercise reasonable control over the mode and order of interrogating witnesses and presenting evidence so as to (1) make [it] effective for the ascertainment of the truth, (2) avoid needless consumption of time, and (3) protect witnesses from harassment or undue embarrassment." While courts should be reluctant to interfere with counsel's control over the presentation of their case and should ensure that each side has the opportunity to present its case fully and fairly, judicial intervention may become necessary if evidence exceeds reasonable bounds and does not contribute to the resolution of the issues presented. Thus, courts should consider limiting or barring the examination of witnesses whose testimony is unnecessary or would be merely cumulative and calling for stipulations where a number of witnesses would testify to the same facts. The court may also review the order in which witnesses are to be called, to determine if it would interfere with an orderly trial (as when counsel tries to call an adversary's expert witness before critical evidence has been presented and before the party's own expert has testified). When particular, clearly defined subject matter requiring the testimony of two or more persons is involved, it may be efficient to examine the witnesses simultaneously, allowing the more knowledgeable witness to answer. This may require consent of counsel, in view of the parties' right under Fed. R. Evid. 615 to have witnesses excluded.[399] Opposing expert witnesses may be examined one after the other in order to clearly frame their agreements and disagreements for the trier of fact.

Judges generally refrain from interfering with counsel's mode of questioning, except when called on to rule on objections. But when the questioning is confusing, repetitive, or irrelevant and threatens to delay the trial, the court may need to limit the examination by acting under Fed. R. Evid. 611(a) and under Fed. R. Evid. 403, which permits exclusion even of relevant testimony "if its probative value is substantially outweighed by . . . considerations of undue delay, waste of time, or needless presentation of cumulative evidence." The court should consider intervening, even without objection, to (1) bar testimony on undisputed or

---

398. *See* Parker, *supra* note 376, at 553–54.

399. Expert witnesses needed to advise counsel are not subject to exclusion. *See* Fed. R. Evid. 615(3) advisory committee's note.

clearly cumulative facts,[400] or matters beyond the scope of the examination; (2) clarify confusing questions or answers; (3) prohibit repeated paraphrasing of answers into new, duplicative questions;[401] and (4) encourage stipulations by opposing counsel to avoid routine testimony, such as the date of a document. Some courts have found it effective to issue guidelines providing, among other things, that the court will:

- refrain from instructing witnesses to answer "yes or no" to questions that are (1) compound, (2) require a witness to make or accept a characterization rather than testify to a fact, or (3) are argumentative in form or substance;

- bar questions framed as arguments rather than requests for testimony that the witness is competent to give;

- prohibit questions asking one witness to comment on the credibility of another, unless prior request is made outside of the jury's presence; and

- sustain objections on the ground that an answer is nonresponsive only when made by interrogating counsel.

As noted in *supra* section 21.643, time limits (if imposed) should usually be established before trial. The burdens on jurors and on the public's access to the court when a trial grows unduly long, however, may require the court to consider setting limits during trial, taking care to avoid prejudicing either side. The mere threat of such limits may cause counsel to expedite the trial. If limits are imposed, they may grant each party a specified number of hours for all direct and cross-examination, restrict the time for specific arguments, or limit the time for examination of particular witnesses. Once limits have been imposed, extensions should be granted only for good cause, taking into account the requesting party's good faith efforts to stay within the limits and the degree of prejudice should an extension be denied.

At times it may be appropriate for the judge, exercising the authority under Fed. R. Evid. 614, to question witnesses called by the parties. In jury trials, this authority should be exercised with restraint to avoid the appearance of partiality or interference with counsel's trial strategy, and should be limited to clarifying matters on which the jury may be confused.[402] Rule 614 also gives the court authority to call its own witnesses (subject to cross-examination by the parties), an au-

---

400. Testimony may be disallowed as cumulative if it relates to evidence to be covered in later testimony.

401. Typical examples include questions that begin "Do I understand you to mean that . . ."; "Is it your testimony then that . . ."; "Is it fair to say that . . ."; and the like.

402. The advisory committee's note to Rule 614 state that "the authority [to question witnesses] is . . . abused when the judge abandons his proper role and assumes that of advocate," and point out that such abuse may be grounds for reversal.

thority that should rarely be exercised other than with respect to an expert appointed by the court under Fed. R. Evid. 706 (see *supra* section 21.51). An alternate approach might be for the judge to suggest questions to counsel outside the hearing of the jury, or inquire whether the matter will be clarified or addressed by another witness.

22.4 Jury Trials

Jury trials in complex cases place a heavy responsibility on the judge, who must ensure not only that the parties receive a fair trial but also that the jurors are treated with courtesy and consideration, are not burdened more than necessary, and are given the help they need to perform their task adequately. Jury management raises a number of issues which, though discussed in the following sections, should also be taken up at the final pretrial conference.

Aside from the largely mechanical matters here discussed, it is well for court and counsel to have in mind the critical role jurors play in the justice process. Although they are the decision makers, they are often made to feel like the forgotten participants in the trial: evidence is presented with little attention to the jurors, they are kept in the dark about much of what is happening in court, and frequently they are left to wait while the judge and counsel are busy with other matters. High on the judge's list of concerns, therefore, should be the considerate and courteous treatment of jurors by counsel, staff, and the court itself.

22.41 Impaneling the Jury[403]

Size of the venire and the panel. To minimize the burden on citizens and the cost to the court, the number of prospective jurors summoned should be no greater

---

403. *See generally* Bench Book, *supra* note 42, §§ 2.02–2.03.

than is reasonably necessary, taking into account such factors as the size of jury panel desired for trial, the nature of the case, and the number of jurors likely to be excused. Enough persons must be called, however, so that the court will not run out of prospective jurors in the course of the selection process. Under Fed. R. Civ. P. 48, between six and twelve jurors must be selected for a civil trial.[404] Though jurors may be excused during trial for good cause,[405] federal courts no longer seat alternates in civil trials; all jurors not excused participate in deliberations. Absent stipulation,[406] the court may not accept a verdict from a jury of fewer than six.[407] The court should seat enough jurors to minimize the risk of a mistrial, considering the probability of incapacity, disqualification, or other developments requiring the excuse of jurors during trial. The primary factor, of course, is the expected length of trial. One rule of thumb is to select eight jurors for a trial expected to last up to two months, ten jurors for a trial expected to last four months, and twelve jurors for a longer trial. In determining the appropriate size of the jury, the judge may also consider asking the parties if they will stipulate that in the event of a hung jury they will accept a verdict from a less than unanimous jury[408] or allow the case to be decided on the record by the court.[409] The parties may be more amenable to entering such agreements before voir dire than after the jury has been selected.

Voir dire. The court may examine prospective jurors itself or allow the parties to do so.[410] If the court conducts the examination, it must "permit the parties or their attorneys to supplement the examination by such further inquiry as it deems proper or . . . itself submit to the prospective jurors such additional questions of the parties or their attorneys as it deems proper."[411] Where the judge conducts voir dire, the attorneys should also be invited to submit proposed questions in

---

404. Local rules may also address jury size. Criminal cases require a jury of twelve, but before verdict the parties may stipulate to a jury of fewer than twelve and a verdict returned by fewer than twelve. Fed. R. Crim. P. 23(b).

405. Fed. R. Civ. P. 47(c).

406. While the parties may stipulate to the return of a verdict by a jury of fewer than six, *cf.* Colgrove v. Battin, 413 U.S. 149, 164 (1973) (referring to possibility without comment), the advisory committee's note to Rule 48 suggests that this be avoided. In addition to raising constitutional issues, smaller juries may be less reliable. There is considerable support for seating a jury of twelve, particularly in complex cases. See the discussion and citations in Ballew v. Georgia, 435 U.S. 223 (1978) (criminal conviction by jury of fewer than six violates due process).

407. The *Colgrove* court held that a six-person jury satisfied the Seventh Amendment, but explicitly declined to comment on the constitutionality of a smaller number. 413 U.S. at 159–60.

408. *See* Fed. R. Civ. P. 48.

409. *See* Fed. R. Civ. P. 39(a)(1).

410. Fed. R. Civ. P. 47(a); Fed. R. Crim. P. 24(a).

411. Fed. R. Civ. P. 47(a). Fed. R. Crim. P. 24(a) is similar, but applies to the defendant, defense counsel, and the government's attorney.

advance of trial and to conduct reasonable follow-up questioning of the jurors after the judge has finished. The court may allow counsel to conduct the entire voir dire, subject to reasonable control necessary to avoid extending the process unduly and to limit the attorneys to inquiring about juror qualifications rather than arguing the case. In light of constitutional restrictions on the use of peremptory challenges on discriminatory grounds, greater leeway may need to be given to counsel in voir dire to lay the foundation for appropriate challenges.

Procedures for the conduct of voir dire vary widely. Inquiries may be directed to the venire, to smaller panels, to jurors one at a time, or by a combination of these methods; challenges may then be exercised privately or before the prospective jurors. Challenges may be made by alternate strikes or presentation of lists, simultaneously or alternating, and the parties may or may not know the identity, order, and other information about replacement jurors before making a challenge.[412] Whatever method the court decides to use, to avoid confusion and prejudice counsel should be informed before trial begins.

In cases involving potentially large jury venires, pre-voir dire jury questionnaires are often mailed to prospective jurors to elicit basic information and identify prospective jurors unable to serve. This procedure avoids unnecessary trips to court, but may lead to an excessive number of requests to be excused and to inappropriate inquiries about the case. An alternative is to have prospective jurors complete a questionnaire in court before voir dire.[413]

During voir dire, prospective jurors should be informed of the expected length of trial, the trial schedule, and other facts that may bear on a juror's ability and qualifications to serve. The prospect of a long trial may produce many requests to be excused, creating the risk of a jury consisting predominantly of persons who are retired or otherwise not employed outside their home. The judge can reduce requests for excuses by making introductory comments emphasizing the responsibilities of citizenship, stressing the importance of juries being composed of a representative cross-section of the population, describing the litigation so as to point out the challenge and opportunity of service, and reminding the venire of the fact that only a few will be selected to serve.

---

412. While the struck panel system allows the attorneys to make more informed challenges, it has been criticized as encouraging improperly motivated challenges and increasing the likelihood of objections based on Edmonson v. Leesville Concrete Co., 111 S. Ct. 2077 (1991) (prohibiting private litigants from exercising race-based peremptory challenges). *See* Leonard B. Sand & Steven A. Reiss, *A Report on Seven Experiments Conducted by District Court Judges in the Second Circuit*, 60 N.Y.U. L. Rev. 423, 425 & nn.16–17 (1985). *See also* J.E.B. v. Alabama, 114 S. Ct. 1419 (1994) (gender-based peremptory challenges violate equal protection).

413. See Sample Jury Questionnaire *infra* § 41.7.

Some judges permit counsel to deliver opening statements to the entire venire, to enable prospective jurors to respond to voir dire questions more intelligently.

Peremptory challenges. In civil (and misdemeanor) cases, each party is allowed three peremptory challenges.[414] Several plaintiffs or several defendants may be considered a single party for that purpose, but the court may allow additional challenges, depending on whether parties' interests conflict or diverge significantly. Additional challenges should be granted sparingly because they will increase the size of the venire and lengthen voir dire and the jury-selection process. Presumptively, each side should have the same number of challenges.[415]

22.42 Juror Note Taking/Notebooks/Questions

Note taking. Permitting jurors to take notes, once discouraged, has now become widely accepted. The arguments in favor of permitting it are particularly compelling in long and complicated trials.[416] Concerns over note taking are minimized by the fact that many jurors will not take notes, but denying them permission to do so is demeaning and inconsistent with the large measure of responsibility the system places on jurors, and it may hamper their performance. Jurors should be provided with paper (or notebooks with space for notes, see *supra* section 22.32) and pens. Some judges instruct jurors that notes are only for the individual juror's use and should not be shown or read to others, that note taking should not distract them from observing the witnesses, and that notes should be left in the jury room during recesses.

Juror notebooks. In addition to holding exhibits provided to individual jurors during the trial (see *supra* section 22.32), notebooks may provide jurors with information that will be helpful to them to organize and retain the information adduced during the trial, such as witness and exhibit lists, pictures of witnesses, chronologies and time lines, glossaries (see *supra* section 22.31), and excerpts from instructions.[417] The court should control the amount of material in the notebooks to ensure that they remain clear and useful.

---

414. 28 U.S.C. § 1870; Fed. R. Civ. P. 47(b). In felony cases, defendants are allowed ten challenges jointly and the government six (with additional challenges for alternates, if selected); the court may allow additional defense challenges if there are multiple defendants. Fed. R. Crim. P. 24(b).

415. Some judges have used unconventional methods of jury selection in complex cases to increase the participation of relatively more experienced and educated jurors. Different techniques have been used with the consent and cooperation of counsel. For a description, see William W Schwarzer, *Reforming Jury Trials*, 132 F.R.D. 575, 580–81 (1991).

416. *See id.* at 590–91.

417. *See* Parker, *supra* note 376, at 550. Preliminary and interim instructions are discussed in *infra* §§ 22.432–22.433.

Juror questions. Some judges have found that permitting jurors to ask questions in open court (in civil cases) can be helpful to jury comprehension. Others require that any questions be submitted in writing for consideration by the judge and counsel. The judge may say nothing on this subject, or may inform jurors that questions are permitted at the conclusion of a witness's examination, for the purpose of helping them understand the evidence; jurors may be cautioned, however, that it is for the lawyers to try the case and that matters occurring to them during one witness's examination may later be covered by another's.[418]

22.43 Jury Instructions[419]

22.431 General Principles

Jurors cannot be expected to render an intelligent verdict if the instructions are unintelligible to them. When a trial is complex and protracted, the need for instructions the jury will understand is particularly compelling. Instructions should therefore use language that lay persons can understand, be concise, concrete, and simple, use the active voice, avoid negatives and double-negatives, and be organized in logical sequence for the reader. As discussed in *supra* section 21.65, the court should direct counsel to submit proposed instructions at the final pretrial conference to focus the attention of the court and counsel on the issues to be tried.

Substantive instructions should be tailored to the particular case, avoiding generalized pattern instructions. Propositions of law should be explained with reference to the facts and parties in the case; illustrations familiar to jurors may also help. Instructions phrased in the language of appellate opinions are not likely to be meaningful to jurors. Most judges reword counsel's proposed instructions, which tend to be argumentative and one-sided, into language of their own, or at least edit them substantially. Simply combining the proposals submitted by counsel for each side is unlikely to produce sound and intelligible instructions. Instructions should be read to the jury with appropriate emphasis and variation

---

418. The pros and cons of juror questioning, and the procedures to follow if it is allowed, are discussed in United States v. Johnson, 914 F.2d 136, 137–39 (8th Cir. 1990) (criminal); DeBenedetto v. Goodyear Tire & Rubber Co., 754 F.2d 512, 513–17 (4th Cir. 1985); Schwarzer, *supra* note 415, 132 F.R.D. at 591–93 (also providing sample instruction).

419. *See generally* Bench Book, *supra* note 42, §§ 2.04–2.05.

in tone, to enhance comprehension and retention; rarely should the reading take much more than a half hour. One or more copies of the instructions should then be sent into the jury room (see *infra* section 22.434).

22.432 Preliminary Instructions

It is difficult for jurors to deal effectively with the evidence presented during a lengthy trial if they have no framework of the factual and legal issues to give structure and context to what they see and hear. Moreover, the jurors should understand the trial process in which they are about to participate and what they can expect. Preliminary instructions provide context and basic guidance for the conduct of jurors. They will typically cover the following subjects:

- **Preliminary statement of legal principles and factual issues.** The instructions should summarize the key factual issues, including a statement of the facts and the parties' major contentions (which may be drafted jointly by the parties), and explain briefly the basic legal issues and principles, such as the elements of claims and defenses to be proved. The court should emphasize that these instructions are preliminary—that no effort is made to cover all of the issues or principles—and that deliberations will be governed by the final instructions to be given at the conclusion of the case. Since one purpose of these instructions is to prepare jurors for opening statements, they are usually given first, with counsel permitted to refer to them in their opening statements. The judge may, however, defer instructions until after opening statements or give supplemental preliminary instructions at that time.

- **The conduct of the trial.** Jurors should be informed of the course of the trial from opening statements to verdict, the methods by which evidence is presented, and the procedure for raising and resolving objections. In some cases, such as those involving charges of conspiracy, the court may wish to inform the jury that cooperation among the litigants at trial has been urged by the court and should not be taken as evidence of concerted action with respect to the matters at issue in the litigation.

- **Schedule.** In addition to the hourly and daily schedule established for the trial of the case, jurors should be advised of any holidays or other planned recesses.

- **Precautions to prevent mistrial.**[420] The court should direct jurors not to discuss the case or communicate with trial participants. It should warn against exposure to publicity and attempts at independent fact-finding,

---

420. See also *infra* § 22.44 (avoiding mistrial).

such as viewing the scene of some occurrence or undertaking experiments or research.

- **Pretrial procedures.** The judge should consider describing briefly the various discovery devices that have been used during the pretrial stage of the litigation, such as depositions, document production, and interrogatories. Not only will this information be helpful when such evidence is later introduced, but it also serves to explain why parties have possession of, or know about, various matters involving other persons.

- **The functions and duties of the jury.** The instructions might also include such matters as the jury's role as fact-finder, the burden of proof, assessing the credibility of witnesses, the nature of evidence, including circumstantial evidence and the purpose of rules of evidence, and the jurors' need to rely on their recollection of testimony (including any special instructions about the use of juror notebooks, note taking, or questions). Most of these instructions should be repeated in the final jury charge, supplemented by any special explanations (such as use of convictions to impeach credibility) warranted by developments at trial or the use of special verdicts or interrogatories.[421]

22.433 Interim and Limiting Instructions

Developments in the course of trial will from time to time create the need for additional instructions. Under Fed. R. Evid. 105, when evidence is admitted that is admissible as to some but not all parties or for a limited purpose only, the court must, upon request, instruct the jury accordingly. At counsel's request, the court may repeat such limiting instructions at the close of trial. Where the offer of such evidence is contemplated, counsel should raise the issue with the court promptly (if possible, before trial) and submit proposed instructions.

The judge should also consider giving instructions at any point in the trial where they might be helpful to the jury; an explanation of applicable legal principles may be more helpful when given at the time the issue arises than if deferred until the close of trial. It is advisable to permit counsel to comment or object before the court gives an instruction. As with preliminary instructions, the court should caution the jury that these are only interim explanations, and that the final, complete instructions on which they will base their verdict will be given at the close of trial. If the parties are presenting their evidence according to a prescribed sequence of issues (see *supra* section 22.34), the judge may structure instructions accordingly.

---

421. See *infra* §§ 22.435 (supplemental instructions), 22.45 (verdicts).

22.434 Final Instructions

Although proposed instructions should generally be submitted to the court in connection with the final pretrial conference, developments during the trial may require that they be revised or supplemented. Counsel are entitled to file written requests for instructions "at the close of the evidence or at such earlier time as the court reasonably directs," and are entitled to notice of the judge's proposed action on them before closing arguments.[422] Most judges, rather than responding to particular requests, prefer to provide counsel with the entire charge they propose to give. The court will then hold a charge conference to consider counsel's objections and requests; generally there will be little controversy if the instructions have been prepared by the court.[423] The judge may expedite the process by asking that proposed instructions be submitted on disks in compatible word-processing programs for ease of editing.

Final instructions may be given before or after closing arguments, or both.[424] Though traditionally instructions have been given after, there are advantages to giving the bulk of the instructions before argument.[425] Instructions on the law may make closing arguments easier to understand, and counsel, instead of previewing the court's instructions during argument, can refer to instructions already given in arguing their application to the facts. Hearing the instructions may also help counsel structure their arguments. The court should, however, reserve the final closing instruction until after arguments, reminding the jury of the instructions previously given and instructing them about the procedures to be followed in deliberations.[426]

Most judges provide jurors with copies of the instructions for use during deliberations.[427] If this is done, jurors should be informed in advance so that they can listen to the charge for a general understanding rather than try to memorize it. Some judges consider it preferable for jurors not to have the written charge in hand while the court is delivering the instructions, lest their attention be diverted by their own reading. Others consider it helpful to permit the jurors to follow the text, or at least to give them a brief topical outline with which they can follow the

---

422. Fed. R. Civ. P. 51; Fed. R. Crim. P. 30.

423. For a general discussion of procedures and options, see Bench Book, *supra* note 42, § 3.07.

424. Fed. R. Civ. P. 51; Fed. R. Crim. P. 30.

425. *See* Fed. R. Civ. P. 51 advisory committee's note.

426. *See* Stonehocker v. General Motors Corp., 587 F.2d 151, 157 (4th Cir. 1978); Babson v. United States, 320 F.2d 662, 666 (9th Cir. 1964).

427. Some courts have also experimented with providing jurors with a tape recording of their charge for use during deliberations. *See* Sand & Reiss, *supra* note 412, at 456–59. Access to desired passages may be facilitated by recording designated portions on separate tapes, or maintaining a record of the counter number where different portions begin. *See id.* at 458.

instructions as they are given. Jurors should be given any special verdict form or interrogatories for use during deliberations.

The oral charge, which is normally transcribed by the court reporter, should be complete within itself (i.e., the judge should not merely refer to writings that the jury may be given). When delivering the charge, the judge should maintain eye contact with the jurors, sensing when to depart from the prepared text to repeat, rephrase, or elaborate as seems necessary. Jurors should be told that, in the event of any variations between the oral and written charge, the oral charge controls and governs their deliberations. Some judges record the oral charge and send the tape into the jury room for reference.

In complex litigation, it may sometimes be helpful for the judge to comment on evidence to explain subject matter foreign to jurors and to keep them from being confused or misled by adversarial presentations. Such comments can and should be made without taking sides, solely to assist comprehension. The judge should avoid expressing a personal opinion on disputed facts,[428] and should always be and appear impartial. Before commenting on the evidence, the judge may submit the proposed language to counsel for comment and objections. The judge's comments may be included with the written instructions given to the jury, but it may be preferable not to do so to avoid giving them undue weight.

After all instructions have been given, counsel is entitled to record any objections to the charge outside the presence and hearing of the jury and before it retires.[429] Objections and the grounds therefor must be stated distinctly or are deemed waived.[430] The judge can then give corrective or supplemental instructions (see *infra* section 22.435) before deliberations begin.

All exhibits received in evidence except items such as currency, narcotics, weapons, and explosive devices may be sent directly to the jury room for the jurors' reference during deliberations, or the court may await requests from the jury. Another alternative is for the court to withhold some items—such as those received for impeachment or another limited purpose—until requested by the jury, when limiting instructions should be repeated. If the exhibits are voluminous, the jury should be given an index or other finding aid to assist their examination (see *supra* section 22.31). Materials not received in evidence, but that might be helpful in managing the evidence—such as tape players, projectors, magnifying glasses, calculators, diagrams, charts, and pleadings—may be sent into the jury room if their potential utility outweighs the risk that, even with pre-

---

428. *See Quercia* v. *United States*, 289 U.S. 466, 469 (1933). *Quercia*, in which Chief Justice Hughes discusses judicial comments on evidence in detail, is still cited as the leading case on the issue. *See, e.g.,* United States v. Beard, 960 F.2d 965, 970 (11th Cir. 1992).

429. Fed. R. Civ. P. 51; Fed. R. Crim. P. 30.

430. Fed. R. Civ. P. 51; Fed. R. Crim. P. 30.

cautionary instructions, their presence could be unfairly prejudicial or subject to misuse. Because the volume of exhibits may make them unmanageable for the jury, counsel may agree to withhold some voluminous materials until specifically requested, particularly if they are mainly for background.

22.435 Supplemental Instructions and Readbacks

Requests by the jury for supplemental instructions during deliberations should be handled in much the same manner as final instructions; the judge should determine the appropriate response after consulting with counsel and permitting counsel to object to the proposed instruction on the record. Instructions should be given orally in open court and should include a reminder that the jury should consider them as a part of those previously given, which remain binding.

The final instructions should advise the jurors that in deliberating on their verdict, they will not have a transcript available but will have to rely on the exhibits and their recollection of the testimony. Nevertheless, it is likely that after a long and complex trial the jury will request readbacks of testimony. The court should ask the jury to make their request as specific and narrow as possible to avoid excessively long readbacks. The judge should then confer with the attorneys to reach agreement, if possible, on the portions of the testimony to be read. If counsel have any objections, they should be permitted to state them on the record.

Care should be taken during the readback to avoid unduly emphasizing any part of the evidence.[431] Some judges decline to authorize readbacks altogether, partly to save time and partly to avoid potentially unfair distortions of the record, but as a result make the jury's task more difficult. A readback can sometimes be avoided, however, by an agreed statement of the parties' positions on the matter at issue.

22.44 Avoiding Mistrial

The potential for and consequences of mistrial, serious in all litigation, are aggravated in complex trials. The most obvious risk is the jury's failure to reach a verdict. A stipulation permitting return of a less than unanimous verdict can reduce that risk. Using special verdicts and interrogatories (see *infra* section 22.451) and permitting juries to return a partial verdict on issues as to which they are able to reach agreement can also help. Most importantly, the facts and the law should be presented in ways that maximize jury comprehension.

The risk of mistrial will also be reduced by taking precautions to shield the jury from improper contacts or exposure. The jury deliberation room should be "sanitized" before the jury retires, and all counsel should review all material before it is sent into the room, to ensure that nothing extraneous is inadvertently

---

431. *See* United States v. Hernandez, 27 F.3d 1403, 1408–09 (9th Cir. 1994).

included. Precautions that can reduce the likelihood of a mistrial include the following:

- **Cautionary instructions.** As discussed in *supra* section 22.432, the jurors should be given, at the outset and periodically during the trial, appropriate instructions regarding improper conduct. The final instructions may also include a brief explanation of the consequences of a mistrial.

- **Sequestration.** Sequestration of jurors should be considered only in extraordinary cases where public interest and media coverage are so intense as to jeopardize the fairness of the trial. See *infra* section 32.31.

- **Stipulations on verdict.** In advance of trial, the court should encourage the parties to stipulate under Fed. R. Civ. P. 48 to accept a majority (i.e., not unanimous) verdict, or under Rule 39(a)(1) to accept a nonjury decision on the same evidence if a verdict cannot be obtained (see *supra* section 21.62). Such stipulations may be made during trial or deliberations—indeed, the parties may not seriously consider them until actually faced with the possibility of mistrial caused by the need to remove a juror—but are generally easier to obtain in advance.

- **Loss of jurors during deliberations.** As long as six jurors will remain, having to excuse or disqualify a juror during deliberations need have no effect.[432] If the loss of one or more jurors would reduce the jury to fewer than six members, however, the court cannot accept the resulting verdict (absent a stipulation, which should be sought before trial).[433] The court should try to avoid this situation by seating a sufficient number of jurors (see *supra* section 22.41).

22.45 Verdicts

22.451 Special Verdicts and General Verdicts with Interrogatories

Special verdicts and interrogatories are commonly used in complex trials. As discussed in *supra* section 21.633, they help jurors organize their deliberations, simplify instructions, facilitate partial verdicts, isolate issues for possible appellate review, and reduce the costs and burdens of a retrial. A verdict form should at

---

432. The rules for criminal cases are different; see *infra* § 32.32.

433. Rule 48 permits the parties to stipulate to accept a verdict from a jury of fewer than six. *See supra* notes 406 & 407 (citing Supreme Court cases on constitutional requirements regarding jury size).

least require separate verdicts on each claim and on damages, but must be drafted so as to prevent duplicate damage awards. Counsel and the court should consider the form of verdict during pretrial.

Special verdicts may require the jury to return findings on each issue of fact, leaving the court to apply the law to the jury's findings.[434] The preparation of special verdict forms can be complicated.[435] The language needs to be concise, clear, comprehensive,[436] and crafted to minimize the risk of inconsistent verdicts.[437] The judge should instruct the jury on how to complete the verdict form properly, as Rule 49 requires, including both the procedure for rendering special verdicts and the specific substantive issues to be decided. To simplify the process, the judge may have the jury return partial verdicts seriatim, instructing on each issue individually before the jury deliberates on it.

Alternatively, the court may submit a general verdict with interrogatories. The jury both determines the facts and applies the law, but in addition makes findings on "issues of fact the decision of which is necessary to a verdict."[438] Some consider this procedure an attractive compromise between a simple general verdict and special verdicts, in that it maintains the traditional role of the jury while potentially avoiding the need to relitigate factual issues if an error of law taints the general verdict. On the other hand, interrogatories increase the length and complexity of deliberations and are more likely to produce inconsistencies. When the interrogatory answers are consistent with each other but inconsistent with the general verdict, the court may simply enter judgment according to the

---

434. Some cases have held that the court may also amend special verdict responses to conform them to the jury's obvious intention or correct a manifest error. *See* Aquachem Co., Inc. v. Olin Corp., 699 F.2d 516, 520 (11th Cir. 1983); Shaffer v. Great Am. Indem. Co., 147 F.2d 981 (5th Cir. 1945), *but cf.* Austin-Westshore Const. Co. Inc. v. Federated Dept. Stores, Inc., 934 F.2d 1217, 1224 (11th Cir. 1991) (*Aquachem* does not apply to general verdict with interrogatories).

435. Under Fed. R. Civ. P. 49(a), the court may use any "method of submitting the issues and requiring the written findings thereon as it deems most appropriate," as an alternative to the rule's suggested methods of submitting "written questions susceptible of categorical or other brief answer," or "written forms of the several special findings which might properly be made under the pleadings and evidence."

436. If any issue of fact raised by the pleadings is omitted, the parties will waive their right to a jury trial on that issue if they fail to demand its submission before the jury retires. If an issue is omitted without such demand, the court may make its own findings. Fed. R. Civ. P. 49(a).

437. Inconsistent verdicts are a concern even with standard verdict forms; careful structuring and instructions should minimize this risk. For a stark example of the danger of ambiguously drafted verdict forms, see Schiro v. Farley, No. 92-7549, slip. op. (Sup. Ct. Jan. 19, 1994), particularly Justice Stevens' dissent at 2–4 & n.2, in which the Court upheld a death sentence based, in part, on a finding that the killing was intentional, despite the fact that the jury left blank the square on the verdict sheet that they were to check if they found the defendant guilty of intentional murder.

438. Fed. R. Civ. P. 49(b).

answers, or may return the jury for further deliberation or order a new trial.[439] The court may not accept the verdict if the answers are inconsistent with each other and at least one is also inconsistent with the general verdict; it must first try to reconcile the answers, ordering further deliberations or a new trial if it cannot.[440] It is therefore particularly important after return of special verdicts or a general verdict with interrogatories that the judge give counsel an opportunity to be heard before the jury is discharged, to allow inconsistencies to be cured by further deliberation following supplemental instructions, and, perhaps, by amendment of the verdict form.[441]

22.452 Judgment as a Matter of Law

The court may grant judgment as a matter of law (formerly directed verdict) on a claim or defense during the trial. Under Fed. R. Civ. P. 50(a)(1), once a party has been fully heard on an issue, the court may determine the issue against that party if "there is no legally sufficient evidentiary basis for a reasonable jury to find for that party on that issue." The court may grant a motion for judgment as a matter of law on any "claim or defense that cannot . . . be maintained or defeated without a favorable finding on that issue." The motion must "specify the judgment sought and the law and the facts on which the moving party is entitled to the judgment," in order to allow the opposing party an opportunity to correct any deficiencies in its proof. While it is appropriate in the interest of economy to grant such motions, when warranted, as soon as a party has completed presentation on a fact essential to one or more of its claims or defenses, the court should not do so until the party has been apprised of the materiality of the fact and afforded an opportunity to supplement its evidence on that fact.[442]

A motion for judgment as a matter of law must be made before submission to the jury. Judges therefore frequently deny or submit such motions initially, even when they believe them to have merit, preferring to defer their resolution until after the jury renders a verdict. In this way, if the jury "gets it right" the judge need not disturb the verdict; any question of invading the province of the jury is avoided, and the verdict will be more difficult to overturn on appeal than would a judgment rendered on motion. If the jury instead renders a verdict lacking sufficient evidentiary support, the judge may then grant the motion upon its re-

---

439. *Id.*

440. *See id.;* Atlantic & Gulf Stevedores v. Ellerman Lines, 369 U.S. 355, 364 (1962).

441. Case law on the court's authority to amend or supplement verdict forms after the jury has returned a verdict is scarce; for a case holding it permissible to amend interrogatories, see United States v. 0.78 Acres of Land, More or Less, Situate in Berks County, Pa., 81 F.R.D. 618, 622 (E.D. Pa.), *aff'd,* 609 F.2d 504 (3d Cir. 1979) (mem.).

442. Fed. R. Civ. P. 50 advisory committee's note.

newal (formerly a judgment notwithstanding the verdict, or J.N.O.V.);[443] if this decision is later overturned, there will be a jury verdict for the appellate court to reinstate if it chooses. Offsetting these advantages is the time and expense that might be saved by granting a meritorious motion.

Motions for judgment as a matter of law may effectively be combined with the procedure discussed in *supra* section 22.34 for sequencing issues for trial. If issues likely to be dispositive are scheduled first, a ruling may reduce or obviate further proceedings. Thus, the judge may chose to deny a pivotal summary judgment motion during pretrial if its correct resolution is doubtful, while scheduling the trial to begin with presentation of the facts in issue (or scheduling a separate trial).[444] Even if not dispositive, early judicial resolution of issues unsubstantiated by facts or law may significantly reduce the scope of evidence, argument, and instructions. An order granting a motion for judgment as a matter of law should be in writing or read into the record, and should state the court's reasoning.

22.453 Return of Verdict[445]

When the jury has returned a special verdict or a general verdict with interrogatories, the judge and counsel should promptly review it for inconsistencies, in order that appropriate steps can be taken before the jury is discharged. The court should then, after consultation with counsel, promptly approve a form of judgment for entry by the clerk.[446] If the judgment does not resolve all aspects of the litigation, the court should consider entering final judgments as to some claims or parties to allow appeal to be taken.[447]

Where issues have been bifurcated or submitted to the jury for seriatim verdicts, the jury may need to resume hearing evidence and further instructions or begin deliberations on other issues.[448] If a recess is called, the judge should instruct the jurors that they remain under the restrictions originally imposed; if the recess extends more than a few days, a supplementary examination of jurors may be necessary on their return to determine whether grounds for disqualification have arisen in the interim.

If the jury is deadlocked, the judge will need to consider appropriate inquiries and instructions. Although the large investment in a long trial makes a mistrial

---

443. The judge may order a new trial or enter judgment as a matter of law. Fed. R. Civ. P. 50(b). If the latter, the judge must still rule on the motion (if any) for a new trial, to assist the appellate court in determining the relief to grant if the judgment is reversed. *See* Fed. R. Civ. P. 50(c)(1).

444. Fed. R. Civ. P. 50 advisory committee's note.

445. For general procedures for receipt of civil verdicts, see Bench Book, *supra* note 42, § 2.06.

446. *See* Fed. R. Civ. P. 58.

447. *See* Fed. R. Civ. P. 54(b); 28 U.S.C. § 1291; see also *infra* § 25.1.

448. See *supra* §§ 21.632 (separate trials), 22.34 (sequencing of evidence and arguments).

costly, the judge should avoid exerting undue pressure on jurors to reach agreement.[449]

22.5 Nonjury Trials

Nonjury trials may take less time to try but, unless well managed, may take longer to decide. Although nonjury trials may be conducted with less formality, procedures to promote clarity and expedition are still important. The court, for example, should not simply receive vast volumes of documents in the expectation that they will be sorted out during the decision process following trial; redaction, summaries, sampling, and other techniques should be considered here as in jury trials. This section discusses additional options for nonjury trials; the absence of a jury gives the judge greater freedom to exercise control over the conduct and shape of the trial.

22.51 Adopted Prepared Statements of Direct Testimony

Where credibility or recollection is not at issue, and particularly when the evidence is complicated or technical, the court may order that the direct testimony of witnesses under the parties' control be presented in substantial part through written statements prepared and submitted in advance of trial.[450] At trial, the witness is sworn, adopts the statement,[451] may supplement the written statement orally, and is then cross-examined and perhaps questioned by the judge. The statement is received as an exhibit and is not read into the record.

This procedure, particularly appropriate for expert witnesses, witnesses called to supply factual background, or those needing an interpreter, has several advantages. The proponent can ensure that it has made a clear and complete record; the judge and opposing counsel, having read the statement, are better able to understand and evaluate the witness's testimony; opposing counsel can prepare for more effective cross-examination; and the reduction of the amount of live testimony saves time.

---

449. The law of the circuit needs to be consulted for appropriate instructions.

450. *See* Charles. R. Richey, *Requiring Direct Testimony to be Submitted in Written Form Before Trial*, 72 Geo. L.J. 73 (1983). Circuit law should be consulted on whether the consent of parties is required.

451. The statement is received as an exhibit; as with all exhibits, objections should be resolved before trial. Because the witness adopts the statement orally in open court, Fed. R. Civ. P. 43 is not violated. *See In re* Adair, 965 F.2d 777 (9th Cir. 1992).

22.52 Findings of Fact and Conclusions of Law[452]

Each party should be directed to submit proposed findings of fact and counter-findings responding to opposing counsel's submissions, unless the pretrial briefs and statements of agreed and disputed facts serve this purpose. Some judges require counsel to exchange proposed findings and conclusions before submission to the court, marking for the court the portions disputed and those not disputed. Findings should be drafted in neutral language, avoiding argument and conclusions, and identify the evidence expected to establish each finding. Proposed findings allow the judge to follow the evidence during trial, adopting, modifying, or rejecting findings as it proceeds. This process simplifies the court's preparation of findings of fact, which, along with its conclusions of law, are required by Fed. R. Civ. P. 52(a).[453] Although the court's preparation of findings is aided by the parties' proposals (some judges require that they be submitted on computer disk for ease of adaptation), appellate courts frown on verbatim adoption of the parties' findings.[454]

Under Rule 52(a), the court's findings of fact and conclusions may be filed as an opinion or memorandum of decision or read into the record in open court. The latter procedure accelerates the time of decision while enabling the court to refine its opinion later as needed. The court may defer the decision until after receiving post-trial briefs. Briefs may not be necessary, however, if adequate pretrial memoranda have been filed. Some judges call for closing arguments immediately after the close of evidence, as in jury trials, and render their decisions promptly following the arguments.

Whatever time savings may be realized by a bench trial can easily be lost if the case is not decided promptly. Decisions become more difficult as the record grows cold with the passage of time, and long delay undermines public confidence in the justice system. Many judges avoid this problem by ruling from the bench whenever possible (preparing their ruling as the trial progresses) or by

452. For general guidance, see Bench Book, *supra* note 42, § 2.07; Litigation Manual, *supra* note 5, at 303.

453. Findings of fact and conclusions of law are also required if the judge renders judgment as a matter of law on a claim (see *supra* § 22.452). Fed. R. Civ. P. 52(c) (judgment on partial findings).

454. *See* Falcon Const. Co. v. Economy Forms Corp., 805 F.2d 1229, 1232 (5th Cir. 1986) (court that adopts findings verbatim leaves doubt whether it has discharged its duty to review the evidence itself and reached its decision on basis of own evaluation of evidence). Verbatim adoption of proposed findings may lead to more searching review at the appellate level. *See, e.g.,* Andre v. Bendix Corp., 774 F.2d 786, 800 (7th Cir. 1985); *In re* Las Colinas, Inc., 426 F.2d 1005, 1010 (1st Cir. 1970). Compare the Seventh Circuit's opinion in *Andre* with that in Scandia Down Corp. v. Euroquilt, Inc., 772 F.2d 1423, 1429 (7th Cir. 1985) (despite verbatim adoption, no special scrutiny required where judge paid careful attention to evidence and wrote own opinion).

setting a deadline for their decision (forcing themselves to arrange their calendar to allow sufficient time).

22.53 Procedures When Combined with Jury Trial

As discussed in *supra* section 21.63, the court may choose to try jury and nonjury issues concurrently (occasionally with an advisory jury, whose verdict is not binding). Evidence admissible only on a nonjury issue may have to be presented without the jury present. The court must also consider the proper sequencing of the jury and nonjury decisions to comply with *Beacon Theatres, Inc. v. Westover*, under which the right to a jury trial on legal claims may not be lost by a prior determination of equitable claims, except under "the most imperative circumstances."[455]

22.6 Inability of Judge to Proceed

Should the trial judge become unable to proceed after trial has begun, Fed. R. Civ. P. 63 permits any other judge to proceed with the trial upon certifying familiarity with the record[456] and determining that the parties will not be prejudiced. Fed. R. Crim. P. 25(a) is similar, but it (1) is limited to inability to proceed because of death, sickness, or "other disability," (2) requires that the successor judge be from the same court, and (3) does not expressly require a finding of lack of prejudice (though constitutional considerations may require it). Fed. R. Crim. P. 25(b) makes more lenient provision for replacement of a judge after a verdict or finding of guilt.

The rule requires the successor judge in a civil nonjury trial, upon request, to recall any witness whose testimony is material and disputed, and who is available to testify again without "undue burden," and permits the recall of any other witness.[457] As a practical matter, it is unlikely that a successor judge will wish to decide a complex case without having heard all the direct and cross-examination of witnesses, unless the parties stipulate to a decision on the record.

Whether a judge unable to proceed in a jury trial should be replaced to avoid mistrial in a complex case is a difficult question, depending in part on how close the trial is to completion. If the disability occurs near the start of the trial, declaring a mistrial may be the preferable course. On the other hand, if a large investment of resources (not only the parties' but also the jurors' time) has been made in the trial, a mistrial should be avoided if the replacement judge has confidence that the trial can go forward without sacrificing fairness; note that one

---

455. 359 U.S. 500, 510–11 (1959).

456. This will, of course, require the availability of a transcript or videotape of the prior trial proceedings; if these are not promptly available, it may be impossible to avoid prejudicing one or more parties. Fed. R. Civ. P. 63 advisory committee's note.

457. Fed. R. Civ. P. 63. *See also id.*

of the reasons for the 1991 amendment liberalizing Rule 63 was "the increasing length of federal trials."[458]

---

458. Fed. R. Civ. P. 63 advisory committee's note.

23. Settlement

Like litigation generally, complex cases are more frequently resolved by settlement than trial. Indeed, the high stakes increase the incentive to avoid the risk of trial, and the burgeoning cost of pretrial activity places a premium on settling early in the litigation. At the same time, however, the large sums, high number of parties and counsel, and complexity of the issues magnify the difficulty of achieving settlement.

This chapter addresses issues encountered in the settlement of complex litigation and suggests options for dealing with them. It focuses on the role of the trial judge, general principles and techniques to promote settlement, and special problems that may arise. Settlement of specific types of litigation is covered in *infra* section 30.4 (class actions), section 33.29 (mass tort litigation), section 33.36 (securities litigation), and section 33.55 (employment discrimination).

23.1 Trial Judge's Role

23.11 General Principles

The parties must negotiate the settlement, but the judge can serve as a catalyst for settlement discussions, create an atmosphere conducive to compromise, and make suggestions helpful to the litigants. Beginning with the first conference, and from time to time throughout the litigation, the court should encourage the settlement process. The judge should raise the issue of settlement at the first opportunity, inquiring whether any discussions have taken place or might be scheduled. As the case progresses, and the judge and counsel become better informed, the judge should continue to urge the parties to consider and reconsider their positions on settlement in light of current and anticipated developments.

The judge's initiatives can facilitate negotiations by removing the obstacles created by attorneys' reluctance to show weakness—to their clients or their opponents—by a willingness to compromise. Moreover, the court's comments can help overcome the intransigence or militance of clients. The judge can assist the parties, without touching on the merits, by focusing their attention on the likely cost of litigating the case to conclusion, in fees, expenses, time, and other resources. The judge can be helpful in other ways, such as scheduling settlement conferences, directing or encouraging reluctant parties, insurers, and other potential contributors to participate, suggesting and arranging for the presence of a neutral person to assist negotiations, targeting discovery at information needed for settlement, and promptly deciding motions whose resolution will lay the groundwork for settlement.[459]

The judge may be particularly helpful in identifying and encouraging consideration of nonmonetary solutions. Where, for example, the parties contemplate a continuing relationship, the judge may stimulate thought about innovative and mutually beneficial arrangements for the future that may pave the way for agreement on monetary terms. Drawing on experience and common sense, a judge may see opportunities for compromise not apparent to the parties and guide their negotiations toward solutions they might not otherwise have discovered.

In some instances, one side may not want the litigation resolved by settlement, even on favorable terms, preferring to have their "day in court"; indeed, some cases involve important questions of law or public policy that are best resolved by public, official adjudication. Sometimes, however, resistance to settlement arises instead from unreasonable or unrealistic attitudes. The judge can help influence counsel or the parties to reexamine their premises and assessments.

Important as is the judge's role as a catalyst for settlement, it must not be permitted to interfere with the steady progress of the case toward trial. Settlement efforts should not be permitted to delay or divert the pretrial process. Both can and should operate effectively on parallel tracks.

---

459. *See* Litigation Manual, *supra* note 5, at 36–39.

Nor should settlement efforts be permitted to impair the parties' perception of the assigned judge's fairness and impartiality. Some judges are able to participate actively in settlement discussion as well as pretrial activity and trial if necessary. Occasionally, the parties request the assigned judge's direct participation, waiving the right to seek recusal.[460] There is a danger, however, that such involvement will affect the parties' confidence in the judge's ability to try the case impartially. For this reason, many judges prefer not to engage in substantive settlement negotiations in cases they are expected to try, particularly if there is to be a bench trial,[461] instead bringing in another judge or other neutral person for that purpose. In some large litigation, the parties will be willing to pay for the services of a skilled mediator. See *infra* section 23.15.

If the judge participates in settlement negotiations, patience and a willingness to listen are essential. Settlement negotiations in complex litigation are not a sport for the short-winded. An obstacle may be removed only to reveal another; the judge should not become, or allow counsel and the parties to become, discouraged. By careful attention, the judge may spot openings and opportunities not readily apparent. To retain room to maneuver, parties may signal their expectations and limits in subtle ways. Often their true objectives remain hidden from all but the most attentive listener. An observant judge can open channels for effective communication.

23.12 Timing/Relationship to Discovery

The subject of settlement should be broached at the initial scheduling conference.[462] Counsel should prepare by discussing the possibility of settlement during the Rule 26(f) conference, as the rule requires, and becoming informed of their clients' positions. Though the parties may lack sufficient information to begin serious discussions, the judge should use the conference to explore the prospects for settlement, as well as the possibility of reference to extrajudicial procedures (see *infra* section 23.15). The judge may be able to schedule negotiations and periodic progress reports and assist counsel in developing a format for them.[463] Counsel should be required to attend settlement conferences with full settlement authority or with immediate access to their client.[464] Any impending or finalized settlement should be disclosed to the court promptly (see also *infra* section 23.23). If negotiations founder, the judge may play a vital role in encour-

---

460. *See id.* at 36.

461. *See* D. Marie Provine, Settlement Strategies for Federal District Judges 28 (Federal Judicial Center 1986).

462. *See* Fed. R. Civ. P. 16(a)(5), (c)(9) (pretrial conferences may be used to consider settlement).

463. *See* Litigation Manual, *supra* note 5, at 16.

464. *See* Fed. R. Civ. P. 16(c).

aging their resumption. Settlement should be on the agenda of every conference, particularly the final pretrial conference.

Although settlement should be explored early in the case, when the uncertainties of litigation and the potential savings of time, effort, and money are the greatest, the parties may be unwilling or unable to settle until they have more information. While some discovery may therefore be needed, the benefits of settlement are diminished if it is put off until discovery has been completed. The judge should instead work with the parties to identify and narrow issues, and then target early discovery at information needed for settlement negotiations.[465] Ordinarily, the court should not stay discovery or other pretrial proceedings based on the pendency of settlement discussions. Maintaining the momentum of the litigation and keeping trial preparation on schedule can create a powerful impetus for settlement. Once the parties are close to agreement, however, if a particular activity or deadline could affect their positions a short extension, monitored by the court, may be warranted. Avoiding the expense of imminent discovery can be an inducement to settle, but a settlement precluding or limiting further discovery should not be allowed to interfere with discovery needed by other parties (see *infra* section 23.22).

23.13 Specific Techniques to Promote Settlement

A number of techniques have proven successful in promoting settlement. The list below is not intended to be exhaustive; creativity in this aspect of the litigation process has few risks and should be encouraged. Among the techniques that have been productive are the following:

- **Firm trial date.** Setting a firm trial date is generally the most effective means to motivate parties to settle. To keep the date credible, the court must ensure that the case proceeds on schedule through pretrial; early settlement discussions should therefore generally not be allowed to delay pretrial proceedings.

- **Reference to another judge or magistrate judge.** To avoid the appearance of partiality, the assigned judge may refer the parties to another judge or magistrate judge in the court to conduct settlement negotiations. Many courts have reciprocal arrangements by which judges assist in settlement negotiations in cases assigned to other judges. Generally, the settlement judge will be expected to maintain the confidentiality of the discussions with the parties.

---

465. Targeted discovery is discussed in *supra* § 21.422.

- **Participation by parties.** The court may request or require that the parties attend settlement conferences.[466] Participation by parties or their representatives may expedite negotiations, avoiding the delays involved in seeking authority. In any event, the attending parties will become better informed of the strengths and weaknesses of each side's case and the costs and risks of pursuing the litigation. The parties' presence may, however, inhibit frank discussion by counsel, who may feel obliged to keep up appearances for the benefit of their clients.

- **Confidential discussions with judge.** Meeting with each party (or side) separately for confidential discussions, with their mutual consent, may help the judge find common ground. The parties may be more willing to speak candidly outside of the adversarial setting, and the judge can point out weaknesses without fear of compromising a party's position in the eyes of opposing counsel. After such discussions, the judge may be able to suggest areas of possible agreement, without revealing confidences. The court may also ask counsel to submit confidential memoranda outlining their settlement posture.

- **Settlement counsel, special masters, or experts.** Despite their familiarity with the case, the attorneys conducting the litigation may not be those best suited to conduct settlement discussions. They are generally selected for their ability as litigators, while others may possess superior negotiation skills. They may also be hampered by personal antagonisms developed in the course of the litigation. The judge may therefore suggest that one or more of the parties engage special counsel for the purpose of conducting settlement negotiations, or designate settlement counsel separate from lead and liaison counsel (see *supra* section 20.222). Judges have also used special masters to assist in settlement of complex litigation and in post-settlement claims-resolution proceedings. Arrangements for compensation of the special master must be made with the agreement of the parties, and selection should be made from a list provided by them (see *supra* section 21.52).

- **Contribution bar orders.** To facilitate partial settlements in multiparty cases, the court may (unless prohibited by the underlying statute) approve as a term of the settlement an order barring claims for contribution or indemnification by nonsettling defendants. To ensure binding effect, the parties affected (or those representing their interests) should be be-

---

466. *See* Fed. R. Civ. P. 16(c) (court may require party or its representative to be present or available by telephone).

fore the court, and their rights should be protected.[467] Courts generally require that the order contain a formula for calculating a setoff for non-settling defendants based on the settlement amount or the settlors' adjudged proportion of fault.[468]

· **Offer of judgment.** Under Fed. R. Civ. P. 68, a party defending against a claim may serve an offer of judgment upon the adverse party at any time more than ten days before trial (or proceedings to determine damages, if liability has already been adjudged). The party served has ten days to accept. If it does not, it will be liable for all costs incurred after the offer was made unless it obtains a more favorable judgment.[469] Invoking this procedure can create an added incentive to accept a reasonable offer in litigation (such as antitrust) where taxable costs may be high, particularly where the underlying statute defines costs to include attorneys' fees.[470]

· **Representative case(s).** The results of a trial of one or a few representative lead cases can provide information and motivation helpful to settlement of related cases.

· **Severance.** The early resolution of one or more issues by separate trial may provide a basis for settlement of others. The resolution of liability, damage, or other pivotal issues can provide the parties with the information or incentive needed for a comprehensive settlement.[471]

---

467. *See, e.g., In re* Masters Mates & Pilots Pension Plan and IRAP Litig., 957 F.2d 1020, 1031 (2d Cir. 1991); *In re* Jiffy Lube Sec. Litig., 927 F.2d 155, 160 (4th Cir. 1991); Franklin v. Kaypro Corp., 884 F.2d 1222, 1229 (9th Cir. 1989); McDonald v. Union Carbide Corp., 734 F.2d 182, 184 (5th Cir. 1984) (per curiam).

468. *See* McDermott v. AmClyde, 114 S. Ct. 1461 (1994) (admiralty).

469. Local or state rules may include similar provisions, see Rule 16.2.5 of the Local Rules for the Central District of California, possibly harsher than Rule 68. *See* Yohannon v. Keene Corp., 924 F.2d 1255, 1263–69 (3d Cir. 1991) (upholding application of Rule 238 of the Pennsylvania Rules of Civil Procedure, which predicates penalty, *inter alia*, on failure to obtain judgment of more than 125% of offer). In deciding whether such state rules or statutes apply in diversity cases, the court should consider Burlington N. R.R. Co. v. Woods, 480 U.S. 1 (1987), in which the Court held inapplicable an Alabama statute imposing a mandatory penalty against appellants obtaining a stay pending an unsuccessful appeal, on the ground that it conflicted with Fed. R. App. P. 39.

470. *See* Marek v. Chesny, 473 U.S. 1, 7–12 (1985).

471. A federal court cannot enforce agreements settling claims lacking an independent basis for federal subject matter jurisdiction, unless the court embodies the settlement in the dismissal order at the request of the parties. Kokkonen v. Guardian Life Ins. Co., 114 S. Ct. 1673 (1994).

23.14 Review and Approval

Ordinarily, settlement does not require judicial review and approval.[472] There are a number of exceptions to this rule, however, many of particular relevance to complex litigation. The Federal Rules require court approval of settlements in class actions (including actions brought by or against an unincorporated association as a class),[473] shareholder derivative actions,[474] and actions in which a receiver has been appointed.[475] The antitrust laws require court approval of consent judgments proposed by the United States in actions it has instituted.[476] Common law may call for review and approval in a variety of contexts where the settlement requires court action, particularly if it affects the rights of nonparties or nonsettling parties,[477] or where the settlement is executed by a party acting in a representative capacity.[478]

Although the standards and procedures for review and approval of settlements vary, in general the court is required to scrutinize the proposed settlement to ensure that it is fair to the persons whose interests the court is to protect. Those affected may be entitled to notice[479] and an opportunity to be heard.[480] This usually involves a two-stage procedure. First, the court reviews the proposal preliminarily to determine whether it is sufficient to warrant public notice and a hearing. If so, the final decision on approval is made after the hearing.

The court must be given enough information to be able to fully and fairly consider the proposed settlement. All terms must be disclosed to enable the court to understand its effect on those not party to the settlement, and to prevent collusion and favoritism.[481] The court needs to be sensitive to the possibility that

---

472. *In re Masters,* 957 F.2d at 1025–26; *see* Fed. R. Civ. P. 41(a)(1)(ii) (voluntary dismissal by stipulation signed by all parties).

473. Fed. R. Civ. P. 23, 23.2. Settlement in class actions is discussed in *infra* §§ 30.212, 30.4.

474. Fed. R. Civ. P. 23.1.

475. Fed. R. Civ. P. 66.

476. 15 U.S.C.A. § 16(e) (West Supp. 1994) (review of proposed antitrust consent judgment to determine if in public interest).

477. *See, e.g., In re Masters,* 957 F.2d at 1025–26 (parties unwilling to settle unless court enforced terms); TBG Inc. v. Bendis, 811 F. Supp. 596, 600 (D. Kan. 1992) (settlement required bar order affecting rights of nonsettling parties).

478. *See, e.g.,* Gaxiola v. Schmidt, 508 F. Supp. 401 (E.D. Tenn. 1980) (action brought on behalf of minors). State law, when applicable in a diversity case, may require approval in similar contexts. *See, e.g.,* Owen v. United States, 713 F.2d 1461, 1464–68 (9th Cir. 1983) (applying California law requiring approval of certain settlements in cases involving joint tortfeasors); Soares v. McCloskey, 466 F. Supp. 703 (E.D. Pa. 1979) (applying Pennsylvania estate statute).

479. *See, e.g.,* Fed. R. Civ. P. 23.1.

480. *See, e.g.,* Michaud v. Michaud, 932 F.2d 77, 81 (1st Cir. 1991); Garabedian v. Allstates Eng'g Co., 811 F.2d 802 (3d Cir. 1987).

481. *See In re* Warner Comm. Sec. Litig., 798 F.2d 35, 37 (2d Cir. 1986).

attorneys or parties have conflicts of interest. The proponents should explain why the proposed settlement is preferable, for those not party to it, to continuation of the litigation, and should respond to objections they may raise. When settlement is proposed early in the litigation, before the court has become knowledgeable about the case, the court should ask for whatever additional information is necessary for its review.

The judge must guard against the temptation to become an advocate—either in favor of the settlement because of a desire to conclude the litigation, or against the settlement because of the responsibility to protect the rights of those not party to it. Neither the proponents of the settlement nor those who are opposed or absent should be favored. The court should be open to hearing the views of those who may be affected by the settlement, whether or not they have legal standing to be heard. Notice to absent parties may be advisable even if not required by governing law. In some cases, the court may appoint an expert under Fed. R. Evid. 706 to provide a neutral assessment,[482] or special counsel to represent the interests of persons who are absent or under a legal disability.

The trial court may not rewrite a settlement agreement; if it is unacceptable, the court must disapprove it.[483] The proponents may revise their agreement to overcome the court's objections and resubmit it; if the changes are substantial, it may be necessary to begin the notice and review process anew. An order approving a settlement should be supported by a statement of the court's reasoning, to create a record for appellate review.[484]

23.15 Alternative Processes to Encourage Settlement

A number of processes outside of the traditional litigation process have proved effective in helping parties reach settlement. These processes are generally described as forms of alternative dispute resolution (ADR), but this is a broad term, applying to a variety of processes that may be used for purposes ranging from

---

482. Some judges report that merely raising the possibly of such an appointment encourages the parties to settle or at least back down from extreme positions. Cecil & Willging, *supra* note 302, at 17.

483. *See* Evans v. Jeff D., 475 U.S. 717, 727 (1986); Jeff D. v. Andrus, 899 F.2d 753, 758 (9th Cir. 1989); *In re Warner*, 798 F.2d at 37. The court may, however, suggest changes. *See* Cotton v. Hinton, 559 F.2d 1326, 1331 (5th Cir. 1977) (discussing process of reviewing proposed settlement).

484. *See Cotton*, 559 F.2d at 1331. An order rejecting a proposed settlement or consent decree is generally not immediately appealable, but may be if the proposal includes injunctive relief. *See* Carson v. American Brands, Inc., 450 U.S. 79 (1981); 28 U.S.C. § 1292(a)(1).

case management to binding adjudication.[485] This section discusses some of the more commonly used processes that may facilitate settlement of complex litigation;[486] innovative judges may develop other methods appropriate for the litigation before them.

23.151 Mediation[487]

Mediation is an informal nonbinding process in which a neutral person[488] facilitates settlement negotiations among the parties. The mediator may be an outside attorney or retired judge selected by the judge or the parties, an expert in some relevant discipline, or another judge or magistrate judge.[489] Several national nonprofit organizations, including the CPR Institute for Dispute Resolution, Inc., and the American Arbitration Association, as well as several for-profit enterprises, maintain panels of experienced lawyers, law professors, and retired judges available to serve as mediators or other ADR neutrals in complex disputes. In addition, a number of district courts maintain court-based ADR programs that provide rosters of court-certified neutrals and guidelines for conducting the mediation process. Mediators should be experienced in federal litigation and should possess communication and negotiation skills; training in mediation skills is available, and it is desirable that a mediator selected for complex litigation has either been trained or has had relevant experience.

The mediator helps the parties communicate not only their positions but also their underlying interests and concerns. The mediation process is seen as interest-based as opposed to rights-based arbitration. By helping the parties understand each other's true interests and objectives, the mediator helps counsel and their clients devise mutually acceptable options for resolving their dispute. Mediators may also facilitate more traditional forms of settlement, by applying their experience to probe each side's position and suggest a fair valuation of the case. To en-

485. *See* Litigation Manual, *supra* note 5, at 62–65. See generally the Judge's Deskbook on Court ADR (1994) [hereinafter Deskbook], published jointly by CPR Institute for Dispute Resolution, Inc. ("CPR") and the Federal Judicial Center. For more information on alternative dispute resolution, contact CPR at 366 Madison Ave., New York, NY 10017, or the National Institute for Dispute Resolution, Suite 500, 1726 M Street, N.W., Washington, DC 20036.

486. Others include early neutral evaluation (ENE) and arbitration (see Deskbook, *supra* note 485) and the trial of selected bellwether cases to develop a pattern for evaluation.

487. *See generally* Deskbook, *supra* note 485, at 3–7.

488. Outside persons who preside over ADR proceedings are called "neutrals"; if they assist the parties in negotiations, they may be called "facilitators." *See* Deskbook, *supra* note 485, at 31.

489. Some courts maintain panels of mediators who usually work on a volunteer basis or may sometimes be compensated from public funds. In complex litigation, however, courts generally require the parties to pay the mediator's fees at rates approved by the court. Deskbook, *supra* note 485, at 5.

courage candor, the mediator may also meet with the parties separately; in any event, mediation sessions are confidential.[490]

The judge may direct the parties to participate in mediation, with or without their consent. Though mediation is generally ineffective if the parties are not motivated to participate in good faith, a court order makes it possible for them to participate without appearing to show weakness.

Opinions differ about the types of cases suitable for mediation; some believe it appropriate for simpler cases only, while others support its use in complex litigation. While in complex litigation, the judge must determine suitability on a case-by-case basis, the following factors generally indicate suitability:

- trial will be to the court and referral will avoid judicial involvement in settlement discussions;
- creative, nontraditional solutions are needed;
- the parties have an interest in maintaining an ongoing relationship;
- public policy or public interest considerations are minor;[491] and
- the dispute is caused or exacerbated by poor communication among the parties.[492]

Some judges initiate mediation after substantially all discovery has been completed (sometimes not until at or after the final pretrial conference), on the theory that the parties need the information acquired during discovery to discuss settlement intelligently. Others have had success initiating it earlier, before the parties' positions have hardened and substantial costs have been incurred; this may be particularly appropriate for cases that appear to require nontraditional resolution. If the parties need certain information or legal rulings before entering mediation, the judge can order targeted discovery and promptly resolve the necessary motions.

Mediation is relatively inexpensive, has had a high rate of success, and has met with substantial litigant satisfaction. If should not be used, however, simply to add a layer to the pretrial process, increasing cost and delay. Before making a referral to mediation, the court should take into account the suitability of the dispute, the parties' attitudes, the likelihood of settlement, and the availability of a suitable mediator. Once a matter is referred to mediation, the judge should not interfere with the process but may set a time limit.

---

490. If the court has rules for a local mediation program, they may affect the conduct of the mediation, for example, with respect to confidentiality; parties should become familiar with such rules (for a sample, see Deskbook, *supra* note 485, at 69–82) or ask the court to establish ground rules for the particular mediation.

491. For discussion of public policy issues, see Deskbook, *supra* note 485, at 59–60, 87.

492. This list is not intended to be exhaustive. *See id.* at 6.

23.152 Summary Jury Trial[493]

A summary jury trial (SJT) produces an advisory jury verdict in a trial-ready case for use by the parties as a basis for settlement negotiations (a variation, the summary *bench* trial, produces an advisory opinion from the presiding judicial officer). A jury is chosen from the court's regular pool, after abbreviated voir dire.[494] A judge or magistrate judge presides. Counsel are allotted a fixed time, generally one to a few hours, to make an abbreviated presentation of their case to the jury, including opening and closing statements as well as evidence. While most SJTs take one to two days, in complex multiparty cases they have been known to take up to two weeks. The type of evidence allowed must be determined by the court in light of the time constraints and is generally limited by the rules of evidence, though they may be relaxed. As with trial and other hearings, objections to admissibility should be made and resolved in advance. The court may also require advance submission of proposed questions for voir dire, jury instructions, and, where relatively extensive presentations are anticipated, lists of exhibits and witnesses. To keep the procedure streamlined, counsel usually summarize proposed witnesses' testimony rather than calling them. After brief instructions, the jurors deliberate for a short period of time and return a consensus verdict or, if unable to agree, individual verdicts. The jury may be asked to answer interrogatories as well, to provide the parties with more specific information. In some courts, the judge and counsel may question the jurors after they deliberate, to delve further into their evaluation of the case. Settlement discussions may be conducted before, during, and after the hearing phase; negotiations may commence as soon as the advisory verdict is returned, or there may be a "cooling-off" period of several days or weeks. If no settlement can be reached, the case is tried as originally scheduled, before different jurors.

SJTs can encourage settlement by (1) suggesting the probable outcome of a trial; (2) giving clients their "day in court" (albeit abbreviated); (3) exposing clients to the opposing side's evidence; (4) highlighting the expense and uncertainty of a jury trial, and, perhaps most importantly; (5) placing a specific (and credible) dollar amount on the table. Client participation is necessary to accomplish many of these ends; executives or other principals authorized to settle therefore must attend the SJT.

Since they require a trial-ready case, SJTs are generally held after discovery. Unlike mediation, SJTs consume significant resources and should therefore be limited to litigation in which:

- the trial will be lengthy and the potential savings substantial;

---

493. *See generally id.* at 19–23.

494. The Deskbook, *supra* note 485, at 20, suggests a six-person jury without alternates. The court may or may not tell the jurors of their advisory role before the proceeding.

- there is wide disagreement between the parties as to how a jury will evaluate their case;
- one or more parties hold an unrealistic view of the merits; and
- one or both parties are unwilling to settle without their "day in court."[495]

Two circuits have held that parties may not be required to participate in an SJT, at least where no local rule authorizes mandatory SJTs.[496] Because of the time and expense involved, and because the process is less likely to be productive with unwilling parties, it is not advisable to hold an SJT without the parties' consent. One circuit has held that the court may close an SJT to the press and public, reasoning that it is more like a settlement conference than a trial, and that publicity might interfere with settlement.[497]

23.153 Minitrial

A minitrial, like an SJT, involves summary presentations of each side's case followed by settlement negotiations. Unlike an SJT, however, the parties present their cases directly to a panel of authorized client representatives, usually senior executives. Though a judicial officer or outside neutral presides, the objective is not to produce an advisory opinion but to launch meaningful settlement negotiations. The parties may, however, ask the presiding neutral to deliver an opinion or act as facilitator in subsequent negotiations. Witnesses are usually not called and the rules of evidence are relaxed; objections may be entirely prohibited.[498] The minitrial itself should take only one or two days, though settlement discussions may take longer. Usually, minitrials are arranged and conducted privately, sometimes even before litigation has commenced, but some federal judges have taken an active role in arranging or officiating at "court minitrials."[499] In either case, the process is flexible enough to allow numerous variations in form (nomenclature varies as well; one judge calls minitrials "conditional summary trials," while the Western District of Michigan uses the term "mini-hearings").

---

495. *See id.* at 21.

496. *See In re* NLO, Inc., 5 F.3d 154 (6th Cir. 1993); Strandell v. Johnson County, 838 F.2d 884 (7th Cir. 1988). *See also* McCay v. Ashland Oil Co., 120 F.R.D. 43 (E.D. Ky. 1988) (court rule provided for mandatory SJTs). Several district courts have held otherwise. *See* Federal Reserve Bank of Minneapolis v. Carey-Canada, Inc., 123 F.R.D. 603, 604–07 (D. Minn. 1988); Arabian American Oil Co. v. Scarfone, 119 F.R.D. 448 (M.D. Fla. 1988); Home Owners Funding Corp. v. Century Bank, 695 F. Supp. 1343, 1347 n.3 (D. Mass 1988). *See also* Charles R. Richey, *Rule 16: A Survey and Some Considerations for the Bench and Bar*, 126 F.R.D. 599, 608 (April 3, 1989) (disagreeing with *Strandell* and supporting mandatory SJT).

497. *See* Cincinnati Gas and Elec. Co. v. General Elec. Co., 854 F.2d 900 (6th Cir. 1988); *but see* Richey, *supra* note 496, at 609 (expressing doubt that *Cincinnati* would stand the test of time).

498. *See* Provine, *supra* note 461, at 79.

499. *Id.* at 76–77. *See* Deskbook, *supra* note 485, at 25.

Participation should normally be voluntary, though mandatory minitrials may be authorized by local rule.[500]

Because of the time and effort they require, court minitrials are generally reserved for complex cases in which a lengthy trial is expected. They have been utilized in cases involving products liability, government and private contracts, regulatory agencies, labor disputes, and complex antitrust cases.[501] In general, however, they are most suitable for large commercial litigation that may become a "battle of experts" at trial.[502] They offer clients a quick, relatively inexpensive look at the strength of each side's case and a means to enter settlement negotiations without appearing to show weakness.[503]

23.2 Special Problems

23.21 Partial Settlements

In litigation involving numerous claims and parties, it is not uncommon for litigants to seek settlement limited to particular claims, defenses, or issues, or with less than all of the parties. Such partial settlements may provide funds needed to pursue the litigation, limit the extent of exposure, reduce the scope of discovery or trial, aid the parties in obtaining evidence, and facilitate later settlements on other issues and with other parties. On the other hand, partial settlements can, because of their timing or terms, interfere with the ultimate resolution of the litigation. A partial settlement on terms that prove too generous, for example, may create resistance to later, more reasonable settlement offers. To avoid such problems, settling parties may adopt a general formula for all settlements; if adhered to, this may discourage adverse parties from prolonging litigation to get better terms.

Late partial settlements in multiparty cases present a number of potential problems.[504] Attorneys with assigned responsibilities at trial may drop out when

---

500. *See* Rule 44 of the Local Rules for the Western District of Michigan.

501. *See* Provine, *supra* note 461, at 78–79. For examples, see the following issues of *Alternatives to the High Cost of Litigation*, a CPR publication: July 1993 ($17 million settlement of environmental litigation); June 1993 ($150 million, environmental); Sept. 1992 ($130 million, utilities); July 1992, at 98 (complex contract); May 1992, at 71 ($30 million, antitrust).

502. *See* Provine, *supra* note 461, at 79.

503. *See id.*

504. Partial settlements in class actions are discussed in *infra* § 30.46.

their client's case has been settled, requiring reorganization of counsel and disrupting trial planning. While it is a common and legitimate litigation strategy to settle with one adverse party to weaken another's position, when done on the eve of trial it may seriously disrupt the progress of the case. While both the power to shift costs for such conduct and the desirability of doing so are unclear, the judge can discourage belated and potentially disruptive settlements; if necessary to reduce the prejudice to nonsettling parties, the judge can grant a continuance. Moreover, lead counsel, members of a trial team, and other attorneys who have accepted responsibilities on behalf of other parties and attorneys should bear in mind that their fiduciary obligations may survive the dismissal of their own clients.

Partial settlements can affect the issues and parties not covered. A partial settlement may (by law) release certain nonsettling parties or entitle them to a setoff for amounts received in settlement from coparties; in some areas of law, this may depend on the settling parties' intention.[505] The agreement must therefore indicate clearly the parties and claims it is intended to cover, making plain the relationship between the damage items covered and those that may later be awarded by judgment. The court needs to consider whether and in what manner payments made under the settlement agreement will be treated as offsets against future awards,[506] and how the settlement will be treated at trial.

The parties may attempt to apportion the settlement among different claims, sometimes for tax purposes[507] and sometimes to enhance their position against nonsettling parties. When partial settlements are submitted for judicial approval, apportionment clauses need to be examined for their effect on further proceedings and other parties. The court should not approve an agreement that does not permit appropriate modification of such clauses if justified by later developments.

Evidence of the settlement of a claim is inadmissible at trial "to prove liability for or invalidity of the claim or its amount," though not for other purposes.[508] There is disagreement over whether this rule prohibits the introduction of evidence of a partial settlement for the purpose of allowing the jury, in determining damages, to consider the amount already recovered from other sources.[509] As an

---

505. *See* Zenith Radio Corp. v. Hazeltine Research, 401 U.S. 321, 343–47 (1971) (discussing subject generally and adopting intention of parties rule for release of antitrust coconspirators).

506. *See* McDermott, Inc. v. AmClyde, 114 S. Ct. 1461 (1994) (admiralty).

507. Several U.S. Tax Court decisions hold that agreements apportioning liability solely to create a tax deduction should not be approved. *See* Federal Paper Board Co., Inc. v. Commissioner, 90 T.C. 1011, n.33 (1988); Metzger v. Commissioner, 88 T.C. 834, 849–50 (1987); Fisher Cos., Inc. v. Comm'r, 84 T.C. 1319, 1340 (1985).

508. Fed. R. Evid. 408.

509. Though federal law disfavors admission, in diversity cases the court may be obliged to apply state law to the contrary. *See, e.g.,* United States v. Johnson, 893 F.2d 448 (1st Cir. 1990); *see also*

alternative, the court may make an appropriate reduction in any judgment recovered against nonsettling parties.[510] The court may, however, inform the jury of the fact (not the amount) of settlement where necessary to explain a party's absence.[511]

23.22 Agreements Affecting Discovery

One of the major incentives to settle is to avoid the cost and burden of further discovery. Settlement agreements may therefore contain provisions purporting to relieve a settling party from further discovery, at least in part. Such agreements may be problematic if other parties need discovery from a settling party, particularly in light of the limits on nonparty discovery. They should therefore be drafted so as to take other parties' continuing need for discovery into account.[512]

A settlement agreement may also purport to require a party not to disclose its terms, or to return, destroy, or keep confidential discovery materials previously obtained.[513] The effect, if not the purpose, of such an agreement may be to forestall or frustrate other litigation, pending or anticipated. For this and other public policy reasons, including the protection of First Amendment interests, and under state law, such agreements may be invalid, unenforceable, or simply not entitled to approval. Where such an agreement may be appropriate (e.g., to protect trade secrets), the court should consider requiring that the materials be preserved for a reasonable period of time. The relevant analysis is similar to that employed when considering issuance of a protective order (see *supra* section 21.43).

23.23 Side Agreements

Agreements allocating financial responsibility among persons or entities are common; contracts of insurance and indemnification are prime examples. Occasionally, however, litigants enter into side agreements apportioning damages that supplement their formal settlement agreements but are not intended to be disclosed to others. These agreements may not of themselves be unlawful or un-

---

McHann v. Firestone Tire & Rubber Co., 713 F.2d 161, 166 n.10 (5th Cir. 1983). If such evidence is received, the court should give appropriate limiting instructions.

510. *See, e.g.,* Jackson v. Johns-Manville Sales Corp., 727 F.2d 506, 531–32 (5th Cir. 1984), *modified on other grounds,* 757 F.2d 614 (1985) (en banc); *McHann,* 713 F.2d at 166.

511. *Jackson,* 727 F.2d at 531.

512. Though nonsettling defendants usually lack standing to appeal orders approving partial settlements, they may appeal if they suffer formal legal prejudice. *See, e.g.,* Zupnik v. Fogel, 989 F.2d 93 (2d Cir. 1993); Mayfield v. Barr, 985 F.2d 1090, 1092–93 (D.C. Cir. 1993); Agretti v. ANR Freight Sys. Inc., 982 F.2d 242, 247 (7th Cir. 1992) (defining "formal legal prejudice"); Alumax Mill Prods., Inc. v. Congress Financial Corp., 912 F.2d 996, 1002 (8th Cir. 1990) and cases cited therein.

513. So-called "sunshine" legislation, adopted in several states and pending in Congress, may make such agreements unenforceable. See *supra* § 21.43.

ethical, and on occasion there may be legitimate reasons for not disclosing them to other parties. In presenting settlement agreements for judicial approval, however, the parties are obliged to make full disclosure to the court of all terms and understandings, including any side agreements. The settling parties may request that certain terms not be disclosed to other parties, but must justify this to the court.[514]

Common types of side agreements include the following:

- **"Mary Carter" agreements.** In return for a settlement payment, the plaintiff may agree to release a particular defendant from liability though the defendant remains party to the suit, with the further provision that the defendant will be reimbursed in some specified manner out of any recovery against other defendants.[515] Many varieties of such agreements have developed, including loan-receipt agreements and agreements to dismiss during the case or not to execute on a judgment if the defendant does not take an aggressive posture against the plaintiff's claims.[516] This type of agreement, which derives its name from *Booth v. Mary Carter Paint Co.*,[517] has been criticized as unfair to nonsettling defendants,[518] since it has the effect of aligning the interests of the "settling" defendant, who remains in the litigation, with those of the plaintiff (usually covertly), eliminating their normal adversarial relationship.[519] Nevertheless, courts have rarely rejected a settlement on this basis,[520] though it has been suggested that they should give such agreements particular scrutiny.[521]

  The primary problem raised by "Mary Carter" agreements is disclosure. Typically, parties entering into such an agreement do so secretly, or they request that the court not disclose the terms of the agreement. Nondisclosure, however, magnifies the prejudice to other parties, since neither the jury nor the defense can take the agreement into account when considering the testimony of the settling defendant; it may there-

---

514. *See, e.g., In re* Braniff, Inc., 1992 WL 261641, at *5 (Bankr. M.D. Fla. 1992) (parties must disclose to court and, unless good cause shown, other parties all agreements settling or limiting liability, whether "formal or informal, absolute or conditional").

515. *See* Marathon Oil Co. v. Mid-Continent Underwriters, 786 F.2d 1301, 1303 n.1 (5th Cir. 1986); Wilkins v. P.M.R. Sys. Eng'g, Inc., 741 F.2d 795, 798 n.2 (5th Cir. 1984); Quad/Graphics, Inc. v. Fass, 724 F.2d 1230, 1236 (7th Cir. 1983). For other definitions, see materials cited in Hoops v. Watermelon City Trucking, Inc., 846 F.2d 637, 640 n.3 (10th Cir. 1988).

516. *See* Annot., 65 A.L.R. 3d 602 (1975).

517. 202 So.2d 8 (Fla. Dist. Ct. App. 1967).

518. *See, e.g.,* Bass v. Phoenix Seadrill/78, Ltd., 562 F. Supp. 790, 796 (E.D. Tex. 1983).

519. *See Hoops*, 846 F.2d at 640.

520. *Bass*, 562 F. Supp. at 796.

521. *See Wilkins*, 741 F.2d at 798 n.2.

fore be ground for a new trial.[522] For this reason, case law favors requiring disclosure of such agreements to the court, parties, and jury.[523] The court should, at the outset of the litigation, impose a continuing duty on counsel to promptly disclose all such agreements without need for a motion or discovery request.

- **Sharing agreements.** Defendants sometimes agree in advance to allocate responsibility for damages among themselves according to an agreed formula (often based on market share). These agreements serve the legitimate purposes of controlling parties' exposure and preventing plaintiffs from forcing an unfair settlement by threats to show favoritism in the collection of any judgment that may be recovered. They may, however, expressly prohibit or indirectly discourage individual settlements. They also create a disincentive for defendants to make available evidence indicating liability on the part of codefendants. Therefore, while they are generally appropriate, the court may refuse to approve or enforce such agreements where they would violate public policy or prejudice other parties in these or other ways.[524]

  Sharing agreements should be discoverable. Once the agreement is made known, it may be possible to structure partial settlements to take its terms into account. It is less clear when and whether they should be admissible in evidence. Since Fed. R. Evid. 408 does not require exclusion of settlement agreements when offered for purposes such as proving bias, they may be admitted to attack a witness's credibility or demonstrate that formally opposing parties are not in fact adverse, accompanied by a limiting instruction that the agreement is not to be considered as proof or disproof of liability or damages.[525] The court should not allow them to be admitted, however, when they are of little relevance and may be prejudicial[526] (e.g., by suggesting a conspiracy to the jury).

- **"Most-favored nation" clauses.** Settlement agreements proposed early in the litigation often contain a "most-favored nation" clause, intended to encourage early settlement by protecting parties against being prejudiced by later, more favorable settlements with others. Such a clause typically

---

522. *See, e.g.,* Leger v. Drilling Well Control, Inc., 69 F.R.D. 358, 361 (W.D. La. 1976), *aff'd*, 592 F.2d 1246 (5th Cir. 1979); *cf.* Reichenbach v. Smith, 528 F.2d 1072 (5th Cir. 1976) (error found harmless).

523. *See, e.g., Hoops*, 846 F.2d at 640; *Reichenbach*, 528 F.2d at 1076 (dictum).

524. *See In re* San Juan Dupont Plaza Hotel Fire Litig., 1993 U.S. Dist. LEXIS 14191 (Sept. 14, 1993).

525. *See* Brocklesby v. United States, 767 F.2d 1288, 1292–93 (9th Cir. 1985).

526. *See* Fed. R. Evid. 403.

obligates a signatory plaintiff to give signatory defendants a proportionate refund if the former settles with other defendants for less, or a signatory defendant to make additional payments to signatory plaintiffs if the former settles with other plaintiffs for more.

Such clauses have several drawbacks: (1) the potential liability under them is indeterminate, making them risky; (2) the additional recovery they may produce for some plaintiffs without any effort by their attorneys makes fees difficult to fix; and (3) the factors that induce parties to settle with different parties for different amounts, such as the time of settlement and the relative strength of claims, are nullified. Such clauses can provide an incentive for early settlement as well as an obstacle to later settlements. To limit their prejudicial impact, such clauses should terminate after a specified length of time (to prevent one or more holdouts from delaying final implementation), impose ceilings on payments, and allow flexibility to deal with changed circumstances or with parties financially unable to contribute proportionately.[527] The court may have to consider voiding or limiting them if enforcement becomes inequitable.[528]

- **Tolling agreements.** Parties may enter into agreements under which one side promises not to assert a statute of limitations defense in return for some consideration. These should generally be disclosed to the court and other parties to avoid disruption of the case-management plan and frustration of the goals of court-imposed deadlines.

23.24 Ethical Considerations

Settlement discussions and agreements can raise a number of ethical issues even if not kept secret:

- **Communications with represented parties.** Attorneys may not communicate directly with a party represented by counsel (absent that counsel's presence or consent).[529] This rule prohibits attorneys from directly ne-

---

527. *See In re* Corrugated Container Antitrust Litig., 752 F.2d 137, 139 n.3 (5th Cir. 1985); Fisher Bros. v. Phelps Dodge, Indus., Inc., 614 F. Supp. 377, 381–82 (E.D. Pa. 1985), *aff'd mem.* 791 F.2d 917 (3d Cir. 1986).

528. If this determination involves disputed questions of fact, the court may have to hold an evidentiary hearing, possibly allowing additional discovery. *See In re Corrugated Container*, 752 F.2d at 142–43 (5th Cir. 1985); *Fisher Bros.*, 614 F. Supp. at 381 & n.8.

529. Model Rules of Professional Conduct 4.2; Model Code of Professional Responsibility DR 7-104. For the purposes of this rule, class members are considered parties represented by class counsel. For further discussion and citations, see *infra* § 30.24.

gotiating settlement with adverse parties.[530] The parties themselves are free to engage in direct settlement discussions without their attorneys.[531]

- **Agreements foreclosing other representation.** Defendants have attempted to condition settlement on an agreement that plaintiff's counsel will not represent other persons with similar claims, but it is an ethical violation for an attorney to enter into or propose such an agreement.[532] A variation, also ethically dubious, is so-called "futures deals," in which the settling attorney agrees to process similar claims of future clients according to the settlement terms, or to advise clients to accept those terms.

- **Negotiations regarding attorneys' fees.** In routine nonclass litigation, in which each party is responsible for its own attorneys' fees, settling defendants customarily pay a negotiated sum, leaving counsel and their clients to settle their fees. Problems may arise, however, in cases where the court must approve settlements containing provisions for attorneys' fees, as in class actions (see *infra* section 30.24) or in cases, such as civil rights actions, in which the losing side is liable for the adversary's attorneys' fees.

One issue is whether settlement negotiations involving attorneys' fees may or should be conducted simultaneously with negotiations on the merits. When a defendant offers to settle for a lump sum covering both damages and fees, negotiating the allocation may create a conflict of interest for the plaintiff's attorney.[533] The problem is acute when the plaintiffs are represented by legal aid or another nonprofit group that has agreed with the clients to seek fees only from the opposing parties.[534] The Supreme Court, while recognizing that "such situations may raise difficult ethical issues for a plaintiff's attorney," has declined to prohibit this practice, reasoning that "a defendant may have good reason to demand to know his total liability."[535] Indeed, the Court has stated that settlement of civil rights cases would be impeded by rules prohibiting si-

---

530. *See, e.g.,* Walker v. Kotzen, 567 F. Supp. 424, 426–27 (E.D. Pa. 1983), *appeal dismissed,* 734 F.2d 9 (3d Cir. 1984). For settlement and related communications in class actions, see *infra* §§ 30.2, 30.4.

531. It may be an ethical violation, however, for an attorney to use their client or a third party to violate the prohibition on direct communication with represented parties. Model Rules of Professional Conduct 8.4(a) & comment (professional misconduct for lawyer to attempt to violate rule through another person).

532. Model Rules of Professional Conduct 5.6(b) & comment; Model Code of Professional Responsibility DR 2-108(b); ABA Comm. on Ethics, Informal Op. 1039 (1968).

533. *See* White v. New Hampshire Dept. of Employment, 455 U.S. 445, 453 n.15 (1982).

534. *See* Evans v. Jeff D., 475 U.S. 717, 721 (1986).

535. *White,* 455 U.S. at 453 n.15; *see Evans* at 732–34; Marek v. Chesny, 473 U.S. 1, 6–7 (1985).

multaneous negotiations of fees.[536] While proposed settlements arising out of such negotiations should therefore not be rejected out of hand, the court should review the fairness of the allocation between damages and attorneys' fees.[537] The ethical problem will be eased if the parties agree to have the court make the allocation.

A further problem may be presented if a defendant conditions a settlement favorable to plaintiffs on an agreement to waive attorneys' fees, particularly if the relief sought is primarily or entirely nonmonetary. Plaintiffs' attorney, having an ethical obligation to obtain the most favorable relief for the client without regard to the attorney's interest in a fee, may thereby be coerced into giving up all fees.[538] This in turn may discourage other attorneys from representing civil rights claimants.[539] Some bar associations have ruled it unethical for defendants to request fee waivers in exchange for relief on the merits.[540] The Court, however, has approved the practice, reasoning that a prohibition on fee waivers would discourage settlement, since, because of the "potentially large and typically uncertain magnitude" of fee awards, defendants are unlikely to settle until the issue of fees has been resolved.[541] The court is therefore free to approve such settlements,[542] though counsel may be prohibited by state rules from proposing them.[543]

- **Failure to submit offers to client.** Attorneys have an obligation to promptly submit nonfrivolous offers of settlement to the client, unless prior discussions have made clear that the proposal will be unacceptable.[544] Breach of this duty is egregious if counsel will be compensated in whole or in part on the basis of the number of hours expended in the litigation, as in the case of defense counsel or when fees are awarded or approved by the court on a lodestar basis.

---

536. *Evans,* 475 U.S. at 736–37 & nn.28–29 (1986).

537. *See id.* at 754, 765 (Brennan, J., dissenting); *but see id.* at 738 n.30.

538. *See id.* at 727–30 & nn.14, 16.

539. *Id.* at 754–59 (Brennan, J., dissenting).

540. *Id.* at 728 n.15.

541. *See id.* at 732–38.

542. The court is not required to do so; in dictum, the Supreme Court suggested that disapproval might be appropriate if the defendant had no realistic defense on the merits or if the waiver was a "vindictive" act designed to discourage counsel from bringing such cases. *Id.* at 739–40 & n.32.

543. *See id.* at 765 (Brennan, J., dissenting).

544. *See* Model Rules of Professional Conduct 1.2(a), 1.4 & comments; ABA Comm. on Ethics, Formal Op. 326 (1970); Deadwyler v. Volkswagen of Am., 134 F.R.D. 128, 140 (W.D.N.C. 1991), *aff'd,* 966 F.2d 1443 (4th Cir. 1992).

24. Attorneys' Fees[545]

Under the American Rule, parties generally bear their own costs of litigation.[546] The amount of attorneys' fees is therefore ordinarily determined by agreement between attorney and client. Much complex litigation, however, arises under statutes or common law rules that require the court to determine the amount of fees, as well as expenses, to be paid to attorneys. The rules that govern the award of attorneys' fees and expenses are not always clear and settled, and involve a large measure of discretion.[547] Moreover, because of the sums involved, the calculation of awards is often complex, burdensome, and bitterly contested, sometimes leading to satellite litigation. Efficient and fair management of the process of

---

545. The subject is treated at length in Alan Hirsch & Diane Sheehey, Awarding Attorneys' Fees and Managing Fee Litigation (Federal Judicial Center 1994). See also *supra* § 23.24 (negotiation of fees and settlement) and *infra* § 30.42 (fees in class actions).

546. *See, e.g.*, Alyeska Pipeline Serv. Co. v. Wilderness Soc'y, 421 U.S. 240 (1975).

547. *See generally* 7A Charles A. Wright & Arthur R. Miller, Federal Practice & Procedure § 1803 (2d ed. 1986 & Supp. 1993).

awarding fees and expenses is therefore essential to the just, speedy, and inexpensive determination of litigation.[548]

24.1 Eligibility for Court-Awarded Fees

24.11 Types of Cases—Overview

The initial determination, to be made early in the case, is whether the prevailing party may be entitled to court-awarded fees. The nature of the award will depend on the type of case and recovery and the governing rules in the jurisdiction. Appropriate management measures should be instituted early, depending on the nature of a party's prospective entitlement, to avoid unnecessary controversy and litigation at later stages.

The following are the principal types of cases and situations in which courts may award attorneys' fees:

- **Common fund cases.** If attorneys' efforts preserve or create a fund or benefit for others in addition to their own clients, the court is empowered to award fees from the fund.[549] The award may be made from recoveries obtained by settlement or by trial. Common fund cases are predominantly, though not exclusively, class actions, but some class actions may also be brought under fee-shifting statutes.[550]

  A variant on the traditional common fund case occurs frequently in mass tort litigation—both class actions and large consolidations—where a fund to pay attorneys' fees is created as a part of a settlement and the court must distribute it among the various plaintiffs' attorneys, including class counsel, court-designated lead and liaison counsel, and individual plaintiffs' counsel.[551]

- **Statutory fees cases.** Over 150 statutes, covering actions ranging from antitrust and civil rights to little known types of claims, authorize courts

---

548. *See* Hensley v. Eckerhart, 461 U.S. 424, 437 (1988).

549. *See, e.g.,* Boeing Co. v. Van Gemert, 444 U.S. 472 (1980); Mills v. Elec. Auto-Lite Co., 396 U.S. 375 (1970); Sprague v. Ticonic Nat. Bank, 307 U.S. 161 (1939); Central R.R. & Banking Co. v. Pettus, 113 U.S. 116 (1885); Trustees of the Internal Improvement Fund v. Greenough, 105 U.S. (15 Otto) 527 (1882).

550. See generally *infra* § 30 (class actions).

551. *See In re* Nineteen Appeals, 982 F.2d 603 (1st Cir. 1992).

to depart from the American Rule and award attorneys' fees to a prevailing party.[552] Whether the award is mandatory or permissive depends on the terms of the particular statute and applicable case law, and may depend on whether the prevailing party is the plaintiff or the defendant.[553]

- **Designated counsel.** The court may award fees to lead counsel, liaison counsel, and other attorneys designated to perform tasks on behalf of a group of litigants (see *supra* section 20.22).[554]

- **Special parties.** Under the common law and many state statutes, court approval is required for the payment of fees charged by counsel for minors, incompetents, and trusts.

- **Sanctions.** The court has inherent power to award fees against a litigant who conducts litigation in bad faith or vexatiously.[555] A statutory counterpart, 28 U.S.C. § 1927, provides for awards against an offending attorney. Various provisions of the Federal Rules of Civil Procedure authorize the award of fees against parties who have failed to comply with rules or orders with respect to discovery and other pretrial proceedings. For a detailed discussion of sanctions, see *supra* section 20.15.

24.12 Common Fund Cases

24.121 Percentage Fee Awards

The common fund exception to the American Rule is grounded in the equitable powers of the courts under the doctrines of *quantum meruit* and unjust enrichment.[556] It applies where a common fund has been created by the efforts of plaintiffs' attorney[557] and rests on the principle that "persons who obtain the

---

552. *See* Ruckelshaus v. Sierra Club, 463 U.S. 680, 684 (1983).

553. Hensley v. Eckerhart, 461 U.S. 424, 429 n.2 (1983) ("A prevailing defendant may recover an attorney's fee only where the suit was vexatious, frivolous, or brought to harass or embarrass the defendant."). *See also* Christiansburg Garment Co. v. EEOC, 434 U.S. 412 (1978); *but cf.* Fogerty v. Fantasy, Inc., 114 S. Ct. 1023 (1994).

554. *In re* Air Crash Disaster at Florida Everglades, 549 F.2d 1006 (5th Cir. 1977) (relying on "common fund" principles and inherent management powers of court in complex litigation).

555. *See* Alyeska Pipeline Serv. Co. v. Wilderness Soc'y, 421 U.S. 240, 258–59 (1975); Ellingson v. Burlington N., Inc., 653 F.2d 1327 (9th Cir. 1981).

556. Trustees of the Internal Improvement Fund v. Greenough, 105 U.S. (15 Otto) 527, 536 (1882).

557. *Compare* Blum v. Stenson, 465 U.S. 886, 900 n.16 (1984); Camden I Condominium Assoc., Inc. v. Dunkle, 946 F.2d 768 (11th Cir. 1991); *and* Court Awarded Attorneys Fees, Report of the

benefit of a lawsuit without contributing to its cost are unjustly enriched at the successful litigant's expense."[558] Historically, attorneys' fees were awarded from a common fund based on a percentage of that fund.[559] At the present time, however, the court must first determine whether the jurisdiction requires use of the lodestar method or whether it requires,[560] permits,[561] or has yet to rule upon[562] the propriety of a percentage fee award.

Prior to 1973, determination of the magnitude of a fee award in both common fund and statutory fee cases was left to the sound discretion of the trial court, with the general standard being reasonableness under the circumstances.[563] In *Lindy Bros. Builders, Inc. v. American Radiator & Standard Sanitary Corp.* ("*Lindy I*"),[564] the Court of Appeals for the Third Circuit vacated a percentage fee award in a common fund case and created what has become known as the *Lindy* lodestar method for calculating fee awards. The Third Circuit gave additional

Third Circuit Task Force, *reprinted in* 108 F.R.D. 237 (1985) [hereinafter Task Force Report] *with* Lindy Bros. Builders, Inc. of Phila. v. American Radiator & Standard Sanitary Corp., 487 F.2d 161 (3d Cir. 1973), *appeal following remand*, 540 F.2d 102 (3d Cir. 1976).

558. Boeing Co. v. Van Gemert, 444 U.S. 472, 478 (1980). *See also* Mills v. Electric Auto-Lite Co., 396 U.S. 375, 392 (1970).

559. *See, e.g.*, Central R.R. & Banking Co. v. Pettus, 113 U.S. 116 (1885); Sprague v. Ticonic Nat. Bank, 307 U.S. 161 (1939). The rationale differs significantly from that on which statutory fee awards rest. *See* Brown v. Phillips Petroleum Co., 838 F.2d 451, 454 (10th Cir. 1988) ("[S]tatutory fees are intended to further a legislative purpose by punishing the nonprevailing party and encouraging private parties to enforce substantive statutory rights."). *See also In re* SmithKline Beckman Corp. Sec. Litig., 751 F. Supp. 525, 532 (E.D. Pa. 1990).

560. *See* Swedish Hosp. Corp. v. Shalala, 1 F.3d 161, 1271 (D.C. Cir. 1993); *Camden I*, 946 F.2d at 774 ("Henceforth in this circuit, attorneys' fees awarded from a common fund shall be based upon a reasonable percentage of the fund established for the benefit of the class."). *See also* the Civil Justice Expense and Delay Reduction Plan for the United States District Court for the Eastern District of New York at V(A)(1) and (2) (requiring an award of attorneys' fees in common fund cases to be based on a percentage of the fund).

561. *See, e.g., In re* Continental Ill. Sec. Litig., 962 F.2d 566, 572 (7th Cir. 1992) (fee award simulating "what the market in fact pays not for the individual hours but for the ensemble of services rendered in a case of this character" would be appropriate); Harmon v. Lymphomed, 945 F.2d 969, 975 (7th Cir. 1991); Weinberger v. Great Nekoosa Corp., 925 F.2d 518, 526 n.10 (1st Cir. 1991); Six (6) Mexican Workers v. Arizona Citrus Growers, 904 F.2d 1301, 1311 (9th Cir. 1990) (allowing use of either percentage or lodestar calculation method in common fund case); Paul, Johnson, Alston & Hunt v. Graulty, 886 F.2d 268 (9th Cir. 1989) (same); *Brown*, 838 F.2d at 454 (award of attorney's fees in common fund case on percentage basis not abuse of discretion).

562. *Compare* Cosgrove v. Sullivan, 759 F. Supp. 166, 168 (S.D.N.Y. 1991) ("While we are sympathetic to the defects in the lodestar approach, we do not have the authority to abandon it completely even in what is realistically a common fund case.") *with* Chatelain v. Prudential-Bache Sec., Inc., 805 F. Supp. 209, 215 (S.D.N.Y. 1992) ("This court declines to apply the lodestar method, and instead favors the use of the straight percentage of recovery method.").

563. Task Force Report, *supra* note 557, 108 F.R.D. at 242.

564. 487 F.2d 161 (3d Cir. 1973).

guidance for implementing the *Lindy* lodestar method on appeal after remand ("*Lindy II*").[565] Thereafter, courts throughout the country abandoned the percentage fee award in both statutory and common fund cases in favor of the lodestar method.[566]

In practice, the lodestar method proved difficult to apply, time-consuming to administer, inconsistent in result, and capable of manipulation to reach a predetermined result. Accordingly, it has been criticized by courts, commentators, and members of the bar.[567] Despite application by courts nationwide, the Supreme Court never formally adopted the lodestar method in a common fund case. In recent years, the trend has been toward the percentage of the fund method.[568]

Courts applying the percentage method have generally awarded attorneys' fees in a range from 25% to 30% of the fund.[569] Several courts have concluded that 25% should be a "benchmark" for such awards, subject to upward or downward adjustment depending on the circumstances of the case.[570] Where the fund is unusually large, however, the application of a benchmark percentage may result in a windfall to counsel.[571] Some courts have therefore used a sliding scale, with the percentage decreasing as the magnitude of the fund increased,[572] or have used the lodestar method.[573]

---

565. 540 F.2d 102 (3d Cir. 1976). Similarly, the Fifth Circuit, in a statutory fee-shifting case, adopted what is commonly referred to as the twelve-factor *Johnson* test to be utilized in determining fee awards. *See* Johnson v. Georgia Highway Express, Inc., 488 F.2d 714 (5th Cir. 1974). "[M]ost commentators consider *Johnson* to be little different from *Lindy* because the first criterion of the *Johnson* test, and indeed the one most heavily weighted, is the time and labor required. Similarly, many of the *Johnson* factors are subsumed within the initial calculation of hours reasonably expended at a customary hourly rate." Task Force Report, *supra* note 557, 108 F.R.D. at 244.

566. *See, e.g.,* Detroit v. Grinnell Corp., 495 F.2d 448 (2d Cir. 1974) (adopting *Lindy* method); Grunin v. International House of Pancakes, 513 F.2d 114 (8th Cir. 1975) (same); Kerr v. Screen Extras Guild, Inc., 526 F.2d 67 (9th Cir. 1975) (adopting *Johnson* test).

567. *See* Task Force Report, *supra* note 557, 108 F.R.D. at 246–53.

568. *See, e.g., Camden I,* 946 F.2d at 775; *Brown,* 838 F.2d at 454; *Paul, Johnson,* 886 F.2d at 272; Bebchick v. Washington Metro. Area Transit, 805 F.2d 396, 407 (D.C. Cir. 1986).

569. *See, e.g., In re* Businessland Sec. Litig., [Current Transfer Binder] Fed. Sec. L. Rep. (CCH) ¶ 96,059 (N.D. Cal. 1991) (30%); Antonopulos v. North Am. Thoroughbreds, Inc., [Current Transfer Binder] Fed. Sec. L. Rep. (CCH) ¶ 96,058 (S.D. Cal. 1991) (33%); *In re* SmithKline Beckman Corp. Sec. Litig., 751 F. Supp. 525 (E.D. Pa. 1990) (25%); *In re* Union Carbide Corp. Consumer Prods. Bus. Litig., 724 F. Supp. 160 (S.D.N.Y. 1989) (30%); *In re* GNC Shareholder Litig., 668 F. Supp. 450, 452 (W.D. Pa. 1987) (25%).

570. *See, e.g., Paul, Johnson,* 886 F.2d at 272; Mashburn v. National Healthcare, Inc., 684 F. Supp. 679, 692 (M.D. Ala. 1988).

571. *See In re* Washington Pub. Power Supply Sys. Sec. Litig., No. 91-16669 (9th Cir. March 23, 1994).

572. *See* Task Force Report, *supra* note 557, 108 F.R.D. at 256; *In re* First Fidelity Bancorporation Sec. Litig., 750 F. Supp. 160 (D.N.J. 1990) (30% of first $10 million, 20% of next $10 million, 10% of any recovery greater than $20 million); Sala v. National R.R. Passenger Corp., 128 F.R.D. 210

An award of attorneys' fees in a common fund case is committed to the sound discretion of the trial court, considering the unique factors in the case.[574] The court awarding such a fee should articulate reasons for the selection of the given percentage sufficient to enable a reviewing court to determine whether the percentage selected is reasonable.[575] The factors used in making the award will vary,[576] but may include one or more of the following:

- the size of the fund created and the number of persons benefited;
- the presence or absence of substantial objections by members of the class to the settlement terms and/or fees requested by counsel;
- the skill and efficiency of the attorneys involved;
- the complexity and duration of the litigation;
- the risk of nonpayment;
- the amount of time devoted to the case by plaintiffs' counsel; and
- the awards in similar cases.

Unlike in a statutory fee analysis, where the lodestar is generally determinative,[577] in a percentage fee award the amount of time may not be considered at all,

---

(E.D. Pa. 1989) (33% of first $1 million, 30% of amount between $1 and $2 million). *But see In re* American Continental Corp. Lincoln Savings and Loan Sec. Litig., MDL Docket No. 834 (D. Ariz. July 25, 1990) (25% of first $150 million, 29% of any recovery greater than $150 million plus additional incentives for prompt resolution of case).

573. *In re* Washington Pub. Power Supply Sys. Sec. Litig., No. 91-16669 (9th Cir. March 23, 1994).

574. *Brown*, 838 F.2d at 453; *Camden I*, 946 F.2d at 774.

575. This may include the identification of the factors relied on, coupled with an explanation of how these factors affected selection of the percentage awarded. *Camden I*, 946 F.2d at 775. *See also Paul, Johnson*, 886 F.2d at 272–73.

576. For instance, the Tenth Circuit in *Brown*, 838 F.2d at 454, endorsed the use of the *Johnson* factors in determining a reasonable percentage fee. Similarly, the Eleventh Circuit instructed the district courts within that circuit to apply the *Johnson* factors plus other pertinent factors such as "the time required to reach a settlement, whether there are any substantial objections by class members or other parties to the settlement terms or the fees requested by counsel, any non-monetary benefits conferred upon the class by the settlement, and the economics involved in prosecuting a class action." *Camden I*, 946 F.2d at 775. In contrast, the Ninth Circuit established a 25% benchmark for such awards, subject to upward or downward adjustment "to account for any unusual circumstances involved in this case." *Paul, Johnson*, 886 F.2d at 272. *See also In re* Activision Sec. Litig., 723 F. Supp. 1373, 1378 (N.D. Cal.. 1989) ("absent extraordinary circumstances that suggest reasons to lower or increase the percentage, the rate should be set at 30%"); RJR Nabisco, Inc. Sec. Litig., [Current Transfer Binder] Fed. Sec. L. Rep. (CCH) ¶ 96,984 at 94,268 (S.D.N.Y. 1992) ("What should govern such awards is not the essentially whimsical view of a judge, or even a panel of judges, as to how much is enough in a particular case, but what the market pays in similar cases . . . .").

577. *See* Hensley v. Eckerhart, 461 U.S. 424, 434 (1983).

or may be only one of many factors to be considered.[578] Indeed, one purpose of the percentage method is to encourage early settlements by not penalizing efficient counsel, ensuring that competent counsel continue to be willing to undertake risky, complex, and novel litigation.[579] Generally, the factor given the greatest emphasis is the size of the fund created, because "a common fund is itself the measure of success . . . [and] represents the benchmark from which a reasonable fee will be awarded."[580]

24.122 Lodestar Fee Awards

While the trend has been toward the percentage method, courts continue to award attorneys' fees in some common fund cases based on the lodestar or a combination of the two methods. Use of the lodestar may be more appropriate than the percentage of the fund method where the fund is extraordinarily large.[581] As with percentage fees, an award of attorneys' fees under the lodestar method should fairly compensate the attorney for the reasonable value of the services beneficially rendered, based on the circumstances of the particular case.[582]

The lodestar method may also be appropriate for distributing attorneys' fees out of a common fund created for that purpose, as in the case of a settlement of mass tort litigation. Such cases may require allocation of fees among different sets of plaintiffs' lawyers, such as those designated by the court to serve on a steering committee (and entitled to compensation for that service) and those who only represent individual plaintiffs. Because compensation directed to the former will reduce the amount available to satisfy contingent fee arrangements, the court will need to resolve conflicts between these groups in determining a fair allocation.[583]

The lodestar calculation begins with the multiplication of the number of hours reasonably expended by a reasonable hourly rate.[584] The number of hours reasonably expended and the reasonable hourly rate must be supported by adequate records and other appropriate evidence. Thus, counsel intending to seek

---

578. *Brown*, 838 F.2d at 456.

579. *See* 3 Herbert B. Newberg & Alba Conte, Newberg on Class Actions, § 14.03 at 14-3 through 14-7 and cases in footnotes 17–20 (3d ed. 1992). *See also* Deposit Guaranty Nat. Bank v. Roper, 445 U.S. 326, 338–39 (1980) (recognizing the importance of a financial incentive to entice qualified attorneys to devote their time to complex, time-consuming cases in which they risk nonpayment).

580. Newberg & Conte, *supra* note 579, at 14-4. *See also Brown*, 838 F.2d at 456; *Camden I*, 946 F.2d at 774.

581. *See* Washington Pub. Power Supply Sys. Sec. Litig., No. 91-16669 (9th Cir. March 23, 1994).

582. *See Lindy I*, 487 F.2d 161.

583. *See In re* Nineteen Appeals, 982 F.2d 603 (1st Cir. 1992).

584. Blum v. Stenson, 465 U.S. 886, 897 (1984); *Hensley*, 461 U.S. at 433. A number of the additional factors set forth in *Johnson* will usually be subsumed in the determination of the reasonableness of the time spent and the hourly rate.

a fee award should maintain time records in a manner that will identify specifically the various tasks and the amount of time spent on them. The failure to keep contemporaneous time records may justify an appropriate reduction in the award.[585] Lawyers should make a good faith effort to exclude excessive, redundant, or otherwise unnecessary hours from a request for attorneys' fees, just as a lawyer in private practice would do in billing clients.[586]

The court must also determine what constitutes a reasonable hourly rate. This will vary according to the geographic area and the attorney's experience, reputation, practice, qualifications, and customary charge, and is intended to encompass the rate that the attorney would normally command in the relevant marketplace in which the services are offered.[587]

The resulting lodestar figure may be adjusted, either upward or downward,[588] to account for several factors including, *inter alia*, the quality of the representation, the benefit obtained for the class, the complexity and novelty of the issues presented, the risk of nonpayment,[589] and the delay in payment.[590] Use of current rather than historic hourly rates[591] or an award of interest[592] is permitted as an appropriate adjustment for delay in payment. Whether enhancements for the risks assumed by plaintiffs' attorneys are permissible in common fund cases is presently an unresolved question.[593]

24.13 Statutory Fee Cases

The analysis of attorneys' fees in a statutory fee (or fee-shifting) case differs philosophically and jurisprudentially from that which applies to a common fund

---

585. *Hensley*, 461 U.S. at 433. Some circuits require contemporaneous time records as a condition to an award of fees. *See* New York State Ass'n for Retarded Children, Inc. v. Carey, 711 F.2d 1136 (2d Cir. 1983); National Ass'n of Concerned Veterans v. Secretary of Defense, 675 F.2d 1319 (D.C. Cir. 1982); 5th Cir. R. 47.8.1 (1983) (absent contemporaneous records, fee based on minimum time necessary).

586. *Hensley*, 461 U.S. at 434; Copeland v. Marshall, 641 F.2d 880, 891 (D.C. Cir. 1980) (en banc).

587. *Blum*, 465 U.S. at 895 ("[R]easonable fees . . . are to be calculated according to the prevailing market rates in the relevant community"); *Lindy I*, 484 F.2d at 167.

588. *See* Newberg & Conte, *supra* note 579, § 14.03.

589. *See In re* Washington Pub. Power Supply Sys. Sec. Litig., No. 91-16669 (9th Cir. March 23, 1994).

590. *See generally Lindy I*, *supra* note 564, and *Lindy II*, *supra* note 565. *But see* Burlington v. Dague, 102 S. Ct. 2638 (1992) (barring use of multiplier in statutory fee case). This bar has been held not applicable to common fund cases. *In re* Washington Pub. Power Supply Sys. Sec. Litig., No. 91-16669 (9th Cir. March 23, 1994).

591. Missouri v. Jenkins, 491 U.S. 274, 283–84 (1989).

592. *In re* Continental Ill. Sec. Litig., 962 F.2d 566, 571 (7th Cir. 1992).

593. *See Burlington*, 112 S. Ct. 2638 (no enhancement in statutory fee cases).

case.[594] The shifting of attorneys' fees in a statutory fee case serves the public policy of encouraging private enforcement of substantive rights created by Congress or the Constitution. For that reason, the lodestar is the appropriate method.[595]

The lodestar calculation—reasonable hours multiplied by a reasonable rate—usually provides an appropriate estimate of the value of a lawyer's services.[596] Enhancements available in common fund cases, such as for results obtained,[597] novelty and complexity of the issues presented,[598] and the contingent nature of the litigation, are not appropriate enhancements in a statutory fee award case.[599] Only in the rare case may exceptional results or quality of representation warrant an upward adjustment.[600] A delay in payment may be taken into account by applying current rates or factoring in an interest adjustment.[601]

A downward adjustment of the lodestar figure may be required when the prevailing party achieved only "limited success."[602] Where plaintiff recovered only nominal damages, for example, the court may award "low fees or no fees."[603]

The court should not award more than the amount that is "reasonable in relation to the results obtained."[604] In applying the lodestar, therefore, the court may also consider counsel's level of effort given the issues at stake, its degree of success in the litigation, and the efficiency and economy with which it handled the litigation.

---

594. *See* Blum v. Stenson, 465 U.S. 886, 900 n.16 (1984).

595. Blanchard v. Bergeron, 489 U.S. 87, 94 (1989) (lodestar approach is the centerpiece of attorneys' fee awards).

596. *Stenson*, 465 U.S. at 897; Pennsylvania v. Delaware Valley Citizens' Council for Clean Air, 478 U.S. 546, 565 (1986).

597. *Stenson*, 465 U.S. at 900 ("Because acknowledgment of the results obtained generally will be subsumed within other factors used to calculate a reasonable fee, it normally should not provide an independent basis for increasing the fee award.").

598. *Id.* at 898–99 (novelty and complexity will be reflected either in an increase in the number of hours or, for especially experienced attorneys who would thus expend fewer hours, in an increased hourly rate).

599. Burlington v. Dague, 112 S. Ct. 2638 (1992).

600. *Stenson*, 465 U.S. at 898 (the quality of representation is usually reflected in an attorney's hourly rate).

601. Missouri v. Jenkins, 491 U.S. 274, 283–84 (1989). *See also* Pennsylvania v. Delaware Valley Citizens' Council (Del Val I), 483 U.S. 711 (1987).

602. Hensley v. Eckerhart, 461 U.S. 424, 436 (1983).

603. Farrar v. Hobby, 113 S. Ct. 566, 575 (1992).

604. *Hensley*, 461 U.S. at 440. However, fees should not be reduced simply because plaintiff was not successful on every contention in the litigation. *Id.* at 435.

24.2 Proceedings to Award Fees

24.21 Setting Guidelines and Ground Rules

Fee applications should not be permitted to result in substantial additional litigation. To the extent possible, the parties should attempt to settle disputes regarding the factual basis for the prevailing party's claim for statutory attorneys' fees. While agreement by the parties on the fee amount should be encouraged,[605] such an agreement will not be binding,[606] and although it may reduce controversy, the court will still be called on to decide whether to approve the agreement. In most instances, however, there will be no agreement and the court must determine the fees to be awarded.

Disputes will be reduced if the court advises the parties at the outset of the litigation what method will be used for calculating fees and, if using the percent-

---

605. *Stenson*, 465 U.S. at 902 n.19; *Hensley*, 461 U.S. at 437. Some courts have expressed concern about the simultaneous negotiation of fee issues and settlement of the merits. *See, e.g.*, White v. New Hampshire Dept. of Employment Sec., 455 U.S. 445, 453–54 n.15 (1982); Cheng v. GAF Corp., 713 F.2d 886, 889–90 (2d Cir. 1983); Mendoza v. United States, 623 F.2d 1338, 1352–53 & n.19 (9th Cir. 1980); Prandini v. National Tea Co., 557 F.2d 1015, 1017 (3d Cir. 1977). See also *supra* § 23.24.

606. Jones v. Amalgamated Warbasse Houses, Inc., 721 F.2d 881 (2d Cir. 1983).

age method, the range of likely percentages. This decision will have a substantial effect on incentives in the litigation. At the commencement of the litigation, the court should also establish guidelines, ground rules, and procedures that will lighten the burdens on the participants, clarify expectations, and reduce the opportunities for disputes.[607] This should be done at an early conference after consultation with counsel. Matters such as those discussed in the following paragraphs should be covered; although most of them are relevant primarily to the lodestar method, they may be helpful in making percentage awards as well.

24.211 Maintaining Adequate and Comprehensible Records

When fees are awarded on a lodestar basis, maintaining careful and complete time records is critical; in other cases, it is at least advisable. In large litigation, however, these records may be so voluminous to be beyond the capacity of the judge to review and analyze. That problem should be addressed early in the case by developing means of record keeping that will facilitate judicial review. Records should be maintained currently (not constructed after the fact), disclosing the name of the attorney, the time spent on each discrete activity, and the nature of the work performed. In some large cases, clients require their attorneys to maintain their time and charge records on computers using programs that facilitate analysis of billings and fee requests; such a program should be considered in large litigation. Such programs enable the reviewer to determine, for example, the total time spent on particular matters or activities and the time spent and activities pursued by individual lawyers. Agreed forms of summaries may be used to achieve similar results.

24.212 Submission of Periodic Reports

Some judges require submission of periodic reports in anticipation of an award at the end of the litigation (to protect attorney work product, it may be necessary to submit some of the information under seal or *in camera*). This practice encourages lawyers to maintain current records adequate for the court's purposes and enables the court to spot developing problems, such as the expenditure of excessive time on the case or some aspects of it. Periodic review of time charges may lead the judge to consider establishing a tentative budget for the case, acceptable billing ranges for attorneys, or at least limits on recoverable fees for particular activities, such as discovery.

---

607. *See* Administrative Order re Guidelines for Fees and Disbursements for Professionals in Southern District of New York Bankruptcy Cases (S.D.N.Y. June 24, 1991), *reprinted in* 3 Bankruptcy Local Court Rules 98–98.5 (CBC 1994 Supp.); Hirsch & Sheehey, *supra* note 545. *See also* Bennett Feigenbaum, *How to Examine Legal Bills*, 77 J. Acct. 4 (May, 1994) (listing criteria for testing reasonableness).

24.213 Staffing

One issue in the determination of fees is the level of staffing reasonable and appropriate for the particular litigation. To discharge its responsibility in awarding reasonable fees, the court must concern itself with the reasonableness of the effort expended, as reflected in the staffing of the case. The court should consider setting at least presumptive guidelines at the outset of the litigation, after discussion with counsel. Setting such guidelines at the outset, to the extent possible and subject to revision as may later become necessary, can reduce the potential for later conflicts and disappointment, and can facilitate judicial review of fee applications. Guidelines may address the number of attorneys for whom time spent attending depositions, court hearings, office and court conferences, and trial may be charged. They may also caution against having high-priced attorneys expend substantial time on projects suitable for less senior attorneys. Finally, they may set forth the range of hourly charges for particular attorneys on the case and permissible charges for travel time. In setting such guidelines, the court should take into account the need for a degree of symmetry between the staffing levels of plaintiffs and of defendants.

24.214 Compensation for Designated Counsel

Lead and liaison counsel designated by the court will perform functions necessary for the management of the case but not appropriately charged to their clients or against the fee award. Early in the litigation, the court should define the functions designated counsel are to perform, determine the method of compensation, specify the records to be kept, and establish the arrangements for their compensation, including setting up a fund to which all parties should contribute in specified proportions. Guidelines should cover staffing, hourly rates, and estimated charges for their services and expenses.

24.215 Reimbursement of Expenses

Rules and practices vary widely with respect to reimbursement of expenses incurred by lawyers in the course of the case out of a fee award. Charges for paralegals and law clerks at market rates[608] and the fees of necessary experts are generally reimbursable. Secretarial assistance, on the other hand, is a normal part of overhead, but courts have differed over whether overtime is reimbursable. Similarly, rulings vary on such items as copy and printing costs, certain meals and travel, and fax, telephone, and delivery charges. The determination of these kinds of claims should not be left to costly and time-consuming adversary adjudication at the end of the litigation; ground rules on reimbursement should be established at the outset.

---

608. Missouri v. Jenkins, 491 U.S. 274, 288 (1989).

In some litigation, parties may believe it necessary to incur substantial costs for different kinds of litigation support or services, such as special computer installations, costly expert services, or elaborate trial exhibits or demonstrations. If counsel expect to treat such items as reimbursable expenses (or taxable costs) at the conclusion of the case, they should advise the court and opposing counsel and obtain clearance before the expenses are incurred, and the court may fix ceilings for such expenses. This procedure should also be followed in cases in which the court does not award attorney fees.

24.22 Motion for Attorneys' Fees

24.221 Contents of the Motion

Local rules that lay down the requirements that motions for fees must meet should be the primary source of guidance. If the court expects to depart, it should advise counsel early in the case so they can prepare and maintain records in ways that will facilitate the later preparation of the motion. The court will need to determine what materials in support of the motion should be filed concurrently and what materials may be submitted at or before a hearing. If the court elects to bifurcate the determination of liability for fees from that of the amount, as it may under Rule 54(d)(2)(C), it should give timely notice to counsel to avoid unnecessary work.

Where multiple counsel in the case expect to submit separate motions, they should be required to coordinate their submissions, avoid duplication, and perhaps attempt to resolve disputes among themselves before submission. Lead counsel can be made responsible for overseeing this process.

24.222 Timing

Rule 54(d)(2)(B) requires that motions for the award of attorneys' fees be filed and served no later than fourteen days after entry of judgment unless otherwise provided by statute or order of the court. Prompt filing of the motion enables the opponent, class members, and other interested parties to be informed of the claim before the time for appeal has expired, affords the court an opportunity to rule on the application while the services are still fresh in mind, and allows an appeal to be taken at the same time as an appeal on the merits.

Although such motions are ordinarily made at the end of the case, an interim award of fees and expenses will sometimes be appropriate.[609]

24.223 Supporting Documentation and Evidence

To the extent not previously submitted with the motion, time and expense records must be submitted in manageable and comprehensible form, preferably in advance of any hearing to enable parties to prepare, to reach agreements where possible, and to streamline the hearing. The time records should reflect the time spent by each attorney and the nature of the work performed; where different claims were litigated, the records should identify the claims to which the particular services relate.[610] In addition, the evidence on which counsel will rely in urging the application of particular rates for particular lawyers, or of a particular percentage when that method is to be used, should be submitted. The direct testimony of witnesses in support of the application can be submitted in the form of declarations, with the witnesses available at the hearing for cross-examination if requested.

All agreements or understandings with clients and other attorneys regarding fees in the litigation must be submitted or disclosed.[611]

24.224 Discovery

Discovery in connection with fee motions should rarely be permitted.[612] If appropriate guidelines and ground rules have been established, the materials submitted should normally meet the needs of the court and other parties. If a party requests clarification of material submitted in support of the motion, or additional material, the court should determine what information is genuinely needed and arrange for its informal production.

---

609. *See* Texas State Teachers Ass'n v. Garland Indep. School Dist., 489 U.S. 782, 791–92 (1989).

610. *Hensley*, 461 U.S. at 437 & n.12.

611. Fed. R. Civ. P. 54(d)(2)(B). *See In re* Agent Orange, 818 F.2d 216 (2d Cir. 1987) (secret side agreements among class counsel must be disclosed and may be against public policy); 7A Charles A. Wright & Arthur R. Miller, Federal Practice & Procedure § 1803 (Supp. 1993) (discussing *Agent Orange*). *But see* Six (6) Mexican Workers v. Arizona Citrus Growers, 904 F.2d 1301, 1311 (9th Cir. 1990) (counsel free to divide lump sum award as they see fit without disclosure). See generally *supra* § 23.23 (settlement; side agreements).

612. Discovery may be advisable where attorneys make competing claims to a settlement fund designated for the payment of fees. *See In re* Nineteen Appeals, 982 F.2d 603, 614 n.20 (1st Cir. 1992) (discovery not required, but is one way to afford competing claimants due process).

24.23 Judicial Review/Hearing and Order

24.231 Judicial Review

Reviewing fee applications is the most burdensome and time-consuming part of the process of awarding attorneys' fees. Courts must conduct that process, burdensome though it may be, in a manner that will discharge their obligation that fees awarded are reasonable and consistent with governing law.

Following are several techniques judges have developed to expedite the review process:

- **Sampling.** Some judges, using techniques employed by auditors, select certain blocks of time, at random or at the suggestion of a party, and examine them closely to determine the reasonableness of the hours charged. The results of the sampling are then applied to the entire fee application by extrapolation.[613]

- **Evaluating the request in light of a budget submitted by counsel at the beginning of the case.** Counsel would have to justify substantial departures from the budget.

- **Using computer programs to facilitate analysis of fee requests.** See *supra* section 24.211.

- **Establishing the fees to be earned or the formula on which they are to be awarded at the outset of the case in the order appointing counsel.** The court should routinely specify, at the outset of the litigation, the method of compensation that will be used. Innovative methods used in this connection have included competitive bidding procedures for the selection of class counsel,[614] and appointment of an outside attorney to negotiate a fee arrangement for the class.[615]

- **Having defendants submit billing records.** Where defendants oppose plaintiff's counsel's fee request, records showing defendants' attorneys' fees may provide a reference for determination of the level of reasonable fees.

---

613. Evans v. Evanston, 941 F.2d 473, 476 (7th Cir. 1991), *cert. denied*, 112 S. Ct. 3028 (1992) (approving the process).

614. *See In re* Wells Fargo Sec. Litig., 156 F.R.D. 223, 157 F.R.D. 467 (N.D. Cal. 1994); *In re* Oracle Sec. Litig., 131 F.R.D. 688, *modified*, 132 F.R.D. 538 (N.D. Cal. 1990).

615. *See* ch. III of the Task Force Report, *supra* note 557.

- **Use of magistrate judges, special masters, or experts.**[616] In fee determinations of great complexity, the judge may call on outside assistance. Before doing so, however, the judge should take all reasonable steps to simplify and streamline the process; magistrate judges are also heavily burdened, and retaining special masters or experts adds to the already substantial cost of litigation.

24.232 Hearing and Order

Rule 54(d)(2)(C) requires the court, on request of a party or class member, to "afford an opportunity for adversary submissions with respect to [a] motion" for attorneys' fees. An evidentiary hearing may be required in some cases where significant facts are in dispute, but subsection (D) permits the court to "establish special procedures by which issues relating to such fees may be resolved without extensive evidentiary hearings." Where competing applications are made for fees payable from a common fund, due process may require that claimants be afforded a meaningful opportunity to be heard.[617] When a hearing is anticipated, the court should hold a prehearing conference to narrow the issues and resolve as many disputes as possible. Techniques to expedite bench trials should be used, such as the advance exchange and submission of direct testimony, subject to cross-examination of the witness at the hearing when requested (see *supra* section 22.51).[618]

Rule 54 (c)(2)(C) requires the court to "find the facts and state its conclusions of law as provided in Rule 52(a)," and to issue its judgment in a separate document under Rule 58. The court's order, which should be made public, must "provide a concise but clear explanation of its reasons for the fee award."

---

616. Fed. R. Civ. P. 54(d)(2)(D). *But see* Estate of Conners v. O'Connor, 6 F.3d 656 (9th Cir. 1993) (magistrate judge cannot enter final, appealable order).

617. *In re Nineteen Appeals,* 982 F.2d at 616.

618. *See In re* Fine Paper Antitrust Litig., 751 F.2d 562 (3d Cir. 1984).

25. Judgments and Appeals

25.1 Interlocutory Appeals

25.11 When Permitted

Appeals may generally be taken only from "final decisions."[619] Interlocutory appeals are disfavored because they may increase cost and delay and add to the burden of appellate courts.[620] Nevertheless, there are occasions on which an interlocutory appeal may be permitted and may save time and expense. Following are the principal types of situations in which an interlocutory appeal may be permitted:

- **Orders granting, continuing, modifying, refusing or dissolving, or refusing to dissolve or modify, injunctions.** Appeals as of right from such orders are authorized by 28 U.S.C. § 1292(a)(1),[621] and an appellate court may treat an order as an injunction even if the district court has labeled it otherwise.[622] An interlocutory order that merely has the practical *effect* of

---

619. 28 U.S.C. § 1291.

620. Catlin v. United States, 324 U.S. 229 (1945); Cobbledick v. United States, 309 U.S. 323 (1940).

621. Interlocutory appeals are also authorized from certain orders relating to receiverships and decrees in admiralty. *See* 28 U.S.C. § 1292(a)(2), (3). Section (c) provides for appeals to the Court of Appeals for the Federal Circuit in civil actions for patent infringement prior to an accounting for damages. Appeals in bankruptcy are subject to a complex statutory scheme. *See* 16 Charles A. Wright et al., Federal Practice and Procedure § 3926 (Supp. 1993).

622. Cohen v. Board of Trustees of the Univ. of Medicine & Dentistry of N.J., 867 F.2d 1455, 1466 (3d Cir. 1989) (en banc). *See also* Hersey Foods Corp. v. Hershey Creamery Co., 945 F.2d 1272, 1277 (3d Cir. 1991) (to be deemed an injunction, order must be directed to party, enforceable by contempt, and designed to protect some or all of the substantive relief sought).

denying an injunction is appealable as of right under 28 U.S.C. § 1292(a)(1) upon a showing that the order would have "serious, perhaps irreparable" consequences and can be effectively challenged only by appeal.[623] Section 1292(a)(1) generally does not, however, permit interlocutory appeals from orders granting or refusing to grant stays.[624] An interlocutory appeal should be taken only when there is a good reason for it, since failure to do so does not waive the right to appeal an order after final judgment.[625]

- **Orders not otherwise appealable that "involve a controlling question of law as to which there is substantial ground for difference of opinion . . . [if] an immediate appeal from the order may materially advance the ultimate termination of the litigation."[626]** To give a party an opportunity to seek interlocutory review of an order, the district court may, in its discretion, issue a written order finding that the above standard is met.[627] The order should clearly articulate the reasons and factors underlying the court's decision to grant certification.[628] The court of appeals has discretion to hear or decline the appeal.[629] Adopted with complex litigation in mind,[630] 28 U.S.C. § 1292(b) provides a mechanism for obtaining early review of crucial orders where an appellate ruling may simplify or shorten the litigation.[631] Examples include orders certifying or refusing to certify a class or allocating the cost of notice, granting or denying motions disposing of pivotal claims or defenses, finding a lack of subject matter jurisdiction,[632] or determining the applicable substantive law. The

---

623. Carson v. American Brands, Inc., 450 U.S. 79, 84 (1981). *See also* Gulfstream Aerospace Corp. v. Maycamas Corp., 485 U.S. 271, 287–88 (1988); Sierra Rutile, Ltd. v. Katz, 937 F.2d 743, 749 (2d Cir. 1991). Under 9 U.S.C. § 16, an order refusing a stay to permit arbitration pursuant to a written arbitration agreement is immediately appealable, but one granting such a stay is not. 9 U.S.C.A. §§ 16(a)(1)(A), (b)(1).

624. *Gulfstream Aerospace Corp.,* 485 U.S. at 279–88 (overruling the *Enelow-Ettleson* doctrine).

625. *See, e.g.,* Clark v. Merrill Lynch, Pierce, Fenner & Smith Inc., 924 F.2d 550, 553 (4th Cir. 1991). The issue may, of course, become moot after final judgment.

626. 28 U.S.C. § 1292(b).

627. Interlocutory appeals are not, however, allowed in civil antitrust cases brought by the United States in which equitable relief is sought. 15 U.S.C. § 29(a) (West Supp. 1994).

628. Metro Transp. Co. v. North Star Reinsurance Co., 912 F.2d 672, 677 (3d Cir. 1990).

629. Coopers & Lybrand v. Livesay, 437 U.S. 463, 475 (1978) (appeal may be denied for any reason, including docket congestion).

630. *See* Wright et al., *supra* note 621, § 3929.

631. *See, e.g., In re* Shell Oil Refinery, 979 F.2d 1014, 1016 (5th Cir. 1992) (orders defining class and class issues, designating class representatives, and setting a class trial plan).

632. *See In re* TMI Litig. Cases Consol. II, 940 F.2d 832 (3d Cir. 1991) (order remanding cases to state court upon finding that federal statute providing federal jurisdictional predicate was unconstitutional).

appellant has ten days from entry of the district court's order to file with the court of appeals a petition for permission to appeal.[633]

- **Orders constituting a clear abuse of discretion in circumstances where the court's legal duty is plainly established.** Review may be available by way of extraordinary writ.[634] Appellate courts grant these writs rarely, limiting them to situations in which the trial court has clearly committed legal error, and a party is entitled to relief but cannot obtain it through other means.[635] Writs have been granted to require that a demand for trial by jury be honored,[636] to vacate orders restricting communications with class members,[637] to uphold claims of sovereign immunity,[638] to vacate orders appointing special masters,[639] and to enforce claims of privilege[640] or work-product protection.[641] A writ may be sought as an alternate ground for interlocutory review where review is denied under § 1292(b).[642]

- **Collateral orders which finally determine claims separable from rights asserted in the action and would be effectively unreviewable on appeal from final judgment.** Under the "collateral order" doctrine, certain nonfinal orders may be considered final decisions for purposes of 28 U.S.C. § 1291.[643] Examples are orders denying immunity,[644] preventing

633. 28 U.S.C. § 1292(b); Fed. R. App. P. 5(a). Failure to meet this deadline is a jurisdictional defect and is strictly enforced. *See, e.g.,* Tranello v. Frey, 962 F.2d 244, 247–48 (2d Cir. 1992).

634. *See* 28 U.S.C. § 1651; Fed. R. App. P. 21.

635. Kerr v. United States Dist. Ct., 426 U.S. 394, 402–03 (1976).

636. *See, e.g.,* Dairy Queen, Inc. v. Wood, 369 U.S. 469 (1962); Beacon Theatres, Inc. v. Westover, 359 U.S. 500 (1959).

637. *See, e.g.,* Coles v. Marsh, 560 F.2d 186 (3d Cir. 1977).

638. *See, e.g.,* Spacil v. Crowe, 489 F.2d 614 (5th Cir. 1974).

639. *See, e.g.,* La Buy v. Howes Leather Co., 352 U.S. 249 (1957).

640. Jenkins v. Weinshienk, 670 F.2d 915 (10th Cir. 1982); Rowley v. Macmillan, 502 F.2d 1326 (4th Cir. 1974); Harper & Row Publishers, Inc. v. Decker, 423 F.2d 487 (7th Cir. 1970), *aff'd per curiam,* 400 U.S. 348 (1971).

641. *See, e.g.,* Bogosian v. Gulf Oil Corp., 738 F.2d 587 (3d Cir. 1984).

642. *See, e.g., In re* Cement Antitrust Litig., 673 F.2d 1020 (9th Cir. 1982) (judge's recusal reviewable by mandamus, but not under § 1292(b)), *aff'd under 28 U.S.C. § 2109 sub nom.* Arizona v. Ash Grove Cement Co., 459 U.S. 1190 (1983).

643. *See* Cohen v. Beneficial Indus. Loan Corp., 337 U.S. 541, 546 (1949). *See, e.g.,* Eisen v. Carlisle & Jacquelin, 417 U.S. 156 (1974) (order directing defendants to bear part of cost of class notice held immediately appealable).

644. *See* Puerto Rico Aqueduct & Sewer Auth. v. Metcalf & Eddy, Inc., 113 S. Ct. 684, 687 (1993); Mitchell v. Forsyth, 472 U.S. 511, 524–30 (1985).

intervention,[645] or modifying a protective order.[646] This doctrine is narrowly construed.[647] As an alternative, a writ may be sought.[648] Whether the right to appeal a collateral order is lost if the appeal is not taken immediately is unclear.[649]

- **Where a claim has been resolved while others remain pending, or the rights or liabilities of one party have been determined while others remain in the litigation.** Review may be available under Fed. R. Civ. P. 54(b) if the district court, in its discretion, makes "an express determination that there is no just cause for delay" and has given "an express direction for the entry of judgment." The order should state the court's reasons. The district court has discretion to direct entry of judgment only for those decisions that are "final" within the meaning of 28 U.S.C. § 1291;[650] unlike 28 U.S.C. § 1292(b), Rule 54(b) does not provide for certification of issues.[651] Once judgment has been entered and the certification made, the party affected must perfect its appeal or it is waived.[652] A Rule 54(b) appeal with respect to a particular party or a discrete claim may be appropriate to speed the final resolution of the litigation.[653] On the other

645. *See* Stringfellow v. Concerned Neighbors in Action, 480 U.S. 370, 377 (1987).

646. *See* Beckman Indus., Inc. v. International Ins. Co., 966 F.2d 470, 472 (9th Cir. 1992) and cases cited therein.

647. *See* Coopers & Lybrand v. Livesay, 437 U.S. 463, 469 (1978) (order denying class certification held not immediately appealable). Mindful of the constraints of *Coopers & Lybrand*, appellate courts have declined to review interlocutory orders restricting communications with class members, Lewis v. Bloomsburg Mills, Inc., 608 F.2d 971 (4th Cir. 1979), awarding interim attorneys' fees, Hillery v. Rushen, 702 F.2d 848 (9th Cir. 1983), directing class counsel to create a list of class members at their own expense, Judd v. First Fed. Sav. & Loan Ass'n, 599 F.2d 820 (7th Cir. 1979), and transferring the action to another district court because of a forum selection clause, Nascone v. Spudnuts, 735 F.2d 763 (3d Cir. 1984). *But cf.* Coastal Steel Corp. v. Tilghman Wheelbrator Ltd., 709 F.2d 190 (3d Cir. 1983) (order refusing to enforce contractual forum selection clause held immediately appealable). For cases on interlocutory appeals of orders on motions to disqualify counsel, see *supra* note 75.

648. Some appellate courts will treat appeals outside the scope of the collateral order doctrine as petitions for special writs. *See, e.g.,* Cheyney State College Faculty v. Hufstedler, 703 F.2d 732, 736 (3d Cir. 1983) (discretionary with court of appeals).

649. *See* Exchange Nat. Bank of Chicago v. Daniels, 763 F.2d 286, 290–92 (7th Cir. 1985).

650. Sears, Roebuck & Co. v. Mackey, 351 U.S. 427, 437–38 (1956); Liberty Mut. Ins. Co. v. Wetzel, 424 U.S. 737, 742–44 (1976).

651. Bogosian v. Gulf Oil Corp., 561 F.2d 434, 443 (3d Cir. 1977).

652. *See, e.g.,* Local P-171, Amalgamated Meat Cutters v. Thompson Farms Co., 642 F.2d 1065, 1071 n.7 (7th Cir. 1981).

653. A judgment of liability, without any determination of damages, is generally not appealable under Rule 54(b). *See* Liberty Mut. Ins. Co. v. Wetzel, 424 U.S. 737 (1976). Orders for immediate transfer of title to property may, however, be appealable without awaiting a damage determination

hand, such an appeal should be avoided if it would result in duplication of work for the court of appeals by having to hear separate appeals on the same or similar issues.[654]

- **Reference of controlling questions of state law to a state appellate court.** A number of state appellate courts entertain references from federal courts of questions of state law not previously decided in the jurisdiction.

25.12 Proceedings While Appeal Pending

An interlocutory appeal, whether by right or by permission, does not ordinarily deprive the trial court of jurisdiction except with respect to the matter that is the subject of the appeal.[655] Notwithstanding the pendency of an interlocutory appeal, the litigation should usually proceed as scheduled through discovery and other pretrial steps toward trial. Depending, however, on the nature of the issue before the appellate court, suspending some portion of the proceedings or altering the sequence in which further activities in the litigation are conducted may be appropriate.

25.2 Coordination in Appellate Practice

25.21 Designation of Single Panel

Where complex litigation is likely to generate several appeals to one appellate court, that court, to avoid duplicative effort and expedite appeals, may want to designate a single panel to hear, to the extent possible, all appeals in the litigation.[656] When initiating the first appellate review in a complex case, therefore, counsel should alert the court of appeals to the possibility of later appeals, whether in the same case or in related cases. Information pertinent to the possible disqualification of judges should be provided at the outset with respect to all cases

---

under Forgay v. Conrad, 47 U.S. 201 (1848). *See* Faysound Ltd. v. Falcoln Jet Corp., 940 F.2d 339, 343 (8th Cir. 1991).

654. *See* Curtiss-Wright Corp. v. General Elec. Co., 446 U.S. 1, 8 (1980); *Sears, Roebuck & Co.*, 351 U.S. at 441–44 (Frankfurter, J., dissenting).

655. *See* 9 James W. Moore et al., Moore's Federal Practice § 203.11, at 3-53 through 3-55 (2d ed. 1994); Taylor v. Sterrett, 640 F.2d 663 (5th Cir. 1981).

656. In the Corrugated Container Antitrust Litigation, the Chief Judge of the Fifth Circuit designated the first panel that considered an appeal in the case to hear all subsequent appeals. Following the division of the Fifth Circuit into the Fifth and Eleventh Circuits, all subsequent appeals were directed to a panel of "new" Fifth Circuit judges that considered the first matter to arise in the case after the circuit division. Between 1979 and 1982, these two panels heard a total of ten appeals.

that are part of the litigation, not just those involved in the first appeal. Special problems with regard to disqualification can arise in class actions;[657] if the first appeal is taken before class certification has been considered, some description should be given to the appellate court of the types of persons or companies that would likely be in the class if one were certified.

25.22 Preargument Conferences

Some appellate courts routinely schedule a preargument conference to consider such matters as simplification of issues, coordination of briefs, and briefing schedules. In complex litigation with multiple appeals, such a conference is particularly desirable and, if necessary, counsel should move for one on the filing of the notice of appeal. An early conference may simplify the appeal, allow coordination with related appeals, and reduce the burdens on the court and counsel. The court may use it to establish coordinated briefing and hearing schedules in related appeals and petitions. Briefing of marginal issues and settled propositions may be avoided. The court may be willing to indicate the points that preliminarily appear to be most significant to it and on which counsel should focus their attention in the briefs. Jurisdictional questions, including timeliness, mootness, or lack of finality of the underlying order, can be addressed and perhaps resolved before proceeding with briefs on the merits.

25.3 Entry of Final Judgment

Under Fed. R. Civ. P. 58, the final judgment must be set forth on a separate document identified as such, and separate from any order, memorandum, or opinion; if the final judgment will run to several pages, a single cover sheet referring to and adopting the provisions set forth in an attached appendix may be prepared for signature. The judgment is effective only when entered by the clerk in accordance with Rule 79(a).[658] The time for appeal does not begin to run until both of these conditions have been met.[659] If a party timely files a motion under Rule 50(b) for judgment as a matter of law, under Rule 52(b) to amend or make additional findings of fact, or under Rule 59 for a new trial or to amend the judgment, the time to appeal runs instead from entry of the order denying a new trial or

---

657. *See In re* Cement Antitrust Litig., 688 F.2d 1297 (9th Cir. 1982), *aff'd under 28 U.S.C. § 2109 sub nom.* Arizona v. United States Dist. Ct., 459 U.S. 1191 (1983); 28 U.S.C. § 455 (disqualification generally).

658. This requirement can be waived by the parties. Bankers Trust Co. v. Mallis, 435 U.S. 381 (1978).

659. Fed. R. App. P. 4(a)(7); United States v. Indrelunas, 411 U.S. 216 (1973). Though notice of the entry is not required to start the time for appeal running, see Fed. R. App. P. 4(a)(1), failure to receive notice may support a motion for reopening the time to appeal. *See* Fed. R. App. P. 4(a)(6). Prevailing parties should therefore send their own notice as a supplement to that expected from the clerk. *See* Fed. R. App. P. 4(a)(6) advisory committee's note.

granting or denying any of the other motions.[660] These post-judgment motions should, therefore, be acted on promptly. Post-judgment motions may affect appealability of other cases consolidated for trial.

The final judgment in class actions must describe the class with sufficient specificity to identify those bound by the decision.[661] In actions maintained under Rule 23(b)(3), a list should be compiled, and referred to in the judgment, that identifies the persons who were sent individual notice and did not timely elect to be excluded from the class.

25.4 Disposition of Materials

Materials filed with the court in complex litigation during discovery or trial may be voluminous. Most courts by local rule or order provide that, after the time for appeal has expired, the parties are permitted—if not directed—to remove many of the documents and other exhibits.

Exhibits gathered or compiled at great expense in the case may, however, be needed by parties in other litigation, pending or not. In complex litigation, the court should therefore be hesitant to authorize immediate destruction of documents and other exhibits. Items permitted to be withdrawn from the court should usually be retained by the parties for a reasonable period of time so that, if shown to be needed in other litigation, they can be produced without undue expense or delay.

---

660. Fed. R. App. P. 4(a)(4). A notice filed before disposition of these motions becomes effective upon their disposition. *See* Fed. R. App. P. 4 advisory committee's note on the 1993 amendments. The pendency of a motion for costs or attorneys' fees tolls the time to appeal if the court on timely application delays entry of the underlying judgment. *See* Fed. R. Civ. P. 58 & advisory committee's note.

661. Fed. R. Civ. P. 23(c)(3).

Part III

30. Class Actions

By its nature, litigation in which claims are made by or against a class tends to be complex and require judicial management. Particularly because such litigation imposes unique responsibilities on the court, as well as on counsel, it calls for closer judicial oversight than other types of litigation. The potential for actions, by counsel or parties, that will deliberately or inadvertently result in prejudice to litigants is great. Once class allegations are made, various otherwise routine decisions—such as whether to dismiss or compromise the action or abandon the class claims—are no longer wholly within the litigants' control. The attorneys and parties seeking to represent the class assume fiduciary responsibilities, and the court bears a residual responsibility to protect the interests of class members, for which Rule 23(d) gives the court broad administrative powers.

This chapter addresses issues commonly arising in the course of the management of class actions. Although substantive and procedural rules are, to a degree, implicated in litigation management decisions, those rules are for the most part beyond the chapter's scope.[662] The focus of this chapter is on the typical class action in which plaintiffs are seeking to be recognized as representatives of a plaintiff class. Occasionally a defendant class is sought to be certified or a request for class certification is made by an adversary rather than by the putative class representatives; the case-management principles discussed here are generally applicable to those and other variants, including derivative actions brought under Fed. R. Civ. P. 23.1.

The organization of this chapter should not be permitted to obscure the fact that the various aspects of managing class action litigation are closely intertwined, and that following cross-references between sections will therefore frequently be helpful.

30.1 Certification

Whether a class is certified and how its membership is defined can often have a decisive effect not only on the outcome of the litigation but also on its management. It determines the stakes, the structure of trial and methods of proof, the scope and timing of discovery and motion practice, and the length and cost of the litigation. The decision on whether or not to certify a class, therefore, can be as important as decisions on the merits of the action and should be made only after consideration of all relevant evidence and arguments presented by the parties.[663]

---

662. For reference to the law of class actions, see generally Herbert B. Newberg & Alba Conte, Newberg on Class Actions (3d ed. 1992 and 1994 Supp.); Carl Aron, Class Actions: Law and Practice with Forms (1987–1988).

663. As to whether the court may act on its own initiative in making this determination, *compare* Citizens Envtl. Council v. Volpe, 364 F. Supp. 286, 288 (D. Kan. 1973), *aff'd*, 484 F.2d 870 (10th Cir. 1973) *and* Huff v. N. D. Cass Co., 485 F.2d 710, 712 (5th Cir. 1973) (en banc) *with* Wilson v. Zarhadnick, 534 F.2d 55 (5th Cir. 1976).

30.11 Timing

Fed. R. Civ. P. 23(c)(1) directs the court to determine "as soon as practicable" whether an action is to be maintained on behalf of or against a class (commonly called "certifying" the class, although Rule 23 does not use the term). Early certification or denial can be crucial, because it substantially affects such fundamental matters as:

- the structure and the stakes of the litigation;
- who the parties are;
- how discovery is conducted;
- the procedure for motion practice;
- the application of ADR procedures; and
- the approach to settlement negotiations.

Denial of class certification has the immediate effect of restarting the running of the statute of limitations against unnamed plaintiffs.[664]

When an action has been filed as a class action, the court must treat it as one until it has determined otherwise. It should therefore take up the matter at the initial scheduling conference, calling on the attorneys to address the issues bearing on certification and establishing a schedule for ruling on the motion for class certification. While the presumption should be in favor of an early resolution, the appropriate timing will vary with the circumstances of the case. Some district courts have local rules that specify a short period—typically thirty to ninety days—within which the plaintiff must file its motion.[665] Such rules, though consistent with Rule 23 in calling for an early class action decision, may not allow sufficient time to develop an adequate record, particularly in complex cases. Requests for modifying such time periods should be made at the initial conference or as soon thereafter as the need is known. Failure to comply with such a rule should not be treated as an absolute bar to certification, though it may be relevant to the determination of adequacy of representation under Rule 23(a)(4).[666]

The court's principal concern should be to develop a record adequate to enable it to decide whether the prerequisites of Rule 23 have been met. While determining numerosity and adequacy of representation may be relatively simple, determining whether common questions exist and predominate and whether the

---

664. For those excluded from the class, the statute of limitations, which was tolled by the filing of the class complaint, begins to run again when the election to be excluded is filed. *See* Chardon v. Fumero Soto, 462 U.S. 650 (1983); Crown, Cork & Seal Co. v. Parker, 462 U.S. 345 (1983); American Pipe & Constr. Co. v. Utah, 414 U.S. 538 (1974). See *infra* § 30.213.

665. *See, e.g.*, Local Rule 27 of the U.S. District Court for the Eastern District of Pennsylvania.

666. *See* McGowan v. Faulkner Concrete Pipe Co., 659 F.2d 554 (5th Cir. 1981); Castro v. Beecher, 459 F.2d 725 (1st Cir. 1972).

class plaintiff's claims are typical of the class may require a more extensive examination. Of course, where a plaintiff's claim is plainly idiosyncratic, or where, on the other hand, the action challenges the legality of a statute or regulation applicable to a definable class, the determination may be sufficiently clear as not to require developing a record for decision. For the court to be able to decide issues of commonalty and typicality, it will generally need to have a clear understanding of the nature of the claims and defenses, and at least a general understanding of the relevant facts and applicable substantive law. Although the court should not at this stage assess the merits of the underlying claim(s),[667] these determinations cannot always be made on the bare allegations of the pleadings, and some discovery may be needed.[668] Moreover, in determining under Rule 23(b)(3) whether class action treatment "is superior to other available methods for the fair and efficient adjudication of the controversy," the court should consider alternatives, such as consolidation, intervention, and the use of test cases.[669]

The court may also need to consider whether to entertain motions to dismiss or for summary judgment pending class certification. Courts have been divided over whether an action may be dismissed on the merits before certification. The court should rarely postpone a ruling on subject-matter jurisdiction or jurisdiction of the parties. Similarly, defects in venue or service of process should ordinarily be raised so that they may be timely corrected before the case is permitted to proceed. A precertification ruling on the merits, however, raises concerns. While it binds only the individual parties,[670] it may have precedential effect on the putative class members. When it is clear that the action lacks merit, dismissal will avoid unnecessary expense for the parties and burdens for the court,[671] but the court should consider whether the interests of putative class members may be prejudiced.[672]

---

667. Eisen v. Carlisle & Jackelin, 417 U.S. 156 (1974) (reversing order requiring defendant to pay for class notice based on preliminary assessment of probabilities of plaintiff's success).

668. Sirota v. Solitron Devices, Inc., 673 F.2d 566 (2d Cir. 1982).

669. *See* Katz v. Carte Blanche Corp., 496 F.2d 747 (3d Cir. 1974).

670. Dismissal before certification is *res judicata* only as to the class representatives, not class members. Wright v. Schock, 742 F.2d 541 (9th Cir. 1984).

671. *See, e.g.,* Roberts v. American Airlines, Inc., 526 F.2d 757 (7th Cir. 1975); Jackson v. Lynn, 506 F.2d 233 (D.C. Cir. 1974); *cf.* Haas v. Pittsburgh Nat'l Bank, 381 F. Supp. 801 (W.D. Pa. 1974), *rev'd on other grounds*, 526 F.2d 1083 (3d Cir. 1975). Courts occasionally have granted summary judgment in favor of a class representative before considering the question of class certification. This practice should usually be avoided. Post-judgment certification in favor of the class may not be possible. Moreover, the potential use of collateral estoppel may have inequitable consequences similar to those of one-way intervention, a practice that Fed. R. Civ. P. 23(c)(3) was intended to prevent.

672. *Compare* Adamson v. Bowen, 855 F.2d 668, 677 n.12 (10th Cir. 1988) *and* Wright v. Schock, 742 F.2d 541 (9th Cir. 1984) (upholding precertification rulings) *with* Bieneman v. Chicago,

Although Fed. R. Civ. P. 23(c)(1) permits entry of a "conditional" class determination order and amendment before the decision on the merits, that procedure should not be used to defer a final class ruling. Undesirable consequences may follow when an expansive class, formed on insufficient information, is later decertified or redefined. Substantial time and expense may be wasted on discovery with respect to matters affecting persons who are later excluded. Those eliminated from the litigation as a result of decertification or reduction in the size of a class may be confused at best or prejudiced at worst. If relief is obtained for a reduced class, those who were initially in the larger class may attempt to reverse the decision that excluded them from the class; such a reversal may be particularly troublesome if the relief was obtained by settlement.

30.12 Discovery

Precertification discovery should be structured to facilitate an early certification decision while furthering efficient and economical discovery on the merits. The determination whether the prerequisites of Rules 23(a) and (b) are satisfied can generally be made on the pleadings and declarations, with relatively little need for discovery. To the extent discovery is needed prior to the certification hearing, it should be directed at the named parties; only upon a demonstration of need—for example, where persons are identified as having information relevant to certification issues—should discovery of putative class members be permitted.[673] If discovery is needed, the court may want to (1) impose appropriate limitations on the number and scope of depositions and other discovery directed at class representatives, and (2) establish a limited time period within which to conduct specific class-related discovery.

Bifurcating class and merits discovery can at times be more efficient and economical (particularly when the merits discovery would not be used if certification were denied), but can result in duplication and unnecessary disputes among counsel over the scope of discovery. To avoid this, the court should call for a specific discovery plan from the parties, identifying the depositions and other discovery contemplated and the subject matter to be covered. Discovery relating to class issues may overlap substantially with merits discovery. A key question in class certification may be the similarity or dissimilarity between the claims of the representative parties and those of the class members—an inquiry that may re-

838 F.2d 962, 964 (7th Cir. 1988) (questioning the procedure since the class representative who has lost on the merits may then have a duty to oppose subsequent class certification).

673. See Campbell v. AC Petersen Farms, Inc., 69 F.R.D. 457 (D. Conn. 1975); Pearlman v. Gennaro, 17 Fed. R. Serv. 2d 666 (S.D.N.Y 1973).

quire discovery on the merits and development of basic issues.[674] If merits discovery is stayed, the discovery plan should make appropriate provision for the lifting of the stay after completion of class discovery.

When discovery is needed on the claims of one or more of the representative parties and the status of some of the members of the putative class, it should be directed at the named plaintiffs. Discovery from class members (see *infra* section 30.232) is susceptible to being used by parties opposing class certification as a device to harass and embarrass, and should be necessary only in unusual circumstances. Precertification inquiries into the financial arrangements between the class representatives and their counsel respecting the expenses of the litigation are rarely appropriate,[675] particularly in view of the ethical rule permitting attorneys to "advance court costs and expenses of litigation, the repayment of which may be contingent on the outcome of the matter,"[676] though these arrangements may later become relevant in awarding fees. See *supra* section 24.12.

Potential problems with class discovery should be addressed early in the litigation. At the initial conference in a case with class allegations, and as a part of planning the schedule for a certification ruling, the judge should inquire whether any discovery from the class is contemplated, either on Rule 23 issues or on the merits of the case, and should make appropriate provisions in the discovery plan.

30.13 Hearings

The nature and scope of the dispute over class certification determines the kind of hearing to be held under Fed. R. Civ. P. 23(c). Although the rule does not specifically require a hearing, one will generally be desirable; some courts have held that a hearing is required before a denial of certification,[677] and one may also be necessary where the factual basis for a class action is challenged.[678] When the facts are not in dispute, oral argument will suffice. Potential disputes of fact may be narrowed or eliminated by the use of stipulations, requests for admission, or uncontradicted affidavits. The parties may be directed to submit a statement of

---

674. *See* Chateau de Ville Prod., Inc. v. Tams-Witmark Music Library, 586 F.2d 962 (2d Cir. 1978); Douglas M. Towns, *Merit-Based Class Action Certification: Old Wine in a New Bottle*, 78 Va. L. Rev. 1001 (1992).

675. *See, e.g.,* Sanderson v. Winner, 507 F.2d 477 (10th Cir. 1974); Kamens v. Horizon Corp., 81 F.R.D. 444 (S.D.N.Y. 1979).

676. Model Rules of Professional Conduct 1.8(e)(1). *See* Paul E. Iacono Structural Eng'g, Inc., v. Humphrey, 722 F.2d 435 (9th Cir. 1983); *In re* Workers Compensation, 130 F.R.D. 99, 108 (D. Minn. 1990).

677. Guerine v. J&W Investment, Inc., 544 F.2d 863, 865 (5th Cir. 1977); Shepard v. Beaird-Poulan, Inc. 617 F.2d 87, 89 (5th Cir. 1980); Jaffree v. Wallace, 705 F.2d 1526 (11th Cir. 1983); Woodworkers v. Georgia-Pacific Corp., 568 F.2d 62 (8th Cir. 1977).

678. *See* General Tel. Co. v. Falcon, 457 U.S. 147, 157–60 (1982).

contested and uncontested facts relevant to Rule 23 issues, using the procedure described in *supra* section 21.47.

When an evidentiary hearing on class certification is necessary, it should not be a minitrial to adjudicate the merits of the class or individual claims.[679] The court may, however, need a detailed explanation from the parties regarding these claims and how they will be presented and defended at a trial on the merits—not to assess the merits of the claims, but to project the type of trial that likely will take place if the case proceeds as a class action. To make the hearing more efficient, the court may limit the number of witnesses, require depositions to be summarized, call for the presentation of the direct evidence of witnesses by written statements, and use other techniques described in *supra* section 22.5 for non-jury trials.

The judge should enter findings and conclusions after the hearing, addressing each of the applicable criteria of Rule 23. Failure to do so may result in reversal, while an order applying these criteria to the facts will generally be given broad deference.[680] Findings are particularly important if the decision rests on credibility assessments.

30.14 Class Definition

Class definition is of critical importance because it identifies the persons (1) entitled to relief, (2) bound by a final judgment, and (3) entitled to notice in a Rule 23(b)(3) action. It is therefore necessary to arrive at a definition that is precise, objective, and presently ascertainable. For example, the class may be defined as consisting of those persons and companies (other than the defendants) that purchased specified products from the defendants and other specified sellers during a specified time period. Because of the notice requirement and the frequent necessity of having to deal with individual damage claims, greater precision is required in (b)(3) actions than in those brought under (b)(1) or (b)(2).[681] Definitions, particularly under (b)(3), should avoid criteria that are subjective (e.g., a plaintiff's state of mind) or that depend on the merits (e.g., persons who were discriminated against). Such definitions frustrate efforts to identify class members, contravene the policy against considering the merits of a claim in deciding whether to

---

679. Eisen v. Carlisle & Jacquelin, 417 U.S. 156 (1974).

680. *See* Marshall v. Kirkland, 602 F.2d 1282, 1301 (8th Cir. 1979) (failure to make findings made review of class treatment impossible); Price v. Lucky Stores, Inc., 501 F.2d 1177 (9th Cir. 1974); 3B James W. Moore & John E. Kennedy, Moore's Federal Practice, ¶ 23.50, at 23-411 to 23-412 (2d ed. 1993).

681. Rice v. Philadelphia, 66 F.R.D. 17 (E.D. Pa. 1974). A class action seeking injunctive and declaratory relief may, however, also include an incidental claim for monetary relief where damages flow automatically from the granting of injunctive relief. *See, e.g.,* Society for Indiv. Rights, Inc. v. Hampton, 528 F.2d 905, 906 (9th Cir. 1975).

certify a class, and create potential problems of manageability.[682] Similarly, objective terms should be used in defining persons to be excluded from the class, such as affiliates of the defendants, residents of particular states in diversity cases, or persons who have filed their own actions or are members of another class. The judge should consider whether the definition will serve the purpose for which the class is certified (i.e., the resolution of common questions of fact and law in a single proceeding). The definition should not, therefore, exclude a substantial number of persons with claims similar to those of persons included in the class. The appropriate scope of a class may also be affected by the applicable substantive law and choice-of-law considerations, which may, among other things, require subclasses.[683]

The definition may be qualified by adding appropriate language describing the claims made on behalf of the class in the litigation, such as allegations of denial of employment on account of race.[684] The class representatives and all members of the class must, however, meet the commonalty and typicality requirements of Rule 23(a), even in cases based on claims of class discrimination.[685] These considerations may make it appropriate for the judge to consider whether class action treatment of the particular litigation would be "superior" to consolidation.[686]

A class may be defined to include future members, but in the case of a Rule 23(b)(3) class, membership should ordinarily be ascertainable as of the time of judgment. There is no need to ascertain individual members in (b)(2) class actions for injunctive relief.[687] When an action is certified as a class action under Rule 23(c)(4) with respect to a particular issue only, the class may be defined in ways that would not otherwise be appropriate if it were certified for all purposes. See *infra* section 30.17.

When a class action may qualify under Rule 23(b)(3) as well as Rule 23(b)(1) or 23(b)(2), it is necessary to specify the particular provision of the rule under which it is certified. Members of a (b)(3) class are entitled to notice and an op-

---

682. *See* Fed. R. Civ. P. 23(b)(3)(D); Simers v. Rios, 661 F.2d 655 (7th Cir. 1981).

683. *See* Phillips Petroleum v. Shutts, 472 U.S. 797 (1985) (due process clause may limit application of state law to multistate classes).

684. A description of the claims made on behalf of or against the class will be useful if *res judicata* questions are presented in later litigation. *See* Dorre v. Kleppe, 522 F.2d 1369 (5th Cir. 1975); *cf.* Cooper v. Federal Res. Bank of Richmond, 464 U.S. 808 (1984) (judgment against class bars only "class claims" and individual claims actually tried).

685. General Tel. Co. v. Falcon, 457 U.S. 147 (1982) (rejecting across the board discrimination claim classes).

686. *See In re* Fibreboard Corp., 893 F.2d 706 (5th Cir. 1990); Cimino v. Raymark Indus., Inc., 751 F. Supp. 649 (E.D. Tex. 1990). See *infra* § 33.2.

687. Robertson v. National Basketball Assoc., 389 F. Supp. 867 (S.D.N.Y. 1975).

portunity to opt out.[688] Rules 23(b)(1) and (b)(2) do not mandate such notice and opportunity, but in an appropriate case the court, under Rule 23(d)(2), may nevertheless require notice and allow exclusion on timely request.[689]

30.15 Multiple Cases and Classes/Subclasses

In certification proceedings, the court may confront a number of conflicting claims. There may be several cases with similar class allegations, each of which might be appropriately certified under Rule 23. These various possibilities are, under Fed. R. Civ. P. 23(b)(3)(B), to be considered in deciding whether to certify a (b)(3) action. Competing claims for certification may be pressed by different class representatives and their attorneys.[690] Rarely should more than one be certified, although under appropriate circumstances subclasses may be considered, as discussed below. The designation of several persons as representatives of the class is, however, often desirable to make plaintiffs more representative of the diverse interests involved; if not already parties, the additional representatives may sometimes be added to the action by joinder, intervention, or filing a consolidated complaint. In the interest of manageability, however, rarely should more than ten persons or firms be named as class representatives. At times, counsel request certification of multiple classes and subclasses to gain appointment to positions of leadership in conducting the litigation (see *infra* section 30.16). Creation of unnecessary classes and subclasses to accommodate an excessive number of attorneys in the litigation leads to confusion, conflict, and excessive attorneys' fees and should be avoided.

In deciding which of several related cases to certify as a class action—assuming that each meets the requirements of Rule 23—the court has broad discretion. A number of factors are relevant. Under Rule 23(b)(3)(B), the court is to consider the pendency of other litigation concerning the controversy, in both state and federal courts, by or against members of the class.[691] If the cases were transferred to the court after having been initially filed in different districts, there may be choice-of-law consequences. The court should consider whether persons who are class members under the allegations of one complaint are also members under those of another. Certifying an earlier case may avoid statute of limitations problems that cannot be cured by amendment of the second complaint. In such cir-

---

688. Fed. R. Civ. P. 23(c)(2).

689. A court is not precluded from defining a class under Rule 23(b)(1) or (b)(2) to include only those putative class members who do not opt out of the litigation. Such a definition may be appropriate in some (b)(2) cases or in a (b)(1)(B) case in which the class was formed merely because separate actions by class members might impede their ability to protect their interests. *See, e.g.,* Penson v. Terminal Transp. Co., 634 F.2d 989 (5th Cir. 1981).

690. *See* Woolen v. Surtran Taxicabs, Inc., 684 F.2d 324 (5th Cir. 1982).

691. *See* Califano v. Yamasaki, 442 U.S. 682 (1979) (need to consider whether proposed nationwide class would improperly interfere with similar pending litigation in other courts).

cumstances, certification of more than one class action may be necessary if class members are to have the benefit of tolling based on the class allegations. Some cases may have impediments to the granting of full relief, such as the failure or inability to join or serve all defendants, or the limited scope of the allegations in the complaint. In addition, the court should consider the quality of representation offered by competing counsel and class representatives (see *infra* section 30.16).

During certification proceedings—or even after a class has been certified—the court may discover differences in the positions of class members, differences that may cause conflicts in the conduct of the litigation or in settlement. Although all members of the class may challenge the same conduct of the defendants, class members' specific interests and legal theories may be different,[692] or the relief sought by some may be inconsistent with or competitive with that sought by others, even though they have a common position on liability.

While the existence of conflicting interests does not alone preclude class certification, it may have a bearing on whether the class meets the prerequisites of Rule 23, in particular the requirements of adequacy of representation and the predominance of common questions. To avoid such problems, the court may define the issues or the controlling theories of recovery—such as those governing damages—so as to avoid or minimize conflicts.[693] The court may also certify more than one class or split a class into subclasses.[694] Each class or subclass must independently satisfy the prerequisites of Rules 23(a) and (b).[695] If too many subclasses are sought, some may not contain enough members to satisfy the numerosity requirement.[696]

Federal class actions may encompass plaintiffs who are also parties to individual or class actions pending in state court. The existence of parallel state court actions does not preclude certification but should be taken into account in arriving at a definition of the class. Because a prior resolution of the federal action may have a preclusive effect on claims pending in state courts, it is important at least

---

692. Different state laws may, for example, govern the claims of class members residing in different states. *See* Phillips Petroleum Co. v. Shutts, 472 U.S. 797 (1985).

693. *See* Blackie v. Barrack, 524 F.2d 891 (9th Cir. 1975).

694. *See, e.g.,* Monarch Asphalt Sales Co. v. Wilshire Oil Co., 511 F.2d 1073 (10th Cir. 1975); Wellman v. Dickinson, 79 F.R.D. 341, 345 (S.D.N.Y. 1978); Tober v. Charnita, Inc., 58 F.R.D. 74 (M.D. Pa. 1973); Siegel v. Chicken Delight, Inc., 271 F. Supp. 722 (N.D. Cal. 1967).

695. Fed. R. Civ. P. 23(c)(4)(B).

696. Defense counsel may advocate subclasses for just that purpose. *Cf.* Green v. Santa Fe Indus., 88 F.R.D. 575 (S.D.N.Y. 1980). Denial of class status in such circumstances may well be appropriate; if conflicts and differences among class members are so sharp that a number of small subclasses result, class treatment may not have been justified in the first place.

that adequate notice be given to enable state plaintiffs to opt out if they wish.[697] Conversely, to the extent a state court class action has progressed further than the federal action, the court may want to consider an appropriate definition to exclude the members of that class. See *infra* section 30.3.

30.16 Selection of Counsel and Representatives

In the selection of a class to be certified or the selection of lead counsel from among those representing different individuals or groups of plaintiffs making up the certified class, the court will often be faced with having to select both counsel for the class and the class representative. The court has wide discretion in making these selections. It is not limited to those who are appearing for the class representatives; if necessary to ensure adequacy of representation, the court may appoint different attorneys as class counsel or may condition class certification on the employment of other or additional counsel (see *supra* section 20.22).

The relative competence, experience, dedication, reliability, and resources of the attorneys who appear on behalf of the different persons seeking to become class representatives are important factors. Attorneys often engage in lively competition for the appointment, and to reach an informed decision the court may require them to make a substantial showing. An important element in the selection process is economy; the court should scrutinize the way in which attorneys propose to bill and the amounts of fees or percentages of the recovery they intend to collect. The court may lay down conditions for appointment designed to control the costs and fees of the litigation—some courts have called for competitive bidding.[698]

The selection of the class representatives is perhaps less critical, depending on the nature of the case; in certain types of fact-intensive cases, such as employment discrimination cases, the representatives should be knowledgeable. In any case, the representatives must be free of conflicts. The court should ensure that they understand their responsibility to remain free of conflicts and to "vigorously pursue" the litigation in the interests of the class,[699] including subjecting themselves to discovery. Later replacement of a class representative may become necessary when, for example, the representative's individual claim has been mooted or otherwise significantly affected by intervening events, such as decertification, or

697. But note that a federal non-opt-out Rule 23(b)(1) or (b)(2) class has the practical effect of an injunction against the state court proceeding. *See In re* Federal Skywalk Cases, 680 F.2d 1175 (8th Cir. 1982).

698. *See In re* Wells Fargo Sec. Litig., 156 F.R.D. 223, 157 F.R.D. 467 (N.D. Cal. 1994); *In re* Oracle Sec. Litig., 131 F.R.D. 688, 132 F.R.D. 538 (N.D. Cal. 1990), 136 F.R.D. 639 (N.D. Cal. 1991). See also *supra* § 20.224. *See generally* Steven A. Burns, *Setting Class Action Attorneys' Fees: Reform Efforts Raise Ethical Concerns*, 6 Geo. J. of Legal Ethics 1161 (1993); Hirsch & Sheehey, *supra* note 545.

699. *See* 1 Herbert B. Newberg, Newberg on Class Actions § 3.22 (2d ed. 1985).

where the representative has engaged in conduct prejudicial to the interests of the class, or is no longer interested in pursuing the litigation.[700] If replacement is needed, the court may permit intervention by a new representative. Formal intervention by class members is usually unnecessary and inadvisable. Class members in Rule 23(b)(3) actions may, however, appear by their own attorneys, subject to the court's power to adopt appropriate controls regarding the organization of counsel. If no appropriate substitute is immediately available, notice may be given to the class under Rule 23(d)(2), inviting intervention as a named party. The notice may provide that, unless a new party seeks by a specified date to intervene to represent the class, the class will be decertified. Because of the potential prejudice to class members, it is important that the notice adequately inform them of the anticipated action and allow sufficient time for a response.[701] To protect the interests of the class, class counsel should make reasonable efforts to recruit a new representative.

30.17 Classes for Special Issues

Under Rule 23(c)(4)(A), "an action may be brought or maintained as a class action with respect to particular issues." Thus, a class may be certified for only certain issues or claims in the litigation.[702] Selectively used, this provision enables a court to achieve the economies of class action treatment for portions of a case, the balance of which may either not qualify under the rule or be unmanageable as a class action. The court may, moreover, certify a (b)(3) class for certain claims, allowing class members to opt out, while creating a (b)(1) or (b)(2) class for other claims, from which opt outs may not be permitted.

The provision authorizing a class for specific common "issues" does not require that an entire claim by or against a class be certified. Although so far little used, several courts have assumed that (c)(4) authorizes class certification of one or more issues relating to liability while certification of other issues affecting liability or damages is denied or deferred.[703] In considering such an approach, the

---

700. *See* Greenfield v. United States Healthcare, Inc., 146 F.R.D. 118 (E.D. Pa. 1993).

701. Lynch v. Baxley, 651 F.2d 387, 388 (5th Cir. 1981). *See* Armour v. Anniston, 654 F.2d 382, 384 (5th Cir. 1984); *cf.* Payne v. Travenol Lab., Inc., 673 F.2d 798 (5th Cir. 1982).

702. *See, e.g.,* Jenkins v. Raymark, 782 F.2d 468 (5th Cir. 1986) (class to adjudicate "state of the art" defense); Weathers v. Peters Realty Corp., 499 F.2d 1197 (6th Cir. 1974) (class for injunctive relief); Nix v. Grand Lodge of Int'l Ass'n of Machinists, 479 F.2d 382 (5th Cir. 1973) (class to determine validity of disciplinary procedures); Chicken Delight, Inc. v. Harris, 412 F.2d 830 (9th Cir. 1969) (class to challenge portions of standard franchise agreement).

703. *See, e.g.,* Halderman v. Pennhurst State School & Hosp., 612 F.2d 84 (3d Cir. 1979) (dictum), *rev'd on other grounds*, 451 U.S. 1 (1981). This appears to have been the intention of the drafters of the clause. *See* Fed. R. Civ. P. 23(c)(4) advisory committee's note. Courts have, for example, considered the propriety of post-verdict proceedings in class actions under the securities acts in which, after the jury has determined liability, individual plaintiffs could seek recovery for qualify-

court should be satisfied that common questions predominate with respect to the certified issues and that those issues are sufficiently separate from other issues that a severed trial will not infringe the constitutional right to jury trial.[704]

30.18 Reconsideration

Although an order of certification under Rule 23(c)(1) "may be conditional, and may be altered or amended before the decision on the merits," it should not be treated as tentative and should be made only after consideration of all available relevant information. Once such an order is issued, the parties can be expected to rely on it and conduct discovery, prepare for trial, and engage in settlement discussions on the assumption that in the normal course of events it will not be altered except for good cause. Sometimes, however, developments in the litigation, such as the discovery of new facts or changes in parties or in the substantive or procedural law, will necessitate reconsideration of the earlier order and the granting or denial of certification or redefinition of the class.

Reconsideration under Rule 23(c)(1) may be on motion of any party or *sua sponte* by the court issuing a show cause order. The procedure to be followed is similar to that for the original hearing under Rule 23(c)(1), although in the later stages of the litigation there may be less need for an evidentiary hearing. In deciding whether to modify its original decision, the court should consider not only the requirements of Rule 23(a) and (b) in the light of the facts and issues of the case, but also whether the parties or the class would be unfairly prejudiced by a change in the proceedings at that point.

30.2 Communication with Class Members

Communication with the class is a major concern in the management of class actions. The court and counsel will need to develop appropriate means for provid-

---

ing shares. *See* Jaroslawicz v. Englehard Corp., 724 F. Supp. 294 (D. N.J. 1989); Biben v. Card, 789 F. Supp. 1001 (W.D. Mo. 1992).

704. *See* Gasoline Prods. Co., Inc. v. Champlin Refining Co., 283 U.S. 494, 500 (1931); Alabama v. Blue Bird Body Co., 573 F.2d 309, 318 (5th Cir. 1978). See also *supra* § 21.632.

ing information to, and obtaining it from, members of the class, and for handling inquiries from potential or actual class members while avoiding communications that may interfere with the conduct of the litigation. The law provides little definitive guidance in this area, so much is left to the court's judgment.

30.21 Notices from the Court

Notice to class members is mandated in two circumstances: (1) when a class is certified under Rule 23(b)(3); and (2) when the parties propose to dismiss or compromise (settle) a class action. Because Rule 23(c)(2) provides that "the court shall direct [notice of a (b)(3) action] to the members of the class," notice is generally given in the name of the court and appears as notice from the court, although typically prepared and distributed by one of the parties. Notice under Rule 23(e) of a proposed dismissal or compromise must be given "as the court directs," and the same procedure is generally followed. In addition, the court may require notice to be given as directed whenever needed "for the protection of class members or otherwise for the fair conduct of the action."[705] Notice is closely related to other aspects of the management of class actions, in particular certification and settlement; this section should therefore be read in conjunction with the rest of this chapter.

30.211 Certification Notice

Notice that the case has been certified as a class action, required for (b)(3) actions, may at times be advisable for (b)(1) and (b)(2) classes as well. As discussed in *supra* section 30.14, many cases meet the standards of Rule 23(b)(3) as well as those of (b)(1) or (b)(2). No generalization can be made as to whether or when the provisions of Rule 23(c)(2) (individual notice and right of exclusion) apply in such circumstances. Giving notice may help bring to light conflicting interests or antagonistic positions within the class conflicts of which the court was not aware at the time of the certification hearing, and dissatisfaction with the fairness and adequacy of representation. Notice will lessen the vulnerability of the final judgment to collateral attack by class members.[706]

While Rule 23 gives no specific guidance on the timing of notice to class members, notice should ordinarily be given promptly after the certification order is issued. Sometimes, as when the parties are nearing settlement or developments

---

705. Fed. R. Civ. P. 23(d).
706. *See* 7A Charles A. Wright & Arthur R. Miller, Federal Practice and Procedure, §§ 1789, 1793 (Supp. 1993).

indicate that it may be necessary to revise the certification, it may be reasonable to delay the notice temporarily. The court should not permit delay, however, if statute of limitations problems could result. If the court certifies a class more narrow than that set forth in the complaint, the statute of limitations will again start to run against those excluded from the class, and delay in giving notice of the class definition may prejudice them.

Rule 23(c)(2) specifies the content of the notice in (b)(3) actions: (1) the right of any class member to opt out if request is made by a specified date; (2) the binding effect of the judgment, favorable or unfavorable, on all class members who do not opt out; and (3) the right of any class member to appear through counsel. In addition, sufficient information about the case should be provided to enable class members to make an informed decision about their participation. Thus, the notice should:

- describe succinctly and simply the substance of the action and the positions of the parties;
- identify the opposing parties, class representatives, and counsel;
- indicate the relief sought;
- explain any special risks of class members, such as being bound by the judgment, while emphasizing that the court has not ruled on the merits of any claims or defenses; and
- describe clearly the procedures and deadlines for opting out.

A simple form for exercising this right of exclusion should be attached to the notice.[707] Counsel usually submit a draft of the proposed notice to the court for its review, revision, and approval. The notice should be accurate, objective, and understandable to class members, which may require that it be printed in more than one language.[708]

Rule 23(c)(2) requires that individual notice in (b)(3) actions be given to class members "who can be identified through reasonable effort," with others given "the best notice practicable under the circumstances."[709] When the names and addresses of most class members are known, notice by mail (generally first-class mail[710]) is usually required. Publication in newspapers or journals may be advisable as a supplement; it is necessary if class members are not identifiable af-

---

707. See Sample Notice and Form *infra* § 41.41.

708. *See, e.g.,* Mendoza v. United States, 623 F.2d 1338 (9th Cir. 1980).

709. Due process does not require actual notice to parties who cannot reasonably be identified. *See* Mullane v. Central Hanover Bank & Trust Co., 339 U.S. 306, 313–19 (1950); Silber v. Mabon, 18 F.3d 1449 (9th Cir. 1994); Weinberger v. Kendrick, 698 F.2d 61 (2d Cir. 1982); Grunin v. International House of Pancakes, 513 F.2d 114 (8th Cir. 1975).

710. Oppenheimer Fund, Inc. v. Sanders, 437 U.S. 340, 355 n.22 (1978), speaks favorably of the use of second-class mail.

ter reasonable effort. Publications that are likely to be read by class members should be selected. Financial and legal journals or sections of newspapers, while useful to a degree, are not likely to be read by many members of the general public. The determination of what efforts to identify and notify are reasonable under the circumstances of the case rests in the discretion of the judge before whom the class action is pending; notification may ultimately become an issue if the estoppel effect of the class action judgment is challenged in other litigation.

The manner in which notice is given can be a source of controversy in class actions. It implicates issues of cost and fairness to the parties and class members, and potential prejudice to one side or the other. The manner of giving notice can encourage or discourage the assertion of certain claims, or can be so costly and burdensome as to frustrate plaintiffs' ability to maintain the action.[711]

In securities cases, for example, the shares of many class members may be held in street name by brokers or financial institutions as nominees, and, depending on the circumstances, giving notice to these nominees alone may not suffice to give notice to the class members.[712] The class representatives are usually able to make satisfactory financial arrangements with the nominees for the class members to forward the notices or at least provide a list of the names and addresses of the beneficial owners. If the nominees are not willing and are not parties to the litigation, a subpoena *duces tecum* can be issued directing them to produce the records from which the class representatives can compile a mailing list. If the litigation is eventually terminated favorably to the class, the representatives may be entitled to reimbursement for these expenses, from either the entire fund recovered for the class, that part of the fund recovered on behalf of security holders whose shares were held in street names, or perhaps the defendants.[713]

The problems of notice may be even more critical with classes composed of individual purchasers of goods or services, since sales records may be lacking or be incomplete and unreliable. Creativity is often needed in devising an effective means of notifying class members.[714] On occasion, notice has been distributed with a defendant company's mailings to shareholders, credit card holders, or customers, or in its employees' pay envelopes, but such procedures have been

---

711. Ordinarily, the time and expense of identifying and notifying class members must be borne, at least initially, by the class representatives. *See Oppenheimer Fund,* 437 U.S. 340 (noting, however, that in some circumstances court might order defendants to assist in identifying class members or even to give notice to the class).

712. *Compare In re* Franklin Nat'l Bank Sec. Litig., 574 F.2d 662 (2d Cir. 1978), *modified* 599 F.2d 1109 (1979) *with In re* National Student Mktg. Litig. v. Barnes Plaintiffs, 530 F.2d 1012 (D.C. Cir. 1976).

713. *See In re* Penn Central Sec. Litig., 560 F.2d 1138 (3d Cir. 1977).

714. *See, e.g.,* Arizona Dairy Prods. Litig., 75-2 Trade Case, ¶ 60,555, 1975 WL 966 (D. Ariz.) (notice printed on milk cartons).

questioned, not only because of the administrative burden they can impose but also because of the potential of prejudice to a defendant from having to publicize an action against itself.[715] Before such means are approved, class counsel should be required to show either a substantial cost saving, other significant advantages over the use of the mail, or the absence of feasible alternatives. Any increased administrative costs to the defendant caused by the alternative means of notice should be taken into account.

The parties seeking class certification must initially bear the cost of preparing and distributing the certification notice required by Rule 23(c)(2)[716] and the expense of identifying the class members.[717] Individual class representatives are, however, responsible only for their pro rata share,[718] and counsel for the class may properly advance such costs with repayment contingent on recovery.[719] The court should require class counsel to keep accurate and complete records of the steps taken to give notice, providing documentation not only if costs are ultimately taxed against the defendants but also if post-judgment attacks are made on the adequacy of notice.

Class representatives may also be required to pay the initial cost of preparing and distributing certification notice when it is ordered in (b)(1) and (b)(2) actions. The class representatives, however, are not required by Rule 23 to pay this cost; courts sometimes have required that these costs be borne by the defendants, particularly when such notice is given at their request (for greater assurance that the judgment will be binding on class members).

30.212 Settlement Notice

Rule 23(e) states that class actions "shall not be dismissed or compromised without the approval of the court, and notice of the proposed dismissal or compromise shall be given to all members of the class in such manner as the court directs." Settlement notices are subject to many of the same considerations outlined above for certification notices. The cost of such notices is, however, often allocated to the defendants by the settlement agreement, and the parties are usually able to agree on a proposed form of notice. Moreover, the court may consider requiring class counsel to use follow-up procedures to contact class members where

---

715. See Pacific Gas & Elec. Co. v. Public Utilities Comm'n, 475 U.S. 1 (1986); Katz v. Carte Blanche Corp., 496 F.2d 747 (3d Cir. 1974) (noting that credit card customers might refuse to pay their regular bills as a result).

716. See Eisen v. Carlisle & Jacquelin, 417 U.S. 156 (1974) (interpreting Rule 23).

717. Oppenheimer Fund, Inc. v. Sanders, 437 U.S. 340 (1978).

718. Rand v. Monsanto Co., 926 F.2d 596 (7th Cir. 1991).

719. Model Rules of Professional Conduct § 1.8(e)(1) (1993).

only a few have filed claims, to ensure that as many as possible of those entitled to share in the settlement will be given the opportunity to do so.[720]

The notice should announce the proposed settlement and state that, if approved, it will bind all class members. It should

- describe the essential terms of the proposed settlement;
- disclose any special benefits provided to the class representatives;
- provide information regarding attorneys' fees (see *supra* section 24.1);
- indicate the time and place of the hearing to consider approval of the settlement, and the method for objecting to (or, if permitted, for opting out of) the settlement;
- explain the procedures for allocating and distributing settlement funds, and, if the settlement provides different kinds of relief for different categories of class members, clearly set out those variations; and
- prominently display the address and phone number of class counsel and the procedure for making inquiries.[721]

If the details of a claims procedure have been determined, claims forms may be included with the settlement notice. Often, however, the details of allocation and distribution are not established until after the settlement is approved. The text of the proposed settlement may or may not be included in the notice, depending on its length and clarity. If the agreement itself is not distributed, the notice must contain a clear, accurate description of the key terms and tell class members where they can examine or secure a copy, such as from the clerk's office, class counsel, or a defendant's employment office.

If a class settlement is tentatively approved before notice of certification has been given, certification and settlement notices should be combined, reducing the expense of notice and avoiding the confusion that separate notification of certification and settlement would produce.[722] If the class has been certified only conditionally for settlement purposes, that fact should be disclosed. Even though a settlement is proposed, the original claims, relief sought, and defenses should be outlined; such information is necessary for class members to make an informed decision. The notice should describe clearly the options open to the class members and the deadlines for taking action.

Settlement by the class representatives of their claims before the court has ruled on certification presents difficult questions. Courts have generally held that,

---

720. See Fed. R Civ. P. 23(d)(2); Zimmer Paper Prods., Inc. v. Berger & Montague, 758 F.2d 86, 91–93 & nn.6, 8 (3d Cir. 1985) (dicta).

721. See Sample Notice *infra* § 41.42.

722. See Sample Notice *infra* § 41.43. See, e.g., In re Nissan Motor Corp. Antitrust Litig., 552 F.2d 1088 (5th Cir. 1977).

prior to a ruling on certification of an action with class allegations, the action will be treated as a class action and Rule 23(e) will preclude any settlement, dismissal, or deletion of class claims without notice to the putative class and approval by the court.[723] Where the representative parties settle only their individual claims and dismiss the class action without prejudice, courts generally require prior approval but may not require notice under Rule 23(e).[724] The court should hold a fairness hearing under its 23(d)(2) authority, consider whether the settlement may be collusive or otherwise prejudicial to the putative class, and determine whether notice should be given.[725] While notice may be costly, it is valuable in providing protection to the parties, counsel, and the court. Similar problems may arise where counsel for the class take procedural actions prior to certification that may affect the members of the class, such as amending the pleadings to delete certain parties or claims, dismissing the action without prejudice, or failing to oppose a summary judgment motion (see *infra* section 30.213).[726]

30.213 Other Court Notices

Rule 23(d)(2) authorizes the court to require that notice be given:

> for the protection of the members of the class . . . of any step in the action, or of the proposed extent of the judgment, or of the opportunity of members to signify whether they consider the representation fair and adequate, to intervene and present claims or defenses, or otherwise to come into the action.

A number of circumstances may make it appropriate for the court to determine that protection of the class or putative class, or the fair conduct of the action, requires that notice be given to some or all of the members. For example, if the court decides not to certify a class, to certify only a smaller class, or to decertify a previously certified class, that decision can have a significant impact on the rights of those thereby excluded. The statute of limitations on their claims, tolled during the pendency of the class action, commences to run again.[727] Because putative class members are entitled to the tolling as a matter of law and will in

---

723. *See* Philadelphia Elec. Co. v. Anaconda Am. Brass Co., 42 F.R.D. 324 (E.D. Pa. 1967). The right of the parties to dismiss under Fed. R. Civ. P. 41(a)(1) is expressly made subject to the provisions of Rule 23(e).

724. *See* Jean W. Burns, *Decorative Figureheads: Eliminating Class Representatives in Class Actions*, 42 Hastings L.J. 165, 177 (1990).

725. *See, e.g.,* Diaz v. Trust Territories of Pac. Islands, 876 F.2d 1401, 1409 (9th Cir. 1989); Shelton v. Pargo, Inc., 582 F.2d 1298 (4th Cir. 1978).

726. *See, e.g.,* Papilsky v. Berndt, 466 F.2d 251 (2d Cir. 1972); Certain-Teed Prods. Corp. v. Topping, 171 F.2d 241 (2d Cir. 1948); Partridge v. St. Louis Joint Stock Land Bank, 130 F.2d 281 (8th Cir. 1942).

727. *See* American Cast Iron Pipe & Constr. Co. v. Utah, 414 U.S. 538 (1974); Crown, Cork & Seal Co. v. Parker, 462 U.S. 345 (1983).

most cases not have actual knowledge of the change in their status, some courts have held that they should be given notice of such action, advising them of the opportunity to join or intervene in the original action or commence a separate action.[728] In bifurcated proceedings, notice of the results of the liability adjudication should be given to class members, providing them an opportunity to file claims for individual relief in the second stage (see, e.g., *infra* section 33.54). The court may also require notice to certain class members to correct misinformation or misrepresentations, or to inform them of a significant change in class counsel or representatives.

The type and contents of the notice and who should bear the cost depend on the circumstances that give rise to the need for it—what prompted it, who should be notified, whose duties it discharges, and when it is given. Thus, the cost of a notice to correct misstatements made by defense counsel should be borne by defendants. Named plaintiffs should usually be required to pay for a notice to announce a change in class representation. In some situations, costs should be divided.

30.22 Communications from Class Members to the Court

Since the court is generally identified in the notices that go to putative or actual class members, the court in the normal course can expect to receive inquiries about the litigation from them and from members of the public. The court should establish a procedure for the clerk's office to handle such inquiries. A routine procedure should be set up for referring inquiries from persons who may have claims in the action to counsel for the class. To the extent that the clerk's office itself has been assigned specific responsibilities, such as handling claims or requests to be heard, it needs to set up procedures to handle such matters efficiently and fairly. There should rarely be any reason for the judge to be involved.

If communications from the class—such as assertions that counsel have refused to respond to their inquiries—indicate the possibility of inadequate representation, the court may take appropriate steps, such as holding a hearing, admonishing counsel, or substituting new class counsel (see *supra* section 30.16).

---

728. *See* Williams v. NOPSI, 30 Fair Empl. Prac. Cas 1127 (BNA) (E.D. La. 1982); Gilford v. Wilson Indus., Inc., 30 Fed. R. Serv. 2d 1211 (S.D. Tex. 1980). *See also* IMPACT v. Firestone, 893 F.2d 1189, 1190–91 (11th Cir. 1990) (describing proceedings below).

30.23 Gathering Information from Class

30.231 Opting Out

In Rule 23(b)(3) actions, class members must be given the option to exclude themselves from the litigation, and they may be given this option in other types of class actions (see *supra* section 30.14). The procedure for making the election should be made simple, and class members should be afforded a reasonable time to exercise their option. Courts usually establish a period of thirty to sixty days following mailing of the notice, or longer if appropriate, for filing the election. A form for use by putative class members who wish to opt out may be included with the notice; it should explain, in clear and concise language, the available alternatives and their consequences. Typically, the court directs that the notices be filed with the clerk, although in large class actions the court may arrange for a special mailing address and designate a committee of counsel to assume responsibility for receiving, time-stamping, tabulating, and entering into a database the information from responses (such as name, address, and social security number).

The court may, in its discretion, treat as effective a tardy election to opt out. In exercising its discretion, the court should consider the reasons for the delay, whether there was excusable neglect, and whether prejudice resulted.[729] Relief from deadlines, however, should ordinarily be granted only if the delinquency is not substantial or if there is good cause; the parties should be entitled to rely in their conduct of the litigation on the state of the class as of the end of the opt-out period. A general extension of time for making the election may be appropriate if, due to logistical problems, a further mailing or publication is needed.

Counsel should maintain careful records of those who opt out and when, both to comply with Rule 23(c)(3) and for use in allocating and distributing funds obtained in the litigation for the class. A computer database will be helpful if the class is large.

30.232 Discovery from Class Members

Post-certification discovery directed at individual class members (other than named plaintiffs) should be permitted only to the extent necessary and should be carefully limited to ensure that it serves a legitimate purpose and is not used to harass either the class representatives or the class members (see *supra* section 30.12). One of the principal advantages of class actions over massive joinder or consolidation would be lost if class members were routinely subjected to discov-

---

729. Silber v. Mabon, 18 F.3d 1449, 1455 (9th Cir. 1994).

ery: "[i]f discovery from absent members of the class is permissible at all, it should be sharply limited and allowed only on a strong showing of justification."[730] The court will need to consider whether the information sought through interrogatories from absent class members is unavailable from other sources,[731] and whether the proposed interrogatories will not require class members to obtain legal or technical counsel.[732] Some courts have held that class members are not parties for the purpose of discovery by interrogatories.[733] Others have permitted limited numbers of interrogatories to be served upon a showing of need,[734] have limited the number of class members to whom they may be directed,[735] or have imposed the cost of mailing otherwise permissible interrogatories to absent members of a plaintiff class on defendants.[736] Attempts to depose class members should require greater justification than interrogatories.[737]

Class members are sometimes called on to provide the court with information regarding their individual claims. This may be appropriate in connection with preparation for the second stage of a bifurcated trial (with adequate time allowed for discovery) or the determination of entitlement to individual relief under a judgment or settlement (see *infra* section 30.47). Class members should not, however, be required to submit proofs of claim as a condition of membership in the class, which would be equivalent to establishing an opt-in procedure.[738] Nor should such claims forms or questionnaires be used to evade the general limitation on discovery from class members.

30.24 Other Communications

Under the broad supervisory authority granted by Rule 23(d), the court may enter appropriate orders to regulate communications with members of the class. Because First Amendment principles are implicated,[739] however, the court should

---

730. 8 Charles A. Wright et al., Federal Practice and Procedure § 2171 (2d ed. 1994).

731. *See* Dellums v. Powell, 566 F.2d 167, 187 (D.C. Cir. 1977).

732. *See* Clark v. Universal Builders, Inc., 501 F.2d 324, 340–41 n.24. (7th Cir. 1974). *Cf.* Robertson v. National Basketball Assoc., 67 F.R.D. 691 (S.D.N.Y. 1975).

733. Wainwright v. Kraftco Corp., 54 F.R.D. 532, 534 (N.D. Ga. 1972); Fisacher v. Wolfinbarger, 55 F.R.D. 129 (W.D. Ky. 1971).

734. *Dellums,* 566 F.2d 167; Brennan v. Midwestern Life Ins. Co., 450 F.2d 999, 1005 (7th Cir 1971); Bisgeier v. Fotomat Corp, 62 F.R.D. 118 (N.D. Ill. 1973); Gardner v. Awards Mktg. Corp., 55 F.R.D. 460, 452 (D. Utah 1972).

735. Transamerican Refining Corp. v. Dravo Corp., 139 F.R.D. 619, 621 (S.D. Tex. 1991) (permitting discovery from 50 of 6,000 class members).

736. Alexander v. Burrus, Cootes & Burrus, 24 Fed. R. Serv. 2d 1313 (4th Cir. 1978).

737. *See Clark,* 501 F.2d at 340–41 (indicating that greater showing of need is required for depositions than for interrogatories).

738. Cox v. American Cast Iron Pipe Co., 784 F.2d 1546 (11th Cir. 1986).

739. *See* Zauderer v. Office of Disciplinary Counsel, 471 U.S. 626 (1985).

not restrict communications between the parties or their counsel and actual or potential class members, except when justified to prevent serious misconduct.[740] Local rules or standing orders automatically prohibiting or limiting such communications should not be relied on.

Although no formal attorney–client relationship exists between class counsel and the putative members of the class prior to class certification, there is at least an incipient fiduciary relationship between class counsel and the class he or she is seeking to represent.[741] While notice from the court to class members is intended to provide them with all the information they need (and should be carefully drafted with this in mind), counsel are free to provide additional information, respond to inquiries, and seek information needed to represent the class.[742] The court may want to admonish counsel, early in the proceeding, about the importance of fairness and accuracy in communications with class members and make clear that misrepresentations or other misconduct in dealing with the class would impair the fairness and adequacy of representation under Fed. R. Civ. P. 23(a)(4). Defendants ordinarily are not precluded from communications with putative class members, including discussions of settlement offers with individual class members before certification,[743] but may not give false or misleading information or attempt to influence class members in making their decision whether to remain in the class.

Such direct communications, whether by plaintiffs or defendants, create a potential for abuse.[744] Judicial intervention may be justified, but only on "a clear record and specific findings that reflect a weighing of the need for a limitation and the potential interference with the rights of the parties"—this weighing "should result in a carefully drawn order that limits speech as little as possible, consistent with the rights of the parties under the circumstances."[745] Even then,

---

740. Gulf Oil Co. v. Bernard, 452 U.S. 89 (1981).

741. Knuth v. Erie-Crawford Diary Coop. Ass'n, 463 F.2d 470 (3d. Cir. 1972). *See* Newberg & Conte, *supra* note 662, § 15.14 (some courts have stated that constructive attorney–client relationship exists between putative class members and class counsel prior to certification); Thomas A. Dickerson, Class Actions: The Law of 50 States § 4.06[2] (1994) ("members of the purported class . . . are deemed represented by counsel for the class representatives as of the time the complaint is filed with the court").

742. *See* Oppenheimer Fund, Inc., v. Sanders, 437 U.S. 340, 354 n.20 (1978).

743. See *Gulf Oil*, 452 U.S. 89, where, after a class action had been commenced, defendant continued to deal directly with members of the putative class concerning an offer of settlement that had been earlier negotiated with the Equal Employment Opportunity Commission (EEOC).

744. *See id.*; Waldo v. Lakeshores Estates, Inc., 433 F. Supp. 782 (E.D. La. 1977); Kleiner v. First Nat'l Bank of Atlanta, 751 F.2d 1193 (11th Cir. 1985); Impervious Paint Indus., Inc. v. Ashland Oil Co., 508 F. Supp. 720, 723 (W.D. Ky.), *appeal dismissed*, 659 F.2d 1081 (6th Cir. 1981) (attorneys should have advised client against improper contact with putative class members).

745. *Gulf Oil*, 452 U.S. at 101–02.

less burdensome remedies may suffice, such as requiring parties to file copies of all nonprivileged communications to class members.[746] If class members have received communications containing misinformation or misrepresentations, a curative notice from the court, at the expense of those at fault, may be appropriate.

Once a class is certified, the rules governing communications apply as though each class member is a client of class counsel. Under accepted ethical principles, defendants and their attorneys may communicate on matters regarding the litigation with class members who have not opted out, but only through class counsel.[747] Communications with class members in the ordinary course of business, unrelated to the litigation, are not barred. Moreover, where appropriate, defendants' counsel may by court order be authorized to answer inquiries from class members about a proposed class settlement. If improper communications occur, curative action may be necessary, such as extending deadlines for opting out, intervening or responding to a proposed settlement, or voiding improperly solicited opt outs. Other sanctions, such as disclosure of information gained in violation of the attorney–client relationship,[748] contempt and fines,[749] assessment of fees, or, in an egregious situation, the replacement of counsel or of a class representative, may be justified.[750]

The restrictions on communications may create problems in some cases. For example, in employment discrimination class actions, key individuals in supervisory positions, on whom the employer must rely both for evidence and for assisting its attorneys, may be members of the class. The employer's defense would be seriously handicapped if direct communications were barred. In such circumstances, the court may consider certification under Rule 23(b)(3) (enabling class members to opt out), exclusion of such persons from the class if they have no genuine claims, certification of a subclass, or entry of an order under Rule 23(d) permitting individuals, although remaining as class members, to renounce representation by class counsel and thereby become directly accessible to the employer's attorneys.

30.3 Relationship to Other Cases

Claims identical or similar to those made in a class action may be the subject of other litigation, either in the same court or in other federal or state courts.

---

746. *See id.* at 104 n.20.

747. *Kleiner,* 751 F.2d at 1207 n.28; Resnick v. American Dental Ass'n, 95 F.R.D. 372 (N.D. Ill. 1982); *see also Gulf Oil,* 452 U.S. at 104 n.21.

748. *Resnick,* 95 F.R.D. at 379; Pollar v. Judson Steel Corp., 33 Fair Emp. Prac. Cas. 1870 (BNA) (N.D. Cal. 1984).

749. *In re* Federal Skywalk Cases, 97 F.R.D. 375 (W.D. Mo. 1983).

750. *Kleiner,* 751 F.2d 1193; Haffer v. Temple Univ., 115 F.R.D. 506 (E.D. Pa. 1987).

Manual for Complex Litigation, Third

Individual suits may be filed either before or after certification by persons who do not wish to be members of the class, or who fear that a class may not be formed or may be dissolved. Other class actions may be filed, or even certified, with proposed classes that overlap or are even identical. The pendency of such cases is a relevant consideration in deciding whether to certify a class and how to define it (see *supra* section 30.15).

Class actions should be coordinated with related individual cases pending in the same court, including adversary proceedings in bankruptcy.[751] When (b)(3) classes are being certified, the court should plan for the possibility that persons may opt out to file their own cases. Planning should include coordination of discovery (making discovery taken or to be taken available and usable in other cases) and trials, including (if trials are not consolidated) sequencing of trials. Consolidation for trial of class and individual actions may be useful,[752] both to avoid duplicative trials and to prevent inequitable nonmutual collateral estoppel.[753] Where cases are pending in different courts, coordination can be accomplished using techniques described in *infra* section 31.

Persons who are members of a class may nevertheless pursue their own separate actions in the same court or in others. This may occur when a class member is too late to opt out of a (b)(3) action or wants to pursue a damage claim not encompassed in a (b)(2) class. The pendency of a certified class action does not preclude the prosecution of such individual actions. The first judgment binding a party will ordinarily be given preclusive effect in other actions. A judgment in the class action adverse to the class will, however, bar only "class claims" or individual claims actually addressed and resolved in the class action.[754] Moreover, questions concerning the court's jurisdiction over class members outside of the jurisdiction and the adequacy of notice raise complex due process issues affecting the binding effect of a judgment in the class action.[755] Prejudgment attempts to enjoin ongoing state court actions are generally barred by 28 U.S.C. § 2283,[756] but it may be possible to enjoin anticipated state litigation if the requisite showing of

---

751. *See, e.g., In re* Flight Trans. Corp. Sec. Litig., 730 F.2d 1128 (8th Cir. 1984).

752. *In re* Shell Oil Refinery, 136 F.R.D. 588 (E.D. La. 1991), *aff'd*, 979 F.2d 1014 (5th Cir. 1992).

753. *See* Premier Elec. Const. Co. v. National Elec. Contractors Ass'n, 814 F.2d 358, 367 (7th Cir. 1987); Sarasota Oil Co. v. Greyhound Leasing & Fin. Corp., 483 F.2d 450 (10th Cir. 1973); Williams v. Lane, 829 F.R.D. 656 (N.D. Ill. 1990); *In re* Transocean Tender Offer Sec. Litig., 455 F. Supp. 999 (N.D. Ill. 1978).

754. *See* Cooper v. Federal Res. Bank of Richmond, 464 U.S. 808 (1984).

755. *See* Phillips Petroleum Co. v. Shutts, 472 U.S. 797 (1985).

756. *See, e.g., In re* Glenn W. Turner Enter. Litig., 521 F.2d 775 (3d Cir. 1975); *In re* Federal Skywalk Cases, 680 F.2d 1175 (8th Cir. 1982).

irreparable injury can be made.[757] An injunction or extraordinary writ may also be available to protect the integrity of settlement.[758]

30.4 Settlements

The class action device may also be used as a vehicle for settlement of large-scale litigation.[759] Classes may be proposed and are sometimes certified in connection with a settlement that might not pass muster in the traditional litigation context. While it may be easier for settlement classes to satisfy Rule 23(a), its requirements should not be ignored, lest relaxing of standards eviscerate the protection of absentees that the rule is intended to afford. Hence, settlements within the class action framework impose a particular responsibility on the court. The substantive terms of the settlement, the procedures for implementing it, and its impact on affected parties require scrutiny to ensure fairness. This may be a time-consuming and demanding task for the judge, but it is essential and no one else can perform it.

This section addresses settlement issues peculiar to class actions. Settlement in complex litigation generally is discussed in *supra* section 23.

30.41 Procedure for Review and Approval

Approval of class action settlements involves a two-step process. First, counsel submit the proposed terms of settlement and the court makes a preliminary fairness evaluation. In some cases this initial evaluation can be made on the basis of information already known to the court, supplemented as necessary by briefs, motions, or informal presentations by the settling parties. The court may want to

---

757. *See* Bruce v. Martin, 680 F. Supp. 616 (S.D.N.Y. 1988).

758. *See* Carlough v. Amchem Prods., Inc., 10 F.3d 189, 201–04 (3d Cir. 1993); *In re* Baldwin-United Corp., 770 F.2d 328 (2d Cir. 1985); *In re* Corrugated Container Antitrust Litig., 659 F.2d 1332 (5th Cir. 1981). See also *infra* § 31.32.

759. *See, e.g., In re* Chicken Antitrust Litig. (American Poultry), 669 F.2d 228 (5th Cir. 1982); Plummer v. Chemical Bank, 668 F.2d 654 (2d Cir. 1982); Parker v. Anderson, 667 F.2d 1204 (5th Cir. 1982); *In re* Fine Paper Antitrust Litig., 632 F.2d 1081 (3d Cir. 1980); *In re* Equity Funding Corp., 603 F.2d 1353 (9th Cir. 1979); *In re* General Motors Corp. Engine Interchange Litig., 594 F.2d 1106 (7th Cir. 1979); Shelton v. Pargo, Inc., 582 F.2d 1298 (4th Cir. 1978).

hear not only from counsel but also from the named plaintiffs, from other parties, and from attorneys who did not participate in the negotiations. The judge may also, at this preliminary stage or later, hear the views of the parties' experts or seek the advice of a court-appointed expert or special master. If the court has reservations, it may advise the parties, who may wish to resume negotiations in an effort to remove potential obstacles to approval.

If the preliminary evaluation of the proposed settlement does not disclose grounds to doubt its fairness or other obvious deficiencies, such as unduly preferential treatment of class representatives or of segments of the class, or excessive compensation for attorneys, and appears to fall within the range of possible approval, the court should direct that notice under Rule 23(e) be given to the class members of a formal fairness hearing, at which arguments and evidence may be presented in support of and in opposition to the settlement. For economy, courts have in appropriate cases permitted the notice under Rule 23(c)(2) to be combined with the Rule 23(e) notice. Approval is required of the settlement of any action brought as a class action, regardless of whether the settlement occurs prior to certification, and even if the only claims being settled are those of the individual plaintiffs, with the class claims being dismissed without prejudice. Notice is required of any settlement of class claims and is considered advisable even if only the individual claims of the named plaintiffs are settled (see *supra* section 30.212).[760]

The notice of the fairness hearing should direct persons wishing to do so to file statements of their objections with the clerk of court by a specified date in advance of the hearing. Opportunity should be provided at the hearing for all objections to the settlement to be presented to the court whether a written statement has been filed previously or not. The same objection need not be heard more than once, although the court may wish to ascertain how many of those in attendance agree or disagree with some proposition. If the subsequent goodwill of class members will be critical to the successful implementation of the proposed settlement, an extended fairness hearing, enabling individuals to express their frustrations or concerns, may be advisable.

Objections may be raised not only by class members but also by parties seeking to intervene under Fed. R. Civ. P. 24. They may claim inadequate representation by class counsel or the named plaintiffs. They may seek intervention where a

---

760. Notice of a precertification voluntary dismissal of a complaint with class action allegations need be given only when such dismissal is likely to prejudice the putative class. Dias v. Trust Territory of Pacific Islands, 876 F.2d 1401, 1408 (9th Cir. 1989); *Shelton*, 582 F.2d at 1303; Newberg & Conte, *supra* note 662, § 8.19. In most instances, notice and court approval of a voluntary dismissal will not be given or obtainable because the members of the putative class will not yet have been determined. Moore & Kennedy, *supra* note 680, ¶ 23.80 at p. 23-480.

class lacks adequate resources to undertake discovery to demonstrate the inadequacy of the settlement.

The proponents of the settlement should be required to satisfy their burden of showing "that the settlement is fair, adequate and reasonable."[761] Even if no objections have been filed and no adverse appearances made, the court should make a sufficient record and enter specific findings to satisfy a reviewing court that it has made the requisite inquiry and has considered the diverse interests and the factors implicated in the determination of fairness, adequacy, and reasonableness.

30.42 Role of the Court

Rule 23(e) states that a "class action shall not be dismissed or compromised without the approval of the court." Rule 23.1 contains a similar direction for shareholder derivative actions. In determining whether a settlement should be approved, the court must decide whether it is fair, reasonable, and adequate under the circumstances and whether the interests of the class as a whole are better served if the litigation is resolved by the settlement rather than pursued. Although settlement is favored, court review must not be perfunctory; the dynamics of class action settlement may lead the negotiating parties—even those with the best intentions—to give insufficient weight to the interests of at least some class members. The court's responsibility is particularly weighty when reviewing a settlement involving a non-opt-out class or future claimants.

Generally, the court will first consider whether counsel had sufficient information to arrive at an informed evaluation, the likelihood of success at trial, and the range of possible recovery. The extent of discovery may be relevant in determining the adequacy of the parties' knowledge of the case. In cases seeking primarily monetary relief, this analysis entails a comparison of the amount of the proposed settlement with the present value of the damages plaintiffs would likely recover if successful, appropriately discounted for the risk of not prevailing. The defendant's inability to pay a greater amount may be a relevant factor, as may the plaintiffs' need for immediate relief. Expert testimony may assist the court in making its evaluation.[762]

Where settlement is proposed early in the litigation, before significant discovery, the court and class counsel may have a limited factual basis for assessing its merits. In some cases, the court may require further discovery to justify the settlement or to secure information needed to implement it, such as determining a fair allocation. Because this will increase attorneys' fees and expenses—the avoid-

---

761. Cotton v. Hinton, 559 F.2d 1326 (5th Cir. 1977); Grunin v. International House of Pancakes, 513 F.2d 114 (8th Cir. 1975).

762. *See In re* Corrugated Container Antitrust Litig., 643 F.2d 195, *on second appeal,* 659 F.2d 1322 (5th Cir. 1981).

ance of which was an inducement for settlement—and may produce evidence whose trustworthiness is suspect, it should be kept to a minimum. If attorneys' fees will be awarded out of a settlement fund, the court should ascertain when the settlement was effectively reached; discovery undertaken after that time may have been unnecessary. The court should monitor post-settlement discovery and limit it to that genuinely needed.

The settlement cannot be evaluated simply by reference to a mathematical yardstick. Other relevant factors that may be taken into account in the determination of the settlement's fairness, adequacy, and reasonableness include whether:

- the named plaintiffs are the only class members to receive monetary relief, or are to receive relief that is disproportionately large;[763]

- the settlement amount is much less than that sought in the complaint or indicated by preliminary discovery;

- major claims or types of relief sought in the complaint have been omitted from the settlement;

- particular segments of the class are treated significantly differently from others;

- claimants who are not members of the class are treated significantly differently;

- many class members object to the settlement; and

- apparently cogent objections have been raised.

Provisions in the settlement for the payment of class counsel's fees also require attention. In class actions whose primary objective is the recovery of money damages, settlements may be negotiated on the basis of a lump sum that covers both class claims and attorneys' fees. Although there is no bar to such arrangements,[764] the simultaneous negotiation of class relief and attorneys' fees creates a potential for conflict.[765] Separate negotiation of the class settlement before an agreement on fees is generally preferable to avoid conflicts of interest between the attorneys and their clients, the class (see generally *supra* sections 24.22, 24.23, on court-awarded attorneys' fees). This procedure does not entirely eliminate the risk of conflict, and, if negotiations are to be conducted in stages, counsel must scrupulously avoid making concessions affecting the class for personal advantage. If an agreement is reached on the amount of a settlement fund and separately

---

763. Differentials are not necessarily improper, but call for judicial scrutiny. Compensation for class representatives may sometimes be merited for time spent meeting with class members or responding to discovery. *In re* Dun & Bradstreet Credit Serv. Customer Litig., 130 F.R.D. 366 (S.D. Ohio 1990).

764. *See* Evans v. Jeff D., 475 U.S. 717 (1986); Marek v. Chesny, 473 U.S. 12 (1985).

765. *See, e.g.,* Malchman v. Davis, 761 F.2d 893 (2d Cir. 1985).

providing an amount for attorneys' fees and expenses, both amounts should be disclosed to the class. Moreover, the sum of the two amounts ordinarily should be treated as a settlement fund for the benefit of the class, with the agreed-on fee amount constituting the upper limit on the fees that can be awarded to counsel. In any event, the judge may condition approval of the settlement on independent review of the agreed attorneys' compensation.

Class members should be advised of the potential impact of the fee determination on the amount available to satisfy the class claim. Unless an upper limit is set, class members will not be adequately advised of what they can expect from the proposed settlement. Courts sometimes require that fee applications be submitted before notice of the proposed settlement is sent to the class, so that the notice can contain full information about the fee requests. The need for close review of provisions for attorneys' fees is particularly acute where the settlement provides for distribution in kind to the plaintiff class in lieu of money. Attorneys may receive large sums out of a settlement that provides only speculative benefits to the class.[766] Depending on the law in the jurisdiction, the court may need to be concerned with agreements among counsel allocating fees.[767]

Another potential source of conflict exists when class counsel concurrently settle cases of individual plaintiffs. The court should examine the fee arrangements to ensure that they do not result in some plaintiffs being favored over others.

The court's role in settlement is limited, however. The court may only approve or disapprove the settlement; it is not empowered to rewrite the agreement between the parties. A statement of the judge's reasons for disapproval, however, may lead to revisions that satisfy the objections (see *supra* section 23.14). In evaluating the settlement, the judge should keep in mind the unique ability of class and defense counsel to assess the potential risks and rewards of litigation; a presumption of fairness, adequacy, and reasonableness may attach to a class settlement reached in arms-length negotiations between experienced, capable counsel after meaningful discovery.[768] If the court makes suggestions at the time the settlement agreement is submitted for tentative approval, the parties may be willing to make changes prior to the time the agreement is submitted to the class members for their consideration. If substantial changes adversely affecting some members of the class are made at the time of the settlement hearing, a new hearing and additional notice may be necessary.

---

766. *See In re* Cuisinart Food Processor Antitrust Litig., 38 Fed. R. Serv. 2d 446 (D. Conn. 1983).

767. *Compare In re* "Agent Orange" Prod. Liab. Litig., 818 F.2d 216 (2d Cir. 1987) *with* Six Mexican Workers v. Arizona Citrus Growers, 904 F.2d 1301 (9th Cir. 1990). For more on side agreements, see *supra* § 23.23.

768. *See, e.g.,* Wellman v. Dickinson, 497 F. Supp. 824, 830 (S.D.N.Y. 1980), *aff'd,* 647 F.2d 163 (2d Cir. 1981); Galdi Sec. Corp. v. Propp, 87 F.R.D. 6 (S.D.N.Y. 1979).

30.43 Role of Counsel

Counsel representing a class are responsible for communicating an offer to the class representatives and ultimately to the members of the class. But they are also responsible for protecting the interests of the class, even in circumstances where the class representatives—their direct clients—take a position that counsel consider contrary to those interests.[769] Class counsel must discuss with the class representatives the terms of any settlement offered to the class, but rejection of the offer by the representatives does not end the attorneys' obligations, since they must act as they believe to be in the best interests of the class as a whole.[770] If counsel for the class doubt the desirability of a settlement offer but have little reason to believe a better offer will soon be made, they should communicate the proposal to the court for a determination of whether it should be submitted to the class and the court for approval. Similarly, class counsel should bring to the court's attention any settlement offer that the class representatives approve, even if, as attorneys for the entire class, they believe it should not receive court approval.

Counsel for the parties are the court's main source of information concerning the settlement. They must fully disclose all agreements and understandings and be prepared to explain how the settlement was reached and why it is fair and reasonable. They must also disclose any facet of the settlement that may adversely affect any member of the class or may result in unequal treatment of members of the class. The judge should ensure that these obligations are met.

Ordinarily, counsel should confer with the court to develop an appropriate program for the two-step process of approval (see *supra* section 30.41). Based on information from counsel, the court will be able to determine the nature of the hearing and the kind of proof indicated for preliminary approval. The submission to the court will consist of the settlement documents and a draft order setting a hearing date and prescribing the notice to be given to class members and the procedure for presenting objections. The court may also call for statements covering such matters as the status of discovery, the identity of those involved in the settlement discussions, the arrangements and understandings about attorneys' fees, and an explanation why the settlement is believed to be in the best interests of the class. Any benefits to be received only by the class representatives should also be disclosed and explained.

At the hearing to consider final approval of the proposed settlement, counsel for the settling parties will be called on to make an appropriate showing on the record why the settlement should be approved. How detailed these explanations

---

769. *See, e.g.,* Flinn v. FMC Corp., 528 F.2d 1169 (4th Cir. 1975); *cf.* Saylor v. Lindsley, 456 F.2d 896 (2d Cir. 1972); Parker v. Anderson, 667 F.2d 1204 (5th Cir. 1982).

770. *See, e.g.,* Kincade v. General Tire & Rubber Co., 635 F.2d 501 (5th Cir. 1981).

should be depends on the circumstances of the case—e.g., the extent of disaffection within the class with respect to the settlement, whether counsel are being paid on a percentage basis or whether relief to the class is in-kind only, whether individual cases are being settled concurrently, and the extent to which allocations among groups of claimants and attorneys must be made.

Counsel's task in justifying the proposed settlement after having vigorously advocated their respective positions is challenging but no less important. Counsel owe a duty of candor to the court to disclose all information relevant to the fairness of the settlement. If the class was certified in adversary proceedings, counsel need also to take into account their ongoing obligation to their clients and the need to protect their position should the settlement fail. In evaluating the settlement, the court may want to take into account not only the presentations of counsel but also information from other sources, such as comments from class representatives and class members, the judge's own knowledge of the case obtained during pretrial proceedings, and information provided by persons who in unusual cases may be appointed by the court as special masters or as experts to assess the settlement.

If the proposed settlement is to be implemented through a settlement class (see *infra* section 30.45), counsel have a heightened duty to the court, since the proceedings are, in effect, ex parte. They must disclose all facts bearing on the fairness of the settlement, including those that may be adverse to their position. The court may need to appoint a special master to examine the settlement on its behalf, particularly where complicated mathematical calculations or other tasks requiring special expertise are involved.

Class counsel should make themselves available to answer questions from class members in the interval between notice of the settlement and the settlement hearing. The notice may advise that questions be directed to class counsel and give counsel's address and telephone number. When most of the class members reside in the same locale—for example, in employment discrimination cases—a meeting may be scheduled at which the class attorneys and class representatives personally explain the terms and consequences of the proposed settlement.

30.44 Role of Class Representatives

Class counsel should consult the class representatives during negotiations. The representatives' views may be important in shaping the agreement and will usually be presented at the fairness hearing; they may be entitled to special weight because the representatives may have a better understanding of the case than most members of the class. Their objections to a settlement, moreover, may be symptomatic of strained attorney–client relations that may have affected settlement negotiations. Accordingly, opposition by class representatives to a proposed settlement needs to be taken seriously by the court, and the notice of the settlement hearing should usually indicate any terms about which class counsel and class representatives differ.

Although rejection of a proposed settlement by a class representative may lead class counsel not to present the matter to the court, a class representative cannot veto a settlement that has been presented to and approved by the court.[771] The court should not permit representatives, in violation of their fiduciary responsibilities, to place their individual interests ahead of the class's and impede a desirable settlement on behalf of the class. Therefore, while the objections of class representatives must be considered by the court, they do not preclude a settlement that resolves the claims of the class, including those of the representatives.

When class representatives favor acceptance of a settlement offer that class counsel believe is inadequate, they should be permitted to submit it to the court for preliminary approval and, if the court so orders, a fairness hearing. Although the court will ordinarily not approve a settlement that counsel do not recommend, class counsel—like class representatives—have no veto power over settlement of class actions.

30.45 Settlement Classes

Occasionally, before a class is certified, parties enter into settlement agreements, which provide for certification of a class as defined therein, for settlement purposes only. Such settlement classes facilitate global settlements. They also permit defendants to settle while preserving the right to contest the propriety and scope of the class allegations if the settlement is not approved and, in Rule 23(b)(3) actions, to withdraw from the settlement if too many class members opt out. The costs of litigating class certification are saved and litigation expense is generally reduced by an early settlement.[772]

For these reasons, courts permit the use of settlement classes and the negotiation of settlement before class certification.[773] Approval under Rule 23(e) of settlements involving settlement classes, however, requires closer judicial scrutiny than approval of settlements where class certification has been litigated. As noted in *supra* section 30.42, an early settlement will find the court and class counsel less informed than if substantial discovery had occurred. As a result, the court will

---

771. *See, e.g.,* Laskey v. International Union (UAW), 638 F.2d 954 (6th Cir. 1981); *Kincade,* 635 F.2d 501.

772. But see *supra* § 24.12 (attorneys' fees in common fund cases), noting the desirability of fee arrangements that reward counsel for efficiency.

773. *See, e.g.,* Weinberger v. Kendrick, 698 F.2d 61 (2d Cir. 1982); *In re* Beef Indus. Antitrust Litig., 607 F.2d 167 (5th Cir. 1979); *cf.* Plummer v. Chemical Bank, 668 F.2d 654 (2d Cir. 1982); *In re* Franklin Nat'l Bank Sec. Litig., 574 F.2d 662 (1978), *modified,* 599 F.2d 1109 (2d Cir. 1979). For an analysis of the factors affecting formation of a settlement class, see *In re* Baldwin-United Corp., 105 F.R.D. 475 (S.D.N.Y. 1984). See also *infra* § 33.29 (mass tort settlements).

find it more difficult to assess the strengths and weaknesses of the parties' claims and defenses, determine the appropriate membership of the class, and consider how class members will benefit from settlement. The court should provide an adequate opportunity for proponents and opponents to make a full showing of all relevant matters.

Settlement classes can raise numerous issues, including conflicts of interest. Some of these issues are the following:

- **Conflicts between class counsel and counsel for individual plaintiffs.** Approval of the class will in effect largely convert individual claimants falling within its definition from clients of their attorneys into clients of class counsel. It will also effectively terminate their pending individual and class actions. Because of these effects, divergent interests must be taken into account and fairly accommodated. The court should consider whether the group of counsel who have negotiated the settlement has fairly represented the interests of all.

- **Protection of future claimants.** The court should consider the impact of the settlement on persons who may not currently be aware that they have a claim or whose claim may not yet have come into existence. Since they cannot be given meaningful notice, they may be particularly prejudiced by the settlement, and their opt-out rights (in a Rule 23(b)(3) action) may be illusory.

- **Administration of claims procedure.** The court should consider whether the persons chosen to administer the procedure are disinterested or have conflicts arising from their representation of individual claimants.

- **Partial settlements.** Settlement classes present special problems when used with partial settlements. Members of the settlement class may have difficulty understanding their position in the litigation. Moreover, since they will not know whether they will be members of a class with respect to claims against nonsettling defendants, they may be unable to make an informed decision regarding the adequacy of the settlement. (See *infra* section 30.46.)

- **Conditional settlements.** The parties may propose a precertification settlement that permits the settling parties to withdraw from the settlement if a specified number of persons opt out of the class or of the settlement. Although this may promote settlement by giving a defendant greater assurance of ending the controversy and avoiding the expense of litigating numerous individual claims, it may also prolong uncertainty by delaying a final settlement. An alternate approach is to provide that the benefits paid to the class will be reduced in proportion to the number of opt outs or the total amount of their claims.

- **Additional barred claims.** Some settlements, particularly in securities litigation, are conditioned on settlors waiving claims for additional time periods not covered by the pleadings or waiving additional potential claims against the settling defendants. Because such waivers raise a potential for abuse, they should be reviewed to ascertain their justification and the compensating benefit to the class for surrendering such claims.

A settlement will occasionally cover a class different from that certified. Typically, the parties propose to enlarge the class—or the claims of the class—to give the settling defendants greater protection against future litigation, although sometimes they may seek to reduce the class. The problem presented by these requests is not the lack of sufficient information and scrutiny, but rather the possibility that fiduciary responsibilities of class counsel or class representatives may have been compromised. The parties should be required to explain in detail what new facts, changed circumstances, or earlier errors support the alteration of the original definition. If a (b)(3) class is enlarged, notice must be given to the new members of their right to opt out; if a class is reduced, notice should be given under Rule 23(d) to those being excluded, since the statute of limitations will begin to run again on their claims.

30.46 Partial Settlements

The fairness of partial settlements may be particularly difficult to evaluate. Because the litigation may continue against others, the parties may be reluctant to disclose fully and candidly their assessment of strengths and weaknesses that led to the settlement. Moreover, the adequacy of the settlement depends in part on the relative exposure of other parties; an apparently generous settlement offer from a single defendant may be questionable if there are no realistic prospects of recovery against nonsettling defendants and, conversely, a partial settlement providing little relief may be entirely satisfactory if the settling defendant has strong defenses or is impecunious. An informed evaluation may be almost impossible if discovery is incomplete or has been conducted against only a few of the defendants; subsequent discovery may reveal that a proposed settlement is not in the best interests of the class. Consideration must also be given to whether the settling defendant may be liable to the class as a whole or only to certain members of the class.

Despite these problems, partial settlements are common in resolving class actions and may be entitled to approval. If several such settlements are being negotiated, the court should ordinarily defer consideration until all are submitted, saving the time and expense of successive notices and hearings, and allowing the court and class members to assess the adequacy of the settlements as a whole. Funds received from the settlements typically are placed in income-producing trusts established by class counsel for the benefit of the class, and held until the case is fully resolved.

Partial settlements shortly before trial may disrupt the trial plan; they may, for example, result in the departure of a lead counsel. The court should usually set a deadline for the presentation of partial settlements sufficiently in advance of trial so that fairness hearings may be completed while allowing the parties sufficient time to prepare for trial whether the settlements are approved or not (see *supra* section 23.21).

The court should be reluctant to approve partial settlements containing provisions that might interfere with further proceedings, such as those attempting to limit further discovery (see *supra* section 23.22). A provision under which the class agrees to a refund if it later settles on terms more favorable to other defendants is particularly inappropriate, since the adequacy of the proposed settlement cannot be fairly determined when its amount is uncertain. Similarly, a defendant's agreement to increase the settlement fund if individual plaintiffs later settle for a greater amount does not diminish the court's responsibility to evaluate the adequacy of the amount offered to the class (see *supra* section 23.23). Although the court may give some deference to provisions purporting to allocate a settlement fund according to particular theories of recovery, claims, or time periods, it should reserve the power to make modifications when warranted by further developments (see *supra* section 23.21).

30.47 Administration

Class settlements are rarely self-executing; various problems may arise in their administration, not limited to clerical or ministerial matters. Sometimes a settlement fund is to be divided equally among all class members who meet specified criteria (for example, employees who sought promotion during a specified period) or allocated in proportion to some measure of damage or injury (for example, the price paid for particular securities). In such cases, the class members are in potentially conflicting roles, since increasing one claimant's benefits will reduce another's. In cases where the settlement provides for a specified payment to each qualifying class member—either a flat sum or an amount determined according to a formula—settling defendants will have an interest in maximizing the extent to which class members are found to be disqualified or have their claims reduced, diminishing the total amount to be paid.

Class members are usually required to file claim forms providing details about their claims and other information needed to administer the settlement.[774] Verification under oath or affirmation pursuant to 28 U.S.C. § 1746 may be required, and in some cases it may be appropriate to require substantiation of the

---

774. See Sample Order *infra* § 41.44.

claims—for example, through invoices, confirmations, or brokers' records. Completion and documentation of the claim forms should be made no more burdensome than necessary to implement the settlement. Nor, for purposes of administering a settlement, should the court necessarily require the same amount and specificity of evidence that might be needed to establish damages at a trial; secondary forms of proof and estimates derived from other sources should generally be acceptable. In order to achieve the intended distribution to beneficiaries, additional mailings, telephone calls, and investigative searches may be needed if notices to class members are returned or if class members fail to submit claim forms. In some cases, as where the defendants' records provide a satisfactory, inexpensive, and accurate method for determining the distribution of a settlement fund, there will be no need to require action by class members.

A procedure should be established for recording receipt of the claim forms and tabulating their contents. These arrangements are usually made by class counsel and approved by the court. If the class is large, forms are customarily sent to a separate mailing address and the essential information is recorded on computers. Form letters may be prepared to answer common inquiries from class members and to deal with recurring errors in completing the claim forms. These activities should be memorialized to minimize subsequent disputes.

The audit and review procedures needed will depend on the nature of the case. Claims of modest amounts are frequently accepted solely on the basis of the verified claim forms.[775] Medium-sized claims—or some of them selected by statistical sampling—may be subjected to telephone audit inquiries or cross-checks against other records. Large claims may warrant a field audit.

A claims committee or special master may be appointed to take custody of settlement funds and administer the distribution procedure. The committee or special master may be charged with reviewing all claims or those that are late, deficient in documentation, or questionable for other reasons. This review may be made merely by considering the materials submitted or may involve a hearing at which the claimant and other interested parties may present additional information bearing on the claim. Provision should be made for judicial review of the findings of the committee or special master unless the terms of the settlement provide that these findings are final under Fed. R. Civ. P. 53(e)(4). Periodic reports should be made to the court of the interest earned, distributions made, allowance and disallowance of claims, and other matters involving the status of administration.

---

775. See *infra* § 41.44.

The settlement may provide for disposition of unclaimed or undistributable funds.[776] Judicial approval is required for such disposition, and the parties may want to provide guidance on whether the funds should be returned to the settling defendant, escheat to the government, be paid to other class members, or be distributed to a charitable or nonprofit institution. Adequate time should be allowed for late claims before any refund or other disposition of settlement funds occurs. A reserve for late claims may also be established.

The equitable powers of the court may be invoked to deal with other problems that commonly arise during administration of settlement but may not be covered by the terms of the agreement, such as:

- the impact of divorce, death, incompetence, claims by minors, and dissolution of business entities or other organizations;
- investment of settlement funds (security of settlement funds is critical—the court should permit these funds to be held in only the most secure investments);
- interim distributions and partial payments of fees and expenses; and
- procedures for handling lost or returned checks (although checks should ordinarily be stamped with a legend requiring deposit or negotiation within ninety days, counsel should be authorized to grant additional time).

The court and counsel should be alert to the possibility of persons soliciting class members after the settlement, offering to provide "collection services" for a percentage of the claims; such activities may fraudulently deprive class members of benefits provided by the settlement and impinge on the court's responsibility to control fees in class actions.[777]

776. Although disfavored in a fully tried class action, "fluid recovery," in which damages are paid in the aggregate without individual proof, may be permissible in a settlement. *See In re* "Agent Orange" Prod. Liab. Litig., 818 F.2d 179, 184–84 (2d Cir. 1987); Beecher v. Able, 575 F.2d 1010, 1016 n.3 (2d Cir. 1978).

777. Jack Faucett Assoc. Inc. v. American Tel. & Tel. Co., 1985-2 Trade Cas. (CCH) ¶ 66,830 (D. D.C. 1985).

31. Multiple Litigation

Multiplication of cases within the federal system or across the federal and state systems is a common characteristic of complex litigation. Multiple claims may, of course, be aggregated in a single class action if the prerequisites of Rule 23 are met. Frequently, though, separate lawsuits are initiated asserting similar claims, or class members opt out to file their own cases. Occasionally, peripheral claims in complex litigation will lead to multiple cases, as in the case of insurance coverage litigation or reactive litigation motivated by forum preferences. Control of the proliferation of cases and coordination of multiple claims is crucial to effective management of complex litigation. When the limitations of federal jurisdiction preclude control, voluntary means may nevertheless be available to achieve coordination and thereby reduce duplicative activity, minimize the risks of conflict, and avoid unnecessary expense. This chapter addresses some of the means of control and coordination available in multiple litigation.

The most powerful device for aggregating multiple litigation pending in federal and state courts—the bankruptcy law[778]—is beyond the scope of this manual. Where related adversary proceedings are pending in bankruptcy court, however, the court should consider having them reassigned, at least tentatively, to the district judge handling related litigation.[779]

---

778. *See* A.H. Robins Co. Inc. v. Piccinin, 788 F.2d 994 (4th Cir. 1986).
779. *See, e.g., In re* Flight Trans. Corp. Sec. Litig., 730 F.2d 1128 (8th Cir. 1984).

31.1 Related Federal Civil Cases

31.11 Cases in Same Court

All related civil cases pending in the same court should ordinarily be assigned at least tentatively to a single judge to determine whether consolidation, or at least coordination of pretrial proceedings, is feasible and will reduce conflicts and duplication (see *supra* section 20.12). If it appears that the cases involve common questions of law or fact, and that consolidation may tend to reduce cost and delay, they may be consolidated under Fed. R. Civ. P. 42(a) (see *supra* section 21.631). Cases pending in different divisions of the court may be transferred upon request under 28 U.S.C. § 1404(b). Cases should not be consolidated, however, where it would result in increased and unjustified burdens on parties, such as requiring them to participate in discovery irrelevant to their cases.[780]

Whether cases should be coordinated or consolidated for pretrial proceedings or for all purposes should be considered at the initial conference, even if the final decision must be deferred pending the development of additional information. When cases are coordinated or consolidated, an order should be entered establishing a master file for the litigation in the clerk's office, relieving the parties from multiple filings of the same pleadings, motions, notices, orders, and discovery materials, and providing that documents need not be filed separately in an individual case file unless applicable to a particular case only.

31.12 Cases in Different Federal Courts

Related cases pending in different federal courts may be consolidated in a single district by a transfer of venue. Under 28 U.S.C. § 1404(a), the court may, "[f]or the convenience of parties and witnesses, in the interest of justice . . . transfer any civil action to any other district or division where it might have been brought."[781] Plaintiffs' choice of forum is, however, entitled to substantial deference.[782]

---

780. *In re* Repetitive Stress Injury Litig., 11 F.3d 368 (2d Cir. 1993).
781. For the implications of the phrase "where it might have been brought," see *supra* note 14.
782. *See* Gulf Oil Co. v. Gilbert, 330 U.S. 501, 508 (1947).

31.13 Multidistrict Transfers Under § 1407

Under 28 U.S.C. § 1407, the Judicial Panel on Multidistrict Litigation is authorized to transfer civil actions pending in more than one district involving one or
more common questions of fact to any district for coordinated or consolidated
pretrial proceedings upon its determination that transfer "will be for the convenience of the parties and witnesses and will promote the just and efficient conduct
of such actions." The panel's authority is not subject to venue restrictions,[783] but
extends only to civil actions[784] and only to transfer for pretrial.[785] Counsel who
seek or oppose transfer before the panel should familiarize themselves with
§ 1407, the panel's rules of procedure,[786] and the panel's decisions in similar
cases.[787]

31.131 Requests for Transfer

Proceedings for transfer of actions by the panel may be initiated by one of the
parties or by the panel itself, although the latter procedure is ordinarily used only
for "tag-along" cases.[788] The panel evaluates each group of cases proposed for
multidistrict treatment on its own facts in light of the statutory criteria, mindful
that the objective of transfer is to eliminate duplication in discovery, avoid
conflicting rulings and schedules, reduce litigation cost, and save time and effort
on the part of the parties, the attorneys, the witnesses, and the courts.[789] As few as

---

783. *In re* New York City Mun. Sec. Litig., 572 F.2d 49 (2d Cir. 1978).

784. Antitrust actions brought by the United States are exempt from the panel's power, 28
U.S.C. § 1407(g), as are injunctive actions instituted by the Securities and Exchange Commission
unless the SEC consents to consolidation. 15 U.S.C. § 78u(g).

785. Although transfer by the panel under § 1407 is only for pretrial purposes, the transferee
court may find it appropriate to transfer cases to itself for trial under 28 U.S.C. § 1404 or § 1406.
Parens patriae antitrust actions brought by states under 15 U.S.C. § 15(c) may be transferred by the
panel for both pretrial and trial. 28 U.S.C. § 1407(h). Under 28 U.S.C. § 2122(a)(3), the panel also
designates the circuit court to hear appeals of federal agency rulings in certain instances in which
petitions for review have been filed in multiple circuits.

786. The panel's rules are found in U.S.C.A. following § 1407 and in U.S.C.S. following the
Federal Rules of Civil Procedure.

787. Opinions of the panel are reported in the Federal Supplement. For a general discussion of
the panel, see Robert A. Cahn, *A Look at the Judicial Panel on Multidistrict Litigation,* 72 F.R.D. 211
(1976).

788. The panel may order transfer on the request of a person not a party in one or more of the
cases. *See, e.g., In re* Equity Funding Corp. Sec. Litig., 375 F. Supp. 1379, 1390 n.4 (J.P.M.L. 1974).

789. *See In re* Plumbing Fixture Cases, 298 F. Supp. 484 (J.P.M.L. 1968).

two cases may warrant multidistrict treatment,[790] although when there are only a few actions, particularly if the same parties and counsel are involved, those advocating transfer bear a heavy burden of persuasion.[791]

The timing of a motion to transfer may be important. In some cases (e.g., large aircraft disasters) the need for multidistrict treatment may be apparent at the outset, and counsel should initiate proceedings before the panel shortly after the second case is filed. Sometimes, however, the justification for transfer may not arise until later in the proceedings, either because additional cases have been filed unexpectedly or because efforts to achieve voluntary coordination have proved ineffective in reducing conflicts and duplication. Counsel should file their motion as soon as the need for transfer can be demonstrated; the panel is reluctant to transfer a case after significant proceedings have occurred or if the motion appears to be motivated by a desire for delay or a change of judges.

Once a transfer under § 1407 becomes effective—when the order granting the transfer is filed in the office of the clerk of the transferee court—the jurisdiction of the transferor court ceases and the transferee court has exclusive jurisdiction.[792] During the pendency of a motion (or show cause order) for transfer, however, the court in which the action was filed retains jurisdiction over the case.[793] The transferor court should not automatically stay discovery (provisions in local rules or expense and delay reduction plans that may mandate early commencement of discovery need to be taken into account and an order modifying their impact on the litigation may be necessary), postpone rulings on pending motions, or generally suspend further proceedings upon being notified of the filing of a motion for transfer.[794] Matters such as motions to dismiss or to remand, raising issues unique to the particular case, may be resolved before the panel acts on the motion to transfer. Sometimes the panel has concluded that it should delay its ruling on transfer until critical motions have been decided by the court in which the case is pending. The pendency of motions raising questions common to related actions, however, can be an additional justification for transfer.[795] At the same time, it may be advisable to defer certain matters until the panel has the opportunity to rule on transfer. For example, there would be little purpose in entering a scheduling order while a conditional order of transfer is pending. The

---

790. *See, e.g., In re* Clark Oil and Ref. Corp. Antitrust Litig., 364 F. Supp. 458 (J.P.M.L. 1973).

791. *See, e.g., In re* Scotch Whiskey, 299 F. Supp. 543 (J.P.M.L. 1969).

792. *In re* Plumbing Fixture Cases, 298 F. Supp. 484 (J.P.M.L. 1968). Unless altered by the transferee court, orders entered by the transferor court remain in effect.

793. Rule 18, Rules of Procedure of the J.P.M.L.; *In re* Four Seasons Sec. Laws Litig., 362 F. Supp. 574 (J.P.M.L. 1973).

794. A copy of the motion is to be filed with the court where the action is pending. *See* Rule 7(c), Rules of Procedure of the J.P.M.L.

795. *See, e.g., In re* Ivy, 901 F.2d 7, 9 (2d Cir. 1990).

court should, however, modify any previously scheduled dates for pretrial or trial as may be necessary to avoid giving the panel a misleading picture of the status of the case.

No single factor determines which district is selected as the one to which the actions will be transferred.[796] The panel will consider the district where the largest number of cases is pending, where discovery has occurred, and where cases have progressed furthest, as well as the site of the occurrence of the common facts and the district in which cost and inconvenience will be minimized. The panel will also consider the experience and skill of available judges. Based on its consideration of these factors, the panel will designate a judge (on rare occasions, the panel has assigned the litigation to two judges) to whom the cases are then transferred for pretrial proceedings. The litigation is usually transferred to a judge in the transferee court, but occasionally the panel has selected a judge designated to sit specially in the transferee district on an intracircuit or intercircuit assignment.

31.132 During Period of Transfer

After the transfer, the transferee judge[797] exercises not only the judicial powers in the transferee district but also "the powers of a district judge in any district for the purpose of conducting pretrial depositions in such coordinated or consolidated proceedings."[798] This supervisory power over depositions in other districts may be exercised in person or by telephone.[799] The transferee judge may vacate or modify any order of a transferor court, including protective orders;[800] until altered, however, orders of the transferor court remain in effect.[801]

Although the transferee judge has no jurisdiction to conduct a trial in the transferred cases, the judge may terminate actions by ruling on motions to dismiss or for summary judgment or pursuant to settlement and may enter consent decrees.[802] Complexities may arise where the rulings turn on questions of substantive law. In diversity cases, the law of the transferor district follows the case to

---

796. *See* Cahn, *supra* note 787, 72 F.R.D. at 214–15.

797. The panel has no authority to direct transferee judges in the exercise of their powers and discretion in supervising multidistrict proceedings. *In re* Plumbing Fixture Cases, 298 F. Supp. 484, 489 (J.P.M.L. 1968).

798. 28 U.S.C. § 1407(b).

799. *See In re* Corrugated Container Antitrust Litig., 662 F.2d 875 (D.C. Cir. 1981); *In re* Corrugated Container Antitrust Litig., 644 F.2d 70 (2d Cir. 1981); *In re* Corrugated Container Antitrust Litig., 620 F.2d 1086 (5th Cir. 1980).

800. *See, e.g., In re* Upjohn Co. Antibiotic Cleocin Prods. Liab. Litig., 664 F.2d 114 (6th Cir. 1981).

801. *See In re* Master Key Antitrust Litig., 320 F. Supp. 1404 (J.P.M.L. 1971).

802. *See, e.g., In re* Trump Casino Sec. Litig., 7 F.3d 357, 367–68 (3d Cir. 1993).

the transferee district.[803] Where the claim or defense arises under federal law, however, the court must consider whether to apply the law of its circuit or that of the transferor court,[804] keeping in mind that statutes of limitations may present unique problems.[805] An action is closed by appropriate orders entered in the transferee court, without further involvement by the panel or the original transferor court.[806] Likewise, the transferee judge may transfer cases for trial to any district, including the § 1407 transferee district, permitted by 28 U.S.C. § 1404.[807]

The transferee court's management plan for the litigation should include provisions for handling tag-along actions transferred by the panel after the initial transfers. Ordinarily, it is advisable to provide that (1) tag-along actions shall be automatically made part of the centralized proceedings upon transfer to the transferee court, (2) rulings on common issues—for example, on the statute of limitations—shall be deemed to have been made in the tag-along action without the need for separate motions and orders, and (3) discovery already taken shall be available and usable in the tag-along cases.[808] Consideration should also be given to means of reducing duplicative discovery activity and expediting later trials by measures such as videotaping key depositions or testimony given in bellwether trials, particularly of expert witnesses, for use at subsequent trials in the transferor courts after remand.

One of the values of multidistrict proceedings is that they bring before a single judge all of the cases, parties, and counsel comprising the litigation. They therefore afford a unique opportunity for the negotiation of a global settlement. Experience shows that few cases are remanded for trial; most multidistrict litigation is settled in the transferee court. In managing the litigation, therefore, the transferee judge should take appropriate steps to make the most of this opportu-

---

803. Van Dusen v. Barrack, 376 U.S. 612 (1964); *In re* Dow Co. "Sarabond" Prods. Liab. Litig., 666 F. Supp. 1466, 1468 (D. Colo. 1987).

804. *Compare In re* Korean Air Lines Disaster, 829 F.2d. 1171 (D.C. Cir. 1987), *aff'd on other grounds sub nom.* Chan v. Korean Air Lines Ltd., 490 U.S. 122 (1989) *with In re Dow Co. "Sarabond,"* 666 F. Supp. 1466 and cases cited therein.

805. *See, e.g.,* Berry Petroleum Co. v. Adams & Peck, 518 F.2d 402, 406 (2d Cir. 1975).

806. Whether under § 1404(a) a case may be transferred only for the determination of certain issues and whether a retransfer or second transfer may be ordered is not clear. *Compare In re* Air Crash Disaster Near Hanover, N.H., 342 F. Supp. 907 (D.N.H. 1971) *and* Starnes v. McGuire, 512 F.2d 918 (D.C. Cir. 1974) *with* Technitrol, Inc. v. McManus, 405 F.2d 84 (8th Cir. 1968).

807. See *supra* note 14, discussing the limitation on where cases may be transferred under § 1404. Even if all cases cannot be transferred to a single district for trial, transfer to a limited number of districts may be useful in facilitating coordination of further proceedings. This procedure may enable the transferee judge to transfer some or all of the cases to the judge's own court for trial.

808. For a discussion of the use of supplemental depositions, see *supra* § 21.453. See also Sample Order *infra* § 41.38.

nity and facilitate the settlement of the federal and any related state cases. See *infra* section 31.31.

31.133 Remand

Under 28 U.S.C. § 1407, actions not filed or terminated in the transferee court or transferred under § 1404 or § 1406 to that or another court are to be remanded by the panel, after appropriate pretrial proceedings, to the respective transferor courts for further proceedings and trial. When this should be done will depend on the circumstances of the litigation. In some cases, remands have been ordered relatively early, while substantial discovery remained to be done; in others, virtually all discovery had been completed and the cases were ready for trial at the time of remand to the transferor districts. Some of the constituent cases may be remanded, while others are retained for further centralized pretrial proceedings.

The panel looks to the transferee court to suggest when remand should be ordered; that court needs to consider at what point remand will best serve the expeditious disposition of the litigation. Under its rules, the panel may also order remand on its own initiative or on the motion of a party.[809] Although authorized to "separate any claim, cross claim, counter-claim, or third-party claim and remand any of such claims before the remainder of the action is remanded," the panel has rejected most requests to exclude portions of a case from transfer under § 1407,[810] believing that such matters may be given individualized treatment by the transferee court if warranted, and has concluded that it has no power to transfer (or sever and remand) particular "issues," as distinguished from particular "claims."[811]

After remand, the transferor court has exclusive jurisdiction and further proceedings in the transferee court with respect to a remanded case are not authorized absent a new transfer order by the panel.[812] Further pretrial proceedings, as needed, are then conducted in the transferor court; all cases remanded to the same court for additional proceedings and trial should be assigned at least initially to a single judge for coordination or consolidation in the transferor court. Although the transferor court has the power to vacate or modify rulings made by

809. Rule 14, Rules of Procedure of the JPML. Great deference is given to the views of the transferee judge. *See, e.g., In re* IBM Peripheral EDP Devices Antitrust Litig., 407 F. Supp. 254, 256 (J.P.M.D.C. 1976). Efforts by parties to use the panel as a substitute for appellate review, by seeking premature remand, have been uniformly rejected.

810. *But see In re* Hotel Tel. Charge Antitrust Litig., 341 F. Supp. 771 (J.P.M.L. 1972); *cf. In re* Midwest Milk Monopolization Litig., 386 F. Supp. 1401 (J.P.M.L. 1975).

811. *In re* Plumbing Fixture Case, 298 F. Supp. 484, 489–90 (J.P.M.L. 1968).

812. *See, e.g., In re* The Upjohn Co. Antibiotic Cleocin Prods. Liab. Litig., 508 F. Supp. 1020 (E.D. Mich. 1981). In unusual circumstances, the panel has by a new order again transferred a remanded case to the transferee district or transferred it to a new district as part of another multidistrict proceeding.

the transferee court, subject to comity and "law of the case" considerations, doing so in the absence of a significant change of circumstances would frustrate the purposes of centralized pretrial proceedings.[813]

The complete pretrial record is sent to the transferor court upon remand of the case. One of the final actions of the transferee court should be entry of a pretrial order that fully chronicles the proceedings, summarizes the rulings that will affect further proceedings, outlines the issues remaining for discovery and trial, and indicates the nature and expected duration of further pretrial proceedings; transferee courts are not expected to provide transferor courts with status reports during the pretrial proceedings. This order will assist the transferor courts in planning further proceedings and trial. In a few cases, the transferee judge has received intracircuit or intercircuit assignments under 28 U.S.C. § 292(b) and (d) to preside at trials of cases remanded to the transferor courts.

31.14 Coordination Between Courts

When related cases are pending in different districts and cannot be transferred to a single district, judges should consider taking steps to coordinate proceedings in their respective courts to avoid or minimize duplicative activity and conflicts in the proceedings and actions of the courts. Coordination may lead to substantial savings in cost and time, but depends on effective communication between judges and among judges and counsel.

Steps that may be taken include the following:

- **Special assignment of judge.** All cases may be assigned to a single judge designated under 28 U.S.C. §§ 292–293, 296 to sit temporarily in other districts where the cases are pending. Judges may be designated to serve in districts both within and outside of their own circuit.

- **Lead case.** Counsel in the various cases may agree with the judge to treat one as the "lead case." The agreement may provide for staying proceedings in the other cases pending resolution of the lead case, or rulings in the lead case may be given presumptive, though not conclusive, effect in the other courts.

- **Joint conferences and orders.** Joint hearings or conferences may be held and may be attended by all judges in person or by telephone.[814] The joint hearings may be followed by joint or parallel orders by the several courts in which the cases are pending.

---

813. *See* Stanley A. Weigel, *The Judicial Panel on Multidistrict Litigation, Transferor Courts and Transferee Courts*, 78 F.R.D. 575, 577 (1978).

814. Under Fed. R. Civ. P. 77(b), consent of the parties is required before trials or hearings may be conducted outside the district; consent is not required for other proceedings, such as conferences.

- **Joint appointments.** The several courts may coordinate the appointment of joint experts under Fed. R. Evid. 706, or special masters under Fed. R. Civ. P. 53, to avoid duplicate activity and inconsistencies. This may be useful in resolving numerous claims of privilege made in a number of cases on similar facts, or where global settlement negotiations are undertaken. The courts may also coordinate in making appointments of lead or liaison counsel.

- **Avoiding duplicative discovery.** Techniques to coordinate discovery and avoid duplication, such as those discussed in *supra* sections 21.423, 21.443, 21.452, and 21.464, should be considered. Deposition notices, interrogatories, and requests for productions should be filed or cross-filed in related cases to make the product of discovery usable in all cases and to avoid duplicative activity. Relevant discovery already completed should ordinarily be made available to litigants in the other cases.[815] If the material is subject to a protective order, the court usually may accommodate legitimate privacy interests by amending the order to include the new litigants within its restrictions,[816] and the party seeking the discovery may be required to bear an appropriate portion of the cost incurred in initially obtaining the information. Document production should be coordinated and joint depositories established.[817] To the extent practicable, the resolution of discovery disputes should be coordinated (e.g., by referring them to a single magistrate judge or special master).

- **Clarifying class definitions.** Conflicts between class actions, or between a class action and individual actions, can be avoided by coordination in drafting class definitions when actions are certified. See *infra* section 31.32.

- **Stays.** In appropriate cases, a judge may order an action stayed pending resolution of a related case in a federal court. See *infra* section 33.63.

---

815. *See* Wilk v. American Medical Ass'n, 635 F.2d 1295, 1299 (7th Cir. 1980) ("Where an appropriate modification of a protective order can place private litigants in a position they would otherwise reach only after repetition of another's discovery, such modification can be denied only where it would tangibly prejudice substantial rights of the party opposing modification. . . . Once such prejudice is demonstrated, however, the district court has broad discretion in judging whether that injury outweighs the benefits of any possible modification of the protective order.").

816. *Id.* at 1301.

817. *See* Fed. R. Civ. P. 26(b)(2) ("The frequency or extent of use of [discovery] . . . shall be limited by the court if it determines that: (i) the discovery is unreasonably . . . duplicative, or is obtainable from some other source that is more convenient, less burdensome, or less expensive. . . .").

31.2 Related Criminal and Civil Cases

Major problems of management arise in concurrent criminal and civil cases involving the same persons. Witnesses may claim the Fifth Amendment privilege in the civil actions, especially if examined prior to final resolution of the criminal proceedings,[818] and serious questions may arise as to the propriety of requiring an accused during the pendency of criminal charges to produce in civil proceedings either adverse (although nonprivileged) evidence or exculpatory evidence to which the prosecution would not be entitled under Fed. R. Crim. P. 16. The criminal proceeding should ordinarily have first priority because of the short pretrial period allowed under the Speedy Trial Act[819] and because of the potential impact of a conviction.[820] Suspending all pretrial activities in civil litigation until the criminal proceeding has been concluded, however, may be unnecessary and inadvisable, since it may be possible to conduct major portions of the discovery program in the civil cases without prejudice before completion of the criminal proceedings.[821]

Because of the need for careful coordination, related criminal and civil cases should be assigned, if possible, to the same judge (though, as noted in *supra* section 20.12, circumstances may exist that make assignment to the same judge inadvisable). Although the MDL panel has no authority to transfer criminal cases, it has frequently ordered transfer of civil actions to the location of related criminal proceedings. If the cases are assigned to different judges, the judges should at least communicate and coordinate informally. If grand jury materials from another court are sought, the two-step procedure described in *Douglas Oil Co. of Cal. v. Petrol Stops Northwest*[822] must be followed.

---

818. Termination of the criminal case will not necessarily result in testimony becoming available. *See* Pillsbury Co. v. Conboy, 459 U.S. 248 (1983) (witness compelled by grant of "use immunity" to give testimony to grand jury does not waive right to claim Fifth Amendment in subsequent civil litigation).

819. The complexity of the case may be a ground for extending the statutory time limits. 18 U.S.C. § 3161(h)(8)(B). See *infra* § 32.22.

820. Even if conviction will not preclude relitigation of issues raised in the civil proceeding, it may be admissible in the civil case as substantive evidence of the essential elements of the offense under Fed. R. Evid. 803(22) or as impeachment evidence under Fed. R. Evid. 609.

821. *See* Landis v. North Am. Co., 299 U.S. 248, 254–55 (1936); Texaco, Inc. v. Borda, 383 F.2d 607 (3d Cir. 1967).

822. 441 U.S. 211 (1979).

31.3 Related State and Federal Cases

31.31 Coordination

Increasingly, complex litigation involves related cases brought in both federal and state courts. Such litigation may involve numerous claims arising from a single event, such as a plane crash or a hotel fire, or from use of or exposure to harmful products or substances over a period of time (see *infra* section 33.2). Unless the defendant files for bankruptcy, no legal basis exists for the exercise of federal control over such litigation. Nevertheless, the cost and delay generated by such proliferation has led judges to undertake innovative efforts to bring about coordination of parallel or related litigation.[823] The approach to coordination will differ depending on the nature of the litigation; whether, for example, it arises out of a single event or out of a series of occurrences, and whether cases are pending within a single state or are dispersed across the country.

Where all of the cases are pending in a single state, coordination is relatively easy to accomplish. States increasingly have adopted procedures for the assignment of complex multiparty litigation to a single judge or judicial panel,[824] facilitating coordination between state and federal courts. Although the multidistrict litigation panel has no power over cases pending in state courts, it sometimes transfers federal cases to a district where related cases are pending in the state courts, in order to facilitate coordination. In such situations, judges have at times been able to achieve substantial coordination of various aspects of pretrial: coordinating scheduling of discovery, motions, and other pretrial events; appointing lead or liaison counsel; developing a coordinated management plan for the entire litigation; providing for joint discovery, such as by cross-noticing of depositions and making discovery taken in one case available in other cases (reciprocity, cost-sharing, and future cooperation may be required as conditions to obtaining discovery for use in other litigation); coordinating rulings on discovery disputes,

---

823. *See generally* William W Schwarzer et al., *Judicial Federalism in Action: Coordination of Litigation in State and Federal Courts*, 78 Va. L. Rev. 1689 (1992) (reporting on a study of eleven notable instances of state–federal coordination in litigation arising from (1) 1972 Federal Everglades Air Crash, (2) 1977 Beverly Hills Supper Club Fire, (3) 1979 Chicago Air Crash, (4) 1980 MGM Grand Hotel Fire, (5) 1981 Hyatt Skywalk Cases, (6) 1986 Technical Equities Fraud, (7) 1987 L'Ambience Plaza Collapse, (8) 1989 Exxon-Valdez Oil Spill, (9) 1989 Sioux City Air Crash, (10) Ohio asbestos litigation, and (11) Brooklyn Navy Yard asbestos litigation). See *infra* § 33.23.

824. Pennsylvania established a three-judge panel to manage and coordinate all breast implant litigation in its state courts, with power to stay, vacate, or modify any orders of any other Pennsylvania state trial court.

such as the assertion of privilege and using parallel orders to promote uniformity to the extent possible;[825] jointly considering class certification and other motions; and jointly conducting comprehensive settlement negotiations. Some courts have considered the possibility of conducting a joint trial, at which separate state and federal juries would sit in the same courtroom and hear common evidence, but substantial procedural and practical difficulties would have to be overcome.[826] Judges might agree that rulings on discovery or procedural matters of the court where a majority of the cases is pending be given presumptive effect by the other courts, or that the court with most of the cases take the lead in certain proceedings, such as class certification.[827] Coordination on a more limited basis can be achieved by designating the same attorneys to serve as lead counsel, appointing the same special master to resolve discovery disputes or facilitate settlement discussions, or using joint document depositories. The common experience of judges is that the willingness and ability to communicate effectively with each other is critical to the success of coordination. Counsel, however, can contribute substantially by initiating the effort and cooperating with it as it proceeds. Differences in procedure between state and federal courts have not been impediments to useful coordination.

Coordination becomes much more difficult and complex when cases are dispersed across a number of states, even where the federal cases are all centered in a single MDL transferee court. Clearly, the federal MDL judge cannot impose coordinated management on widely dispersed state courts; it is difficult even to obtain and communicate information about such widespread litigation. The greatest need, therefore, is for an information network that could form the basis for voluntary coordinated action by state court judges to the extent feasible under and consistent with their rules and procedures. The federal judge can serve as a catalyst for the development of an information network from which eventually some degree of state–federal coordination may emerge. In some litigation, coordinating committees of state court judges handling related cases have been formed with the support of the State Justice Institute. Such committees, with the help of the federal transferee judge, can serve as a channel of communication. They may also allow the development of a framework for coordination (perhaps including suggested forms of orders) to be recommended to the state judges assigned to the litigation in the various states.[828] Coordination may involve inviting state courts to participate in a program for coordinated national discovery while reserving to

825. See Sample Order *infra* § 41.51.

826. *See Judicial Federalism in Action, supra* note 823, at 1727–32.

827. *See, e.g.,* Union Light, Heat & Power Co. v. United States Dist. Ct., 588 F.2d 543 (6th Cir. 1979).

828. In the Silicone Breast Implant Litigation, a special master was appointed to serve as liaison between the federal and state judges and facilitate coordination.

them control of local discovery. Any coordination plan must take into account that cases in some state courts will reach trial sooner than those in others and needs, therefore, to retain substantial flexibility. It should be possible, however, to reach agreements that will minimize duplicative discovery activity, such as consolidated depositions of experts who will testify in numerous cases and maintaining document depositories. Coordination planning should also take into account that rulings of a single court have the potential of becoming preemptive; for example, the first court to reject a particular privilege claim will cause the material sought to be protected to become available for the entire litigation.[829]

31.32 Jurisdictional Conflicts

The pendency of related actions in state and federal courts can cause jurisdictional complexities and conflicts, leading to requests in the federal court either to stay or dismiss its proceeding or, conversely, to enjoin proceedings in the state court.

Generally, federal courts have a duty to exercise their jurisdiction. The mere pendency of parallel or related litigation in state court is not a basis for a refusal to exercise jurisdiction. Discretion to stay or dismiss the federal proceedings exists, however, in a limited number of circumstances. The court may stay its proceedings where a pending state proceeding may decide a pivotal question of state law, the decision of which may obviate the need for the federal court to decide a constitutional issue before it.[830] The court may dismiss an action in the interest of comity where state law claims are alleged and federal court litigation would impair a comprehensive state regulatory scheme.[831] And in exceptional circumstances, the federal court may dismiss an action to avoid piecemeal litigation where the state court has previously acquired jurisdiction of the *res* and is the more convenient forum.[832]

Where the action alleges both federal claims and related state law claims joined on the basis of supplemental jurisdiction, the district court may decline to exercise jurisdiction over a state law claim if the claim raises a novel or complex issue of state law, if it substantially predominates over the federal claims, if the district court has dismissed all federal claims, or, in exceptional circumstances, if there are compelling reasons for declining jurisdiction.[833] In making the decision

---

829. See *infra* § 33.22 for relevant provisions of case-management orders in the Silicone Breast Implant Litigation implementing state–federal coordination of multiple actions in many states.

830. Railroad Comm'n of Texas v. Pullman, 312 U.S. 496 (1941).

831. Burford v. Sun Oil Co., 319 U.S. 315 (1942).

832. Colorado River Water Conservation Dist. v. United States, 424 U.S. 800 (1976); *see also* Moses H. Cone Memorial Hosp. v. Mercury Constr. Corp., 460 U.S 1 (1983).

833. 28 U.S.C. § 1367. The court's discretion to dismiss claims entertained under its supplemental jurisdiction may be narrower than under the former doctrine of pendent jurisdiction. *See* Executive Software N. Am., Inc. v. District Ct., 15 F.3d 1484, 1491–97 (9th Cir. 1994) and cases

whether to retain the state law claims, the court should consider whether dismissal or remand will result in substantially duplicative litigation and unnecessary burdens on parties, witnesses, and the courts.

The federal court's power to interfere with parallel or related proceedings in state court is limited. The Anti-Injunction Act prohibits federal courts from enjoining or staying proceedings in a state court[834] except as expressly authorized by an Act of Congress,[835] or where necessary in aid of its jurisdiction, or to protect or effectuate its judgments. The exceptions under the Act are narrowly construed. The pendency of a parallel state court action does not warrant issuance of an injunction even though an earlier judgment in that action would be *res judicata* in the federal action.[836] Therefore, the fact that persons who fall within the scope of a class certified in a federal court action are maintaining parallel actions in state court does not afford a basis for interference with the state court actions during the pendency of the federal action. In arriving at an appropriate definition of a proposed class, however, the court may want to consider whether it can be drawn so as to avoid unnecessary conflict with state court actions.[837]

Courts have used the All Writs Act[838] to effectuate global settlements in large scale litigation. The Act enables the court to issue orders directed to nonparties in the pending litigation.[839] Under the Act, courts have enjoined or removed to federal court parallel state court litigation that would have frustrated comprehensive class settlements approved by the federal court binding on the parties to the state court litigation,[840] or that would have required relitigation in state court of a matter finally decided in federal court.[841]

---

cited therein. Where a case has been removed under 28 U.S.C. § 1441(c), discretion to remand the separate and independent state law claim may be broader.

834. 28 U.S.C. § 2283. *See also* Younger v. Harris, 401 U.S. 37 (1971).

835. The prime example of such authorizing legislation is 42 U.S.C. § 1983. *See* Mitchum v. Foster, 407 U.S. 225 (1972).

836. Vendo Co. v. Lektro-Vend Corp., 433 U.S. 623, 642 (1977).

837. Where the class is certified under Fed. R. Civ. P. 23(b)(3), class members have the right to opt out and litigate their claims independently in state or federal court.

838. 28 U.S.C. § 1651 authorizes federal courts to "issue all writs necessary or appropriate in aid of their respective jurisdictions and agreeable to the usages and principles of law."

839. *See* United States v. New York Tel. Co., 434 U.S. 159 (1977).

840. *In re* Baldwin-United Corp., 770 F.2d 328 (2d Cir. 1985); *In re* "Agent Orange" Prod. Liab. Litig., 996 F.2d 1425 (2d Cir. 1993), *cert. denied sub nom.* Ivy v. Diamond Shamrock Chem. Co., 114 S. Ct. 1125 (1994). *But cf. In re* Real Estate & Settlement Servs. Antitrust Litig., 869 F.2d 760 (3d Cir. 1989); Brown v. Ticor Title Ins. Co., 982 F.2d 386 (9th Cir. 1992), *cert. dismissed as improvidently granted*, 114 S. Ct. 1359 (1994) (due process requires that plaintiffs with monetary claims be given right to opt out of class action settlement).

841. *See* Kelly v. Merrill Lynch, 985 F.2d 1067 (11th Cir. 1993).

32. Criminal Cases

32.1 General Principles

Criminal cases differ significantly from civil cases, primarily because the defendant's liberty is at stake but also because of the procedural protections to be observed, the limited right to discovery, and the special problems concerning publicity and security. Nevertheless, complex criminal cases—cases involving numerous defendants or counts, voluminous evidence, complex or novel issues, unusual public interest, or a lengthy trial—require management. The general principles of early and active judicial involvement, creation of a plan for pretrial and trial, and professionalism of counsel therefore apply to complex criminal litigation as well, although their implementation will generally be different than in civil litigation.

This chapter discusses management techniques and practices that have been found useful in complex criminal litigation. As previously pointed out, there is no bright line dividing complex from other criminal cases; much of what is said in this chapter may therefore apply also to cases that may not be considered complex. At the same time, however, this chapter does not purport to be a comprehensive manual on the management of criminal litigation.[842] It is intended to provide a reference that judges and attorneys will find useful in developing and implementing the management of complex criminal litigation.

32.11 Early Judicial Supervision

When an indictment is returned in a potentially complex criminal case, the clerk's office, the U.S. Attorney's Office, and defense counsel should promptly notify the assigned judge.[843] The judge will want to review the indictment and consider the following matters:

- whether to alter the procedures by which routine criminal cases are handled—for example, whether to conduct or attend the arraignment if it would ordinarily be handled by a magistrate judge;

- whether to depart from any standing order or practice used by the judge in order to specially set significant dates—for arraignment, filing of motions, providing discovery, holding pretrial conferences, and starting trial;

- whether other commitments of the judge might conflict with the setting of an early trial date;[844] and

- whether the anticipated length of trial may require adjustment of normal case assignment procedures during the time before trial and while it is in progress.

Effective judicial supervision requires that the judge set the appropriate tone from the outset of the proceedings. This may be accomplished by:

- maintaining order and consistency in the conduct of the proceedings; when ground rules are laid down, such as for the filing of papers, the start of the trial day, and the taking of recesses, they should be observed;

- conducting the litigation in ways that will instill confidence in all parties that they will get a fair trial;

- communicating to the attorneys what the court expects of them and insisting on compliance with rules and directions governing the course of the proceedings, particularly when attorneys participating in the case come from other jurisdictions and may be unfamiliar with local practice;

---

842. The Federal Judicial Center is working with Judicial Conference committees to assess the need and appropriate focus for such a manual.

843. In courts in which criminal cases are not assigned to a judge until after arraignment, an individual assignment should nevertheless be specially made upon the filing of an indictment in a complex case. Some courts also have special assignment procedures designed to avoid assignment of complex criminal cases to judges already involved in a lengthy trial. *See, e.g.,* Local General Rule 2.11, U.S. District Court for the Northern District of Illinois.

844. In complex cases, the court has discretion, upon making appropriate findings, to extend the time for trial mandated by the Speedy Trial Act. 18 U.S.C. §§ 3161–3174. See *infra* § 32.22.

- insisting, within the limits demanded by fairness, that the case move expeditiously to conclusion; and

- encouraging cooperation among counsel; while recognizing counsel's obligation of zealous advocacy, the court can encourage them to confine themselves to issues that are reasonably disputable and not to assert rights that will have no impact on the outcome but whose exercise can cause delay.

In many courts, magistrate judges conduct most pretrial proceedings. In a complex case, the judge should consider whether, and to what extent, to instead conduct those proceedings personally. By holding the initial pretrial conference and hearing applications and motions, the judge will gain valuable early insight into the strategies and personalities of the attorneys and defendants, get a head start on identifying and addressing the issues and problems likely to arise as the case progresses, and save time that might have to be spent reviewing magistrate judges' rulings. On the other hand, experienced magistrate judges are competent to conduct criminal pretrial proceedings and can thereby free the judge's time for other pressing commitments. It may be advisable to consider the division of duties between judge and magistrate judge on a case-by-case basis to arrive at the most appropriate arrangement for the particular case.

While severance of counts and defendants for trial is common in complex cases, it may be advisable to defer that issue and conduct unified pretrial proceedings for the entire case. Similarly, where related criminal cases are pending in the court, pretrial proceedings—motion hearings and pretrial conferences—may be coordinated, whether or not the cases will be consolidated for trial.[845] Coordination is facilitated if all such cases in the same court are assigned to a single judge, at least for pretrial purposes.[846]

32.12 Representation

The Criminal Justice Act (CJA) requires that the court "furnish[] representation for any person financially unable to obtain adequate representation."[847]

---

845. Joint pretrial hearings of related criminal and civil cases may also be useful, particularly to deal with the sequence of discovery and trial and to avoid potential conflicts in the proceedings. See *supra* § 31.2.

846. Local rules ordinarily provide for assignment of related cases to a single judge, but even in the absence of such assignment, consolidation for limited purposes, such as ruling on challenges to a warrant or wiretap that resulted in multiple indictments, may be feasible.

847. 18 U.S.C.A. § 3006A(a) (West Supp. 1994). The statute contains detailed provisions as to which "financially eligible" persons must or may be provided representation—those who *must* be provided representation include all such persons charged with felonies or Class A misdemeanors, while those who *may* be provided representation include those charged with Class B or C misdemeanors and habeas petitioners. See *id.* § 3006A(a)(1)–(2). See also Fed. R. Crim. P. 44 (a) and (b)

"Representation" includes not only counsel, but "investigative, expert and other services necessary for adequate representation."[848] Making an appointment under the CJA[849] therefore requires two inquiries for each defendant: first, whether the defendant meets the criteria for financial eligibility,[850] and second, what services beyond those of counsel the defendant may require. Because costs escalate rapidly in complex litigation, the requirements of the Act must be closely observed.

The first inquiry is usually conducted without assistance of counsel; in a multidefendant case, each defendant must be questioned separately. If the information available to the court at the outset is insufficient to determine a defendant's entitlement conclusively, the court may appoint counsel but reserve the right to charge the defendant with some or all of the fees and costs should it later appear that the defendant is able to pay. In lengthy cases, courts usually approve periodic interim payments to counsel to avoid financial hardship.

If fees and the cost of other services authorized by the CJA are expected to be substantial,[851] it is advisable for counsel to submit estimates to the court early in the proceedings. Requests for services by investigators, interpreters, and other nonlawyers should be submitted early for court approval; payments for such services exceeding the maximum statutory amount (currently $1,000) require certification by the court and approval from the chief judge of the circuit.[852] In some cases, very large fees may be generated; the judge should receive from counsel all information necessary to review billings and exercise reasonable control of expenditures. Review of requests for investigatory, expert, or other trial-preparation expenses should usually be conducted ex parte in order to maintain the confidentiality of the defense's work product.

Cases involving non-English-speaking defendants (or defendants suffering from hearing impairment) are likely to require funds to compensate interpreters.[853] Where non-English-speaking defendants understand the same lan-

---

(dealing with appointment of counsel only); Bench Book, *supra* note 42, § 1.02 (assignment of counsel or pro se representation).

848. 18 U.S.C.A. § 3006A(a) (West Supp. 1994).

849. Although most districts have CJA implementation plans establishing a panel of attorneys eligible for appointment, the publicity generated by some criminal cases may lead attorneys who are not on the panel to seek appointment under the CJA. Appointment of nonpanel attorneys could harm the integrity of the plan and discourage others from serving on the panel.

850. 18 U.S.C.A. § 3006A(b) (West Supp. 1994).

851. *Id.* § 3006A(e). Certain services may be available under the CJA even if the defendant is not represented by counsel appointed under the Act.

852. *Id.* § 3006A(e)(3). Where large expenditures are anticipated, it may be advisable for the court to alert the chief judge and the Defender Services Division of the Administrative Office as soon as possible, particularly in districts without a federal defender office.

853. *See generally* the Court Interpreters Act, 28 U.S.C. § 1827.

guage, one interpreter may be used for all;[854] if, on the other hand, defendants understand only different languages or dialects, multiple interpreters may be needed.[855] Only qualified and reliable interpreters should be used; certified interpreters are available in most courts for the more common languages. The extent to which translation will be needed will vary, depending on such factors as the defendant's competency in English, the level of hearing impairment, and the complexity of the proceedings and testimony. The court has broad discretion over the manner in which interpreters are used, so long as the fairness of the trial is preserved.[856]

The CJA directs that the court "shall appoint separate counsel for persons having interests that cannot properly be represented by the same counsel."[857] When two or more defendants who are jointly charged or joined for trial are represented by the same counsel or counsel associated in the practice of law (whether appointed under the CJA or not), the court is required under Fed. R. Crim. P. 44(c) to "promptly inquire" about the joint representation, "personally advise each defendant of the right to . . . separate representation," and, unless no conflict is likely to arise, "take such measures as may be appropriate to protect each defendant's right to counsel."[858] Although the rule does not specify the procedure, case law generally requires a "searching inquiry" on the record in which the judge (1) personally advises each defendant of the potential dangers of joint representation, (2) allows the defendants to question the court as to the nature and consequences of joint representation, and, most importantly, (3) elicits a narrative response from each defendant (as opposed to simple assent to a series of questions from the bench) establishing that he or she has been advised of his or her rights, understands the potential conflict and its possible dangers, and voluntarily waives his or her rights in this regard in clear, unequivocal, and unambiguous words after consultation with his or her attorney or another counsel.[859] For specifics, the

854. See *infra* § 34.39 for a description of available technology.

855. Multiple reporters may also be needed if, because of fatigue or strain, they must work in shifts.

856. See Valladares v. United States, 871 F.2d 1564, 1566 (11th Cir. 1989).

857. 18 U.S.C.A. § 3006A(b) (West Supp. 1994).

858. See also ABA Standards Relating to the Function of the Trial Judge § 3.4(b) (Approved Draft, 1972). The duty to avoid conflicts of interest falls initially on counsel. Model Code of Professional Responsibility EC 5-15; ABA Standards for Criminal Justice: Prosecution Function and Defense Function, Standard 4-3.5(b) (3d ed. 1993). Attorneys representing joined defendants should promptly inform the court if they are associated in the practice of law or are being compensated by the same party. When a corporation or other business entity is a defendant, the same attorney should not ordinarily represent the entity and individual officers. See, e.g., In re Gopman, 531 F.2d 262, 266 (5th Cir. 1976) (union and its officials).

859. See United States v. Garcia, 517 F.2d 272, 278 (5th Cir. 1975).

law of the circuit should be consulted.[860] This inquiry should be made as soon as the possibility of joint representation becomes apparent in order to minimize delay should new counsel have to be retained. This inquiry is necessary even if the case is not going to trial[861] or the defendants initially consent to the joint representation.[862] Though substantial deference should be paid to defendants' right to counsel of their choice, the court may prohibit joint representation presenting a substantial possibility of conflict of interest even if the defendant waives the right to conflict-free representation.[863] Such possible conflicts of interest may arise in a variety of contexts, including where an attorney has represented multiple clients during a grand jury investigations where an attorney's former client is a codefendant or potential witness,[864] and where an attorney received privileged information as the result of a joint defense agreement with a codefendant or potential witness.[865]

In multiparty cases the court needs to consider whether to call on defense counsel to organize themselves for pretrial and trial; the use of lead and liaison counsel furthers the efficient and economical conduct of the litigation but may be inadvisable in a criminal case in the face of objection by a party.[866] It may, however, be possible for counsel to avoid duplicate work by dividing various trial preparation tasks, such as reviewing or translating documents, listening to and transcribing tapes, interviewing witnesses, conducting investigations, preparing expert testimony, and preparing demonstrative evidence for use at trial.[867] Where appropriate, defense motions should be filed jointly, avoiding the preparation of duplicate paper work. In particularly complex cases, some courts have appointed coordinating counsel for the defense, not to represent any defendant but to assist in the administration of the case and serve as a communication link between the

---

860. *See also* Bench Book, *supra* note 42, § 1.22 (Supp. June 1989) (problems with and procedures for joint representation), § 1.23 (3d ed. 1986) (form for waiver of conflict of interest).

861. United States v. Mari, 526 F.2d 117, 121 (2d Cir. 1975) (Oakes, C.J., concurring).

862. United States v. Dolan, 570 F.2d 1177 (3d Cir. 1978).

863. United States v. Wheat, 486 U.S. 153 (1988).

864. *See* United States v. Kenny, 911 F.2d 315, 320–21 (9th Cir. 1990) (potential conflict required disqualification where attorney represented two business associates, both under investigation, and government had approached each for information about the other).

865. *See* Wilson P. Abraham Constr. Corp. v. Armco Steel Corp., 559 F.2d 250, 253 (5th Cir. 1977) (breach of fiduciary duty for attorney to use confidential information received pursuant to joint defense agreement to later detriment of codefendant).

866. See *supra* § 20.22 for discussion of the appointment and duties of lead and liaison counsel.

867. Should an emergency require the temporary absence of a defense attorney during a lengthy trial, the court may, with the consent of the affected parties, permit another attorney to represent the excused attorney's client during this absence.

court and the various defense counsel.[868] The appointment may be made under the CJA, and the court must determine how such counsel is to be compensated.[869]

A defendant has a constitutional right to proceed pro se,[870] but waiver of the right to counsel must be made knowingly and intelligently.[871] Before allowing a defendant to proceed pro se, the court must conduct an on-the-record colloquy (similar to that conducted in the case of joint representation) in which the defendant is made aware of the nature of the charge, the range of penalties, the dangers and disadvantages of self-representation,[872] the fact that specialized training and expertise are generally required to conduct an effective defense, the possibility that an attorney might be better able to develop and present defenses to the charge, and the fact that the judge believes it to be in defendant's best interest to be represented by counsel.[873] Most judges have found it advisable to appoint standby counsel, even over defendant's objection, to assist a pro se defendant and protect codefendants from prejudice.[874] Standby counsel may advise and assist the defendant in any way, but decisions must be left to the defendant, and counsel's presence must not be so intrusive as to destroy the jury's perception that the defendant is representing himself.[875] A pro se defendant should be instructed to comply with and observe applicable rules and refrain from speaking in the first person as though he or she were testifying; if the pro se defendant violates the rules, curative instructions to the jury may be necessary.[876]

On occasion, a defendant will be unwilling to continue with present counsel, even after the trial has started. If there is good cause, the court should first seek substitute counsel, who must be given sufficient time to prepare, but may have to grant a defendant's request to proceed pro se.[877] Once trial begins, however, the defendant's right to self-representation is qualified; at that point, the judge must

---

868. For a description of the use of coordinating counsel, see United States v. Mosquera, 813 F. Supp. 962 (E.D.N.Y. 1993).

869. *See id.* at 968 (holding it proper to compensate such counsel under § 3006A of the CJA).

870. Faretta v. California, 422 U.S. 806 (1975). For case law on the numerous issues raised by pro se representation, see Manual on Recurring Problems in Criminal Trials § I(A) (Federal Judicial Center 3d ed. 1990).

871. *Faretta*, 422 U.S. at 835.

872. *Id.*

873. *See* Manual on Recurring Problems in Criminal Trials, *supra* note 870, § I(A)(1) (citing cases); for a sample procedure, *see* Bench Book, *supra* note 42, § 1.02(3).

874. McKaskle v. Wiggins, 465 U.S. 168 (1984); Manual on Recurring Problems in Criminal Trials, *supra* note 870, § I(A)(3) (citing *McKaskle* and other cases on standby counsel).

875. *McKaskle,* 465 U.S. at 178.

876. United States v. Sacco, 563 F.2d 552, 556 (2d Cir. 1977) (also discussing other suggested measures).

877. For case law addressing the issues involved in substitution of counsel, see Manual on Recurring Problems in Criminal Trials, *supra* note 870, § I(B).

weigh the prejudice to defendant from denying his request against the disruptive effect on the trial if the request is granted.[878]

A defendant may at times seek to break away from counsel to conduct personal negotiations with the prosecution. Ethical rules generally prohibit attorneys from communicating with a represented adverse party about the subject matter of the representation without the consent of that party's attorney.[879] Circumstances may arise in criminal cases, however, that make it imperative for a defendant to seek to communicate directly with the prosecution.[880] When such a situation arises, it should be promptly brought to the judge's attention. To protect the defendant's legitimate interests, the judge should probably question the defendant about his or her unwillingness to be represented by current defense counsel during the communication with the prosecution, and ensure that this decision is not the product of coercion or other improper influences. Depending on the results of this questioning, the judge may direct the prosecution not to confer with the defendant until new counsel, even if only temporary, has been secured. If the judge finds that improper communications between the prosecution and a defendant have already occurred, sanctions may be appropriate, such as suppression of evidence obtained through the improper contact, reprimand of the prosecutor or a contempt citation, reference to the state bar for possible disciplinary proceedings, request for appropriate action by the Department of Justice, or, in an extreme case, dismissal of the indictment.[881]

---

878. Sapienza v. Vincent, 534 F.2d 1007, 1010 (2d Cir. 1976); *see also* Chapman v. United States, 553 F.2d 886, 893 (1977) (citing cases).

879. *See* Model Rules of Professional Conduct 4.2; Model Code of Professional Responsibility DR 7-104. Every state and the District of Columbia have adopted a version of the rules or the code. Courts have unanimously held that federal prosecutors are not exempt from Rule 4.2 and DR 7-104, but disagree as to when the prohibition applies. *See, e.g.,* United States v. Powe, 9 F.3d 68, 69 (9th Cir. 1993) (communication permissible before indictment in noncustodial context); United States v. Lopez, 4 F.3d 1455, 1461 (9th Cir. 1993) (prosecution's duty to refrain from communication begins "at the latest" upon indictment); United States v. Hammad, 858 F.2d 834, 837–40 (2d Cir. 1988) (dicta) (applicability of prohibition not bound to moment of indictment, but generally inapplicable to preindictment, noncustodial context, absent misconduct); Annotated Model Rules of Professional Conduct Rule 4.2 comment at 432–34 (2d ed. 1992). The Justice Department has promulgated a regulation, opposed by the National Conference of Chief Justices and others, which would allow government attorneys to communicate with represented persons in certain circumstances. *See* 28 C.F.R. § 77 (1995); 59 Fed. Reg. 39910 (Aug. 4, 1994). *See also Justice Department Contacts with Represented Persons,* 78 Judicature 136 (Nov.–Dec. 1994).

880. *See Lopez,* 4 F.3d at 1461 (dicta) (in appropriate case, court may order prohibition lifted).

881. *See* United States v. Lopez, 765 F. Supp. 1433, 1461 (N.D. Cal. 1991) (citing cases); *Lopez,* 4 F.3d at 1464 (reversing dismissal of indictment but approving other sanctions).

32.2 Pretrial

32.21 Conferences

An early initial pretrial conference is an important element of effective case management. Fed. R. Crim. P. 17.1 authorizes the judge, at any time after the filing of an indictment, to order one or more conferences "to consider such matters as will promote a fair and expeditious trial."[882] This is the judge's first opportunity to organize the case and set the tone for its conduct, as previously discussed.[883] In addition to establishing a schedule and addressing the various pretrial issues discussed below, the following matters may be considered:

- calling on the prosecution to describe succinctly the substance of the charges and substance of the evidence against defendants, the nature of discovery materials, the estimated length of trial, and anticipated procedural problems; and to identify any related cases; and inviting defense counsel to do the same to the extent they are willing;

- beginning the process of identifying and narrowing issues;

- inviting counsel to submit stipulations on uncontested matters before trial (e.g., that a bank is a national bank, that the handwriting is the defendant's, that commerce is involved, or that a substance is what it is alleged to be);

- inviting recommendations or proposals from counsel for the management of the case;

- advising counsel of standing orders or special procedures that will apply to the case;

- where attorneys participating in the case are from outside the jurisdiction or are unfamiliar with federal court procedure, alerting them to critical

---

882. Although by its terms the rule applies only if the defendant is represented by counsel, courts schedule pretrial conferences in cases where defendants represent themselves. In such cases, no sanctions should be imposed for nonattendance, nor any attempt made to obtain stipulations.

883. See *supra* § 32.11.

requirements and ensuring that they are prepared and competent to practice in the court;[884] and

- informing appointed counsel of the procedures for payment of interim fees and expenses and the need to obtain advance approval for investigative and expert services.[885]

A criminal defendant has a constitutional right to be present at all critical stages of the proceedings against him if his presence would contribute to the fairness of the proceedings.[886] Therefore, although Fed. R. Crim. P. 43(c)(3) provides that a defendant need not be present "at a conference or argument upon a question of law," and a defendant may specifically waive attendance, it is generally inadvisable to hold a conference in the absence of a defendant. Even a conference intended only to address a point of law might lead to a discussion at which the defendant should be present. If the defendant is in pretrial detention, arrangements for conferences need to be made so as to minimize the complications and delays involved in transporting him to the courthouse; advance notice to and coordination with the marshal are advisable as well as efforts to have the defendant held at a nearby location. Security and space considerations will often make it advisable, especially in multidefendant cases, to hold conferences in the courtroom rather than in chambers. Arrangements must also be made to permit private consultation between defendants and their attorneys or among counsel.

All conferences should be held on the record to avoid later confusion or disagreement and to preserve a record for appellate review. Fed. R. Crim. P. 17.1 requires that the court, at the conclusion of every pretrial conference, prepare and file a memorandum of all matters agreed on. The court has broad authority to issue orders "not inconsistent with" the federal and local rules that will expedite the litigation.[887]

---

884. The court should also be alert to any sign that counsel may fail to meet minimum standards of competent representation satisfying the Sixth Amendment. McMann v. Richardson, 397 U.S. 759, 771 (1970). Signs of possible inadequacy include lack of preparation, failure to make appropriate requests to the prosecution for exculpatory materials, and failure to preserve important rights of the defendant. William W Schwarzer, *Dealing with Incompetent Counsel—The Trial Judge's Role*, 93 Harv. L. Rev. 633, 656–58 (1980). If these raise concerns about counsel's competence, the judge may give counsel assistance (on the record and before opposing counsel), admonish counsel, allow defendant to change counsel, appoint advisory counsel, or require substitution of counsel, using the least obtrusive means necessary to remedy observed deficiencies. *Id.* at 650, 659.

885. *See* 18 U.S.C.A. § 3006A(e) (West Supp. 1993).

886. Kentucky v. Stincer, 482 U.S. 730, 745 (1987). A waiver by defendant of this right must be on the record. Presence by remote video transmission is discussed in *infra* § 34.31.

887. Fed. R. Crim. P. 57 allows judges to "regulate their practice in any manner not inconsistent with" federal and local rules.

32.22 Schedules

Although criminal cases are subject to the time limits of the Speedy Trial Act, the exception for complex cases, coupled with the exclusion of time during the pendency of motions, can lead to substantial delays.[888] While the Act is intended to allow defendants sufficient time to prepare adequately for trial in a complex case, it requires cases to be tried as expeditiously as is consistent with fairness to the parties. The complexity of a case is a relevant consideration in establishing a fair schedule for pretrial and trial, but it is not a license for automatic and indefinite delay. If the case is to move expeditiously to conclusion, it is essential that the court establish a schedule for all important events at the initial conference, or in any event as early as possible, and enforce compliance with it. The schedule should be established only after consultation with counsel. In complex cases involving a number of criminal defense attorneys, the court will inevitably have to accommodate various conflicting commitments.[889] Once the schedule has been worked out, however, counsel should understand that they will be bound by it and no continuances will be granted for personal or professional conflicts. The following matters should be considered in establishing the schedule:

- Setting a firm trial date—when that is not feasible at the early conference because not enough is known about the case, a date should at least be fixed for the setting of a trial date.

- Setting firm dates for the filing and hearing of motions—different dates may be set for different motions (in limine motions, for example, may be filed in connection with the final pretrial conference), and a terminal date may be set at which time all motions not filed are deemed waived.

- Setting a firm date for the delivery of discovery by the respective parties—generally disclosure should be made by the government soon after the arraignment to enable the defendant to prepare his defense and evaluate any proffered plea agreement (see *infra* section 32.24).

- Setting a firm date for giving notice of any defense based on alibi, mental condition, or public authority.[890]

32.23 Pretrial Hearings

Evidentiary hearings on motions should ordinarily be scheduled well in advance of trial, particularly those that may take substantial time to hear or that, if granted, will significantly affect the scope or course of trial. Apart from avoiding

---

888. 18 U.S.C. § 3161(h). The time limits are not subject to being waived by the defendant. For discussion of the Act, see Bench Book, *supra* note 42, § 1.19.

889. When those commitments are in state court cases, the judge may want to contact the state court judge to coordinate the respective calendars.

890. Fed. R. Crim. P. 12.1, 12.2, 12.3.

interruptions of the trial, an early hearing has several advantages. If the motion is decided in favor of the defendant, an appeal may be taken by the prosecution with little or no delay of the trial. If the motion is decided in favor of the prosecution, the defendant can enter a conditional guilty plea under Fed. R. Crim. P. 11(a)(2), preserving the right to appeal the ruling. Pretrial hearings on motions in limine under Fed. R. Evid. 104 enable the court to rule on various evidentiary issues, such as the use of convictions under Fed. R. Evid. 609 and evidence of other acts under Fed. R. Evid. 404(b), and (in rare cases) the admissibility of coconspirator statements under Fed. R. Evid. 801(d)(2)(E), thereby streamlining the trial.[891] Pretrial rulings on pivotal evidentiary issues are facilitated if the prosecution is required to give advance notice of its intent to offer such evidence, along with a supporting memorandum. Addressing these issues before trial allows the judge and attorneys to give them more deliberate consideration than during trial, although it may be impossible to decide certain issues, such as relevance, without taking into account evidence received at trial and the posture of the parties at that time.[892] If pretrial rulings are made, the court should indicate whether they are final (not renewable at trial) or provisional (subject to modification or requiring formal renewal at trial as a condition to any claim of error).

Pretrial hearings are also an appropriate occasion for receiving status reports from counsel, inquiring about the progress of the various phases of the case, such as production of discovery material, monitoring the government's compliance with its obligations to produce exculpatory and other material matter, determining whether any problems have arisen affecting the schedule for the case, and reminding counsel of upcoming scheduled events in the case.

32.24 Discovery

Pretrial discovery in criminal cases, unlike that available in civil litigation, is limited. Fed. R. Crim. P. 16 requires the government on request to produce statements of the defendant and his criminal record; on request the government must also produce relevant documents and tangible objects, reports of examinations and tests, and a summary of the prospective testimony of expert witnesses, but such a request obligates the defense to make reciprocal disclosure.[893] A motion for

---

891. See generally Manual on Recurring Problems in Criminal Trials, supra note 870, § V(A) (evidence; admissibility); United States v. N.L. Indus., Inc., 1990–1991 Trade Cas. (CCH) ¶ 69,036 (E.D. La. 1990) (requiring government to proffer conspiracy evidence at pretrial hearing for ruling on hearsay objection).

892. For example, the balancing of probative value and prejudicial effect of a prior conviction under Fed. R. Evid. 609(a) may require consideration of trial testimony. Note that a pretrial ruling admitting a defendant's prior conviction for impeachment will not be reviewable on appeal if the defendant as a result decides not to testify. See Luce v. United States, 469 U.S. 38 (1984).

893. In multiparty cases, a request by one defendant will be treated as made on behalf of all defendants, imposing the reciprocal obligations on each defendant.

a bill of particulars under Fed. R. Crim. P. 7(f) is limited to clarification of the charges against the defendant and cannot be used for discovery of supporting evidence.[894] The parties have no right to take depositions for discovery purposes[895] except that under Fed. R. Crim. P. 15, "in exceptional circumstances," the court may permit a party to take the deposition of one of its own witnesses to preserve the testimony for trial.[896] The parties have no right to obtain in advance of trial the names of their adversaries' witnesses, except to the extent provided in Rule 12.1 when an alibi defense is raised and Rule 12.3 when the defense of public authority is asserted.[897] Under the Jencks Act, the defendant is entitled to production of statements of a prosecution witness, but only after completion of the witness's direct examination; under Rule 26.2, the prosecution has similar access to statements of defense witnesses other than the defendant.[898]

Fed. R. Crim. P. 17(c) allows the use of subpoenas to compel third-party production of documents and objects. While the court should not allow this procedure to be used for "fishing expeditions," it may permit parties to use it to marshal and organize documents in the possession of third parties when such evidence is relevant, not otherwise reasonably obtainable, and needed to prepare properly for trial.[899] Depending on how much judicial control is needed, the court may require prior approval of subpoenas, or of certain categories of subpoenas, or give the parties general authority to issue them. Such authority does not

894. See, e.g., United States v. Davis, 582 F.2d 947, 951 (5th Cir. 1978).

895. The parties may, however, arrange for the defense to conduct informal pretrial interviews of consenting prosecution witnesses. See Manual on Recurring Problems in Criminal Trials, supra note 870, § V(B)(4). This may significantly improve trial preparation; the court should therefore encourage the practice subject only to legitimate needs to protect witnesses' safety.

896. The court may order depositions on motion in criminal cases only when "due to exceptional circumstances in the case it is in the interest of justice that the testimony of a prospective witness of a party be taken and preserved for use at trial," or the witness is detained pursuant to 18 U.S.C. § 3144 (release or detention of a material witness). Fed. R. Crim. P. 15(a). See also 18 U.S.C. § 3503.

897. Fed. R. Crim. P. 12.1 requires the defendant to give notice of an alibi defense and provide a list of the witnesses on whom he intends to rely to establish the alibi, and imposes on the prosecution a reciprocal duty to provide a list of the witnesses on whom it intends to rely to establish the defendant's presence at the scene of the offense or to rebut the defense witnesses' alibi testimony. In addition, Fed. R. Crim. P. 12.3 requires the defendant to give notice of a defense of public authority and allows the government to demand a list of the witnesses on whom the defendant intends to rely to establish the defense, triggering a reciprocal duty to disclose witnesses the government intends to rely upon in opposing the defense.

898. 18 U.S.C. § 3500; Fed. R. Crim. P. 26.2. Disputes may arise over what constitutes a "statement" for Jencks Act purposes. See Manual on Recurring Problems in Criminal Trials, supra note 870, § III(A).

899. See United States v. Iozia, 13 F.R.D. 335, 338 (S.D.N.Y. 1952), cited with approval in United States v. Nixon, 418 U.S. 683, 699 (1974).

constitute a ruling on the admissibility of the evidence thereby obtained, and does not preclude a motion to quash.

Although involuntary discovery from parties in criminal cases is limited, broad disclosure is possible if the parties consent. For example, the Jencks Act does not prevent the voluntary early production of the statements of prosecution witnesses; prosecutors can generally be persuaded to make early production since, by giving the defense an opportunity to prepare, it will avoid interruptions at trial and may lead to a plea. As an inducement to broadened pretrial discovery, the defense may be willing to agree not to raise objections regarding authenticity or to contest certain readily provable facts (e.g., interstate commerce; see *supra* section 32.21). Such issues can be resolved without formal motions at a pretrial hearing—called an "omnibus hearing" in some districts. In many districts the U.S. Attorney, frequently at the urging of the court, has adopted an "open file" policy for most criminal cases. Other courts by local rule require counsel to meet and exchange discoverable information before filing pretrial motions.

The judge should encourage such voluntary disclosures, subject to the defendant's right not to commit to a defense until the end of the prosecution's case. Voluntary disclosure, and often exchange, is particularly appropriate in cases charging "white collar" crimes, such as securities fraud or antitrust violations, that typically involve voluminous documents and accounting and other technical data. Discovery in such cases may be managed much as it is in complex civil litigation, with the court taking early and active control.[900] The parties should produce documents, including indexes and other finding guides, in a manner that will facilitate efficient review. The court should set an early date by which each party must identify the exhibits it intends to use in its case in chief, with additional exhibits allowed subsequently for good cause only. In producing documents pursuant to Rule 16(a)(1)(c) that are "material to the preparation" of the defense, the prosecution may be asked to separately identify those materials it *will* use and those it *may* use at trial. While all relevant documents should be produced, excessive production may hamper the defense by burying it under marginally relevant material. Documents should be marked for production and consecutively numbered to prevent later disputes over whether a document was produced.

In the absence of cooperation by the government, the judge needs to take steps to ensure that the defendant's rights to disclosure are observed in meaningful ways. The defendant is entitled to the timely production of exculpatory and other material matter in the government's possession that will assist in the preparation of the defense, and judicial oversight may be necessary to ensure that the

---

900. See *supra* § 21.4.

government complies with its obligation.[901] The judge may enter a specific order requiring the government to produce all such materials and specifying the date for compliance.[902] The court may also, in the exercise of its inherent supervisory power, require the prosecution to provide lists of witnesses and exhibits in advance of trial.[903] Early disclosure of such materials is important because it may be critical to the defendant's strategic decisions. Because the government often establishes a deadline for the acceptance of a proffered plea bargain, fairness requires that the disclosure to which defendant is entitled be made in a timely manner. Moreover, such disclosure facilitates counsel's preparation for trial and avoids unnecessary work. It will also enable the judge to conduct a more effective pretrial conference, which can eliminate unnecessary witnesses, encourage stipulations, and generally streamline the trial.

Under the Jencks Act, both the prosecution and the defense are required to produce all witness statements that relate to the subject matter concerning which the witness has testified. Although the government is under no duty to produce the material before the witness has testified, many prosecutors will do so, particularly when urged by the court and given to understand how denying the defendant a recess to examine a statement until after the direct testimony of each af-

---

901. Brady v. Maryland, 373 U.S. 83 (1963), requires the prosecution to disclose exculpatory and other material evidence upon specific request from the defense. United States v. Agurs, 427 U.S. 97 (1976), extended this requirement to cases where the defense has made no request or only a general request for *Brady* material. In United States v. Bagley, 473 U.S. 667 (1985), a majority of the Court adopted a unified test of materiality for specific, general and no request cases, requiring disclosure whenever there is a "reasonable probability" that the evidence would affect the result of the proceeding; the existence of a specific request may, however, be relevant to this analysis. *See* 2 Wayne R. LaFave & Jerold H. Isreal, Criminal Procedure § 19.5 at 181–83 (West Supp. 1991). The disclosure requirement extends to matters affecting the credibility of key prosecution witnesses, such as inducements given to obtain their testimony. *See Bagley,* 473 U.S. at 676–77; Giglio v. United States, 405 U.S. 150 (1972). The judge should caution the prosecution that failure to comply with its disclosure obligations may result in a mistrial or dismissal, even where extensive time and effort have already been expended. *See, e.g.,* United States v. Boyd, 833 F. Supp. 1277 (N.D. Ill. 1993) (granting new trials after multiyear prosecutions primarily on ground of failure to disclose inducements given to government witnesses). Prosecutors should resolve doubts in favor of disclosure or consult with the judge. See *Agurs,* 427 U.S. at 108, and other cases cited in Manual on Recurring Problems in Criminal Trials, *supra* note 870, § III(B)(2).

902. The court has the authority to direct when *Brady* material must be disclosed. United States v. Starusko, 729 F.2d 256, 261 (3d Cir. 1984). The government should make disclosure in time "to allow the defense to use the favorable material effectively in the preparation and presentation of its case." United States v. Pollack, 534 F.2d 964, 973 (D.C. Cir. 1976). For additional case law on the timing of disclosure of *Brady* material, see Manual on Recurring Problems in Criminal Trials, *supra* note 870, § III(B)(4).

903. *See, e.g.,* United States v. Napue, 834 F.2d 1311, 1318 (7th Cir. 1987); United States v. Higgs, 713 F.2d 39, 44 n.6 (3d Cir. 1983) (citing cases).

fected witness will disrupt the trial.[904] While the Jencks Act entitles the government to withhold such material, there is nevertheless little reason to do so—it disrupts and delays the litigation—in the absence of legitimate security or perjury concerns, particularly if the government has pressured the defendant by imposing a deadline for accepting a plea bargain.

Discovery in criminal cases should be coordinated with that in related civil litigation.[905] As discussed in *supra* section 31.2, a stay of some discovery in the civil litigation will sometimes be needed. The prosecution may ask the court trying the civil case to stay discovery to prevent defendants from taking advantage of it in the criminal case. Similarly, the defense may ask the court to stay the civil case to avoid the prejudice of having to assert the Fifth Amendment privilege during the pendency of the criminal case. The discovery available in civil cases may, however, occasionally be used to obtain information that will allow the related criminal proceedings to be conducted more effectively and efficiently.

32.25 Electronic Surveillance

Complex criminal cases frequently involve extensive electronic surveillance. The legality of the surveillance and the admissibility of its product must be determined by pretrial motions.[906] The government should promptly produce all underlying documentation necessary to determine whether the surveillance was properly authorized and conducted. If the same surveillance material is at issue in more than one case, the court should consider consolidation of the motion hearings.

Extensive electronic surveillance presents significant logistical problems, particularly in multidefendant cases and cases involving non-English speaking defendants. Defense counsel must be given adequate time to review the prosecution's recordings. In order to expedite trial preparation, the prosecution should identify as soon as possible conversations that it anticipates offering at trial and promptly make available logs or indices identifying the participants and any defendants the government contends are referred to or mentioned. Defense counsel should coordinate and divide the responsibility of reviewing and transcribing the tapes.

The prosecution should also promptly produce transcripts of any recordings it expects to present at trial, upon defendants' agreement that any differences

---

904. *See* United States v. Minsky, 963 F.2d 870, 876 (6th Cir. 1992) (while government cannot be required to make early disclosure of Jencks Act material, it should nevertheless do so to allow defense opportunity to review undisputed material and court to rule on remainder).

905. See *supra* §§ 21.455, 31.2.

906. Under 18 U.S.C. § 3504, if the defense claims that evidence is inadmissible as the product of allegedly unlawful electronic surveillance, the prosecution must affirm or deny the occurrence of the allegedly unlawful act.

between the drafts produced and the versions presented at trial will not be commented on. The parties should be asked to reach agreement in advance of trial on the text of transcripts, including the proper translation of any material in a foreign language. Only to the extent that there are material disagreements should multiple versions be presented at trial. The process of reviewing tapes and producing transcripts may be quite lengthy.[907]

Prior to trial, tapes and transcripts should be organized for quick reference and efficient presentation. Entering transcripts into a computer database, for example, facilitates finding particular words or names. The equipment to be used for jury presentation should be tested in advance of trial to eliminate any glitches. Stipulations should be sought as to chain of custody and foundation.

32.26 Classified Information

The Classified Information Procedures Act[908] defines classified information and establishes procedures for cases potentially involving such information. After filing of the indictment, any party may move under the Act for a pretrial conference to consider matters relating to classified information. Following such a motion, or upon its own motion, the court must then "promptly" hold such a conference.[909] At this conference, the judge must establish the timing of (1) requests for discovery, (2) defendant's required giving of notice of intent to disclose classified information,[910] and (3) the commencement of the procedure under section 6 of the Act (discussed below) for reviewing and ruling on evidence involving classified information.[911] The court should also take steps to obtain expedited security clearances for the defendants, their attorneys, and court personnel (clearance is not required for the judge and jurors).[912] Once it is established that classified information issues will arise, the Department of Justice will appoint a court security officer, who will work with the court and parties on security mat-

---

907. Even recordings in a foreign language should, upon a party's request, be played for the jury, since the tone of a conversation may have evidentiary value. The jury can evaluate, for example, whether a statement reported in a transcript was made jokingly. The judge should ask the jurors whether any of them understand the foreign language. *See* Hernandez v. New York, 500 U.S. 352 (1991) (no violation of *Batson* where attorney exercised peremptory challenges against Spanish-speaking jurors indicating possible difficulty in following official translation, but might be impermissible to challenge all jurors who understand the language at issue); Pemberthy v. Beyer, 19 F.3d 857 (3d Cir. 1994) (permissible to use peremptory challenges against Spanish-speaking jurors). Such jurors should be instructed that only the translation is evidence that they may consider. *Hernandez*, 500 U.S. at 369 (Stevens, J., dissenting).

908. 18 U.S.C.A. App. at 621 (West 1985).

909. *Id.* § 2.

910. *See id.* § 5. If the court does not set a time, notice must be given thirty days before trial. *Id.*

911. *Id.* § 2.

912. *See id.* at note following § 9.

ters.[913] This officer, although employed by the Justice Department, is independent from the prosecution.

Other security measures specified in the Act will apply, including limitations on the public disclosure of court filings.[914] As stated above, the defense must notify the court and the government if it expects to disclose or cause the disclosure of classified information, whether at trial or during pretrial, including in the notice a brief description of the information.[915] The government may require the court to "conduct a hearing to make all determinations concerning the use, relevance or admissibility of classified information."[916] This hearing must be held *in camera* upon certification of the Attorney General.[917] The court must make specific written determinations as to each item on which it has been asked to rule.[918] To the extent the court finds particular classified information relevant, the government may move for the substitution of a statement admitting relevant facts or a summary.[919] If the court finds that these alternatives do not adequately protect the defendant's rights—and the government refuses to authorize disclosure of the information—the court may dismiss the entire indictment or specific counts, or impose other sanctions upon the prosecution.[920]

The Act is designed to require the judge to pass on relevance, use, and admissibility of classified information *prior to* trial. Although this may run counter to the court's preference to rule on admissibility in context at trial, it allows the government to evaluate the classified information "costs" of proceeding with a particular prosecution. If the prosecution goes forward, the court may take steps at trial to prevent the unnecessary disclosure of classified information.[921]

913. *Id.*

914. See *id.* § 3, requiring the court, upon motion of the United States, to issue an order protecting against disclosure of any classified information disclosed to the defendant by the United States, and § 6(e)(1), imposing the same requirement if, after review, the court denies a government motion to provide the information by alternate means and the government files an affidavit of the Attorney General objecting to disclosure. See also *id.* § 6(d), requiring sealing of the record of an *in camera* hearing at which the court determines that the information at issue may not be disclosed or elicited.

915. *Id.* § 5. Under the Act, the government has a duty of pretrial notification only when it must establish that the material relates to classified information or the national defense as an element of the offense. *Id.* § 10.

916. *Id.* § 6(a).

917. *Id.*

918. *Id.*

919. *Id.* § 6(c).

920. *Id.* § 6(e)(2). The prosecution has the right to an immediate expedited appeal from any such order, *id.* § 7, and the order does not take effect until it has had that opportunity. *Id.* § 6(e).

921. *Id.* § 8.

32.27 Publicity[922]

Complex criminal trials often involve personalities or events that command widespread public interest and attract extensive attention from the news media. In such cases, the court has a special responsibility to assure that jurors unbiased by pretrial publicity are available for selection and that the jurors chosen are appropriately shielded during the trial from publicity that might impair their fairness and objectivity.[923]

The options available to the court for avoiding prejudicial publicity range from restrictions on trial access and extrajudicial statements to closing the courtroom. Such severe measures should be avoided, however, if more traditional measures, such as extensive voir dire, jury sequestration, continuance, or change of venue, will be adequate.[924] Court should utilize the least restrictive measures adequate for the purpose to avoid First Amendment problems and maintain public confidence in the fairness and openness of judicial proceedings.

Criminal proceedings generally may not be closed to the public.[925] The court may order closure only in the rare case where an "overriding interest" exists, supported by specific findings made on the record, and no alternative will suffice.[926]

The law is more tolerant, however, of orders prohibiting extrajudicial statements concerning the proceedings by attorneys, court personnel, parties, witnesses, and law enforcement officials involved in the case. While such prohibitions implicate First Amendment concerns, and therefore should not be imposed

---

922. Much of the material in this section and *infra* § 32.31 is drawn from Managing Notorious Cases (Timothy R. Murphy ed., SJI 1992), which is published by the National Center for State Courts and provides additional detail on the issues discussed in this section.

923. Some courts have adopted the *Revised Report of the Judicial Conference Committee on the Operation of the Jury System on the "Free Press—Fair Trial" Issue, reprinted in* 87 F.R.D. 519 (1980) [hereinafter *Revised Report*]. Judges in courts that have not adopted the report may wish to study its recommendations and implement its suggestions by special order in appropriate cases. *See also* I ABA Standards for Criminal Justice, Fair Trial and Free Press (3d ed. 1991) [hereinafter ABA Standards]. For a general discussion of the court's duty to protect criminal defendants from the prejudicial effects of publicity, see Sheppard v. Maxwell, 384 U.S. 333 (1966).

924. For the standard for change of venue because of prejudice, see Fed. R. Crim. P. 21(a).

925. *See* Richmond Newspaper, Inc. v. Virginia, 448 U.S. 555 (1980); Globe Newspaper Co. v. Superior Court, 457 U.S. 596 (1982) (trial); Press-Enterprise Co. v. Superior Court, 464 U.S. 501 (1984) (voir dire); Waller v. Georgia, 467 U.S. 39 (1984) (suppression hearing); El Vocero de Puerto Rico v. Puerto Rico, 113 S. Ct. 2004 (1993) (preliminary hearing); United States v. Antar, 63 U.S.L.W. 2299 (3d Cir. Oct. 25, 1994) (reversing order sealing transcript of jury voir dire).

926. *Richmond Newspaper,* 448 U.S. at 580–81; *see also* Gannett Co. v. DePasquale, 443 U.S. 368 (1979) (upholding state court closure of suppression hearing); ABA Standards, *supra* note 923, at 8-3.2; *Revised Report, supra* note 923, Recommendation C(4), 87 F.R.D. at 534–35 (closure restricted to pretrial proceedings). For a discussion of times when closure may be appropriate and the procedure to be followed, see Bench Book, *supra* note 42, § 3.10.

---

indiscriminately, the court may order them when there is a likelihood of prejudice to the accused's right to a fair trial.[927] The court should, however, seek voluntary cooperation before resorting to coercive measures.

Problems with extrajudicial speech most commonly arise from attorneys' attempts to continue their advocacy outside the courtroom. To avoid prejudice resulting from attorneys' comments to the media, the court may consider imposing guidelines limiting such comments and suggesting appropriate responses to impromptu questioning by the media as well as ground rules for scheduled press conferences. The court may remind counsel of local disciplinary rules[928] and propose agreement to limits on extrajudicial statements, making its expectations clear while restricting threats of disciplinary referrals or contempt to egregious circumstances.

If the judge finds it necessary to issue an order restricting attorneys' speech, it must be narrowly drawn. The general standard for restraint of attorney speech allows the court to prohibit only speech that "will have a substantial likelihood of materially prejudicing" the proceeding.[929] Statements falling into this category include comments on:

- the prior criminal record of a suspect or defendant;
- the character or reputation of a suspect or defendant;
- an attorney's opinion on the guilt of a suspect or defendant, the merits of a case, or the evidence presented;
- the existence or contents of any admission, confession, or statement of a suspect or defendant, or the refusal or failure to make a statement;
- the results of examinations or tests administered, or the refusal to submit to them;
- the identity, testimony, or credibility of prospective witnesses;

---

927. *See* Dobbert v. Florida, 432 U.S. 282, 302 (1977) (favorably referring to gag order placed on "all participants" of trial); *Sheppard*, 384 U.S. at 359–63 (suggesting propriety of gag order on attorneys, accused, witnesses, court staff, coroner, and law enforcement officials); Nebraska Press Ass'n v. Stuart, 427 U.S. 539, 601 n.27 (1976) (Brennan, J., concurring) (favorably quoting *Sheppard* on same issue); Dow Jones & Co., Inc. v. Simon, 842 F.2d 603 (2d Cir. 1988) (permissible to place gag order on "trial participants"); Radio & Television Ass'n v. District Ct., 781 F.2d 1443, 1444 (9th Cir. 1986) (same); Levine v. District Ct., 764 F.2d 590, 601 (9th Cir. 1985) (upholding gag order on attorneys, court personnel, law enforcement officers, and witnesses).

928. *See, e.g.,* Model Rules of Professional Conduct 3.6 (trial publicity).

929. Gentile v. State Bar of Nev., 111 S. Ct. 2720, 2725 (1991) (upholding constitutionality of standard). Recommendation A of *Revised Report, supra* note 923, uses a "reasonable likelihood" standard. 87 F.R.D. at 525. ABA Standard 8-1.1 adopts the more protective "substantial likelihood" test, as does Model Rule of Professional Conduct 3.6. *See* United States v. Cutler, 815 F. Supp. 599, 612–16 (E.D.N.Y. 1993) (both standards consistent with *Gentile*).

- the possibility of a guilty plea or other disposition; and
- information that the attorney knows or should know will likely be inadmissible at trial.

In contrast, protected statements include:

- the general nature of the charges;
- the general nature of any defense to the charges or other public accusations, including the fact that the suspect or defendant has no prior criminal record;
- the name, age, occupation, or family status of the suspect or defendant;
- information necessary to aid in the apprehension of the suspect or defendant or to warn the public of any dangers that may exist;
- requests for assistance in obtaining evidence;
- the existence of an investigation in progress, including generally its length and scope, the charge or defense involved, and the identity of the investigating agency;
- the facts and circumstances of the arrest, including the time and place and the identity of the arresting agency;
- the identity of the victim, where such disclosure is not prohibited by law and would not be harmful to the victim;
- at the time of seizure, a description of physical evidence seized;
- information in the public record; and
- the scheduling or result of any step in the judicial process.

To withstand appellate review, an order restricting extrajudicial speech should be (1) based on a clearly articulated finding of fact, (2) made after an evidentiary hearing at which all parties are given an opportunity to be heard, (3) drawn narrowly to address a particular problem posing a substantial likelihood of prejudicing the proceedings, and (4) imposed only when no practical alternative is available.

Orders prohibiting the media from publishing or broadcasting information relating to a criminal case are unlikely to be upheld.[930] The court should therefore seek, through informal agreement, voluntary media compliance with necessary

---

930. *See Nebraska Press Ass'n*, 427 U.S. 539; *In re* Providence Journal, 820 F.2d 1342, *modified en banc*, 820 F.2d 1354 (1st Cir. 1986). *See also Revised Report, supra* note 923, Recommendation C(3), 87 F.R.D. at 533–34 (no direct restraints on media); ABA Standards, *supra* note 923, at 8-3.1 (direct restraint on media permissible only if "clear and present danger to the fairness of the trial or other compelling interest").

restrictions. Judges report that this is generally obtainable if the media are allowed reasonable access[931] and identical standards are applied to all media sources.

The court may, however, impose "reasonable limitations" on media access to trial "in the interest of the fair administration of justice."[932] The court should set clear and fair ground rules at the outset, disseminate them broadly, and enforce them consistently. While the judge should make every reasonable effort to allow the media to obtain information essential to the performance of their job, the media must be given to understand that the judge is in control of the trial and the courtroom, and will not allow or negotiate deviations from the ground rules. Usually, the court will find it advisable to restrict media representatives to a designated section of the courtroom. To the degree possible, this section should be far from the jury and out of their sightlines to minimize distraction. Use of photography and electronic recording and broadcasting devices in criminal cases is currently prohibited in federal courts.

The court may also consider instructing court personnel, parties, counsel, and witnesses[933] not to speak to the press, and appointing a court employee[934] (or media representative)[935] as a liaison to provide a single channel for communication between the court and the media.[936] This liaison may disseminate information on such administrative matters as scheduling, seating, and court

---

931. For example, if seating capacity is limited, the court may provide preferential seating for media representatives, including in-court artists.

932. *Richmond Newspaper*, 448 U.S. at 581–82 n.18; *see Sheppard*, 384 U.S. at 358.

933. Jurors are always prohibited from discussing the case during trial. They may, however, be sought out by attorneys, parties, or the media for post-verdict questioning. Opinions differ as to the desirability of orders prohibiting or restricting this practice, see United States v. Antar, 839 F. Supp. 293 (D.N.J. 1993) (order issued), and as to the court's authority to issue such orders. *See* United States v. Antar, 63 U.S.L.W. 2299 (3d Cir. Oct. 25, 1993) (reversing the district court's order in part and affirming it in part). *See generally* Abraham S. Goldstein, *Jury Secrecy and the Media: The Problem of Postverdict Interviews*, 1993 U. Ill. L. Rev. 295, 303–07. The validity of such an order may depend on factors such as (1) the persons to whom it is directed, (2) its scope, (3) whether the case may be retried on remand or after a mistrial, or whether related cases are pending or anticipated, and (4) the need for the order in the particular case. *See* Goldstein at 303–07. At a minimum, the court should inform jurors that they are under no obligation to speak to anyone about the case. *See* Handbook for Trial Jurors (prepared under the supervision of the Judicial Conference and published by the Administrative Office) at 13 (also noting that court may direct jurors not to reveal information on other jurors' votes). Local rules may also impose restrictions. *See* Goldstein, at 305 & n.45.

934. The judge may designate a staff member or an experienced employee in the office of the clerk of court.

935. This was done by the judge in United States v. Poindexter, Cr. No. 88-80 (D.D.C.). For a detailed account, see Managing Notorious Cases, *supra* note 922, at app. 4.

936. Then-Justice Rehnquist denied an application for a stay of an order making such an appointment in KPNX Broadcasting Co. v. Arizona Super. Ct., 459 U.S. 1302 (1982).

---

procedures. The court should not hold press conferences. Ordinarily it is best for the court to communicate with the public only through statements and rulings on the record.

32.28 Severance and Joinder

Complex cases are frequently brought on indictments that join numerous counts and defendants. Improperly joined counts or defendants are subject to severance under Fed. R. Crim. P. 8. But the judge may also determine that severance is appropriate[937] when the multiplicity of defendants, counts, evidence, and necessary instructions would jeopardize the jury's ability to comprehend and deal separately with each defendant's case, make it difficult for the court to conduct a fair and efficient trial,[938] or result in an excessively long, costly, and cumbersome trial. The prosecution may, at the judge's suggestion, be willing to sever counts and defendants, particularly where the outcome of the first trial may determine the disposition of severed counts and defendants, through dismissal or plea bargains.[939] Severance is appropriate of peripheral defendants, against whom the charges are narrow, and who should not fairly be required to prepare for and attend a long trial. Severing particular defendants or counts can reduce the cost and time required to prepare for trial, and the presence of fewer defendants and attorneys can expedite the trial.[940]

Conversely, separate criminal cases may be joined for trial under Fed. R. Cr. P. 13 "if the offenses, and the defendants if there is more than one, could have been joined in a single indictment." In combination with the power to sever, this enables the court to structure the case for the efficient trial of related indictments.[941]

---

937. The law of the circuit needs to be consulted. Generally, granting of a severance is committed to the discretion of the court. United States v. Casamento, 887 F.2d 1141, 1149 (2d Cir. 1989); United States v. Lurz, 666 F.2d 69, 77 (4th Cir. 1981). The court may order severance even if the counts or defendants were properly joined under Rule 8 and applicable case law. *See* United States v. Andrews, 754 F. Supp. 1161 (N.D. Ill. 1990); United States v. Shea, 750 F. Supp. 46 (D. Mass. 1990). For a discussion of procedures and standards to be used in determining whether to sever, see *Casamento*, 887 F.2d at 1151–53.

938. *See* United States v. Harris, 458 F.2d 670, 672–72 (5th Cir. 1972); Fed. R. Crim. P. 14 (relief from prejudicial joinder). *See also* United States v. Baker, 10 F.3d 1374, 1389–93 (9th Cir. 1993) (dicta; criticizing "mega-trials"); United States v. Zafiro, 945 F.2d 881, 885 (7th Cir. 1991) (advisable to sever trials of peripheral defendants).

939. *See* United States v. Gay, 567 F.2d 916, 919 (9th Cir. 1978).

940. Shortening the trial also reduces the risk of a mistrial through the loss of a juror or other trial participant and can increase diversity in the juror pool. *See* United States v. Vastola, 670 F. Supp. 1244, 1262–63 (D.N.J. 1987).

941. *See* United States v. Halper, 590 F.2d 422, 428 (2d Cir. 1978); United States v. Haygood, 502 F.2d 166, 169 n.5 (7th Cir. 1974). The court may suggest issuance of a superseding indictment, but this can cause delay.

Where *Bruton v. United States*[942] would normally call for severance of defendants, the court may try the case with separately impaneled juries.[943] Most of the evidence will be heard at the same time by both juries, sitting separately in the same courtroom. The jury considering the charges against a defendant implicated by the confession of a nontestifying codefendant is excused from the courtroom when evidence of that confession is presented.[944] Although this may take extra time at trial, elimination of the need to conduct separate trials may result in net savings.

32.3 Trial

32.31 Physical Arrangements and Security

Complex criminal cases will often create a need to accommodate a large number of defendants and counsel, a high degree of public and media interest, and security concerns. This may require substantial changes in the physical arrangements of the courthouse and courtroom and in the court's routine procedures. Plans for physical changes should be made well in advance of trial.[945] Similarly, plans for accommodating the public and media and for dealing with security concerns should be in place before the trial begins. Some aspects of such plans may be incorporated in a court order.[946] Some relevant considerations are the following:

- Courtroom seating of defendants in multidefendant cases should take into account security concerns and minimizing of disruptions. If there are many defendants and counsel, name signs may be placed on the tables except when in-court identifications will be made.[947] Arrangements may have to be made for secure and private conference facilities for defendants and counsel, and for secure witness waiting rooms. A portion of

---

942. 391 U.S. 123 (1968).

943. This step is necessary only when redaction of the confession at issue to eliminate reference to the name or existence of the nontestifying coconspirator is inadequate. Richardson v. Marsh, 481 U.S. 200, 211 (1986).

944. *See* United States v. Lebron-Gonzalez, 816 F.2d 823, 830 (1st Cir. 1987) (approving procedure and citing cases in which other circuits have done so).

945. Prefabricated components may be available from other courts that have conducted mass trials.

946. For sample security orders, see Managing Notorious Cases, *supra* note 922, at app. 9.

947. To further facilitate individual consideration of each defendant, the jurors can be given pictures identifying them. These must not be prejudicial as, for example, mug shots would be.

the public section of the courtroom may be reserved for the media. Artists making sketches should be located so they do not distract the jury and, if the jury is anonymous, admonished not to sketch jurors.

- In multidefendant cases, special arrangements may be needed for transporting defendants in custody to and from the courtroom and holding them during recesses in order to ensure their timely appearance in court. Handling large numbers of incarcerated defendants can result in trial delays unless adequate provision is made.

- Cases involving defendants charged with violent or violence-related crimes require special attention to security issues.[948] A security plan should be prepared to deal both with routine procedures and with contingencies (such as the need to evacuate in case of emergency).[949] The plan should be prepared in consultation with the court's security committee, the marshal, and other court personnel concerned, as well as with counsel for the parties. Following are some of the issues relevant to a security plan:

  –the identity of persons and agencies having specified responsibilities;

  –the identity of persons to be contacted in the event of particular contingencies;

  –lines of communication for participants in the security plan;

  –plans for dealing with disruptions by spectators or defendants;

  –provisions for reporting and dealing with threats to trial participants;

  –the need for particular security features in the courtroom (such as bullet-proof shields);

  –the availability of operative alarms;

  –the availability of adequate communication facilities;

  –coordination with local law enforcement authorities;

  –the availability of security personnel in sufficient numbers;

  –the adequacy of equipment and facilities to screen for bombs and firearms; and

  –the availability of video and other monitoring devices for public areas.

---

948. While safety is the overriding concern, the court should be aware that highly visible and extensive security measures may prejudice the defendants' right to a fair trial by leading jurors to believe that the accused are known to be violent and dangerous. For discussion of the balance between defendants' rights and the need for security, see Holbrook v. Flynn, 475 U.S. 560 (1986).

949. For a sample security plan, see Managing Notorious Cases, *supra* note 922, at app. 10.

- Cases with high public interest may require plans for crowd control addressing points such as the following:
    - –appropriate control of access to the courthouse and courtroom;
    - –contingency plans for control of demonstrations in or around the courthouse;
    - –requiring identification of courthouse or courtroom visitors;
    - –a procedure for screening at the courtroom entrance;
    - –securing other courthouse or courtroom entrances or exits against public access;
    - –procedures for emergency evacuation;
    - –control of parking in or around the courthouse; and
    - –appropriate arrangements for media representatives.
- Jury management in high profile or high security cases may require special arrangements, such as:
    - –secure and nonpublic access to the courthouse and courtroom;
    - –enhanced privacy and protection for jurors; and
    - –measures to avoid alarming or distracting jurors or otherwise prejudicing defendants.[950]

32.32 Jury Selection[951]

The publicity generated by certain complex criminal cases creates special problems in the selection of an impartial jury. Indeed, an otherwise ordinary criminal case may become complex because of the publicity generated by the facts or personalities involved. This may require a large pool of prospective jurors and painstaking examination of the individuals. Some of the considerations in the management of jury selection follow:

- Jury questionnaires are frequently used to eliminate from the jury pool persons who will obviously have to be excused for disqualification, hardship, or inability to serve in a long trial.[952] The responses will also be helpful to counsel in preparing for voir dire of individual jurors and the exercise of peremptory challenges. Pretrial distribution of questionnaires may, however, tend to produce an excessive number of requests to be excused and failures to appear. One alternative is to have jurors complete such questionnaires at the courthouse after they have reported for service

---

950. Jurors can be instructed that security procedures are a normal part of trials and that they should not draw any inferences adverse to defendants.

951. *See generally* Bench Book, *supra* note 42, § 1.13 (Supp. July 1993).

952. For a sample questionnaire, see Litigation Manual, *supra* note 5, Sample Form 37 at 317.

and have received preliminary instructions from the judge about the case. Another alternative is to simply give potential jurors a list of questions that will be asked on voir dire, to allow them time to prepare to answer. Whatever approach is used, attorneys should be consulted about the instrument to be used and given an opportunity to make suggestions and objections.

- Voir dire may be and generally is conducted by the judge, although many judges permit counsel to supplement the court's questions.[953] Counsel should be asked to submit proposed voir dire questions; where counsel conduct the examination, reasonable time limits may be imposed. The jurors should receive information about the case before voir dire to enable them to give more informed responses.[954] Probing for bias, especially in a high publicity case, requires care and patience. Perfunctory catch-all questions (e.g., "Do you believe that you can be fair and impartial?") cannot be depended on to be effective. Many judges believe that eliciting narrative answers at least on some important points is necessary. Where the case has received extensive publicity, it may be advisable to question jurors at the outset about their exposure and reaction to it to eliminate quickly those disqualified from serving;[955] follow-up questioning of those who have been exposed may be conducted individually in chambers.[956] Jurors are not automatically disqualified for having read or heard about a case (any more than they are for holding opinions about drugs or crime); circuit law needs to be consulted on the controlling standards.

- Where a long trial is expected, jurors should be advised at the start of voir dire of the anticipated schedule to eliminate early those unable to serve.

- The decisions in *Batson v. Kentucky*[957] and its progeny barring the discriminatory exercise of peremptory challenges have complicated jury selection. If the defendant makes a prima facie showing in objecting to a challenge, the burden shifts to the government to set forth a reasonably specific race and gender-neutral explanation for its challenge. When a *Batson*-type objection is raised and not immediately granted, the state-

953. Fed. R. Crim. P. 24. For voir dire procedures and standard questions, see Bench Book, *supra* note 42, § 1.14.

954. The court or counsel may read the indictment or an agreed summary to be read to the jury before the voir dire examination. Some courts have counsel deliver opening statements to the entire jury pool before voir dire.

955. *See* ABA Standards, *supra* note 923, at 8-3.5.

956. *See* Nebraska Press Ass'n v. Stuart, 427 U.S. 539, 564 (1976); United States v. Parker, 877 F.2d 327, 331 (5th Cir. 1989). For discussion of different methods of jury selection, see Gordon Bermant, Jury Selection Procedures in United States District Courts (Federal Judicial Center 1982).

957. 476 U.S. 79 (1986).

ments of defense and government counsel should be made on the record (though out of the hearing of the jury) to preserve a record for appeal. When the possibility of such a challenge exists, the court or deputy clerk may want to keep a running tally identifying jurors who have been excused by the parties.

- The court must impanel twelve jurors,[958] and may impanel up to six alternates to replace those who are excused or disqualified before the jury retires to deliberate.[959] How many alternates to seat will depend on the judge's experience with juries under similar circumstances, considering the estimated length of the trial, the time of the year and the incidence of sickness, and other potential causes of interference. While avoiding mistrial is a prime consideration, the court needs also to consider the burdens imposed on alternate jurors, the drain of available jurors for other trials, and the cost of the additional jurors.

- In some high-profile cases, judges, instead of sequestering the jury, have adopted the less onerous option of seating an anonymous jury. Anonymity helps protect the jurors' safety and privacy,[960] but may intimidate jurors and complicate voir dire. Factors relevant to the determination whether an anonymous jury is necessary include (1) whether any defendant has participated in "dangerous and unscrupulous conduct," (2) whether there is evidence of a past attempt by any defendant to interfere with the judicial process, and (3) the extent of pretrial publicity and the possibility that the jurors' identities will become public.[961] To maintain anonymity, potential jurors are identified only by a preassigned number. The attorneys are given lists cross-referencing these numbers with the jurors' questionnaire responses, including only that information necessary for voir dire.[962] The number of lists cross-referencing juror numbers with jurors' names and addresses should be kept to a minimum

---

958. Fed. R. Crim. P. 23(b).

959. Fed. R. Crim. P. 24(c). See also *infra* § 32.33 (loss of juror during deliberations).

960. United States v. Thomas, 737 F.2d 1359, 1364–65 (2d Cir. 1985); United States v. Barnes, 604 F.2d 121, 140–41 (2d Cir. 1979). *See also* Bench Book, *supra* note 42, at 1.13–2 (discussing anonymous juries generally).

961. United States v. Persico, 832 F.2d 705, 717 (2d Cir. 1982). In cases in which the prosecution seeks the death penalty, 18 U.S.C. § 3432 requires disclosure to the defense of the names and addresses of witnesses and potential jurors three days prior to trial.

962. Many courts prefer not to use questionnaires with an anonymous jury to avoid accidental disclosure of their identities. If they are used, the judge should review the answers before turning them over to counsel.

and their distribution closely controlled.[963] The jurors should be given an explanation of the procedure and the reasons for it and, again, cautioned against drawing adverse inferences.[964] Anonymous juries generally meet at a designated place, remote from the courthouse, from which they are transported to court. At the courthouse their movements need to be controlled so as to avoid contact with the public and to protect their anonymity. Managing such a jury is complicated and requires advance planning.

- Only in rare cases, when the court concludes that no alternative will sufficiently protect jurors' security and shield them from improper influence, are juries sequestered.[965] The decision should be made well in advance of trial to give the marshal time to make the arrangements for lodging, meals, transportation, and security.[966] Particularly in long trials, attention needs to be given to such matters as recreation, family contacts, emergencies, medical care, and personality conflicts.[967] A less intrusive alternative is limited sequestration. Although the jury is not held overnight, they are sequestered while at the courthouse, provided with a private dining area, and escorted to and from the courtroom. When jurors are sequestered, they should be cautioned against drawing adverse inferences.[968]

- Once the jury is impaneled, no matter what procedures are adopted, care should be taken that the jurors receive proper treatment from responsible court personnel. Jury service in lengthy cases is particularly arduous and requires personal sacrifices from jurors. It is well for the court to communicate to jurors the court's and parties' appreciation for their service; some judges visit the jury room after the verdict has been returned and thank jurors personally. Jurors should be reminded of the important role they are playing in the justice process. Their needs should be accommodated to the extent feasible and courtesy and consideration shown by court personnel in contact with them. As elsewhere discussed, the pro-

---

963. Even the judge and other jury members may be kept unaware of the jurors' names. Paul Riley, Handbook on Management of Large Jury Trials at 14 (S.D.N.Y. monograph, undated).

964. For sample instructions, see United States v. Tutino, 883 F.2d 1125, 1133 (2d Cir. 1989) (quoting Judge Leval), and *Thomas*, 757 F.2d at 1365 n.1 (quoting Judge Pollack).

965. The decision to sequester is discretionary with the court. 2 Charles A. Wright, Federal Practice and Procedure § 389 at 398–99 & n.11 (citing cases) (2d ed. 1982).

966. The decision should usually be made before trial, but the court may order sequestration during trial when the situation warrants. United States v. Gay, 522 F.2d 429, 435 (6th Cir. 1975).

967. For more on sequestration, see Judge's Manual for the Management of Complex Criminal Cases, distributed by the Administrative Office of the United States Courts in November 1982.

968. *See Thomas*, 757 F.2d at 1364–65 & n.1 (providing sample instruction).

ceedings should be moved along to minimize the length of time when the jurors will be needed. Jurors should not be kept waiting and interruptions requiring them to be excused from the courtroom should be avoided.

32.33 Managing the Trial

Because of the high stakes involved, criminal trials will generally be more hard-fought and sometimes more contentious than civil trials and therefore present challenging management problems for the judge. Fairness to the participants in the process—as well as to the jurors—requires that such trials be conducted in an orderly and expeditious fashion. Although criminal trials require greater circumspection in the exercise of judicial control than civil trials, the judge should not hesitate to exercise such control as is necessary to maintain order and momentum. Unless the judge does so, such a trial may take on a life of its own, jeopardizing due process rights and imposing unreasonable costs and burdens. This section discusses problems that commonly arise in connection with complex criminal trials. Reference should also be made to the discussion of relevant generic issues affecting the conduct of trials in complex cases, in *supra* sections 22.13–22.15, 22.21–22.23, 22.31–22.32, and 22.42–22.43.

- **Expediting the trial.** The seriousness of the issues at stake may lead the attorneys to try the case leaving no stone unturned. This requires the judge to assert and retain control of the proceedings in order to move them to an expeditious conclusion (see *supra* sections 32.11, 32.22). The trial schedule is an important aspect of that control; some judges believe that a full trial day, with no unnecessary interruptions, for as many days each week as possible, is effective. Others schedule trials from 8:00 A.M. to 1:00 P.M. each day, giving them time to attend to other important matters. Whatever the schedule, interruptions should be avoided; evidentiary or other problems can usually be taken up during recesses or in conferences at the start or the end of the trial day instead of at sidebar conferences or special recesses. Hearings on motions during the trial should be scheduled so as not to interrupt the trial. A conference at the end of each trial day is useful also to address problems arising during the trial and to plan the witnesses and exhibits for the next day, making for a well-prepared and orderly trial.

- **Defendants and witnesses in custody.** Courtroom security arrangements appropriate for the defendants (and occasionally witnesses) need to be made with the marshal, taking into account the magnitude of the risk presented. Incarcerated defendants are usually escorted to their seats before the jury is brought into the courtroom and not removed until after the jury has been excused. If shackles are used, they should be concealed. Deputy marshals in attendance should also be as unobtrusive as possible (some judges have them remove their badges).[969] Security precautions, because they may create a risk of prejudice to the defendant's right to a fair trial, should be no more visible than necessary.[970]

- **Cumulative evidence.** Fed. R. Evid. 611 directs the court to "exercise reasonable control over the mode and order of interrogating witnesses . . . to . . . avoid needless consumption of time." Unnecessary witnesses and exhibits should be eliminated as much as possible during pretrial; some may, however, become unnecessary only after developments at trial. The judge should exclude witnesses or exhibits that are obviously redundant or otherwise unnecessary, and should curtail redundant and needlessly lengthy interrogation.

- **Recalcitrant witnesses.** When a witness refuses to testify, the grounds for the refusal, whether a Fifth Amendment claim or other ground, need to be established on the record outside the hearing of the jury. To the extent possible, counsel should inform the judge of such a claim in advance so that the proceedings can be scheduled without interrupting the trial.[971] It is improper for counsel knowingly to cause a witness to invoke the Fifth Amendment before the jury.

- **Absence of defendant or counsel.** The absence of any one of the defendants and attorneys in a complex criminal trial can cause serious and costly disruptions. Under Fed. R. Crim. P. 43, a defendant may waive his right to be present at the trial, except at the impaneling of the jury and return of the verdict. Such a waiver should not be accepted, however, unless genuinely voluntary. When a defendant is absent, the court should attempt to discover the explanation before deciding whether to proceed. Similarly, an attorney's unexplained or unavoidable absence may require a delay in the trial. In multidefendant cases, however, a defendant and his counsel may be excused from phases of the trial not affecting that defendant, with appropriate explanation given to the jury.

- **Absence of juror during trial.** Whether a juror who fails to appear or asks to be excused during the trial should be replaced by an alternate is a difficult call. It is best to conserve alternates in the early stages of the trial. Moreover, fairness to the juror and possibly the parties requires that the

---

969. *See* United States v. Ferguson, 758 F.2d 843, 854 (2d Cir. 1985).

970. *See* Holbrook v. Flynn, 475 U.S. 560 (1986). In the rare case where the judge allows the defendant to be dressed in a manner that reveals the fact of incarceration, the reasons therefor should be stated on the record, and the jury advised to draw no adverse inference. *See* ABA Standards for Criminal Justice: Trial by Jury, Standard 15-3.2 (approved draft, August 1993).

971. *See* Bench Book *supra* note 42, §§ 3.05–3.06.

judge not be too quick to replace a juror who may only briefly be unavailable.

- **Publicity during trial.** If potentially prejudicial publicity appears during the trial, the judge will need to consider three steps: (1) determine whether the article or broadcast could have a prejudicial effect on jurors; (2) determine whether any of the jurors saw or heard it; and (3) question any exposed juror individually about how it affected the juror, whether he or she discussed it with others, and whether it might affect the juror's ability to be fair and impartial. The judge will then need to consider whether to excuse the juror and, in any event, whether to give a cautionary instruction. Similar steps need to be taken where an attempt has been made to communicate with a juror or the juror has heard something touching the case.

- **Guilty pleas during trial.** In a multidefendant case, a defendant's plea should be taken outside the presence of the jury and at a time when it will not interrupt the trial. The defendant should continue to participate in the trial until the plea has actually been entered. The jury should be appropriately instructed not to speculate about the absence of the defendant from the trial and to ignore evidence received against that defendant only.

- **Improper behavior by the defendants, attorneys, or others.** While adequate latitude must be given for vigorous advocacy[972] and reasonable allowance made for the stress placed on all participants by the trial, the judge needs to deal promptly with improper behavior, taking what steps are necessary to maintain order while avoiding overreaction to offensive conduct. For relatively minor improprieties, particularly those due to ignorance or misunderstanding, a mild admonition and explanation of the required standards of conduct—given outside the hearing of the jury—will usually suffice.[973] For repeated or deliberate misconduct, the court should consider more severe measures, including citing the individual for contempt.[974] In the event of courtroom disturbances that must be dealt with immediately to preserve order and prevent disruption of the pro-

---

972. *See In re* McConnell, 370 U.S. 230, 236 (1962).

973. In cases with a potential for disruptive conduct, the judge may provide guidance in advance on proper courtroom decorum expected of defendants, counsel, and spectators.

974. *See* 18 U.S.C. § 401; *see also* Fed. R. Crim. P. 42; Bench Book, *supra* note 42, § 1.24 (criminal contempt). A citation for contempt requires intentional obstruction of court proceedings; it is generally not appropriate for occasional disrespect or unintentional transgression of court directives stemming from vigorous advocacy. *See McConnell*, 370 U.S. at 236; Pennsylvania v. International Union of Operating Eng'rs, 552 F.2d 498, 509 (3d Cir. 1977).

ceedings, the judge may summarily impose punishment for contempt under Rule 42(a).[975] Obstreperous spectators may be removed from the courtroom, and, if necessary as a last resort, defendants who persist in disruptive conduct may be bound and gagged or removed while the trial is in progress until they are willing to conduct themselves in an orderly manner.[976]

- **Expedited transcripts.** In unusually lengthy and complex cases, an expedited transcript may be valuable to counsel in preparing for cross-examination and for the examination of later witnesses, to the jurors in refreshing their memories about the testimony,[977] and to the court in avoiding delays if there are post-trial motions or appeals. However, daily or expedited copy is costly and will not necessarily be approved under the CJA.[978] If the court chooses to order expedited transcripts, it may order payment for daily copy under section 3006A of the CJA if such transcripts are needed by defense counsel. If expedited copy is requested by someone other than counsel appointed under the CJA, the CJA counsel are entitled to copies at the copy rate.[979]

- **Loss of a juror after deliberations have begun.** To avoid a mistrial,[980] the parties may stipulate to a verdict by a jury of fewer than twelve. Even in the absence of a stipulation, the court under Fed. R. Crim. P. 23(b) may excuse a juror for just cause during deliberations and receive a verdict by the eleven remaining jurors. Ordinarily the court should not do so except where the trial has been lengthy and a mistrial would be costly; if the

---

975. The maximum punishment for summary contempt is six months' imprisonment. *See* Codispoti v. Pennsylvania, 418 U.S. 506 (1974). If the misconduct involves contemptuous remarks directed toward the trial judge personally, but does not merit immediate punishment, the contempt proceedings should be conducted before another judge. Fed. R. Crim. P. 42(b); United States v. Meyer, 462 F.2d 827 (D.C. Cir. 1972).

976. Illinois v. Allen, 397 U.S. 337 (1970). If such problems are anticipated, or if the defendant's absence may be prolonged, arrangements may be made for a remote loudspeaker or closed-circuit television in order to keep the defendant informed about the proceedings. The court should advise the defendant of his right to return to the courtroom upon an agreement to behave properly. *See* Scurr v. Moore, 647 F.2d 854, 858 & n.5 (8th Cir. 1981).

977. The transcript cannot be made available to the jurors until after it has been redacted. Circuit law varies as to the extent that the jury may be given all or part of the transcript on request during deliberations.

978. *See* Resolution of the Judicial Conference of the United States, Reports of the Judicial Conference 1980, at 19.

979. *Id.*

980. Before ordering a mistrial, the court must give each side an opportunity to comment, including stating their consent or objection to the order, and to suggest alternatives. Fed. R. Crim. P. 26.3.

juror expects to be able to return shortly, a brief interruption of the deliberations may be acceptable. If the full jury had reached a verdict as to any defendant before the juror was lost, the judge may accept that verdict,[981] but should not announce it until all deliberations have concluded.[982]

- **Recall of alternate juror.** Although Fed. R. Crim. P. 24(c) provides that alternate jurors "shall be discharged" when the jury retires to deliberate, some circuits have upheld the use of alternates to replace jurors during deliberations.[983] Others have held that this is permissible only if the defendant expressly and knowingly consents.[984] If an alternate juror is recalled and substituted after deliberations have begun,[985] the judge must instruct the jury to begin deliberations anew, starting with election of a foreperson. To prepare for this eventuality, the court may instruct alternate jurors before discharging them that, because they may be recalled, they remain subject to the constraints imposed on them at trial until deliberations have concluded.

- **Readback of testimony.** When the jury requests a readback, the court should take care to avoid giving undue emphasis to particular testimony.[986] Generally, only the portion of the transcript agreed to by the parties should be read.

- **Return of the jury's verdict.** In cases where the return of the verdict may be expected to provoke a strong emotional response in the courtroom or

---

981. Fed. R. Crim. P. 31(b) allows the court to receive a verdict at any time during deliberations with respect to any defendant as to whom the jury has agreed.

982. *See generally* Bench Book, *supra* note 42, § 17.1 (Supp. July 1993) (receipt of verdict in criminal trial).

983. *See* United States v. Hillard, 701 F.2d 1052 (2d Cir. 1983); United States v. Phillips, 664 F.2d 971 (5th Cir. 1981); *but see* United States v. Lamb, 529 F.2d 1153 (9th Cir. 1975). Alternate jurors who are not replacing other jurors should not be present during deliberations, but violation of this rule is not "plain error" under Fed. R. Crim. P. 52(b), and is therefore not cognizable when raised for the first time on appeal. United States v. Olano, 113 S. Ct. 1770 (1993). It may, however, be permissible for the parties to stipulate to the presence of an alternate juror so long as that juror does not participate in the deliberations unless ordered to do so by the court in the event a regular juror is lost.

984. *See* United States v. Baccari, 489 F.2d 274 (10th Cir. 1973); United States v. Davis, 608 F.2d 698, 699 (6th Cir. 1979); United States v. Evans, 635 F.2d 1124, 1126–28 (4th Cir. 1980); United States v. Kaminski, 692 F.2d 505, 517–18 (8th Cir. 1982). Some judges routinely offer the parties an opportunity to stipulate to such a procedure before deliberations begin. *See* United States v. Foster, 711 F.2d 871, 885 (9th Cir. 1983).

985. Alternates should be substituted in the order in which they were seated. *See* Fed. R. Crim. P. 24(c).

986. United States v. Hernandez, 27 F.3d 1403, 1408–09 (9th Cir. 1994).

the community, the court should consider the optimum timing for the return. The public announcement may be delayed until the jury has been safely removed. Sufficient lead time should be given local law enforcement officers to make necessary plans.

- **Jury deadlock.** When the jury appears unable to reach a verdict, the judge may give appropriate instructions governed by the law of the particular circuit. Before declaring a mistrial, counsel should be consulted and given the opportunity to make suggestions.[987]

32.34 Sentencing Hearings

The complexities of the sentencing guidelines and other rules governing sentencing are beyond the scope of this manual.[988] The principles concerning the need to maintain control and seek an expeditious resolution, however, apply here as well. Disputed issues relevant to imposition of sentence may be resolved without hearing, either on the papers submitted by the parties or the affidavits of witnesses. Only serious and difficult questions of fact require a hearing. Hearings do not require the formality of a trial and the rules of evidence are not binding.

---

987. Fed. R. Crim. P. 26.3.
988. *See generally* Fed. R. Crim. P. 32 and the Guidelines Manual.

33. Application in Particular Types of Litigation

33.1 Antitrust

Claims or defenses arising under the antitrust laws do not invariably require treatment as complex litigation. A two-party distributor termination action, for example, is unlikely to need intense judicial management. Antitrust litigation can, however, involve voluminous documentary and testimonial evidence, extensive discovery, complicated legal, factual, and technical (particularly economic) questions, numerous parties and attorneys, and substantial sums of money, calling for the application of techniques and procedures for the management of complex litigation.[989] Antitrust claims are not limited to complaints, but are also fre-

---

989. Many of the principles and practices of judicial management and of the procedures discussed in this Manual were initially developed in antitrust litigation. *See* William W Schwarzer,

quently raised in counterclaims, particularly in patent litigation. They are often brought as class actions, and may be filed in several federal and state courts concurrently with or following criminal or administrative proceedings. Lengthy trials are not unusual, nor are controversies over settlements and attorneys' fees. The earlier sections of this manual will therefore be relevant to many of the issues that arise in the management of complex antitrust litigation, both civil and criminal. In particular, some of the procedures used to manage mass tort and securities cases (see *infra* sections 33.2, 33.3) may also be of value in multiparty antitrust litigation.

33.11 Managing the Issues

Effective management of antitrust litigation requires that the pivotal factual and legal issues be identified, clarified, and narrowed as soon as practicable (see generally *supra* section 21.3). Unless the judge and the attorneys give early attention to the issues, substantial time may be wasted on claims subject to summary dismissal, on class action disputes not critical to the ruling on class certification, and on discovery not relevant to the later-refined issues regarding liability or damages. By carefully defining the issues at an early stage, the court may be able to structure the litigation so as to limit the scope and volume of discovery, reducing cost and delay, facilitating the prospects of settlement, and shortening and improving the trial.

The procedures for pretrial management of complex litigation discussed in *supra* section 21 apply generally to antitrust litigation. General principles relevant to structuring trials apply to antitrust litigation, although particular care must be taken when considering severance of damage issues from other elements of the claim (see *supra* sections 21.631–21.632).[990]

Issues that may arise in antitrust litigation and may, depending on the circumstances, be appropriate for pretrial resolution include the following:

- **Subject matter jurisdiction.** Whether the requisite effect on interstate commerce can be established[991] and whether the claim is within the reach

---

Managing Antitrust and Other Complex Litigation (1982); ABA Antitrust Section, Monograph No. 3, Expediting Pretrial and Trial of Antitrust Cases (1979); Report, National Commission for the Review of Antitrust Laws and Procedures (1979).

990. *Compare* Alabama v. Blue Bird Body Co., 573 F.2d 309, 318–19, 328 (5th Cir. 1978) (disapproving of bifurcation of liability and damages) *and* Windham v. American Brands, Inc., 565 F.2d 59, 70–72 (4th Cir. 1977) (upholding denial of bifurcation) *with In re* Plywood Antitrust Litig., 655 F.2d 627, 631–36 (5th Cir. 1981) (permissible to try issue of statutory violation, including existence of injury and method of calculating damages, separately from amount of individual damages) *and* Franklin Music Co. v. American Broadcasting Co., 616 F.2d 528, 538 (3d Cir. 1979) (upholding bifurcation). Bifurcation of liability and damages issues "must be approached with trepidation." Response of Carolina, Inc. v. Leasco Response, Inc., 537 F.2d 1307, 1324 (5th Cir. 1976).

991. *See, e.g.*, McLain v. Real Estate Bd. of New Orleans, Inc., 444 U.S. 232 (1980).

of the antitrust laws[992] are jurisdictional issues that may be capable of summary resolution under Fed. R. Civ. P. 56 or by a separate evidentiary hearing under Rule 42.

- **Standing.** Whether the claimant has the necessary standing to maintain a claim for damages[993] and whether injury to competition can be demonstrated are legal issues that can sometimes be resolved by motion under Rule 12 or 56 or by a separate trial under Rule 42.

- **Exemptions, immunities.** The application of antitrust laws may be barred or limited by statutory exemptions or immunities, such as those applicable to the insurance industry[994] or organized labor,[995] where restraints are imposed or authorized by state action,[996] or where collective solicitation of governmental action has occurred.[997] The application of the antitrust laws may also be circumscribed by the primary or exclusive jurisdiction of a regulatory agency.

- **Statute of limitations.** Whether an action or claim is time-barred may be appropriate for early resolution by summary judgment.[998]

- **Market definition.** The definition of the relevant geographic and product market, which may determine the existence of market power requisite to proof of liability and the scope of relevant evidence, can be a critical element. The parties may be willing to stipulate to or to narrow the range of dispute over the facts, and at least some facts may be subject to judicial

992. *Compare* Hunt v. Mobil Oil Corp., 550 F.2d 68 (2d Cir. 1977) (pretrial dismissal based on "act of state" doctrine) *with* International Ass'n of Machinists & Aerospace Workers v. Organization of the Petroleum Exporting Countries, 649 F.2d 1354 (9th Cir. 1981) (act of state doctrine applied after trial).

993. *See, e.g.,* Kansas v. Utilicorp. United, Inc., 497 U.S. 199 (1990) (actions by states and utilities consolidated after summary judgment as to standing); Associated Gen. Contractors v. California State Council of Carpenters, 459 U.S. 519 (1983) (standing requires analysis of relationship between defendants' conduct and plaintiff's injury); Illinois Brick Co. v. Illinois, 431 U.S. 720 (1977) (no federal antitrust damages for "indirect" purchases); Brunswick v. Pueblo Bowl-O-Mat, Inc., 429 U.S. 477 (1977) ("antitrust injury" requirement); Zenith Radio Corp. v. Hazeltine Research, Inc., 395 U.S. 100 (1969) ("direct injury" requirement).

994. *See* 15 U.S.C. §§ 1011–1015; Group Life and Health Ins. Co. v. Royal Drug Co., 440 U.S. 205 (1979) (narrow construction of insurance exception).

995. United States v. Hutcheson, 312 U.S. 219 (1941); 29 U.S.C. §§ 101–110, 113–115.

996. *See* FTC v. Ticor Title Ins. Co., 112 S. Ct. 2169 (1992); Patrick v. Burget, 486 U.S. 94 (1988); Southern Motor Carriers Rate Conf. v. United States, 471 U.S. 48 (1985); California Retail Liquor Dealers Ass'n v. Midcal Aluminum, Inc., 445 U.S. 97 (1980); Parker v. Brown, 317 U.S. 341 (1943).

997. Eastern R.R. Presidents' Conf. v. Noerr Motor Freight, Inc., 365 U.S. 127 (1961); United Mine Workers v. Pennington, 381 U.S. 657 (1965).

998. *See, e.g.,* Norton-Children's Hosp. v. James E. Smith & Sons, 658 F.2d 440 (6th Cir. 1981); Dayco Corp. v. Goodyear Tire & Rubber Co., 523 F.2d 389 (6th Cir. 1975).

notice. The dispute over the market may be susceptible to resolution under Rule 56 in the absence of disputed evidentiary facts (see *supra* section 21.34), or through a separate bench or jury trial under Rule 42. Where extensive fact finding is required, the issue may be referred to a special master, magistrate judge, or court-appointed expert for a report and recommendation (see *supra* section 21.5).

- **Theory and proof of damages.** The attention given to liability issues in antitrust cases may lead to neglect of injury and damage issues. Early consideration of the proposed theory of damages and proof of cognizable injury may significantly affect the conduct of the litigation. The alleged injury may not qualify as antitrust injury, or the damages claimed may, in whole or in part, not be recoverable under the antitrust laws; if so, claims may be subject to dismissal, the scope of discovery reduced, or the method for proving damages otherwise altered. The extent to which injury and damages will require individualized proof can be critical in determining whether a class of antitrust claimants should be certified or whether a consolidated trial of separate but related claims is feasible. Early scrutiny of the claimed damages can facilitate settlement, either because of the magnitude of the potential exposure or because provable damages are too small to justify the cost of pursuing the litigation. Indeed, in some cases the court may conclude that the initial discovery should be focused on the fact and amount of damages, perhaps leading to a separate trial on such issues before extensive discovery and trial on liability issues, such as the existence of a conspiracy (see discussion of sequencing discovery in *supra* section 21.424). If the time needed for discovery and trial of the issues of impact and damages caused by a particular practice would be relatively short, substantial savings may be effected by postponing significant discovery on liability issues, since the damage verdict, if any, could pave the way to an early settlement. If the practice in question is well defined in scope and time, such "reverse bifurcation" may be feasible, subject, however, to substantive rules of antitrust law. In any event, the court should require the pretrial exchange of expert reports, computations, and exhibits regarding injury and damages (see *supra* section 21.48), whether a separate trial is held or not.

The court should consider establishing a schedule for early completion of motion-related discovery and the submission and decision of motions. Merits discovery should be stayed only to the extent that the outcome of a motion will significantly affect the scope of that discovery.

33.12 Transactional and Economic Data, and Expert Opinions

Antitrust cases often involve the collection, assimilation, and evaluation of vast amounts of evidence regarding numerous transactions and other economic data. Some of this material may be entitled to protection as trade secrets or confidential commercial information. Effective management of such cases depends on the adoption of pretrial procedures to facilitate the production and utilization of this material and its efficient presentation at trial. Among the measures that may be useful are the following:

- **Limiting scope of discovery.** Early attention to the issues may make feasible establishment of reasonable limits on the scope of discovery. Limits may be fixed with reference to the transactions alleged to be the subject matter of the case, to the relevant products or services, or to geographical areas and time periods. Limits should, however, be subject to modification if a need for broader discovery later appears. See generally *supra* section 21.423.

- **Confidentiality orders.** Protective orders may facilitate the expeditious discovery of materials that may be entitled to protection as trade secret or other confidential commercial information (see *supra* section 21.431). Especially if the parties are competitors, provisions may be included that preclude or restrict disclosure by the attorneys to their clients. Particularly sensitive information, such as customer names and pricing instructions, may be masked by excision, codes, or summaries without impairing the utility of the information in the litigation.

- **Summaries; computerized data.** The court should direct the parties to work out arrangements for the efficient and economical exchange of voluminous data. Where feasible, data that exist in computerized form should be produced in computer-readable format. Identification of computerized data may lead to agreement on a single database on which all expert and other witnesses will rely in their testimony. Other voluminous data can be produced by way of summaries or tabulations, subject to appropriate verification procedures to minimize, and more quickly resolve, disputes about accuracy, and obviating extensive discovery of source documents. Such exhibits should be produced well in advance of trial. See generally *supra* sections 21.446 (discovery of computerized data) and 21.492 (summaries).

- **Other sources.** Relevant economic data may be obtainable from government or industry sources more quickly and cheaply than through discovery from the litigants. Accordingly, the court may wish to make an early determination regarding the admissibility of such evidence under Fed. R. Evid. 803(8), (17), and (18).

- **Expert opinions.** Economists may be employed to study such topics as the relevant market, concentration of economic power, pricing structures, elasticity of demand, barriers to entry, marginal costs, and the effect of the challenged practices on competition and the claimants. Early in the litigation, the court should call for an identification of the subjects on which expert testimony will likely be offered, determine whether such testimony is necessary, rule at least preliminarily on the appropriate scope of expert testimony, and establish a schedule for disclosure of experts' reports, recognizing that some studies may require considerable time both to prepare and to review. Agreement on a common database to be used by all experts is desirable, and the court may require the parties to agree on methodology and form before surveys or polls are conducted (see *supra* section 21.493).[999] Objections to the admissibility of experts' opinions should be heard and decided in advance of trial under Fed. R. Evid. 104(a).[1000] If significant conflicts exist between the parties' experts on matters of theory, the court may wish to appoint an expert under Fed. R. Evid. 706 (see *supra* section 21.51). See generally *supra* section 21.48.

33.13 Conflicts of Interest

Attention should be given early in the litigation to possible conflicts of interest that may lead to disqualification of attorneys[1001] (see *supra* section 20.23) or recusal of the judge (see *supra* section 20.121). These problems may be acute in antitrust actions brought on behalf of large classes of purchasers because (unless special steps are taken) the identification of class members—which can result in disqualification of the judge under 28 U.S.C. § 455[1002]—may not occur until after substantial proceedings have taken place. The court may wish to consider the feasibility of asking the parties to provide a list of known class members.

33.14 Related Proceedings

Antitrust litigation sometimes involves a number of individual and class actions for damages filed in several federal and state courts, and may involve criminal or administrative proceedings as well. The effect of such parallel or related proceed-

---

999. *See also* Reference Manual on Scientific Evidence (Federal Judicial Center 1994).

1000. *See, e.g.,* Daubert v. Merrell-Dow Pharmaceuticals, 113 S. Ct. 2786 (1993).

1001. *See, e.g,* Westinghouse Elec. Corp. v. Gulf Oil Corp., 588 F.2d 221 (7th Cir. 1978); Westinghouse Elec. Corp. v. Kerr-McGee Corp., 580 F.2d 1311 (7th Cir. 1978).

1002. *See In re* Cement Antitrust Litig., 688 F.2d 1297 (9th Cir. 1982), *aff'd under 28 U.S.C. § 2109 sub. nom.* Arizona v. United States Dist. Ct., 459 U.S. 1191 (1983). Note that § 455(f), added following this decision, allows a judicial officer who discovers a financial interest after devoting "substantial judicial time" to a case to avoid recusal by divestment, unless the interest "could be substantially affected by the outcome." 28 U.S.C. § 455(f).

ings must be taken into account when developing and implementing a management plan for the litigation.

Recognizing the desirability of centralized management, the Judicial Panel on Multidistrict Litigation commonly transfers civil antitrust cases for pretrial purposes under 28 U.S.C. § 1407, usually to a district in which related civil cases, and sometimes also criminal or civil proceedings brought by the United States, are pending (§ 1407 does not apply to criminal cases or civil antitrust actions brought by the United States[1003]). If centralized management of the entire litigation is impossible or impractical, the affected courts should nevertheless attempt to coordinate proceedings through procedures such as those described in *supra* sections 20.123 and 31.14. Injunctions against or stays of parallel actions are generally not available (see *supra* section 31.32).

Special problems are presented when conduct that is the basis for civil antitrust claims is also the subject of criminal or administrative proceedings. Indeed, disclosure of a criminal or administrative investigation frequently triggers the filing of civil actions (see *supra* section 31.2). The criminal charges should ordinarily be tried first, not only because of the requirements of the Speedy Trial Act but also because Fifth Amendment claims tend to disrupt civil discovery.[1004] A general stay of all activities in the civil litigation pending completion of the criminal case will rarely be appropriate, however.[1005] Similarly, although a decision by the Federal Trade Commission or some other agency may narrow the issues or reduce the scope of discovery,[1006] the court should carefully weigh the rights and interests of all parties before deciding whether to defer any of the proceedings in the civil actions.

Special problems are also presented where parallel litigation is brought in federal and state courts (see *supra* section 31.3) alleging violations of federal and state antitrust laws arising out of substantially the same conduct. While neither

---

1003. 28 U.S.C. § 1407(g).

1004. Completion of a witness's testimony in the criminal case will not necessarily preclude that witness from invoking the Fifth Amendment in the civil proceedings. *See* Pillsbury Co. v. Conboy, 459 U.S. 248 (1983).

1005. *See* Landis v. North Am. Co., 299 U.S. 248, 254–55 (1936); Texaco, Inc. v. Borda, 383 F.2d 607 (3d Cir. 1967).

1006. For example, enforcement proceedings may result in collateral estoppel. *See, e.g.,* Parklane Hosiery Co. v. Shore, 439 U.S. 322 (1979). Moreover, the findings of an agency may be admissible under Fed. R. Evid. 803(8)(C), perhaps eliminating the need for certain discovery. *See, e.g., In re* Japanese Elec. Prods. Antitrust Litig., 723 F.2d 238 (3d Cir. 1983), *rev'd on other grounds sub. nom.* Matsushita Elec. Indus. Co. v. Zenith Radio Corp., 475 U.S. 574 (1986); *In re* Plywood Antitrust Litig., 655 F.2d 527 (5th Cir. 1981).

removal of,[1007] nor an injunction against,[1008] the state court proceedings is normally available, the judges involved may coordinate the proceedings informally. See *supra* section 31.31.

The availability to different classes of purchasers of separate and distinct remedies in state and federal court, along with the general unavailability of injunctions against state proceedings, can create serious problems in achieving global settlements.[1009] In some circumstances, however, a court may enjoin state proceedings under the All Writs Act[1010] to effectuate a global settlement of complex litigation.[1011]

1007. Although state and federal claims may substantially overlap, federal antitrust law does not preempt state law, *see* California v. ARC Am. Corp., 490 U.S. 93 (1989), and removal is not permissible except in the unusual case where the court finds that the claim asserted is simply a disguised federal claim. *See* Federated Dep't Stores v. Moitie, 452 U.S. 394, 397 n.2 (1981) (reaching merits of defense in antitrust action removed from state court).

1008. *See* 28 U.S.C. § 2283 (Anti-Injunction Act); Younger v. Harris, 401 U.S. 37 (1971) (federal courts should ordinarily not enjoin pending state criminal proceedings).

1009. Antitrust claims are frequently brought under state antitrust laws that permit indirect purchasers to recover or provide a more favorable measure of damages. *See* Alton Box Board Co. v. Esprit De Corps, 682 F.2d 1267 (9th Cir. 1982); *In re* Corrugated Container Antitrust Litig., 659 F.2d 1332, 1336 (5th Cir. 1981). Thus, a settlement with the federal plaintiffs (direct purchasers) will not bar later state law claims by indirect purchasers. *ARC Am. Corp.*, 490 U.S. 93. *See* Philip. E. Areeda & Herbert Hovencamp, Antitrust Law ¶¶ 337.4 (indirect purchasers under federal and state law), 323.1 (*res judicata* and state law) (Supp. 1992).

1010. 28 U.S.C. § 1651. *See* FTC v. Dean Foods Co., 384 U.S. 597, 603–04 (citing cases interpreting Act).

1011. *See, e.g.*, Battle v. Liberty Nat. Life Ins. Co., 877 F.2d 877 (11th Cir. 1989), *aff'g* 600 F. Supp. 1449 (N.D. Ala. 1987); *In re Corrugated Container*, 659 F.2d 1332. *Cf. In re* Real Estate Title & Settlement Servs. Antitrust Litig., 869 F.2d 760 (3d Cir. 1989) (vacating injunction for lack of personal jurisdiction); *Alton Box*, 682 F.2d at 1270–73 (upholding denial of injunction sought against nonparty to federal action in different court). See *supra* § 31.32 (jurisdictional conflicts in related state and federal cases).

33.2 Mass Torts

Courts have long recognized the need for special procedures in litigation involving multiple tort claims arising from a mass disaster, such as a hotel fire, the crash of a commercial airliner, or a major chemical explosion or oil spill. More recently, the need for special procedures has been starkly demonstrated by the rapidly increasing volume of litigation involving new types of disasters—numerous claims arising from discrete uses of or exposures to widely distributed products or substances, usually over an extended period of time.[1012] Such claims have led to the recognition of a new type of mass tort, sometimes called a latent toxic tort or simply a toxic tort. Examples include claims associated with exposure to asbestos, Dalkon Shield IUDs, silicone gel breast implants, and pharmaceutical products such as MER/29. Mass torts may also involve alleged defects in mass-produced mechanical products, such as a heart valve, a computer keyboard, or an automobile. The key element of such claims is generally the similarity of activity connected with the design and manufacture of a product, leading to a high volume of repetitive litigation.

Mass tort litigation has stimulated a considerable amount of creativity and experimentation by attorneys and judges pressed to find ways of coping with the volume of litigation, much but not all of it in federal district courts. The ALI Complex Litigation Project found that "[c]reative lawyers and judges have shown

---

1012. See generally American Law Institute, Complex Litigation Project 6–23 [hereinafter ALI Project], for a succinct history of some major events in the history of mass torts; see also Francis E. McGovern, *Resolving Mature Mass Tort Litigation*, 69 B.U. L. Rev. 659 (1989) [hereinafter *Mature Mass Torts*].

that both justice and efficiency can be achieved by those willing to stretch the bounds of the existing procedural scheme to expedite the handling of these cases."[1013] Some of the methods used, including some described in this section, have not been considered, much less approved, by appellate courts. Many innovative approaches raise fundamental questions about whether specific procedures, especially procedures that aggregate or segment claims, are fair to one or another group of litigants.[1014] Discussion in this manual should not be construed as asserting a position on the legality, constitutionality, or fairness of disputed practices. Courts and attorneys should assess independently the legal authority for and against some of the more novel procedures and the often interrelated factors affecting fairness and efficiency.

On the other hand, in addressing novel problems for which legislative and rule-making solutions have not been found, the absence of precedent should not foreclose innovation and creativity. Indeed, the lack of such solutions makes innovation and creativity imperative if the aim of the Federal Rules of Civil Procedure, the "just, speedy, and inexpensive determination of every action," is to be realized.

Mass disaster litigation is distinct from mass toxic tort or defective product litigation. In mass disaster litigation, the injuries occur at a single site and usually manifest themselves immediately; in mass toxic tort or defective product litigation injuries may occur in numerous, widely dispersed locations, at different times, and their full effect may remain hidden for years. All three types of litigation require courts to deal with multiple personal injury and damage claims, but management of mass toxic tort and defective product litigation is substantially more complex and demanding. This section addresses all three types of litigation, identifying different approaches as appropriate.

Management of mass tort litigation is complicated by many factors. Related cases may be filed in different courts, both federal and state, often with multiple plaintiffs and defendants.[1015] Some defendants may be in bankruptcy under either

---

1013. ALI Project, *supra* note 1012, at 9.

1014. For a discussion of the interplay between considerations of efficiency and fairness in deciding whether or not to aggregate claims, see ALI Project, *supra* note 1012, at 53–64.

1015. Complaints with hundreds, or even thousands, of named plaintiffs are sometimes filed, but courts have limited this practice, for example by strict application of the "same transaction or occurrence or series of transactions or occurrences" test of Fed. R. Civ. P. 20(a). *See, e.g.,* Ali Abdullah v. ACandS, Inc., No. 94-1085, 1994 U.S. App. LEXIS 19760 (1st Cir. August 1, 1994) (affirming the dismissal of a complaint on behalf of 1,000 plaintiffs against 93 defendants on grounds that the complaint did not meet Fed. R. Civ. P. 20's prerequisites for joinder—the "same transaction, occurrence, or series of transactions or occurrences" rule—and that its filing did not comply with local rules regarding the specificity of pleading for asbestos complaints); *see also* Aaberg v. ACandS Inc., No S-93-2185, 1994 U.S. Dist. LEXIS 116 (D. Md. Jan. 7, 1994) (complaint attempting to join 1,000 maritime asbestos plaintiffs against 93 defendants).

Chapter 11 reorganization or Chapter 7 liquidation, sometimes at different stages. The ability of future claimants to obtain compensation may be at risk. Cases may be governed by different state laws regarding such issues as liability, the measure of compensatory damages, the standards for award of punitive damages, the statute of limitations, insurance coverage, and rights of contribution or indemnification. Pronounced conflicts may exist among the defendants, and the filing of third-party complaints may result in the joinder of numerous additional parties. Highly technical expert testimony is usually needed, and its admissibility often disputed, calling into play the judge's role as the gatekeeper in reviewing novel scientific evidence.[1016] Conflicts may arise for judges and lawyers out of the complexity and volume of present and future claims, the need to adapt traditional procedures to new contexts, and the need for the judge to assume an active role in managing the litigation.[1017]

The ability to consolidate separate cases for joint trial may be hampered by the sheer numbers of cases and the practical limits of consolidated proceedings; moreover, consolidation of cases on all issues may not be feasible because of individualized disputes as to causation and damages. If available funds are insufficient to cover all claims, groups of plaintiffs may compete to obtain an early trial or settlement. Certain cases—for example those in which the plaintiff is severely disabled, hospitalized, or near death—may involve claims for priority.[1018]

1016. See *supra* §§ 21.48, 21.64. In Daubert v. Merrell Dow Pharmaceuticals, Inc., 113 S. Ct. 2786 (1993), the Court stated that the trial judge is responsible for determining the relevance of expert testimony and the reliability of the methodology upon which the expert relies. *Id.* at 2799. The Supreme Court also identified four illustrative factors for the trial judge to consider when assessing the methodology underlying expert testimony:
  1. whether a scientific theory or principle can be and has been tested;
  2. whether the theory or technique has been subjected to peer review and publication;
  3. whether the known or potential rate of error indicates reliability; and
  4. whether the theory or technique has gained general acceptance in the scientific community.

See Reference Manual on Scientific Evidence (Federal Judicial Center 1994).

1017. *See generally* Jack B. Weinstein, *Ethical Dilemmas in Mass Torts Litigation,* 88 Nw. U. L. Rev. 469 (1994); Geoffrey Hazard, *Commentary, Reflections on Judge Weinstein's Ethical Dilemmas in Mass Torts Litigation,* 88 Nw. U. L. Rev. 569 (1994).

1018. *See generally* 28 U.S.C. § 1657; Fed. R. Civ. P. 40. To preserve the authority of judges to establish priorities on a case-by-case basis, the Judicial Conference has generally opposed *statutory* priorities other than those embodied in 28 U.S.C. § 1657. *See, e.g.,* Report of the Proceedings of the Judicial Conference of the United States 80 (September 1990) (reiterating "strong opposition to legislative provisions imposing statutory litigation priority"). The conference acted on the recommendation of its Committee on Federal–State Jurisdiction, which articulated the above policy in part because "individual cases within a class of cases inevitably have different need of priority treatment" and because "priorities are best set on a case by case basis as dictated by the exigent circumstances of the case and the status of the court docket." Report of Committee on Federal–State

To insure the existence of funds to compensate future claimants, payment of damage awards may have to be deferred or apportioned.

33.21 Centralized Management

All related litigation pending in the same court, including actions regarding insurance coverage, suits for indemnification, and adversary proceedings in bankruptcy,[1019] should ordinarily be assigned to the same judge, at least for pretrial management.[1020] Similarly, if several cases are remanded to a transferor court for trial after a period of multidistrict supervision under 28 U.S.C. § 1407,[1021] they should all be assigned to one judge, at least initially, to coordinate such further discovery as may be needed and to determine the most appropriate trial structure and schedule.

The duration of unitary judicial supervision will depend on the circumstances of the litigation. After a period of centralized management, the court may conclude that the trial of some issues—for example, disputes over insurance coverage—may be conducted just as efficiently by another judge. The court may determine that separate trials should be held of individual actions, or of groups of individual actions, or of particular common issues, such as exposure and damages, and may need to arrange for assignments to several judges after common discovery has been completed.

Jurisdiction to the Judicial Conference 5 (September 1990) (unpublished manuscript on file with the Office of the Judicial Conference secretariat, Administrative Office of the U.S. Courts). See also the discussion of the deferred or dormant docket in *infra* § 33.253.

1019. References to bankruptcy judges of proceedings to determine the dischargeability of tort claims may be withdrawn by the district court and assigned to the judge supervising the underlying claims. 28 U.S.C. § 157(d). The court may also decide to defer transfer of multiple claims for personal injury or wrongful death under 28 U.S.C. § 157(c)(5) until after a period of centralized pretrial management. In some mass tort contexts, district judges and bankruptcy judges have presided jointly and issued joint opinions and orders. *See, e.g., In re* A.H. Robins Co., Inc. (Carolyn C. v. Dalkon Shield Claimants Trust, 158 Bankr. 640), 1993 Bankr. LEXIS 1335 (Bankr. E.D. Va. August 31, 1993); *In re* Joint E. & S. Dist. Asbestos Litig. (Estate of Findley), NYAL Index No. 4000, CV 90-3973, 1993 U.S. Dist. LEXIS 7843 (E.D.N.Y., S.D.N.Y. June 10, 1993).

1020. Supervision of all cases by one judge can provide centralized management of the cases pending in that court and also can facilitate coordination with other courts. Assignment to a single judge may, however, have the effect of delaying disposition and of limiting the judicial resources available for managing mass tort litigation. For a discussion of various approaches and their effects, see Thomas E. Willging, Trends in Asbestos Litigation 31–46 (Federal Judicial Center 1987) [hereinafter Trends].

1021. See *supra* § 31.13. The general intent underlying 28 U.S.C. § 1407 is to eliminate duplicative discovery, reduce excessive litigation costs, and reduce or prevent inconsistent rulings from different courts. *See In re* Plumbing Fixtures Cases, 298 F. Supp. 484, 499 (J.P.M.L. 1968).

33.22 Case-Management Orders

When responsibility for numerous related cases is centralized in a single judge, continuous, active case management is imperative. Case-management plans and orders must be promptly developed, updated, and modified as the litigation unfolds. An initial, interim case-management order will set the stage for the ongoing management process. That order should, among other things, help organize the cases and counsel, preserve evidence, set priorities for pretrial pleadings and other activity, defer unnecessary pleadings, identify preliminarily the legal and factual issues, outline preliminary discovery and motions, and direct counsel to coordinate the implementation of the order. The order should take into account the proposals of counsel and should encourage collaboration among counsel and the parties.[1022]

Items that may be covered in initial and follow-up case-management orders in mass tort litigation are illustrated by the orders issued in one major product liability litigation.[1023] The initial case-management order in that litigation,[1024] issued shortly after the Judicial Panel on Multidistrict Litigation transferred the cases to the transferee judge, contained provisions which:

- set the agenda and ground rules for the initial conference, notified parties that attendance would not be necessary and that parties with similar interests would be expected to agree to be represented at the conference by a single attorney;

- established an initial service list of counsel;

- urged counsel to familiarize themselves with the *Manual for Complex Litigation, Third* and "be prepared at the conference to suggest procedures that will facilitate the expeditious, economical, and just resolution of this litigation";

- directed counsel for each side to meet, confer, and seek consensus on all agenda items and, specifically, to propose a discovery plan, including methods to obtain expert discovery, a timetable for considering motions,

---

1022. See generally *supra* §§ 21.2 and 21.3.

1023. *In re* Silicone Gel Breast Implant Prods. Liab. Litig., MDL No. 926, 793 F. Supp. 1098 (J.P.M.L. 1992) (transferring federal breast implant cases to the U.S. District Court for the Northern District of Alabama). The Mass Tort Case-Management Order presented *infra* § 41.52 was derived in large part from orders issued in the breast implant litigation. Judge Raymond L. Acosta prepared a comprehensive set of case-management orders dealing with a common disaster mass tort trial in *In re* San Juan Dupont Plaza Hotel Fire Litig., MDL No. 721. Most, perhaps all, of the orders issued in that litigation are available through LEXIS and Westlaw.

1024. *In re* Silicone Gel Breast Implant Prods. Liab. Litig., MDL No. 926, Order No. 1 (N.D. Ala. June 26, 1992).

and a proposal addressing whether to maintain one or more cases as class actions;

- called for consolidated (1) preliminary reports on the critical factual and legal issues, (2) lists of all affiliated companies and counsel (to assist the court in addressing recusal or disqualification questions), (3) lists of pending motions, and (4) summaries of the nature and status of similar litigation pending in state courts;

- directed attorneys interested in serving as lead, liaison, or coordinating counsel to "submit information showing how and at what rates they will be expected to be compensated" and to disclose any "agreements or commitments they have made respecting the role and responsibility of other attorneys in conducting pretrial proceedings, discovery, and trial";

- consolidated all cases for pretrial proceedings, created a master docket and file, and established a case caption format;

- barred motions under Rule 11 or 56 without leave of court and ordered that counsel meet and attempt to resolve other motions (except Rule 12 motions to dismiss);

- ordered the parties to preserve all documents and records containing relevant information and established ground rules for any routine purges of computer records;

- stayed formal discovery and granted extensions of time for responding to complaints and motions, pending establishment of a schedule; and

- announced the judge's intention to handle all matters personally and designated a magistrate judge to handle matters requiring immediate judicial attention when the district judge was unavailable.

After the initial conference, the court issued a revised case-management order[1025] which:

- permitted the admission *pro hac vice* of any attorney licensed to practice in another federal court;

- reaffirmed the consolidation of all cases for pretrial purposes only;

- finalized the procedures for filing materials in the master file or in separate case files and for corresponding with the court;

- provided a list of counsel for defendants, all of whom were authorized by their clients to accept service of process by certified mail;

1025. *Id.*, Order No. 5 (Revised Case-Management Order), entered September 15, 1992.

- granted leave for plaintiffs' counsel to add, without further motion or order, additional plaintiffs from the same state as parties with pending claims against the same defendants;
- designated liaison counsel and established a procedure for serving orders, pleadings, and other documents;
- established a master pleading system for complaints and answers;
- deemed that any motion or order applied to each similarly situated party unless that party disavowed it;
- continued to bar filing of Rule 11 and Rule 56 motions without leave of court;
- entered a comprehensive discovery order with the objectives of
     – producing discovery that would support separate trials for each case,
     – using discovery from prior federal and state trials and depositions,
     – preparing videotaped depositions for witnesses who will testify more than once,
     – making all discovery readily accessible to federal and state litigants by creating a joint plaintiff–defendant, federal–state library,
     – keeping claims of confidentiality and protective orders to a minimum,
     – accommodating discovery in federal and state courts, and
     – dividing discovery into national, regional, and case-specific categories;
- defined the role of the plaintiffs' steering committee;
- established preliminary guidelines for conducting depositions, provided a system for resolving disputes arising during depositions,[1026] and fixed a procedure for use of depositions at trial;
- appointed a special master to assist the court in coordinating federal and state discovery and enjoined any party from objecting to use of a federal deposition in a state court action based on the fact that the deposition was not taken in the state court action;
- extended indefinitely the time for opting out of a provisionally certified class action and stated that the pendency of that action would toll the statute of limitations for members of that class; and
- kept open the question of trial structure and schedule.

1026. Later, the judge issued a 27-page order expanding on the deposition guidelines issued in Order No. 5. *Id.*, Order No. 11 (deposition guidelines), entered June 29, 1993.

These orders were subject to modification throughout the course of the litigation. The court scheduled and conducted monthly status conferences to consider problems, hear and rule on motions, and when necessary modify or supplement case-management orders. Later the court created an electronic bulletin board to facilitate communication[1027] and initiated a procedure to use CD-ROM technology to image and store defendants' discovery documents, making them accessible to parties at a modest cost.[1028]

Effective management requires constant attention to developments in the litigation. Problems—including difficulties in implementing current orders—need to be promptly identified and resolved. By soliciting feedback on the operation of the case-management plan on a continuous basis, the judge is able to obtain the information necessary to adjust case-management procedures as needed.

33.23 State–Federal Coordination

Mass tort litigation frequently involves filings in both federal and state courts. While multidistrict treatment of the federal cases under 28 U.S.C. § 1407 may be possible,[1029] some state court cases may not have been removed—or may not be removable—and therefore are not subject to § 1407 transfer. When consolidated treatment in a single court is not possible, state and federal judges should coordinate the proceedings.

Coordination between state and federal courts has the potential of reducing duplication of effort, with the resulting waste of resources, and of minimizing conflicts between jurisdictions. Courts have been able to coordinate scheduling and discovery plans, to appoint joint special masters and lead counsel, to create federal–state depositories, to preside jointly at hearings, and to conduct joint settlement and alternative dispute resolution procedures.[1030] The difficulty of co-

1027. *Id.*, Order No. 7, entered October 6, 1992, which served as the model for the Electronic Bulletin Board Order, *infra* § 41.39.

1028. *Id.*, Order No. 4, entered September 9, 1992.

1029. See *supra* § 31.13. The Judicial Panel on Multidistrict Litigation has consolidated a number of mass tort cases for centralized pretrial management. After initially rejecting applications to consolidate asbestos personal injury actions, see, e.g., *In re* Asbestos & Asbestos Insulation Material Prod. Liab. Litig., 431 F. Supp. 906 (J.P.M.L. 1977), the panel later transferred all pending federal asbestos personal injury claims in the Eastern District of Pennsylvania. *In re* Asbestos Prods. Liab. Litig., 771 F. Supp. 415 (J.P.M.L. 1993); *In re* Silicone Gel Breast Implant Prods. Liab. Litig. (MDL Docket No. 926), 793 F. Supp. 1098 (J.P.M.L. 1992); *see also In re* Swine Flu Immunization Prod. Liab. Litig., 464 F. Supp. 949 (1979); *In re* A.H. Robins Co. "Dalkon Shield" IUD Prod. Liab. Litig., 406 F. Supp. 540 (J.P.M.L. 1975).

1030. William W Schwarzer et al., *Judicial Federalism in Action: Coordination of Litigation in State and Federal Courts*, 78 Va. L. Rev. 1689, 1700–06 (1992), documents eleven case studies of such cooperation. Most of the cases involved mass torts, including three major air crashes, two groups of asbestos cases, two hotel fires, two building collapses, an investment fraud case, and an oil spill.

ordination increases, however, with the degree of dispersion of the cases; coordination within one or two states is much more readily accomplished than national coordination, though an effort should be made in the latter situation as well, especially when the MDL process has been used to consolidate federal cases.

The following are some of the steps a judge may consider to coordinate cases with state court judges:

- direct counsel to identify the names of all similar cases that have been filed in state court, the judges to whom they are assigned, and their state of pretrial preparation;

- contact judges with significant numbers of cases in each state and encourage those judges to establish lines of communication within their state, such as designating a liaison attorney and judge to communicate with federal counterparts;

- appoint one or more attorneys to serve as liaison with each state court in which a significant number of similar cases have been filed;

- appoint a special master with primary responsibility for monitoring, coordinating, and disseminating information about state and federal activities;

- send sample or model case-management orders, master pleadings, questionnaires, and discovery protocols to state judges with similar cases and encourage them to adopt the same or similar approaches to discovery and pretrial management;

- establish a mechanism to coordinate trial dates or to conduct joint trials;

- create joint federal–state, plaintiff–defendant document depositories that will be accessible to attorneys in all states;

- schedule joint federal–state depositions;

- hold joint pretrial conferences;

- order discovery materials from prior state and federal cases to be included in the document depository;

- enjoin attorneys who conduct federal discovery from objecting to its use in state proceedings on the grounds that it originated in a federal court;

- issue joint orders for the preservation of evidence and coordinate the examination of evidence by experts in both state and federal proceedings; and

- preside jointly at status conferences, motion hearings, and perhaps even at trial.[1031]

By initiating communications with the judge's state or federal counterpart, the judge creates an opportunity for cooperation that can lead to innovative and effective methods for the management and disposition of the litigation.

33.24 Organization of Counsel[1032]

Several factors may complicate efforts to coordinate the attorneys' activities through appointment of lead counsel and committees. The same factors, however, also increase the need for coordination among attorneys and for judicial involvement in organizing counsel for efficient conduct of the litigation.

Attorneys representing the plaintiffs may be unaccustomed to working as part of a litigation team; often they will have highly individualistic styles and different approaches toward discovery and trial.[1033] Incentives to cooperate may, however, be created by pretrial rulings. If, for example, the cases are certified as class actions, judicial control over the award of attorneys' fees permits the judge to influence directly the organization of counsel.[1034] By scheduling consolidated cases for an early trial, the court may give plaintiffs' counsel incentives to join in consolidated pretrial preparation. Requiring attorneys on the same side to meet and confer regarding common positions on motions can also further cooperation.

Conflicts in legal and strategic positions may make appointment of lead counsel for the defendants difficult. Nevertheless, a number of common defenses are likely, and the court should consider creating incentives for the parties to confer with lead counsel before embarking on any separate course of action. For example, the judge may require that individual arguments be submitted to lead counsel for consideration prior to the lead argument to the court and that lead counsel present all individual arguments that are not inconsistent with the lead argument.

At a minimum, the court should designate one or more attorneys for the plaintiffs and defendants to present motions and arguments during coordinated

---

1031. See generally the orders issued in *In re* Silicone Gel Breast Implant Prods. Liab. Litig., MDL No. 926 (N.D. Ala. July 23, 1992).

1032. See *supra* § 20.22.

1033. Cooperation among plaintiffs' counsel through formation of national professional associations to share discovery materials, technical studies, and legal research is, however, increasingly common in major mass tort litigation. Through such efforts, the time and expense of discovery in individual cases can be substantially reduced. Protective orders covering confidential information obtained during discovery in one case may be drafted to enable disclosure to attorneys for use in the other related cases, subject to appropriate restrictions precluding use or disclosure for nonlitigation purposes.

1034. See *supra* §§ 30.16, 30.42.

pretrial proceedings and to conduct common discovery.[1035] Disagreements among the parties and counsel should not prevent designation of an attorney to act as liaison counsel in distributing documents and developing joint discovery requests.

33.25 Parties, Pleading, Docketing, and Issues

33.251 Parties

Management of mass tort cases may be complicated by the addition of new parties. New actions may be commenced throughout the course of the litigation, particularly in cases involving latent toxic torts. Moreover, as discovery progresses additional defendants may be joined by amendments to plaintiffs' complaints or by a succession of third-party complaints.

Pursuant to Fed. R. Civ. P. 16(b)(1), the court should establish at the initial pretrial conference a schedule for joinder of additional parties and amendment of pleadings. The parties should be afforded a reasonable opportunity for discovery before the deadline for adding parties or amending pleadings, but the schedule should not be modified without a showing of good cause. The court may establish a presumptive period for later-added parties to join other parties—usually sixty days from service—subject to their right to seek additional time.

The court should also develop a system for incorporating new plaintiffs into the structure of the litigation. For example, if prior cases are consolidated into clusters by worksite, disease, or some other feature, a system needs to be devised

---

1035. The cost of these services may be apportioned among all parties who benefit from the services. *See* Smiley v. Sincoff, 958 F.2d 498 (2d Cir. 1992); *In re* Air Crash Disaster at Fla. Everglades, 549 F.2d 1006 (5th Cir. 1977); *In re* Silicone Gel Breast Implant Prods. Liab. Litig., MDL No. 926, Order No. 13 (N.D. Ala. July 23, 1992). Any process established to determine or change the allocation of fees must afford those affected an opportunity to be heard. *In re* Nineteen Appeals Arising out of the San Juan Dupont Plaza Hotel Fire Litig., 982 F.2d 603 (1st Cir. 1992). Objections to fees and assessments, and proposals to amend the fee structure, can be assigned to a special master. *In re* Shell Oil Refinery, Civil Action No. 88-1935, Order and Reasons (E.D. La. January 13, 1989).

Once made aware of the court's powers, counsel have usually been able to agree on an equitable method for making such payments, either by establishing a fund through advance assessments or by periodic billings. Contributions may be required from parties subsequently settling and from those in later-filed cases. See *supra* § 20.223; *In re* Swine Flu Immunization Prod. Liab. Litig., 89 F.R.D. 695 (D.D.C. 1981); *cf.* Vincent v. Hughes Air W., Inc., 557 F.2d 759 (9th Cir. 1977) (improper to assess persons settling before appointment of lead counsel or without filing suit).

for assigning new cases to appropriate groups or for creating new groups. Such a system may entail the collection of information about the characteristics of each new case. Necessary data could be collected at filing and could be used to create a database that would provide a continuous flow of the type of information needed to manage the litigation.

The court may also wish to consider directing the defendants to compile information, such as the dates on which and areas in which each defendant marketed a particular product, so that plaintiffs can determine the appropriate defendants to sue. Such records might forestall claims against the entire universe of defendants.[1036]

Discovery should not ordinarily be postponed until all parties have been joined; indeed, some discovery often will be needed before all potential parties can be identified. Interrogatories may be served on the existing parties; their answers will be available to, and usable by, any parties later added to the litigation. Similarly, new parties may use documents produced in response to requests by others and should ordinarily be given access to document depositories.[1037] To facilitate the use of depositions by new parties, the court may adopt the procedures described in *supra* section 21.453 (deferred supplemental depositions).

33.252 Pleadings

Particularly if the litigation will involve a number of actions filed, removed, or transferred over a period of time, the court should consider establishing a master file with standard pleadings, motions, and orders.[1038] Answers, third-party complaints, and motions contained in the master file may be "deemed" automatically filed in each new case to the extent applicable.[1039] Similarly, rulings on motions under Fed. R. Civ. P. 12 and 56 may be deemed to apply in the new cases, as may a pretrial order establishing a standard plan and schedule for discovery. These procedures will expedite proceedings in the later-filed cases, while preserving the parties' rights to claim error from adverse rulings. The parties should not, however, be precluded from presenting special issues or requests in individual cases by supplemental pleadings, motions, and arguments.

33.253 Docketing

In latent toxic torts, exposure to the product and the early manifestation of injuries may precede functional disability and loss of earnings by years or even decades. Nevertheless, parties may file cases to prevent statutes of limitations

---

1036. *See In re* Coordinated Breast Implant Litig., No. JCCP-2754-0001 (Cal. Super. Ct., San Diego County).

1037. See *supra* § 21.444.

1038. See Sample Order *infra* § 41.52.

1039. See *supra* § 21.32 (pleading and motion practice).

(which run from discovery or the time the claim arises) or statutes of repose (which run from the occurrence of the actionable event) from extinguishing their claims. Some courts, generally with the consent of the parties affected, have established dormant or inactive dockets to register such claims with the court, deferring their consideration until the injuries become manifest.[1040]

33.254 Issues

Identifying the issues—and the governing statutory or decisional law—is critical in developing a plan for the efficient resolution of complex tort litigation. Multiple tort cases frequently involve claims and defenses asserted under various federal and state laws. In an early conference, the court may be able to persuade the parties to agree to streamline their claims and defenses, for example, by trading off a weak claim against a weak defense.

Some legal issues may be capable of being resolved and reviewed on interlocutory appeal relatively early in the litigation.[1041] This procedure has been used to decide whether claims were cognizable under federal common law,[1042] barred by the statute of limitations,[1043] or governed by collateral estoppel.[1044] Major disputes over insurance coverage, which can frustrate management of the underlying claims, may also warrant early attention and appellate review.[1045] Interlocutory certification of controlling but unresolved questions of state law to state courts may also be feasible.[1046]

Differences in the substantive law governing liability and damages may substantially affect discovery, trial, and settlement. In mass disaster litigation, the court may find upon analysis of the applicable choice-of-law rules[1047] that the

---

1040. *See, e.g., In re* Asbestos II Consolidated Pretrial, 142 F.R.D. 152 (N.D. Ill. 1991). *See generally,* Trends, *supra* note 1020 at 51–54; *see also* the discussion of priorities, *supra* note 1018.

1041. See *supra* §§ 25.11–25.12.

1042. *See In re* "Agent Orange" Prod. Liab. Litig., 635 F.2d 987 (2d Cir. 1980).

1043. *See* Neubauer v. Owens-Corning Fiberglas Corp., 686 F.2d 570 (7th Cir. 1982).

1044. *See* Miller v. Delta Air Lines, Inc., 861 F.2d 814 (5th Cir. 1988); *In re* Asbestos Litig. (Raymark Indus., Inc.), 829 F.2d 1233, 1242 (3d Cir. 1987); Hardy v. Johns-Manville Sales Corp., 681 F.2d 334 (5th Cir. 1982); Ezagui v. Dow Chem. Corp., 598 F.2d 727 (2d Cir. 1979). *See also* Michael Green, *The Inability of Offensive Collateral Estoppel to Fulfill Its Promise: An Examination of Estoppel in Asbestos Litigation,* 70 Iowa L. Rev. 141 (1984).

1045. *See, e.g.,* Keene Corp. v. Insurance Co. of N. Am., 667 F.2d 1034 (D.C. Cir. 1981) (appeal under 28 U.S.C. § 1292(b)).

1046. See *supra* § 25.1.

1047. In diversity cases, the federal court must apply the choice-of-law rules of the state in which it sits. Klaxon Co. v. Stentor Elec. Mfg. Co., 313 U.S. 487 (1941). In a case transferred under 28 U.S.C. § 1404(a), the transferee court must apply the choice-of-law rules that would have governed in the transferor court. Ferens v. John Deere Co., 494 U.S. 516 (1990); Van Dusen v. Barrack, 376 U.S. 612 (1964). If, however, venue is improper or personal jurisdiction is lacking in the transferor court, transfer must be made pursuant to 28 U.S.C. § 1406, Goldlawr, Inc. v. Heiman, 369 U.S. 463

---

same state law governs all cases[1048] or that subclasses or other consolidated groups can be created.[1049] In national toxic tort and defective products class action litigation, choice-of-law issues will be more problematic because there may be a wide range of applicable laws and the state in which the action is filed may not have a significant relationship with many of the class members, with the defendants, or with the activities that are subject to the litigation.[1050] To protect against a lack of claim or issue preclusion, the court may have to ensure that—in addition to giving notice and an easy-to-execute right to opt out—it applies state law having a significant relationship to the litigation or explicitly consented to by the parties.[1051]

The following are some of the issues to be addressed early in the litigation: (1) whether to certify one or more classes generally or for particular claims or issues;[1052] (2) whether to consolidate groups of cases under Fed. R. Civ. P. 42(a) for pretrial management; (3) whether punitive damages may be claimed;[1053] and (4) whether plaintiffs' claims are barred by limitations or other legal bars.

(1962), and the choice-of-law rules of the transferee court apply. *See, e.g.,* Tel-phonic Servs., Inc. v. TBS Intern., Inc., 975 F.2d 1134, 1141 (5th Cir. 1992); Manley v. Engram, 755 F.2d 1463, 1467 (11th Cir. 1985). See *supra* note 14. These statutes should not be confused with 28 U.S.C.A. § 1631 (West. Supp. 1993), which provides for transfer of cases from courts lacking subject-matter jurisdiction.

1048. As a threshold matter, there "can be no injury in applying . . . [the forum state's law] if it is not in conflict with that of any other jurisdiction" connected with the litigation. Phillips Petroleum Co. v. Shutts, 472 U.S. 797, 816 (1985). *See also, e.g., In re* Air Crash Disaster near Chicago, Ill., 644 F.2d 594 (7th Cir. 1981) (punitive damages); *In re* Air Crash Disaster near Chicago, Ill., 644 F.2d 633 (7th Cir. 1981) (prejudgment interest).

1049. *In re* School Asbestos Litig., 977 F.2d 796–98 (3d Cir. 1992) (division of state laws into four categories that encompass the variations in the product liability laws of the states may prove successful; plaintiff's proposal to pursue the strictest state standards of liability would raise constitutional issues about whether class members from a state with a less strict law could be precluded from challenging an adverse decision based on another state's stricter standard).

1050. *Phillips Petroleum,* 472 U.S. at 821–22 (where a state does not have significant contacts with the claims asserted by each member of the plaintiff class, the application of that state's law to all members of the class is arbitrary, unfair, and hence unconstitutional); *see also In re* Real Estate Title and Settlement Servs. Antitrust Litig., 869 F.2d 760 (3d Cir. 1989) ("if the [putative class] member has not been given the opportunity to opt out in a class action involving both important injunctive relief and damage claims, the member must have minimum contacts with the forum or consent to jurisdiction" to be precluded from litigating its claims in its own forum).

1051. For discussion of the need for and a proposal for a federal choice-of-law standard to apply in mass tort contexts, see ALI Project, *supra* note 1012, at 375–98.

1052. See *supra* § 30.1. *See also* Fed. R. Civ. P. 23(c)(4)(A); Jenkins v. Raymark, 782 F.2d 468 (5th Cir. 1986) (approving certification of class to determine viability of "state of the art" defense and other specified issues).

1053. *See generally* Dunn v. Hovic, 1 F.3d 1371 (3d Cir. 1993) (en banc); Simpson v. Pittsburgh Corning Corp., 901 F.2d 277 (2d Cir. 1990).

33.26 Consolidation/Class Action

Aggregation of claims can be a major factor in the fair and efficient management of mass tort litigation. It can facilitate centralized decision making, minimize duplication, reduce cost and delay, further consistency in outcomes and fairness to the parties, and enhance the prospect of settlement. Implementation of aggregation in mass tort litigation, however, confronts the court with often very difficult problems that should be addressed early in the litigation.[1054] Moreover, because of the magnitude of the exposure, the complexity of management, and the predominance of individual issues, aggregation, whether through consolidation or class action treatment, may not be appropriate for some litigation.[1055] In general, those mass torts in which general causation has become relatively clear over time are likely to be candidates for large consolidations or even class action treatment. Fairness may demand that mass torts with few prior verdicts or judgments be litigated first in smaller units—even single-plaintiff, single-defendant trials—until general causation, typical injuries, and levels of damages become established.[1056] Thus, "mature" mass torts like asbestos or Dalkon Shield may call for procedures that are not appropriate for incipient mass tort cases, such as those involving injuries arising from new products, chemical substances, or pharmaceuticals.[1057]

33.261 Consolidation

In mass disaster or toxic tort litigation, consolidation of all or most of the individual cases may be feasible and efficient.[1058] In other mass tort litigation, consolidation may be feasible by subdividing cases into clusters that raise similar issues or present similar case-management needs. Consolidation may be limited to

---

1054. For a discussion of the structural differences between class actions and consolidations, see Charles Silver, *Comparing Class Actions and Consolidations,* 10 Rev. Litig. 495 (1991).

1055. *See, e.g., In re* Repetitive Stress Injury Litig., 11 F. 3d 368 (2d Cir. 1993); Kranz v. National Gypsum, 995 F.2d 346 (2d Cir. 1993).

1056. Empirical research suggests that decisions to consolidate or bifurcate trials may affect jury decisions about liability and damages. Irwin A. Horowitz & Kenneth S. Bordens, *Mass Tort Civil Litigation: The Impact of Procedural Changes on Jury Decisions,* 73 Judicature 22 (1989).

1057. Litigation is "mature" if through previous cases (1) discovery has been completed, (2) a number of verdicts have been received indicating the value of claims, and (3) plaintiffs' contentions have been shown to have merit. *See* McGovern, *Mature Mass Torts, supra* note 1012, at 659. Typically, in such litigation little or no new evidence is likely, appellate review of novel legal issues has been completed, and a full cycle of trial strategies has been exhausted; examples include the asbestos and Dalkon Shield litigation. *Id.* at 659.

1058. *See id.* at 687, 690. *But see supra* note 1055 and accompanying text.

discovery or motion activity, or it may extend to trial. In dealing with novel claims, however, it may be advisable to postpone deciding on a trial structure until the issues have been clarified through discovery and motions; consolidation should not be ordered until it is sufficiently clear that genuine common questions of fact or law exist.[1059]

When different state laws apply, as in most multidistrict proceedings, organizing cases by state or groups of states should be considered.[1060] Courts should also consider whether the cases have the same counsel on one or both sides and whether the cases are at similar stages of discovery and other pretrial development. In some instances, cases having substantially the same evidence, particularly expert and fact witnesses, may be combined. In cases with large numbers of plaintiffs, the court may want to consider directing the parties or a special master to create a database containing relevant identifiable characteristics of the parties that might affect settlement, discovery, or trial. In toxic tort litigation, a database might store information such as (1) the circumstances of exposure to the toxic product (e.g., the worksite or other locus, time span, amount of exposure), (2) the types of diseases or injuries attributable to the exposure (e.g., asbestosis, lung cancer, pleural thickening), (3) relevant and distinguishing characteristics of multiple products, and (4) commonalty of occupations or other roles (e.g., consumer, bystander, spouse).[1061]

Cases may be consolidated for pretrial proceedings, and even for trial, notwithstanding differences in the applicable substantive law. The evidence on liability that will be sought during discovery and presented at trial is often the same whether claims are premised, for example, on negligence, breach of warranty, or strict liability. Jurors in a single trial may be asked to resolve by special verdict such questions as whether a product was negligently designed or manufactured, whether it was reasonably suited for its intended use, whether it presented an unreasonable danger to consumers, and whether adequate warnings were given about its use. Differences in the defenses and the measure of damages should create no major problems during discovery. They need to be taken into account, however, in structuring the trial; in appropriate circumstances, a joint trial of common issues may be feasible, followed by separate trials of remaining issues.[1062]

1059. See In re Repetitive Stress Injury Litig., 11 F.3d 368 (2d Cir. 1993).

1060. See In re School Asbestos Litig., 789 F.2d 996, 1010–11 (3d Cir. 1986).

1061. See Johnson v. Celotex, 899 F.2d 1281 (2d Cir. 1990); Hendrix v. Raybestos-Manhattan, Inc., 776 F.2d 1492 (11th Cir. 1985); see also Trends, supra note 1020, at 104–07.

1062. To avoid inconsistent adjudication and duplicative presentation of evidence, punitive damage claims should ordinarily be tried to the same jury that determined liability.

33.262 Class Action[1063]

Despite the Advisory Committee's 1966 caveat,[1064] courts have increasingly utilized class actions to avoid duplicative litigation in mass tort cases, although primarily in the context of settlement (see *supra* section 30.45); few mass tort class actions have gone to trial and judgment. "Opt-out" classes have been certified under Rule 23(b)(3) in litigation arising from mass disasters[1065] and from exposure to toxic substances.[1066] In appropriate cases, common issues of fact or law have been carved out for class certification under Rule 23(c)(4)(A).[1067] Certification has been on both an intradistrict[1068] and on a nationwide basis.[1069] Courts have continued, however, to exercise their discretion to decline certification when class treatment does not appear to be "superior to other available methods,"[1070] such as consolidation or individual treatment.[1071]

1063. See generally *supra* § 30 re class actions.

1064. "A 'mass accident' resulting in injuries to numerous persons is ordinarily not appropriate for a class action because of the likelihood that significant questions would be present, not only of damages but also of liability and defenses of liability, affecting the individuals in different ways. In these circumstances an action conducted nominally as a class action would degenerate in practice into multiple lawsuits separately tried." Fed. R. Civ. P. 23 advisory committee's note, *reprinted in* 39 F.R.D. 69, 103 (1966). For a detailed discussion of the trend away from this view, see *In re* A.H. Robins Co., Inc., 880 F.2d 709, 729–38 (4th Cir. 1989).

1065. Watson v. Shell Oil Co., 979 F.2d 1014, 1020–21 (5th Cir. 1992) (personal injury and property damage claims arising from oil refinery explosion); Coburn v. 4-R Corp., 77 F.R.D. 43 (E.D. Ky. 1977) (Beverly Hills Supper Club fire), *mandamus denied sub nom.* Union Light, Heat & Power Co. v. District Ct., 588 F.2d 543 (6th Cir. 1978); *In re* Federal Skywalk Cases, 95 F.R.D. 483 (W.D. Mo. 1982) (certifying opt-out class of business invitees injured in collapse of hotel skywalk after mandatory class was vacated).

1066. Sterling v. Velsicol Chem. Corp., 855 F.2d 1188 (6th Cir. 1988) (opt-out class of water contamination victims in vicinity of a landfill); *In re* School Asbestos Litig., 789 F.2d 996, 1009 (3d Cir. 1986) (nationwide 23(b)(3) class of schools seeking compensatory damages associated with the presence of asbestos-containing building materials); Jenkins v. Raymark Indus., 782 F.2d 468, 473 (5th Cir. 1986) (districtwide class of asbestos personal injury claimants to resolve specific issues, including the "state of the art" defense); *In re* "Agent Orange" Prod. Liab. Litig., 100 F.R.D. 718 (E.D.N.Y. 1983) (nationwide class of Viet Nam veterans exposed to dioxins certified under Rule 23(b)(3) for compensatory relief and under Rule 23(b)(1)(B) for punitive damages), *mandamus denied sub nom. In re* Diamond Shamrock Chem. Co., 725 F.2d 858 (2d Cir. 1984).

1067. See Wadleigh v. Rhone-Poulenc Rorer, Inc., 157 F.R.D. 410 (N.D. Ill. 1994) (negligence liability for infected blood); *In re* Copley Pharmaceutical, Inc. "Albuteral" Prods. Liab. Litig., 1994 WL 605613 (D. Wy. Oct. 28, 1994) (negligence, breach of warranty claims for contamination of bronchodilator); *supra* note 1052 and accompanying text.

1068. *See, e.g., Sterling*, 855 F.2d 1188; *Jenkins*, 782 F.2d 468.

1069. *See, e.g., School Asbestos*, 789 F.2d 996; *Agent Orange*, 100 F.R.D. 718.

1070. Fed. R. Civ. P. 23(b)(3).

1071. See, e.g., *In re* Fibreboard Corp., 893 F.2d 706, 712 (5th Cir. 1990), recognizing, however, that class action treatment is appropriate for the trial of common defenses and punitive damages. In addition, class action treatment of both liability and damage issues may even be feasible where the

Except in a settlement context, mandatory classes under Fed. R. Civ. P. 23(b)(1) or (2) have rarely been certified in tort cases.[1072] In adversarial (nonsettlement) contexts, courts have disagreed as to the standard for certifying a "limited fund" non-opt-out class under Rule 23(b)(1)(B).[1073] Since mass tort actions usually involve individual claims for monetary relief, courts have held that they fail to satisfy the "incompatible standards of conduct" requirement of Rule 23(b)(1)(A),[1074] or the "injunctive relief" requirement of Rule 23(b)(2).[1075]

33.27 Discovery

Discovery in mass tort cases frequently has two distinct dimensions: that involving the conduct of the defendants, and that relating to the individual plaintiffs' activities and injuries. Sometimes—particularly in multidistrict litigation—the court directs that discovery first be conducted regarding those matters that bear on the defendants' liability to all plaintiffs,[1076] deferring discovery into the details of each plaintiff's unique claims. In other cases, however, recognizing the need to obtain plaintiff-specific information for settlement purposes, the court may order that such discovery be conducted concurrently with, or even preceding, discovery from the defendants.[1077] Federal or local rules may specify information that must

parties stipulate to procedures for the allocation of damages among members of the class, as in the Exxon Valdez litigation.

1072. *See Robins,* 880 F.2d at 738–40 (discussing trend). *But see In re* Joint E. & S. Dist. Asbestos Litig. (Manville Corp.), 982 F.2d 721, 735–45 (2d Cir. 1992) (vacating district court approval of a settlement class in which competing interests of subgroups of personal injury claimants and codefendants were combined and represented collectively). See also *infra* § 33.29 (settlement).

1073. Under Fed. R. Civ. P. 23 (b)(1)(B), the test is whether the adjudication of separate actions would create a risk of the early claims disposing of the interests of later claimants. *Compare In re* Northern Dist. of Cal., Dalkon Shield IUD Prods. Liab. Litig., 693 F.2d 847, 852 (9th Cir. 1982) (Rule 23(b)(1)(B) certification proper only where disposition of early claims "necessarily" will affect later claims) *with Agent Orange,* 100 F.R.D. at 726 ("the proper standard is whether there is a substantial probability . . . that if damages are awarded, the claims of earlier litigants would exhaust the defendants' assets") *and In re* Jackson Lockdown/MCO Cases, 107 F.R.D. 703, 713 (E.D. Mich. 1985) (disagreeing with *Dalkon Shield* and adopting "probable risk" standard).

1074. *See, e.g., In re* Bendectin Prods. Liab. Litig., 749 F.2d 300, 305 (1984). *But see In re* Fernald Litig., 1989 U.S. Dist. LEXIS 17764 (S.D. Ohio Sept. 29, 1989).

1075. *See, e.g.,* Lukens v. Bryce Mountain Resort, Inc., 538 F.2d 594, 595–96 (4th Cir. 1976). Damages incidental to injunctive relief may be awarded in a Rule 23(b)(2) class action. *See* Pettaway v. American Cast Iron Pipe Co., 494 F.2d 211, 256–58 (5th Cir. 1974) (employment discrimination; back pay).

1076. Videotaped depositions are particularly useful in multidistrict litigation where the testimony of key witnesses may have to be presented at trial in numerous, geographically dispersed transferor—or state—courts after remand. See generally *supra* § 21.452.

1077. Interrogatories inquiring into the extent of the plaintiffs' damages may be useful early in the litigation even if depositions of the plaintiffs are to be delayed. Answers to such interrogatories may be prepared without disrupting the schedule for discovery from the defendants, and may be a

be disclosed in advance of discovery; the judge may alter these requirements to fit the particular litigation.[1078]

To avoid multiple requests for the same information, the court should encourage or require parties with similar interests to meet and fashion joint standard interrogatories and document requests.[1079] Answers to interrogatories should generally be made available to other litigants, who in turn should generally be permitted to ask only supplemental questions. In lieu of interrogatories, questionnaires directed to individual plaintiffs in standard, agreed-upon form have been used successfully. The court may order that standard discovery requests be automatically deemed filed as new parties are joined or new actions filed. The court should also consider establishing document depositories,[1080] instituting procedures to facilitate the use of depositions against parties later added to the litigation,[1081] and providing counsel in related cases in other courts with access to relevant confidential materials covered by protective orders.[1082] Courts may wish to consider vacating any protective orders issued in individual cases prior to their consolidation and taking other actions to promote access to materials from other litigation.[1083]

In cases that involve a massive number of claims for damages for similar injuries, sampling techniques can streamline discovery relating to individual plaintiffs' activities and injuries.[1084] Sampling and surveying can be used to obtain information useful both for settlement and for bellwether trials of the sample cases or for a class trial.[1085] Whether the aim is settlement or trial, the court

---

valuable starting point for settlement discussions. For example, in the Ohio Asbestos Litigation, special masters worked with the parties to develop standard forms with information that would be relevant to both settlement and trial. *See* Francis E. McGovern, *Toward a Functional Approach for Managing Complex Litigation*, 53 U. Chi. L. Rev. 440, 478–91 (1986); Wayne D. Brazil, *Special Masters in Complex Case: Expanding the Judiciary or Reshaping Litigation*, 53 U. Chi. L. Rev. 399–402 (1986); Trends, *supra* note 1020, at 60–69.

1078. See *supra* § 21.13 (prediscovery disclosure).

1079. Trends, *supra* note 1020, at 47–50. Alternative forms of interrogatories might be drafted to deal with variations, such as differences in the use of a toxic product or in the measure of damages for various plaintiffs.

1080. See *supra* § 21.444.

1081. See *supra* §§ 21.453, 21.445.

1082. See *supra* § 21.43.

1083. *See, e.g., In re* Silicone Gel Breast Implant Prods. Liab. Litig., MDL No. 926, Order No. 5 at 9 (N.D. Ala. Sept. 15, 1992). In that order the court indicated that it expected parties to the litigation to waive rights under protective orders issued in cases that were not consolidated under the MDL order. The court also required applications for protective orders to specify the materials to be protected and the terms and conditions of any proposed limits to the protection.

1084. See *supra* § 21.493.

1085. See *supra* §§ 21.423, 21.443, 21.464. *See also* Brazil, *supra* note 1077, at 402–06 (discussing sampling and surveying techniques used by special master as settlement aid in Alabama DDT case);

should ensure that the sample is representative of all claims encompassed in the particular proceeding with respect to relevant factors, such as the severity of the injuries, the circumstances of exposure to the product or accident, applicable state law, and the products and defendants alleged to be responsible.

In mass accident cases, it may be advisable, depending on the type and location of the disaster and the availability and adequacy of a public investigation, for the court to direct the taking of control of the physical evidence and of immediate discovery at the disaster site. This type of discovery may require participation by experts from both sides—and perhaps a court-appointed expert or special master—sifting through evidence at the site, documenting and preserving samples for common testing and use at trial, and videotaping and photographing the scene.[1086] A joint committee of experts may be formed and directed to coordinate the collecting, recording, and testing of evidence.[1087] As soon as practical, the court should establish a central location, accessible to all parties, for storage and preservation of evidence. In mass disasters occurring on a defendant's property or involving a mechanical product, the court may require the defendant to produce blueprints or other technical drawings to enable plaintiffs to investigate the site or product adequately.

In planning discovery, the court should ascertain from the parties what information may be available as a result of government investigations[1088] and from prior litigation of similar cases. Reports from the National Transportation Safety Board, the Federal Aviation Administration, or other public agencies may help identify witnesses and documents. Agency findings may substantially reduce the need for discovery on certain issues.[1089] Before approving the discovery plan, the judge should also ascertain the extent to which discovery materials may be available as a result of litigation in other courts.[1090]

Expert opinions play a vital role in many mass tort cases, both during the discovery process and at trial. The court should ordinarily establish early in the litigation a schedule for disclosing expert opinions in the form of a written report and for deposing the experts.[1091] An early deadline for the experts' "final" opinions may be needed to avoid the confusion that often results if opinions are

---

Cimino v. Raymark, 751 F. Supp. 649, 653, 664–65 (E.D. Tex. 1990) (discussing selection of sample and use in structuring trial and in extrapolating damages and applying formula to class). *See also infra* note 1094. Appointment by the court of a statistics expert may be advisable.

1086. *See In re* Shell Oil Refinery, 132 F.R.D. 437 (E.D. La. 1990).

1087. See *infra* § 33.73 (discussing use of databases in Superfund litigation); see also *infra* § 41.52 (Mass Tort Case-Management Order) at ¶¶ 3, 4.

1088. See generally *supra* § 21.491.

1089. Such findings may be admissible under Fed. R. Evid. 803(8)(C).

1090. See *supra* § 21.423.

1091. See *supra* § 21.48.

altered as trial approaches. An early deadline also permits the court to timely rule on admissibility and decide whether an independent expert should be appointed under Fed. R. Evid. 706.[1092]

33.28 Trial[1093]

The structuring of the trial should be addressed as early in the pretrial process as is feasible. To illustrate, if the trial of a mass tort case is to proceed by using bellwether plaintiffs, identification of those plaintiffs and discovery as to their exposure and injury should occur at the earliest opportunity. If the trial is to be of consolidated groups of claimants with comparable exposure or injuries, the composition of those groups should be defined during discovery and motion practice and should be consistent with the organization of counsel. The court's decisions should be informed by proposals and comments of counsel.

In mass tort cases involving large numbers of plaintiffs, a single trial of all issues before a single jury may be impractical, at least in the absence of special procedures.[1094] Courts have, however, experimented with various approaches to structuring trials to achieve greater efficiency and expedition in the resolution of mass tort cases. The approaches include: (1) a series of traditional trials, each with an individual plaintiff against an individual defendant on all issues, tried with the expectation that a few verdicts will establish parameters for the settlement or trial of all remaining cases; (2) a series of consolidated trials on all issues,[1095] each with groups of plaintiffs against an individual defendant or multiple defendants;[1096] (3)

1092. See generally *supra* § 21.51. For an example of the use of court-appointed experts in a mass tort context, see Carl B. Rubin & Laura Ringenbach, *A Role for the Court's Expert in Asbestos Litigation*, 137 F.R.D. 35 (1991). For a discussion of a pretrial procedure to assist in determining the need for a court-appointed expert, see Joe S. Cecil & Thomas E. Willging, Court-Appointed Experts: Defining the Role of Experts Appointed Under Federal Rule of Evidence 706 at 83–95 (Federal Judicial Center 1993).

1093. For discussion of complex trials generally, see *supra* § 22.

1094. In *Cimino, supra* note 1085, for example, the court tried the common issues to a jury verdict and later impaneled two juries to hear the individual issues presented by a statistically representative sample of 160 plaintiffs. Using statistical techniques, the court extrapolated the verdicts from representative cases and applied the average verdicts to cases of the same disease type. For a discussion of the scientific and legal bases for the approach, see Michael Saks & Peter Blanck, *Justice Improved: The Unrecognized Benefits of Aggregation and Sampling in the Trial of Mass Torts*, 44 Stan. L. Rev. 815 (1992). *See also* Edward F. Sherman, *Aggregate Disposition of Related Cases: The Policy Issues*, 10 Rev. Litig. 273 (1991) (discussing economy, efficiency, consistency, fairness, and constitutional values). *See generally* Mullenix, *supra* note 8.

1095. The court must ensure that cases to be consolidated involve issues that are sufficiently "common." *See* Malcolm v. National Gypsum Co., 995 F.2d 346 (2d Cir. 1993) (reversing joint trial of forty-eight asbestos cases on ground that lack of commonality resulted in jury confusion).

1096. Consolidation of fewer than ten cases has been called "extremely effective." *See Mature Mass Torts, supra* note 1012, at 687.

a consolidated trial with all or most plaintiffs against all or most defendants on common issues only, reserving the individual issues for individual or smaller consolidated trials;[1097] (4) a consolidated trial on common issues followed by a stipulated binding procedure (e.g., arbitration) to resolve individual issues[1098] or by some other approach to the individual issues (e.g., bellwether trials, extrapolation, special master); (5) a consolidated trial of all issues of a representative sample of cases in which the trier of fact establishes a lump sum damage award for all plaintiffs;[1099] and (6) bellwether trials on all issues of a limited number of selected cases representative of the total mix, to establish a foundation for resolving the balance.[1100]

1097. *See* Jenkins v. Raymark Indus., 782 F.2d 468 (5th Cir. 1986) (single class action trial of punitive damages and state-of-the-art defense followed by joint trials on individual issues with seven to ten plaintiffs). The individual issues may also be resolved through the procedures discussed immediately below involving trials of representative cases. *See also* Watson v. Shell Oil Co., 979 F.2d 1014, 1017–20 (5th Cir. 1992), *rehearing granted*, 1993 WL 133329 (case settled before rehearing; panel affirmed a trial plan for determination of liability and punitive damages in conjunction with compensatory damages in twenty fully tried sample cases to be followed by full trials of other individual claims by a different jury). In that case, the first stage of the trial plan included the apportionment of liability between the two primary defendants. *In re* Shell Oil Refinery, 136 F.R.D. 588, 593 (E.D. La. 1991).

Issues relating to liability may be severed under Fed. R. Civ. P. 42(b) from issues relating to causation or damages, and then consolidated under Rule 42(a) for a joint trial. See *supra* §§ 21.632, 22.34. State laws precluding bifurcation may not be binding upon the federal courts. *See* Rosales v. Honda Motor Co., 726 F.2d 259 (5th Cir. 1984).

1098. The court should ensure that the parties' waiver of the right to a jury trial is knowing and intelligent. After the settlement of the class claims in *Jenkins* (discussed above), the court created a voluntary alternative dispute resolution procedure to handle future claims. The program had some initial success but the court later judged it to be ineffective, in part because some parties failed to cooperate. Cimino v. Raymark, 751 F. Supp. 649, 651 (E.D. Tex. 1990). It may therefore be advisable to require parties to decide at the outset whether they are willing to enter into and be bound by the result of an ADR process. For discussion of ADR in general, see *supra* § 23.15.

1099. *See Cimino*, 751 F. Supp. at 664. The Fifth Circuit rejected such a trial plan in *In re Fibreboard Corp.*, 893 F.2d 706 (5th Cir. 1990), in part on the ground that a lump sum award would not satisfy the Texas substantive law requirement of a finding of individual damages as an element of each tort claim. *See also* Charles A. Wright et al., Federal Practice and Procedure § 1784 (1986 ed.) ("One possibility is to try the damage issue only once, making a single award for the class, and then develop an expeditious administrative means of dividing the lump sum among the class members.").

1100. *See, e.g.,* Sterling v. Velsicol, 855 F.2d 1188 (6th Cir. 1988) (bench trial of five representative plaintiffs used to determine liability, punitive damages, and individual causation and damages for the five, deferring causation and damages for the balance of the class). Special verdicts or a general verdict with interrogatories under Fed. R. Civ. P. 49 are likely to be helpful in establishing a basis for settling the other cases or narrowing the remaining liability issues on principles of collateral estoppel. *See also* Note, *Using the Special Verdict to Manage Complex Cases and Avoid Compromise Verdicts,* 21 Ariz. St. L.J. 297 (1989) (discussing use of special verdicts to enhance jury competence).

Bellwether trials can be combined with one of the following procedures to re-solve the remaining claims: (1) extrapolation of the average of the verdicts to all similar cases;[1101] (2) referral to a special master for application of the liability and damages verdicts;[1102] (3) consolidated follow-up trial or trials; or (4) a stipulated procedure to resolve individual claims according to a formula or by a hearing before an arbitrator, special master, or magistrate judge.

In pursuing traditional or bellwether trials, the court will need to decide whether to have a unitary trial, or to bifurcate liability and damages, or to trifur-cate liability, general causation, and individual causation. Reverse bifurcation or trifurcation, starting with damages, has been used when the court determines that degree of injury and the amount of damages are the primary issues in dispute.[1103]

Traditional or bellwether trials of mass torts can benefit from many of the standard practices for managing trials of complex litigation.[1104] Similarities among the cases tried and cases awaiting trial may make feasible the development and use of a standard pretrial order, including generally applicable rulings on evi-dentiary and trial issues. The repetitive presentation of the same evidence may be streamlined by the use, for example, of videotaped expert testimony and standard exhibits.[1105]

33.29 Settlement[1106]

Settlement activity in mass tort litigation tends to parallel pretrial and trial orga-nization. Consolidated cases tend to generate settlement-related information at the same time and follow a settlement timetable driven by pretrial and trial dead-lines.[1107] In general, organization of cases along individual plaintiff lines can be

---

Compare Ezagui v. Dow Chem. Corp., 598 F.2d 727 (2d Cir. 1979) (defendant precluded in second trial from contesting inadequacy of warning) *with* Hardy v. Johns Manville Sales Corp., 681 F.2d 334 (5th Cir. 1982) (defendant not collaterally estopped under circumstances of case) *and In re* Asbestos Litig. (Raymark Indus., Inc.), 829 F.2d 1233, 1242 (3d Cir. 1987). Each side may be invited to select a specified number of cases for trial.

1101. *Cimino,* 751 F. Supp. at 664–65.

1102. *See* Foster v. Detroit, 254 F. Supp. 655 (E.D. Mich. 1966), *aff'd,* 405 F.2d 138 (6th Cir. 1968); *see also* Samuel Issacharoff, *Administering Damage Awards in Mass Tort Litigation,* 10 Rev. Litig. 463, 471–80 (1991) (discussing administrative models for apportioning damage awards in mass contract-based, Title VII, and tort cases).

1103. *See* Trends, *supra* note 1020, at 102–04.

1104. See generally *supra* § 22 (trials).

1105. See generally *infra* § 34 (technology).

1106. See generally *supra* § 23 (settlement).

1107. As suggested above, encouraging early settlement may require special discovery ap-proaches and other pretrial involvement. *See* Trends, *supra* note 1020, at 55–86.

expected to lead to individual settlements, and organization along aggregated lines can be expected to produce aggregated settlements.[1108]

Although most defendants prefer to avoid bankruptcy, the bankruptcy process appears to be used with increasing frequency to achieve and implement settlement in mass tort litigation.[1109] Bankruptcy alone permits a federal court to marshal all claims against a defendant and to control both state and federal litigation. It is of limited utility, however, in disposing of litigation against numerous defendants who are unlikely to choose the same course. As an alternative to bankruptcy, it may be possible to set a ceiling on damages by certifying a mandatory "limited fund" settlement class that includes future claimants, obtaining court approval of the proposed settlement fund as fair to all members of the class, and, so long as a procedure is provided to protect future claimants, enjoining the filing of additional actions. This approach has been used in some mass tort actions, but because of the difficulty in protecting the interests of future claimants, its legality is questionable.[1110] The Fourth Circuit approved such a

---

1108. *See, e.g.,* special master Francis McGovern's description of the settlement in *Jenkins v. Raymark* in *Mature Mass Torts, supra* note 1012, at 663–75 (1989); Mullenix, *supra* note 8, at 550–69 (discussing settlement activity and trial plans in *Cimino v. Raymark* and the *School Asbestos Litig.*); Trends, *supra* note 1020, at 87. A notable exception is the "global settlement" reached in the breast implant litigation that arose out of a pretrial structure designed to support individual trials within an MDL consolidation.

1109. *See generally In re* A.H. Robins Co., Inc., 880 F.2d 709 (4th Cir. 1989) (Dalkon Shield); Kane v. Johns-Manville Corp., 843 F.2d 636, 638–41 (2d Cir. 1988) (asbestos); *In re* UNR Indus., Inc., 725 F.2d 1111 (7th Cir. 1984) (asbestos), all of which review the history of the litigation.

1110. *In re* Joint E. & S. Dist. Asbestos Litig. (Keene Corp.), 14 F.3d 726 (2d Cir. 1993) (vacating preliminary injunction enjoining pending and future asbestos-related litigation against an asbestos manufacturer–plaintiff in a nationwide mandatory 23(b)(1)(B) class action filed to protect settlement discussions; the action did not present a case or controversy under Article III and was a "a self-evident evasion of [the Bankruptcy Code, which is] the exclusive legal system established by Congress for debtors to seek relief."). *Cf.* Carlough v. Amchem Prods., Inc., 10 F.3d 189 (3d Cir. 1993) (affirming subject-matter jurisdiction of district court in nationwide opt-out settlement class action involving future asbestos personal injury claims and affirming the issuance of a preliminary injunction against competing state class action as necessary in aid of the court's jurisdiction); *In re* Baldwin United Corp. 770 F.2d 328 (2d Cir. 1985) (impending settlement of consolidated securities litigation supported injunction against threatened actions by state attorneys general); *In re* Corrugated Container Antitrust Litig., 659 F.2d 1332 (5th Cir. 1981) (state proceedings enjoined to preserve federal jurisdiction in multidistrict antitrust litigation); *In re* Silicone Gel Breast Implants Prods. Liability Litig., MDL No. 926, Order No. 14 (N.D. Ala. Sept. 10, 1993) (finding a limited fund based on examining defendant's assets and insurance and defining a settlement class that includes future "claims for injuries not yet known or manifest"). Note that the *Breast Implant* and *Carlough* (later known as *Georgine* after a substitution of the first named plaintiff) actions were brought by personal injury claimants whereas the *Keene* action was brought by a manufacturer against personal injury claimants, seeking the court's assistance in achieving settlement. This difference in claims may affect the analysis.

procedure in *In re A.H. Robins, Co., Inc.,*[1111] in which the district court had certified a nationwide class under Fed. R. Civ. P. 23(b)(1)(B). That case may have paved the way for similar actions, but, as noted above, at least one court of appeals has expressed the opinion that bankruptcy provides the exclusive remedy for an insolvent defendant.[1112]

Certification of settlement classes involving unidentified class members with latent injuries from exposure to toxic products raises questions of fairness and requires careful consideration by the court (see *supra* section 30.45).[1113] The interests of future claimants may well conflict with the interests of present claimants who seek the maximum recovery on their claims and of defendants who seek to obtain the widest possible preclusive effect of the settlement so that they can continue doing business without the threat of future litigation. Courts have taken steps to protect the interests of future claimants by obtaining estimates of the number, quality, and value of outstanding and anticipated claims; estimation of such claims may require expert study and testimony covering such areas as statistics and epidemiology.[1114] Conflicts may also exist between plaintiffs and their counsel, among defendants, and between defendants and their insurers, adding complexity and risk to settlement efforts.

1111. 880 F.2d 709 (1989). The court found that due process was satisfied by the settlement's provision of a right to jury trial for class members who did not accept an arbitration award.

1112. *In re Joint E. & S. Dist. Asbestos Litig. (Keene Corp.),* 14 F.3d at 732–33.

1113. For an opinion addressing fairness issues in the context of a controversial mass tort settlement proposal, see Georgine v. Amchem Prods., Inc., 157 F.R.D. 246 (E.D. Pa. 1994) (on appeal) (memorandum opinion approving class settlement); *In re* Silicone Breast Implant Prods. Liab. Litig., 1994 WL 578353 (N.D. Ala) (same).

Occasionally, courts have found it beneficial to use an expert appointed pursuant to Fed. R. Evid. 706 to evaluate a proposed settlement. *See* Williams v. City of New Orleans, 543 F. Supp. 662, 670 (E.D. La. 1982), *rev'd on other grounds,* 694 F.2d 987, 996 (5th Cir. 1983), *aff'd en banc,* 729 F.2d 1554, 1564 (1984); Ohio Pub. Interest Campaign v. Fisher Foods, Inc., 546 F. Supp. 1, 4, 11 (N.D. Ohio 1982); Morales v. Turman, 569 F. Supp 332, 338–39 (E.D. Tex. 1983); Alaniz v. California Processors, 73 F.R.D. 269, 274 (N.D. Cal. 1976).

1114. *See, e.g., In re* Joint E. & S. Dist. Asbestos Litig., NYAL Index No. 4000, Memorandum and Order on Motion to Quash Notice of Subpoena (E.D.N.Y., S.D.N.Y Nov. 5, 1993) (discussing appointment of panel of experts under Fed. R. Evid. 706 to estimate number of future claims expected to be filed against the Manville Personal Injury Trust). *See also In re* Joint E. & S. Dist. Asbestos Litig. (Eagle-Picher Indus., Inc.), 134 F.R.D. 32, 34–35 (E.D.N.Y. 1990) (special master found that assets of Eagle-Picher were so limited that there was substantial risk that payments for claims would be in jeopardy; court certified mandatory class under Fed. R. Civ. P 23(b)(1)(B) and stayed all pending proceedings in federal and state courts pending approval of proposed settlement of pending and future claims). Estimation proceedings in a settlement class action are analogous to those that a bankruptcy court would use to estimate personal injury claims. *See Robins,* 880 F.2d at 719–20; *see also* Note, *The Manville Bankruptcy: Treating Mass Tort Claims in Chapter 11 Proceedings,* 96 Harv. L. Rev. 1121, 1128–29, 1132–33 (1983).

In mass tort litigation, collecting information about past, pending, and future claims is integral to reviewing settlement. The court can often organize pretrial data-gathering so that it supports settlement as well as trial. In litigation with thousands of personal injury claims, courts have appointed special masters to assemble databases that document the main features of claims.[1115] In consolidated cases, computer-based data have been used to match individual pending cases with closed cases having similar characteristics to provide guidance for settlement.[1116]

The parties should attempt to achieve, to the extent feasible, a "global" settlement, resolving not only the defendants' potential liability to the plaintiffs, but also their liability to one another for indemnification or contribution.[1117] If the entire litigation cannot be resolved through a single settlement, partial settlements—by some defendants with all plaintiffs, by all defendants with some plaintiffs, or by some defendants with some plaintiffs—should be explored.[1118] If all efforts fail, the parties may be able to resolve a significant portion of the litigation through a series of case-by-case, party-by-party settlements.[1119] In the absence of bellwether trials or their equivalent, taking a representative sample of claims through mediation, arbitration, or another form of alternative dispute resolution can generate evaluations supporting further settlements.

1115. In *Jenkins v. Raymark*, the special master used the same database to support settlement discussions and to demonstrate to the jury the array of claims. *Mature Mass Torts, supra* note 1012, at 669–70, 674. *See also id.* at 682–88 (describing the $5 million data-collection process established to estimate the value of Dalkon Shield personal injury claims under § 502(c) of the Bankruptcy Code).

1116. *See* Brazil, *supra* note 1077, at 399–402 (1986) (describing the computer-based data-collection procedures used by special masters Francis McGovern and Eric Green in the Ohio Asbestos Litigation); *see also* Trends, *supra* note 1020, at 60–69 (discussing and evaluating the use of computer data in the Ohio Asbestos Litigation).

1117. In Ahearn v. Fibreboard, No. 93cv526 (E.D. Tex. Sept. 9, 1993) (order provisionally certifying class for settlement purposes), for example, the parties included a (co)defendant settlement class and negotiated a contribution and indemnity agreement with one codefendant acting as a representative of the class. The proposed settlement would include an order barring contribution and indemnity claims by other asbestos products producers and manufacturers. An alternative is for the defendants to agree to contribute specified amounts to a settlement fund, while reserving the right to litigate their respective obligations to one another.

1118. The hazards of partial settlements are discussed in *supra* § 23.21.

1119. The court should consider requiring that a specified amount or percentage be set aside from such settlements to compensate plaintiffs' lead attorneys and steering committee members for their services on behalf of all plaintiffs. *See In re* Silicone Gel Breast Implant Prods. Liab. Litig., MDL No. 926, Order No. 13 (N.D. Ala. July 23, 1993); *In re* San Juan Dupont Plaza Hotel Fire Litig., MDL No. 721 (D. P.R. March 18, 1987); *In re* Swine Flu Immunization Prod. Liab. Litig., 89 F.R.D. 695 (D.D.C. 1980).

Various provisions can be made in a settlement for future claims. A portion of the settlement funds may be set aside to purchase an annuity or to fund a trust to pay future benefits or provide diagnostic services to plaintiffs, depending on such factors as medical developments and expenses and economic losses after the date of the settlement.[1120] Similarly, if the defendants are concerned about the possibility of actions being instituted after the settlement—for example, by minors with respect to whom the statute of limitations may be tolled—some of the settlement funds may be reserved for a period of time contingent on such claims.[1121]

As in other types of litigation, the assigned judge should be wary of extensive involvement in settlement.[1122] Although some judges participate actively in settlement negotiations,[1123] others take care to insulate themselves from the negotiations, leaving this activity to a special master or settlement judge;[1124] where judges have been involved, they have turned over to another judge the responsibility for review and approval of the settlement.[1125]

1120. *Cf.* Friends for All Children, Inc. v. Lockheed Aircraft Corp., 746 F.2d 816 (D.C. Cir. 1984) (affirming preliminary injunction requiring a corporate defendant that had conceded liability and settled some cases to provide funds for diagnostic, treatment, and educational services for plaintiffs awaiting trial).

1121. *See In re* MGM Grand Fire Hotel Litig., 570 F. Supp. 913 (D. Nev. 1983).

1122. See *supra* § 23.11. *See, e.g.,* Carlough v. Amchem Prods., Inc., No. 93-215, slip op. at 10–22 (E.D. Pa. April 15, 1993) (denying motion to recuse MDL transferee judge).

1123. *See e.g., In re* "Agent Orange" Prod. Liab. Litig., 597 F. Supp. 740, *aff'd,* 818 F.2d 145 (2d Cir. 1987). For an assessment of the risks of such judicial involvement in settlement, see Peter Schuck, *The Role of Judges in Settling Complex Cases: The Agent Orange Example,* 53 U. Chi. L. Rev. 337, 359–65 (1986).

1124. *See e.g., In re* Silicone Gel Breast Implants Prods. Liab. Litig., MDL No. 926 (in which the transferee judge appointed three judges to act as mediators to assist in discussing a global settlement); *In re* MGM Grand Fire Hotel Litig., 570 F. Supp. 913 (D. Nev. 1983). In response to a motion for recusal, the MDL transferee judge described his role as limited to reviewing documentary evidence supporting plaintiffs' damage claims; a special master had been appointed to assist with negotiations related to examining defendants' solvency and the transferee judge avoided receiving reports related to defendants' liability. *MGM Grand Fire* at 924–26. In *In re* San Juan Dupont Plaza Hotel Fire Litig., MDL No. 721, 1988 U.S. Dist. LEXIS 17332 at 201 (D. P.R. Dec. 2, 1988), the transferee judge appointed the former transferee judge from the *MGM Grand* litigation to serve as settlement coordinator while the transferee judge managed the litigation. In two major asbestos class actions the trial judges "remained relatively detached from settlement discussions." Mullenix, *supra* note 8, at 551.

1125. Carlough v. Amchem Prods., Inc., No. 93-215 (E.D. Pa. January 29, 1993) (order appointing second district judge to conduct hearings on fairness of class settlement), *settlement approved sub nom.* Georgine v. Amchem Prods., No. 93-215 (E.D. Pa. August 16, 1994).

33.3 Securities

Cases alleging securities fraud under federal and state laws can present many of the same problems that arise in mass tort litigation, discussed in *supra* section 33.2. The principles and techniques of litigation management discussed elsewhere in this manual are also generally applicable. This section discusses issues and problems peculiar to securities litigation.

33.31 Coordination and Consolidation

At the initial conference, as well as at later conferences, the judge should inquire about any related litigation pending or expected. All related litigation in the same court, including pertinent aspects of bankruptcy proceedings, should ordinarily be assigned or transferred to one judge for initial supervision and planning. The extent to which the cases should be formally consolidated for further pretrial proceedings and trial will depend on the circumstances; after a period of centralized management, some cases may be appropriately reassigned to other judges of the court for further proceedings and trial.

The judge should be alert to the possibility that in addition to private actions, proceedings may be initiated by the Securities and Exchange Commission (SEC) or state administrative agencies. In addition, parties may be debtors in bankruptcy, which may lead to automatic stays, removal of cases, related adversary proceedings, and objections to the discharge of debts. Separate actions regarding fidelity bonds and other insurance coverage are common. Suits may also be brought to prevent foreclosure of security interests.

Because the conduct alleged in securities fraud litigation often affects persons in many states, related cases—occasionally competing or conflicting—may be filed in a number of courts. Centralized pretrial management of the federal litigation may be effected through transfers by the Judicial Panel on Multidistrict Litigation under 28 U.S.C. § 1407.[1126] If cases remain in different courts, the judges should attempt to coordinate the proceedings, formally or informally, to minimize the risk of conflicts (see *supra* section 31.14; see also *supra* section 31.31 (coordination with related actions in state courts)). If one court authorizes an ac-

---

1126. *See, e.g., In re* Washington Pub. Power Supply Sys. Sec. Litig., 568 F. Supp. 1250 (J.P.M.L. 1983).

tion to proceed derivatively under Fed. R. Civ. P. 23.1 or on behalf of a class under Rule 23, especially one certified under Rule 23(b)(1) or (b)(2), other courts may conclude that a deferral of proceedings involving similar issues is justified though not required. Similarly, the judges may, after consultation with counsel, determine that one of the cases may appropriately serve as the "lead case" for purposes of discovery or trial.[1127]

33.32 Issues

Pleadings. Complaints in securities fraud cases typically assert numerous claims under federal and state statutes and common law against various defendants, usually including the company whose securities are involved, its officers and directors, independent accountants and attorneys, and brokerage firms.[1128] In addition to claims under the 1933 and 1934 Acts, plaintiffs may include claims under the Racketeer Influenced and Corrupt Organizations Act, 18 U.S.C. §§ 1961–1968 (see *infra* section 33.8). Complaints may be lengthy, in part because of the requirement of Fed. R. Civ. P. 9(b) that fraud be pleaded with particularity.[1129] Defendants frequently need substantial time to respond to the complaint and to decide whether to file counterclaims, cross-claims, and third-party complaints. And the plaintiffs, after some initial discovery, may be willing to dismiss some of the claims and defendants.

For these reasons, the judge should consider entering an order immediately after assignment of the litigation suspending the time for all defendants to respond to the complaint. At the initial conference, the court should, after consulting with counsel, establish a schedule for filing motions and additional pleadings. If there is reason to expect that plaintiffs may be able to cure apparent defects in the complaint and comply with Rule 9(b), the judge may decide to suspend the time for filing some motions and pleadings until after the plaintiffs have conducted limited, relevant discovery and filed amended complaints. The order should allow for timely filing of pleadings containing claims that could otherwise

---

1127. The first case, even if resolved by a nonjury trial, may result in collateral estoppel even as to issues that would otherwise be tried to a jury in the subsequent litigation. *See* Parklane Hosiery Co. v. Shore, 439 U.S. 322 (1979) (defendant precluded by adverse decision in proceeding brought by SEC for equitable relief from relitigating in action for monetary relief whether proxy statement was misleading). For further discussion of coordination, see *supra* §§ 31.14, 31.31.

1128. In light of the Supreme Court's holding in Central Bank of Denver v. First Interstate Bank of Denver, No. 92-854 (April 19, 1994), that private plaintiffs may not maintain aiding and abetting claims under § 10(b) of the 1934 Act, the inclusion of "secondary actors" such as attorneys, accountants, and brokers may be less frequent, though such actors can still be held liable for primary violations of § 10(b). *See Central Bank of Denver,* at 1994 U.S. LEXIS 3120, *51.

1129. Rule 9(b) applies to complaints alleging federal securities fraud. *See, e.g.,* Greenstone v. Cambex Corp., 975 F.2d 22 (1st Cir. 1992); Whalen v. Carter, 954 F.2d 1087, 1097–98 (5th Cir. 1992).

be barred by statutes of limitations. In some cases, defendants have by letter advised plaintiffs of deficiencies in their pleadings, giving an opportunity for correction without the cost and delay of a formal motion. If several complaints have been filed, consideration may be given to filing of a single consolidated complaint. Ordinarily, the court should also set a deadline after which new claims, defenses, and parties may be added only upon a showing of good cause. In deciding on an appropriate schedule for filing and refining the pleadings, the court should weigh the desirability of early identification of the issues against the possibility that pleadings filed too soon may be imprecise and overly broad, or may need to be amended later as a result of information obtained during discovery.

Defining and narrowing the issues. As soon as practical, counsel and the court should begin the process of issue definition and clarification described in *supra* section 21.3. Among issues that may be susceptible to early resolution under Fed. R. Civ. P. 12 or 56 are the following:

- whether an instrument constitutes a "security" subject to registration;[1130]
- whether a claim is barred by the statute of limitations;[1131]
- whether a statement or omission is "material";[1132]
- whether a demand must be made on a corporation's directors;[1133]
- whether the "business judgment" rule allows the directors or a committee they have established to dismiss or settle the action,[1134] or provides a defense to liability;[1135]
- whether "controlling person" liability may be imposed;[1136]

1130. *See, e.g.,* Associates in Adolescent Psychiatry v. Home Life Ins. Co., 941 F.2d 561, 564–64 (7th Cir. 1991).

1131. *See* Lampf, Pleva, Lipkind Prupis & Petigrow v. Gilbertson, 501 U.S. 350 (1991). In some cases, plaintiffs must affirmatively plead compliance with the statute of limitations, with supporting facts. *See, e.g., In re* Chaus Sec. Litig., 801 F. Supp. 1257 (S.D.N.Y. 1992).

1132. *See* Basic, Inc. v. Levinson, 485 U.S. 224, 230–41 (1988).

1133. *See, e.g.,* Daily Income Fund, Inc. v. Fox, 464 U.S. 523 (1984).

1134. *See* Burks v. Lasker, 441 U.S. 471 (1979) (state law controls issue of board's power to discontinue derivative action on federal claim). *See, e.g.,* RCM Sec. Fund, Inc. v. Stanton, 928 F.2d 1318 (2d Cir. 1991); Joy v. North, 692 F.2d 880 (2d Cir. 1982); Clark v. Lomas & Nettleton Fin. Corp., 625 F.2d 49 (5th Cir. 1980); Abbey v. Control Data Corp., 603 F.2d 724 (8th Cir. 1979); Zapata Corp. v. Maldanado, 430 A.2d 779 (Del. 1981).

1135. *See, e.g.,* Hanson Trust PLC, HSCM v. ML SCM Acquisition Inc., 781 F.2d 264 (2d Cir. 1986).

1136. *See, e.g.,* Martin v. Shearson Lehman Hutton, Inc., 986 F.2d 242 (8th Cir. 1993); Hollinger v. Titan Capital Corp., 914 F.2d 1564, 1572–76 (9th Cir. 1990) (en banc).

- whether and when a "sale" or "purchase" occurred;[1137]
- whether the disclosure documents "bespeak caution";[1138]
- whether "forward looking" statements are actionable;[1139]
- whether public availability of material information excuses nondisclosure in an action relying on the "fraud on the market" theory;[1140]
- whether loss causation can be established;[1141]
- whether scienter is alleged and can be established;[1142]
- whether the elements of secondary liability claims have been established;[1143] and
- whether a defendant may be held liable as a "seller."[1144]

In addition, the resolution of various issues—for example, whether the plaintiffs may proceed on a "fraud on the market" theory[1145]—will be relevant to whether individual cases may be consolidated for joint trial or should proceed as a class action (see *infra* section 33.33).[1146]

33.33 Class and Derivative Actions

At the initial conference, the court should set a schedule for determining whether one or more of the cases should proceed as a class action under Fed. R. Civ. P. 23 or a derivative action under Rule 23.1. Although the discussion in *supra* section 30—including the desirability of an early determination of these questions— is generally applicable, in securities litigation some clarification of the issues and discovery on the merits of the case will often be needed before these determina-

---

1137. *See, e.g.,* Frankel v. Stratton, 984 F.2d 1328, 1333 & n.3, 1337–38 (2d Cir. 1993); Colan v. Mesa Petroleum Co., 951 F.2d 1512 (9th Cir. 1991); Freeman v. Decio, 584 F.2d 186, 200 (7th Cir. 1986).

1138. *See, e.g., In re* Casino Sec. Litig., 7 F.3d 357, 371–73 (3d Cir. 1993).

1139. *See, e.g., In re* Verifone Sec. Litig., 11 F.3d 865, 870–71 (9th Cir. 1993); *In re* Convergent Technologies Sec. Litig., 948 F.2d 507, 517 (7th Cir. 1991).

1140. *See In re* Apple Computer Sec. Litig., 886 F.2d 1109, 1115 (9th Cir. 1989).

1141. *See, e.g.,* McGonigle v. Combs, 968 F.2d 810, 819–22 (9th Cir. 1992); Bastian v. Petren Resources Corp., 892 F.2d 680, 685–86 (7th Cir. 1990).

1142. *See* Ernst & Ernst v. Hochfelder, 425 U.S. 185 (1976). *See, e.g.,* Hollinger v. Titan Capital Corp., 914 F.2d 1564, 1568–72 (9th Cir. 1990) (en banc).

1143. The Supreme Court's decision in *Central Bank of Denver* "leaves little doubt that the Exchange Act does not even permit the [SEC] to pursue aiders and abettors in civil enforcement actions under § 10(b)," and "at the very least casts serious doubts . . . on other forms of secondary liability" such as conspiracy. 1994 U.S. LEXIS 3120, *65–67 & n.12 (Stevens, J., dissenting).

1144. *See* Pinter v. Dahl, 486 U.S. 622, 641–47 (1988).

1145. *See Basic, Inc.,* 485 U.S. at 241–49.

1146. *See, e.g.,* Mirkin v. Wasserman, 858 P.2d 568 (Cal. 1993); *In re* LTV Sec. Litig., 88 F.R.D. 134 (N.D. Tex. 1980).

tions are made. Discovery from the representative parties (and even from some members of the putative class) may also be warranted, although the court should limit such discovery appropriately. See *supra* sections 30.12, 30.232.

Class definition. Various relevant matters will need to be resolved before a class can be defined. The initial complaint will occasionally include some claims—for example, reliance upon oral misrepresentations or the breach of a "suitability" standard—that rarely would be susceptible to class action treatment, along with other claims—such as an omission of a material fact from a proxy statement—that may well be presented on behalf of a class. The dates when the plaintiffs bought or sold the securities, and what information they had on those dates, may not be clear from the complaint, yet may be critical to a decision regarding the class of persons they might properly represent. Whether the plaintiffs are able to proceed on a "fraud on the market" theory may depend both on matters developed during discovery and on what claims will be pursued in the case. See *supra* section 33.32. The court may need to determine whether a particular claim is made derivatively or individually[1147] and whether the same plaintiff may assert both derivative and class claims.[1148]

In deciding whether a class should be certified, what class the plaintiffs may represent, and whether multiple classes or subclasses should be formed, the court may need to consider sources of potential conflict and their effect, among different participants in the action:

- holders of different types of securities;[1149]
- those who took some action and those who did not;[1150]
- those who bought or sold before an alleged misstatement and those who did so after (or continued to hold the security);[1151]
- those who had inside information and those who did not;[1152]

1147. *See Daily Income Fund,* 464 U.S. at 527–34.

1148. *Compare* Hawk Indus., Inc. v. Bausch & Lomb, Inc., 59 F.R.D. 619, 623–24 (S.D.N.Y. 1973) *and* Ruggiero v. American Bioculture, Inc., 56 F.R.D. 93 (S.D.N.Y. 1972) *with* Keyser v. Commonwealth Nat. Fin. Corp., 120 F.R.D. 489, 492–93 (M.D. Pa. 1988) *and In re* Dayco Sec. Litig., 102 F.R.D. 624 (S.D. Ohio 1984) *and* Bertozzi v. King Louie Int'l, Inc., 420 F. Supp. 1166 (D. R.I. 1976). The court may choose to address any actual conflict arising between the claims at the remedy stage. *Keyser,* 120 F.R.D. at 492 n.8 (*citing Bertozzi,* 420 F. Supp. at 1180).

1149. *See, e.g.,* Margolis v. Caterpillar, Inc., 815 F. Supp. 1150, 1157 (C.D. Ill. 1991) (buyers of call options and sellers of put options); Deutschman v. Beneficial Corp., 761 F. Supp. 1080, 1082–83 (D. Del. 1990) (common stock and call options).

1150. *See, e.g., In re* Bally Mfg. Sec. Litig., 141 F.R.D. 262, 270 (N.D. Ill. 1992) (those who sold during class period and those who did not).

1151. *See, e.g.,* Kovaleff v. Piano, 142 F.R.D. 406 (S.D.N.Y. 1992); Deutschman v. Beneficial Corp., 132 F.R.D. 359, 382–83 (D. Del. 1990); *In re* LTV Sec. Litig., 88 F.R.D. 134 (N.D. Tex. 1980).

1152. *See, e.g.,* Dubin v. Miller, 132 F.R.D. 269, 274–75 (D. Colo. 1990).

- those who purchased at different times based on different information;[1153] and

- those seeking damages and those seeking rescission.[1154]

Such differences in the situations of various groups of plaintiffs and putative class members require the court's early attention. They may be argued by defendants in opposing class action treatment, and while sometimes they may justify denial of class certification, at other times they may be resolved by appropriately limiting the definition of the class or classes that the plaintiffs may represent, by creating additional classes or subclasses, or by tailoring the relief afforded plaintiffs. For example, the court may define a class to exclude (or treat as a subclass) those who, as often occurs in complex securities litigation, are also defendants in the class action or in related litigation. If a subclass should be formed and no representative of that subclass is a party, the court may direct notice to the unrepresented class members, giving them time to have a representative intervene.[1155] Although, as discussed in *supra* section 30.15, unnecessary classes should generally be avoided, in some securities cases multiple classes or subclasses may be needed to ensure that the interests of all class members are fairly and adequately protected, particularly during settlement negotiations. Occasionally a mandatory class under Fed. R. Civ. P. 23(b)(1) or (b)(2) may be proper, but generally classes in securities litigation will be certified under Rule 23(b)(3), with the right to notice and an opportunity to opt out. The right of class members to opt out of a (b)(3) class, if adequately disclosed, may cure some conflicts.

Notices. Absent special circumstances, the class representatives must bear not only the cost of providing notice to the class under Rule 23(c)(2) but also the expense of obtaining the names and addresses of the class members, which frequently are in the possession of the defendants or a transfer agent.[1156] When securities are registered in street names with brokerage houses, the assistance of the brokerage houses will be needed.[1157] Sometimes—for example, in a class action on behalf of holders of bearer bonds—the identity of class members may not be ascertainable. In such a case, notice should be given by publication in media likely to be seen by the class members (see *supra* section 30.211).

1153. *See, e.g.,* Hoxter v. Simmons, 140 F.R.D. 416, 421–22 (D. Ariz. 1991); Alfus v. Pyramid Tech. Corp., 765 F. Supp. 598, 605–06 (N.D. Cal. 1991).

1154. *See, e.g.,* Larson v. Dumke, 900 F.2d 1363, 1366–68 (9th Cir. 1990); Davis v. Comed, Inc., 619 F.2d 588, 592–98 (6th Cir. 1980).

1155. *See* Fed. R. Civ. P. 23(d)(2).

1156. Oppenheimer Fund, Inc. v. Sanders, 437 U.S. 340 (1978).

1157. *See* Silber v. Mabon, No. 92-56004 (3d Cir. March 15, 1994) (no due process violation where notice mailed to broker holding stock in street name was not sent to class member until after opt-out period, but court should have considered allowing late opt out).

33.34 Discovery

The principles and procedures discussed in *supra* section 21.42 for controlling discovery are generally applicable to securities litigation. Ordinarily, plaintiffs' counsel should begin by ascertaining the categories and locations of relevant documents and the potential witnesses, deferring depositions until after these documents have been produced and reviewed. Reciprocal prediscovery disclosure appropriately directed by the court to avoid wasted effort can expedite and reduce the amount of discovery needed (see *supra* section 21.13). Interrogatories may be useful to identify sources of information and objective background facts and data, facilitating and expediting depositions. Discovery by plaintiffs and defendants may be conducted concurrently, particularly if information from both sides will be needed to determine whether the litigation should proceed as a derivative or class action; it may also assist the parties in entering into early settlement negotiations.

To avoid duplicative discovery in multiple litigation, the court should require that plaintiffs in related cases prepare a single set of interrogatories to be propounded to each defendant, and that the parties coordinate discovery plans. Consideration should be given to establishing a common document depository and cross-noticing depositions of common witnesses for use in all cases.[1158] The court should ascertain at the initial conference whether claims of attorney–client privilege or other requests for protective orders are likely to arise during the course of discovery, and should attempt to resolve them before they can disrupt the discovery schedule (see *supra* section 21.43). The court should establish early in the litigation a schedule for the exchange of expert reports and the taking of depositions, and also should adopt procedures to facilitate discovery and use at trial of summaries and computerized data.[1159] As in other cases, counsel should be expected to stipulate facts not genuinely in controversy and may be directed to develop a joint statement of agreed (or uncontroverted) facts.[1160]

33.35 Court-Appointed Special Masters and Experts

Securities cases frequently present complex factual disputes over matters of accounting, corporate finance, and market analyses. Such disputes, or the negotiation or implementation of settlement, sometimes may be appropriately referred to a magistrate judge, special master, or court-appointed expert. See *supra* section 21.5.

1158. See *supra* §§ 21.444 (document depositories), 21.455 (depositions, coordination with related litigation). See generally *supra* § 31 (multiple litigation).

1159. See *supra* §§ 21.48 (discovery of expert opinions), 21.446 (discovery of computerized data), 21.492 (discovery, special problems, summaries), 22.32 (trial, use of exhibits).

1160. See *supra* §§ 21.641 (statements of facts and evidence), 21.47 (requests for admission).

33.36 Trial and Settlement

Procedures similar to those used for trial and settlement of mass tort litigation (see *supra* sections 33.28–33.29) may also be appropriate for securities litigation. Related cases—both class actions and individual cases—may be consolidated for a joint trial on specified issues, such as the defendants' respective liabilities for alleged misrepresentations and omissions, while leaving for subsequent separate trials other issues, such as damages and individual defenses. Class or derivative actions may not be settled without court approval; the court should apply the principles and procedures governing settlements of class actions in general (see *supra* section 30.4). Nonmonetary benefits—such as a change in corporate management or policies—may play a significant role in derivative actions.[1161]

33.4 Takeover

Takeover litigation—actions brought in connection with the attempted acquisition or transfer of control of a corporation by obtaining securities, assets, or stockholder support—presents special problems for the court, counsel, and parties. Several actions and counteractions may be filed almost simultaneously in different courts to enjoin or remedy alleged violations of federal antitrust and securities laws and state statutes. Major decisions must often be made rapidly about complex factual, legal, and economic issues that involve large amounts of money and would ordinarily take months or even years to resolve. Fortunately, such litigation typically involves only a few parties, represented by experienced attorneys accustomed to working under severe time constraints and other pressures. The existence of state statutes and corporate defenses, such as shareholders rights plans ("poison pills"), may render time constraints less severe than suggested by the Williams Act.[1162]

The court should be aware that the litigants' positions are often influenced by effects anticipated outside the courtroom—on shareholders, other potential purchasers, financial institutions, and the media—and that even the timing of hearings and rulings may have strategic importance to the parties.

1161. *See* Bell Atlantic Corp. v. Bolger, 2 F.3d 1304, 1310–12 (3d Cir. 1993) and cases cited therein.

1162. 82 Stat. 454, *codified as amended at* 15 U.S.C.A. § 77m(d)–(e) (West 1981 and Supp. 1994) and 15 U.S.C. § 77n(d)–(f).

33.41 Immediate Control and Planning

As soon as possible after the commencement of takeover litigation—preferably within a day or two after the complaint is filed—the judge should hold a preliminary conference with counsel. Plaintiff's counsel will usually know or be able to ascertain the identity of counsel for the defendants. Attorneys for other companies with an interest in the litigation, either as potential intervenors or as parties in related cases, may be requested to participate in the conference. In appropriate circumstances, the court may also invite counsel for government enforcement agencies, such as the Securities and Exchange Commission or the Antitrust Division of the Department of Justice. Conferences may be held by telephone to accommodate attorneys who are not available on short notice for a conference in chambers. Although the complaint will typically include a request for a temporary restraining order (TRO) and an application for a preliminary injunction, a TRO—or, indeed, any order in takeover litigation—should almost never be granted ex parte, particularly given the opportunity for a telephone conference.

Among the agenda items that may be appropriate for consideration at this initial conference, whether held in person or by telephone, are the following:

- **Preliminary issues.** If serious questions will be raised about standing, personal jurisdiction, venue, or other threshold matters that, if resolved promptly, might reduce or eliminate the need for discovery, the court should establish a schedule for expedited resolution of these issues. Counsel or the court should ascertain the status of other related cases, including times set for hearings, and make plans to coordinate the proceedings to the extent possible. If jurisdiction and venue will not be contested, the judge may require the parties to include any related claims that may arise and enjoin them from instituting new litigation in other courts. Because of time constraints, multidistrict transfer under 28 U.S.C. § 1407 is rarely feasible. Transfer of cases to a single district under 28 U.S.C. § 1404 or 1406 may, however, be appropriate; if so, such transfers should be ordered as expeditiously as possible. If the cases remain in separate courts, the judges should confer and attempt to avoid conflicts in schedules and rulings.

- **Time and form of hearing.** The most significant hearing in takeover litigation is usually that on the preliminary injunction. The court's ruling may moot or resolve other issues. Depending on the date of the hearing, the court may, under Fed. R. Civ. P. 65(a)(2), order the trial on the merits to be advanced and consolidated with the hearing. In some cases, the plaintiff may not seek a preliminary injunction if a hearing on a permanent injunction can be held expeditiously. Before deciding when to hear the application for a preliminary injunction, the judge should determine whether there is a critical date by which a ruling on the application must be rendered and ascertain from counsel all dates important to the litigation, including those on which any statutory waiting periods expire or significant events (such as a stockholders' meeting or the commencement of acquisition of shares by a competing offeror) are scheduled to occur. Because of the prevalence of state statutes, such as Control Share Acquisition Acts and Business Combination statutes, as well as shareholders' rights plans (poison pills), the federal statutory waiting period may not be controlling. The court should question counsel about the interplay of such laws and corporate defenses and the effect they will have on the date to be set for the hearing. If the deadline for a ruling cannot be met because of requirements of other litigation, such as criminal proceedings subject to the Speedy Trial Act, the court should consider reassignment of the case to another judge. The court should also obtain counsel's views about the minimum time needed to conduct essential discovery and the hearing itself. The court may make a tentative determination on the form of the hearing—for example, whether the motion will be decided on affidavits, depositions, and documents alone, or whether witnesses will be heard in person and, if so, whether their direct testimony will be presented by prepared statements and reports (see *supra* section 22.51).

- **Scheduling.** The court should establish a schedule for filing responsive pleadings and motions, defining and narrowing issues, conducting necessary discovery, and holding the next conference. The schedule depends on the date set for the hearing, and will usually be substantially compressed compared to those typical of other litigation. For example, the court may require that the answer be combined with any motions and filed well before the twenty-day period prescribed by Fed. R. Civ. P. 12(a) (as the rule authorizes) and that the parties serve papers by personal delivery rather than through the mail. In setting the schedule, the judge should take into account the suggestions and requests of counsel; although the schedule should be regarded as firm, unforeseen events may require revision. The attorneys should confer in advance of each conference, seeking through discussion and compromise to narrow, if not eliminate, disagreements on the matters to be considered by the court. The court may also, after some discussion, adjourn the conference for a day or two to permit counsel to develop more detailed proposals for management of the case.

- **Emergency matters.** Any pending request for a TRO should generally be resolved at the initial conference, and the court should establish a procedure—such as telephonic conference calls or setting aside a period before or after normal office hours for a conference in person—for attending to other matters that may arise and require an immediate ruling, such as critical discovery disputes that the parties are unable to resolve. The judge should, however, caution the parties that unnecessary "emergency" motions, whose primary purpose may be to influence the market, may subject offending counsel or their clients to appropriate sanctions.

All orders in takeover litigation involving entities with publicly traded securities should, to the extent feasible, be announced after the market closes. These rulings may have a substantial impact on the market for both plaintiffs' and defendants' stock and are sometimes monitored by securities professionals in an attempt to take immediate action in response to the court's actions, often to the disadvantage of less sophisticated market participants. In unusual situations involving important confidential information, the court may also consider holding certain proceedings *in camera* or receiving some evidence under seal. Expecting counsel, however, to defer disclosing the results of a court conference, even if so ordered, is probably unrealistic, and such an order could conflict with the disclosure requirements of the federal securities laws.

Because of the limited time within which rulings must be made, the need for the judge to be personally involved in management and supervision is greater here than in other complex litigation. The court should avoid referral to a magistrate judge or special master—such a referral may result in critical delays while rulings are reviewed.

33.42 Discovery

The discovery program for this type of litigation must be carefully planned; counsel should be encouraged to submit a jointly agreed plan for the court's approval. The potential scope of disputed issues can lead to excessive discovery demands, both for documents and depositions, creating unreasonable burdens on the parties considering the brief time usually available for compliance. The court should therefore stress the need to identify and narrow the disputed issues (see *supra* section 21.33) and see that the discovery plan is narrowly tailored in light of the issues (see *supra* section 21.41).

Discovery should begin with an expedited procedure for the identification of relevant files, records, and documents necessary for the resolution of the issues. Steps should be taken to avoid excessively voluminous production that will burden rather than assist the parties. The court should consider the following:

- limiting the relevant periods of time for discovery requests (see *supra* section 21.424);
- having documents and files redacted to eliminate extraneous matter (see *supra* section 21.44);

- requiring that relevant documents be exchanged before depositions (see *supra* section 21.452);
- setting time limits for depositions (see *supra* section 21.451);
- encouraging counsel and the parties to consider alternative means of obtaining testimony in the limited time available, such as through statements and interviews of witnesses (see *supra* section 21.452) or discovery in related litigation (see *supra* section 21.423);
- having expert opinions produced in the form of a signed report, which may avoid the need for depositions (see *supra* section 21.48); and
- encouraging and approving stipulated protective orders (see *supra* section 21.43).

33.43 Additional Conferences; Preparation for Trial

One or two additional conferences will usually be needed before the hearing, each conference preceded by a meeting (or conference call) among counsel. The primary purposes of these conferences are to assure that schedules are being met, to narrow or revise the issues based on intervening circumstances (such as an offer being made by another company for the "target" company's stock, or other defensive measures adopted or proposed to be adopted by the "target" company), and to make final preparations for the hearing.

Complaints in takeover litigation frequently include a number of claims that, after further exploration, the plaintiffs may be willing to eliminate, at least for purposes of the preliminary injunction. Similarly, defenses and counterclaims may be abandoned as the hearing date approaches. The court should encourage the parties to narrow the scope of the case to the most important issues, setting a date by which they are to specify those allegations the parties will press at the hearing.

Various steps may be taken to expedite and streamline the hearing:
- where no substantial factual disputes exist, the hearing may be held on affidavits alone;
- where there are disputes, the parties may be directed to submit statements of undisputed facts (see *supra* section 21.641) or requests for admission (see *supra* section 21.47) to narrow the scope of the hearing;
- if witnesses are to be heard, they should be identified in advance along with the substance of their testimony and the exhibits they will sponsor (see *supra* section 22.23);
- where credibility is not a substantial factor, the court may require that direct testimony be offered in the form of adopted narrative statements, exchanged in advance and subject to cross-examination and motions to strike at the hearing (see *supra* section 22.51);

- proposed exhibits should be exchanged in advance of the hearing and objections should be made in writing in advance of the hearing or deemed waived;
- objections to foundation should be resolved before the hearing;
- if deposition testimony is to be used, counsel should present stipulated summaries or extracts in lieu of lengthy readings of transcripts (see *supra* sections 22.331–22.332);
- briefs should be submitted in advance of the hearing, along with proposed findings of fact and conclusions of law (see *supra* section 22.52) and proposed forms of order; and
- where time is of the essence, the court may rule from the bench at the conclusion of the hearing, dictating findings and conclusions into the record, directing counsel to prepare and submit formal findings and conclusions based on the record.

33.5 Employment Discrimination

Individual actions alleging employment discrimination generally are not considered complex.[1163] But complexity may be introduced into such litigation by class action allegations, the scope of potential discovery, the technical nature of expert testimony, and the complications that may arise from the granting of relief, whether by way of judgment or consent decree. When there are related actions against the same employer, including "pattern and practice" actions by a government agency, they should ordinarily be assigned to the same judge for coordinated pretrial proceedings and perhaps consolidated trial.

33.51 Issues and Parties

At the initial pretrial conference (see *supra* section 21.21), the court should attempt to identify the specific acts of discrimination each plaintiff (or intervenor) claims to have suffered and the particular relief sought. The court should also ascertain that the administrative prerequisites to the filing of an action have been

---

1163. But note that under 42 U.S.C. § 2000e-5(f)(5), such cases are to be heard "at the earliest practicable date and in every way expedited." If the case is not scheduled for trial within 120 days after joinder of issues, a special master may be appointed under Fed. R. Civ. P. 53.

timely satisfied by named plaintiffs.[1164] Early identification of the individual claims that may be pursued in the litigation is needed as a foundation for a determination whether they qualify for class certification[1165] and for development of an appropriate plan for discovery and trial. The initial narrowing of issues may usually be accomplished without discovery; if jurisdictional facts are disputed— such as when a plaintiff received a "right to sue" letter—they can be resolved through an expedited hearing, evidentiary if necessary.

Plaintiffs in employment discrimination cases often seek relief that might adversely affect other employees or putative employees of the defendant employer. Where potentially affected employees are represented by a labor organization, even if only the employer was named in the administrative charges or is alleged to have been guilty of discrimination, it may be advisable to join the organization as a necessary party or to have it intervene in order to make the decree binding if plaintiffs are successful.[1166] Similarly, in some cases joinder of or intervention by other employees who would be adversely affected by plaintiffs' relief may also be warranted to ensure that all competing interests are adequately represented and to protect against subsequent claims of reverse discrimination[1167] (see also *infra* section 33.55).

33.52 Class Actions

Employment discrimination cases that meet the prerequisites of Rule 23(a) may qualify as class actions under Rule 23(b)(2) where the defendant "has acted . . . on grounds generally applicable to the class, thereby making appropriate final injunctive relief with respect to the class as a whole." They may also qualify under Rule 23(b)(3) on the ground that a common question of fact or law predominates; indeed, where monetary relief is sought, a (b)(3) class is generally the appropriate vehicle. Whether the action is maintained under (b)(2) or (b)(3) will make a significant difference with respect to various aspects of class action litigation, in particular the definition of the class, entitlement to damages, class notice, and opt-out rights (see *supra* sections 30.14, 30.231).

Members of a Rule 23(b)(2) class generally are not entitled to recover other than incidental damages (i.e., damages to which plaintiffs would be automatically entitled once liability is established).[1168] For that reason, and because *res judicata*

1164. Harriss v. Pan Am. World Airways, Inc., 74 F.R.D. 24 (N.D. Cal. 1977). Claims under Title VII require the prior filing by the individual claimant of a charge with the EEOC. Claims under 42 U.S.C. § 1981 (racial discrimination) and 42 U.S.C. § 1983 (discrimination by governmental employers) do not require filing of an administrative charge, but are subject to state statutes of limitations.

1165. *See* General Tel. Co. v. Falcon, 457 U.S. 147 (1982).

1166. *See* Fed. R. Civ. P. 19, 24.

1167. *See* Martin v. Wilks, 490 U.S. 755 (1989).

1168. *See* Simer v. Rios, 661 F.2d 655 (7th Cir. 1981).

considerations with respect to individual claims are not significant, less precision is required in the definition of the class. On the other hand, in a (b)(3) action, where plaintiffs' primary claim is for damages, the class must be defined with more specificity and the court must satisfy itself that the determination of individual claims does not preclude the existence of a predominant common question. Because Rule 23(c)(4) permits an action to be maintained as a class action with respect to particular issues, a (b)(3) or (b)(2) class may be certified for bifurcated adjudication of a common issue (stage I), to be followed by separate trials (coordinated or consolidated as may be appropriate) to adjudicate individual damage claims (stage II) (see *infra* section 33.54).

In addressing a motion for class certification, the court needs to consider whether the complaint challenges an employment practice affecting a class of employees or whether instead it primarily challenges the individual treatment of employees. A complaint alleging a policy and practice of racial discrimination may satisfy the requirements for a (b)(2) action.[1169] Where, however, plaintiffs seek class-wide relief on the basis of the impact of such a policy on their individual employment conditions, they must also show that their claims are sufficiently related to those of the putative class members that they meet the requirements of commonality and typicality for the class.[1170] In determining the appropriate class, the court must ascertain whether the practice or conduct complained of involves the entire operation of the employer, or only a specific facility, department, or individual supervisor.

To ascertain the precise nature of the class claim and whether it meets the prerequisites of Rule 23(a), the court should in the first instance probe beneath the pleadings to identify the particular practice or procedure complained of and the extent to which the evidence that will be offered to support the class plaintiffs' claims will also support the claims of members of the class. Some discovery may be needed although, as noted, precertification discovery should be held to a minimum (see *supra* section 30.12). Occasionally, as indicated, the class claims will be consolidated with individual claims and there may be reasons for proceeding with merits discovery on the latter. Where that is the case, an effort should be

1169. *General Tel. Co.*, 457 U.S. at 159, n.15 (class members need not be identically situated and a class action of both applicants and incumbents might be justified if a general policy of discrimination were shown to manifest itself in both hiring and promotional practices in the same general fashion); *see, e.g.*, McKenzie v. Sawyer, 684 F.2d 62 (D.C. Cir. 1982).

1170. *General Tel. Co.*, 457 U.S. at 147 (emphasizing the need for careful attention to the requirements of Rule 23 in the light of the legal and factual issues underlying plaintiff's cause of action and rejecting the approach that one who claims injury from an employer's alleged ethnic discrimination is automatically qualified to represent all others adversely affected by any manifestation of that discrimination ("across the board discrimination")). *See also* Harriss v. Pan Am. World Airways, Inc., 74 F.R.D. 24 (N.D. Cal. 1977).

made to organize discovery so as to avoid duplication. Disposition of the individual claims should not, however, affect the ruling on the class motion; the merits of the individual claims will not determine whether the class action can go forward and certification is appropriate.

The court's ruling on certification should describe the class (and any subclasses) as precisely as possible, both to facilitate planning for discovery, trial, and settlement and to define the persons (and claims) that will be entitled to relief under and barred by a final judgment in the action.[1171] A precise definition of the issues to be tried is important for, among other things, *res judicata* and collateral estoppel. This definition should be stated in objective terms to the extent feasible—for example, all female applicants during a specified time who, like the plaintiffs, failed to meet the employer's height and weight requirements. If not clear from the description of the class itself, the nature of the claimed class discrimination should be indicated—for example, all persons of color employed by the defendant during a specified period who allege that they were denied promotion during that period on account of their race. Definitions should exclude criteria that are subjective or depend on the merits of the claim (see *supra* section 30.14). Although the court is authorized under Rule 23(c)(1) to enter a conditional order of certification and modify it prior to final judgment, later modifications can be prejudicial to class members and interfere with the effective management of the action, and should therefore be avoided. See *supra* section 30.11.

Rule 23 does not provide for opt out by members of a (b)(2) class. If the court determines that certain members of the class should be excluded, perhaps because their interests are aligned with management (see *supra* section 30.24) or to avoid conflicts within a class, it may tailor the class definition appropriately to exclude certain persons from the class or create one or more subclasses.[1172]

Notice to class members must be given when a (b)(3) class is certified. It is not required for a (b)(2) class, but may be advisable for a number of reasons, such as to bring to light possible conflicts and to ensure the *res judicata* effect of a judgment. The form of notice—individual mailing, posting on bulletin boards, or inclusion in pay envelopes—will depend on the circumstances of the case (see *supra* section 30.2). While the cost of notice is generally borne by plaintiffs,[1173] in employment litigation relatively cost-free methods of reaching at least current

1171. *See* Cooper v. Federal Res. Bank of Richmond, 467 U.S. 867 (1984) (related "individual" claims of discrimination not precluded by a finding of no "class" discrimination).

1172. *See* Penson v. Terminal Transp. Co., 634 F.2d 989 (5th Cir. 1981).

1173. *See* Eisen v. Carlisle & Jacquelin, 417 U.S. 156 (1974) (plaintiff must bear cost of notice required for class actions under Rule 23(b)(3)).

employees are usually available. Moreover, where notice is being given in a (b)(2) action at the employer's request, it may be required to bear the cost.

Collective actions are authorized to be brought by employees asserting claims under the Age Discrimination in Employment Act (ADEA), 29 U.S.C. § 626(b), or the Fair Labor Standards Act (FLSA), 29 U.S.C. § 216(b). While all included plaintiffs need to be similarly situated, the possibility of varying defenses does not vitiate a collective action.[1174] The requirements that apply to class actions under Rule 23 need not be met,[1175] although notice should be given of ADEA collective actions.[1176]

33.53 Discovery

In planning the discovery program for employment discrimination litigation, five characteristics should be taken into account:

1. many aspects of the company's employment practices and its workforce may be potentially relevant as circumstantial evidence;
2. most of the information will be within the control of the employer, often in computerized form;
3. except for actions brought by the government, plaintiffs usually have limited resources;
4. expert testimony and complex statistical evidence will play an important role at trial; and
5. trial will often be conducted in stages.

Identification of source materials. Discovery can be greatly simplified and expedited if the parties are directed to exchange core information before discovery begins. That information should include not only that required under Rule 26(a)(1) and the district's local rules or expense and delay reduction plan, but also potentially relevant documentary materials such as statements of employment policies, policy manuals and guides, and an identification and general explanation—perhaps with samples—of the types of records that contain data that may be relevant to the issues in the case. After obtaining this information, plaintiffs may need to depose or interview informally the personnel director or other person responsible for maintaining these records in order to clarify the nature of the information contained in these records, how the information is coded or compiled, and how data may be extracted from the various sources. Employers frequently maintain the same or similar information in different forms. For ex-

1174. *See* Lockhart v. Westinghouse Credit Corp., 879 F.2d 43 (3d Cir. 1989).
1175. *See* Anson v. University of Tex. Health Science Ctr., 962 F.2d 539 (5th Cir. 1991); Owens v. Bethlehem Mines Corp., 108 F.R.D. 207 (S.D. W. Va. 1985).
1176. *See* Hoffman-LaRoche, Inc. v. Sperling, 493 U.S. 165 (1989).

ample, earnings information may be kept in a personnel file, in tax records, and in payroll records. Job histories of employees may be determined from periodic transfer and promotion records, from individual work record cards, or from personnel files. The company may also have compiled relevant data regarding its workforce and employment practices for reporting to governmental agencies or for use in other litigation. The parties can then determine the most efficient and economical method for the employer to produce, and plaintiffs to obtain, the most relevant information. Because many aspects of the company's employment practices may have some potential relevance as circumstantial evidence, and various records may contain information about these practices, judgment needs to be exercised in deciding what information is necessary and how that information may be most efficiently produced. Under Fed. R. Civ. P. 26(g), counsel are required to weigh the potential value of particular discovery against the time and expense of production, and under Rule 26(b)(2) the judge is expected to limit discovery to avoid duplication and unjustified expense.

Computerized records. The time and expense of discovery may usually be substantially reduced if pertinent information can be retrieved from existing computerized records. Moreover, production in computer-readable form of relevant files and fields (or even of an entire database) will reduce disputes over the accuracy of compilations made from such data and enable experts for both sides to conduct studies using a common set of data. The parties' computer experts should informally discuss, in person or by telephone, procedures to facilitate retrieval and production of computerized information; the attorneys can then confirm these arrangements in writing. See *supra* section 21.446.

Confidential information. The privacy interests of employees may be protected by excluding from production records or portions of records the contents of which are irrelevant to the litigation (employees' medical histories, for example, are rarely of significance in a discrimination case) or by masking the names of individuals in particular compilations. If the company fears exposure to privacy claims were it to disclose personal information voluntarily, the parties may draft an order for entry by the court, directing the employer to provide the information. A protective order barring unnecessary disclosure of sensitive items may also be useful in facilitating the production of relevant information. The persons to whom plaintiffs' counsel will be permitted to disclose confidential materials will depend on the circumstances. For example, counsel might be allowed to disclose some sensitive information to the plaintiffs or even to class members, but permitted to disclose information about tests only to an expert. See *supra* section 21.43.

Preservation of records. Equal Employment Opportunity Commission (EEOC) regulations require that, when a charge of discrimination or a civil action has been filed, the "employer shall preserve all personnel records relevant to the charge or action until final disposition of the charge or action." 29 C.F.R.

§ 1602.14. The parties may disagree on which records are covered by this mandate, particularly with respect to computerized data that may be periodically erased as new information is electronically stored. A separate order of the court may be needed both to clarify what records must be preserved and to provide relief from unduly burdensome retention requirements. See *supra* section 21.442.

Statistical evidence and expert testimony. Employment discrimination litigation frequently involves the collection and presentation of voluminous data regarding characteristics of the company's workforce and its employment practices. In addition to using data already computerized by the company, the parties often prepare new databases, electronically storing information manually extracted from other records. To eliminate disagreements about the accuracy of these new databases and to reduce the time and expense otherwise involved in preparing and verifying separate databases, the parties may—with the court's encouragement—be able to agree on joint development of a common database on which their respective experts will conduct their studies. If agreement on a common database cannot be obtained, pretrial verification procedures should be used to eliminate (or quantify) errors in the different databases (see *supra* sections 21.446, 21.493). As discussed in *supra* section 21.492, this information should, whenever possible, be presented at trial through summaries, charts, and other tabulations,[1177] and pretrial procedures should be adopted to facilitate this presentation and reduce disputes over the accuracy of the underlying data and the compilations derived from such data. Indeed, to the extent practicable, disputes at trial regarding statistical evidence should be limited to its interpretation, relevance, and weight, not its accuracy. Experts who will present statistical studies or express opinions should be required to prepare and disclose a written report containing a complete statement of all opinions to be expressed and all exhibits to be used, the basis and reasons for them, and the data and information considered in arriving at them.[1178] The parties' experts' reports should be exchanged before expert depositions are taken.[1179] After reviewing these reports and considering the comments of counsel, the court may conclude that it should appoint an independent statistical expert under Fed. R. Evid. 706. The court should, however, be

1177. In discrimination cases, the parties sometimes attempt to introduce in bulk numerous personnel files, work history cards, and other similar documents. The court may insist on compilations and is not required to "[wade] through a sea of uninterpreted raw evidence." *See, e.g.,* Crawford v. Western Elec. Co., 614 F.2d 1300, 1319 (5th Cir. 1980).

1178. Fed. R. Civ. P. 26(a)(2). See *supra* § 21.48.

1179. For further discussion of discovery from experts, including establishing schedules, see *supra* § 21.48.

wary of making an appointment under Rule 706 if the plaintiffs will be able to pay their share of any assessed fees only if they prevail (see *supra* section 21.51).[1180]

Discovery from class members. The extent to which discovery from class members should be permitted, as well as the timing and form of such discovery, will depend on the circumstances of the case. Court approval should usually be required before any discovery from class members is undertaken, and the judge should limit such discovery to that which is genuinely needed and ensure that it is not used to harass either the members or the representatives of the class (see *supra* sections 30.12, 30.232). As noted in *supra* section 33.52, depositions of a limited number of putative class members are sometimes needed prior to a ruling on class certification. In some cases, limited discovery from class members may be conducted before a stage I trial on liability to the class, with the rest deferred (see *supra* section 33.54).[1181] Each party should ordinarily be permitted to depose any class member whom the other party plans to call as a witness, and discovery may also be appropriate of a class member whose employment history will be used as evidence showing the existence (or non-existence) of the alleged discrimination. Whether anecdotal experiences of individual class members are relevant at a stage I trial will depend on the circumstances of the particular case (see *supra* section 33.54). If such evidence will become relevant at subsequent proceedings only if liability to the class is established at the stage I trial, discovery from those class members may be deferred until after the first trial. Similarly, class members on whose behalf claims for individual relief are presented after a finding of class-wide liability may be treated as subject to discovery.

33.54 Trial

Employment discrimination class actions have commonly been tried in separate stages under Rule 42(b).[1182] In some cases the class issues may themselves be severed, with the stage I trials of different class issues conducted separately. The stage I trial determines whether the defendants have discriminated against the class. Whether the merits of the individual claims of the class representatives should be tried in stage I depends on whether proof of those claims is essential to establishing liability on the class claim. If class-wide discrimination is found, issues of relief are tried in stage II. Since the 1991 amendment of Title VII, parties in disparate treatment cases are entitled to request a jury trial. If a jury is demanded, the bifurcation of class actions will be substantially more complicated.

1180. *See generally* Joe S. Cecil & Thomas E. Willging, Court-Appointed Experts: Defining the Role of Experts Appointed Under Federal Rule of Evidence 706 (Federal Judicial Center 1993); Reference Manual on Scientific Evidence (Federal Judicial Center 1994).

1181. *See, e.g.,* Western Elec. Co. v. Stern, 544 F.2d 1196 (3d Cir. 1976).

1182. *See* United States v. United States Steel Corp., 520 F.2d 1043 (5th Cir. 1975); Johnson v. Goodyear Tire & Rubber Co., 491 F.2d 1364 (5th Cir. 1974).

Although the class-wide issue of discrimination is readily tried to a jury in stage I, the trial of individual damage claims to a jury in stage II will result in potentially lengthy trials since in some cases Title VII permits recovery of back pay as well as compensatory damages, including future loss and pain and suffering. Moreover, the court must consider whether fairness to the parties requires that both liability and relief be tried to a single jury. In view of these complexities, the class certification may be limited to the (b)(2) issue (class-wide liability and injunctive relief), with all other claims proceeding as separate actions but contingent on the outcome of the (b)(2) trial (see *supra* sections 30.17, 33.52).

Where the case is tried to the court instead, the court in stage I determines the appropriateness of class-wide injunctive relief. An immediate appeal from the ruling on injunctive relief is permissible under 28 U.S.C. § 1292(a). Because resolution of claims for individual relief can be an expensive and time-consuming process, such an appeal may be desirable as a means for obtaining early appellate review of a finding of liability. If an appeal under § 1292(a) is unavailable, the court can consider certifying its ruling on class liability for appeal under 28 U.S.C. § 1292(b) (see *supra* section 25.11). The award of attorneys' fees may be deferred until completion of proceedings for individual relief; an interim award, however, is frequently made after a grant of injunctive relief.[1183] In stage II the court, perhaps after a period for additional discovery, resolves the individual damage claims of the class members. In this second stage, the claimants—who, by proof of their membership in the class, are presumed to have been subjected to the discrimination practiced against the class[1184]—are permitted to present their individual claims of injury,[1185] subject to the right of the employer to raise defenses to those claims that were not resolved during the stage I proceedings. Further severance may be useful at the individual remedy stage. For example, the court may identify those entitled to relief before the parties proceed with discovery and possible trial regarding the amount of damages. The court may require class members to complete information forms disclosing the critical facts—e.g., the job bids that they assert were discriminatorily rejected by the company—on which their claim of individual injury is based. The court may establish a claims

---

1183. *See* Fed. R. Civ. P. 54(d).

1184. McKenzie v. Sawyer, 684 F.2d 62 (D.C. Cir. 1982); Pettway v. American Cast Iron Pipe, 494 F.2d 211 (5th Cir. 1974); King v. Trans World Airlines, Inc., 738 F.2d 255 (8th Cir. 1984); Cox v. American Cast Iron Pipe Co., 784 F.2d 1546 (11th Cir. 1986).

1185. As to whether the amount of damages each class member has sustained must be individually determined or whether damages may be assessed on a class-wide basis, *compare* Mitchell v. Mid-Continent Spring Co., 583 F.2d 275, 283 n.11 (6th Cir. 1978) (individual damages must be proved) *with* Pettway v. American Cast Iron Pipe Co., 494 F.2d 211, 259–63 (5th Cir. 1974) (class-wide formula permissible).

resolution procedure administered by a magistrate judge or special master under Rule 53.

When the trial of the action is bifurcated into stages, the court should define precisely the issues to be resolved at the stage I trial, as well as those to be decided in subsequent proceedings if class-wide discrimination is found at stage I. Although this delineation will not eliminate all duplicative evidence—for example, anecdotal testimony may be admissible as circumstantial evidence at the first trial and, if liability is established, be offered as direct evidence on individual claims in later proceedings—it will enable counsel to prepare more effectively for both stages of the litigation. Issues are generally separated according to the extent they depend on the particular circumstances of individual employees; for example, defenses such as "business necessity" and "bona fide occupational qualification" are usually resolved at stage I, while the issue of whether employees may be excused from making applications for a position is generally reserved for decision in later proceedings.

The focus of the stage I trial, whether to the court or the jury, will frequently be on statistical evidence and expert testimony. Pretrial planning should consider the extent to which "anecdotal" evidence regarding the individual experiences of various employees, union stewards, supervisors, and managers will also be received. Such evidence may be offered by plaintiffs or defendants to provide illustrative support for their respective positions and for the studies conducted by their experts. Some limits on the number of witnesses may be appropriate, however, to avoid unnecessary duplication,[1186] and pretrial disclosure should be required of their names and the general subject matter of their expected testimony.[1187]

33.55 Settlement

Timing. Precertification settlements of discrimination cases brought as class actions present special problems and should be approached with great caution (see generally *supra* section 30.45). Similarly, if the parties propose settlement of only the individual claims of the named plaintiffs and abandonment of the class claim, the court should take the steps necessary to ensure that members of the putative class are not prejudiced. The court may decide that the putative class should be notified of the proposed settlement and given an opportunity to intervene to pursue the class claims (see *supra* section 30.212). Settlement negotiations in class actions should ordinarily be deferred until the court has ruled on class certification; in employment discrimination litigation, the parties should explore settlement possibilities as the case proceeds toward trial after the certification

---

1186. *Cf.* Watkins v. Scott Paper Co., 530 F.2d 1159, 1172 (5th Cir. 1976).
1187. Fed. R. Civ. P. 26(a)(3).

ruling, and, if those initial efforts are unsuccessful, they should renew their discussions after the stage I trial.

Affirmative relief. Many employment discrimination cases terminate in consent decrees or in litigated judgments that order implementation of certain employment practices that may be seen as constituting affirmative action. Such provisions raise difficult issues concerning their effect on groups of employees that may be adversely affected by them and their vulnerability to subsequent legal challenge.[1188] The Civil Rights Act of 1991 establishes procedures for precluding subsequent challenge by persons who (1) prior to entry of the order, had actual notice of the potential adverse effect and an opportunity to object, or (2) who were adequately represented.[1189] Parties to the decree may also seek intervention or joinder of persons who may claim to be adversely affected.

Attorneys' fees. Ethical concerns may be raised by parties' attempts to settle claims for attorneys' fees before a settlement of the class claims has been effected or, indeed, if the defendants offer to settle class claims by payment of a lump sum on condition that attorneys' fees be waived Although the parties should be encouraged to settle claims regarding attorneys' fees, these negotiations preferably should not be commenced until the class claims have been resolved by trial or settlement. See *supra* sections 23.24, 24.21, 30.42.

Settlement hearing. Hearings on approval of class action settlements in employment discrimination litigation may generate vigorous objections.[1190] Because such opposition often stems from misunderstandings about the terms of the proposed settlement, the notice of settlement should provide full information in comprehensible form. Class counsel may also schedule, in advance of the hearing, meetings with the class at which counsel and the class representatives can explain in person the terms of the agreement and can answer questions. At the outset of the hearing, before the court proceeds to hear objections from class members or others, counsel should again describe in plain language the key features of the settlement, clarify misunderstandings, and indicate why they believe it to be advantageous to the class (see *supra* section 30.43). The judge may also explain portions of the proposed settlement that may have been confusing to members of the class. In its notice to the class of the proposed settlement, the court should usually require that any objections or requests to be heard be filed in writing by a specified date. It is advisable, however, to permit persons who have not filed timely objections to express their views at the hearing, including representatives

---

1188. Martin v. Wilks, 490 U.S. 755 (1989).

1189. 42 U.S.C. § 2000e-2(n).

1190. Opposition to the settlement does not, however, mean that it should necessarily be rejected by the court. *See, e.g.,* Cotton v. Hinton, 559 F.2d 1326 (5th Cir. 1977). See also *supra* §§ 30.41–30.44.

of employees not members of the class who claim they will be adversely affected by the settlement.

Implementation. Settlements of employment discrimination cases sometimes specify the persons to whom awards will be made and the amount each person is to be paid. More frequently, however, settlements have provided only the basic principles for determining these awards, contemplating further proceedings to ascertain the factual matters on which the awards depend. The settlement may, for example, establish one or more funds to be shared by persons satisfying prescribed criteria; in this situation the court may require class counsel after the settlement to preliminarily identify those class members eligible to participate in distribution, and provide those found ineligible an opportunity to present their claims to the court or a special master. If the settlement provides for a specified payment—whether a flat sum or an amount determined under a formula—to be made to each class member meeting specified criteria, the defendants may have a financial interest in challenging the claims of class members, and the court may refer such matters to a magistrate judge or special master under Rule 53 for individual hearings as necessary (see *supra* section 30.47). The court may also decide to appoint a special master under Rule 53 to monitor future implementation of injunctive features of the settlement (see *supra* section 21.52).

33.6 Patent

The principal source of complexity in patent litigation generally is the technical nature of the subject matter. Its unfamiliarity poses unique problems for judges and juries. Expert witnesses often have a dominant role. While general principles of effective case management (discussed elsewhere in this manual) apply to patent cases, primary attention must be directed to the management of the technical aspects of patent cases.

In that respect, patent litigation has much in common with other types of litigation that increasingly require courts to deal with technical subject matter, such as copyright and trademark, mass tort, employment discrimination, and even criminal litigation. The principal focus of this chapter, therefore, is on the management of the technical aspects of patent litigation.

Patent cases generally have only one party, or a few interrelated parties, on each side of a case. Litigation over a patent or a series of related patents may, however, proliferate and lead to multiforum litigation in federal courts requiring resort to procedures for coordination through MDL proceedings, the imposition of stays on redundant actions, or informal arrangements.

33.61 Technology

The judge will often need some general explanation of the substance and terminology of the science or technology involved in the subject matter of the patent before attempting to deal with the issues in the case or develop a plan for discovery and trial.[1191] Therefore, at an early stage, typically at or before the initial conference, the court may ask counsel to provide a concise and objective overview, orally or in writing, of the technical matters, including a definition of key terms and concepts. To encourage candor, the court may direct that these statements will not bind the parties and may not be used against them later in the proceedings. The court may also ask the parties jointly to develop a glossary of terms and concepts, using a procedure similar to that described in *supra* section 21.47 for developing a joint statement of uncontested and contested facts.

The judge may also convene an informal pretrial conference with both sides' experts present at which the experts are called on to explain the reasons for their different opinions or conclusions. The judge should not hesitate to ask questions to probe behind their opinions and seek explanations in order to identify, narrow, and understand the issues. The judge will be able to prepare for the conference by reading the reports prepared by the parties' experts for the trial (see *supra* section 21.48).

Increasingly, judges seek additional pretrial briefing on technological or scientific issues involved in the case. Although experts will in their trial testimony address those issues, judges look for a more nonadversarial setting to learn the fundamentals—the vocabulary and general intellectual framework of the subject matter—in order to deal more intelligently with issues arising during the trial. In some cases, jurors have been included in what is sometimes called a tutorial. It may be given at the outset of the trial by experts selected by the opposing sides or by a court-appointed expert, preferably selected from a list submitted by the parties (see *supra* section 21.51). Limiting the use of the court-appointed expert to explaining the general subject matter, without becoming involved in the disputes of the parties, will make it easier to maintain neutrality. Unless the parties con-

---

1191. Some helpful published material may be available. *See* Reference Manual on Scientific Evidence (Federal Judicial Center 1994).

sent, the court-appointed expert should have no ex parte communications with the judge.

Caution should be exercised by the judge in making demands on the parties for pretrial educational materials or services. Because they may be quite costly, the court should inquire about the prospective cost before issuing directions.

33.62 Defining the Issues

The typical patent case involves a number of separate, but related, claims and defenses. In addition to seeking injunctive relief and damages for the alleged infringement, plaintiffs often assert claims of unfair competition, wrongful business interference, and other similar state law tort claims. Defendants may plead specially several of the statutory bars under 35 U.S.C. §§ 102 and 103 or other sections of Title 35, as well as assert misuse of the patent or other equitable defenses and counterclaim for violations of antitrust laws. Although a sufficient basis for these contentions may exist for purposes of Fed. R. Civ. P. 11, many may prove to be without merit and may be abandoned by the time of trial.

The court should consider requiring the parties to submit detailed statements of their claims and defenses early in the litigation. Sometimes statements of claims can be supplied at the outset of the case. At other times, when the accused product is not available or not subject to examination, some discovery may be required. The statement submitted by plaintiff should contain a detailed explanation of the infringement contentions; it may be an element-by-element claims chart for each claim asserted. It should also specify which claims are alleged to have been infringed wantonly or willfully. The defendant should be required to respond to the claims chart at the same level of detail. This will help narrow the issues.

The court should set a date by which the defendant will be required to state those defenses it expects to litigate. The court should allow reasonable time for discovery to determine which defenses have factual support. The court should also set a date for the disclosure of all prior art that defendant will use to challenge the patent. Under 35 U.S.C. § 282, disclosure must be made "at least thirty days before the trial," but the court should generally fix an earlier deadline to allow adequate time for trial preparation.

With encouragement from the court, counsel may be willing to drop marginal claims or defenses at the time of the initial conference, or at least agree that discovery on them should be deferred while attention is given to the significant issues. Some of these issues may, of course, also be subject to early resolution by motion under Fed. R. Civ. P.12 or 56.

Assertions that the patentee is guilty of unclean hands or fraud on the Patent and Trademark Office—typically based on an alleged misrepresentation or failure to disclose pertinent prior art or test results—merit attention by the court.[1192] If the allegations have substance, discovery into matters otherwise protected by the attorney–client privilege may be warranted; on the other hand, pending some substantiation of these charges, the privilege should be respected and, therefore, the court may need to control the scope of discovery from counsel or clients. Particularly in nonjury cases, the trial judge may call on another judge to conduct any *in camera* inspections that are needed to determine whether sufficient evidence of fraud exists for the privilege to be waived.

In this connection, the court needs to be concerned with whether litigation counsel was involved in the prosecution of the patent before the patent office or provided prelitigation advice regarding validity, in particular giving a noninfringement letter. Where a willful infringement claim is asserted, if the alleged infringer continued to market a product after notice of a patent, it may be required to waive its privilege with respect to advice letters from counsel.[1193] Even in other circumstances, discovery from the attorney who prosecuted the patent is common. Because this will greatly complicate discovery and may undermine the effectiveness of litigation counsel, the court should determine early in the case what role counsel played with respect to the challenged patent, consider the potential ethical and practical problems, and determine whether to obtain the client's written consent to the representation after full disclosure.

Bifurcation for trial under Rule 42(b) may be advisable to avoid unnecessary time and expense of discovery and trial (note, however, that the Supreme Court has indicated a preference that the district court resolve invalidity issues even if no infringement is found[1194]). In most cases, damages should be severed from other issues to simplify the task of the fact finder. Sometimes trifurcation of the statutory issues, equitable defenses, and damages may be advisable. Some defenses—for example, an "on sale" bar—may be dispositive and suitable for early trial. Discovery and trial with respect to claims of unfair competition and antitrust counterclaims frequently are deferred until resolution of the patent issues, at which time these claims are often resolved by voluntary dismissal or settlement.

1192. Fraud may be asserted not only as a defense to the infringement claim, but also as part of the foundation for an antitrust counterclaim. *See* Walker Process Equip. Inc. v. Food Mach. & Chem. Corp., 382 U.S. 172 (1965).

1193. Fromson v. Western Litho Plate & Supply Co., 853 F.2d 1568, 1572–73 (Fed. Cir. 1988); Underwater Devices, Inc. v. Morrison-Knudsen Co., 717 F.2d 1380, 1389–90 (Fed. Cir. 1983). The Federal Circuit has recommended that the willfulness issue be bifurcated for later trial to avoid unfairness. Quantum Corp. v. Tandon Corp., 940 F.2d 642, 643–44 (Fed. Cir. 1991).

1194. Cardinal Chem. Co. v. Morton Int'l, Inc., 113 S. Ct. 1967 (1993).

33.63 Related Litigation

Patent litigation frequently involves a series of cases brought in different districts. Sometimes transfer is ordered to a single court under 28 U.S.C. § 1407 for centralized pretrial proceedings, although the Judicial Panel on Multidistrict Litigation may decline to order such transfers on the ground that coordination can be achieved through the cooperative efforts of the affected courts and counsel (often the real parties in interest and the attorneys are the same, or at least related, in all cases). It is common practice to stay all pending litigation except the first suit between the patent owner and a manufacturer or high-level distributor. Later suits against customers are routinely stayed, and a declaratory judgment suit by the manufacturer of the claimed infringing product is preferred over even an earlier filed suit by the patent owner against a customer.[1195] In the absence of a stay, techniques such as those described in *supra* section 31.13 may be used to avoid or minimize duplicative discovery and potential conflicts in pretrial and trial schedules.

Decisions by other courts involving the same patent require careful study. A final decision holding the patent invalid will preclude further efforts to enforce the patent against others—provided the patentee "had a full and fair chance to litigate" its validity.[1196] In such circumstances, however, the patentee must be given the opportunity to demonstrate under the factors outlined in *Blonder-Tongue* that "in justice and equity" it should not be collaterally estopped by the adverse decision. Although a decision upholding the validity of the patent will not bar a new defendant from attacking the patent and, indeed, is not necessarily binding even on the same court under the doctrine of stare decisis, the decision is nevertheless entitled to appropriate weight in a subsequent case, the weight depending primarily on the degree of similarity of the prior art and other evidence introduced in the two cases.[1197]

33.64 Discovery

Discovery frequently is conducted according to a prescribed sequence of issues, particularly if severed trials under Fed. R. Civ. P. 42(b) are contemplated. This approach, however, may cause extra expense and delay if discovery regarding the priority issues will involve examination of many of the same witnesses and exhibits as discovery on the subsequent issues. Moreover, deferral of discovery regarding damages may complicate efforts to evaluate the litigation for settlement.

1195. William Gluckin & Co. v. International Playtex Corp., 407 F.2d 177 (2d Cir. 1969).

1196. Blonder-Tongue Lab., Inc. v. University of Ill. Found., 402 U.S. 313 (1971). This principle applies not only when the first decision holds the patent invalid but also when, after rulings upholding its validity, a decision is subsequently made that it is invalid. *See* Stevenson v. Sears, Roebuck & Co., 713 F.2d 705 (Fed. Cir. 1983).

1197. *Stevenson*, 713 F.2d at 711 n.5.

Parties are free to use nonstenographic means of taking depositions and expert depositions are often taken using videotape to avoid potential problems in securing the expert's attendance at trial.[1198]

Protective orders of the type described in *supra* section 21.432 will usually be appropriate in patent cases.[1199] Disclosure of particularly sensitive information—such as production processes and customer information—may be restricted to counsel and their experts, but counsel should exercise restraint in designating materials as confidential. In some cases the parties prefer that inspection of such facilities and exhibits be done by a court-appointed expert or special master, rather than by someone associated with their adversary. For further protection, filing of sensitive documents may either be waived under Fed. R. Civ. P. 5(d) or be made under seal.

At the initial conference, the court should ascertain the extent to which discovery will be sought of matters that may be protected by the attorney–client privilege or work-product doctrine and, if so, whether disclosure will be resisted (see *supra* section 33.62). Use of a special master may be warranted if such disputes will be extensive and cannot be resolved by considering a few specimen documents.

Early inquiry should also be made about use of out-of-court tests or in-court demonstrations. If tests are contemplated, protocols should be set up at an early conference with respect to who may attend or observe, what criteria must be met to permit use of the results in court, and when disclosure of the results must be made. The court should set a deadline for pretrial disclosure of any such tests or proposed demonstrations and may wish to consider before trial objections to the admissibility of such evidence.

The parties should not undertake formal discovery outside the country without prior approval from the court, and any requests for documentary evidence in such countries should be precisely and narrowly drafted (see *supra* section 21.494). If the parties are unable to agree on a translation or translator for documents in foreign languages, the court may appoint an expert under Fed. R. Evid. 706.

Discovery of experts specially retained to testify at trial is governed by Rule 26(a)(2); discovery of nontestifying experts is governed by Rule 26(b)(4)(B) (see *supra* section 21.48).

1198. Fed. R. Civ. P. 30(b)(3).
1199. See Sample Form *infra* § 41.36.

33.65 Expert Opinions

33.651 *Control of Expert Testimony*

While expert testimony will generally be essential to patent litigation, the court should control the subject matter of expert testimony and the number of experts the parties will be permitted to call. The court should require the parties to identify the technical experts they propose to present and the subject matter to be covered by each. Compliance with the requirements of Rule 26(a)(2) will routinely lead to such disclosure, but it is advisable for the court, after having heard from counsel, to determine as early as possible what witnesses will be permitted to testify in order to avoid the expense of complying with the disclosure rule with respect to experts who will be barred.

Technical experts are those whose special training or experience in the applicable technology or science qualifies them to express opinions bearing on the validity or invalidity of the patent—such as the scope and content of the prior art, the level of skill in the art, and the obviousness or non-obviousness of the claimed invention in view of the prior art[1200]—and on the alleged infringement. Some witnesses testifying to some of this subject matter—for example, the history of the invention—may be percipient witnesses testifying to fact rather than opinion. Some witnesses may testify both as experts and fact witnesses. The nature of a witness's testimony should therefore be clearly identified for purposes of the discovery rules and the rules of evidence.

Patent law experts—patent attorneys, patent law professors, or former officials of the Patent and Trademark Office—are frequently offered to express opinions on legal issues, such as alleged estoppel arising from the prosecution of the application for the patent in question, the duty of disclosure to the patent office, and whether or not that duty has been violated by particular acts or omissions during such prosecution. Because this testimony relates to legal issues that counsel for the parties are able to argue, the need for it should be questioned by the judge.

Because of the cost and time consumed by expert discovery and expert testimony at trial, the court should place appropriate limits on the number of experts parties will be permitted to use at trial. Rarely should it be necessary to have more than one expert witness with respect to any particular technological or scientific discipline.

1200. *See* Graham v. John Deere Co., 383 U.S. 1, 17–18 (1966).

33.652 Admissibility of Expert Testimony

Opinion testimony must comply with the requirements of Rules 702 and 703 of the Federal Rules of Evidence. Under *Daubert v. Merrell Dow Pharmaceuticals, Inc.*,[1201] the reasoning or methods underlying the testimony must be scientifically valid and relevant to the facts at issue. While questions of the weight and credibility of testimony are for the jury, the court must rule on objections— generally by way of a pretrial motion under Fed. R. Evid. 104(a)—going to the scientific reliability and relevance of proffered evidence.

33.653 Court-Appointed Experts

After consideration of the subject matter of the litigation, the court may con- clude—particularly if the subject matter is complex and the differences between the experts are not attributable to factual disputes that a trial can readily re- solve—that an independent expert should be appointed under Fed. R. Evid. 706. Such an expert may also be helpful if the parties' facilities or processes need to be inspected and they are reluctant to permit access by the opposing experts. A number of issues, including the timing, selection, discovery, and compensation of court-appointed experts, their specific duties, and the handling of communica- tions with them, all require consideration by the court. See *supra* section 21.51.

Consideration may also be given to referring the patent for reexamination by the patent office under 35 U.S.C. § 302, with citations of prior art furnished under 35 U.S.C. § 301. In unusual cases, reference to a special master under Fed. R. Civ. P. 53 (see *supra* section 21.52) may be warranted.

33.66 Trial

To ensure a fair trial, whether it is by the court or a jury, comprehension of the is- sues and the evidence is critical. Comprehension will be enhanced by limiting the length of the trial and the volume of evidence, and by conducting the trial in ways that will further understanding. See generally *supra* section 22.

33.67 Appeals

The Court of Appeals for the Federal Circuit has exclusive jurisdiction of appeals in patent infringement cases from all district courts.[1202] Decisions by this court

---

1201. 113 S. Ct. 2786 (1993). *Daubert* overruled Frye v. United States, 293 F. 1013 (D.C. Cir. 1923), which established the "general acceptance" test for the admissibility of expert opinions. *Daubert* continues to be widely followed by state courts. *See generally* Reference Manual on Scientific Evidence (Federal Judicial Center 1994).

1202. *See* 28 U.S.C. §§ 1292(c)(2), 1295(a)(1), 1338(a). 28 U.S.C. § 1295(a)(1) provides that this jurisdiction is exclusive if the jurisdiction of the district court "was based, in whole or in part, on [28 U.S.C. § 1338(a)]."

are therefore controlling in patent litigation,[1203] and earlier opinions of other courts should be viewed with caution. Interlocutory appeals may be available prior to resolution of all issues under 28 U.S.C. § 1292(c)(1) (interlocutory appeal from orders granting or denying preliminary injunctions), 28 U.S.C. § 1292(c)(2) (judgments in patent infringement cases appealable if "final except for an accounting"), and Fed. R. Civ. P. 54(b). See *supra* section 25.1.

33.7 CERCLA (Superfund)

The Comprehensive Environmental Response, Compensation, and Liability Act (CERCLA, also known as "Superfund"), 42 U.S.C. §§ 9601–9675, was designed to create a comprehensive approach to cleaning up hazardous waste sites, an approach that has in turn led to complex litigation unique in character.[1204] The plaintiff may be the U.S. Environmental Protection Agency (EPA), a private party, or a state or local environmental protection office. A case may involve scores of defendants and third-party defendants, with numerous counterclaims and cross claims seeking indemnification and contribution.[1205] Defendants are frequently corporations, including foreign corporations and defunct corporations, and, in cases involving larger sites, are likely to be geographically dispersed. The act provides for nationwide service of process.[1206] U.S. district courts have exclusive original jurisdiction over all controversies arising under CERCLA.[1207] These cases differ from mass tort claims in that they do not involve personal injuries,[1208] but they may be related to, and require coordination with, mass tort

---

1203. *See, e.g.,* Weinar v. Rollform, Inc., 744 F.2d 797 (Fed. Cir. 1984) (guidelines for instructions and interrogatories).

1204. This chapter addresses CERCLA as it stood as of September 30, 1994. Subsequent legislative changes may affect its provisions in ways that cannot presently be foreseen.

1205. *See, e.g.,* New York v. Exxon Corp., 744 F. Supp. 474, 476, 479 (S.D.N.Y. 1990) (15 primary corporate defendants and approximately 300 third-party defendants); United States v. Kramer, 770 F. Supp. 954, 960 (D.N.J. 1991) (50 primary defendants and approximately 300 third-party defendants); United States v. Stringfellow, 661 F. Supp. 1053, 1055–58 (C.D. Cal. 1987) (more than 100 parties).

1206. 42 U.S.C. § 9613(e). See *infra* note 1234 and accompanying text for discussion of problems relating to the application of nationwide service to pendent (now "supplemental," *see* 28 U.S.C. § 1367) state law claims. Section 9613(e) does not authorize service of process in foreign countries. United States v. Ivey, 747 F. Supp. 1235 (E.D. Mich. 1990). Problems relating to serving foreign defendants are addressed in *supra* § 21.494.

1207. 42 U.S.C. § 9613(b).

1208. See *supra* § 33.2.

claims arising from the same release of hazardous substances into the environment. The number of parties and issues typically calls for treating CERCLA cases as complex litigation.

Many of the general principles applicable to complex litigation apply to CERCLA cases.[1209] This subchapter concentrates on the special features of CERCLA cases. Other federal environmental statutes, such as the National Environmental Policy Act, the Clean Air Act, and the Safe Drinking Water Act, may involve similar management issues. Consequently, the discussion in this section may suggest approaches to analogous problems arising under those statutes, although it does not directly address issues under statutes other than CERCLA.

33.71 Statutory Framework

Pursuant to CERCLA, the EPA develops and promulgates standards and goals for cleaning up hazardous waste sites across the country. The results of EPA's efforts are published as federal regulations, which include the National Contingency Plan (NCP), the Hazardous Ranking System (HRS), and the National Priority Listing (NPL). Using the standards set forth in the NCP and the HRS, the EPA lists "facilities" on the NPL that contain "hazardous substances" and that may represent a danger of "release" of those substances into the environment.[1210] CERCLA imposes joint and several liability, with rights of contribution, on the following types of entities associated with a hazardous disposal facility: current owners or operators of the facility, past owners or operators, those who arranged for disposal of hazardous waste (usually referred to as "generators" of hazardous materials), and transporters of such materials.[1211] Collectively, these groups are referred to as "potentially responsible parties," or PRPs. Federal, state, and local governments have been held includable as defendants under the large CERCLA umbrella.[1212] Liability is strict, with relatively few and narrow statutory defenses (e.g., that a third-party or an act of God was the *sole* cause of the discharge).[1213]

1209. See *supra* § 20 (general principles). For an excellent overview, see Ridgway M. Hall, Jr., et al., *Superfund Response Cost Allocation: The Law, The Science and The Model*, 49 Bus. Law. 1489 (Aug. 1994).

1210. 42 U.S.C. § 9605. The terms in quotes are defined at 42 U.S.C. § 9601.

1211. 42 U.S.C. § 9607(a).

1212. *See generally* Kyle E. McSlarrow et al., *A Decade of Superfund Litigation: CERCLA Caselaw from 1981–1991*, 21 Envtl. L. Rep. 10367, 10368–10370 (July 1991) [hereinafter McSlarrow].

1213. 42 U.S.C § 9607(b). In addition, courts have interpreted the statute to provide a "useful product defense" that applies if a seller sold a substance in the normal course of business, had no control over where the substance went, and did not have a contractual relationship with the facility from which the substance was released. *See generally*, Allan J. Topol & Rebecca Snow, Superfund Law & Procedure § 3.8.E.2 (1992). *But see* United States v. Aceto Agric. Chems. Corp., 872 F.2d 1373, 1381–82 (8th Cir. 1989) (complaint against manufacturers of pesticides for wastes generated by independent contractor in the process of converting technical grade pesticides into commercial

Liability is also retroactive; activities that predate the complaint by decades or more and that may have been legal when undertaken can be the subject of the action.[1214]

The act authorizes the EPA or private parties who have incurred "response costs" in cleaning up a hazardous-waste facility to bring actions to recover such costs.[1215] The EPA also has the power to order responses administratively[1216] and can seek injunctive relief in the district in which a release of a hazardous substance is occurring or threatening to occur.[1217]

The act adopts an expansive view of liability designed to place responsibility for remedying problems arising out of the disposal of hazardous wastes on those who contributed in some way to the harmful conditions. When a major landfill is involved, the wide sweep of coverage tends to draw in a large number of geographically dispersed defendants. The key issue becomes how to allocate the clean-up costs among defendants, any of whom may believe that they are being singled out to pay more than their fair share. The breadth of the statute and its recognition of contribution claims encourages lawyers and their clients to search out all PRPs and thereby reduce a client's portion of the response costs. EPA typically sues a limited number of PRPs, perhaps those it considers to be the major contributors who are able to pay. This approach leaves it to those parties to pursue their own third-party or contribution claims. CERCLA affords the district courts considerable discretion to allocate costs among parties according to equitable principles,[1218] applying broad guidelines found in the legislative history and

grade pesticides for defendants states a claim for relief under CERCLA); Louisiana-Pacific Corp. v. ASARCO, Inc., 6 F.3d 1332, 1340–41 (9th Cir. 1993) (a jury finding that slag, a by-product of copper smelting with a nominal commercial value, was a product under state law did not preclude the court from finding it to be a hazardous waste under CERCLA).

1214. See, e.g., Allied Corp. v. Acme Solvents Reclaiming, Inc., 691 F. Supp. 1100, 1103 (N.D. Ill. 1988) (relevant conduct spans nearly thirty years and operation closed for fifteen years before court's ruling).

1215. 42 U.S.C. § 9607(a). Response costs have to be consistent with the NCP and may include damages resulting from injuries to natural resources as well the costs of health assessments or health effect studies. See, e.g., United States v. Ottati & Goss, 900 F.2d 429 (1st Cir. 1990) (EPA action); Louisiana-Pacific Corp. v. ASARCO, Inc., 6 F.3d 1332, 1336–37 (9th Cir. 1993) (private party action). Attorneys' fees incurred in prosecuting an action against a potentially responsible party and in negotiating a consent decree will generally not be recoverable as necessary response costs. Key Tronic Corp. v. United States, 114 S. Ct. 1960 (1994). Attorneys' fees for services incurred in connection with identifying other PRPs, however, are recoverable because such activity increases the probability that a cleanup will be effective and get paid for. Id.

1216. 42 U.S.C. § 9604.

1217. Id. § 9606(a).

1218. Id. § 9613(f)(1); see generally Rhode Island v. Picillo, 883 F.2d 176 (1st Cir. 1989) (courts have discretion to allocate responsibility according to combination of equitable factors).

known as the "Gore factors."[1219] These factors are not exclusive; they include the volume and toxicity of each party's hazardous waste, the degree of involvement and the degree of care exercised by a party, and the extent to which a party cooperated with public officials to prevent harm to the public. The act offers a party that settles with the United States protection against liability for contribution claims by others that relate to the subject of the settlement.[1220]

33.72 The Three Phases of CERCLA Litigation

CERCLA litigation can be divided into three interrelated phases—liability, determination of remedy and damages, and allocation of response costs—each of which has implications for case management. In practice, issues may cut across these phases. For example, liability and allocation of damages may be determined by the same evidence.

Liability. Liability issues concern (1) whether the defendant is a present or former owner or operator of a facility or generator of hazardous waste, or a contractor or a transporter, (2) who is in some way responsible for the disposal of a hazardous substance at a facility, (3) from which there has been a release or threatened release of the substance into the environment, (4) leading the plaintiff to incur response costs consistent with the National Contingency Plan. Generally, there is little doubt about liability under CERCLA because, as outlined above, statutory defenses are quite narrow and because the act does not set a minimum threshold for liability. Disputes about whether a particular defendant qualifies as an owner, operator, arranger, or hauler may, of course, require factual development.

Determination of remedy and damages. EPA has authority to issue an administrative order requiring parties to clean up the site, or EPA itself may clean up the site. If the site has been partially or fully cleaned up, EPA or a private party who incurred costs in cleaning a site may bring an action to recover those "response costs." EPA administrative action in selecting a remedy is likely to be determinative, but there may be questions about whether costs incurred were necessary and there may be judicial review, based on the record at the agency level, of EPA's choice of a cleanup plan.[1221] Disputes over damages may focus on whether the EPA remedy was necessary, that is, whether the costs of hiring an inspector or monitor to oversee the cleanup are recoverable, whether EPA's over-

---

1219. The "Gore factors" originally appeared in section 3071(a) of H.R. 7020, which was passed by the House in 1980, but not enacted as part of CERCLA. *See* 126 Cong. Rec. 26,779, 26,781 (1980); *see also* Amoco Oil Co. v. Borden, Inc., 889 F.2d 664, 672–73 (5th Cir. 1989); United States v. R.W. Meyer, Inc., 932 F.2d 568, 571 (6th Cir. 1991); Topol & Snow, *supra* note 1213, § 6.4.

1220. 42 U.S.C. § 9613(f)(2).

1221. For an example of a finding that an EPA decision was arbitrary and capricious, see *In re* Bell Petroleum Servs., Inc., 3 F.2d 889, 904–05 (5th Cir. 1993).

head costs can be reduced because EPA was at fault in delaying the litigation,[1222] or whether the response was consistent with the requirements of the NCP.

Allocation of response costs. Because allocation decisions depend on applying a host of factors to a complex factual record involving a large number of parties, such decisions often represent the most challenging aspects of CERCLA cases. Allocation decisions will include addressing all cross claims and contribution claims. The Gore factors, noted above, are generally applied to guide the equitable allocation among the responsible parties.[1223]

33.73 Case Management

Preserving evidence. Because relevant evidence in CERCLA cases may be decades old, occasions may arise for the parties to seek to preserve evidence before filing a complaint. In such cases, it may be appropriate for the court, pursuant to Fed. R. Civ. P. 27, to authorize the taking of prefiling depositions of percipient witnesses (and, when feasible, the production or preservation of documents and other tangible things).[1224] The same considerations may also persuade a court, once an action has been filed, to order the parties to preserve documents, records, and other tangible evidence and to make exceptions to a discovery plan and permit such depositions to be taken out of turn.[1225]

Joining new parties. Incentives for defendants to round up all potentially responsible parties (PRPs) can lead to a continuous parade of new parties. As a result, the court will need to guard against indiscriminate joinder, perhaps by requiring the parties to set forth the factual basis for each joinder motion.

The court may also need to control the timing of joinder. Each new party can be expected to want to catch up with discovery and motion practice, thereby delaying trial. Furthermore, entry of a new party may create a conflict of interest for counsel or grounds for recusal by the judge.[1226] Controlling the entry of new parties will permit the court to control the size and shape of the litigation. Judges have used at least two approaches to address this problem.

The recommended approach is to target the first phase of discovery at identifying all PRPs and developing information about the quantity and quality of waste that each produced during the history of the site. The court should set a

---

1222. *See, e.g.,* United States v. Ottati & Goss, 900 F.2d 429, 443–45 (1st Cir. 1990).

1223. *See, e.g., R.W. Meyer,* 932 F.2d 568.

1224. *See In re* Petition of Delta Quarries & Disposal, Inc., 139 F.R.D. 68 (M.D. Pa. 1991) (granting petition to depose ailing witness alleged to have personal knowledge of identity of companies that disposed hazardous substances at landfill fifteen years earlier).

1225. For an example of such an order, see Sample Order *infra* § 41.53.

1226. *See* United States v. New Castle County, 116 F.R.D. 19, 24 (D. Del. 1987) (denying motion to name and realign various parties; court notes that adding new parties after deadline would likely produce conflicts of interest for current counsel, would interfere with pretrial and trial case-management plans, and would likely disrupt settlement efforts).

reasonable but firm deadline, which could be as long as a year, for adding parties or cross claims or counterclaims. Once the deadline is reached, the parties and the court will have an overview of the size and scope of the litigation. Creating a central document depository or a computerized document storage system can help ensure that the newly joined parties have access to the product of prior discovery and can hold demands for additional discovery to a minimum. Once a court-imposed deadline for joining new parties has passed, pretrial, settlement, and trial plans can proceed, addressing issues relating to all the parties, while consideration of late presented claims is deferred.[1227] This approach may be conducive to reaching a global disposition of the entire litigation.

Another approach is to postpone joinder issues, contribution claims, and other cross claims until after the litigation against the initial defendants has been resolved. In cases involving large numbers of PRPs, this approach may have the advantage of keeping the organization relatively simple while devising a plan to remedy the site or determine the costs of the remedy. The disadvantage, however, is that parties joined later may wish to relitigate those issues or reopen discovery. On the other hand, once the cases have been resolved as to the initial defendants, those defendants may be able to reach out-of-court settlements with third parties without the expense of litigation.

CERCLA encourages the expedited settlement of disputes with parties whose contributions to the site have been minimal in terms of volume and toxicity or who are innocent purchasers that did not contribute to the problem ("*de minimis*" parties).[1228] Pressing the EPA to define *de minimis* levels early may help control the size of the litigation and serve the congressional purpose of limiting transaction costs for such parties.

Gathering related cases. The court and parties may need to make special efforts to identify cases and claims that are related to the CERCLA case. The initial pretrial order should call for the parties to identify and report any proceeding arguably related to the CERCLA case. Such proceedings may include state judicial or administrative proceedings to enforce CERCLA-type state laws,[1229] private claims for personal injury, property damage, nuisance, and the like, insurance coverage disputes in federal or state court, and bankruptcy proceedings.[1230] While

---

1227. *Id.*

1228. 42 U.S.C. § 9622(g). For examples of *de minimis* settlements, see United States v. Cannons Eng'g Corp., 720 F. Supp. 1027 (D. Mass. 1989), *aff'd*, 899 F.2d 79 (1st Cir. 1990); United States v. Rohm & Haas Co., 721 F. Supp. 666 (D.N.J. 1989).

1229. For a discussion of preemption issues, see McSlarrow, *supra* note 1212, at 10373–74; Topol & Snow, *supra* note 1213, § 2.2.

1230. Generally, governmental regulatory actions, such as EPA actions under CERCLA, are exempt from the automatic stay provisions of the Bankruptcy Act, 11 U.S.C. § 362(b)(4), but a money judgment obtained in a CERCLA proceeding cannot be executed without approval from the

some related cases may be in state courts, coordinated proceedings, including trials and settlement conferences, may be possible.[1231] Some courts have exercised supplemental (formerly called "pendent") subject-matter jurisdiction over state law claims,[1232] perhaps in an effort to bring together all parties who might contribute to cleaning up the site. Other courts have rejected supplemental jurisdiction for state law claims to avoid unduly complicating the litigation.[1233] In considering whether to exercise supplemental jurisdiction in a case involving out-of-state defendants, the court should be aware of the constitutional, statutory, and fairness issues that arise when nationwide service of process is used to obtain personal jurisdiction over parties to supplemental state law claims lacking an independent basis for federal jurisdiction.[1234] The court should also consider the problems resulting from trying state and CERCLA claims together; a right to a jury trial may attach to state law claims, and the jury's findings of fact may affect the outcome of what would otherwise be nonjury issues.[1235] In addition, the elements of state and CERCLA claims, while related, may be quite different.

Courts differ in their approaches to linking insurance coverage litigation involving some parties to a CERCLA case. While some might seek to join the insurance litigation to a CERCLA case, others avoid any formal linkage because the principal issues in these two types of complex actions are distinct. Insurance litigation turns on contractual arrangements and is often fact intensive and hotly contested, involving numerous carriers, parties, and waste sites. Bringing insurers into settlement discussions of a CERCLA case, however, may enhance the prospects of settlement of both groups of cases while avoiding an unwieldy consolidated trial.

---

bankruptcy court. *See, e.g.,* United States v. Nicolet, Inc., 857 F.2d 202, 209–10 (3d Cir 1988); *see also* Topol & Snow, *supra* note 1213, § 7.7.7.

1231. See *supra* § 31.3 (state–federal coordination).

1232. *See, e.g.,* New York v. Shore Realty Corp., 759 F.2d 1032, 1050 (2d Cir. 1985) (nuisance claim); *see also* New Jersey Dept. of Envtl. Protection v. Gloucester Envtl. Man. Servs., Inc., 719 F. Supp. 325 (D.N.J. 1989) (court exercised jurisdiction over state claims even after EPA, which had removed case from state court, was dismissed from the litigation). *See* 28 U.S.C. § 1367 (creating supplemental jurisdiction for claims related to federal question actions).

1233. *See, e.g.,* Commerce Holding Co. v. Buckstone, 749 F. Supp. 441, 446–47 (E.D.N.Y. 1990) (differences in legal issues, standards of proof, right to jury trial, and remedies warrant exercise of discretion to dismiss pendent state claims without prejudice); *see generally,* Topol & Snow, *supra* note 1213, § 7.3, n.29 and cases cited therein.

1234. *See* Jon Heller, *Pendent Personal Jurisdiction and Nationwide Service of Process,* 64 N.Y.U. L. Rev. 113 (1989); James J. Connors, *Nationwide Service of Process Under the Comprehensive Environmental Response, Compensation, and Liability Act: The Need for Effective Fairness Constraints,* 73 Va. L. Rev. 631 (1987).

1235. Lytle v. Household Mfg., 494 U.S. 545 (1990); Dollar Sys. v. AVCAR Leasing Sys., 890 F.2d 165 (9th Cir. 1989).

Manual for Complex Litigation, Third

Using special masters and magistrate judges.[1236] Special masters and magistrate judges may be needed to cope with the extraordinary pretrial demands of CERCLA litigation. Courts have approved their use for limited pretrial purposes.[1237] Use of special masters to preside at trial may be disapproved unless the parties consent.[1238] As discussed below in connection with settlement, the use of a magistrate judge, special master, or settlement judge may serve to insulate the judge from settlement negotiations in nonjury CERCLA cases.

Organizing counsel.[1239] At the outset, the court will want to familiarize itself with the parties' own efforts to organize themselves in response to EPA's prelitigation investigation of the site. EPA sometimes encourages defendants to organize by refusing to entertain settlement discussions with individual PRPs.[1240] Such efforts may lead to a site study and settlement discussions with EPA.

Faced with hundreds of parties in some CERCLA cases, organization of counsel is essential in order for the court to be able to communicate effectively with all parties. Because the ultimate issue turns on allocation of responsibility for response costs, and cross claims are the norm, conflicting interests are common and the court and the parties will need to be sensitive to the problems arising when parties with adverse claims (e.g., a third-party plaintiff and the third-party defendant it brought into the litigation) are included within the same group of parties.

The type of organization may vary with its purpose and the issues in dispute. If the purpose is to organize parties with similar interests with respect to the legal issues, the court may want to use the groups identified in the statute: owners, operators, generators, contractors, and transporters, and, perhaps, subgroups based on the nature of the site, the time of use, the hazardous substances, or some other feature.[1241] Subject-matter subcommittees can be created to work on issues such

---

1236. See generally *supra* §§ 21.52 and 21.53.

1237. *In re* Armco, Inc., 770 F.2d 103, 105 (8th Cir. 1985) (mandamus issued to revoke authority of special master to preside at trial and mandamus rejected in relation to reference of pretrial activity to master, including making recommendations on dispositive motions); *see also* New Jersey Dept. of Envtl. Protection v. Gloucester Envtl. Man. Servs., Inc., 719 F. Supp. 319, 330–31 (D.N.J. 1989) (appointment of a magistrate judge for pretrial management and settlement negotiations); *cf. In re* United States, 816 F.2d 1083 (6th Cir. 1987) (mandamus issued to vacate portion of order of reference authorizing special master to make recommendations on dispositive motions, but approving reference for other pretrial matters, including discovery).

1238. *In re* Armco, Inc., 770 F.2d 103, 105 (8th Cir. 1985); United States v. Stringfellow, 1990 U.S. Dist. LEXIS 19001 (C.D. Cal.) (consent).

1239. See generally *supra* § 20.22.

1240. Section of Litigation, American Bar Association, Environmental Litigation 2–4 (1991).

1241. *See, e.g.,* New Jersey Dept. of Envtl. Man. Servs., Inc., No. 84-0152 (D.N.J. April 3, 1987) (case-management order appointing five liaison counsel for the plaintiff, the owner, the alleged operators, the alleged generators, and the alleged transporters).

as joinder of parties, jurisdiction, discovery, liability, *de minimis* status, remediation, and contribution.

If the purpose is to create groups to facilitate settlement, relevant communities of interests may be defined by the type of substance a group of parties sent to a site, the amount of hazardous wastes associated with the parties, the time periods a group of parties used a site, or other common factors relating to geography, expert witnesses, records, or the like. For example, the court may want to consider combining all the major contributors in one tier, followed by a mid-level tier, and a *de minimis* tier.[1242]

Organizing counsel and parties will avoid duplicate discovery and motion practice and give the court an individual liaison, or, at most, one for each group, to contact about scheduling and other nonsubstantive matters. One approach is to allow the parties to organize themselves, nominate lead and liaison counsel, propose a mode of payment, and tentatively define the authority of lead and liaison counsel and a committee structure. It may be sufficient for the court to suggest these topics as an agenda for a meeting of counsel, review the results of the meeting, and issue an appropriate order implementing the results or modifying them as necessary. The court may also advise counsel of its guidelines, such as the avoidance of duplicative efforts (e.g., providing in a case-management order that a party waives its right to raise an issue unless it is first presented to a committee of counsel). This approach may be particularly suitable where the parties have organized themselves to deal with the EPA before the litigation. The court should, however, independently review and evaluate any organizational arrangement among counsel to ensure that it meets the needs of the court for managing the litigation. For example, the judge may want to be sure that lead counsel for a group in fact represents one of the primary PRPs in that class. The judge, of course, retains the final authority whether to enter an order adopting the parties' recommendations.

Narrowing the issues.[1243] Case law allows courts to dispose summarily of many legal issues arising in CERCLA litigation,[1244] possibly including constitutional claims.[1245] Judicial decisions have given meaning to arcane terminology in the statute. Many, perhaps most, of the initial ambiguities about the wide scope

---

1242. *See, e.g.,* Denver v. Adolph Coors Co., 829 F. Supp. 340 (D. Colo. 1993) (order regarding approval of *de minimis* and mid-tier settlements).

1243. See also *supra* § 21.33.

1244. One commentator summarizes that federal courts "are shaping CERCLA by judicial interpretation to a degree rarely if ever seen for any other statute." In the first ten years after the enactment of the Superfund, more than 1,000 reported decisions were handed down that bear on Superfund issues. Topol & Snow, *supra* note 1213, at vi.

1245. *Id.* at 21 (referring to retroactive liability claims).

of liability and the narrow range of defenses have been resolved.[1246] Form complaints and answers, however, may not have caught up with the case law and parties may routinely plead defenses that they do not intend to pursue seriously. The initial conference generally should prune such dead wood. Standard rulings on identical issues raised by different parties may reduce duplication of effort.

Requiring each side or group to meet and develop an agreed-on statement of the factual and legal issues in dispute and using the Rule 16 conference to clarify the factual and legal bases for the disputes should assist in identification of the genuinely controverted issues and the abandonment of marginal issues. Pressing the lawyers to identify facts supporting each element of each claim or defense and to tie the claim or defense to the legal framework of CERCLA may also help to reveal the strengths and weaknesses of parties' positions. Issues can then be outlined in a statement, rostered for the litigation in a logical and practical sequence, such as addressing first issues that might dispose of all or part of the litigation (e.g., whether the substances found at the site are hazardous, whether the government's proposed remedy is reasonable and based on the record of decision, whether there is a nexus between actions of alleged generators of hazardous waste and the disposal of hazardous wastes at the specific site in question). Second- and third-tier issues can then be identified and incorporated into the case-management plan, which may also include a proposed structure for settlement discussions and for trial. Issues may be organized to conform to the liability, remediation, and allocation phases of CERCLA litigation described above.

Managing motion practice. Building on the statement defining the issues, judges may group types of motions and call for filing of consolidated motions on similar issues according to a time schedule that will avoid duplicative and piecemeal motions. For example, the court may establish a brief window within which particular types of motions may be filed.[1247] The court may also want to direct that certain motions and third-party complaints be "deemed" to include all defendants (as it may want to direct that answers to third-party complaints be "deemed" to include cross claims and counterclaims against those defendants by third-party plaintiffs).[1248]

1246. Some useful resources in finding the law relating to CERCLA include a three-volume loose-leaf set, Environmental Law Institute, Law of Environmental Protection (1993), and a two-volume set edited by private attorneys, Topol and Snow, *supra* note 1213. For brief summaries of the field, see Andrew H. Perellis & Mary E. Doohan, *Superfund Litigation: The Elements and Scope of Liability, in* Section of Litigation, American Bar Association, Environmental Litigation 1–21 (1991), and McSlarrow, *supra* note 1212.

1247. For an example of such a window of time for filing motions to join additional parties, see Sample Order *infra* § 41.53, ¶¶ 3, 4.

1248. See also *supra* §§ 21.32, 33.252, and sample Mass Tort Case-Management Order *infra* § 41.52, ¶¶ 5, 6. The court should, however, consider the impact of "deeming" cross claims and

The organization of counsel can be used to filter all claims relating to a particular issue, with assigned counsel being responsible for including in briefs and arguments the claims of individual defendants that call for an individual analysis or for separate application of a general rule to a peculiar fact pattern. At the liability phase of the litigation, motions for partial summary judgment may be a way to weed out unmeritorious claims or defenses[1249] or, in a rare case, even to allocate responsibility for paying the response costs.[1250] Evidentiary hearings under Rule 43(e) may be used to determine if there is a genuine issue of material fact.

Prompt rulings on motions are particularly important in CERCLA litigation because they can clarify liability and clear the path for the parties to allocate damages among themselves. Where a primary party's liability turns on a legal issue of first impression, the district court should consider the advantages of certifying its order on liability for interlocutory appeal before allocating damages against the disadvantages of delaying the progress of the case.[1251] When the subject of the interlocutory appeal is not central to the entire case, the court may decide to continue with other aspects of the litigation while the appeal is pending.[1252]

Informal exchanges. The EPA will often generate useful information before filing suit. This may take the form of the parties' responses to requests for information under section 104(e) of CERCLA or even the official record of decision (ROD) created to determine the appropriate response under section 113(k). Ordering the EPA to produce this data will contribute to developing a database.

CERCLA cases also present opportunities for courts to encourage or direct the parties to share information. For example, information relevant to the site provided to the EPA or another government agency will generally be available for immediate exchange. In cases with complex technical issues, it may be particu-

---

counterclaims on parties whose liability is determined to be *de minimis*. To avoid imposing disproportionate risks of extensive liability on *de minimis* defendants, the court might consider exempting such parties from a "deeming" order. Another option would be to defer the time for filing cross claims until after *de minimis* parties have settled the claims against them and generally obtained the benefit of a bar against contribution claims as permitted under 42 U.S.C. § 9622(g)(2), (5).

1249. For example, the question of whether or not a harm is capable of apportionment among multiple defendants is a question of law. *In re* Bell Petroleum Servs., Inc., 3 F.3d 889, 896 (5th Cir. 1993). *See also* United States v. Wade, 577 F. Supp. 1326 (E.D. Pa. 1983) (granting summary adjudication that certain defendants are liable under CERCLA, but requiring a trial to determine whether to impose joint and several liability and to allocate liability).

1250. *See* United States v. R.W. Meyer, Inc., 932 F.2d 568 (6th Cir. 1991) (affirming summary judgment allocating response costs among three entities).

1251. *See* United States v. Fleet Factors Corp., 901 F.2d 1550 (11th Cir. 1990) (interlocutory appeal taken to obtain ruling on whether district court correctly interpreted and applied CERCLA provision in denying motion for summary judgment by a holder of a security interest in contaminated real property).

1252. See *supra* § 25.1.

larly useful for the technical experts on remediation to give informal presentations of data and proposed plans to the other experts. To promote candid discussion, a case-management order can provide that discussions among groups of litigants will not constitute evidence of a conspiracy and that an expert's inadvertent disclosure of confidential information during such discussion will not waive trade-secret or attorney work-product protections.[1253]

Managing discovery. CERCLA cases generally require structured discovery. Discovery should be planned to produce data that can be used for both settlement and trial. Creating a credible and accurate database with clear documentation of the problems at a site is a critical element of managing Superfund litigation. Such a database can be expected to provide a means of persuading parties to assume responsibility for their documented contribution to the problem. Without a credible database, the parties and the court cannot determine whether the proposed remedy is based on faulty assumptions about the nature of the problems, and the parties are not likely to accept proposed settlement allocations.[1254] The court may want to consider whether the complexity and demands of the case justify the appointment of a magistrate judge or special master to oversee discovery, applying the criteria discussed in *supra* sections 20.14 and 21.5.

The need for data about who contributed what to the problems at the facility coincides with the need to identify PRPs promptly. At an early stage, the court probably should focus the parties' attention on identifying all PRPs and the bases of their liability. Later stages can concentrate on damages, methods of remediation, and cleanup costs. All stages of discovery should be coordinated with plans for resolving motions and for structuring the trial (e.g., on a bifurcated or trifurcated basis). Stages should not be so rigid as to require multiple depositions of the same parties or multiple searches for similar records.

Centralized discovery management. The number of defendants in a typical case requires measures to avoid duplicative discovery, such as use of a master set of interrogatories for plaintiffs and defendants and prohibiting duplicative depositions.[1255] Centralized document management, in the form of document depositories or computerized data storage and retrieval, will generally be necessary in CERCLA litigation because of the need to make past discovery easily accessible to new parties. Electronic technology now provides the capacity for large

---

1253. For an example of such an order, see Sample Order *infra* § 41.53, ¶¶ 18–19. See also ¶ 17 for language protecting defendants against claims of conspiracy for cooperating in the litigation.

1254. For a judge's perspective on the elements of a database that focuses on settlement (but could apply in large part to preparation for trial), see Jerome B. Simandle, *Resolving Multi-Party Hazardous Waste Litigation*, II Vill. Envtl. L. J. 111, 127–32 (1991).

1255. For an example of an order directing the EPA to produce its administrative record and ordering the parties to use master interrogatories and to coordinate depositions, see Sample Order *infra* § 41.53, ¶¶ 2, 10, and 12–13. See also *supra* §§ 21.45 and 21.46.

volumes of documents to be imaged optically and distributed economically to the parties.[1256] Central document management may also provide a mechanism for allocating the cost of discovery fairly among its users.

Managing expert testimony. CERCLA cases are prone to lead to battles of experts in highly technical areas, such as chemistry, hydrology, and geology. Continuous testing and sampling the soil and wastes at a given site may be necessary. At a minimum, courts should consider adopting procedures that will produce a common database for the experts to analyze. For example, appointing an experts' committee with responsibility for jointly defining issues, testing soil and allegedly hazardous materials, creating joint databases, developing proposed factual stipulations, and splitting samples among the experts will help reduce unproductive adversariness and keep the focus on genuine issues.[1257] Some judges have directed the parties to have their experts meet without counsel to identify and consider the technical issues relating to the proposed remedial design.[1258] Such a meeting can uncover erroneous assumptions and avoid wasting resources on a remedy that might be technically flawed.

Structuring the trial. CERCLA cases rarely go to trial, but when they do, the trial is likely to be complicated.[1259] Bifurcation or trifurcation into two or three phases—liability (if necessary), damages (remediation plans), and allocation of damages—should be considered.[1260] The order of trial (and of the corresponding settlement discussions) can be varied to address dispositive issues first. Addressing challenges to the proposed remedy may crystallize issues relating to response costs and how they should be allocated. The EPA ordinarily has to determine the scope of proposed cleanup efforts before the court can allocate responsibility for remediation.

Except for natural resource damage claims, courts have held that parties are not entitled to a jury trial in CERCLA cases.[1261] One approach used in a case involving damages to natural resources, was to focus case management on

---

1256. See *infra* § 34 (courtroom technology) and *supra* § 21.44 (documents).

1257. *See* United States v. Price, 20 E.R.C. 2229 (D.N.J. 1984). See also *supra* § 21.48.

1258. Simandle, *supra* note 1254, at 132 (1991).

1259. See, *e.g.*, United States v. Ottati & Goss, Inc., 630 F. Supp 1361 (D.N.H. 1985) (liability); 694 F. Supp. 977 (D.N.H. 1988) (remedy and allocation of damages), *aff'd in part & vacated in part*, 900 F.2d 429 (1st Cir. 1990).

1260. In United States v. Hardage, 750 F. Supp. 1460, 1463 (W.D. Okla. 1990), the court divided the trial into four phases, starting with the remedy, then liability, and splitting the allocation phase into a third-party claims phase and a cost-allocation phase.

1261. *See* United States v. NEPACCO, 810 F.2d 726, 749 (8th Cir. 1986); United States v. Northernaire Plating Co., 685 F.2d 1410, 1413 (W.D. Mich. 1988) (citing cases).

preparing a single case involving a primary defendant for a jury trial.[1262] To ascertain the universe of facts at issue, the litigants were ordered to make requests for admission of any fact on which they intended to offer evidence and were precluded from offering any evidence that was not subject of such a request. Each request had to be detailed "to the level of specificity of a patent claim."[1263]

Special verdict forms (see *supra* section 22.451), jury notebooks (see *supra* section 22.42), time limits for each side (see *supra* section 22.35), interim instructions (see *supra* section 22.433), and other jury aids may also be necessary. Setting firm trial dates and using other trial management procedures is presumed.[1264] See generally *supra* section 22.

Facilitating settlements.[1265] CERCLA expressly encourages settlement, and the EPA has generally sought consent decrees to conclude CERCLA litigation. Judicial involvement may be needed to structure cases for settlement; organizing counsel as described above, for example, can be essential for creating a framework for bringing representatives of various interest groups together. Discovery should be designed to give the groups the information necessary to assess their liability, for example, to determine the volume and toxicity of substances sent to the site or to identify the costs and contributions of various parties to remedies.

CERCLA cases present unique settlement challenges. A case does not end when the court determines or the parties agree as to the amount of damages or response costs. The court or the parties must allocate the total damages among a host of parties with different levels of responsibility. Allocations may have to account for the reasonable cost of actions taken by some defendants to clean up the facility. To complicate matters further, the assessment and allocation of damages may not be final. The act limits the ability of the government to settle claims relating to future liability that might result from an unforeseen release of hazardous substance at the facility, for example, during the cleanup process.[1266] Thus, a settlement can generally be expected to include "reopeners."

A global settlement of a CERCLA claim resolves not only the parties' monetary liability to each other but also their obligations to undertake remedial activities at the site. In cases involving complex remediation plans, it may be useful for

---

1262. The district court in *In re* Acushnet River & New Bedford Harbor: Proceedings Re Alleged PCB Pollution, 712 F. Supp. 994 (D. Mass. 1989), held that there is a right to trial by jury in cases involving recovery of damages to natural resources because such cases are a form of statutory tort.

1263. *In re* Acushnet River & New Bedford Harbor: Proceedings Re Alleged PCB Pollution, 712 F. Supp. 1019, 1030–31 (D. Mass. 1989).

1264. See generally *supra* § 21.212

1265. See generally *supra* § 23.

1266. 42 U.S.C. § 9622(f).

a portion of the negotiations about cleanup options to be conducted by the parties' experts and technical representatives without participation by counsel.[1267]

As noted above, CERCLA singles out *de minimis* parties for expedited settlements.[1268] Frequently the EPA makes an effort to settle with such parties in a fixed amount at an early stage. The Act permits the EPA to offer a covenant not to sue as well as a statutory bar against liability for contribution claims.[1269] If the EPA has not identified *de minimis* parties, the court may want to encourage the agency or the parties to do so and to define a *de minimis* volume of disposal. The statutory goal is to release such parties before transaction costs accumulate.

As with most complex litigation, judicial approaches to use of settlement techniques or ADR differ widely.[1270] The magnitude of these cases and the possibility that recusal would impose a serious hardship on the entire court suggest that the trial judge should not be directly involved in settlement negotiations.[1271] Referral of settlement and pretrial management to a magistrate judge or a special master should be considered. Ruling on motions and facilitating discovery on central issues of liability and damages may promote settlement by giving parties the information needed to evaluate cases.

A settlement approach developed by one judge includes four major elements:[1272]

1. **Setting the stage.** The initial question is whether the parties have sufficient interest in pursuing settlement. If this process of "agreeing to seek to agree" succeeds, it will produce a written good faith agreement of most parties to pursue settlement of specified issues.

2. **Organizing counsel and defining a timetable.** Groups would be created along the lines discussed under "Organizing counsel" above (i.e., by selecting settlement liaison for each group of defendants and defining the authority of the liaisons). The initial task of the liaison and the groups is to define a timetable for the process. The timetable should be coordinated with the pretrial process and should adapt the discovery program to settlement needs. Whether to participate in the EPA's formulation of the remedial design or to devise an alternative design is a threshold issue for consideration by the group.

1267. Simandle, *supra* note 1254, at 132 ("topics of such dialogue can involve the proposed remedial design, the on-site and off-site degradation, ground water monitoring and modeling, projected remedial costs, and projected operations and maintenance costs for the remedial action").

1268. 42 U.S.C. § 9622(g).

1269. 42 U.S.C. § 9622(g)(2), (5).

1270. See also *supra* § 23.15 (discussing some ADR techniques).

1271. See *supra* § 23.11.

1272. For a discussion of the settlement model, see Simandle, *supra* note 1254.

3. **Joining additional parties and creating a database.** The database would consist primarily of data about the contributions of each party to the landfill along the lines discussed under "Managing discovery," above. Here, the emphasis is on identifying parties who contributed substantially to the problems and can be expected to contribute substantially to a financial settlement. The parties would then identify the information needed and develop the structure of a database, perhaps with the help of consultants hired jointly by the parties. Generally, information about insurance would also be collected.

4. **Allocating responsibility.** This stage involves the hard negotiations. Using outside assistance—a special master, court-appointed mediator, or a consultant hired by the parties—in analyzing the data and recommending allocations may lend objectivity to the process.

This process appears to have proved successful in major Superfund litigation. The role of the district court in the process is to rule promptly on those motions that define the liability of the parties and the contours of the issues. The district judge remains insulated from settlement discussions and is able to preside at a bench trial, if necessary.

33.8 Civil RICO[1273]

33.81 Pleadings

The pleadings play an especially important role in civil RICO[1274] cases. Because RICO applies to a broad range of conduct, often occurring over an extended period of time and involving a large number of people or entities, the complaint will often assert numerous claims against numerous parties. Since most RICO complaints allege underlying acts of mail, wire, or securities fraud, which must be pleaded with particularity under Fed. R. Civ. P. 9(b), the complaint may be lengthy and complex. The strict pleading requirements peculiar to RICO (discussed further below) may result in extensive motion practice directed at dismissing all or parts of the complaint. Decision of these motions can

---

1273. With acknowledgment to Edward F. Mannino, Esq.
1274. Racketeer Influenced and Corrupt Organizations Act, 18 U.S.C. §§ 1961–1968.

significantly affect the scope of the litigation; eliminating claims will not only obviate discovery and other proceedings related to the claims themselves, but may remove the jurisdictional predicate for supplemental state law claims,[1275] allowing them to be dismissed as well (usually without prejudice).[1276] The court should therefore adopt procedures for RICO cases designed to test the sufficiency of the pleadings early on, before other significant litigation activity commences. Some courts have standing orders requiring parties alleging RICO claims to file RICO case statements, amplifying and clarifying the allegations in the pleading. In courts that do not, the court may adopt a case order requiring submission of such statements before responsive motions or pleadings are due.[1277] These statements, together with a careful reading of the complaint, will help narrow the issues and allow early identification of claims insufficient on their face, which may be dismissed (with or without prejudice) before significant time and effort is spent on them.

The length and complexity of RICO complaints may justify granting defendants additional time to respond. The court should consider entering an order immediately following assignment of the litigation suspending the time for defendants to respond until after the initial conference. At the conference, counsel and the court may be able to narrow the issues, avoiding unnecessary motion practice. At the conclusion of the conference or shortly thereafter, the court should set a schedule for filing motions and opposing and reply briefs, as well as responsive pleadings.

33.82 Defining and Managing the Issues

Efficient management of RICO litigation requires that the disputed legal and factual issues and the precise statutory violations alleged be identified and, where possible, narrowed, as early as possible. This is made difficult by the complexity of the RICO statute and the fact that the terms it employs, such as "person," "enterprise," "conduct," and "pattern," have been given varying and sometimes confusing interpretations. Reference to the four categories of unlawful conduct specified in 18 U.S.C. § 1962 will assist the process:

1. **Section 1962(a): Investment of income.** This subsection makes it unlawful for "any person who has received any income derived . . . from a pattern of racketeering activity . . . to invest . . . any part of such income . . . in acquisition of an interest in, or the establishment or operation of, any enterprise . . . ." Most courts have ruled that the only injury compensable under § 1962(a) is that resulting from a defendant's *investment* of racke-

---

1275. *See* 28 U.S.C. § 1367 (supplemental jurisdiction).

1276. *See, e.g.,* Parker & Parsley Petroleum Co. v. Dresser Indus., 972 F.2d 580, 584–90 (5th Cir. 1992); Spiegel v. Continental Ill. Nat. Bank, 790 F.2d 638, 649–50 (7th Cir. 1986).

1277. See Sample Form *infra* § 41.54.

teering income.[1278] Therefore, claims under § 1962(a) alleging injury resulting from racketeering activity alone, rather than from the investment of income so derived, may be subject to early dismissal.

2. **Section 1962(b): Interest/control.** This subsection makes it unlawful for a person "to acquire or maintain . . . any interest in or control of any enterprise" through a pattern of racketeering activity. Most courts have required that the alleged injury to the plaintiff proximately result from the defendant's acquisition of an interest in, or control over, an enterprise.[1279] If the complaint does not allege injury arising specifically from such an acquisition, § 1962(b) claims may be subject to dismissal.

3. **Section 1962(c): Conduct of an enterprise.** Most civil RICO claims are filed under § 1962(c), which makes it unlawful to "conduct or participate, directly or indirectly, in the conduct" of an enterprise through a pattern of racketeering activity. The four primary elements of this subsection, as set out by the Supreme Court, are "(1) conduct (2) of an enterprise (3) through a pattern (4) of racketeering activity."[1280] The interpretation of the first three of these requirements (the fourth is relatively uncontroversial) is shrouded in considerable uncertainty, only some of which has been resolved by the Court. The judge should therefore give early attention to determining the definitions applied in the circuit.

• **"Conduct."** The Supreme Court has ruled that liability for "participat[ing]" in the "conduct" of the enterprise extends only to those who "have some part in directing [the enterprise's] affairs," adopting the "operation or management" test articulated by the Eighth Circuit.[1281] The defendant need not be in upper management; liability may extend to lower-level employees under the direction of upper management, persons associated with the enterprise who exert control over it (for example, by bribery), and outsiders who participate in the operation or management of the enterprise.[1282] Nevertheless, the al-

---

1278. *See, e.g., Parker & Parsley*, 972 F.2d at 584; Danielsen v. Burnside-Ott Aviation Training Ctr., Inc., 941 F.2d 1220, 1229–30 (D.C. Cir. 1991); Craighead v. E. F. Hutton & Co., 899 F.2d 485, 494 (6th Cir. 1990); Ouaknine v. MacFarlane, 897 F.2d 75, 82–83 (2d Cir. 1990); Rose v. Bartle, 871 F.2d 331, 356–58 (3d Cir. 1989); Grider v. Texas Oil & Gas Corp., 868 F.2d 1147, 1149–51 (10th Cir. 1989). *Contra* Busby v. Crown Supply, Inc., 896 F.2d 833, 837 (4th Cir. 1990) (en banc).

1279. *See, e.g.,* Danielsen v. Burnside-Ott Aviation Training Center, Inc., 941 F.2d 1220 (D.C. Cir. 1991); Kehr Packages, Inc. v. Fidelcor, Inc., 926 F.2d 1406 (3d Cir.), *cert. denied*, 111 S. Ct. 2839 (1991); Airlines Reporting Corp. v. Barry, 666 F. Supp. 1311, 1315 (D. Minn. 1987).

1280. Sedima, S.P.R.L. v. Imrex Co., 473 U.S. 479, 496 (1985).

1281. Reves v. Ernst & Young, 113 S. Ct. 1163, 1168–70 (1993), referring to Bennett v. Berg, 710 F.2d 1361, 1364 (8th Cir. 1983) (en banc).

1282. *Reves*, 113 S. Ct. at 1173.

---

legations against at least some defendants, particularly outsiders (such as accountants, attorneys, or lenders), may fail to satisfy the conduct requirement. In some cases, a Rule 12 motion or a motion for summary judgment may be an appropriate vehicle to resolve this issue.[1283]

• **"Enterprise" and "Person."** Most courts have ruled that § 1962(c) was designed to punish only the persons who run an enterprise illegally and not the enterprise itself, which often will be an innocent victim of the racketeering activity.[1284] Therefore, § 1962(c) requires pleading and proof of two separate entities—a "person" and an "enterprise"—with only the "person" being liable for damages.[1285] Three different theories have been used to attempt to reach the assets of a corporate enterprise despite this requirement: (1) affiliated corporations; (2) vicarious liability; and (3) association-in-fact enterprises. Circuit law has been divided on these issues. Some courts have ruled that a subsidiary is an "affiliated corporation," which conducts the affairs of its separate parent corporation, and thus can be held liable for damages under § 1962(c).[1286] By contrast, all of the federal appeals courts that have considered the issue have held that an employer alleged to be the RICO "enterprise" cannot be held vicariously liable under § 1962(c) for the acts of its employees.[1287] Claims alleging the existence of "association-

1283. Outsiders may still be liable as conspirators (under § 1962(d)) or under an "aiding and abetting" theory, which has been recognized by two federal appeals courts. *See* Petro-Tech, Inc. v. Western Co., 824 F.2d 1349, 1356, 1359–60 (3d Cir. 1987); Armco Indus. Credit Corp. v. SLT Warehouse Co., 782 F.2d 475, 485–86 (5th Cir. 1986).

1284. *See, e.g.,* Board of County Comm'rs v. Liberty Group, 965 F.2d 879, 885 (10th Cir.), *cert. denied,* 113 S. Ct. 329 (1992); Yellow Bus Lines, Inc. v. Local Union 639, 883 F.2d 132, 139–40 (D.C. Cir. 1989); Schofield v. First Commodity Corp., 793 F.2d 28, 29–30 (1st Cir. 1986); Bennett v. United States Trust Co., 770 F.2d 308, 315 (2d Cir. 1985); B.F. Hirsch v. Enright Refining Co., 751 F.2d 628, 634 (3d Cir. 1984); Rae v. Union Bank, 725 F.2d 478, 481 (9th Cir. 1984).

1285. *See, e.g.,* Bennett v. Berg, 685 F.2d 1053, 1061–62 (8th Cir. 1982).

1286. *See, e.g.,* Haroco, Inc. v. American Nat. Bank & Trust Co., 747 F.2d 384, 402–03 (7th Cir. 1984), *aff'd on other grounds,* 473 U.S. 606 (1985); Center Cadillac, Inc. v. Bank Leumi Trust Co., 808 F. Supp. 213, 236–37 (S.D.N.Y. 1992). *Contra* NCNB Nat'l Bank v. Tiller, 814 F.2d 931, 936–37 (4th Cir. 1987), *overruled on other grounds,* Busby v. Crown Supply, Inc., 896 F.2d 833, 840–41 & n.8 (4th Cir. 1990) (en banc); *In re* Tucker Freight Lines, Inc., 789 F. Supp. 884, 893 (W.D. Mich. 1991).

1287. *See* Parker & Parsley Petroleum Co. v. Dresser Indus., 972 F.2d 580, 584 (5th Cir. 1992); Board of County Comm'rs v. Liberty Group, 965 F.2d 879, 885, 886 (10th Cir.), *cert. denied,* 113 S. Ct. 329 (1992); Miranda v. Ponce Fed. Bank, 948 F.2d 41, 45 (1st Cir. 1991); Brittingham v. Mobil Corp., 943 F.2d 297, 300–03 (3d Cir. 1991); Landry v. Air Line Pilots Ass'n Int'l, 901 F.2d 404, 425 (5th Cir. 1990); Yellow Bus Lines, Inc. v. Local Union 639, 883 F.2d 132, 140 (D.C. Cir. 1989); D & S Auto Parts, Inc. v. Schwartz, 838 F.2d 964, 967–68 (7th Cir. 1988); Petro-Tech, Inc. v. Western Co., 824 F.2d 1349, 1359–60 (3d Cir. 1987); Luthi v. Tonka Corp., 815 F.2d 1229, 1230 (8th Cir. 1987); Schofield v. First Commodity Corp., 793 F.2d 28, 32 (1st Cir. 1986). Note, however, that in-fact enterprises" pose a more difficult problem, and may not be appropriate for summary resolution under Rule 12(b)(6) or 56. RICO provides that an enterprise may be composed of "any union or group of individuals associated in fact although not a legal entity."[1288] A RICO enterprise must, however, be a continuing unit that has some type of organization and constitutes an entity separate and apart from the alleged pattern of racketeering;[1289] claims alleging association-in-fact enterprises have been dismissed on pretrial motions for failure to allege the requisite continuity, or for failure to identify an enterprise that is more than a corporate entity and its agents conducting their regular business.[1290]

- "Pattern." The Supreme Court's most recent attempt to define the "pattern" requirement was in *H.J. Inc. v. Northwestern Bell Telephone Co.*, in which it ruled that proving a pattern requires showing that the racketeering acts "are related" and "amount to or pose the threat of continued criminal activity."[1291] The Court defined "related" acts as those "that have the same or similar purposes, results, participants, victims, or methods of commission, or otherwise are interrelated by distinguishing characteristics and are not isolated events."[1292] The Court defined "continuity" to require either "a closed period of repeated

---

some courts permit vicarious liability where an employer is benefited by its employees' § 1962(c) violations, if the employer is distinct from the enterprise. *See, e.g.,* Brady v. Dairy Fresh Prods. Co., 974 F.2d 1149, 1154 (9th Cir. 1992); *Petro-Tech,* 824 F.2d at 1361–62. Vicarious liability has also been found proper under other subsections of § 1962. *See, e.g.,* Quick v. Peoples Bank of Cullman County, 993 F.2d 793, 797–98 (11th Cir. 1993) (§ 1962(b)). *See generally* A Proposal for the Application of Vicarious Liability Under Civil RICO (American College of Trial Lawyers 1994).

1288. 18 U.S.C. §1961(4). While some have argued that this definition limits associations-in-fact to groups of individuals, that argument has found little support in the decisions. *See, e.g.,* Atlas Pile Driving Co. v. DiCon Fin. Co., 886 F.2d 986, 995 n.7 (8th Cir. 1989); Shearin v. E.F. Hutton Group, Inc., 885 F.2d 1162, 1165–66 (3d Cir. 1989). *But see In re* Tucker Freight Lines, Inc., 789 F. Supp. 884, 893 (W.D. Mich. 1991).

1289. United States v. Turkette, 452 U.S. 576, 583 (1981).

1290. *See, e.g., Parker & Parsley,* 972 F.2d at 583; Brittingham v. Mobil Corp., 943 F.2d 297, 300–03 (3d Cir. 1991) ("a § 1962(c) enterprise must be more than an association of individuals or entities conducting the normal affairs of a defendant corporation"); *Yellow Bus Lines,* 883 F.2d at 141 ("allowing plaintiffs to generate such 'contrived partnerships' consisting of an umbrella organization and its subsidiary parts, would render the non-identity requirement of section 1962(c) meaningless. We decline to permit such an 'end run' around the statutory requirements."); Atkinson v. Anadarko Bank & Trust Co., 808 F.2d 438 (5th Cir. 1987); *Haroco,* 747 F.2d at 401, *aff'd on other grounds,* 473 U.S. 606 (1985). *But see Atlas Pile Driving,* 886 F.2d 986 (two members of "association in fact" enterprise could also be "persons" liable).

1291. 492 U.S. 229, 239 (1989).

1292. *Id.* at 240.

conduct" or "past conduct that by its nature projects into the future with a threat of repetition."[1293] Whether the acts "establish a threat of continued racketeering activity depends on the specific facts of each case."[1294] Following *H.J.*, courts have dismissed § 1962(c) claims in two overlapping areas for failure to satisfy the pattern requirement. First, where the allegations involve completed ("closed-ended") conduct lasting twelve months or less, and where there is no threat of future criminal conduct, courts have dismissed the claims on motions to dismiss or for summary judgment.[1295] Second, courts have held that claims involving only a single (or a few) victims cannot pose a threat of long-term criminal conduct, and should be dismissed even where the conduct complained of lasted for many months or even years.[1296] In other cases, courts have applied a multifactor test to determine whether a pattern of racketeering activity has been pleaded or proved. The factors considered typically include the nature, number, and variety of predicate acts; the duration or time span involved;[1297] the number of victims; the number of separate transactions involving unlawful conduct; and the presence of distinct injuries.[1298]

1293. *Id.* at 241.

1294. *Id.* at 242.

1295. *See, e.g.*, Midwest Grinding Co. v. Spitz, 976 F.2d 1016 (7th Cir. 1992); Uni*Quality, Inc. v. Infotronx, Inc., 974 F.2d 918 (7th Cir. 1992); Tel-Phonic Servs., Inc. v. TBS Int'l, Inc., 975 F.2d 1134 (5th Cir. 1992); Hughes v. Consol-Pennsylvania Coal Co., 945 F.2d 594, 609–11 (3d Cir. 1991), *cert. denied*, 112 S. Ct. 2300 (1992) (holding that "twelve months is not a substantial period of time" for continuity purposes in a closed-ended scheme); Feinstein v. RTC, 942 F.2d 34 (1st Cir. 1991); Kehr Packages, Inc. v. Fidelcor, Inc., 926 F.2d 1406 (3d Cir.), *cert. denied*, 111 S. Ct. 2839 (1991); Pyramid Sec., Ltd. v. IB Resolution, Inc., 924 F.2d 1114 (D.C. Cir.), *cert. denied*, 112 S. Ct. 85 (1991); American Eagle Credit Corp. v. Gaskins, 920 F.2d 352 (6th Cir. 1990); Delta Pride Catfish, Inc. v. Marine Midland Bus. Loans, Inc., 767 F. Supp. 951, 967–68 (E.D. Ark. 1991); Johnston v. Wilbourn, 760 F. Supp. 578, 588–89 n.16 (S.D. Miss. 1991) (collecting cases and concluding that in no case in which predicate acts spanned less than one year in a closed-ended scheme had courts found a pattern).

1296. *See, e.g.*, Boone v. Carlsbad Bancorporation, Inc., 972 F.2d 1545, 1556 (10th Cir. 1992); Hindes v. Castle, 937 F.2d 868, 872–76 (3d Cir. 1991) ("[i]t remains an open question whether RICO liability is ever appropriate for a single-scheme, single-victim conduct threatening no future harm"); Lange v. Hocker, 940 F.2d 359 (8th Cir. 1991); Banks v. Wolk, 918 F.2d 418, 422 (3d Cir. 1990); United States Textiles, Inc. v. Anheuser-Busch Cos., 911 F.2d 1261, 1267–69 (7th Cir. 1990); Sil-Flo, Inc. v. SFHC, Inc., 917 F.2d 1507, 1516 (10th Cir. 1990).

1297. In gauging the duration in cases charging mail or wire fraud, some courts have held that only the duration of the fraudulent acts is relevant, and that innocent mailings may not be considered. *See, e.g.*, Feinstein v. RTC, 942 F.2d 34, 46 (1st Cir. 1991); *Kehr Packages*, 926 F.2d at 1418, *cert. denied*, 111 S. Ct. 2839 (1991).

1298. *See, e.g.*, *Midwest Grinding*, 976 F.2d at 1023–25. These factors are followed by courts which established this test before *H.J.* While that test was not followed in *H.J.*, and while some

4. **Section 1962(d): Conspiracy.** This subsection makes it unlawful to conspire to violate the previous three. To state a claim under § 1962(d), a plaintiff must plead that the defendant agreed to join the conspiracy, agreed to commit predicate acts, and knew that those acts were part of a pattern of racketeering activity.[1299] The agreement to commit predicate acts, standing alone, is not enough.[1300] There is a circuit split on two important issues under § 1962(d). First, some courts have held that a RICO conspiracy claim may be stated where a plaintiff is injured by any acts that further a RICO conspiracy,[1301] while others require that the acts complained of all be predicate acts as defined by § 1961.[1302] Second, some courts require that a defendant agree to commit at least two predicate acts,[1303] while others hold that it is sufficient if a defendant agreed that some member of the enterprise would commit the predicate acts.[1304]

- **Additional issues.** The following issues may also arise in RICO litigation:

    –standing: whether a RICO plaintiff has the necessary standing to sue may be appropriate for resolution under Rule 12 or 56;[1305]

courts have since found it no longer permissible, see, e.g., Fleet Credit Corp. v. Sion, 893 F.2d 441, 445–46 (1st Cir. 1990), other courts still utilize it. *See, e.g.,* Banks v. Wolk, 918 F.2d 418, 423 (3d Cir. 1990); *United States Textiles,* 911 F.2d at 1267–69.

1299. *See, e.g.,* Glessner v. Kenny, 952 F.2d 702, 714 (3d Cir. 1991); Reddy v. Litton Indus. Inc., 912 F.2d 291 (9th Cir. 1990); Hecht v. Commerce Clearing House, Inc., 897 F.2d 21 (2d Cir. 1990).

1300. *See, e.g.,* Seville Indus. Mach. Corp. v. Southmost Mach. Corp., 742 F.2d 786, 792 n.8 (3d Cir. 1984).

1301. Schiffels v. Kemper Fin. Servs., Inc., 978 F.2d 344, 348–51 (7th Cir. 1992); Shearin v. E.F. Hutton Group, Inc., 885 F.2d 1162, 1169 (3d Cir. 1989).

1302. Bowman v. Western Auto Supply Co., 985 F.2d 383 (8th Cir.), *cert. denied,* 113 S. Ct. 2459 (1993); Reddy v. Litton Indus., Inc., 912 F.2d 291 (9th Cir. 1990); *Hecht,* 897 F.2d 21.

1303. *See, e.g.,* Miranda v. Ponce Fed. Bank, 948 F.2d 41 (1st Cir. 1991); United States v. Rastelli, 870 F.2d 822 (2d Cir. 1989).

1304. *See, e.g.,* United States v. Pryba, 900 F.2d 748 (4th Cir. 1990); United States v. Kragness, 830 F.2d 842, 860 (8th Cir. 1987); United States v. Joseph, 835 F.2d 1149 (6th Cir. 1986); United States v. Neapolitan, 791 F.2d 489, 494–98 (7th Cir. 1986); United States v. Adams, 759 F.2d 1099 (3d Cir. 1985); United States v. Tille, 729 F.2d 615, 619 (9th Cir. 1984); United States v. Carter, 721 F.2d 1514 (11th Cir. 1984).

1305. *See, e.g., In re* Sunrise Sec. Litig., 916 F.2d 874 (3d Cir. 1990); Mid-State Fertilizer Co. v. Exchange Nat. Bank, 877 F.2d 1333, 1334–36 (7th Cir. 1989); Warren v. Manufacturers Nat. Bank, 759 F.2d 542 (6th Cir. 1985). *See also* Ceribelli v. Elghanayan, 990 F.2d 62 (2d Cir. 1993).

–proximate cause: whether a claimed injury is sufficiently related to the claimed RICO violation may be appropriate for resolution under Rule 12 or 56;[1306]

–propriety of damage claims: some categories of damages, such as claims for personal injury, may not be allowable under RICO;[1307]

–statute of limitations: although the appeals courts have divided on when a RICO claim accrues,[1308] the issue may be appropriate for early resolution;

–availability of equitable relief: although the RICO statute provides for certain equitable remedies,[1309] these may not be available to private litigants;[1310]

–arbitration: since an arbitration clause in an agreement between the parties will be enforced by a federal court to require arbitration of RICO claims,[1311] the court should determine early on whether such an agreement exists—the right to arbitrate may be lost if not promptly invoked;[1312] and

–miscellaneous defenses: in some RICO cases, dismissal may be appropriate under theories of preemption,[1313] abstention,[1314] act of

---

1306. *See, e.g.*, Holmes v. Securities Investor Protection Corp., 112 S. Ct. 1311 (1992); Imagineering, Inc. v. Kiewit Pac. Co., 976 F.2d 1303, 1311–12 (9th Cir. 1992), *cert. denied*, 113 S. Ct. 1644 (1993); Zervas v. Faulkner, 861 F.2d 823 (5th Cir. 1988); Brandenburg v. Seidel, 859 F.2d 1179 (4th Cir. 1988).

1307. *See, e.g.*, Genty v. RTC, 937 F.2d 899, 918–19 (3d Cir. 1991); Grogan v. Platt, 835 F.2d 844 (11th Cir. 1988); Drake v. B.F. Goodrich Co., 782 F.2d 638 (6th Cir. 1986).

1308. *See, e.g.*, McCool v. Strata Oil Co., 972 F.2d 1452, 1464–66 (7th Cir. 1992); Bivens Gardens Office Bldg., Inc. v. Barnett Bank, 906 F.2d 1546, 1554–55 (11th Cir. 1990); Keystone Ins. Co. v. Houghton, 863 F.2d 1125, 1130 (3d Cir. 1988).

1309. 18 U.S.C. §1964(a).

1310. *Compare In re* Fredeman Litig., 843 F.2d 821 (5th Cir. 1988) *and* Religious Technology Ctr. v. Wollersheim, 796 F.2d 1076 (9th Cir. 1986) *with* Aetna Casualty & Surety Co. v. Liebowitz, 570 F. Supp. 908, 910 n.11 (E.D.N.Y. 1983), *aff'd on other grounds*, 730 F.2d 905 (2d Cir. 1984).

1311. *See, e.g.*, Shearson/American Express, Inc. v. McMahon, 482 U.S. 220 (1987); Kerr-McGee Ref. Corp. v. M/T Triumph, 924 F.2d 467 (2d Cir.), *cert. denied*, 112 S. Ct. 81 (1991).

1312. *See, e.g.*, Van Ness Townhouses v. Mar Indus. Corp., 862 F.2d 754, 758–59 (9th Cir. 1988); Faircloth v. Jackie Fine Arts, Inc., 682 F. Supp. 837, 841 (D.S.C. 1988), *modified on other grounds*, 938 F.2d 513 (4th Cir. 1991). *See also* Nesslage v. York Sec., Inc., 823 F.2d 231, 234 (8th Cir. 1987).

1313. *See, e.g.*, Smith v. Fidelity Consumer Discount Co., 898 F.2d 907 (3d Cir. 1989).

1314. Coopers & Lybrand v. Sun-Diamond Growers, 912 F.2d 1135 (9th Cir. 1990); *Brandenburg*, 859 F.2d at 1190–95.

state,[1315] primary jurisdiction,[1316] and *res judicata* or collateral estoppel (discussed further below).[1317]

33.83 Related Litigation

Because the "pattern" pleaded may involve activities in several states, related RICO actions may be filed in several districts. The procedures for consolidation or coordination discussed in *supra* section 31 should therefore be considered, as appropriate. Because criminal racketeering activity is an element of civil RICO liability, civil RICO defendants will often be, or have been, the subject of criminal investigation or prosecution. The court should determine the existence and status of any related criminal proceedings, which may have an effect on pretrial and trial planning. Where criminal and civil RICO cases are proceeding concurrently, the criminal charges should ordinarily be tried first, without a general stay being imposed in the civil action (see *supra* section 31.2).

If related cases have been concluded, the trial judge must consider potential claim and issue preclusion. RICO provides that a final judgment in favor of the United States in a criminal proceeding shall estop the defendant from denying the essential allegations of the criminal offense in any civil proceeding brought by the United States.[1318] The statute is silent on the use of such convictions in civil cases brought by private parties, but courts may still apply claim and issue preclusion.[1319] Preclusion may also arise from prior civil litigation, whether in federal or state court.[1320] Prior administrative proceedings[1321] or arbitration awards[1322] may also be accorded preclusive effect. Some courts, however, have held that prior adjudications in bankruptcy court will not bar subsequent civil RICO actions based on claims which could have been raised in bankruptcy.[1323]

1315. W.S. Kirkpatrick & Co. v. Environmental Tectonics Corp., Int'l, 110 S. Ct. 701 (1990).

1316. *See, e.g.*, H.J. Inc. v. Northwestern Bell Tel. Co., 734 F. Supp. 879 (D. Minn. 1990), *aff'd*, 954 F.2d 485 (8th Cir.), *cert. denied*, 112 S. Ct. 2306 (1992).

1317. *See, e.g.*, Saud v. Bank of New York, 929 F.2d 916 (2d Cir. 1991). See *supra* § 33.82.

1318. 18 U.S.C. § 1964(d).

1319. *See, e.g.*, Appley v. West, 832 F.2d 1021 (7th Cir. 1987); Roso v. Saxon Energy Corp., 758 F. Supp. 164, 167–70 (S.D.N.Y. 1991); Anderson v. Janovich, 543 F. Supp. 1124, 1132 (W.D. Wash. 1982).

1320. *See, e.g.*, *Saud*, 929 F.2d 916; Polur v. Raffe, 912 F.2d 52, 56–57 (2d Cir. 1990); Evans v. Dale, 896 F.2d 975, 977–78 (5th Cir. 1990); McCarter v. Mitcham, 883 F.2d 196, 199–201 (3d Cir. 1989).

1321. *See* Fry v. General Motors Corp., 728 F. Supp. 455, 459–60 (E.D. Mich. 1989).

1322. *See, e.g.*, Central Transport, Inc. v. Four Phase Sys., Inc., 936 F.2d 256 (6th Cir. 1991); Benjamin v. Traffic Executive Ass'n E. R.R., 869 F.2d 107 (2d Cir. 1989); Rudell v. Comprehensive Accounting Corp., 802 F.2d 926 (7th Cir. 1986); Greenblatt v. Drexel Burnham Lambert, Inc., 763 F.2d 1352, 1360–62 (11th Cir. 1985).

1323. Barnett v. Stern, 909 F.2d 973, 978–82 (7th Cir. 1990); Howell Hydrocarbons, Inc. v. Adams, 897 F.2d 183 (5th Cir. 1990).

While claim and issue preclusion ordinarily bar the parties or those in privity with them from relitigating claims or defenses which were, or which could have been, litigated in a prior proceeding, and from relitigating factual or legal issues which were actually litigated and essential to a final judgment, there are considerations common to civil RICO cases that may operate to bar application of these doctrines in some cases. Different burdens of proof,[1324] inability to litigate the issue in the prior proceeding,[1325] or lack of knowledge regarding the facts required to allege a RICO violation[1326] may prevent application of preclusion doctrines in a civil RICO action.

33.84 Discovery

The specific elements required to prove a RICO violation may pose special problems in discovery. The "pattern" requirement may involve discovery into a RICO defendant's conduct and practices over an extended period of time and with respect to numerous transactions. The existence of related criminal proceedings may raise issues such as the defendant's Fifth Amendment privilege against self-incrimination and the discoverability of grand jury material (see *supra* section 21.491). Civil RICO claims may also require discovery involving foreign countries (see *supra* section 21.494). These issues must be addressed early in the litigation, before depositions begin, in order to avoid unnecessary conflict and discovery motions.

To establish a pattern of racketeering activity, a civil RICO plaintiff must allege separate predicate acts that are both related and pose a threat of continuity.[1327] While discovery into unrelated alleged criminal acts should therefore ordinarily not be permitted,[1328] courts must be careful not to curtail unduly a plaintiff's discovery into alleged wrongdoing, especially where it relates to other alleged victims of the same pattern of racketeering activity or to acts within the exclusive knowledge of the defendant.[1329]

33.85 Final Pretrial Conference[1330]

It may not be possible to determine the sufficiency of some RICO claims until the parties have conducted discovery. Prior to the final pretrial conference, the court

---

1324. *See, e.g.*, Wilcox v. First Interstate Bank, 815 F.2d 522 (9th Cir. 1987).

1325. *See, e.g.*, George v. United Ky. Bank, Inc., 753 F.2d 50 (6th Cir. 1985).

1326. *See, e.g.*, Norris v. Wirtz, 703 F. Supp. 1322 (N.D. Ill. 1989).

1327. H.J. Inc. v. Northwestern Bell Tel. Co., 492 U.S. 229 (1989). See *supra* § 33.81.

1328. *See, e.g.*, Jolley v. Welch, 904 F.2d 988, 992 (5th Cir. 1990); Olive Can Co. v. Martin, 906 F.2d 1147, 1152–53 (7th Cir. 1990); Zerman v. E.F. Hutton & Co., 628 F. Supp. 1509, 1512 (S.D.N.Y. 1986); PMC, Inc. v. Ferro Corp., 131 F.R.D. 184 (C.D. Cal. 1990).

1329. *See, e.g.*, Michaels Bldg. Co. v. Ameritrust Co., N.A., 848 F.2d 674, 679–81 (6th Cir. 1988); Halperin v. Berlandi, 114 F.R.D. 8, 11–13 (D. Mass. 1986).

1330. See generally *supra* § 21.6.

should require the parties to file statements and memoranda setting out the claims and defenses that remain viable and the factual and legal bases therefor. The parties should attempt to reach stipulations where possible; where disagreements remain, motions for summary judgment, filed in advance by a specified deadline, can be resolved or at least considered at the conference. If the elimination of RICO or other federal claims removes the jurisdictional basis for supplemental state law claims, the court should decide whether it will retain jurisdiction over those claims.

33.86 Trial

Some of the technical issues in civil RICO trials may be particularly confusing to lay jurors. The court should therefore explain to the jurors the general nature of the claims. This should be done at an early stage, either during voir dire or before the parties' opening statements (see *supra* sections 22.41, 22.43). In addition to briefly noting the general nature of the case, the court should outline some of the characteristics and elements of a civil RICO case. These include the fact that the case is a civil action, not a criminal proceeding; that the burden of proof is by a preponderance of the evidence, not beyond a reasonable doubt;[1331] and that the plaintiff need not prove that the defendant is a "racketeer" in the everyday sense of that term or is associated with "organized crime." The court should urge the parties to submit a joint set of preliminary comments or instructions for this purpose.

To avoid confusion, and to direct the jurors' attention to the sufficiency of each separate statutory and common law claim submitted for their decision, special verdicts or a general verdict with interrogatories should usually be employed (see *supra* sections 21.633, 22.34, 22.451). Issues may be submitted to the jury for decision sequentially, both to simplify deliberations and to obviate deliberation on issues rendered moot by an earlier verdict. Some courts have held that the jury should not be informed that damages awarded on a RICO verdict will automatically be trebled.[1332]

1331. *See, e.g.*, Sedima, S.P.R.L. v. Imrex Co., 473 U.S. 479, 491 (1985); *In re* EDC, Inc., 930 F.2d 1275, 1280 (7th Cir. 1991); Wilcox v. First Interstate Bank, N.A., 815 F.2d 522, 530–32 (9th Cir. 1987).

1332. *See* Lerchen v. Merrill Lynch, Pierce, Fenner & Smith, Inc., No. 86-1158 (E.D. Mich. 1985), *aff'd*, 817 F.2d 756 (6th Cir. 1987). *See also* Pollock & Riley, Inc. v. Pearl Brewing Co., 498 F.2d 1240 (5th Cir. 1974) (antitrust).

34. Courtroom Technology[1333]

Courtroom technology is increasingly coming into use in litigation, and that use can be expected to expand as the technology develops, creating additional applications, increasing speed and accuracy, and reducing cost. While the impetus for the use of technology in a given case will generally come from counsel, the judge can both encourage and control it as appropriate. Considerations such as the desirability of technology in presenting the issues effectively and the balance of costs and benefits will come into play. Where substantial disparity exists in the litigants' respective resources, fairness will be an important consideration. If technology is to be shared or used for common benefit, arrangements for the allocation of costs may be needed. Deploying technology will often require physical arrangements as well; the court should ensure coordination among the parties in making the necessary arrangements, including adequate opportunity to install and test equipment. Ground rules to address such matters should be developed early in the litigation, before substantial investments have been made.

What follows is a basic description of some of the technologies becoming available for courtroom use, along with ways in which they can be used, their advantages and disadvantages, and related considerations. The speed with which technology advances could render any more specific information obsolete by the time it is published; additional, more specific, and current information may be available to judges from the Office of Judges' Programs of the Administrative Office of the U.S. Courts.

1333. With acknowledgments to Donald E. Vinson, Ph.D., and Roger L. McCarthy, Ph.D.

34.1 Functions and Benefits

- **Promoting economy.** Litigation often requires the processing and use of vast amounts of information. Technology allows great quantities of data to be efficiently stored, transported, and accessed.

- **Aiding analysis.** Litigation requires not only the collection of facts but also their analysis and interpretation. Technology can improve the speed and accuracy of factual analysis.

- **Fostering visual perception.** Technology has led the public to depend on and expect the sophisticated production and display of visual information. In general, visual displays convey more information than audio recordings or writings read aloud (e.g., a deponent's demeanor) and increase jury attention, comprehension, and retention. For example, computer-aided simulation substantially aids witnesses, juries, and judges in reconstructing events with precision and in detail.

34.2 Safeguards

Courtroom technology may be subject to abuse and manipulation; basic safeguards should be employed to ensure integrity and fairness:

- **Judicial training.** Familiarity with the capabilities of various technological aids will help judges anticipate pitfalls and potentials for abuse.

- **Independent experts.** Courts may call on independent experts for advice on questions pertaining to specific uses of technology (see *supra* section 21.51).

- **Guidelines.** Explicit guidelines should be developed to govern the use of technology in the courtroom. Judges have substantial discretion to exclude inappropriate or misleading technological applications.

34.3 Technologies Available for Courtroom Use

.31 Video 395
.32 Computer Animation 397
.33 Laser Discs 398
.34 CD-ROM 400
.35 Electronic or Digitized Still Photographs 401
.36 Photogrammetry 402
.37 Personal Computers 403
.38 Computer-Aided Transcription (CAT) 404
.39 Simultaneous Distributed Translation (SDT) 405

34.31 Video

What it is:

Among the technologies available for courtroom use, video technology may be the most familiar to, and widely used by, the public. Video camera recorders (VCRs) and videotape recorders (also usually called VCRs in lay terminology) are widely available and come in "VHS" and "8 mm" format; the primary difference between the two is the smaller size of the 8 mm tapes. The two formats and their hardware are currently incompatible; most VCRs in the home and office are VHS.

How it is used:

Video camera recorders are the functional equivalent of movie cameras, with one key difference: instead of exposing film to light, they translate light into electronic signals which are recorded on videotape or broadcast "live" for display on monitors ("monitors" are video display screens, like television screens but without the "tuners" found in television sets that allow them to pick up broadcast signals—only a monitor is needed to play videotapes; the screens used with personal computers are also "monitors"). In addition to their home and office use, more sophisticated and expensive VCRs are utilized by television news programs for virtually all news stories seen in a broadcast. Videotape recorders can play videotapes and record images and sounds directly from a television broadcast for playback at a later time.

Strengths and benefits of video technology:

- **Cost:** Video camera recorders and videotape recorders are relatively inexpensive.

- **User-friendly:** VCRs are easy to use. Most cameras are auto-focus and can record for several hours at a time on a single battery and tape; many now produce tapes instantly ready for insertion into a videotape player for playback. Even the presence of a human being is not required: video cameras can be set up to record unattended for long periods of time, and videotape recorders can be programmed to record during a specified time period.

- **Low potential for abuse:** The nature of "analog" video technology makes it very difficult to alter video images without leaving a trace. Videotape which has been edited or otherwise tampered with will show obvious signs of alteration. Moreover, the video quality declines with each generation of a copied tape. An original analog videotape is therefore a reliable record. Newer "digital" VCR technology will, however, make alterations harder to detect. (Unlike analog technology, where a signal is recorded or transmitted in essentially its original form, digital recording equipment translates sounds and images into a string of 0s and 1s, which digital playback equipment can read and retranslate for display. This results in a higher quality image, but one that can be edited relatively easily by simply rearranging the sequence of 0s and 1s.)

- **Facilitate court "appearances":** Conferences and hearings can be held by live video conferencing (like a conference call, but with visual display in addition) instead of requiring attorneys or other participants to travel to the courthouse, reducing fees and minimizing inconvenience. In criminal cases, live video conferencing can permit the defendant to participate in a pretrial proceeding without having to be transported from his place of custody, though this may implicate rule-based and constitutional concerns.[1334]

- **Video record of court proceedings:** VCR technology permits the court and the parties to acquire a full video record of the trial proceedings. A video record may be more complete and accurate than a mere transcript. Only a few state courts now permit video recording; it is not currently allowed in federal courts.

- **Presentation of evidence.** When monitors are available in the courtroom, exhibits and other evidence can be conveniently displayed; videotape might be used, for example, to demonstrate the operation of a patented device or the appearance of a scene or location relevant to the litigation.

Potential limitations and abuses:

- **Privacy:** The beneficial attributes of VCR technology—relatively low cost, simple mechanics, and widespread availability—may also prove to be drawbacks, particularly in the area of individual privacy rights. Used as a surveillance tool, the VCR is an efficient method of monitoring various environments for security purposes; this function, however, risks intruding on the privacy interests of employees or innocent bystanders. The court should use its discretion to exclude or require redaction of video recordings that improperly impinge on a person's privacy.

- **Image quality:** Current video technology captures a relatively low quality of image, with less than 1/20th the detail of a 35 mm photograph. Also, the range of video quality varies greatly, depending on the type of equip-

---

1334. *See* Valenzuela-Gonzales v. District Ct., 915 F.2d 1276, 1277–81 (9th Cir. 1990) (arraignment via closed-circuit television violates Fed. R. Crim. P. 43, absent showing of necessity); United States v. Washington, 705 F.2d 489, 497 n.4 (D.C. Cir. 1983) (defendants may be present for voir dire via closed-circuit T.V. if given opportunity to consult with counsel and court finds procedure necessary). *Cf.* Maryland v. Craig, 110 S. Ct. 3157, 3166–70 (1990) (finding of necessity required for witness in criminal trial to testify via closed-circuit T.V.). Proposed amendments to Fed. R. Crim. P. 10 and 43 would allow arraignment and other pretrial proceedings to be conducted with the defendant present via video teleconferencing, but only on defendant's waiver.

ment used, the conditions of taping, and the experience of the person operating the video camera.

- **Durability:** While videotape is a fairly durable medium, it declines in quality with each playing. It does not possess the archival quality of paper, photographs, and film; currently, videotape has a shelf-life of approximately five to ten years.

34.32 Computer Animation

What it is:

Computer-generated animation (or simulation) is similar to the more familiar film animation, which is created by a series of hand-painted scenes on celluloid (later transferred to film) displayed in rapid sequence, creating the illusion of motion. Computer animation achieves the same effect with a series of still images, but without actually filming real events or scenes, avoiding the laborious process of hand painting. Instead, individual frames are generated by a computer and stored in a magnetic or alternative format, and then played back at twenty-four frames per second on a monitor.

How it is used:

Computer animation can be used to create simulations in the form of visual, moving-image reconstructions of actual scenes and events that were not recorded (or recorded insufficiently), or of events that did not actually occur or things that do not currently exist, for example to present a hypothetical scenario or illustrate the design and function of a product not yet manufactured.

Strengths and benefits of computer animation:

- **Creative control:** Computer animation allows the creator to absolutely control what appears—or does not appear—in each computer-generated frame. Even the laws of physics and the constraints of the rational mind can be abandoned to create what the animator desires.

- **Visualization of abstract concepts or difficult-to-observe events:** Since the animator has complete creative control over the images, abstract concepts can be presented visually. Minute, split-second, or slowly occurring physical processes can be presented in a manner that facilitates observation. Abstract or complex scientific processes and evidence can be illustrated clearly, enhancing comprehension.

- **Repeated use:** Libraries of "stock" animation can be developed for ready availability, reducing cost and effort.

Potential limitations and abuses:

- **Cost:** Computer animations require vast amounts of information and detail from the animator, making this technology currently relatively expensive (compared, for example, to video technology). Advances in computer animation will likely reduce the cost.

- **Requires a "guide":** Displaying animation requires a person to access the technology via computer or videotape and then guide the viewers through what they are seeing.

- **Reality compromised:** Computer animation, like its film counterpart, can rarely appear truly "real." Since the animator possesses creative control over the end-product, it must be remembered that computer-animated images are ultimately human-created and thus susceptible to human biases.

- **Foundational requirement:** Computer animation, like any other representational evidence, is inadmissible without a proper foundation (see *supra* section 21.642). The proponent may be required to present both the factual information relied on and the process by which this information was used to produce the animation. Experts such as engineers and scientists may be required to testify about technical and scientific matters. To save trial time, the court should encourage the parties to stipulate to authenticity after making their own examination or resolve the issue by pretrial hearing under Fed. R. Evid. 104. Note that, since animation is merely a series of still pictures, traditional means of establishing a foundation for still images may be employed.

- **Medium overpowers the message?:** The powerful impression left by computer animation may be difficult for an opposing party to overcome. Once jurors view the animation, it can become difficult to persuade them to accept a different version of events. If requested, the judge may caution the jury about the weight to give such evidence. The judge may also need to consider under Fed. R. Evid. 403 whether the prejudicial effect of the evidence outweighs its probative value. Where the opposing party lacks the resources to respond in kind, particular attention needs to be given to the fairness of the presentation.

34.33 Laser Discs

What they are:

Laser discs, like CD-ROMs, are a form of optical disc. Laser disc technology allows an enormous amount of information to be stored in digital form on a portable twelve-inch disc. Approximately 50,000 video frames with audio (about thirty minutes of continuous playing at 30 frames per second) can be conveniently stored on a single disc.

How they are used:

A laser disc player reads this information with a laser beam and reproduces it on a monitor. Because (unlike film or videotape) the information is stored digitally, frame numbers may be coded at the time of production and thereafter retrieved instantaneously by scanning a light pen over a bar code that can be generated by any common laser printer.

Strengths and benefits of laser disc technology:

- **Efficient all-in-one storage:** Virtually any type of documentary, graphic, taped, or animated evidence can be stored on a laser disc. Laser discs streamline the presentation of evidence by eliminating the often unwieldy nature of voluminous papers and bulky trial binders. Charts and graphs are easily called up on the monitor. Laser discs also eliminate the often awkward and time-consuming searches for exhibits and other papers during trial.

- **Recorded testimony:** Videotaped depositions can be stored on laser discs and rapidly retrieved for direct comparison with in-court testimony. This allows selected portions of a deposition to be recalled and shown almost instantly, in any desired order, without the need for pretrial editing or time-consuming fast-forwarding and rewinding at trial.

- **Higher quality display than CD-ROM:** Information on laser discs generally is not "compressed," as it is on CD-ROM, resulting in a higher quality image. Laser discs are therefore superior to CD-ROM for full-screen video display of complex or detailed images.

- **Low cost/user friendly:** Laser disc technology is relatively inexpensive and widely available, and information retrieval is easy, requiring little training or guidance.

Potential limitations and abuses:

- **Less information storage than CD-ROM:** Because information stored on a laser disc is generally not "compressed," a laser disc cannot store as much information as a CD-ROM.

- **Lower image quality than printing:** Images stored on laser discs are retrieved to a monitor, a device inferior in detail to printed charts and graphs. High-definition monitors will ultimately resolve this difference, but the technology is still developing, and is therefore expensive (though it can be rented). In some cases, therefore, charts and graphs may be the preferred medium for displaying important information.

- **Complex production:** Laser disc production is a complex process requiring sophisticated video-editing capabilities. It is almost always performed by a vendor.

34.34 CD-ROM

What it is:

CD-ROMs ("compact disc—read only memory"), like laser discs, are a type of optical disc. Each 12 cm (4.71") disc can store approximately 635 million bytes of digital data—the equivalent of a twenty-four-volume encyclopedia. While information retrieval is easy, discs are difficult to produce—they are usually created at specially equipped facilities, though emerging (and costly) technology allows individual users to create their own. Once information is written onto a disc, it cannot be deleted to make room to store new information, but can only be read (thus "read only" memory). More advanced "rewritable" optical drives allow information to be stored on, and retrieved or erased from, optical discs (as with computer disks).[1335]

How it is used:

CD-ROM technology can be used to store and retrieve audio and video information, including the entire range of documentary data—briefs, business records, charts, graphs, and photographs. As with laser discs, specific information can be accessed quickly, usually by entering a code on the unit or a remote control device. Visual images are retrieved on computer or television monitors.

Strengths and benefits of CD-ROM technology:

- **Affordability/familiarity:** CD-ROM technology has been on the market for several years and is relatively inexpensive. The equipment used for retrieving data from compact discs is widely available and familiar to many consumers, and will soon be available on most personal computers.

- **Easy access:** Data on CD-ROM can be retrieved almost instantly. In conjunction with a computer, the data can be searched (by, for example, name, date, or specific wording) for rapid retrieval of desired information, even if not precoded for retrieval by code.

- **Durability:** Compact discs are highly durable. Unlike with tapes or even floppy disks, the information stored on compact discs is fairly difficult to damage or destroy through everyday use. Compact discs are therefore highly archival.

- **Compactness:** The information on CDs is "compressed" to increase the amount that can be stored. They therefore can hold even more information than current laser discs, despite being much smaller, facilitating transport and storage.

- **Commonplace:** The proliferation of compact discs in the recording industry has made this technology familiar to the American consumer.

1335. *See* Charles Piller, *Optical Update*, MacWorld, Nov. 1992, at 124.

- **User-friendly:** Use of a CD player or personal computer to retrieve information from a CD does not require elaborate training or instructions.

Potential limitations or abuses:

- **No standardized retrieval system:** Each compact disc contains its own access program that must be loaded into the memory of the CD player or computer. Storage and access formats are not yet standardized in CD-ROM technology.

- **Relatively "slow":** By computer standards, CD-ROM retrieval is slow, requiring about a half-second for access to the desired information, although speeds are increasing.

- **Display inferior to laser discs:** Because, unlike on laser discs, information on CD-ROM is "compressed," the video image displayed is less sharp. This may change with advancing technology.

34.35 Electronic or Digitized Still Photographs

What they are:

Electronic (or digitized) "photographs" are images captured on discs rather than on light-sensitive film. These images can then be retrieved on television or computer monitors and transferred to CD-ROM discs for permanent storage. In contrast, conventional photography employs film chemically treated to produce a "negative" when exposed to the proper light conditions, which is then used to produce color or black-and-white prints on paper (the "positive" image).

How they are used:

Electronic/digitized photography serves the same purpose as conventional photography—to capture images—but does not require chemical development and may be reproduced on monitors. The photographs can be easily accessed and enlarged by computer.

Strengths and benefits of electronic photographs:

- **Electronic enhancement:** The primary benefit of this technology is the ability to improve the quality of photographs and manipulate the images in them. Unlike with conventional photography, a poor quality photograph can be "enhanced" by computer to produce a higher quality image.

- **Greater depth of field:** Compared to conventional photography, electronic photographs typically produce clear images of objects located within a greater range of distance.

- **Laser printed:** In addition to video display, electronic photographs can be printed by a personal computer attached to a color laser printer.

- **Efficient storage:** Electronic photographs may be stored on durable discs and quickly retrieved on video display monitors or printed.

Potential limitations and abuses:

- **Reduced image detail:** Compared to conventional photographs, electronic images capture far less detail. The common 35 mm photograph is able to register approximately ten times more image detail than an electronic/digitized image. Technological advances should soon enable electronic photography to match the level of detail achieved by conventional photography.

- **Alteration:** Electronic photographs can be altered without leaving a trace (unlike conventional photographs). The court must therefore use special care when electronic photographs are offered in evidence. As with any photograph, authentication should be made by testimony of a knowledgeable witness that the photograph accurately represents the matter in question. The judge may also, however, require the proponent to establish a chain-of-custody, with each custodian testifying that the photograph was not altered.

- **Expense:** The equipment used to produced electronic photography is currently much more expensive and complex than equipment used in conventional photography.

34.36 Photogrammetry

What it is:

Photogrammetry is not a single technology but rather a method of obtaining quantitative information about physical objects by interpreting photographs. For example, photogrammetric techniques have been used to compile topographic maps from aerial and space photographs. Recent advances in computer software programs make it possible to reconstruct accidents and other events based on an extrapolation of information available in photographs.

How it is used:

Computer-aided photogrammetry is useful in reconstructing accidents by analyzing photographs of the accident site. Software programs use mathematical concepts to establish precise relationships between objects in a photograph and to retrieve three-dimensional data about those objects. Information obtained directly from an accident site can be checked against the data extracted in photogrammetric analysis.

Strengths and benefits of photogrammetry:

- **Permanent record for analysis:** Photographs taken soon after an event may be analyzed at a later date using photogrammetry techniques. Thus, photographs become a permanent record of important information that would otherwise be difficult to obtain long after occurrence.

- **Reconstruction:** Photogrammetry can be used to reconstruct information that might not be available directly from the site. For example, the length of skid marks and the three-dimensional crash profile of vehicles may be determined using photogrammetric techniques.

Potential limitations or abuses:

- **Poor photographic image:** Photogrammetric techniques interpret information provided by a photograph; if the image is poor or otherwise lacking in important data, photogrammetry may be of limited help in extracting the desired information.

34.37 Personal Computers

What they are:

Personal computers (PCs) are desktop or notebook ("laptop") computers that run programs or use communications technology to access online information resources and communicate directly with other PC users. Information storage and retrieval may be on internal "hard" disks or on portable "floppy" disks (floppy disks currently come in two sizes, 5.25" and 3.5", with the former being phased out; the latter-sized disk, despite its name, is nonflexible). The personal computer is used in conjunction with all of the technology discussed above.

How they are used:

In the courtroom, attorneys are increasingly using lap-top computers to take trial notes. Personal computers can also be used to project images on monitors or scan photographs or text. In this respect, a basic personal computer can drive an entire in-court presentation.

Strengths and benefits of personal computers:

- **Versatility/ability to go "online":** PCs can run a wide variety of software programs and, when equipped with a modem (a device that allows a PC to make and receive telephone calls and data transmissions), can access many online information services (Lexis and Westlaw are the two most familiar examples), including entire libraries. Indeed, a database accessible by PC can be created for large-scale litigation to store and provide access to filings, eliminating the need for costly copying and individual service on numerous parties, and to provide an "electronic bulletin board" for low-cost dissemination of other information.[1336] See also *supra* section 21.444 (document depositories).

- **Display:** In a litigation setting, PCs can use monitors to display and highlight evidentiary and demonstrative exhibits.

1336. *See* Robert J. Katzenstein, *CLAD: Delaware's Paperless Docket*, 20 Litig. 37 (ABA Winter 1994).

- **Searchability:** Information stored on a PC can be accessed and retrieved easily and quickly, because of the PC's ability to rapidly search large amounts of data for desired information.
- **Affordability:** PCs and the software they run have become relatively inexpensive.

Potential limitations or abuses:

- **Limited power and memory:** Personal computers are limited in size, memory, and power. Full-screen video, film, and animation cannot be run on most PCs, though this technology is available and developing.
- **Tampering:** Programs that run on PCs can be tampered with, thus altering the computational ability and the results of any analyses.
- **Risk of lost material:** PC users risk accidentally losing their material if it is not properly saved to hard or floppy disks or, for even greater security, backed-up on computer tape. This risk can be reduced by regular saving and backing-up.
- **Viruses:** PCs and their software are vulnerable to "viruses" (programs designed to spread throughout the system) that may interfere with normal computing or destroy data. A range of antiviral programs is available to combat this risk.
- **Distraction:** Some judges find the use of PCs distracting, particularly in a jury trial. Courtroom use of PCs should therefore be cleared in advance.

34.38 Computer-Aided Transcription (CAT)

What it is:

A computer-aided transcription (CAT) system using "realtime" technology can translate a court reporter's keystroke patterns and custom abbreviations to create a readable English transcript of the proceeding almost instantaneously. The text is saved in a computer file for easy search and retrieval, even as the trial is proceeding.

How it is used:

A court reporter using CAT and realtime software can immediately provide counsel and the court (directly if their PCs are on the same network, otherwise on a floppy disk) with all the testimony during that court day, searchable on a key word basis, in highly complete and accurate form. Editing to eliminate "first-cut" errors will be needed to produce a final version, but a draft transcript can be available almost immediately. For greater speed, a "scopist" can work on producing a certified transcript while the court reporter is working in the courtroom. Trial counsel and the court can use this system for speedy review and retrieval of trial testimony, and counsel may even maintain a running electronic transcript of the entire trial on their PC.

Strengths and benefits of computer aided transcription:

- **Faster turnaround:** CAT dramatically increases the speed at which a transcript is produced, permitting prior testimony to be used at trial without a waiting period.
- **More efficient:** A transcript of an entire trial day can be created almost immediately, while daily transcripts have previously required two or three reporters working together.

Potential limitations and abuses:

- **First cut errors:** Even with the best CAT system, the "first cut" of the day's testimony will contain a few errors or incorrect phonic transcriptions. These can generally be corrected easily and quickly.
- **Multiple versions:** If trial counsel is given a copy of the CAT file before the court reporter's edits are incorporated, there will be two (or more) slightly different versions of the transcript in existence, potentially causing confusion.
- **Special system required:** The plain stenograph producing all paper output is unusable in this process. A new stenograph is required that records all the key strokes on a disk, or sends them directly to a computer. Specialized software for the translation of stenographic key strokes is also required. These costs will generally be offset by the resulting savings.

34.39 Simultaneous Distributed Translation (SDT)

What it is:

When a courtroom proceeding involves a number of non-English speaking participants, substantial economies can be achieved with simultaneous distributed translation (SDT) of foreign languages. This translation technique, pioneered by the United Nations, is now in regular use in a number of courts. SDT requires a single translator (for each foreign language) who is present in court translating the proceeding in "real time" by speaking into a "mask" (a microphone with added protection to contain the speaker's voice) of the type traditionally used to produce an audio transcript of court proceedings. The output of the recorder attached to the mask is fed to an amplification and distribution system that permits anyone given headphones to listen to the translation as it is spoken. The headphones are often wireless, facilitating broad distribution.

How it is used:

This technique permits a single translator to translate for many people understanding the same language, at the same time creating a record of the translation. It is used to eliminate multiple translators who inevitably produce multiple, slightly differing translations, and to avoid the distracting, error-prone, and potentially dangerous practice of having translators sit next to the person needing translation and whispering into that person's ear.

Strengths and benefits of simultaneous distributed translations:

- **Economy:** SDT can significantly reduce the number of translators needed. Only one translator is required for each foreign language. Where several foreign languages need to be simultaneously translated and distributed, multiple translators, all speaking into masks, do not interfere with one another.

- **Speed:** When the translation is done audibly by a single translator in open court, the length of the proceeding is extended since every word must be spoken twice; SDT provides simultaneous translation.

- **Uniformity:** SDT ensures that all listeners understanding the same language receive the same translation.

- **Recordability:** Translation given in whispers to a number of different parties is not reflected on the record, whereas with SDT the translator's exact words can be captured for the record.

Potential limitations and abuses:

- **Translator skill:** It requires a particularly skillful translator to listen and translate at the same time. The court should ensure the competence of proposed translators prior to the proceeding. All methods of translation, however, have common problems of lack of accuracy.

- **Custom wiring:** Most courtrooms are not equipped with microphone jacks at counsel tables and other locations where people are seated; these must be installed in advance. The hardware and wiring involved is, however, simple, inexpensive, and readily available. Wireless SDT technology is also widely available.

- **Headphones:** Because the translations are heard via headphones, the court has to speak loudly enough to get the attention of participants wearing headphones who may not be looking at the judge.

34.4 Overview of Issues and Concerns

When considering the use of courtroom technology, judges should keep the following considerations in mind:

- **Unfair advantage:** Whether actual or perceived, the advantages a party may gain by access to expensive, sophisticated devices must be weighed in formulating policies for courtroom use of technology. This is a particular concern when one party can afford to use technology and another cannot. Traditionally, parties able to afford superior representation have been allowed to exercise that advantage freely; indeed, for the court to do otherwise might be considered a violation of the party's rights. Whether this principle extends to the use of technology is a question not yet fully resolved. Nevertheless, because technology can possess persuasive power not always obvious to the observer, the court should be aware of and guard against the risk of unfairness arising from its use.

- **Distraction:** Technology can at times create a spectacle distracting jurors from the legal and factual issues in the case. The court must decide, on a case-by-case basis, whether the proposed use of technology will serve a proper function.

- **Over-reliance:** Technology—especially video technology—captures the imagination. The power and speed of modern communication and computation is impressive. Yet these attributes may also lead to over-reliance on technology in the courtroom. Traditional display boards or paper documents can often accomplish the same evidentiary purposes without the cost, difficulties, and risks of hi-tech devices.

- **Distortion of evidence:** As this chapter has suggested, some technologies are capable of rearranging and enhancing images taken from reality. This creates two concerns: intentional misrepresentation of reality and, more commonly, the potential of confusion of recorded reality with computer-created information. When technology is used to present hypothetical scenarios or alter the appearance of recorded reality, the court must ensure that the jurors are clearly informed about what they are to see and hear, and given the guidance and instruction needed to separate factual evidence from technological creations.

Part IV

40. Checklists

40.1 Early Pretrial

1. Court. [*supra* section 20.1]

__ Early assumption of active supervision over litigation. [*supra* sections 20.1, 20.13]

__ Assignment to single judge. [*supra* section 20.12]

__ Review potential conflicts; recusal/disqualification. [*supra* section 20.121]

__ Related litigation. [*supra* sections 20.123, 31]

    __ Cases pending in same court. [*supra* section 31.11]

    __ Reassignment of cases. [*supra* section 20.123]

    __ Consolidation for pretrial. [*supra* section 31.11]

    __ Coordination of cases not consolidated.

__ Cases pending in other courts. [*supra* sections 31.12, 31.2, 31.3]

__ Civil cases pending in other federal courts. [*supra* sections 31.12, 31.14]

    __ Potential multidistrict transfers under 28 U.S.C. § 1407. [*supra* section 31.13]

    __ Potential transfers under 28 U.S.C. § 1404 or 1406. [*supra* section 20.123]

    __ Potential removal of state cases. [*supra* section 31.32]

    __ Coordination with cases not removed. [*supra* section 31.31]

    __ Related criminal cases. [*supra* section 31.2]

__ Coordination order. [*infra* section 41.51]

    __ Joint hearings.

    __ Joint special master.

    __ Joint appointment of lead counsel.

    __ Designation of lead case.

    __ Deference to prior rulings.

__ Suspension of local rules. [*supra* section 21.12]

__ Procedures for attending to emergency matters; telephonic conferences. [*supra* section 21.422]

__ Referrals to magistrate judges, special masters, and other judges. [*supra* sections 20.122, 20.14]

__ Schedule and set format for initial pretrial conference (see paragraph 3 below). [*supra* sections 21.11, 21.12, 21.21, 33.22]

2. Counsel. [*supra* section 20.2]

___ Admission *pro hac vice.*

___ Present/potential problems of disqualification/withdrawal. [*supra* section 20.23]

___ Responsibilities. [*supra* section 20.21]

___ Coordination of counsel/designated counsel. [*supra* section 20.22]

    ___ Organizational structure. [*supra* section 20.221]

        ___ Liaison counsel.

        ___ Lead counsel.

        ___ Committees.

        ___ Trial counsel.

    ___ Designated counsel.

        ___ Powers and responsibilities. [*supra* section 20.222]

        ___ Compensation. [*supra* section 20.223]

___ Maintenance and submission of time and expense records. [*supra* section 24.211, *infra* section 41.32]

___ Establishing policies and guidelines. [*supra* section 24.21]

    ___ Avoidance of unnecessary attendance or other expenditure of time. [*supra* sections 21.23, 24.223]

    ___ Obligations under Fed. R. Civ. P. 11, 16, 26, and local rules. [*supra* section 20.21]

    ___ Cooperation and courtesy; resolving disputes without resort to court. [*supra* section 20.21]

    ___ Use of *MCL Third.*

___ Responsibility for preparation/maintenance of service list.

3. Initial pretrial conference. [*supra* section 21.21]

___ Appearances. [*supra* section 21.23]

    ___ Counsel.

    ___ Parties.

    ___ Counsel from other cases.

    ___ Others.

___ Agenda. [*supra* sections 21.21, 33.22]

___ Identification and narrowing of issues (see paragraph 5 below). [*supra* section 21.33]

___ Deadlines and limits on joinder and pleadings. [*supra* sections 21.32, 21.33, 33.251]

___ Coordination with related federal or state litigation. [*supra* sections 31, 33.23]

___ Jurisdiction of subject matter and parties.

___ Consolidation and severance (see paragraph 26 below). [*supra* sections 21.631, 21.632, 33.261]

___ Referral to magistrate judge or special master (see paragraph 10 below). [*supra* sections 21.52, 21.53]

__ Organization of counsel and maintenance of time and expense records (see paragraph 2 above).

__ Reducing filing and service (see paragraph 4 below).

__ Suspension/revision of local rules/orders.

__ Reference to ADR procedures. [*supra* section 23.15]

__ Class-action issues (see paragraph 7 below).

__ Disclosure and discovery (see paragraphs 8, 9 below).

__ Preservation orders. [*supra* section 21.442]

__ Experts (see paragraph 10 below).

__ Judge's expectations and practices. [*supra* section 21.21]

__ Case-management plan. [*supra* section 21.211]

__ Scheduling orders. [*supra* section 21.212]

__ Scheduling next conference (see paragraph 12 below).

__ Sanctions. [*supra* section 20.15]

   __ When court will impose.

   __ Requirement of good faith effort to resolve disputes.

   __ Procedure.

__ Settlement (see paragraph 11 below).

4. Filing and service. [*supra* section 21.11]

__ Reducing filing.

   __ Creation of master file. [*supra* sections 21.12, 33.22]

      __ Filing in master file.

      __ When to file in individual cases also.

   __ Nonfiling of discovery except on court order. [*supra* section 21.431]

__ Reducing service under Fed. R. Civ. P. 5. [*supra* section 21.12]

   __ Use of liaison counsel to receive/distribute orders.

   __ Use of liaison counsel to receive/distribute documents from parties.

   __ Parties to be served separately.

__ Maintenance of service list.

5. Issues. [*supra* section 21.3]

__ Preparation for initial conference. [*supra* section 21.12]

__ Identifying, narrowing, and resolving issues. [*supra* sections 21.33, 33.254]

   __ Duplicative, irrelevant, or frivolous issues.

   __ Uncontested issues.

   __ Use of stipulation.

__ Target discovery on issues for early resolution. [*supra* sections 21.31, 21.422, *infra* section 41.33 paragraph 2(b)]

   __ Class certification (see paragraph 8 below).

__ Dispositive motions. [*supra* section 21.34, *infra* section 41.30 paragraph 4(c)]
__ Motions affecting scope of discovery.

6. Pleadings and motions. [*supra* section 21.32]
__ Suspension of time for filing certain pleadings and motions. [*supra* section 21.32]
__ Deadlines. [*supra* sections 21.32, 33.251]
    __ Adding/changing claims or defenses.
    __ Joining additional parties.
    __ Counterclaims, cross claims, third-party complaints.
    __ Relief from deadlines if justified by discovery.
__ Refiling of amended/consolidated complaint after discovery.
__ Procedure for motions.
    __ Requirement of good faith attempt to resolve.
    __ Determine if discovery needed; set scope.
    __ Schedule for submission, argument, and decision.
__ Standard and "deemed" pleadings, motions, and orders. [*supra* sections 21.32, 33.252]
    __ Provision for later filed cases.
    __ Supplementing/revising standard pleadings.
__ Summary judgment. [*supra* section 21.34]
    __ Partial.
    __ Discovery allowed.
    __ Time for filing, argument, and decision.
    __ Alternative early trial of severed issues under Fed. R. Civ. P. 42(b). [*supra* section 21.632]
__ Interlocutory appeal. [*supra* section 25.1]

7. Class certification. [*supra* sections 30.1, 33.262]
__ Time/procedures for presenting certification question. [*supra* section 30.11]
    __ Relation to other proceedings in the litigation.
    __ Whether formal motion required and, if so, when. [*supra* section 30.11]
__ Discovery. [*supra* section 30.12]
    __ Schedule; completion date.
    __ From class representatives.
    __ From class members. [*supra* section 30.232]
__ Briefing; statement of uncontested/contested facts. [*supra* section 30.13]
    __ Schedule.
    __ Identify factual disputes on which evidentiary hearing needed.
    __ Proposed method and form of certification notice. [*supra* section 30.211]
__ Hearings. [*supra* section 30.13]
    __ Dates.

__ Evidence presented by affidavit, witnesses, or other.

__ Need to define class in objective terms and identify particular claims of class. [*supra* section 30.14]

__ Possible class conflicts. [*supra* section 30.15]

    __ Within class.

    __ With other classes sought/certified.

    __ With nonclass actions.

    __ Conflicts involving counsel. [*supra* section 30.16]

__ Communications with class. [*supra* section 30.2]

8. Prediscovery disclosure. [*supra* section 21.13]

__ Meeting of counsel.

__ Modification of requirements of Fed. R. Civ. P. 26(a)(1).

__ Defining/scheduling prediscovery exchange of information.

__ Schedule for supplementation under Fed. R. Civ. P. 26(e).

9. Preliminary plan for discovery. [for complete discovery checklist, see *infra* section 40.2]

__ Obligations under Fed. R. Civ. P. 26(g). [*supra* section 20.21]

__ Discovery plan. [*supra* section 21.421]

    __ Advance meeting of counsel under Fed. R. Civ. P. 26(f). [*supra* section 21.421]

    __ Court adopts discovery plan after conference. [*supra* section 21.421, *infra* section 41.33]

    __ Periodic progress reports by counsel.

__ Limitations. [*supra* section 21.422, *infra* section 41.33]

    __ Time limits and schedules.

    __ Cutoff date for discovery. [*supra* section 21.422]

    __ Limits on quantity.

    __ General limitations under Fed. R. Civ. P. 26(g).

__ Sequencing of discovery. [*supra* section 21.422]

__ Procedures for resolving disputes. [*supra* section 21.424]

    __ Attempts by counsel to resolve voluntarily.

    __ Procedures for obtaining court ruling.

        __ Form of motion—written/oral.

        __ When briefs required/permitted.

        __ Telephonic rulings.

        __ Use of magistrate judges.

    __ Appointment of special master. [*supra* sections 20.14, 21.52, *infra* section 41.37]

__ Special provisions.

__ Confidential information; protective orders. [*supra* section 21.43, *infra* section 41.36]

__ Provisions for allocation of costs. [*supra* section 21.433]

__ Documents. [*supra* section 21.44]

    __ Adoption of identification system. [*supra* section 21.441]

    __ Preservation. [*supra* section 21.442, *infra* section 41.34]

    __ Depositories. [*supra* section 21.444, *infra* section 41.35]

    __ Evidentiary foundation. [*supra* section 21.445]

__ Depositions. [*supra* section 21.45]

    __ Cross-noticing. [*supra* section 21.455]

    __ Coordination with related litigation. [*supra* section 21.455]

    __ Guidelines/time limits. [*supra* sections 21.451, 21.456, *infra* section 41.38]

    __ Timing; scope.

    __ Limits on number. [*supra* section 21.451]

    __ Deferred supplemental depositions. [*supra* section 21.453]

__ Requests for admission. [*supra* section 21.47, *infra* section 41.61]

__ Expert discovery. [*supra* section 21.48]

__ Discovery of class members/representatives. [*supra* section 30.232]

__ Discovery in other countries. [*supra* section 21.494]

__ Governmental investigations/grand jury materials. [*supra* section 21.491]

__ Computerized data. [*supra* section 21.446]

__ Summaries. [*supra* section 21.492]

__ Surveys; other sampling techniques. [*supra* section 21.493]

__ Schedule for amendments under Fed. R. Civ. P. 26(e).

__ Duty to disclose agreements affecting discovery. [*supra* section 23.22]

10. Special appointments and referrals. [*supra* sections 20.14, 21.5, *infra* section 41.37]

__ Court-appointed experts under Fed. R. Evid. 706. [*supra* section 21.51]

__ Magistrate judges. [*supra* section 21.53]

__ Special masters under Fed. R. Civ. P. 53. [*supra* section 21.52]

__ Scope of referral.

__ Timing.

__ Procedure for selection.

    __ Nominations by parties.

    __ Suggestions by other groups; peremptory challenges.

    __ Use of magistrate judge as special master.

__ Compensation.

__ Discovery from court-appointed experts.

__ Communication with parties/experts/court.

__ Agreements as to effect of findings.

__ Report.

__ Referrals to alternative dispute resolutions mechanisms. [*supra* section 23.15]

11. Settlement. [*supra* section 23]

__ Raising settlement with the parties. [*supra* section 21.214]

__ Techniques to encourage settlement. [*supra* section 23.13]

    __ Firm trial date.

    __ Settlement conferences with parties.

    __ Confidential discussions with judge.

    __ Contribution bar orders.

    __ Offer of judgment.

    __ Trial of representative cases.

    __ Severance.

    __ Referral to other judges/magistrate judges/special masters.

    __ Settlement counsel.

__ Use of alternate processes. [*supra* section 23.15]

    __ Mediation.

    __ Summary jury trial.

    __ Summary bench trial.

    __ Minitrial.

__ Special problems.

    __ Class actions. [*supra* sections 30.4, 33.29]

        __ Partial settlements. [*supra* sections 23.21, 30.46]

        __ Settlement classes. [*supra* section 30.45]

    __ Side agreements. [*supra* section 23.23]

        __ "Mary Carter" agreements.

        __ Most-favored-nation clauses.

        __ Agreements affecting discovery. [*supra* section 23.22]

        __ Tolling agreements.

    __ Ethical considerations. [*supra* section 23.24]

12. Subsequent conferences. [*supra* section 21.22]

__ Scheduling the next conference.

__ Interim status reports.

__ Additional conferences.

    __ Prescheduled.

    __ On request.

    __ For emergency matters.

13. Preparation of order. [*supra* section 21.211]

__ Fed. R. Civ. P. 16(e) order stating action taken at conference.

    __ Drafted by counsel.

    __ Dictated into record.

    __ Subject to later refinement.

__ Use of exhibits as attachments to order.

40.2 Disclosure and Discovery

14. Obligations of parties/counsel under Fed. R. Civ. P. 26. [*supra* sections 20.21, 21.13, 21.421]

__ Fed. R. Civ. P. 26(a)(1): prediscovery disclosure.

__ Fed. R. Civ. P. 26(e): supplementation and amendment of responses.

__ Fed. R. Civ. P. 26(f): meet and confer to plan discovery.

__ Fed. R. Civ. P. 26(g): certification of requests, responses.

__ Sanctions under Fed. R. Civ. P. 16, 26, 37 for noncompliance. [*supra* section 20.15]

15. Filing and service.

__ Nonfiling of discovery materials under Fed. R. Civ. P. 5(d).

    __ All discovery requests/responses.

    __ Confidential materials. [*supra* section 21.431]

    __ Filing when needed in connection with motions.

    __ Reports regarding discovery.

    __ Abbreviated notices of discovery requests/responses.

__ Reducing service requirements under Fed. R. Civ. P. 5(c). [*supra* section 21.12]

__ Use of liaison counsel. [*supra* section 20.221]

16. Preclusion.

__ Orders precluding evidence for failure to comply with disclosure or discovery obligations. [*supra* section 20.153]

17. Matters for early discovery. [*supra* sections 21.31, 21.41, 21.422]

__ Sources of information. [*supra* section 21.421, *infra* section 41.33]

    __ Location/form of documents.

    __ Identification/location of witnesses.

    __ Computerized data, summaries. [*supra* sections 21.446, 21.492]

    __ Governmental investigations/grand jury materials. [*supra* section 21.491]

    __ Other litigation. [*supra* section 21.423]

__ Class-action discovery. [*supra* sections 30.12, 30.232]

__ Issues affecting scope of litigation or discovery. [*supra* section 21.41]

18. Discovery control. [*supra* section 21.42]

__ Relationship between discovery and issues. [*supra* section 21.41]
__ Limitations. [*supra* sections 21.421–21.422]
    __ Time limits. [*supra* section 21.422, *infra* section 41.33]
        __ Cutoff date (or firm trial date).
        __ Schedule for completing particular discovery.
    __ Quantity limits. [*supra* section 21.422]
        __ Number/length of depositions. [*supra* section 21.451]
        __ Number of interrogatories. [*supra* section 21.462]
        __ Requiring joint interrogatories/document requests. [*supra* sections 21.423, 21.443, 21.464]
    __ Limiting scope of discovery.
        __ By issues. [*supra* section 21.422]
        __ By time period. [*supra* section 21.422]
        __ Priority to particular claims/defenses. [*supra* section 21.422]
        __ Precluding duplicative or burdensome discovery. [*supra* section 21.422]
__ Sequencing discovery. [*supra* section 21.422]
    __ Targeted discovery.
        __ Focused on information for settlement.
        __ Focused on dispositive motion.
    __ Common vs. individual discovery. [*supra* section 33.25]
    __ Priority/preference according to party.
        __ From one side before other side.
        __ By one side before other side.
        __ Alternatively by weeks/months.
    __ According to form of discovery. [*supra* section 21.422, *infra* section 41.33]
        __ Document production.
        __ Depositions.
        __ Interrogatories.
        __ Requests for admission.
    __ By issues.
    __ By time period.
    __ Geographically.
__ Reducing cost/time of discovery. [*supra* section 21.423]
    __ Cooperation among counsel.
    __ Stipulations.
    __ Informal discovery.
        __ Document inspection.
        __ Interviews of possible witnesses.

__ Consultation before formal discovery requests prepared.

__ Nontechnical reading of discovery requests.

__ Identifying/producing similar information already available.

__ Discovery from other litigation and other sources.

__ Combining forms of discovery into single discovery request.

__ Conference depositions.

__ Limiting number of counsel.

__ Resolving discovery disputes. [*supra* section 21.424, *infra* section 41.38]

__ Good faith effort by counsel to resolve voluntarily.

__ Procedures for obtaining court ruling.

__ Form of motion/request—written or oral.

__ When briefs required/permitted.

__ Telephonic conferences.

__ Reference to magistrates.

__ Use of magistrate judge, special master, or other judge on special matters.

__ Depositions in other districts. [*supra* section 21.424]

__ Acting as deposition judge outside district.

__ Coordination with deposition–district judge.

__ Monitoring progress of discovery. [*supra* section 21.421]

__ Periodic written reports.

__ Reports at conferences.

__ Cost-shifting/allocation. [*supra* section 21.433]

19. Confidential and privileged information. [*supra* section 21.43]

__ Early identification of potential problem areas.

__ Protective orders. [*supra* section 21.432, *infra* section 41.36]

__ Umbrella vs. narrower order.

__ To whom disclosure authorized without prior court approval.

__ Extent of disclosure to clients.

__ Disclosure to experts.

__ Disclosure for trial-support services.

__ Execution of agreements precluding further disclosure.

__ Counsel in related litigation.

__ Copying.

__ Maintaining security.

__ Procedures for challenging confidentiality.

__ Modification of order to allow access by others.

__ Related litigation.

__ News media, public interest groups.

___ Governmental investigations.

___ Special terms regarding depositions. [*infra* sections 41.36, 41.38]

___ Availability of protection to third parties.

___ Subpoenas from other courts/agencies.

___ Claims of privilege, trial preparation materials, work product. [*supra* section 21.43, *infra* section 41.37]

    ___ Possible avoidance by sequencing discovery.

    ___ Need to identify and describe items for which privilege claimed.

    ___ Use of *in camera* inspections.

        ___ By trial judge.

        ___ By special master, magistrate judge, or other judge. [*supra* sections 21.52, 21.53]

___ Consideration of nonwaiver agreements. [*supra* section 21.432]

20. Documents. [*supra* section 21.44]

___ Identification system. [*supra* section 21.441]

    ___ Use of uniform designation throughout litigation.

    ___ Log of documents produced.

___ Preservation orders. [*supra* section 21.442, *infra* section 41.34]

    ___ Modification of interim order against destruction.

        ___ Exemption to avoid unnecessary hardship.

        ___ Limiting scope as issues narrowed.

        ___ Procedure for giving advance notice of proposed destruction.

    ___ Special problems with computerized data; preservation of hard copies.

    ___ Disposition. [*supra* section 25.4]

        ___ After litigation concluded.

        ___ Deferred.

___ Document depositories. [*supra* section 21.444, *infra* section 41.35]

    ___ Location.

    ___ Cost.

        ___ Justified by benefit.

        ___ Allocation.

    ___ Procedures for operation.

        ___ Acquisition of materials.

        ___ Numbering.

        ___ Indexing.

        ___ Storage.

            ___ Hard copies.

            ___ CD-ROM.

    __ Other.
    __ Access. [*infra* section 41.35]
        __ Other litigants.
        __ Confidential documents.
        __ Copying; removal.
        __ Logs.
    __ Notification of additional filings.
  __ Joint use of depository with related litigation. [*supra* section 31.13, *infra* sections 41.35, 41.51]
__ Computerized data. [*supra* section 21.446]
  __ Identification of existing data/printouts.
    __ Description of files/fields/records/other.
    __ Direct communication between parties' experts.
  __ Identification of data prepared/compiled for trial.
    __ Time for disclosure.
    __ Format.
    __ Preservation of source documents.
  __ Verification.
    __ Production of source documents.
    __ Inquiry regarding input, storage, retrieval.
    __ Opportunity for testing.
  __ Production.
    __ Format.
        __ Hard copies.
        __ Computer-accessible form.
        __ Special programming/formats.
    __ Protection of confidential information, including system itself.
  __ Cost.
__ Coordinating requests for documents. [*supra* section 21.443]
  __ Joint requests for production.
  __ Joint inspection and copying.
  __ Court monitoring of requests.
  __ Standard/deemed requests in multiple litigation. [*infra* section 41.52]
__ Discovery from nonparties. [*supra* section 21.447]
  __ Subpoena: duty to avoid undue burden or expense.
  __ Sufficient advance notice.
  __ Applicability of confidentiality orders. [*infra* section 41.36]
  __ Cost-sharing.

___ Alternate sources of obtaining information.

21. Depositions. [*supra* section 21.45]

___ Limitations. [*supra* section 21.451]

    ___ Number/length of depositions.

    ___ Requiring court approval.

        ___ Generally.

        ___ Depositions of class members. [*supra* section 30.232]

        ___ Depositions outside country. [*supra* section 21.494]

___ Cost-saving measures. [*supra* section 21.452, *infra* section 41.38]

    ___ Informal interviews.

        ___ Recorded electronically.

        ___ Converted into nonstenographic deposition.

    ___ Nonstenographic depositions.

        ___ By party taking deposition.

        ___ By other party as additional record.

        ___ Provision for transcription(s).

    ___ Telephonic depositions.

        ___ By stipulation.

        ___ By court order.

        ___ Restrictions on attendance/coaching.

        ___ Providing documents to deponent.

        ___ Safeguards.

    ___ Written questions under Fed. R. Civ. P. 31.

    ___ Conference depositions.

    ___ Representative depositions.

    ___ Affidavit from proposed deponent claiming no knowledge.

    ___ Reduce/eliminate transcripts/copies.

    ___ Limited attendance by counsel.

        ___ Authorizing supplemental examination after review of transcript. [*supra* section 21.453]

        ___ Participation by telephone.

        ___ Providing written questions under Fed. R. Civ. P. 30(c).

___ Videotaped. [*supra* sections 21.452, 22.333, *infra* section 41.38]

    ___ Ground rules/safeguards.

    ___ Edited.

___ Scheduling. [*supra* section 21.454, *infra* sections 41.33, 41.38]

    ___ Concurrent depositions.

        ___ Multiple track.

    __ Preferential/exclusive rights for particular parties.

    __ According to subject matter.

__ Related litigation. [*supra* section 21.455, *infra* section 41.51]

    __ Cross-noticing.

    __ Adoption of previous testimony.

    __ Coordination of scheduling.

    __ Stipulation to use in related cases.

__ Guidelines. [*infra* section 41.38]

    __ Who may be present.

    __ Advance approval for telephonic and nonstenographic depositions.

    __ Confidential information—examination/production.

    __ Providing copies of documents to deponent/other counsel.

    __ Procedures for supplemental examination.

__ Controlling abusive conduct. [*supra* section 21.456, *infra* section 41.38]

    __ Improper objections; suggesting answers.

    __ Instructions not to answer.

    __ Bad faith/oppressive examination.

    __ Procedure to resolve disputes. [*supra* section 21.424]

22. Interrogatories. [*supra* section 21.46]

__ Uses. [*supra* section 21.46]

    __ Identify witnesses/documents.

    __ Obtain specific information known in part by different persons.

    __ Facilitate later discovery.

    __ Explain denials of requests for admission.

__ Contention interrogatories. [*supra* section 21.461]

    __ Timing.

    __ Scope.

__ Limitations. [*supra* section 21.462]

    __ Number.

    __ Showing of need.

__ Practices to save time and expense. [*supra* section 21.464]

    __ Standard/master interrogatories (duplicative requests prohibited).

    __ Use of answers from other litigation.

    __ Nontechnical reading.

    __ Respond with available information similar to that requested.

    __ Prompt response based on information known at time.

    __ Successive responses as information obtained.

    __ Use of conference deposition instead.

__ Schedule dates for supplementation.

23. Admissions. [*supra* section 21.47]

__ Fed. R. Civ. P. 36 procedures. [*supra* sections 21.47]

    __ Timing.

    __ Obligation to clarify denial, admit other parts.

    __ Interrogatories to further clarify.

__ Timing: adequate opportunity for discovery.

__ Acknowledging facts that will not be disputed or contested. [*supra* section 21.47, *infra* section 41.61]

    __ Development of statement of disputed/agreed facts. [*supra* section 21.47]

        __ Sequential preparation.

        __ Timetable.

        __ Scope.

            __ All facts.

            __ Principal facts.

            __ Facts that may be admitted and, if admitted, will reduce scope of trial.

            __ Facts on particular issues (e.g., summary judgment).

            __ Use for special hearings (e.g., class certification, preliminary injunctions).

        __ Annotations by reference to witnesses/documents.

            __ Permissive.

            __ Mandatory, with preclusive effect.

    __ Evidentiary objections.

        __ Not basis for refusing to admit.

        __ Requiring certain objections (e.g., authentication).

        __ Requiring all objections.

    __ Effect.

        __ Admitted for purpose of trial; when independent evidence permitted.

            __ Precluding proof of unlisted facts.

        __ Sanctions under Fed. R. Civ. P. 36 for unwarranted denial.

        __ Withdrawal of admission under Fed. R. Civ. P. 36 standards.

__ Use of judicial notice.

24. Special discovery problems and contexts.

__ Expert opinions. [*supra* sections 21.48, 21.51]

    __ At initial conference:

        __ Identify subjects on which expert opinions may be offered.

        __ Set timetables for:

            __ Identifying experts to be called.

            __ Disclosure of reports/information under Fed. R. Civ. P. 26(a)(2).

__ Deposing experts.

    __ Revisions to opinions/reasons.

__ Materials considered by expert.

    __ General requirement for preservation/disclosure/production.

__ Disclosure of written report of opinions.

__ Critiques of opinions by other experts—time for disclosure.

__ Allocate costs of depositions.

__ Limiting length of depositions.

__ Pretrial consideration of objections to expert's qualifications or opinions.

__ Discovery from nontestifying experts.

__ Discovery from court-appointed experts. [*supra* section 21.51]

__ Discovery of class members/representatives.

    __ Limits on scope of discovery from class representatives and counsel. [*supra* section 30.12]

    __ Court approval before discovery from class members. [*supra* section 30.232]

    __ Limits on quantity/scope/form of discovery from class members. [*supra* section 30.232]

__ Discovery outside country. [*supra* section 21.494]

    __ Advance approval from court required.

    __ Need shown.

    __ Request is specific.

__ Governmental investigations/grand jury material. [*supra* section 21.491]

    __ Early identification of relevant investigations/reports.

    __ Production.

        __ From parties.

        __ From public records.

        __ Subpoena.

        __ Requests under Freedom of Information Act.

        __ Grand jury materials.

    __ Admissibility.

        __ Discovery regarding trustworthiness.

        __ Pretrial consideration of objections.

__ Summaries; compilations. [*supra* sections 21.446, 21.492]

    __ Timetable for disclosure.

    __ Production of underlying data.

    __ Verification procedures.

        __ Detecting/correcting errors.

        __ Stipulation as to estimated range of errors.

__ Polls, surveys, other sampling techniques. [*supra* section 21.493]

    __ Timetable for disclosure of potential use.

    __ Consultation between experts prior to conducting survey.

    __ Disclosure of results/underlying data.

    __ Admissibility.

    __ Discovery.

    __ Pretrial consideration of objections.

__ Discovery relating to settlements.

    __ Discovery regarding fairness/adequacy of proposed class settlements. [*supra* section 30.41, 30.42]

    __ Potential problems with agreements affecting discovery. [*supra* section 23.22]

__ Discovery relating to attorneys' fees. [*supra* section 24.224]

    __ Scope of discovery.

    __ Inquiry into hours/rates of opposing counsel.

__ Discovery in particular litigation.

    __ In criminal cases. [*supra* section 32.24]

    __ In mass tort litigation. [*supra* section 33.27]

    __ Employment discrimination. [*supra* section 33.53]

    __ Patent litigation. [*supra* section 33.64]

    __ Securities litigation. [*supra* section 33.34]

    __ Takeover litigation. [*supra* section 33.42]

    __ Civil RICO litigation. [*supra* section 33.84]

40.3 Final Pretrial Conference and Preparation for Trial

25. Final Pretrial Conference. [*supra* section 21.6]

__ Status of discovery.

__ Status of final pretrial disclosures (witness/exhibit lists, etc.).

__ Requests for relief from deadlines/preclusion orders.

__ Review statements of uncontested/contested facts. [*supra* sections 21.641, 21.65]

__ Status of motions. [*supra* section 21.66]

    __ Challenges to jurisdiction or venue.

    __ Transfer under 28 U.S.C. § 1404 or 1406.

    __ Summary judgment.

    __ Motions seeking to limit scope of proof.

    __ Issues regarding right to jury trial. [*supra* section 21.62]

__ Rulings on objections to evidence resolvable before trial. [*supra* section 21.642]

    __ Hearings under Fed. R. Evid. 104, as necessary.

    __ Review of preclusion orders.

__ Consider whether to recommend remand under 28 U.S.C. § 1407. [*supra* section 31.133]

__ Cutoff for partial settlements in class or other actions. [*supra* sections 23.21, 30.46]

__ Final pretrial order. [*supra* section 21.67]

26. Trial preparation. [*supra* section 21.6]

__ Set/modify/confirm date and place of trial. [*supra* section 21.61]

__ Trial schedule. [*supra* section 22.11]

    __ Normal hours.

    __ Days of no trial or abbreviated hours.

    __ Holidays; recesses.

__ Structure of trial. [*supra* sections 21.63, 33.28]

    __ Consolidation under Fed. R. Civ. P. 42(a). [*supra* section 21.631]

    __ Class action. [*supra* section 30]

    __ Individual actions.

    __ Transfer under 28 U.S.C. § 1404 or 1406.

    __ Severance under Fed. R. Civ. P. 42(b). [*supra* section 21.632]

        __ Define/confirm issues for trial and those severed for later trial.

        __ If both jury and nonjury issues to be tried: [*supra* section 22.53]

            __ Sequence for receiving jury/nonjury evidence.

            __ Use of advisory verdict.

        __ Schedule for subsequent trials of severed issues.

            __ Timing.

            __ Disposition of jury.

    __ Special procedures for nonjury trial. [*supra* section 22.5]

__ Jury selection. [*supra* section 22.41]

    __ Number of jurors to be called/impaneled.

    __ Number to be selected.

    __ Number of peremptory challenges.

    __ Review of practices used in court for exercising challenges.

    __ Submission of suggested voir dire questions.

    __ Written questionnaires.

        __ Before jury reports.

        __ After jurors given initial instructions.

__ Special procedures to handle problems of publicity. [*supra* section 32.27]

__ Jury management. [*supra* section 22.4]

    __ Note taking. [*supra* section 22.42]

    __ Exhibit books. [*supra* section 22.32]

    __ Questions by jurors. [*supra* section 22.42]

__ Jury instructions.
    __ Content. [*supra* sections 21.65, 22.43]
    __ Timing. [*supra* section 22.43]
    __ Preliminary instructions. [*supra* section 22.432]
    __ Interim and limiting instructions. [*supra* section 22.433]
    __ Final instructions. [*supra* section 22.434]
__ Opening and supplemental statements. [*supra* sections 22.21, 22.34]
__ Order of proof/issues/evidence. [*supra* sections 22.23, 22.34]
    __ Order of presentation.
    __ Sequencing of evidence and arguments. [*supra* section 22.34]
__ Schedule for interim conferences during trial. [*supra* section 22.15, *infra* section 41.63 paragraph 19]
__ Verdict. [*supra* section 22.45]
    __ Form: special or general with interrogatories. [*supra* section 22.451]
    __ Sequential verdicts.
    __ Agreement to accept less than unanimous verdict.
    __ Agreement to accept nonjury decision if jury not unanimous.
    __ Agreement on excusing juror after deliberations begin.
__ Mistrial. [*supra* section 22.44]

27. **Witness and exhibit lists.** [*supra* section 22.23]
__ Time for submission. [*supra* section 21.641]
    __ Sequentially.
    __ Concurrently by all parties.
__ Witness lists.
    __ All witnesses that will be called.
        __ Exception for impeachment evidence.
    __ Witnesses that may be called.
    __ Nature of expected testimony.
        __ Subject matter.
        __ Outline of expected testimony.
        __ Estimated length of testimony.
    __ Depositions.
        __ Designation of portions to be offered.
        __ Preparation of agreed summaries of depositions.
__ Exhibit lists.
    __ All exhibits that will be offered.
        __ Exception for impeachment evidence.
    __ Exhibits that may be offered.

__ Procedures for marking exhibits. [*supra* section 22.13]

    __ Provide copies of exhibits not previously produced.

__ Identify evidence to be offered against fewer than all parties.

__ Use of demonstrative evidence. [*supra* sections 22.31, 34]

__ Statements of facts and evidence. [*supra* section 21.641]

    __ Timing.

    __ Objections.

        __ Certain objections (e.g., authenticity, foundation) waived if not raised.

        __ All objections waived if not raised.

__ Effect of pretrial submissions. [*supra* section 21.67]

    __ Precluding witnesses/exhibits/subject matter not listed:

        __ Exception for impeachment.

    __ Precluding all or certain objections not raised.

28. Limitations on trial evidence.

__ Precluding proof of facts not disclosed on statement of contested facts. [*supra* sections 21.47, 21.641]

__ Precluding/limiting proof of facts not in dispute.

__ Precluding expert testimony unless report filed. [*supra* section 21.48]

__ Limits on quantity of evidence. [*supra* section 22.35]

    __ Culling lists of witnesses/exhibits in light of disputed issues.

        __ Redact excessively long exhibits.

    __ Limit number of expert witnesses.

    __ Limit number of lay witnesses/exhibits on particular subjects.

    __ Limit time for presentation by parties. [*supra* section 21.643]

__ Depositions. [*supra* section 22.33, *infra* section 41.38]

    __ Selected extracts, purged of unnecessary materials. [*supra* section 22.332]

    __ Summaries. [*supra* section 22.331]

__ Adoption of prepared reports as direct testimony, subject to cross-examination. [*supra* section 22.51]

__ Permitting all/specified witnesses to remain in courtroom by not invoking Fed. R. Evid. 615. [*supra* section 22.35]

__ Limiting cross-examination on additional subjects under Fed. R. Evid. 611(b).

__ Use of summaries or samples in lieu of voluminous source documents. [*supra* section 22.32]

29. Briefs. [*supra* section 21.66]

__ Avoiding unnecessary briefs/memoranda.

__ Timetable.

    __ Sequential.

___ Concurrent.

___ Supplemental as trial progresses.

___ Contents.

   ___ Specific issues.

   ___ All probable issues.

   ___ Suggested special verdict/interrogatories. [*supra* section 21.633]

   ___ Proposed findings/conclusions in nonjury cases. [*supra* section 22.52]

___ Limitations.

   ___ Length.

   ___ Limit attachments.

30. Procedures for multiparty cases.

___ Designation of lead/trial counsel. [*supra* section 20.22, *infra* section 41.31]

___ Opening statements. [*supra* section 22.21]

   ___ Order.

   ___ Time limits.

   ___ Nonrepetitive statements by other counsel.

___ Order of presentation of evidence; examination of witnesses. [*supra* section 22.23]

   ___ Fixed order throughout trial.

   ___ Rotation.

   ___ Shifting order, based on principal proponent/adversary of each witness.

   ___ Designate attorney to conduct principal examination (direct or cross) of each witness, with standby counsel, supplemental examination by other counsel. [*supra* section 22.22]

___ Objections/motions, deemed made on behalf of all unless disclaimed (supplementation by other counsel). [*supra* section 22.22]

31. Administrative details.

___ Final trial schedule. [*supra* section 22.11]

___ Order of proof. [*supra* section 22.23]

   ___ Advance notice of expected order of presenting witnesses and documents.

   ___ Notify of changes in schedule as soon as known.

   ___ Notify of changes in deposition designations.

   ___ Notify of portion of document to be offered.

___ Exhibits. [*supra* sections 22.13, 22.31, 22.32]

   ___ Premarked and listed on clerk's exhibit sheets.

   ___ Absent objection, deemed as offered and received when identified.

   ___ Notify counsel before using (to avoid interruptions while they review/locate copies).

   ___ Notice and ruling on demonstrative exhibits.

__ Provide copies for court/jurors of:
    __ Glossaries, indexes, demonstrative aids. [*supra* section 22.31]
    __ Exhibit books.
  __ Enlargements/slides.
  __ Representatives assist clerk in maintaining/indexing list of exhibits received.
__ Arrangements for facilities/equipment. [*supra* section 22.12]
  __ Courtroom arrangement, tables, seating, name plates.
  __ Courthouse access.
  __ Witness/exhibit/conference rooms.
  __ Copying, computer, video, or audio display equipment.
  __ Use of courtroom technology. [*supra* section 34]
__ Guidelines/discussion of courtroom protocol/decorum. [*supra* section 22.24]
  __ Examination of witnesses.
  __ Manner of making objections.
  __ Submission of exhibits to witnesses.
  __ Publication of exhibits to jurors.
  __ Sidebar/chambers conferences.
  __ How/when offers of proof made.
__ Transcripts. [*supra* section 22.14]
  __ Expedited.
  __ Whether to permit independent tape recording of proceedings.
__ Interpreters; translation of documents.
__ Special arrangements if jury sequestered. [*supra* sections 22.44, 32.31]
  __ Hotel/meals.
  __ Transportation.
  __ Family visitation.
  __ Recreation.
  __ Security.
__ Awarding attorneys' fees. [*supra* section 24]
  __ Eligibility for court-awarded fees.
    __ Common fund cases. [*supra* section 24.12]
    __ Statutory fee cases. [*supra* section 24.13]
  __ Proceedings to award fees. [*supra* section 24.2]
__ Judgment and appeal. [*supra* section 25]
  __ Interlocutory appeal. [*supra* section 25.1]
  __ Entry of final judgment. [*supra* section 25.3]

41. Sample Orders and Forms

Note: The sample orders and forms in this section are illustrative and suggestive only, and will need to be adapted to the needs and circumstances of each case. Additional sample orders and forms may be found in the *Federal Rules of Civil Procedure Appendix of Forms* and in the *Manual for Litigation Management and Cost and Delay Reduction* (Federal Judicial Center 1992).

41.1 Typical Format—Orders in Multiple Litigation

UNITED STATES DISTRICT COURT
_____ DISTRICT OF _____

In re:) Master File No. _____ [1]
)
_____ [2] LITIGATION)
) This Document Relates To:
) [All Cases]

Order No. _____ [3]

[Preamble]

[Body of Order]

Dated: _____

_____
United States District Judge

Attachments:
_____ [4]

Notes:

1. In its order establishing a master case file—a decision that is frequently deferred until the initial conference—the court should include provisions such as those contained in *infra* section 41.30,

paragraph 1, and specify a master file number. The multidistrict litigation (MDL) number is used if the litigation includes cases transferred under 28 U.S.C. § 1407. Documents that apply generally to all constituent cases are so identified; those that apply only to particular cases should specify in their captions or by a separate list the style or case number of such cases.

2. Courts frequently assign multiple litigation a descriptive name, both to serve as an abbreviated caption in orders, pleadings, and other documents, and to minimize confusion if parties are changed or cases dismissed. In multidistrict proceedings under 28 U.S.C. § 1407, the name given by the Judicial Panel on Multidistrict Litigation is used.

3. If many orders may be entered during the litigation, the court should number its major orders sequentially for convenient reference. An explanatory description of the nature of the order is often added. Transcripts of conferences at which rulings are made should be included in the numerical sequence if no separate order incorporating these rulings will be prepared.

4. For ease of drafting, as well as reference, append lists and lengthy directives (such as a protective order for confidential documents) as attachments rather than including them within the body of an order. Sample orders and other materials from *MCL Third* may be incorporated by reference.

41.2 Sample Order Setting Initial Conference

[caption]

Order No. _____

(Setting Initial Conference)

It appearing that [the above styled case(s)] [the cases listed on Attachment _____] may merit special attention as complex litigation, the court ORDERS:

1. **Initial Conference.** All parties shall appear for a conference with the undersigned on the ____ day of _____ [date] _____ , at ____ A.M./P.M. in [Court]room _____ , United States Courthouse, _____ .

    (a) **Attendance.** To minimize costs and facilitate a manageable conference, parties are not required to attend the conference, and parties with similar interests are expected to agree to the extent practicable on a single attorney to act on their joint behalf at the conference. A party will not, by designating an attorney to represent its interests at the conference, be precluded from other representation during the litigation; and attendance at the conference will not waive objections to jurisdiction, venue, or service.[1]

    (b) **Service List.** This order is being mailed to the persons shown on Attachment _____ , which has been prepared from the list of counsel making appearances with the Judicial Panel on Multidistrict Litigation. Counsel on this list are requested to forward a copy of the order to other attorneys who should be notified of the conference. A corrected service list will be prepared after the conference.

    (c) **Other Participants.** Persons who are not named as parties in this litigation but may later be joined as parties or are parties in related litigation pending in other federal and state courts are invited to attend in person or by counsel.

2. **Purposes; Agenda.** The conference will be held for the purposes specified in Fed. R. Civ. P. 16(a), 16(b), 16(c), and 26(f) and subject to the sanctions prescribed in Rule 16(f). A tentative agenda is appended as Attachment ____.[2] Counsel are encouraged to advise the court as soon as possible of any items that should be added to the agenda.

3. **Preparations for Conference.**

    (a) **Procedures for Complex Litigation.** Counsel are expected to familiarize themselves with the *Manual for Complex Litigation, Third*, and be prepared at the conference to suggest procedures that will facilitate the just, speedy, and inexpensive resolution of this litigation.

(b) **Initial Conference of Counsel.** Before the conference, counsel shall confer and seek consensus to the extent possible with respect to the items on the agenda, including a proposed discovery plan under Rule 26(f) and a suggested schedule under Rule 16(b) for joinder of parties, amendment of pleadings, consideration of any class action allegations, motions, and trial. [The court designates _____ _____ and _____ _____ to arrange the initial meetings of plaintiff's and defendants' counsel, respectively.]³

(c) **Preliminary Reports.** Counsel will submit to the court by____[date]____, a brief written statement indicating their preliminary understanding of the facts involved in the litigation and the critical factual and legal issues. These statements will not be filed with the clerk, will not be binding, will not waive claims or defenses, and may not be offered in evidence against a party in later proceedings.

(d) **List of Affiliated Companies and Counsel.** To assist the court in identifying any problems of recusal or disqualification, counsel will submit to the court by _____[date]_____, a list of all companies affiliated with the parties and all counsel associated in the litigation.

(e) **List of Pending Motions.** Counsel's statement shall list all pending motions.

(f) **List of Related Cases.** Counsel's statement shall list all related cases pending in state or federal court and their current status, to the extent known.

4. **Interim Measures.** Until otherwise ordered by the court:

(a) **Admission of Counsel.** Attorneys admitted to practice and in good standing in any United States District Court are admitted *pro hac vice* in this litigation. Association of local cocounsel is not required.

(b) **Pleadings.** Each defendant is granted an extension of time for responding by motion or answer to the complaint(s) until a date to be set at the conference.

(c) **Pending and New Discovery.** Pending the conference, all outstanding disclosure and discovery proceedings are stayed and no further discovery shall be initiated. This order does not (1) preclude voluntary informal discovery regarding the identification and location of relevant documents and witnesses; (2) preclude parties from stipulating to the conduct of a deposition that has already been scheduled; (3) prevent a party from voluntarily making disclosure, responding to an outstanding discovery request under Rule 33, 34, or 36; or (4) authorize a party to suspend its efforts in gathering information needed to respond to a request under Rule 33, 34, or 36. Relief from this stay may be granted for good cause shown, such as the ill health of a proposed deponent.

(d) **Preservation of Records.** Each party shall preserve all documents and other records containing information potentially relevant to the subject matter of this litigation. Each party shall also preserve any physical evidence or potential evidence and shall not conduct any testing that alters the physical evidence without notifying opposing counsel and, unless counsel stipulate to the test, without obtaining the court's permission to conduct the test. Subject to further order of the court, parties may continue routine erasures of computerized data pursuant to existing programs, but they shall (1) immediately notify opposing counsel about such programs and (2) preserve any printouts of such data. Requests for relief from this directive will receive prompt attention from the court.

(e) **Motions.** No motion shall be filed under Rules 11, 12, or 56 without leave of court and unless it includes a certificate that the movant has conferred with opposing counsel in a good faith effort to resolve the matter without court action.

[(f) **Orders of Transferor Courts.** All orders by transferor courts imposing dates for pleading or discovery are vacated.]

5. **Later Filed Cases.** This order shall also apply to related cases later filed in, removed to, or transferred to this court.

6. **Other Provisions.** [Include any special instructions, such as procedures for presenting emergency matters prior to conference.]

Dated:_____

_____

United States District Judge

Attachments: [Omitted]

Notes:

1. In some cases the court may decide that the parties themselves should attend the conference with their counsel. See *supra* section 21.23.

2. As an alternative, the clause might read, "The items listed in the *MCL Third*, sections 21.21 and 40.1, shall, to the extent applicable, constitute a tentative agenda."

3. Designation of attorneys to organize these initial meetings may be useful both to fix responsibility and to reduce early factionalism among those interested in becoming lead or liaison counsel. The attorneys designated by the court need not be persons who would be considered for appointment as lead or liaison counsel.

41.3 Sample Case-Management Orders

41.30 General

[caption]

Order No. _____

(Initial Case-Management Order)

Having considered the comments and proposals of the parties presented at the initial conference held _____[date]_____, the court ORDERS:

1. **Pretrial Consolidation.** The cases listed on Attachment _____ are, until further order, consolidated for pretrial purposes. This order does not constitute a determination that these actions should be consolidated for trial, nor does it have the effect of making any entity a party to an action in which it has not been joined and served in accordance with the Federal Rules of Civil Procedure.

    (a) **Master Docket and File.** The clerk will maintain a master docket and case file under the style "In re _____ LITIGATION," master file number _____ . All orders, pleadings, motions, and other documents will, when filed and docketed in the master case file, be deemed filed and docketed in each individual case to the extent applicable.

    (b) **Captions; Separate Filing.** Orders, pleading, motions, and other documents will bear a caption similar to that of this Order.[1] If generally applicable to all consolidated actions, they shall include in their caption the notation that they relate to "ALL CASES" and be filed and docketed only in the master file. Documents intended to apply only to particular cases will indicate in their caption the case number of the case(s) to which they apply, and extra copies shall be provided to the clerk to facilitate filing and docketing both in the master case file and the specified individual case files.

(c) **Discovery Requests and Responses.** Pursuant to Fed. R. Civ. P. 5(d), discovery requests and responses will not be filed with the court except when specifically ordered by the court or to the extent offered in connection with a motion.[2]

[(d) **Coordinated Actions.** The actions listed on Attachment _____ are not consolidated for pretrial purposes at the present time, but discovery in such cases shall be coordinated with that in the consolidated actions to prevent duplication and conflicts.][3]

2. **Organization of Counsel.**[4]

(a) **Plaintiffs.** To act on behalf of plaintiffs with the responsibilities prescribed in [Attachment _____] [*infra* section 41.31], the court designates—

(1) as Liaison Counsel:

_____[name, address, telephone number]_____

(2) as Lead Counsel:

_____[name, address, telephone number]_____

(3) as additional members of Plaintiffs' Steering Committee:

_____[names, addresses, telephone numbers]_____

_____

_____

(b) **Defendants.** To act as Liaison counsel on behalf of all defendants [except defendant(s) _____] with the responsibilities prescribed in [Attachment _____] [*infra* section 41.31, paragraph 4], the court designates _____[name, address, telephone number]_____

_____.

(c) **Reimbursement.** If agreement cannot be reached on a method for periodically reimbursing attorneys for expenses incurred and paying them for services rendered as lead or liaison counsel, the matter will be presented to the court for resolution.

(d) **Time Records.** Counsel who anticipate seeking an award of attorneys' fees from the court shall comply with the directives contained in [Attachment _____] [*infra* section 41.32] regarding the maintenance and filing of contemporaneous records reflecting the services performed and the expenses incurred.

3. **Service of Documents.**

(a) **Orders.** A copy of each order will be provided to Plaintiffs' Liaison Counsel and Defendants' Liaison Counsel for distribution as appropriate to other counsel and parties. [A copy shall also be provided to counsel for defendant(s) _____ .]

(b) **Pleadings, Motions, and Other Documents.** Plaintiffs' Liaison Counsel will be provided with ____ copies of each pleading, motion, or other document filed by a party; Defendants' Liaison Counsel will be provided with _____ copies of each such document. [Pursuant to Fed. R. Civ. P. 5, service on Liaison Counsel constitutes service on other attorneys and parties for whom Liaison Counsel is acting, such service being deemed effective seven days after service on Liaison Counsel.[5]]

4. **Refinement of Issues.**

(a) **Rule 12 Motions.** [Include rulings on pending Rule 12 motions if appropriate, or establish dates for filing, briefs, and arguments. For example, "The motions of defendants A.B. and C.D. to dismiss the complaint of plaintiff E.F. for failure to state a claim on which relief may be granted are, upon consideration, DENIED. A similar motion is hereby deemed filed by each other defendant, and the same order deemed made on each such motion."]

(b) **Pleadings.** Each defendant shall have until _____[date]_____ , to file its answer to the complaint, including any cross claims or counterclaims. Answers to any cross claims or counterclaims will be filed by _____[date]_____ . Except for good cause shown, no additional parties may be joined as plaintiff, defendant, or third-party defendant after _____[date]_____ .

(c) **Summary Judgment.** The following issues may be submitted for early resolution on motions under Fed. R. Civ. P. 56: _____
_____
_____ .

Subject to further order of the court, motions seeking summary judgment on these issues will be filed with supporting affidavits and briefs by ___[date]___. Opposing affidavits and briefs will be filed by ___[date]___ , and any reply briefs by _____[date]_____ .

(d) **Class Action.** Plaintiffs will file by ___[date]___ , their motion seeking class certification, identifying the class(es) for which certification is sought, detailing the facts on which satisfaction of the requirements of Fed. R. Civ. P. 23 is asserted, and describing what and how notice will be given to class members. Defendants will file by _____[date]_____ , any objections to class certification, specifying with particularity the factual and legal basis of their objection and identifying any facts on which an evidentiary dispute exists. A hearing will be conducted by the court under Rule 23(c) on ___[date]___ , at which time the parties may present extracts of depositions, responses to interrogatories, and documentary evidence relevant to any factual disputes. Only on a showing of good cause will a party be permitted to call a witness to testify in person at the hearing.

5. **Discovery.**

    (a) **Schedule.** Discovery shall be conducted according to the schedule attached as Attachment _____ [*infra* section 41.33]. All discovery [other than on the issue(s) of _____] shall be completed by _____ [date] _____ .

    (b) **General Limitations.** All discovery requests and responses are subject to the requirements of Fed. R. Civ. P. 26(b)(1) and (2) and (g). Discovery shall not, without prior approval of the court, be taken of putative class members or of persons in countries outside the United States; and any request for such discovery shall indicate why the discovery is needed and the specific information or documents sought.

    (c) **Confidentiality Order.** See Attachment _____ [*infra* section 41.36].

    (d) **Documents.**

        (1) Preservation. See Attachment _____ [*infra* section 41.34].

        (2) Numbering System. Counsel shall develop and use a system for identifying by a unique number or symbol each document produced or referred to during the course of this litigation. All copies of the same document should ordinarily be assigned the same identification number.

        (3) Document Depositories. See Attachment _____ [*infra* section 41.35].

        (4) Avoidance of Multiple Requests. Counsel shall, to the extent possible, coordinate and consolidate their requests for production and examination of documents to eliminate duplicative requests from the same party. No party shall request documents available to it at a document depository or from its own Liaison Counsel.

    (e) **Interrogatories.** Counsel shall, to the extent possible, combine their interrogatories to any party into a single set of questions. No question shall be asked that has already been answered in response to interrogatories filed by another party unless there is reason to believe that a different answer will be given. [Without leave of court, interrogatories shall not include more than _____ separate questions, including subparts.]

    (f) **Depositions.** See Attachment _____ [*infra* section 41.38].

    (g) **Special Agreements.** All parties shall be under a continuing duty to make prompt disclosure to the court (and, unless excused by the court for good cause shown, to other parties) of the existence and terms of all agreements and understandings, formal or informal, absolute or conditional, settling or limiting their rights or liabilities in this litigation. This obligation includes not only settlements, but also such matters as "loan receipt" and "Mary Carter" arrangements, and insurance, indemnification, contribution, and damage-sharing agreements.

6. **Trial.** Subject to further order of the court, the parties are directed to be ready for trial on all issues [except _____] by _____ [date] _____ .

[Counsel are advised that the court will require a listing in advance of trial of the factual contentions each party expects to prove at the trial, identifying the witnesses and documents to be presented in support of each such contention, and may preclude the presentation of any contention, witness, or document not so identified.]

7. **Next Conference.** The next pretrial conference is [tentatively] scheduled for _____ ____ [date] _____ .

8. **Later Filed Cases.** The terms of this order, including pretrial consolidation, shall apply automatically to actions later instituted in, removed to, or transferred to this court (including cases transferred for pretrial purposes under 28 U.S.C. § 1407) that involve claims of _____ .
Objections to such consolidation or other terms of this order shall promptly be filed, with a copy served on liaison counsel for plaintiffs and defendants.

Dated: _____

_____
United States District Judge

Attachments: [Omitted]

Notes:

1. See *supra* section 41.1.

2. As a means of keeping advised of the progress of discovery without unnecessarily burdening the clerk's office, the court may wish to add this provision: "At the time of requesting or responding to discovery, the parties shall file with the clerk a one-page notice indicating the nature of the discovery request or response."

3. Coordination of discovery, including use of joint notices for common depositions, is often appropriate even if consolidation is not warranted.

4. This order provides for appointment of only liaison counsel for defendants while providing for appointment of liaison counsel, lead counsel, and a steering committee for plaintiffs. In many cases, of course, the same organizational structure for both plaintiffs and defendants will be appropriate.

5. To assure that each liaison counsel has a complete file, copies of all documents should be served on both liaison counsel even if individual service is also to be made on other attorneys and parties. If the court directs under Fed. R. Civ. P. 5 that service on all opposing counsel may be made by serving liaison counsel, some additional time should be provided for liaison counsel to make distribution among those counsel and parties interested in a particular document.

41.31 Responsibilities of Designated Counsel

Responsibilities of Designated Counsel

It is ORDERED

1. **Plaintiffs' Lead Counsel.** Plaintiffs' Lead Counsel shall be generally responsible for coordinating the activities of plaintiffs during pretrial proceedings and shall:

   (a) determine (after such consultation with other members of Plaintiffs' Steering Committee and other cocounsel as may be appropriate) and present (in briefs, oral argument, or such other fashion as may be appropriate, personally or by a designee) to the court and opposing parties the position of the plaintiffs on all matters arising during pretrial proceedings;

   (b) coordinate the initiation and conduct of discovery on behalf of plaintiffs consistent with the requirements of Fed. R. Civ. P. 26 (b)(1) and (2), and (g), including the preparation of joint interrogatories and requests for production of documents and the examination of witnesses in depositions;

   (c) conduct settlement negotiations on behalf of plaintiffs, but not enter binding agreements except to the extent expressly authorized;

   (d) delegate specific tasks to other counsel in a manner to ensure that pretrial preparation for the plaintiffs is conducted effectively, efficiently, and economically;

   (e) enter into stipulations, with opposing counsel, necessary for the conduct of the litigation;

   (f) prepare and distribute to the parties periodic status reports;

   (g) maintain adequate time and disbursement records covering services as lead counsel;

   (h) monitor the activities of cocounsel to ensure that schedules are met and unnecessary expenditures of time and funds are avoided; and

   (i) perform such other duties as may be incidental to proper coordination of plaintiffs' pretrial activities or authorized by further order of the court.

   Counsel for plaintiffs who disagree with lead counsel (or those acting on behalf of lead counsel) or who have individual or divergent positions may present written and oral arguments, conduct examinations of deponents, and otherwise act separately on behalf of their client(s) as appropriate, provided that in doing so they do not repeat arguments, questions, or actions of lead counsel.

2. **Plaintiffs' Liaison Counsel.** Plaintiffs' Liaison Counsel shall:

    (a) maintain and distribute to cocounsel and to Defendants' Liaison Counsel an up-to-date service list;

    (b) receive and, as appropriate, distribute to cocounsel orders from the court [and documents from opposing parties and counsel];

    (c) maintain and make available to cocounsel at reasonable hours a complete file of all documents served by or upon each party [except such documents as may be available at a document depository]; and

    (d) establish and maintain a document depository.

3. **Plaintiffs' Steering Committee.** The other members of Plaintiffs' Steering Committee shall from time to time consult with Plaintiffs' Lead and Liaison Counsel in coordinating the plaintiffs' pretrial activities and in planning for trial.

4. **Defendants' Liaison Counsel.** Defendants' Liaison Counsel shall:

    (a) maintain and distribute to cocounsel and to Plaintiffs' Liaison Counsel an up-to-date service list;

    (b) receive and, as appropriate, distribute to cocounsel orders from the court [and documents from opposing parties and counsel];

    (c) maintain and make available to cocounsel at reasonable hours a complete file of all documents served by or upon each party [except such documents as may be available at a document depository];

    (d) establish and maintain a document depository; and

    (e) call meetings of cocounsel for the purpose of coordinating discovery, presentations at pretrial conferences, and other pretrial activities.

5. **Privileges Preserved.** No communication among plaintiffs' counsel or among defendants' counsel shall be taken as a waiver of any privilege or protection to which they would otherwise be entitled.

Dated: _____

_____
United States District Judge

41.32 Attorneys' Time and Expense Records

Attorneys' Time and Expense Records

It is ORDERED:

1. **Maintenance of Contemporaneous Records.** All counsel shall keep a daily record of their time spent and expenses incurred in connection with this litigation, indicating with specificity the hours, location, and particular activity [such as "conduct of deposition of A.B."]. The failure to maintain such records will be grounds for denying court-awarded attorneys' fees, as will an insufficient description of the activity (such as "research" or "review of correspondence").[1]

2. **Filing.**[2] By the fifteenth day of each month, each firm that may seek an award (or approval) of a fee by the court shall file [under seal with the clerk] [with Lead Counsel] a report summarizing according to each separate activity the time and expenses spent by its members or associates during the preceding month (and the ordinary billing rates of such attorneys in effect during such month) and the accumulated total of the firm's time, hourly rates, and expenses to date. [Lead Counsel shall file under seal with the clerk by the last day of the month a report summarizing for all participating counsel such time and expenses reports, arranged according to the particular activities.]

Dated: _____

_____

United States District Judge

Notes:

1. The court may wish to include more specific guidelines concerning staffing, hourly rates, reimbursable expenses, and required documentation. See *supra* sections 24.21–24.22.

2. In cases in which the court may award fees, time and expense records should ordinarily be submitted through lead counsel, if one has been appointed, in order to assist lead counsel in monitoring the activities of cocounsel and in preparing a single, consolidated report for filing with the court. See *supra* section 24.212.

41.33 Scheduling Order

Scheduling Order

It is ORDERED:

1. Discovery[1] shall be conducted according to the following schedule:

Discovery	Time[2]
Interrogatories by all parties to ascertain identity and location of witnesses and documents, including computerized records	_____
Document production by all parties	_____
Lay-witness depositions • noticed by plaintiffs • noticed by defendants	 _____ _____
Expert(s): • plaintiffs: – submission of reports – depositions • defendants: – submission of reports – depositions	 _____ _____ _____ _____
Production of proposed computerized summaries and samples: • by plaintiffs • by defendants	 _____ _____

2. Except for good cause shown—

   (a) relief from the above schedule shall not be granted and all discovery shall be completed by _____[date]_____;[3]

   (b) discovery shall be limited to matters occurring after _____[date]_____ , [and before _____[date]_____];

(c)   no more than _____ interrogatories (including subparts) may be pro-pounded to any party (exclusive of interrogatories seeking the identity and loca-tion of witnesses and documents);

[(d) no more than _____ depositions may be taken by either plaintiffs or defendants, and no single deposition (other than of_____) may take more than _____ hours/days;]⁴ and

(e)   no amendment of pleadings may be made after _____[date]_____ , and no additional parties may be joined as plaintiff, defendant, or third-party defen-dant after ____[date]_____ .

3.   The parties are expected to be prepared for trial on all issues [except_____
_____]
      by_____[date]_____.

Dated: _____

                                        _____
                                        United States District Judge

Notes:

1. Where prediscovery disclosure is to occur, appropriate provision should be made in the order.

2. The time for undertaking or completing some aspect of discovery may be stated either by us-ing specific dates or by reference to completion of discovery that should precede it. The listing in this sample order of certain forms of discovery is not intended to suggest that they should be under-taken in this sequence or that each item should be completed before other discovery is undertaken. For example, in many cases, depositions should be conducted by both sides during the same period of time, during which the parties may also be involved in preparing answers to interrogatories and responses to requests for admission.

3. The extent to which a schedule for all discovery can be established at the initial conference will depend on the circumstances of the litigation. In some complex cases it may be feasible to establish a timetable only for certain portions of discovery, leaving for subsequent conferences the setting of a schedule for other discovery and a final cutoff date for all discovery. In other cases, a comprehensive discovery schedule—which may even include dates for preparation and submission of a joint state-ment of contested and uncontested facts and for identification of trial witnesses and documents—can be established at the initial conference.

4. Other restrictions on discovery may be added.

41.34 Preservation of Records

Order for Preservation of Records[1]

It is ORDERED:

1. **Preservation.** During the pendency of this litigation, and for _____ days after entry of a final order closing all cases, each of the parties herein and their respective officers, agents, servants, employees, and attorneys, and all persons in active concert or participation with them who receive actual notice of this order by personal service or otherwise, are restrained and enjoined from altering, interlining, destroying, permitting the destruction of, or in any other fashion changing any "document" in the actual or constructive care, custody, or control of such person, wherever such document is physically located, or irrevocably changing the form or sequence of the files in which the document is located. Such persons are also enjoined from changing the location of any such documents except to facilitate compilation, review, or production (as by filing in a document depository).

2. **Scope.**

    (a) "Document" shall mean any writing, drawing, film, videotape, chart, photograph, phonograph record, tape record, mechanical or electronic sound recording or transcript thereof, retrievable data (whether carded, taped coded, electrostatically or electromagnetically recorded, or otherwise), or other data compilation from which information can be obtained, including (but not limited to) notices, memoranda, diaries, minutes, purchase records, purchase invoices, market data, correspondence, computer storage tapes, computer storage cards or disks, books, journals, ledgers, statements, reports, invoices, bills, vouchers, worksheets, jottings, notes, letters, abstracts, audits, charts, checks, diagrams, drafts, recordings, instructions, lists, logs, orders, recitals, telegram messages, telephone bills and logs, résumés, summaries, compilations, computations, and other formal and informal writings or tangible preservations of information.

    (b) This order pertains only to documents containing information that may be relevant to, or may lead to the discovery of information relevant to, [_____ _____describe general subject matter of litigation_____] [which have been written or generated after ____[date]___, and before ___[date]___]. Any document described or referred to in any discovery request or response made during this litigation shall, from the time of the request or response, be treated for purposes of this order as containing such information unless and until the court rules such information to be irrelevant.

(c) Counsel are directed to confer to resolve questions as to what documents are outside the scope of this order or otherwise need not be preserved and as to an earlier date for permissible destruction of particular categories of documents. If counsel are unable to agree, any party may apply to the court for clarification or relief from this order upon reasonable notice. A party failing, within 60 days after receiving written notice from another party that specified documents will be destroyed, lost, or otherwise altered pursuant to routine policies and programs, to indicate in writing its objection shall be deemed to have agreed to such destruction.

3. **Implementation.** Each party will, within 10 days after receiving this order, designate an individual who shall be responsible for ensuring that the party carries out the requirements of this order.

Dated: _____

_____
United States District Judge

Note:
  1. See *supra* section 21.442.

41.35 Document Depositories

Order for Establishment of Document Depositories

It is ORDERED:

1. **Establishment of Depositories.** Document depositories shall be established in ____[specify city]____ at such locations as the parties may agree upon. In the absence of agreement, the court upon motion shall designate such locations. Documents produced by plaintiffs pursuant to formal or informal request shall be placed in a plaintiff's depository maintained at the expense of plaintiffs; those produced by defendants pursuant to formal or informal request shall be placed in a defendant's depository maintained at the expense of defendants. Each depository will contain equipment for producing copies and separately counting the copies that are made for each party.

2. **Filing System.** The filing party shall place the documents in the depository in sequential order according to the document numbers, and the documents shall be organized in groups in accordance with the document identification prefixes. Documents without identification numbers shall be organized in an orderly and logical fashion. Existing English translations of all foreign-language documents shall be filed with the documents.[1]

3. **Access, Copying, Log.** Counsel appearing for any party in this litigation and the staffs of their respective law firms working on these cases shall have reasonable access during business hours to each document in any such depository and may copy or obtain copies at the inspecting parties' expense. Such inspection shall not be subject to monitoring by any party. A log will be kept of all persons who enter and leave the depository, and only duplicate copies of documents may be removed from the depository except by leave of court. [Access to, and copying of, confidential documents is subject to the limitations and requirements of the order protecting against unauthorized disclosure of such documents.]

4. **Subsequent Filings.** After the initial deposit of documents in the depository, notice shall be given to both Liaison Counsel of all subsequent deposits.

Dated:_____

_____
United States District Judge

Note:

1. Provision may be made for use of CD-ROM or other appropriate technology. See *supra* section 21.444.

41.36 Confidentiality Orders and Acknowledgment

Confidentiality Order (Form A)

To expedite the flow of discovery material, facilitate the prompt resolution of disputes over confidentiality, protect adequately material entitled to be kept confidential, and ensure that protection is afforded only to material so entitled, it is, pursuant to the court's authority under Fed. R. Civ. P. 26(c) and with the consent of the parties, ORDERED:

1. **Nondisclosure of Stamped Confidential Documents.** Except with the prior written consent of the party or other person originally designating a document to be stamped as a confidential document, or as hereinafter provided under this order, no stamped confidential document may be disclosed to any person.

    [A "stamped confidential document" means any document which bears the legend (or which shall otherwise have had the legend recorded upon it in a way that brings it to the attention of a reasonable examiner) "Confidential—Subject to Protective Order in Civil Action No._____ , United States District Court,_____ District of _____ " to signify that it contains information believed to be subject to protection under Fed. R. Civ. P. 26(c). For purposes of this order, the term "document" means all written, recorded, or graphic material, whether produced or created by a party or another person, whether produced pursuant to Rule 34, subpoena, by agreement, or otherwise. Interrogatory answers, responses to requests for admission, deposition transcripts and exhibits, pleadings, motions, affidavits, and briefs that quote, summarize, or contain materials entitled to protection may be accorded status as a stamped confidential document, but, to the extent feasible, shall be prepared in such a manner that the confidential information is bound separately from that not entitled to protection.]

2. **Permissible Disclosures.** Notwithstanding paragraph 1, stamped confidential documents may be disclosed to counsel for the parties in this action[1] who are actively engaged in the conduct of this litigation; to the partners, associates, secretaries, paralegal assistants, and employees of such counsel to the extent reasonably necessary to render professional services in the litigation; to persons with prior knowledge of the documents or the confidential information contained therein, and their agents; and to court officials involved in this litigation (including court reporters, persons operating video recording equipment at depositions, and any special master appointed by the court). Subject to the provisions of subparagraph (c), such documents may also be disclosed—

(a) to any person designated by the court in the interest of justice, upon such terms as the court may deem proper; and

(b) to persons noticed for depositions or designated as trial witnesses to the extent reasonably necessary in preparing to testify; to outside consultants or experts retained for the purpose of assisting counsel in the litigation; to employees of parties involved solely in one or more aspects of organizing, filing, coding, converting, storing, or retrieving data or designing programs for handling data connected with these actions, including the performance of such duties in relation to a computerized litigation support system; and to employees of third-party contractors performing one or more of these functions; provided, however, that in all such cases the individual to whom disclosure is to be made has signed and filed with the court a form containing—

(1) a recital that the signatory has read and understands this order;

(2) a recital that the signatory understands that unauthorized disclosures of the stamped confidential documents constitute contempt of court; and

(3) a statement that the signatory consents to the exercise of personal jurisdiction by this court.

(c) Before disclosing a stamped confidential document to any person listed in subparagraph (a) or (b) who is a competitor (or an employee of a competitor) of the party that so designated the document, the party wishing to make such disclosure shall give at least 10 days' advance notice in writing to the counsel who designated such information as confidential, stating the names and addresses of the person(s) to whom the disclosure will be made, identifying with particularity the documents to be disclosed, and stating the purposes of such disclosure. If, within the 10-day period, a motion is filed objecting to the proposed disclosure, disclosure is not permissible until the court has denied such motion. The court will deny the motion unless the objecting party shows good cause why the proposed disclosure should not be permitted.

3. **Declassification.** A party (or aggrieved entity permitted by the court to intervene for such purpose) may apply to the court for a ruling that a document (or category of documents) stamped as confidential is not entitled to such status and protection. The party or other person that designated the document as confidential shall be given notice of the application and an opportunity to respond. To maintain confidential status, the proponent of confidentiality must show by a preponderance of the evidence that there is good cause for the document to have such protection.

4. Confidential Information in Depositions.

(a) A deponent may during the deposition be shown and examined about stamped confidential documents if the deponent already knows the confidential information contained therein or if the provisions of paragraph 2(c) are complied with.

Deponents shall not retain or copy portions of the transcript of their depositions that contain confidential information not provided by them or the entities they represent unless they sign the form prescribed in paragraph 2(b). A deponent who is not a party or a representative of a party shall be furnished a copy of this order before being examined about, or asked to produce, potentially confidential documents.

(b) Parties (and deponents) may, within 15 days after receiving a deposition, designate pages of the transcript (and exhibits thereto) as confidential. Confidential information within the deposition transcript may be designated by underlining the portions of the pages that are confidential and marking such pages with the following legend: "Confidential—Subject to Protection Pursuant to Court Order." Until expiration of the 15-day period, the entire deposition will be treated as subject to protection against disclosure under this order. If no party or deponent timely designates confidential information in a deposition, then none of the transcript or its exhibits will be treated as confidential; if a timely designation is made, the confidential portions and exhibits shall be filed under seal separate from the portions and exhibits not so marked.

5. **Confidential Information at Trial.** Subject to the Federal Rules of Evidence, stamped confidential documents and other confidential information may be offered in evidence at trial or any court hearing, provided that the proponent of the evidence gives five days' advance notice to counsel for any party or other person that designated the information as confidential. Any party may move the court for an order that the evidence be received *in camera* or under other conditions to prevent unnecessary disclosure. The court will then determine whether the proffered evidence should continue to be treated as confidential information and, if so, what protection, if any, may be afforded to such information at the trial.

6. **Subpoena by Other Courts or Agencies.** If another court or an administrative agency subpoenas or orders production of stamped confidential documents that a party has obtained under the terms of this order, such party shall promptly notify the party or other person who designated the document as confidential of the pendency of such subpoena or order.

7. **Filing.** Stamped confidential documents need not be filed with the clerk except when required in connection with motions under Fed. R. Civ. P. 12 or 56 or other matters pending before the court. If filed, they shall be filed under seal and shall remain sealed while in the office of the clerk so long as they retain their status as stamped confidential documents.

8. **Client Consultation.** Nothing in this order shall prevent or otherwise restrict counsel from rendering advice to their clients and, in the course thereof, relying generally on examination of stamped confidential documents; provided, however, that in rendering such advice and otherwise communicating with such clients, counsel shall not

make specific disclosure of any item so designated except pursuant to the procedures of paragraphs 2(b) and (c).

9. **Prohibited Copying.** If a document contains information so sensitive that it should not be copied by anyone, it shall bear the additional legend "Copying Prohibited." Application for relief from this restriction against copying may be made to the court, with notice to counsel so designating the document.

10. **Use.** Persons obtaining access to stamped confidential documents under this order shall use the information only for preparation and trial of this litigation (including appeals and retrials), and shall not use such information for any other purpose, including business, governmental, commercial, administrative, or judicial proceedings. [For purposes of this paragraph, the term "this litigation" includes other related litigation in which the producing person or company is a party.]

11. **Non-Termination.** The provisions of this order shall not terminate at the conclusion of these actions. Within 120 days after final conclusion of all aspects of this litigation, stamped confidential documents and all copies of same (other than exhibits of record) shall be returned to the party or person that produced such documents or, at the option of the producer (if it retains at least one copy of the same), destroyed. All counsel of record shall make certification of compliance herewith and shall deliver the same to counsel for the party who produced the documents and not more than 150 days after final termination of this litigation.

12. **Modification Permitted.** Nothing in this order shall prevent any party or other person from seeking modification of this order or from objecting to discovery that it believes to be otherwise improper.

13. **Responsibility of Attorneys.** The attorneys of record are responsible for employing reasonable measures, consistent with this order, to control duplication of, access to, and distribution of copies of stamped confidential documents. Parties shall not duplicate any stamped confidential document except working copies and for filing in court under seal.

14. **No Waiver.**

    (a) Review of the confidential documents and information by counsel, experts, or consultants for the litigants in the litigation shall not waive the confidentiality of the documents or objections to production.

    (b) The inadvertent, unintentional, or *in camera* disclosure of confidential document and information shall not, under any circumstances, be deemed a waiver, in whole or in part, of any party's claims of confidentiality.

15. Nothing contained in this protective order and no action taken pursuant to it shall prejudice the right of any party to contest the alleged relevancy, admissibility, or discoverability of the confidential documents and information sought.

Dated: _____

_____
United States District Judge

Acknowledgment of Protective Order and Agreement To Be Bound

_____ states as follows:

1. That s/he resides at _____
   in the city and county of _____
   and state of _____ ;

2. That s/he has read and understands the protective order dated _____[date]_____ ,
   entered in the _____ litigation;

3. That s/he

   (a) is engaged as a consultant or expert, or

   (b) has been interviewed by _____ on behalf of
   _____ in the preparation and
   conduct of one or more of the cases consolidated under the Transfer Order in
   MDL No. _____ . In re _____litigation;

4. That s/he agrees to comply with and be bound by the provisions of the protective order;

5. That counsel who has retained or consulted with her/him has explained the terms thereof;

6. That s/he will not divulge to persons other than those specifically authorized by paragraph 2 of the protective order, and will not copy or use, except solely for purposes of this litigation, any confidential document or information as defined by the protective order, except as provided therein.

_____
(name of individual to whom disclosure will be made)

Note:

1. The order should indicate whether disclosure may be made to house counsel actively involved in the conduct of the litigation and to attorneys involved in related litigation in other courts.

Confidentiality Order (Form B)

It is hereby ordered that the following provisions shall govern claims of confidentiality in these proceedings:

(a) Only documents containing trade secrets, special formulas, company security matters, customer lists, financial data, projected sales data, production data, matters relating to mergers and acquisitions, and data which touch upon the topic of price may be designated "confidential," provided such documents have not previously been disclosed by the producing party to anyone except those in its employment or those retained by it. Such documents or parts thereof will be designated after review by an attorney for the producing party by stamping the word "confidential" on each page.

(b) If any party believes a document not described in the above paragraph should nevertheless be considered confidential, it may make application to the Court or Special Master. Such application shall only be granted for reasons shown and for extraordinary grounds.

(c) Documents designated "confidential" shall be shown only to the attorneys, the parties, parties' experts, actual or proposed witnesses, and other persons whom the attorneys deem necessary to review the documents for the prosecution or defense of this lawsuit. Each person who is permitted to see confidential documents shall first be shown a copy of this Order and shall further be advised of the obligation to honor the confidentiality designation.

(d) If a party believes that a document designated or sought to be designated confidential by the producing party does not warrant such designation, it shall first make a good faith effort to resolve such dispute with opposing counsel. In the event that such a dispute cannot be resolved by the parties, either party may apply to the Court or Special Master for a determination as to whether the designation is appropriate. The burden rests on the party seeking confidentiality to demonstrate that such designation is proper.

(e) At the time of deposition or within 10 days after receipt of the deposition transcript, a party may designate as confidential specific portions of the transcript which contain confidential matters under the standards set forth in paragraph (a) above. This designation shall be in writing and served upon all counsel. No objection shall be interposed at deposition that an answer would elicit confidential information. Transcripts will be treated as confidential for this 10-day period. Any portions of a transcript designated confidential shall thereafter be treated as confidential in accordance with this Order. In filing materials with the Court in pretrial proceedings, counsel shall file under seal only those specific documents and that deposition testimony designated confidential, and only those specific portions of briefs, applications, and other filings which contain verbatim confidential data, or which set forth the substance of such confidential information.

(f) In any application to the Court or Special Master referred to or permitted by this Order, the Court or Special Master may exercise discretion in determining whether the prevailing party in such a dispute may recover the costs incurred by it and, if so, the amount to be awarded.

Dated: _____

By the Court:

_____
United States District Judge

41.37 Referral of Privilege Claims to Special Master[1]

Referral of Privilege Claims to Special Master

It appearing that submission of claims of privilege to a special master appointed under Fed. R. Civ. P. 53 is warranted by the expected volume of such claims and by the likelihood that *in camera* inspection may be needed to rule on these claims and should be accomplished, to the extent possible, by someone other than the judge to whom this litigation has been assigned, the court hereby [with the consent of the parties] ORDERS:

1. **Appointment.** _____ is appointed under Rule 53 as special master for the purpose of considering all claims of privilege (including claims of protection against disclosure for trial preparation materials) that may be asserted during the course of discovery in this litigation and for such other matters as may be referred to such special master by the court, such as resolution of disputes under the Confidentiality Order.

2. **Procedures.** The special master shall have the rights, powers, and duties provided in Rule 53 and may adopt such procedures as are not inconsistent with that rule or with this or other orders of the court. Until directed otherwise by the special master or the court, any person asserting a privilege shall specifically identify the document or other communication sought to be protected from disclosure, including the date, the person making the statement, the persons to whom or in whose presence the statement was made, other persons to whom the contents were or have been revealed, the general subject matter of the communication (unless itself claimed to be privileged), the particular privilege(s) or doctrine(s) upon which protection against disclosure is based, and any other circumstances affecting the existence, extent, or waiver of the privilege. When appropriate, the special master may require that this documentation of claims of privilege be verified.

3. **Reports.** The special master shall make findings of fact and conclusions of law with respect to the matters presented by the parties and shall report expeditiously to the court pursuant to Rule 53(e) as applicable in nonjury actions. Unless directed by the court or believed advisable by the special master, the report shall not be accompanied by a transcript of the proceedings, the evidence, or the exhibits. Such parts of the report, if any, as may be confidential shall be filed under seal pending further order of the court.

4. **Fees and Expenses.** Compensation at rates mutually agreeable to the special master and the parties shall be paid to the special master on a periodic basis by the parties, together with reimbursement for reasonable expenses incurred by the special master. The special master may employ other persons to provide clerical and secretarial assis-

tance; such persons shall be under the supervision and control of the special master, who shall take appropriate action to insure that such persons preserve the confidentiality of matters submitted to the special master for review. Final allocation of these amounts shall be subject to taxation as costs at the conclusion of the case at the discretion of the court.[2]

5. **Distribution.** A copy of this order shall be mailed by the clerk to the special master and to Liaison Counsel for the parties.

Dated: _____

_____
United States District Judge

Notes:

1. See *supra* section 21.52

2. The order may provide the specific compensation payable to the master and specify the reimbursable expenses.

41.38 Deposition Guidelines[1]

Deposition Guidelines

It is ORDERED that depositions be conducted in accordance with the following rules:

1. **Cooperation.** Counsel are expected to cooperate with, and be courteous to, each other and deponents.

2. **Stipulations.** Unless contrary to an order of the court, the parties (and when appropriate, a nonparty witness) may stipulate in any suitable writing to alter, amend, or modify any practice relating to noticing, conducting, or filing a deposition. Stipulations for the extension of discovery cutoffs set by the court are not valid, however, until approved by the court.

3. **Scheduling.** Absent extraordinary circumstances, counsel shall consult in advance with opposing counsel and unrepresented proposed deponents in an effort to schedule depositions at mutually convenient times and places. [That some counsel may be unavailable shall not, however, in view of the number of attorneys involved in this litigation, be grounds for deferring or postponing a deposition if another attorney from the same firm or who represents a party with similar interests is able to attend.]

4. **Attendance.**

    (a) **Who May Be Present.** Unless otherwise ordered under Fed. R. Civ. P. 26(c), depositions may be attended by counsel of record, members and employees of their firms, attorneys specially engaged by a party for purposes of the deposition, the parties or the representative of a party, counsel for the deponent, and potential witnesses. While a deponent is being examined about any stamped confidential document or the confidential information contained therein, persons to whom disclosure is not authorized under the Confidentiality Order shall be excluded.

    (b) **Unnecessary Attendance.** Unnecessary attendance by counsel is discouraged and may not be compensated in any fee application to the court. Counsel who have only marginal interest in a proposed deposition or who expect their interests to be adequately represented by other counsel may elect not to attend and to conduct pursuant to paragraph 11(b) of this order supplemental interrogation of the deponent should a review of the deposition reveal the need for such examination.

5. **Conduct.**

    (a) **Examination.** Each side should ordinarily designate one attorney to conduct the principal examination of the deponent, and examination by other attorneys should be limited to matters not previously covered. Counsel should cooperate in the allocation of time so that time limits set by the court are complied with.

(b) **Objections and Directions Not to Answer.** Counsel shall comply with Fed. R. Civ. P. 30(d)(1). When a privilege is claimed, the witness should nevertheless answer questions relevant to the existence, extent, or waiver of the privilege, such as the date of a communication, who made the statement, to whom and in whose presence the statement was made, other persons to whom the contents of the statement have been disclosed, and the general subject matter of the statement, unless such information is itself privileged.

(c) **Private Consultation.** Private conferences between deponents and their attorneys in the course of interrogation are improper except for the purpose of determining whether a privilege should be asserted. Unless prohibited by the court for good cause shown, such conferences may be held during normal recesses and adjournments.

(d) **Continuation of Deposition.** If a deposition is not finished on Friday of a deposition week, it will continue on the following Monday, subject to the availability of the witness. If the witness is unavailable, it will resume on a newly noticed date.

6. **Documents.**

(a) **Production of Documents.** Witnesses subpoenaed to produce documents should ordinarily be served at least 30 days before the scheduled deposition. Arrangements should be made to permit inspection of the documents before the interrogation commences.

(b) **Confidentiality Order.** A copy of the Confidentiality Order shall be provided to the deponent before the deposition commences if the deponent is to produce or may be asked about documents that may contain confidential information. [Counsel shall comply with the provisions of the Confidentiality Order when examining a deponent about confidential information.]

(c) **Copies.** Extra copies of documents about which counsel expect to examine the deponent should ordinarily be provided to opposing counsel and the deponent. Deponents should be shown a document before being examined about it except when counsel seek to impeach or test the deponent's recollection.

(d) **Marking of Deposition Exhibits.** Documents shall be referred to by the Bates-stamp number assigned by the document depository.

7. **Depositions of Witnesses Who Have No Knowledge of the Facts.** An officer, director, or managing agent of a corporation or a government official served with a notice of a deposition or subpoena regarding a matter about which such person has no knowledge may submit to the noticing party a reasonable time before the date noticed an

affidavit so stating and identifying a person within the corporation or government entity believed to have such knowledge. Notwithstanding such affidavit, the noticing party may proceed with the deposition, subject to the right of the witness to seek a protective order.

8. **Recording Depositions by Nonstenographic Means.**

   (a) **Tape-Recorded Depositions.** By so indicating in its notice of a deposition, a party may record the deposition by tape recording in lieu of stenographic recording pursuant to Fed. R. Civ. P. 30(b)(2) and (3). Other parties may at their own expense arrange for stenographic recording of the deposition, may obtain a copy of the tape and transcript upon payment of a pro rata share of the noticing party's actual costs, and may prepare and file their own version of the transcript of the tape recording.

   (b) **Videotaped Depositions.** By so indicating in its notice of a deposition, a party may record the deposition by videotape pursuant to Fed. R. Civ. P. 30(b)(2) and (3).

   (1) Rules for Videotaped Reporting.

      (i) *Video Operator.* The operator(s) of the videotape recording equipment shall be subject to the provisions of Fed. R. Civ. P. 28(c). At the commencement of the deposition the operator(s) shall swear or affirm to record the proceedings fairly and accurately.

      (ii) *Attendance.* Each witness, attorney, and other person attending the deposition shall be identified on camera at the commencement of the deposition. Thereafter, only the deponent (and demonstrative materials used during the deposition) will be videotaped.

      (iii) *Standards.* The deposition will be conducted in a manner to replicate, to the extent feasible, the presentation of evidence at a trial. Unless physically incapacitated, the deponent shall be seated at a table or in a witness box except when reviewing or presenting demonstrative materials for which a change in position is needed. To the extent practicable, the deposition will be conducted in a neutral setting, against a solid background, with only such lighting as is required for accurate video recording. Lighting, camera angle, lens setting, and field of view will be changed only as necessary to record accurately the natural body movements of the deponent or to portray exhibits and materials used during the deposition. Sound levels will be altered only as necessary to record satisfactorily the voices of counsel and the deponent. Eating and smoking by deponents or counsel during the deposition will not be permitted.

(iv) *Interruptions.* [The videotape shall run continuously throughout the active conduct of the deposition.] [Videotape recording will be suspended during all "off the record" discussions.][2]

(v) *Index.* The videotape operator shall use a counter on the recording equipment and after completion of the deposition shall prepare a log, cross-referenced to counter numbers, that identifies the positions on the tape at which examination by different counsel begins and ends, at which objections are made and examination resumes, at which exhibits are identified, and at which any interruption of continuous tape recording occurs, whether for recesses, "off the record" discussions, mechanical failure, or otherwise.

(vi) *Filing.* [The operator shall preserve custody of the original videotape in its original condition until further order of the court.] [Subject to the provisions of paragraph 10 of this order, the original of the tape recording, together with the operator's log index and a certificate of the operator attesting to the accuracy of the tape, shall be filed with the clerk.] No part of a videotaped deposition shall be released or made available to any member of the public unless authorized by the court.

(vii) *Objections.* Requests for pretrial rulings on the admissibility of evidence obtained during a videotaped deposition shall be accompanied by appropriate pages of the written transcript. If needed for an informed ruling, a copy of the videotape and equipment for viewing the tape shall also be provided to the court.

(viii) *Use at Trial; Purged Tapes.* A party desiring to offer a videotape deposition at trial shall be responsible for having available appropriate playback equipment and a trained operator. After the designation by all parties of the portions of a videotape to be used at trial, an edited copy of the tape, purged of unnecessary portions (and any portions to which objections have been sustained), [may] [shall] be prepared by the offering party to facilitate continuous playback; but a copy of the edited tape shall be made available to other parties at least ____ days before it is used, and the unedited original of the tape shall also be available at the trial.

9. **Telephonic Depositions.** By indicating in its notice of a deposition that it wishes to conduct the deposition by telephone, a party shall be deemed to have moved for such an order under Fed. R. Civ. P. 30(b)(7). Unless an objection is filed and served within days after such notice is received, the court shall be deemed to have granted the motion. Other parties may examine the deponent telephonically or in person. However, all persons present with the deponent shall be identified in the deposition and shall not by word, sign, or otherwise coach or suggest answers to the deponent.

10. **Waiver of Transcription and Filing.** The parties and deponents are authorized and encouraged to waive transcription and filing of depositions that prove to be of little or no usefulness in the litigation or to agree to defer transcription and filing until the need for using the deposition arises.

11. **Use, Supplemental Depositions.**

    (a) **Use.** Depositions may, under the conditions prescribed in Fed. R. Civ. P. 32(a)(1)–(4) or as otherwise permitted by the Federal Rules of Evidence, be used against any party (including parties later added and parties in cases subsequently filed in, removed to, or transferred to this court as part of this litigation)—

        (1) who was present or represented at the deposition;

        (2) who had reasonable notice thereof; or

        (3) who, within 30 days after the filing of the deposition (or, if later, within 60 days after becoming a party in this court in any action that is a part of this litigation), fails to show just cause why such deposition should not be usable against such party.

    (b) **Supplemental Depositions.** Each party not present or represented at a deposition (including parties later added and parties in cases subsequently filed in, removed to, or transferred to this court) may, within 30 days after the filing of the deposition (or, if later, within 60 days after becoming a party in this court in any action that is a part of this litigation), request permission to conduct a supplemental deposition of the deponent, including the right to take such deposition telephonically and by nonstenographic means. If permitted, the deposition shall be treated as the resumption of the deposition originally noticed; and each deponent shall, at the conclusion of the initial deposition, be advised of the opportunity of nonattending parties to request a resumption of such deposition, subject to the right of the deponent to seek a protective order. Such examination shall not be repetitive of the prior interrogation.

12. **Rulings.**

    (a) **Immediate Presentation.** During depositions, disputes arising that cannot be resolved by agreement and that, if not immediately resolved, will significantly disrupt the discovery schedule or require a rescheduling of the deposition, may be presented by telephone to the court. If the judge is not available during the period while the deposition is being conducted, the dispute may be submitted to Magistrate Judge _____ by telephone or as the judge may direct.[3] The presentation of the issue and the court's ruling will be recorded as part of the deposition.

(b) **Extraterritorial Jurisdiction.** The undersigned will exercise by telephone the authority granted under 28 U.S.C. § 1407(b) to act as district judge in the district in which the deposition is taken.[4]

Dated: _____

_____

United States District Judge

Notes:

1. See *supra* section 21.45.

2. If a simultaneous stenographic transcript is being made, the court may prefer that "off the record" discussions be eliminated from the videotape.

3. See *supra* section 21.456.

4. The power to exercise authority over nonparty deponents outside the district is available only in multidistrict litigation, unless the judge has been given an intracircuit or intercircuit assignment.

41.39 Electronic Bulletin Board

Order No. _____
(Electronic Bulletin Board)

Lead and Liaison Counsel for Plaintiffs and Defendants are directed to meet and confer for the purpose of establishing an informational electronic bulletin board capable of being accessed by computers to obtain notices and announcements relating to proceedings and events in this litigation and also to provide electronic versions of transcripts of status conferences, orders, cases, opinions, schedules of depositions, and some or all of the materials filed with the document depository. Counsel may recommend, by motion, that a portion of the bulletin board be accessible only to counsel for plaintiffs, counsel for defendants, or both. Any limitations, however, should be restricted to (1) matters that represent the work product of attorneys for plaintiffs or defendants and are not otherwise available to other persons, and (2) matters that are confidential under a protective order issued by this court. The bulletin board should be established so that it is compatible with most communications software, with a view toward making it publicly available.

Counsel using computers to prepare documents sent to the clerk or to the judge's chambers are asked to retain computer-readable text files of these documents. [Counsel are expected to use computers to prepare documents sent to the clerk or to the judge's chambers.] The court contemplates that procedures will be established for maintaining an electronic library and bulletin board of these files for quick and inexpensive access by other litigants and interested members of the public.

Dated: _____

_____
United States District Judge

41.4 Sample Class Action Orders

Note: The class action forms have been adapted from antitrust litigation for illustrative purposes and may be adapted for other litigation by appropriate changes.

41.41 Order Certifying Class

[caption]

Order No. _____
(Certifying Class)

In accordance with the findings and conclusions contained in the Opinion filed concurrently herewith [omitted], it is, subject to alteration or amendment under Fed. R. Civ. P. 23(c), conditionally ORDERED:

1. **Class Certification.** Civil Action No. _____ , styled _____
_____ shall be maintained as a class action on behalf of the following class of plaintiffs:

> [Describe class in objective terms to the extent possible. For example, "All persons and entities throughout the United States and its territories (other than widget manufacturers and entities owned or controlled by them) that, since _____[date]_____ , have purchased widgets directly from any of the defendants or from any other widget manufacturer."]

with respect to the following cause(s) of action:

> [Describe class claims as precisely as possible. For example, "Any claims for damages or injunctive relief under federal antitrust laws premised upon an alleged conspiracy among the defendants and other widget manufacturers to restrict competition in the manufacture, distribution, and sale of widgets by setting the minimum prices charged for widgets after _____[date]_____ ."]

2. **Class Representative; Class Counsel.** Subject to further order of the court, [A.B. Co.] is designated as class representative and [X.Y.] is designated as counsel for the class.

3. **Notice.**[1]

   (a) Class counsel shall by _____[date]_____ , cause to be mailed in the name of the clerk by first class mail, postage prepaid, to all class members who can be identified through reasonable efforts, a notice in substantially the form as Attachment A. In addition to class members identified through an examination of defendants' records, this notice will also be mailed to persons who are members of [National Widget Dealers Trade Association].

   (b) Class counsel shall cause to be published in the _____ by ____[date]____, a notice in substantially the form as Attachment B.

4. **Exclusion.** Class members may exclude themselves from the class by filing with the "Committee of Counsel" by ____[date]_____ , the form attached to Exhibit A or some other appropriate written indication that they request exclusion from the class. Class counsel and _____ are designated as a Committee of Counsel to arrange for a post office box and to receive and tabulate requests for exclusion.

5. **List of Class Members.** Class counsel will file with the clerk by_____[date]_____ , an affidavit identifying the persons to whom notice has been mailed and who have not timely requested exclusion.

Dated:_____

_____
United States District Judge

Note:

    1. The circumstances of each case will dictate the form and manner of giving notice.

UNITED STATES DISTRICT COURT
_____ DISTRICT OF_____

In re:)
) Master File No. _____
[WIDGET ANTITRUST] LITIGATION   )

Notice of Class Action

**This notice may affect your rights.
Please read carefully.**

Si usted desea obtener una copia de este documento legal en Espanol, favor de actuar immediatamente y escribir a

> Committee Counsel
> P.O. Box _____
> [city, state, zip]_____

TO: Purchasers of [Widgets]

Your rights may be affected by a lawsuit pending in this court, Civil Action No. ____. [A.B. Co., the company bringing the lawsuit] charges that since _____[date]_____, [C.D. Inc., E.F. Inc., and G.H. Inc.] have unlawfully agreed among themselves and with other [widget] manufacturers to restrict price competition in the sale of [widgets] and that, as a result, buyers of [widgets] have paid higher prices than they otherwise would have paid. It asserts that under the federal antitrust laws these companies are legally responsible to the purchasers for three times the amount of the claimed overcharges, as well as for attorneys' fees and costs. [A.B. Co.] (the plaintiff) also asks that the [three] companies (the defendants) be prohibited from continuing the alleged conspiracy. The defendants deny these claims and charges.

The court has not ruled on the merits of the plaintiff's charges or on the denials and other defenses made by the defendants. However, some matters have arisen during the preparation of this case for trial that affect purchasers of [widgets] who were not previously parties to the lawsuit. The purpose of this notice is to advise you (who have been identified as possibly such a purchaser) of these events and their potential effect on your rights.

Class-Action Ruling

The court has conditionally ruled that this lawsuit may be maintained as a claim for triple damages, injunctive relief, attorneys' fees, and costs not only by [A.B. Co.] but also on behalf of a class consisting of certain other buyers of [widgets]. The court has named [A.B. Co.] as representative of the class and its attorney, [X.Y.,] as counsel for the class. The class consists of those persons and entities throughout the United States and its territories (other than [widget] manufacturers and companies owned or controlled by them) that since _____[date]_____, have purchased [widgets] directly from the defendants or other [widget] manufacturers.

This ruling by the court of a class action does not mean that any money or injunctive relief will be obtained for purchasers of [widgets], because these are contested issues that have not been decided. Rather, the ruling means that the final outcome of this lawsuit—whether favorable to the plaintiffs or to the defendants—will apply in like manner to every class member; that is, to all [widget] buyers described above who do not timely elect to be excluded from the class (see below).

The class is limited to those persons and companies that have made at least one purchase of [widgets] since _____[date]_____, directly from the defendants or some other company that manufactures [widgets]. If you have bought [widgets] during the period only from other sources (for example, from dealers or retailers), you are not a member of the class on whose behalf this suit will be maintained and any claims you desire to make against the defendants must be presented independently by you.

Election by Class Members

If you fit the above description of a class member, you have a choice whether or not to remain a member of the class on whose behalf this suit is being maintained. Either choice will have its consequences, which you should understand before making your decision.

1. If you want to be excluded from the class, you must complete the enclosed form ("Exclusion Request") and return it to the "Committee of Counsel, [Widget] Antitrust Litigation, P.O. Box _____[address]_____," by mail postmarked no later than _____[date]_____. By making this election to be excluded,

(a) you will not share in any recovery that might be paid to [widget] purchasers as a result of trial or settlement of this lawsuit;

(b) you will not be bound by any decision in this lawsuit favorable to the defendants; and

(c) you may present any claims you have against the defendants by filing your own lawsuit, or you may seek to intervene in this lawsuit.

2. If you want to remain a member of the class, you should NOT file the "Exclusion Request" and are not required to do anything at this time. By remaining a class member, any claims against the defendants for damages under the federal antitrust laws arising from the defendants' conduct as alleged by the class representative will be determined in this case and cannot be presented in any other lawsuit.

Rights and Obligations of Class Members

If you remain a member of this class:

1. [A.B. Co. and its attorney, X.Y.,] will act as your representative and counsel for the presentation of the charges against the defendants. If you desire, you may also appear by your own attorney. You may also seek to intervene individually and may advise the court if at any time you consider that you are not being fairly and adequately represented by [A.B. Co. and its attorney].

2. Your participation in any recovery, which may be obtained from the defendants through trial or settlement, will depend on the results of this lawsuit. If no recovery is obtained for the class, you will be bound by that result also.

3. You may be required as a condition to participating in any recovery through settlement or trial to present evidence respecting your purchases of [widgets]. (You should, therefore, preserve invoices and other records reflecting these purchases.)

4. You will be entitled to notice of any ruling reducing the size of the class and also to notice of, and an opportunity to be heard respecting, any proposed settlement or dismissal of the class claims. (For this reason, as well as to participate in any recovery, you are requested to notify the "Committee of Counsel" of any corrections or changes in your name or address.)

Further Proceedings

[As noted, the essential allegations of the charges against the defendants are denied by them. Because of the substantial discovery and other pretrial proceedings that remain to be done, trial of the case is not likely to occur before ____[date]____. You may communicate with Class Counsel if you have evidence you believe would be helpful to establishment of the class claims, and you may be asked by the parties to provide information relevant to the case.]

Additional Information

Any questions you have concerning the matters contained in this notice (and any corrections or changes of name or address) should not be directed to the court but should be directed in writing to:

> Committee of Counsel
> [Widget Antitrust Litigation]
> P.O. Box _____
> [city, state, zip] _____

If you decide to remain a member of the class and wish to communicate with Class Counsel as your attorney in this litigation, you may do so by writing or calling:

> [X.Y., Esq.]
> Attorney at Law
> [street address] _____
> [city, state, zip] _____
> Telephone: _____

You may, of course, seek the advice and guidance of your own attorney if you desire. The pleadings and other records in this litigation may be examined and copied at any time during regular office hours at the office of the clerk, _____ _____ [address] _____ .

Reminder as to Time Limit

If you wish to be excluded from the class on whose behalf this action is being maintained, return the completed "Exclusion Request" to the Committee of Counsel by mail postmarked on or before _____ [date] _____ .

Dated: _____

> _____
> [U.V.], Clerk of Court
> United States District Court
> [address] _____
> [city, state, zip] _____

Enclosure:
Exclusion Request

Request for Exclusion

Read the enclosed legal notice carefully before filling out this form.

The undersigned has read the notice of class action, dated _____, and does NOT wish to remain a member of the plaintiff class certified in the case of [A.B. Co. v. C.D. Inc., et al.], CA _____ , in the United States District Court for the _____ District of _____ .

Date: _____

         [typed name of company]_____

         [typed address of company]_____

         [typed city, state, zip]_____

         [signature]_____

         [typed name of signer]_____

         [typed title of signer]_____

If you want to exclude yourself from the class, you must complete and return this form by mailing before _____ [date] _____ , to:

         Committee of Counsel
         [Widget Antitrust Litigation]
         P.O. Box _____
         [city, state, zip]_____

A separate request for exclusion should be completed and timely mailed for each person or entity electing to be excluded from the class.

UNITED STATES DISTRICT COURT
_____ DISTRICT OF_____

In re:)
)   Master File No. _____
[WIDGET ANTITRUST] LITIGATION   )

Published Notice of Class Action

This notice may affect your rights.
Please read carefully.

TO: Purchasers of [WIDGETS]

Your rights may be affected by a lawsuit pending in this court, Civil Action No. ____ .

The plaintiff, [A.B. Co.], charges that since _____[date]_____, the defendants, [C.D. Inc., E.F. Inc., and G.H. Inc.], have unlawfully agreed among themselves and with other [widget] manufacturers to restrict price competition in the sale of [widgets] and that, as a result, buyers of [widgets] have paid higher prices than they otherwise would have paid. The plaintiff asserts that under the federal antitrust laws these defendants are legally responsible to the purchasers for three times the amount of the claimed overcharges, as well as for attorneys' fees and costs, and the plaintiff also asks that they be prohibited from continuing the alleged conspiracy. The defendants deny these charges. The court has not ruled on the merits of the charges or of the defendants' denials and other defenses.

The court has, however, conditionally ruled that this lawsuit may be maintained as a claim on behalf of a class consisting of all persons and entities throughout the United States and its territories (other than [widget] manufacturers and companies owned or controlled by them) that since _____[date]_____ have purchased [widgets] directly from the defendants or other [widget] manufacturers.

Persons and entities that have been identified as possible members of this class are being advised by mail of their rights with respect to the lawsuit (including the right to exclude themselves from the class if they desire). This notice is being published because some class members may not receive the mailed notice. If you are (or may be) a member

of the class but do not receive individual notice of your rights by _____[date]_____,
you are requested to notify

>Committee of Counsel
>[Widget Antitrust] Litigation
>P.O. Box _____
>[city, state, zip] _____

giving your correct name and current address. You will then be mailed a more detailed explanation of your rights in this litigation and be placed on the mailing list for any future notifications regarding the suit.

Dated: _____

>_____
>[U.V.], Clerk of Court
>United States District Court
>[address] _____
>[city, state, zip] _____

41.42 Order Setting Hearing on Proposed Class Settlement

[caption]

Order No. _____
(Order for Hearing on Proposed Class Settlement)

The court having made a preliminary review of the proposed settlement of this action, it is ORDERED:

1. **Proposed Settlement.** The proposed settlement between the plaintiff class and the defendants appears to be within the range of reasonableness and accordingly shall be submitted to the class members for their consideration and for a hearing under Fed. R. Civ. P. 23(e).

2. **Hearing.** A hearing shall be held in Courtroom _____, United States Courthouse, _____[address]_____ , at ____ A.M./P.M., on _____[date]____ , to consider whether the settlement should be given final approval by the court.

    (a) Objections by class members to the proposed settlement will be considered if filed in writing with the clerk on or before _____[date]_____ .[1]

    (b) At the hearing, class members may be heard orally in support of or in opposition to the settlement, provided such persons file with the clerk by _____[date]_____ , a written notification of their desire to appear personally, indicating (if in opposition to the settlement) briefly the nature of the objection.

    (c) Counsel for the class and for the defendants should be prepared at the hearing to respond to objections filed by class members and to provide other information, as appropriate, bearing on whether or not the settlement should be approved.

3. **Notice.** The parties to the proposed settlement shall by_____[date]_____ , cause to be mailed in the name of the clerk by first class mail, postage prepaid, to members of the class [who did not timely elect to be excluded from litigation] a notice in substantially the form as Attachment A. [Notice of the proposed settlement (and of the rights of class members to object to the settlement) shall also be given by

publication in the following manner: _____

_____

_____.]

Dated: _____

_____
United States District Judge

Attachment A: Notice

Note:

1. In some cases, the court has required that a copy of objections also be mailed to a designated address to facilitate inspection by counsel.

UNITED STATES DISTRICT COURT
_____ DISTRICT OF _____

In re:)
) Master File No. _____
[WIDGET ANTITRUST] LITIGATION)

Notice of Proposed Class Settlement

TO: Purchasers of [Widgets] who are members of the plaintiff class in _____
_____ .

A lawsuit pending in this court (_____) involves a claim by [A.B. Co.] (the plaintiff) that [C.D. Inc., E.F. Inc., and G.H. Inc.] (the defendants) violated federal antitrust laws by conspiring among themselves and with other [widget] manufacturers to the damage of those buying [widgets] after _____[date]_____ . The court ruled that this case was to be maintained on behalf of a class consisting of all persons and entities throughout the United States and its territories (other than [widget] manufacturers and companies owned or controlled by them) that after ____[date]_____ , bought [widgets] directly from a [widget] manufacturer. If you are such a purchaser, you should have received a notice dated_____ , advising you of the certification of this class and of your rights as a member of the class.

The purpose of this notice is to advise you of the status of the lawsuit, including a statement of your rights with respect to a proposed settlement of the case.

Terms of Proposed Settlement

Subject to court approval, the plaintiff and defendants have agreed on a settlement under which [C.D. Inc., E.F. Inc., and G.H. Inc.] will pay the amounts of $_____ , $ _____, and $ _____, respectively. These payments will be in final settlement of all claims by class members against the defendants for violations of federal antitrust laws in the sale of [widgets] from _____[date]_____, to _____[date]_____ . The defendants do not admit any wrongdoing or liability on their part; the proposed settlement with them is a compromise of disputed claims and does not mean that they or any other [widget] manufacturers are guilty of the charges made by the plaintiff.

This settlement fund, totaling $ _____, will, after reduction for such fees and expenses of the Class Counsel as may be allowed by the court, be distributed to class members (who have not elected to be excluded from the class) in a method to be determined by the court. The court has not fixed the amount of fees and expenses to be allowed or determined the precise method of allocating and distributing the net settlement fund to class members. However Class Counsel has indicated that the total fees and expenses to be requested (including amounts in connection with distribution of the settlement fund) will not exceed $_____, and that the method to be proposed for allocating the net settlement funds will be based on the total amount paid to [widget] manufacturers for [widgets] by class members during the period from _____[date]_____, to _____[date]_____. [Although the amount to be distributed to individual class members cannot be accurately determined until fees and expenses have been fixed, the method for allocation has been determined, and more complete information has been obtained regarding (widget) purchases by all class members, Class Counsel estimates that the net recovery by class members should be in the approximate range of ___% to ___% of the gross amounts paid by them to (widget) manufacturers for (widgets) during the applicable period.]

Settlement Hearing

The court will hold a hearing in Courtroom _____ , United States Courthouse _____[address]_____ , at _____ A.M./P.M., on_____[date]_____ , to determine whether, as recommended by both Class Counsel and the class representative, it should approve the proposed settlement.

Objections to the proposed settlement by class members (who have not previously elected to exclude themselves from the class) will be considered by the court, but only if such objections are filed in writing with the clerk by mail postmarked before ___[date]___. Attendance at the hearing is not necessary; however, class members wishing to be heard orally in opposition to the proposed settlement should indicate in their written objection their intention to appear at the hearing.

Class members who support the proposed settlement do not need to appear at the hearing or take any other action to indicate their approval.

Further Proceedings

If the settlement is approved by the court, procedures will be established to ascertain the amounts of [widget] purchases made by class members and any other information needed to apportion and distribute the settlement fund. Class Counsel believes that, unless delayed by appeals or unforeseen events, this distribution may be made by _____[date]_____. You should preserve records relating to your purchases of [widgets] during the period covered by the settlement.

If the settlement is not approved, the case will continue to be prepared for trial or other judicial resolution of the claims and defenses. [Trial (of certain issues in the case) is presently scheduled for _____[date]_____ ; depending on the results of that trial, further proceedings may be necessary before the case is finally resolved.]

Additional Information

Any questions you have about the matters in this notice should *not* be directed to the court, but may be directed by telephone or in writing to:

[X.Y., Esq.]
Class Counsel
[Widget Antitrust] Litigation
[address] _____
[city, state, zip] _____
Telephone: _____
or
[S.T., Esq.]
Defendant's Lead Counsel
[Widget Antitrust] Litigation
[address] _____
[city, state, zip] _____
Telephone: _____

You may, of course, seek the advice and guidance of your own attorney if you desire. The pleadings and other records in this litigation, including a complete copy of the proposed settlement agreement, may be examined and copied at any time during regular office hours at:

Office of the Clerk of Court
United States District Court
[address] _____
[city, state, zip] _____

Reminder as to Time Limits

If you wish to object to the proposed settlement, file your written objection with the clerk of the court by mail postmarked on or before _____[date]_____ . Include any request to be heard orally at the hearing.

Dated: _____

_____
[U.V.], Clerk of Court
United States District Court
[address] _____
[city, state, zip] _____

UNITED STATES DISTRICT COURT
_____ DISTRICT OF _____

In re:)
)   Master File No. _____
[WIDGET ANTITRUST] LITIGATION   )

Notice of Proposed Class Settlement (Partial)

TO: Purchasers of [widgets] who are members of the plaintiff class in _____
_____.

    A lawsuit pending in this court (_____) involves a claim by [A.B. Co.] (the plaintiff) that [C.D. Inc., E.F. Inc., and G.H. Inc.] (the defendants) violated federal antitrust laws by conspiring among themselves and with other [widget] manufacturers to the damage of those buying [widgets] after _____ [date] _____. The court ruled that this case was to be maintained on behalf of a class consisting of all persons and entities throughout the United States and its territories (other than [widget] manufacturers and companies owned or controlled by them) which after _____ [date] _____, bought [widgets] directly from a [widget] manufacturer. If you are such a purchaser, you should have received a notice dated _____, advising you of the certification of this class and of your rights as a member of the class.

    The purpose of this notice is to advise you of the status of the lawsuit, including a statement of your rights with respect to a proposed settlement of the case.

Terms of Proposed Settlement

    Subject to court approval, the plaintiff and [C.D. Inc.], one of the defendants, have agreed on a settlement under which [C.D. Inc.] will pay the amount of $_____. This payment will be in final settlement of all claims by class members against [C.D. Inc.] for violations of federal antitrust laws in the sale of [widgets] from _____ [date] _____, to _____ [date] _____.

    [C.D. Inc.] does not admit any wrongdoing or liability on its part; the proposed settlement with it is a compromise of disputed claims and does not mean that it or any other [widget] manufacturers are guilty of the charges made by the plaintiff.

    The settlement funds will be held for the exclusive benefit of the class members (who have not elected to be excluded from the class), including the payment of class counsel for services rendered on behalf of the class. Distribution to class members will not be made at this time and probably will not be made until resolution of the class claims against the remaining defendants, [E.F. Inc. and G.H. Inc.]. [A portion of the funds may, if permitted by the court, be used to pay the cost of conducting this litigation on behalf of the class members against the remaining defendants.] The fairness and reasonableness of the amount of this settlement, as well as of utilization or distribution of the fund, are subject to the approval of the court; and the manner and method of distribution to the class will be determined at a future time, after providing the class members appropriate notice and an opportunity to be heard.

Settlement Hearing

The court will hold a hearing in Courtroom _____, United States Courthouse, _____[address]_____, at _____ A.M./P.M., on _____[date]_____, to determine whether, as recommended by both class counsel and the class representative, it should approve the proposed settlement.

Objections to the proposed settlement by class members (who have not previously elected to exclude themselves from the class) will be considered by the court, but only if such objections are filed in writing with the clerk by mail postmarked on or before _____[date]_____. Attendance at the hearing is not necessary; however, class members wishing to be heard orally in opposition to the proposed settlement should indicate in their written objection their intention to appear at the hearing.

Class members who support the proposed settlement do not need to appear at the hearing or take any other action to indicate their approval.

Further Proceedings

The claims of the class against [E.F. Inc. and G.H. Inc.] will continue to be prepared for trial or other judicial resolution whether or not the settlement is approved. If the settlement is not approved, [C.D. Inc.] will remain as an additional defendant against whom these claims are made. If the settlement is approved, [C.D. Inc.] will no longer be a defendant, and the amount paid by [C.D. Inc.] will be credited against any judgment obtained in the proceedings from the two remaining defendants. (It should be noted that the claims made on behalf of the class are based not only on purchases made from the three defendants but also on purchases made from other [widget] manufacturers; this will continue to be true whether or not the settlement with [C.D. Inc.] is approved.)

Discovery is expected to be completed by _____[date]_____. Trial [of certain issues in the case] is presently scheduled for _____[date]_____; depending on the results of that trial, further proceedings may be necessary before the case is finally resolved. Each of the defendants (including [C.D. Inc.]) denies the essential allegations made against it; and the court has not determined the merits of these claims or the defenses.

Additional Information

Any questions you have about the matters in this notice should *not* be directed to the court, but may be directed by telephone or in writing to:

> [X.Y., Esq.]
> Class Counsel, [Widget Antitrust] Litigation
> [address] _____
> [city, state, zip] _____
> Telephone: _____
> or
> [S.T., Esq.]
> Defendants' Lead Counsel, [Widget Antitrust] Litigation
> [address] _____
> [city, state, zip] _____
> Telephone:_____

You may, of course, seek the advice and guidance of your own attorney if you desire. The pleadings and other records in this litigation, including a complete copy of the proposed settlement agreement, may be examined and copied at any time during regular office hours at:

> Office of the Clerk of Court
> United States District Court
> [address] _____
> [city, state, zip] _____

Reminder as to Time Limits

If you wish to object to the proposed settlement, file your written objection with the clerk of the court by mail postmarked on or before _____[date]_____. Include any request to be heard orally at the hearing.

Dated: _____

> _____
> [U.V.], Clerk of Court
> United States District Court
> [address] _____
> [city, state, zip] _____

41.43 Order—Combined Certification and Proposed Settlement

[caption]

Order No. _____
(Certifying Class and Setting Hearing on Proposed Settlement)

In accordance with the findings and conclusions contained in the Opinion filed concurrently herewith [omitted], it is ORDERED:

1. **Class Certification.** Civil Action No. _____ , styled _____
_____ , shall be maintained as a
class action on behalf of the following class of plaintiffs:

> [Describe class in objective terms to the extent possible. For example, "All persons and entities throughout the United States and its territories (other than [widget] manufacturers and entities owned or controlled by them) that, between _____[date]_____ , and _____[date]_____ , have purchase [widgets] directly from any of the defendants or any other [widget] manufacturer."]

with respect to the following cause(s) of action:

> [Describe class claims as precisely as possible. For example, "Any claims for damages or injunctive relief under federal antitrust laws premised upon an alleged conspiracy among [widget] manufacturers to restrict competition in the manufacture, distribution, and sale of [widgets] by setting the minimum prices charged for [widgets] between _____[date]_____ , and _____[date]_____ ."]

2. **Class Representative; Class Counsel.** [A.B. Co.] is designated as class representative and [X.Y.] is designated as counsel for the class.

3. **Exclusion.** Class members may exclude themselves from the class by filing with the "Committee of Counsel" by _____[date]_____ , the form appended to Attachment A[1] or some other appropriate written indication that they request exclusion from the class. Class counsel and _____
_____ are designated as a Committee of Counsel to arrange for a post office box and to receive and tabulate requests for exclusion.

4. **Proposed Settlement.** The proposed settlement between the plaintiff class and the defendants appears, upon preliminary review, to be within the range of reasonableness and accordingly shall be submitted to the class members for their consideration and for a hearing under Fed. R. Civ. P. 23(e). The terms of the settlement are as follows:

[describe terms in clear, nontechnical manner]

5. **Hearing.** A hearing shall be held in Courtroom _____, United States Courthouse, _____ , at _____ A.M./P.M., on ____[date]____ , to consider whether the settlement should be given final approval.

(a) Objections by class members (who do not timely elect to exclude themselves from the class) to the proposed settlement should be considered if filed in writing with the clerk on or before _____[date]_____ .

(b) At the hearing, class members (who do not timely elect to exclude themselves from the class) may be heard orally in support of or in opposition to the settlement, provided such persons file with the clerk by _____[date]_____ a written notification of the desire to appear personally, indicating (if in opposition to the settlement) briefly the nature of the objection.

(c) Counsel for the class and for the defendants should be prepared at the hearing to respond to objections filed by such class members and to provide other information, as appropriate, bearing on whether or not the settlement should be approved.

6. **Notice.**

(a) Class Counsel shall by ____[date]____ , cause to be mailed in the name of the clerk by first class mail, postage prepaid, to all class members who can be identified through reasonable efforts, a notice in substantially the same form as Attachment A. In addition to class members identified through an examination of defendants' records, this notice will also be mailed to persons who are members of [National Widget Dealers Trade Association].

(b) Class Counsel shall cause to be published a notice in substantially the same form as Attachment B in the following manner _____ _____ _____ _____ .

7. **List of Class Members.** Class Counsel will file with the clerk by _____[date]_____ , an affidavit identifying the persons to whom notice has been mailed and who have not timely requested exclusion.

Dated: _____

_____
United States District Judge

Attachments:
    A—Notice

Note:

    1. For Attachment A, see *supra* section 41.41. That form should be accompanied by a summary of the relevant information contained in the Notice of Proposed Class Settlement, *supra* section 41.42, Attachment A.

41.44 Order—Approving Settlement/Claims Procedure

[caption]

Order No. _____
(Approving Settlement; Claims Procedure)

In accordance with the findings and conclusions contained in the Opinion filed concurrently herewith [omitted], it is ORDERED:

1. **Approval of Settlement.** The settlement is, after hearing, determined to be fair, reasonable, and in the best interests of the class. It is, therefore, approved. By separate order [omitted], this action will be dismissed with prejudice, each side to bear its own costs.

2. **Award of Fees and Expenses.** In accordance with the findings and conclusions contained in the Opinion [omitted], [X.Y.] is awarded $_____ as compensation and $_____ as reimbursement for expenses, to be paid [from the settlement fund] [by the defendants].[1] [Application for an award from the settlement fund of additional fees and expenses in connection with further proceedings, including administration and distribution of the settlement fund, may be made to the court.]

3. **Administration and Distribution of Settlement Fund.**

    (a) **Investment.** [After payment of counsel fees and expenses as awarded by the court,] the settlement fund shall, pending distribution to class members, be held in interest-bearing investments to be approved by the court from time to time.

    (b) **Allocation.** The [net] settlement fund shall be allocated among the class members in proportion to their "qualified purchase," which means the net price (after discounts and allowances) paid by them to [widget] manufacturers for [widgets] from _____[date]_____, to _____[date]_____.

    (c) **Claims; proof of purchases.** Unless extended by the court (or the special master) class members shall have until _____[date]_____, to submit claims detailing, with appropriate supporting proof, their "qualified purchases."

    (d) **Special master.**[2] _____ is appointed as special master under Fed. R. Civ. P. 53 to review, tabulate, and (as appropriate) audit claims made by class members. The special master shall establish procedures to resolve disputes regarding eligibility of persons to be members of the class and regarding the amount of "qualified purchases" by such persons. The findings and conclusions of the special master identifying the class members, their respective "qualified purchases," and their allocable shares of the settlement fund shall be reported to the court under Fed. R. Civ. P. 53(e)(2) as soon as is practicable. Compensation and expenses of the special master will be paid from the settlement fund in such amount as the court may determine to be fair and reasonable.

    (e) **Distribution.** The net settlement fund, with interest, shall be distributed to class members as soon as practicable after the amount to which each is entitled has been determined. Any funds remaining after distribution has been completed may be distributed as the court may direct.

4. **Notice.** Class counsel shall by _____[date]_____ , cause to be mailed in the name of the clerk by first class mail, postage prepaid, to members of the class [who did not timely elect to be excluded from litigation] a notice in substantially the same form as Attachment A. [Notice in substantially the same form as Attachment B shall also be given by publication in the following manner: _____ _____ .]

5. **Reserved Jurisdiction of Court.** The court retains jurisdiction over the settlement of this case and may enter additional orders to effectuate the fair and orderly administration of the settlement as may from time to time be appropriate, including the determination of persons to whom payment should be made in the event of death or dissolution and the right to set aside a portion of the net settlement fund not exceeding [$_____] [____ % of the net fund] as a reserve for late claims and other contingencies and to determine the appropriate disposition of any portion of the reserve not distributed to the class members.

Dated: _____

_____
United States District Judge

Attachments:
    A—Notice
    B—Published Notice

Notes:

    1. This assumes that an application for attorneys' fees was heard concurrently with the hearing on approval of the settlement.

    2. These sample forms contain provisions generally suitable if a special master is appointed to administer the settlement. In other cases, use of a claims committee or magistrate judge may be appropriate.

UNITED STATES DISTRICT COURT
_____ DISTRICT OF _____

In re:)
) Master File No. _____
[WIDGET ANTITRUST] LITIGATION   )

Notice of Method of Distribution and Claims Procedure

TO: Purchasers of [Widgets] who are members of the plaintiff class in CA _____
_____ .

Status of Proceedings

On _____[date]_____ , all persons believed to be members of the plaintiff class for whom addresses where available and who had not timely elected to exclude themselves from the class were notified of the proposed settlement of this litigation. Following a hearing on _____[date]_____ , this settlement was approved by the court.

The amount received for the class from the defendants, after payment of attorneys' fees and expenses, is $ _____ . Distribution of these funds, which are being held at interest, will be made to class members as soon as feasible after the necessary information has been obtained from the class members and appropriate orders are issued by the court. Barring unforeseen difficulties, this distribution should occur by _____ , 19_____ .

The purpose of this notice is to advise class members of the procedure by which the settlement funds will be distributed and to ascertain data necessary to make this distribution.

Eligibility to Share in the Proceeds

Distribution will be made to a class of persons and entities throughout the United States and its territories (other than [widget] manufacturers and companies owned or controlled by them) that did not timely elect to be excluded from the class and that between _____[date]_____ , and_____[date]_____ , purchased one or more [widgets] directly from a [widget] manufacturer.

You are NOT eligible to file claims in this litigation or to share in the proceeds of the settlement if: (1) you are or have been a [widget] manufacturer or a company owned or controlled by such a manufacturer, or (2) you timely elected to exclude yourself from the class in this case, or (3) you did not during the indicated period purchase [widgets] directly from a [widget] manufacturer. (If, for example, you purchased [widgets] during this period only from a wholesaler or retailer that was not a [widget] manufacturer, you are not eligible to participate in the settlement.)

Plan of Distribution

The net settlement fund will be distributed as follows:

1. The "qualified purchases" of each eligible class member will be determined. A "qualified purchase" means the net price (exclusive of transportation charges and after any discounts or allowances) paid by a class member to a [widget] manufacturer for [widgets] from _____[date]_____, to ____[date]_____. The procedure by which the "qualified purchases" of the class members will be determined is explained below.

2. The "qualified purchaser" by all eligible class members will be totaled.

3. Each eligible class member's share of the net settlement fund to be distributed after payment of fees and expenses will be its fractional share of the fund where the numerator of the fraction will be its "qualified purchases" and the denominator will be the total of the "qualified purchases" by all eligible class members.

Claims; Documentation

To participate in the allocation and distribution of the settlement fund, eligible class members must complete and sign, under penalties of perjury, the claim form attached hereto and mail it, first class mail, postage prepaid, before _____[date]_____, to:

> Special Master
> [Widget Antitrust] Litigation
> P.O. Box _____
> [address]_____
> [city, state, zip]_____

You may be required during audit of the claims to provide appropriate supporting evidence (such as invoices and purchase orders), and should therefore preserve such records.

If any question is raised about your eligibility to participate in the settlement or the amount of your "qualified purchases," you will be provided an opportunity to be heard in an appropriate manner before the special master appointed by the court to review, tabulate, and audit the claims.

Additional Information

Any questions you have about matters contained in this notice (and any corrections or changes of name or address) should NOT be directed to the court, but should be addressed in writing to:

> Special Master
> [Widget Antitrust] Litigation
> P.O. Box _____
> [address] _____
> [city, state, zip] _____

You may also write or telephone:

> [X.Y., Esq.]
> Class Counsel
> [Widget Antitrust] Litigation
> [address] _____
> [city, state, zip] _____
> Telephone: _____

You may, of course, also seek the advice and guidance of your own attorney if you desire. Employment of private counsel is not, however, required as a condition to participation in the settlement, and will be at your own expense.

Jurisdiction

The court has retained jurisdiction over the settlement of this case and may enter appropriate orders to effectuate the fair and orderly administration of the settlement, including setting aside a portion of the settlement fund as a reserve for late claims and other contingencies.

Reminder as to Time Limit

You are not entitled to participate in the settlement unless you file your completed claim form with the special master by mail postmarked on or before _____ [date] _____ .

Dated: _____

> _____
> [U.V.], Clerk
> United States District Court
> U.S. Courthouse
> _____

Attachment:
    Claim Form

UNITED STATES DISTRICT COURT
_____ DISTRICT OF _____

In re:)
)   Master File No. _____
[WIDGET ANTITRUST] LITIGATION   )

Claim Form
(Complete both sides of form)
(See instructions on back)

Section I. Identification

1. Business Name of Claimant _____

2. Address _____
    _____

3. City, State, Zip Code _____

4. Telephone _____

5. Other names and addresses used by claimant (including any predecessors) from
    _____[date]_____ , to _____[date]_____ . (If you received more than one copy
    of the settlement notice, indicate the names and addresses to which they were sent):
    _____
    _____.

(Use Additional Sheets if Necessary)

6. Name, title, address, and telephone number of the individual (if different from the
    person signing this form) who is most knowledgeable about claimant's purchases of
    [widgets] from _____[date]_____ , to _____[date]_____ :
    _____
    _____
    _____.

7. Has claimant ever been owned or controlled by a [widget] manufacturer?
    (if "yes," describe the circumstances below)

Section II. [Widget] Purchases

Manufacturer from Which Purchased	Date of Purchase	Number of [Widgets]	Net Price	Type/No. of Document Reflecting Purchase
_____	_____	_____	$_____	_____
_____	_____	_____	$_____	_____
_____	_____	_____	$_____	_____
_____	_____	_____	$_____	_____

(Use Additional Sheets If Necessary)

I certify under penalty of perjury that to the best of my knowledge, information, and belief the information on the front and back of this claim (and any additional sheets) is true and correct and that this is the only claim being made with respect to these purchases.

Dated: _____

_____

Business name of claimant

By:

_____

(Signature of authorized officer)

_____

(Printed name of officer)

_____

(Title and telephone number)

Instructions

1. Complete all items. Type or print all information (except for signature).

2. Attach additional sheets if space is inadequate.

3. Retain supporting documentation (invoices, purchase orders, etc.).

4. Mail first class, postage prepaid, before _____[date]_____ , to:

> Special Master
> [Widget Antitrust] Litigation
> P.O. Box _____
> [address] _____
> [city, state, zip] _____

UNITED STATES DISTRICT COURT
_____ DISTRICT OF _____

In re:)
)   Master File No. _____
[WIDGET ANTITRUST] LITIGATION   )

Published Notice of Settlement Distribution

TO: Purchasers of [Widgets]

The class action charging [C.D. Inc., E.F. Inc., and G.H. Inc.] with violation of the federal antitrust laws in the sale of [widgets] has been settled. Settlements with the defendants in the total amount of $_____ have been approved by the court.

If you purchased [widgets] directly from a [widget] manufacturer between _____ ____[date]_____, and _____[date]_____, you may be entitled to a share of the proceeds of the settlements. You are not, however, entitled to participate in the settlement if you are or have been a [widget] manufacturer (or a company owned or controlled by such a manufacturer) or if you timely elected to exclude yourself from the class.

Notice of the method by which the funds will be distributed, eligibility requirements, and the action that must be taken by eligible persons to obtain a share of the proceeds was mailed on _____[date]_____, to all persons and entities previously identified as members of the class.

If you are or may be a member of the class but do not receive the mailed notice by _____[date]_____, you should immediately notify the "Special Master, [Widget Antitrust] Litigation, P.O. Box_____, _____," requesting a copy of the notice and a claim form. Delay in filing the claim form described in the notice may result in loss of benefits to which you might otherwise be entitled.

Dated: _____

                              _____
                              [U.V.], Clerk
                              United States District Court, U.S. Courthouse
                              [address]_____

41.5 Sample Orders—Special Cases

41.51 Coordinating Proceedings in Different Courts

[caption]

Order No. _____
(Coordination with Proceedings in Other Courts)

It appearing that [the above-styled cases] [the cases listed on Attachment____] share common issues with, and will involve common discovery with, certain cases pending in _____[list other court(s)]_____ (the "related actions") and that pretrial proceedings in all these cases should be coordinated to avoid unnecessary conflicts and expense, conserve judicial resources, and expedite the disposition of all the cases, this court, after having consulted with counsel [and being advised that similar orders will be entered in such other court(s)[1]], ORDERS:

1. **Designated Counsel.**[2]

   (a) **Plaintiffs' Lead and Liaison Counsel.** _____
   and _____ are designated as Plaintiffs' Lead Counsel and Plaintiffs' Liaison Counsel, respectively, in this court, with the responsibilities prescribed in [Attachment ____] [*supra* section 41.31, paragraphs 1 and 2]. They may serve in similar capacities in the related cases if so authorized or permitted by the courts in which such cases are pending and, in any event, shall endeavor to coordinate activities in these cases with those in the related cases.

   (b) **Defendants' Liaison Counsel.** _____
   is designated to serve as Defendants' Liaison Counsel with the responsibilities prescribed in [Attachment ____] [*supra* section 41.31, paragraph 4]. Defendants' Liaison Counsel may serve in a similar capacity in the related cases if so authorized or permitted by such courts and, in any event, shall endeavor to coordinate activities in these cases with those in the related cases.

   (c) **Compensation.** Attorneys designated as Lead or Liaison Counsel by this court and the other courts shall be entitled to reasonable compensation and reimbursement of expenses for services performed in such capacities, equitably apportioned among the parties in these and the related cases benefiting from such services. This court will cooperate with the other courts in making appropriate orders for such compensation and reimbursement if agreement cannot be reached between such counsel and the parties for whom they are acting.

2. Discovery.[3]

(a) **Joint Document Depositories.** The document depositories prescribed in [Exhibit _____] [*supra* section 41.35] shall be established for the joint use of parties in these related cases. [Subject to agreement regarding the sharing of expenses,] counsel in the related cases shall have access to the documents in such depositories to the same extent as counsel in the cases in this court. Parties will not make new requests for production of documents in these proceedings if such documents have already been produced and are available to them in the related cases.

(b) **Confidential Documents.** Counsel in the related cases shall have access to confidential documents produced under the Confidentiality Order entered in this court [see, e.g., *supra* section 41.36] on the same terms and conditions as counsel in the cases in this court. Counsel in the cases in this court obtaining access to documents marked confidential under similar orders entered in other courts shall be subject to the terms and conditions of such orders.

(c) **Depositions.** Depositions of persons whose testimony will likely be relevant both in these cases and in the related cases should ordinarily be cross-noticed for use in all such cases. [The parties in the cases before this court are directed to show cause within 60 days why the depositions previously taken in the related cases should not be usable in this court, subject to the right to conduct supplemental examination on a showing of need.]

3. **Consistency of Rulings.** To avoid unnecessary conflicts and inconsistencies in the rulings of this and the other courts on matters such as discovery disputes and scheduling conflicts,

[Alternate 1—Deferral to Prior Rulings]

This court will adopt a ruling already made on such matter by another court in a related case unless a different ruling is shown to be mandated by the laws and rules governing this court or justified by particular circumstances of the cases before this court.

[Alternate 2—Lead Case]

Such disputes will initially be presented in case no. _____, pending in _____[name of court]_____ , and the ruling made in that case will be given effect in all [other] cases in this court unless a different ruling is shown to be [mandated by the laws and rules governing this court or] justified by particular circumstances of such cases.

[Alternate 3—Joint Special Master]

_____ is appointed under Fed. R. Civ. P. 53(d) to serve as Special Master in these cases (and, under similar appointments by the other courts, in the related cases) (1) to assist the respective courts in preparing and monitoring schedules and plans for coordinated conduct of discovery and other pretrial proceedings; (2) to recommend to the respective courts appropriate resolution of discovery disputes, including controversies regarding limitations on the scope or form of discovery and questions regarding claims of privilege and confidentiality; and (3) to facilitate proper cooperation and coordination among counsel.

[Alternate 4—Joint Hearings]

This court will be prepared to conduct consolidated hearings and pretrial conferences with judges of the courts where related cases are pending and to enter joint rulings (except to the extent differences may be mandated by different laws or rules governing the courts or justified by special circumstances in the various cases).

4. **Other Litigation.** Upon application, these provisions may be ordered applicable to cases involving the same common issues subsequently filed in other courts.

Dated: _____

_____
United States District Judge

Attachments [omitted]

Notes:

1. The terms of coordination between the affected courts should ordinarily be arranged—either by direct consultation between the judges of the courts or indirectly through counsel—before this type of order is entered, and, if feasible, parallel orders should be entered by the various courts. See *supra* sections 31.14, 31.31.

2. This form provides for appointment of lead counsel and liaison counsel for plaintiffs, but only liaison counsel for defendants. In some cases, the same organizational structure will be appropriate both for plaintiffs and for defendants.

3. Depending on the circumstances, it may be appropriate to condition access to discovery materials either on a reciprocal obligation or on payment of fair compensation for a share of the services involved in gathering the information.

41.52 Mass Tort Case-Management Order[1]

[caption]

Order No. _____
(Standard Procedures)

It appearing that [the above-styled cases] [cases listed in Attachment _____] involve claims of death, personal injury, and other damage arising as a result of [exposure to] [use of] [_____ products] [the incident occurring at _____ on _____[date]_____] and that other similar actions may be filed in or transferred to this court in the future, the court ORDERS:

1. **Filing of Order.** A copy of this Order shall be filed in each such case. In cases subsequently filed, a copy will be provided by the clerk to each plaintiff at the time of the filing the complaint and will be served with the complaint on any defendant not previously a party in these cases. [In cases subsequently removed or transferred to this court, a copy will be provided by the clerk to each new party upon removal or transfer.]

2. **Pretrial Consolidation.** All cases in this litigation are consolidated for pretrial purposes. This is not a determination that any of these actions should be consolidated for trial.

3. **Case Grouping Information.** The cases in this litigation are further consolidated into subgroups for pretrial purposes. Those groups are [describe precisely the subgroups, such as all cases filed by attorney X, Y, and Z; all cases involving injuries or diseases X, Y, and Z; all cases involving exposure to products X, Y, and Z; all cases involving injuries that occurred at worksites X, Y, and Z; all cases involving injuries that occurred in the same state; all cases involving the same set of defendants; all cases involving death, disabling injury, or nondisabling injury; or some combination of characteristics]. To determine the group to which each case should be assigned the court will [accept the designation of plaintiffs' counsel if not disputed by defendants' counsel] [order plaintiffs to submit information regarding case characteristics in a form developed by counsel for plaintiffs and defendants and approved by the court].

4. **Case-Management Data; Special Master or Court-Appointed Expert.** At the time of filing, plaintiffs shall be required to submit information that may be relevant to assigning cases to subgroups, evaluating cases for settlement purposes, and developing a trial plan. Plaintiffs' and defendants' counsel shall meet and confer to identify specific information about individual cases that is likely to affect settlement or trial, including information relating to factors such as described in paragraph 3 and addi-

tional factors relating to each plaintiff's exposure to or use of particular products, the degree of injury, diagnosis and prognosis, loss of employment, medical expenses, and other information relating to the claims and defenses. Plaintiffs' and defendants' counsel should attempt to come to an agreement on a method for entering such information into a standard electronic format that would be available to the parties to the litigation and the court. [The court will entertain nominations of individuals to serve as a special master or court-appointed expert to assist the parties in establishing a database addressing the factors described above.] [If counsel are unable to agree on the factors or the format, the court will entertain nominations of individuals to serve as a special master or court-appointed expert to establish a database addressing the factors described above.]

5. **Filing of Papers with Court.** The purpose of the following instructions is to reduce the time and expense of duplicate filings of documents through use of a master case file, while at the same time not congesting the master case with miscellaneous pleadings and orders that are of interest only to the parties directly affected by them. It is not intended that a party lose any rights based on a failure to follow these instructions.

(a) **Master Docket and File.** The clerk will maintain a master docket and case file under the style "In re _____ Product Liability Litigation (MDL-XXXX)" as master file number [CV NN-1000-X]. Orders, pleadings, motions, and other documents bearing a caption similar to that of this order will, when docketed and filed in the master case, be deemed to have been docketed and filed in each individual case to the extent applicable and will not ordinarily be separately docketed or physically filed in such individual cases. However, the caption may also contain a notation indicating whether the document relates to all cases or only to specified cases.

(b) **Separate Filing.** A document that relates only to a specific case and would not be of interest except to the parties directly affected by it—such as an amended complaint adding a party or a motion to dismiss a party—should bear the caption and case number of that case rather than of the master case file. Such a document will be docketed and filed in that case and not in the master case file. Please note that cases removed or transferred to this court are assigned a new case number in this court.

(c) **Leave to Add Parties.** Until otherwise directed, plaintiffs are granted leave, without need for any special motion or order, to add other plaintiffs to any pending (or subsequently filed, removed, or transferred) case if all plaintiffs in the case (1) will be represented by the same counsel (or if counsel for existing plaintiffs consent to the intervention), (2) all plaintiffs are suing the same defendants, and (3) all plaintiffs [were exposed to defendants' products] in the same state. The purpose of this authorization is to avoid unnecessary filing fees and the delays inherent in 28 U.S.C. § 1407 transfers. The joinder of such parties will not be viewed as affecting subsequent motions by either plaintiffs or defendants for separate trials under Rule 42(b).

6. **Master Pleadings; Motions; Orders.**

    (a) **Master/Sample Complaints.** Plaintiffs' steering committee has filed in [CV NN-10000-X]:

        (1) a master complaint containing allegations that would be suitable for adoption by reference in individual cases, and

        (2) a sample complaint illustrating how allegations from the master complaint can be incorporated into an individual case.

    The allegations of the master complaint are not deemed automatically included in any particular case. However, in order to avoid possible problems with statutes of limitations or doctrines of repose, it shall be deemed (except to the extent a plaintiff thereafter files an amended complaint disavowing such claims and theories or limits its claims and theories to those contained in an amended complaint) that as of this date, for cases now pending in this court (or as of the date other cases are filed in, removed to, or transferred to this court) a motion is filed in each such case to amend the complaint to add any potentially applicable claims and theories from the master complaint not contained in the complaint actually filed in that case.

    (b) **Master Answers.** By _____, each entity listed below will file in [CV NN-1000-X] a master answer that incorporates its defenses in law or fact to claims made against it in the various actions that are presently pending in this litigation, including any cross claims it makes against other defendants. The answer will not attempt to provide a cross-reference to particular paragraphs or counts of the various complaints. The answer will, however, in a "generic" manner admit or deny (including denials based on lack of information and belief) the allegations typically included in claims or cross claims made against it as well as make such additional allegations as are appropriate to its defenses or cross claims. This may be done through allegations such as "It alleges that it is incorporated in State A; that it has its principal place of business in State B; that during the period from (date) to (date) it manufactured, sold, and distributed products intended to be used in _____; that these products were intended to be used only by trained, knowledgeable _____
    and were accompanied by warnings and instructions that adequately explained such risks as were inherent and unavoidable in the products; that these products were not unreasonably dangerous, were suitable for the purposes for which they were intended, and were distributed with adequate and sufficient warnings; that it is without knowledge or information at this time sufficient to form a belief as to any averment that one of its products was used in the procedure on which the

plaintiff's complaint is based; that to the extent the plaintiff makes a claim for X (or under statute Y) it is not liable because _____ ; etc."

(1) When so filed in [CV NN-1000-X], these answers constitute an answer in each constituent case now pending or when hereafter filed in, removed to, or transferred to this court except to the extent the defendant later files a separate answer in an individual case.

(2) A defendant not listed below may also file a master answer in [CV NN-1000-X] by _____[date]_____ , or within 45 days after the first case in which it is named as a defendant is filed in, removed to, or transferred to this court.

(c) **Refinement of Pleadings.** It is anticipated that an amended, more specific complaint and answer may be required before a case is scheduled for trial or remanded to a transferor court, but amendments of pleadings prior to that time should generally be avoided.

(d) **Motions; Orders.** A motion, brief, or response that has potential effect on multiple parties (e.g., documents submitted in connection with a motion for partial summary judgment asserting that punitive damages are not recoverable with respect to [the product's use] in State A) will be deemed made in all similar cases on behalf of, and against, all parties similarly situated except to the extent such other parties timely disavow such a position. Additional motions, briefs, or responses addressed to such issues should not be filed or submitted by other parties except to the extent needed because of inadequacy of the original papers, to present unique facts, or a difference in positions. Orders resolving such motions will likewise be deemed as made with respect to all parties similarly situated unless the order indicates otherwise.

7. **Service of Original Complaints; Amendments Adding Parties.**

(a) **Acceptable Service.** Exhibit _____ is a list of the "National Defendants"—that is, those entities that have frequently been named as defendants in these cases filed throughout the United States—with the name and address of their national counsel and information provided by national counsel indicating the state(s) in which they are incorporated, in which they have their principal place of doing business, and in which they will or may contest personal jurisdiction. To eliminate disputes over service of process and reduce the expense of such service, these defendants [have agreed] [shall inform the court within ___ days as to whether or not they agree] to accept service of process in these cases (without, however, waiving any objections to personal jurisdiction or venue) if a copy of the summons and complaint is sent by certified mail, return receipt requested, to the person or address shown in Exhibit ____. Defendants' agreement [report to the court as noted above should indicate whether it] applies to any case involving [product] claims filed in any federal district court or in any state court of general jurisdiction.

(b) **Extension of Time to Serve.** Notwithstanding Fed. R. Civ. P. 4(m), plaintiffs shall have thirty days after the date of this order (or, if later, thirty days after the date a case is subsequently filed in, removed to, or transferred to this court) in which to effect service on defendants.

(c) **Leave to Add Parties.** Until otherwise directed, plaintiffs are granted leave, without need for any special motion or order, to add other plaintiffs to any pending (or subsequently filed, removed, or transferred) case if all plaintiffs in the case (1) will be represented by the same counsel (or if counsel for existing plaintiffs consent to the intervention), (2) all plaintiffs are suing the same defendants, and (3) all plaintiffs were exposed to [the product] in the same state. The purpose of this authorization is to avoid unnecessary filing fees and the delays inherent in 28 U.S.C. § 1407 transfers. The joinder of such parties will not be viewed as affecting subsequent motions by either plaintiffs or defendants for separate trials under Rule 42(b).

8. **Motions.**

   (a) **Meet and Confer.** To avoid unnecessary litigation concerning motions, including motions relating to discovery disputes, counsel are directed to meet and confer before filing a motion. In any motion filed, counsel for the moving party must certify that a good faith effort was made to resolve the dispute.

   (b) **Motions Under Rule 11, Rule 12, and Rule 56.** No motion shall be filed under Rule 11, 12, or 56 without leave of court.

9. **Inactive [Product] [Incident] Docket.** The purpose of this paragraph is to establish a procedure for separating cases in which the plaintiff has little or no physical impairment from cases with more serious impairments to assist the court in establishing priorities for managing its docket. The intent is to toll the operation of any applicable statutes of limitation or repose while a case is listed as inactive. The clerk shall establish a separate file called the "Inactive [product] [incident] Docket," which shall consist of (1) cases voluntarily dismissed pursuant to a general stipulation prepared by plaintiffs and defendants that will set forth their agreement that such cases can be revived if specific conditions should be met, and (2) claims initiated by a "Notice of Claim" procedure. To invoke the notice procedure, a claimant must file an "Affidavit of Notice of Claim" that includes (1) the name(s), address(es), and marital status of the claimant(s); (2) a brief statement of circumstances of claimant's exposure(s) to the [product] [incident giving rise to the common claims]; (3) a statement of the nature of the injury, disease, or condition alleged to have been caused by the [product] [incident]; and (4) the names of the entities to be given notice and whom the claimant proposes to serve.

Upon certification of the claimant(s) that notice's have been sent to all listed defendants in the manner set forth in the stipulation of agreement signed by plaintiffs' and defendants' representatives, the claims shall be recorded on the inactive docket.

The filing of the Notice of Claim or the voluntary dismissal pursuant to the stipulation shall toll all applicable statutes of limitation or repose regarding any claims of the plaintiff or plaintiff's spouse, children, dependents, heirs, or estates arising relating to the exposure to [product] [incident]. Claims may be removed from the inactive docket at any time by the filing and serving of a complaint. Signing the stipulation referred to above signifies the consent of each signing party to this procedure and to the tolling of the statutes of limitations or repose as described above.

10. **Settlement.**

[Insert any special provisions to facilitate settlement, such as appointment of a settlement judge or special master to assist the parties, a timetable for scheduling settlement conferences, or procedures for using arbitration, minitrials, or summary jury trials. Also include any provision for contributions by later-settling parties to compensate designated counsel for services previously rendered.]

[11. **Discovery.** See separate discovery order.]

Dated: _____

                                                    _____
                                                    United States District Judge

Note:
    1. See *supra* § 33.2

41.53 CERCLA Case-Management Order

[caption]

Order No. _____

(Case-Management Order)

It is ORDERED:

1. **Limited Consolidation.** Until further order of the Court, the above-captioned actions, Civil Action No. _____ and Civil Action No. _____ (collectively, the "Actions"), are consolidated before the undersigned for the limited purposes of coordinated case management and discovery.

2. **Lodging of the Administrative Record; Stay of Administrative Record Discovery.** On or before _____[date]_____, plaintiff, the United States of America, will lodge with the Court the administrative record developed by the Environmental Protection Agency ("EPA") in connection with the initial Remedial Investigations and Feasibility Studies (RI/FS) for the _____ Landfill (the "Landfill"); on or before _____[date]_____, _____ plaintiff, the United States of America, will lodge with the Court the administrative record developed by the EPA in connection with the Record of Decision (including the Supplemental Feasibility Study). No discovery shall be permitted at this time as to what documents constitute or will constitute these administrative records until further Order of the Court.

3. **Temporary Stay of Counterclaims, Cross Claims, and Third-Party Claims.** Until _____[date]_____ , the date established herein for the Second Case-Management Conference, no counterclaims, cross claims, or third-party claims in either of the Actions, and no claims related to the Landfill by defendants in one of the Actions against defendants in the other of the Actions, shall be filed. The stay as to counterclaims and third-party claims shall be addressed at the Second Case-Management Conference. All counterclaims, cross claims, or third-party claims filed prior to the entry of this Order are stayed until the Second Case-Management Conference.

4. **Filing of Claims.** At the Second Case-Management Conference, scheduled herein, the Court will establish a schedule for filing of the claims referred to in the proceeding paragraph. Nothing in this Order shall prejudice the right of any defendant in either of the Actions to assert any such claims, nor shall any such claims be barred by laches or by any statute of limitations by virtue of the delay in filing such claims required by this order.

5. **Realignment of Pleadings.** The United States of America, in Civil No. _____ , and the State Department of Environmental Protection, in Civil No. _____ , are hereby granted

leave to file amended complaints, not later than _____[date]_____ , without the necessity of a motion. The purposes of these amended complaints are to cure misnomer problems, to add defendants, to dismiss defendants already named, without prejudice, to conform the defendants named in the two amended complaints to the degree that the plaintiffs deem appropriate, and to clarify the causes of action, demands, and relief sought in the amended complaints to the degree that the plaintiffs deem appropriate. Existing defendants who have already answered or otherwise responded to the complaint need not answer or otherwise respond to the amended complaint unless they choose to do so. All other defendants shall answer or otherwise respond within the time provided in the Rules.

6. **Joinder of New Parties.** Except as provided herein or by subsequent order, no party may join an additional party in this case. The joinder of new parties may occur through the amendment of the complaints (see _____ above), or by the coordinated efforts of the Defense Litigation Committee to be formalized by the defendants. The Defense Litigation Committee will serve as a clearinghouse for information pertinent to identifying new parties through coordinated discovery efforts. Discovery with respect to joining new parties is discussed in paragraphs _____ below. No later than ____[date]____, the Defense Litigation Committee shall have assembled a list of new parties whose joinder will be considered at the Second Case-Management Conference on _____[date]_____ .

To the extent feasible, this listing shall be selective, seeking joinder of parties with a relatively higher degree of alleged responsibility and continuing viability, and avoiding joinder of parties with a relatively lower degree of alleged responsibility or which are of doubtful viability. It is anticipated that leave to file a consolidated third-party complaint joining the new parties in an orderly fashion, and leave for individual defendants to file contractual indemnification claims, will be granted at the Second Case-Management Conference. [There will be an additional opportunity to join further new parties in the future as the cases unfold.]

7. **Amendments.** The goal of the Amended Complaints and the Consolidated third-party complaint is to have a more unified and orderly set of pleadings and joinders so that these Actions may go forward expeditiously.

8. **Scope of Discovery.** Discovery shall be limited at present to the following issues:

(a) Identification of new parties.

(b) Quantity, quality, and nexus of parties' wastes to the _____ Landfill.

[It is anticipated that parties providing full discovery on these issues and believing themselves to have no nexus of hazardous wastes to the Landfill will be permitted to seek summary judgment in the near future.]

No discovery is permitted at this time regarding issues of "release or threatened release" at the Landfill, or of "the incurring of response costs consistent with the NCP at the Landfill." Enlarging discovery to these issues, and the precise extent, timing, and appropriateness of summary judgment motion practice relating to some or all liability issues, will be considered at the Second Case-Management Conference, following lodging of the Administrative Records under _____ , above.

Forms of Discovery

9. **Document Production.** Production of documents shall be coordinated and go forward promptly and responses shall be served within _____ days of service. The deposition of representatives of EPA, DEP [the State Department of Environmental Protection], or a defendant shall not go forward until that party has responded to the document production request upon it.

10. **Depositions.** Depositions are permitted at this time only with respect to the issue of identification of new parties and quantity, quality, and nexus. Such depositions may be taken, on these issues, of existing parties and nonparties, except that no depositions of representatives of the EPA or the DEP or of a defendant are permitted until that party has timely responded to the document production request upon it. Scheduling of depositions on behalf of defendants will be coordinated between the plaintiffs and the Defense Litigation Committee, endeavoring to conduct not more than one deposition at a time.

11. **Procedure for Scheduling Depositions.**

    ***

12. **Interrogatories to Plaintiffs.** The plaintiffs shall serve certified responses to a common set of interrogatories, derived from the set of interrogatories served by _____ _____ on behalf of fourteen defendants, pertaining to quantity, quality, nexus, and identification of additional parties, within _____ days after service, to the same extent as if served on behalf of all _____ defendants in the United States case and all _____ defendants in the State case. All other interrogatories are stricken, without prejudice, and need not be answered.

13. **Interrogatories to Defendants.** The plaintiffs may propound a set of common interrogatories on the above issues upon each of the defendants, each of whom shall serve certified responses to same within _____ days after service.

14. **Requests for Admission.** Requests for admission shall not be served until further order of the court, to be discussed at the Second Case-Management Conference.

15. **Liaison Counsel for Defendants.** The court recognizes the defendants' selection of _____ , _____ , as Liaison Counsel for Defendants with respect to communications from the court to the defendants.

16. **Service List.** Liaison Counsel for the Defendants shall prepare and promptly file with the clerk, the Service List containing the names, addresses, and telephone and facsimile numbers of attorneys appearing in this case and of unrepresented parties.

17. **Cooperation Among Defendants; Defense Litigation Committee.** Cooperation efforts among defendants in the Actions for the purpose of coordinating discovery, trial, counsel, or otherwise minimizing expenses in the Actions are being conducted at the direction of the Court for its convenience in the resolution of the Actions and they shall not constitute evidence of conspiracy, concerted action, or any other wrongful conduct in this or any other proceeding. The defendants are hereby directed to take reasonable steps to eliminate duplication of effort and redundant discovery. The defendants have also informed the Court that they have selected and will continue to organize a Defense Litigation Committee, the duties of which shall be better defined before the Interim Status Conference on _____ [date] _____ at

_____ .

18. **Privileges Preserved.** All information and/or documents exchanged among the defendants in the Actions shall be communicated for the limited purpose of assisting in a common defense in this litigation only, and such exchange shall not constitute a waiver of any attorney–client work product, trade secret, or other privilege. All discussions will be treated as not admissible into evidence in accordance with the terms of Fed. R. Evid. 408.

19. **Cooperation Between Plaintiffs and Exchange of Information.** Exchange of information and/or documents between the plaintiffs relating to the prosecution of these actions is communication for the limited purpose of assisting in a common cause and shall not constitute a waiver of whatever attorney–client, work product, enforcement-sensitive, or any other privilege, if any, may apply.

20. **Preservation of Documents.** All parties and their counsel are hereby directed to preserve any information in their possession, custody, or control that constitutes or contains material or information that may be relevant in these Actions. All parties and their counsel are directed to take all reasonable steps to communicate the requirements of this provision to the individuals employed by that party who must know of this provision in order for it to be effective. Plaintiffs shall instruct their RI/FS contractors and subcontractors (and any other of plaintiffs' contractors and subcontractors) to preserve all such information.

Dated: _____

_____

United States District Judge

41.54 Civil RICO Case-Statement Order[1]

[caption]

Order No. _____

It is ORDERED:

The proponent of the civil RICO claim shall file and serve [within _____ days of____
_____] a case statement that shall include the facts relied on to initiate the RICO
claim. In particular, the statement shall use the numbers and letters set forth below, unless
filed as part of an amended and restated pleading (in which latter case, the allegations of
the amended and restated pleading shall reasonably follow the organization set out below), and shall state in detail and with specificity the following information:

1. State whether the alleged unlawful conduct is in violation of 18 U.S.C. §§ 1962(a),
   (b), (c), and/or (d). If you allege violations of more than one § 1962 subsection, treat
   each as a separate RICO claim.

2. List each defendant, and state the alleged misconduct and basis of alleged liability of
   each defendant.

3. List the alleged wrongdoers, other than the defendants listed above, and state the alleged misconduct of each wrongdoer.

4. List the alleged victims, and state how each victim allegedly was injured.

5. Describe in detail the pattern of racketeering activity or collection of an unlawful debt
   alleged for each RICO claim. A description of the pattern of racketeering activity
   shall:

   (a) list the alleged predicate acts and the specific statutes allegedly violated by each
       predicate act;

   (b) state the dates of the predicate acts, the participants in the predicate acts, and a
       description of the facts surrounding each predicate act;

   (c) if the RICO claim is based on the predicate offenses of wire fraud, mail fraud,
       fraud in the sale of securities, or fraud in connection with a case under U.S.C.
       Title 11, the "circumstances constituting fraud or mistake shall be stated with
       particularity," Fed. R. Civ. P. 9(b) (identify the time, place, and contents of the
       alleged misrepresentation or omissions, and the identity of persons to whom and
       by whom the alleged misrepresentations or omissions were made);

(d) describe in detail the perceived relationship that the predicate acts bear to each other or to some external organizing principle that renders them "ordered" or "arranged" or "part of a common plan"; and

(e) explain how the predicate acts amount to or pose a threat of continued criminal activity.

6. Describe in detail the alleged enterprise for each RICO claim. A description of the enterprise shall :

    (a) state the names of the individuals, partnerships, corporations, associations, or other entities allegedly constituting the enterprise;

    (b) describe the structure, purpose, roles, function, and course of conduct of the enterprise;

    (c) state whether any defendants are employees, officers, or directors of the alleged enterprise;

    (d) state whether any defendants are associated with the alleged enterprise, and if so, how;

    (e) explain how each defendant participated in the direction of the affairs of the enterprise;

    (f) state whether you allege [(i) that the defendants are individuals or entities separate from the alleged enterprise, or (ii) that the defendants are the enterprise itself, or (iii) that the defendants are] members of the enterprise; and

    (g) if you allege any defendants to be the enterprise itself, or members of the enterprise, explain whether such defendants are perpetrators, passive instruments, or victims of the alleged racketeering activity.

7. State whether you allege, and describe in detail, how the pattern of racketeering activity and the enterprise are separate or have merged into one entity.

8. Describe the alleged relationship between the activities and the pattern of racketeering activity. Discuss how the racketeering activity differs from the usual and daily activities of the enterprise, if at all.

9. Describe what benefits, if any, the alleged enterprise and each defendant received from the alleged pattern of racketeering activity.

10. Describe the effect of the activities of the enterprise on interstate or foreign commerce.

11. If the complaint alleges a violation of 18 U.S.C. § 1962(a), provide the following information:

    (a) State who received the income derived from the pattern of racketeering activity or through the collection of an unlawful debt; and

(b) Describe the use or investment of such income.

12. If the complaint alleges a violation of 18 U.S.C. § 1962(b), provide the following information:

    (a) Describe in detail the acquisition or maintenance of any interest in or control of the alleged enterprise; and

    (b) State whether the same entity is both the liable "person" and the "enterprise" under § 1962(b).

13. If the complaint alleges a violation of 18 U.S.C. § 1962(c), provide the following information:

    (a) state who is employed by or associated with the enterprise; [and]

    (b) state whether the same entity is both the liable "person" and the "enterprise" under § 1962(c).

14. If the complaint alleges a violation of 18 U.S.C. § 1962(d), describe in detail the alleged conspiracy.

15. Describe the alleged injury to business or property.

16. Describe the relationship between the alleged injury and violation of the RICO statute.

17. List the damages sustained by reason of the violation of § 1962, indicating the amount for which each defendant allegedly is liable.

18. Provide any additional information you feel would be helpful to the Court in processing your RICO claim.

Dated: _____

_____
                    United States District Judge

Note:

1. This order has been designed to establish a uniform and efficient procedure for deciding civil actions containing claims made pursuant to 18 U.S.C. §§ 1961–1968 ("civil RICO").

41.6 Sample Pretrial Orders

41.61 Order to Establish Contested and Uncontested Facts[1]

[caption]

Order No. _____

(Statement of Contested and Uncontested Facts)

It is ORDERED:

1. **Development of Joint Statement of Contested and Uncontested Facts.**

    (a) **Plaintiffs' Proposed Facts.** By ____[date]____, plaintiffs shall serve on opposing parties a narrative statement listing all facts proposed to be proved by them at trial in support of their claim(s) as to liability and damages [except on the issue(s) of _____].

    (b) **Defendants' Response and Proposed Facts.** By ___[date]___, defendants shall serve on opposing parties a statement—

        (1) indicating separately as to each numbered statement of fact whether they contest or do not contest it;

        (2) stating all additional facts proposed to be proved by them at trial in opposition to, or in defense against, the plaintiffs' claim; and

        (3) stating all facts proposed to be proved by them at trial in support of their counterclaim(s), cross claim(s), or third-party claim(s).

    (c) **Replies.**

        (1) By _____[date]_____, plaintiffs shall serve on opposing parties a statement indicating separately as to each numbered statement of fact whether they contest or do not contest the fact (including defendants' modifications of the facts initially proposed by plaintiffs) and stating all additional facts proposed to be proved by them at trial in opposition to, or in defense against, the defendants' counterclaims; and

(2) By _____ [date] _____ , defendants to cross claims and third-party claims shall serve on opposing parties a statement indicating separately as to each numbered statement of each whether they contest or do not contest it, and stating all additional facts proposed to be proved by them at trial in opposition to, or in defense against such cross claims or third-party claims.

(d) **Final Response.** By _____ [date] _____ , defendants making counterclaims, cross claims, or third-party claims shall serve on opposing parties a statement indicating which statements of fact they contest and which they do not contest (including modifications of the facts initially proposed by them).

(e) **Joint Statement of Contested and Uncontested Facts.** By _____ [date] _____ , the parties shall file with the court a joint statement separately listing the facts that are not contested and those that are contested, indicating as to the latter the precise nature of their disagreement. These facts, both contested and uncontested, will to the extent practicable be organized and collected under headings descriptive of the claim or defense to which they may be relevant (and, where appropriate, subdivided into factual categories descriptive of particular parties and time periods).

2. **Directions.**

(a) **Narration of Proposed Facts.** In stating facts proposed to be proved, counsel shall do so in brief, simple, declarative, self-contained, consecutively numbered sentences, avoiding all "color words," labels, argumentative language, and legal conclusions. If a fact is to be offered against fewer than all parties, counsel shall indicate the parties against which the fact will (or will not) be offered. [The facts to be set forth include not only ultimate facts, but also all subsidiary and supporting facts except those offered solely for impeachment purposes.]

(b) **Agreement and Disagreement.** Counsel shall indicate that they do not contest a proposed fact if at trial they will not controvert or dispute that fact. In indicating disagreement with a proposed fact, counsel shall do so by deletion or interlineation of particular words or phrases so that the nature of their disagreement (and the extent of any agreement) will be clear.

(c) **Objections.** Objections to the admissibility of a proposed fact (either as irrelevant or on other grounds) may not be used to avoid indicating whether or not the party contests the truth of that fact. [Counsel shall, however, indicate any objections, both to the facts which they contest and those which they do not contest.]

(d) **Individual Positions.** To the extent feasible, counsel with similar interests are expected to coordinate their efforts and express a joint position with respect to the facts they propose to prove and to the facts other parties propose to prove. Subject to the time limits set forth in paragraph 1, each party may, however, list additional proposed facts relating to positions unique to it.

3. **Annotations.** Facts, not evidence, are to be listed by the parties. However, a party may identify in parentheses at the end of a proposed fact the witness(es), deponent(s), document(s), or other evidence supporting the truth of the fact. No party, however, will be required to admit or deny the accuracy of such references.

   [Alternate—Annotation Required.][2] For each proposed fact, the parties shall, at the time of proposing to prove the fact, list the witnesses (including expert witnesses), documents, and (with line-by-line references) any depositions and answers to interrogatories or requests for admission that they will offer to prove that fact. In their response, parties shall, if they object to any such proposed fact or proposed proof, state precisely the grounds of their objection and, if they will contest the accuracy of the proposed fact, similarly list the witnesses, documents, depositions, interrogatories, or admissions that they will offer to controvert that fact. In the joint statement submitted to the court, any objections to each uncontested fact will be shown, and any objections and the listing of evidence will be shown for each contested fact. Except for good cause shown, a party will be precluded at trial from offering any evidence on any fact not so disclosed and from making any objection not so disclosed.

4. **Effect.**

   (a) **Elimination of Proof.** The uncontested facts shall be taken at the trial as established under Fed. R. Civ. P. 36 without the need for independent proof. To the extent relevant to a resolution of contested issues and otherwise admissible, these facts may be read to the jury. Independent proof of uncontested facts will be allowed only if incidental to the presentation of evidence on contested facts or if such proof will better enable the jury to resolve contested facts.

   (b) **Preclusion of Other Facts.** Except for good cause shown, the parties shall be precluded at trial from offering proof of any fact not disclosed in their listing of proposed facts (except purely for impeachment purposes).

5. **Sanctions.** Unjustified refusal to admit a proposed fact or to limit the extent of disagreement with a proposed fact shall be subject to sanctions under Fed. R. Civ. P. 37(c). Excessive listing of proposed facts [or of the evidence to be submitted in support of or denial of such facts] imposing undue burdens on opposing parties shall be subject to sanctions under Rule 16(f).

Dated:_____

_____
United States District Judge

Notes:

1. These statements are sometimes known as statements of contentions (and proof) or as final pretrial statements (FPS). See *supra* §§ 21.47, 21.641.

2. Because it is burdensome, such annotation with preclusive effect should be ordered only in unusually complex cases. For the same reason, the parties are sometimes required to list only the principal facts supporting their claims or defenses or the facts to which the other parties may possibly agree.

41.62 Order for Pretrial Preparation

[caption]

Order No. _____
(Order for Final Pretrial Preparation)

It is ORDERED:

1. **Discovery Cutoff.** All discovery shall be completed, and all responses to discovery requests served, by _____ .

2. **Exchange of Witness Lists and Exhibits.**

   (a) Plaintiff shall serve and submit to the court its list of trial witnesses, listing separately those it will call and those it may call if needed (other than purely for impeachment), and copies of all proposed exhibits consecutively numbered using the blocks of numbers heretofore assigned, and a list of such exhibits, by _____[date]_____ .

   (b) Defendants shall serve and submit to the court its list of trial witnesses, listing separately those it will call and those it may call if needed (other than purely for impeachment), and copies of all proposed exhibits consecutively numbered using the blocks of numbers heretofore assigned, and a list of such exhibits, by _____[date]_____ .

   (c) Voluminous data shall be presented by summary exhibits pursuant to Fed. R. Evid. 1006, and voluminous exhibits shall be redacted to eliminate irrelevant material (which shall remain available for examination by opposing counsel). Where copies of documents are offered, the originals shall be available for examination unless waived by stipulation.

3. **Motions.** The parties shall file all motions for summary judgment and motions in limine, including motions under Fed. R. Evid. 104 (a) and motions to limit or sever issues, by _____[date]_____ . Responses shall be filed by _____[date]_____ . A hearing on all motions will be held on _____[date]_____ at _____ _____ . Objections to evidence not raised by motion, other than objections under Fed. R. Evid. 402 and 403, shall be waived.

4. **Jury Instructions, Forms of Verdict, and Voir Dire Questions.** The parties shall submit proposed jury instructions, forms of verdict, and voir dire questions by _____[date]_____ . The parties shall make a good faith effort to submit at that time a statement of undisputed facts to be read to the jury.

5. **Designation of Discovery Excerpts To Be Offered at Trial.**

   (a) The parties shall submit designations of excerpts from depositions, interrogatory answers, and responses to requests for admissions to be offered at trial (other than purely for impeachment) by _____[date]_____ .

   (b) The parties shall make a good faith effort (i) to prepare a stipulated summary of the relevant substance of deposition testimony to be read to the jury, and (ii) to prepare stipulated excerpts from videotaped depositions to be offered at trial.

6. **Supplementation of Prior Disclosure or Discovery Responses.** All supplemental information required under Fed. R. Civ. P. 26(e), including without limitation supplementation of expert reports or deposition testimony, shall be submitted by _____[date]_____ .

7. **Trial Briefs.** Trial briefs, not to exceed _____ pages including appendices, shall be filed [concurrently] by ____[date]_____ .

8. **Final Pretrial Conference.** A final pretrial conference will be held on _____[date]_____ at _____ .

9. **Trial.** Trial will commence on _____[date]_____ at _____ _____ .

Dated:_____

_____
United States District Judge

41.63 Final Pretrial Order

[caption]

Order No. _____
(Final Pretrial Order)

It is ORDERED:

1. **Rulings on Pending Motions.** The court rules as follows on the pending motions:

   _____
   _____
   _____ .

2. **Consolidation for Trial.** The following cases are consolidated for trial:

   _____
   _____
   _____ .

3. **Issues To Be Tried.**

   (a) The following issues will be tried: _____
   _____
   _____ .

   (b) The following issues are severed for a subsequent trial to be scheduled by the court: _____
   _____
   _____ .

4. **Witnesses.** The witnesses to be called by plaintiff and defendants respectively are those identified on the witness lists attached as Attachment A.

5. **Exhibits.** The exhibits to be offered by plaintiff and defendants, respectively, are those identified on the exhibit lists attached as Attachment B.

6. **Discovery Excerpts.** The excerpts from stenographic and from video depositions, interrogatory answers, and responses to requests for admission identified on Attachment C may be offered at trial.

7. **Undisputed Facts; Judicial Notice.** Facts that have previously been established as undisputed, and facts of which the court will take judicial notice, are set forth on Attachment D.

8. **Order of Proof.** [State any directions concerning the order of proof at trial, such as the defendants making their employees available to be called during plaintiff's case, the sequence of calling opposing expert witnesses, etc.]

9. **Preclusion of Other Proof.** Evidence not identified in this order may not be offered and no issues other than those identified in this order may be tried. The identification of evidence in this order does not commit a party to offering it.

10. **Jury.** A jury of _____ persons shall be seated. Each side shall be permitted three peremptory challenges. Counsel will be permitted a reasonable time to conduct supplemental voir dire following the questioning by the court. All remaining jurors shall participate in deliberations and return of the verdict(s).

11. **Trial.** Trial will commence on _____ [date] _____ at _____ . The jury portion of the trial will be conducted each trial day from _____ to _____ . Trial will be held on the following days: _____ .

12. **Limitations.** [Insert any limitations on the length of the trial, the time available for each side or for any specific part of the trial, or the number of witnesses and exhibits previously established by the court.]

13. **Jury Instructions.** The court will give brief preliminary instructions to the jury and will give most of the jury charge prior to counsel's summation.

14. **Opening Statements.** Opening statements shall be limited to _____ per side, and no exhibits or other visual aids may be displayed to the jury that have not previously been cleared with the court and opposing counsel.

15. **Examination of Witnesses.** [In cases with multiple counsel, provide for the designation of counsel to conduct the principal examination and cross-examination and the right of other counsel to conduct supplemental examination as needed.]

16. **Scheduling of Witnesses.** Counsel shall advise opposing counsel not less than_____ [24 or more] hours before calling a witness or offering an exhibit for direct examination. Counsel will be held responsible for scheduling a sufficient number of witnesses for each trial day to avoid the necessity for an early recess.

17. **Receipt of Exhibits into Evidence.** The clerk will mark all exhibits to which objections have previously been waived or overruled as having been received into evidence at the commencement of trial.

18. **Publication of Exhibits.** Ordinarily, exhibits should be published by visual means that will enable the jury to see the exhibits while the relevant examination is being conducted, and not by being passed among the jurors.

19. **Matters not for the Jury.** Matters to be considered outside of the presence of the jury shall be taken up at a conference with the court to be held at the conclusion of each

trial day, or at such other times as the court may schedule. No recesses for such purposes shall be permitted during the trial day while the jury is sitting.

20. **Verdict.** [The parties have stipulated that a unanimous verdict may be returned by not less than five jurors.]

21. **Jury Conduct.** Jurors wishing to do so will be permitted to take notes.

Dated: _____

_____

United States District Judge

41.7 Jury Questionnaire[1]

Juror No. _____

Name of case: _____

Case number: _____

Nature of case: _____

Trial date: _____

* * *

1. Name: _____

2. Age: _____

3. What community or area do you live in? _____

4. Area lived in before current address: _____

5. Occupation: _____

6. Employer: _____

7. How long? _____

8. Former employer: _____

9. How long? _____

10. Marital Status: ( ) Married ( ) Divorced ( ) Separated ( ) Single

11. Name of spouse: _____

12. Spouse's occupation: _____

13. Spouse's employer: _____

14. How long? _____

15. Spouse's former employer: _____

16 How long? _____

17. Number of children and ages: _____

18. Occupations of adult children: _____

19. If you or your spouse were in the military service, state:

    Yourself: Branch: _____   Dates of service: _____

    Did you serve in combat? ( ) yes ( ) no

    Highest rank attained: _____

Spouse: Branch: _____   Dates of service: _____

    Did your spouse serve in combat? ( ) yes ( ) no

    Highest rank attained: _____

20. Are you, or have you been, employed by a governmental entity? ( ) yes ( ) no

21. If yes, what entity? _____

    Position or job title: _____

    Dates of employment: _____

22. Are members of your family, or have they been, employed by a governmental entity? ( ) yes ( ) no

23. If yes, which family members and what entities? _____
_____

24. Name of high school you attended: _____

    Location: _____

    Number of years attended: _____

25. Name of college or university, if any: _____

    Location: _____

    Major subject: _____

    Year of graduation: _____

    Highest degree attained: _____

26. Have you previously served on a civil trial jury? ( ) yes ( ) no

    If yes, dates of service: _____

    If yes, did the jury reach a verdict in each case? ( ) yes ( ) no

27. Have you previously served on a criminal trial jury? ( ) yes ( ) no

    If yes, dates of service: _____

    If yes, did the jury reach a verdict in each case? ( ) yes ( ) no

28. Have you ever testified as a witness in a case? ( ) yes ( ) no

    If yes, state the nature of the case and your relationship to it: _____
_____

29. Have you every been a party to a lawsuit? ( ) yes ( ) no

    If yes, state the nature of the case and your participation in it:_____
_____

30. Do you have an physical problems which may interfere with your service as a juror? ( ) yes ( ) no

   If yes, state the nature of the problem: _____

   _____

31. Do you have any pressing personal or business obligations which would make jury service of _____ days a week for a trial which may last for a period of _____ weeks difficult at this time? ( ) yes ( ) no

   If yes, state the nature of the difficulty: _____

   _____

32. Have you read, seen, or heard anything about this case from any source ?

   ( ) yes ( ) no

   If yes, describe what you have read, seen, or heard about this case: _____

   _____

33. Are you aware of any reason why you would not be able to serve as a fair and impartial juror in this case if selected? ( ) yes ( ) no

   If yes, state the reason: _____

   _____

   I declare (affirm, certify, verify, or state) under penalty of perjury that the foregoing is true and correct.

_____

(Signature)

_____

(print or type name)

_____

(date signed)

Note:

   1. This questionnaire is necessarily generic and basic. It should be adapted for use in particular litigation by taking into account the facts of that litigation.

Index

Index

All references in this index are to section numbers.

confidential information, 33.12
conflicts of interest, 33.13
conspiracy, 33.11
coordination, 31.13n, 33.14
counterclaims, 33.1
criminal proceedings, related, 33.14
damages, 33.11, 33.14n
discovery limitations, 33.12
disqualification, 33.13
economic data, 33.12
exchange of exhibits/opinions, 33.11, 33.12
experts, 33.12
Federal Trade Commission, 33.14
government reports, 33.12
issues, 33.11
jurisdiction, 33.11
market definition, 33.11
multidistrict transfers, 31.12, 33.14
parens patriae actions, 31.13n
privileges, 33.14
protective orders, 33.12
referral to special master, magistrate judge,
    or court-appointed expert, 33.11
related proceedings, 33.14
removal, 31.32n, 33.14n
SEC, 31.1n
settlement, 23.14, 33.11
severance, 33.12
standing, 33.11
state claims/actions, 33.14
statute of limitations, 33.11
summaries, 33.12
summary judgment, 33.11
trade secrets, 33.12
transfer, 31.13n, 33.14

APPEALS (see also INTERLOCUTORY
    APPEALS)
attorneys' fee, effect of motions for, 25.3n
of attorney disqualification orders, 20.23n
.of liability determination, 25.11n
patent litigation, 33.67
preargument conferences, 25.22
related cases, 25.21
single panel, 25.21
time for, 25.3

ASSESSMENTS to compensate counsel,
    20.223

ASSIGNMENTS OF JUDGES
complex litigation, 20.12, 31.11
criminal cases, 20.123, 31.2, 32.11
inter- and intracircuit, 31.131
multidistrict litigation, 31.13
one judge, 20.12, 31.11, 32.11, 33.21, 33.31,
    33.5
other divisions, 20.123, 31.11
reassignment, 20.121, 21.11, 33.31
related cases, 20.123, 31.14
relief from other cases, 20.12, 32.11

ATTORNEY–CLIENT PRIVILEGE (see
    PRIVILEGES)

ATTORNEYS (see COUNSEL)

ATTORNEYS' FEES, 24
American Rule, 24
appellate review, 24.121
assessments, 20.223, 33.22n, 33.27n
common fund, 24.11
conflicts of interest, 23.24, 30.16, 30.43
contributions by settling parties, 20.223,
    24.23
control of, 21.452, 24.2
court approval, 23.24, 24.11, 24.23
designated counsel, 20.223, 20.225, 24.11,
    24.214
discovery, 24.224
documentation, 24.211
effect on finality, 25.3n
excessive hours, 20.223
guidelines, 24.21
hearings, 24.232
interim awards, 24.222, 32.12
later-filed cases, 20.223
limiting attendance to control, 20.223,
    21.452, 24.213
lodestar, 24.122
losing party liable, 23.24
motion for, 24.22
periodic filing, 24.212
procedures for awarding, 24.2
rates as factor in selecting, 20.224, 24.23
reasonable rates, 24.122

Rule 68, 23.13
sanctions, 24.11
settlements, 23.24
simultaneous negotiations on merits, 23.24,
   30.42, 33.55
statutory fees, 24.11, 24.13
time/expense records, 20.223, 24.211,
   24.223, 24.231
timing, 23.24n, 24.13, 33.54
unnecessary activity, 20.223, 24.122

AUTHENTICATION, 21.445, 21.446, 21.47,
   34.35

BANKRUPTCY (see ADVERSARY
   PROCEEDINGS)

BELLWETHER TRIAL, 31.132, 33.27, 33.28

BRIEFS
   appellate, 25.22
   class action settlements, 30.41
   limits on length, 21.12, 21.32
   post-trial, 22.52
   pretrial, 21.66, 33.61
   proposed findings/conclusions of law,
      22.52, 33.43
   schedule for, 21.211, 33.81
   takeover litigation, 33.43

BUSINESS RECORDS
   exception to hearsay rule, 21.446n
   preservation, 21.442, 33.53, 41.34
   production of, 21.446, 34.31

CASES (see LEAD CASE, RELATED CASES)

CERCLA (Superfund), 33.7
   administrative orders, 33.71, 33.72
   case management, 33.73
   contribution, 33.71, 33.73
   costs, 33.71, 33.72, 33.73
   counsel, organization of, 33.73
   damages, 33.72, 33.73
   database, 33.73
   "deemed" pleadings, 33.73
   defenses, 33.71, 33.73
   de minimus parties, 33.73
   discovery, 33.73
      centralized, 33.73
   document depository, 33.73

Environmental Protection Agency (EPA),
   33.7–33.73
evidence, 33.73
experts, 33.73
generators, 33.71
Gore factors, 33.71, 33.72
insurance coverage litigation, 33.73
interlocutory appeal, 33.73
issues, narrowing, 33.73
joint and several liability, 33.71
judicial review, 33.72
liability, 33.71, 33.72, 33.73
magistrate judges, 33.73
motion practice, 33.73
National Contingency Plan (NCP), 33.71,
   33.72
parties, joinder, 33.73
potentially responsible parties (PRPs),
   33.71, 33.73
pretrial conferences, 33.73
related cases, 33.73
remedy, 33.72
response costs, 33.71, 33.72
   allocating, 33.71, 33.72, 33.73
settlement, 33.73
special masters, 33.73
special verdict, 33.73
statutory framework, 33.71
transporters, 33.71
trial, 33.73
   jury, 33.73

CERTIFICATION
   class (see CLASS CERTIFICATION)
   for appeal, 21.32, 25.11
   questions of controlling state law, 25.11

CHARTS, 22.21, 22.31, 22.434, 34.33, 34.34
   (see also SUMMARIES)

"CHINESE WALL," 20.23n

CHOICE-OF-LAW RULES
   class actions, 30.15
   diversity cases, 33.254n
   mass tort cases, 33.254
   transferee court, 33.254n

CLASS ACTION COMMUNICATIONS

accurate records required of counsel, 30.211

advice, requests by class, 30.22

(b)(1) and (2) classes, 30.14, 30.211, 30.231, 33.52

certification notice, 30.14, 30.211, 30.231, 33.33, 33.52, 41.41
   combined with settlement notice, 30.212, 41.43

claims (see CLASS ACTION SETTLEMENT)

consumer cases, 30.211

content of (b)(3) notice, 30.14, 30.211, 30.231

costs, 30.211, 33.33, 33.52

curative notices, 30.24

dependent upon class definition, 30.14

discovery from class members, 21.451, 30.12, 30.232, 33.33, 33.53
   certification issue, 30.12, 30.233
   court approval, 21.451, 30.232, 33.53
   depositions, 21.451, 30.233, 33.53
   harassment, 30.12, 30.233, 33.33, 33.53
   limitations, 30.12, 30.233, 33.33, 33.53
   merits, 21.451, 30.12, 30.233, 33.53
   need, 30.232, 33.53

distribution of settlement 41.44

drafted by counsel, 30.211

extensions of deadlines, 30.24

individual notice, 25.3, 30.211

information from class, 30.23

intervention, soliciting, 30.213, 33.33

list of class members, 41.41, 41.43

mail, 30.211, 30.231, 41.41

mandatory for (b)(3) actions, 25.3, 30.211, 30.231, 30.14, 30.45

meeting of class, 30.43, 33.55

names and addresses, 33.33

notices from court, 30.14, 30.15, 30.21, 30.213, 30.24, 33.52, 41.41–41.44

opting out (see CLASS ACTIONS)

other court notices, 30.213

other languages, 30.211

partial dismissal of class claims, 30.212

post-judgment attacks, 30.211

presentation of claims (see CLASS ACTION SETTLEMENT)

publication, 30.211, 33.33, 41.41, 41.43

receipt, 30.211

referral of class questions to committee, 30.22, 41.41

res judicata effect, 30.211, 33.52

restrictions on, 25.11, 30.24

review and revision by court, 30.211

securities cases, 30.211, 33.33

settlement notice (see CLASS ACTION SETTLEMENT)

CLASS ACTIONS (see also CLASS ACTION COMMUNICATIONS, CLASS ACTION SETTLEMENT, CLASS CERTIFICATION, CLASS MEMBERS, and CLASS REPRESENTATIVES)

adversary proceedings in bankruptcy, coordination with, 30.3

choice of law, 30.15

class counsel, 30.15, 30.16, 30.22, 30.24, 30.43

collateral estoppel, 30.3

consolidation for trial, 30.3, 33.36

discovery on merits, 21.422, 30.12, 30.232, 33.33, 33.53

dismissal prior to certification, 30.212

disqualification
   class members as parties, 20.23n
   counsel, 20.23, 33.13
   judge, 20.121, 33.13

ethical obligations, 23.24, 30.24, 30.43

fiduciary relationship, 30, 30.24, 30.45

final judgment, 25.3

identification, 20.11

individual cases, 30.3

interlocutory appeal, 25.11n

opting out, 30.14, 30.17, 30.211, 30.231, 30.3, 30.45
   (b)(1) and (b)(2) actions, 30.14, 30.231, 31.32n, 33.52
   employment discrimination, 30.24, 33.52
   extension of time, 30.231, 30.24
   forms, 30.211, 30.231, 41.4
   need to maintain records, 30.231
   procedures, 30.211, 30.231, 41.41, 41.43
   sample request for exclusion, 41.41
   tabulation of responses, 30.231, 41.41
   time limits, 41.41, 41.43

related cases, 30.3, 31.14, 33.31, 33.33

settlement prior to certification, 30.212,
30.45, 33.55
trial (see also TRIAL)
conducted in stages, 33.54
consolidation of related cases, 21.631,
30.3, 33.36
limits on evidence, 33.54

CLASS ACTION SETTLEMENT
administration, 30.47, 33.55
appointment of special master, 21.52,
30.47, 33.55
audit procedures, 30.47
computer, use of, 30.47
investment of funds, 30.46, 30.47, 41.44
payment, 30.47, 33.55
sample order, 41.42, 41.43, 41.44
attorneys' fee approval, 23.24, 24.11, 24.13,
30.42
before certification, 30.212, 30.45, 33.55
claims
forms, 30.212, 30.47, 41.44
individual, 30.232, 33.33, 33.64, 33.55
perjury, 30.47, 41.44
presentation, 30.232, 33.55
procedures, 30.47, 41.44
recording receipt, 30.47
substantiation, 30.47, 33.55, 41.44
class representatives
approval, 30.42, 30.43
fiduciary duties, 30.44, 30.45
opposition to settlement, 30.44, 33.55
witnesses at hearing, 30.44
counsel's role, 30.43
court approval, 23.14, 23.24, 30.212, 30.41,
30.42, 30.44, 33.55
reserved jurisdiction, 41.44
deadline for partial settlement, 23.21, 30.46,
disclosure of offers, 23.24, 30.43
discovery, 30.43
distribution from fund, 30.231, 30.47,
33.55, 41.44
publication, 41.44
sample notice, 41.44
evidence, 30.41, 33.55
experts, 23.14, 30.41, 30.42, 30.43
fairness, 30.41, 30.42, 30.44, 30.45
fund(s), 23.24, 30.212, 30.46, 30.47, 33.55,
41.42

hearings (see judicial review)
individual claims (see claims)
interests of class as whole, 30.41–30.44,
30.46
judicial review, 23.14, 23.21, 23.24, 30.212,
30.4, 30.41, 30.42, 30.44, 30.45, 33.55
class members, objections by, 30.41,
30.42, 30.44, 41.42
court-appointed experts/special masters,
21.51, 21.52, 30.42, 30.47, 33.55
formal hearing after notice to class,
30.212, 30.41–30.44, 33.55, 41.42
sample order for hearing, 41.42
views of others, 23.14, 30.41, 33.55
meeting of class, 30.43, 33.55
monitoring post-settlement discovery,
30.43, 33.55
nonmonetary benefits, 23.11, 33.36, 33.55
notice, 23.14, 30.212, 30.41, 30.45, 33.55,
41.42–41.44
combined with certification notice,
30.212, 41.43
content, 30.212, 33.55, 41.4
draft order, 30.43
publication, 41.43, 41.44
sample order and notice, 41.41, 41.42
objections by class members, 30.41, 30.42,
30.44, 41.42
offers communicated to class, 23.24, 30.43
opposition, 30.44, 33.55
order approving settlement, 41.44
partial settlements, 23.21, 30.45, 30.46,
33.29
funds in income-producing trusts, 30.46
interference with further proceedings,
23.11, 23.21–23.23, 30.46
sample order, 41.42
referral to special masters/experts, 21.51,
21.52, 30.47, 33.65
secret/side agreements, 23.23
settlement classes, 30.45, 33.262, 33.29
suspension of discovery pending
negotiations, 23.12
time limits, 41.42, 41.44
unclaimed funds, 30.47, 41.44

CLASS CERTIFICATION, 30.1–30.18, 33.26,
33.33, 33.52, 41.41
agenda topic at first conference, 21.213

amendment of class orders, 30.11
antitrust cases, 30.14, 33.11
case selection, 30.15
class definition, 30.14, 30.15, 33.52
conditional certification, 30.11, 30.18,
    33.52, 41.41
conferences, 30.11
deadline for motion seeking, 41.30
decertification, 30.11, 30.16
description of claims, 30.11, 30.14, 33.33,
    33.52, 41.44
discovery, 21.213, 30.11, 30.12, 30.232,
    33.33, 33.34, 33.52, 33.53
    bifurcation, 30.12, 33.53
    court approval, 30.232, 33.53
    depositions of putative class members,
        21.451, 30.12, 30.232, 33.53
    limitations, 30.11, 30.12, 30.232, 33.34,
        33.53
    priority, 21.213, 21.422, 30.12
    purposes, 30.12, 33.33, 33.34, 33.52
    structure, 30.12
    unnecessary, 30.11, 30.12, 33.52
early determination, 21.211, 21.213, 30.11,
    30.12, 33.33, 33.62
employment discrimination, 30.11, 33.52
error in certification, 30.11, 30.18
extension of time periods, 30.11
failure to move, 30.11
findings and conclusions, 30.13
hearings, 30.11, 30.13, 30.18
impact on further proceedings, 21.213,
    30.11
issue development, 30.11
list of persons receiving notice, 30.231
management techniques for, 30.1
mass tort cases, 33.26
multiple classes, 30.1, 33.33
notice (see CLASS ACTION
    COMMUNICATIONS)
opposition, 33.33
order, 30.11, 30.18
    conditional until entry of judgment,
        30.11, 30.18, 33.52
    modification, 30.18
    sample, 41.41
precertification
    approval of settlement, 30.212
    motions, 30.11

settlement negotiations, 30.11, 30.45,
    33.55
preliminary inquiry, 30.11
reconsideration, 30.18
rulings on motions, 30.11
schedule, 21.211, 21.213, 30.11
securities cases, 33.33
selection of
    cases, 30.15
    counsel, 30.16
    representatives, 30.16 (see also CLASS
        REPRESENTATIVES)
show cause order, 30.18
specific issues, class for, 30.17
subclasses, 30.15, 30.24, 33.33, 33.52
substitution/replacement of counsel, 30.22,
    30.24
summary judgment motions, 30.11
timing, 30.1, 30.11, 33.33, 33.55

CLASS MEMBERS
advice, requests for, 30.22
as parties for discovery, 30.232
as parties for disqualification, 20.23n
awards after settlement, 30.47, 33.55
claims, 30.232, 33.33, 33.54, 33.55
conflicts, 30.16, 30.47, 33.13, 33.33
definition (see CLASS CERTIFICATION)
deleted before certification, 30.212
depositions after certification, 30.232, 33.53
discovery from, 21.451, 30.12, 30.232,
    33.33, 33.53, 33.64
employee benefits in settlement, 33.55
entitlement to distribution, 33.55
harassment, 30.12, 30.232, 33.33, 33.53
hearings before special master, 30.47
identification, 20.121, 30.211, 33.13
interests of class as whole, 30.41–30.44,
    30.46
intervention, 20.154, 30.15, 30.16, 33.33
    as class representative, 30.15, 30.16
list of, 25.3, 41.41, 41.43
meeting before settlement hearing, 33.55
names and addresses, 30.211, 33.33, 41.41
notice, 25.3, 30.14, 30.21, 30.231, 30.41 (see
    also CLASS ACTION
    COMMUNICATIONS, notices from
    court)
objections to settlement, 30.44, 33.55

innovation, 10.1, 20.13, 20.14, 21.54, 21.631, 21.64, 22.3, 23.11, 23.15, 33.2
interim measures, 21.12
issues—narrowing, 21.33, 21.34, 21.41, 21.641, 33.254, 33.32, 33.82
judicial management, 21.1, 21.12, 21.13
mass torts, 33.2
MCL 3d, 10, 30.21, 33.2, 41.2
multitrack depositions, 21.451n, 21.454
patent litigation, 33.6
pretrial proceedings, 21
reassignment, 20.121
RICO litigation, 33.8
securities litigation, 33.3
takeover litigation, 33.4

COMPUTER-AIDED TRANSCRIPTION, 22.14, 34.38 (see also COURTROOM TECHNOLOGY)

COMPUTER-BASED
document depositories, 21.444, 21.446, 41.35
electronic bulletin board, 41.39
litigation support, 34.37

COMPUTERIZED DATA, 21.446
accuracy, 21.446, 33.53
admissibility, 21.446, 21.483, 33.53
antitrust cases, 33.12
attorney work product, 21.446
authentication, 21.446n
computer-readable form, 21.446, 33.12, 33.53
confidential material, 21.432n
cost of obtaining, 21.433, 21.446, 33.53
discovery, 21.446, 33.12, 33.53
document depository, 21.444
employment discrimination cases, 33.53
erasure, 41.2
error
elimination of, 21.492, 33.53
projected range, 21.446, 33.53
sources of, 21.446
evidence, 21.446, 21.492, 33.53
experts, use by, 21.446, 33.53
hard copies/printouts
discovery, 21.446, 33.12
error, potential, 21.446

hearsay, 21.446n
periodic creation, 21.442
retention, 21.442, 41.2, 41.34
used as "originals," 21.446n
identification, early, 21.446, 33.12
interrogatories, 21.446
jointly developed by parties, 33.53
preservation, 21.442, 33.53, 41.2, 41.34
pretrial rulings, 21.446, 21.492, 33.53
printouts (see hard copies/printouts)
production, 41.31
protective orders, 21.446
sample, 21.446 (see also SAMPLING TECHNIQUES)
storage and retrieval, 21.442, 21.444, 21.446, 21.461, 33.53
summaries, 21.446, 21.492 (see also SUMMARIES)
system and programs, 21.446n, 21.461
tabulations and voluminous information, 21.446, 21.492
trial preparation materials, 21.446n
trial use, 21.446, 21.492, 33.53
verification by sampling, 21.446

COMPUTER TERMINAL
attorneys' offices, 21.452
courtroom, 22.12, 34.37, 34.38

CONFERENCE(S), 21.2–21.23 (see also PRETRIAL CONFERENCE, INITIAL/FINAL)
attendance, 21.23, 33.41
before responsive pleadings, 20.11, 21.11, 33.41
criminal cases, 32.21
joint with other courts, 20.123, 31.14, 31.31
motions, consideration of, 21.32
number of, 21.22
preliminary meetings of counsel, 21.421, 33.41, 33.43
preparation for, 21.11, 21.211, 41.2
related state/federal cases, 33.23
settlement
class actions, 30.41, 30.42, 30.44
promote settlement, 23.11, 23.13
subsequent to initial, 21.22
telephone, 21.22, 31.13, 33.41
transcribing, 21.22

appointment of lead and liaison counsel,
31.31, 33.23, 33.24, 41.51
bankruptcy cases, 30.3
centralized management, 20.123, 33.14,
33.21, 33.31
counsel, 20.123, 20.22, 31.13, 32.12, 33.22,
33.63
court's role, 20.22, 30.3, 31.132, 31.31,
33.21, 33.41
criminal cases, 20.123, 31.2, 32.11, 32.24,
33.14
discovery, 21.423, 31.11, 31.131–31.133,
31.14, 31.2, 31.31, 33.34, 33.63 (see also
JOINT DISCOVERY REQUESTS)
informal, 20.123, 33.31
joint (see JOINT CONFERENCE, JOINT
ORDERS BY SEVERAL COURTS)
judges in state and federal cases, 20.123,
20.225, 31.31
pretrial proceedings, 20.123, 31.11, 31.13,
31.14, 31.31, 32.11, 33.21, 33.31, 41.3
related cases (see RELATED CASES)
sample order, 41.51

COST(S)
apportioned among plaintiffs, 33.24n
attorneys' fees as, 20.152, 20.155n, 21.421,
23.13
cost-shifting sanctions, 20.154, 21.47
identifying class members, 30.211
notice to class members, 30.211
reducing discovery costs, 21.42, 21.423,
21.452, 33.11
reduction as objective of transfer, 31.131
refusal to stipulate provable facts, 21.47
settlement notice borne by defendants,
30.212
sharing as condition for discovery, 21.433,
31.14
shifting, 20.154, 21.433, 21.47
taxable, 21.444n, 22.14n, 23.13

COUNSEL
admission pro hac vice, 33.22, 41.2
admonishment by court, 22.15, 30.22,
30.24, 32.33
appearances at initial conference, 21.12,
21.23, 33.22, 33.41, 41.2
behavior

contentiousness, 20.21, 21.21
depositions, 21.424, 21.451, 21.456, 41.38
trial, 22.15, 22.24
certification by, 20.21, 21.463
committees, 20.221, 33.24 (see also
DESIGNATED COUNSEL)
compensation (see ATTORNEYS' FEES)
competent representation, 32.21n
conflicts (see CONFLICTS OF INTEREST)
conspiracy cases, 22.22
cooperation, 20.13, 20.21, 20.222, 31.31,
33.24, 41.38
coordination, 20.22, 20.225, 31.13, 32.12,
33.24, 33.63
designated (see DESIGNATED COUNSEL)
dilatory tactics, 20.13
disbarment, 20.154
disqualification, 20.23, 33.13 (see also
DISQUALIFICATION)
expenses/fees (see ATTORNEYS' FEES)
joint appointment by several courts, 20.225,
33.23, 33.24, 31.13, 31.31, 41.51
lead (see LEAD COUNSEL)
liaison (see LIAISON COUNSEL)
local, 21.12, 21.494
MCL 3d, use by, 33.22, 41.2
multidistrict transfer, representation after,
21.12n
organization, 20.221, 32.12, 41.2, 41.3,
41.31
preparation for conferences, 21.21, 41.2
pressures in complex litigation, 20.21, 32.33
removal, 20.154, 30.22
reprimand, 20.154
resolving disputes informally, 20.21, 21.424
responsibilities
after settlement, 20.222, 23.21
class action settlements, 30.43, 33.55
conflicts of interest, 20.23
court officer, 20.21, 20.23
identify complex case, 20.11, 32.11
interrogatories, 21.463
other parties, 20.22, 20.221, 20.222, 23.21
plan, developing and implementing,
20.13, 20.21, 21.421
sanctions (see SANCTIONS)
scheduling conflicts, 20.21, 20.221, 22.11
service list—prepare/maintain, 41.31
stipulations, 21.423, 21.47

trial, 20.221, 22.22, 22.24, 32.12
unnecessary duplication of efforts, 20.221,
21.423, 21.452
unprofessional conduct (see behavior)

COURT (see also JUDGE(S))
transferee/transferor, 31.131–31.133,
33.254n
centralized management, 33.21, 33.23n
choice-of-law rules, 31.132, 33.254
complete pretrial record, 31.133
exclusive jurisdiction after remand,
31.133
further pretrial proceedings, 31.133
several cases assigned to one judge, 33.21
videotaped depositions, 31.132, 33.27n

COURT-APPOINTED EXPERTS, 21.51
antitrust litigation, 33.11, 33.12
compensation, 21.51n
computerized data, 21.446
criteria for selection, 21.51
discovery from, 21.48
discovery, use in, 21.48n, 21.51, 33.64
joint appointment, 31.14, 21.52
mass tort litigation, 33.27
patent litigation, 33.61, 33.653
procedures governing, 21.51
securities litigation, 33.35
settlement, 30.41
special master, distinguished from, 21.52
translation of foreign documents, 33.64

COURT OF APPEALS
coordination, 25.21, 25.22
designation of single panel, 25.21
discretion under, 28 U.S.C. § 1292(b),
25.11
disqualification, 25.21
extraordinary writs, 25.11
Federal Circuit, 25.11n
interlocutory appeals, 25.11
jurisdictional questions, 25.22
preargument conference, 25.22
single panel, 25.21
state court, 25.11

COURTROOM TECHNOLOGY, 34
CD-ROM, 21.444, 33.22, 34.34

computer-aided transcription (CAT),
21.452, 22.14, 34.38
computer animation, 21.642, 34.32
electronic photographs, 34.35
laser discs, 34.33
personal computers, 34.37
use of, 21.433, 21.444, 21.446, 22.32,
24.211, 30.47, 32.25, 33.12, 33.53
photogrammetry, 34.36
safeguards, 34.2
simultaneous distributed translation (SDT),
34.39
video, use of, 21.452, 21.46, 22.12, 22.333,
34.31 (see also VIDEOTAPING)

CRIMINAL CASES
alibi defense, 32.22, 32.24
antitrust cases, 33.14
arraignment, 32.11
assignment, 20.123, 31.2, 32.11n
conferences, 32.11, 32.21
during trial, 22.15, 32.33
confession, 32.28
contempt, 32.12, 32.27, 32.33
continuance, 32.22
coordination, 20.123, 31.2, 32.11, 33.14 (see
also related civil proceedings, related
criminal proceedings)
counsel, 32.11, 32.12, 32.21
conflict of interest, 32.12
fees and expenses, 32.12, 32.21
organization, 32.12, 32.21
courthouse facilities, 32.31
dates (see schedules)
depositions, 32.24
discovery, 31.2, 32.11, 32.22, 32.24
stay in related civil case, 21.431n, 31.2,
32.24, 33.14
disruptive conduct, 32.33
documentary evidence, 32.24
exchange of discoverable items, 32.24
grand jury (see GRAND JURY
MATERIALS)
hearings, 32.23
indictment, 32.11, 32.12, 32.28
insanity defense, 32.22
Jencks Act, 32.24
judge's relief from other cases, 32.11
judicial supervision, 32.11, 32.21

jury, 32.25n, 32.27, 32.32, 32.33 (see also
JURY/JUROR(S))
excuse during deliberations, 22.44
magistrate judges, 32.11
MCL 3d, 32.1
media at trial, 32.27, 32.31
mistrial, 32.32, 32.33
motions
bill of particulars, 32.24
in limine, 32.22, 32.23
suppression, 32.23, 32.25
multiple juries, 32.28
objections, 32.24
omnibus hearing, 32.24
orders, 32.21, 32.24, 32.27
pleas, 32.24, 32.22, 32.23, 32.33
pretrial proceedings, 32.11, 32.22, 32.23
privileges, 31.2, 33.14 (see also
PRIVILEGES)
publicity, 32.27, 32.32, 32.33
related civil proceedings, 20.123, 31.2,
21.431n, 32.11n, 32.24, 33.14
related criminal proceedings, 32.11, 32.24
schedules, 32.22, 32.33
security measures, 32.31
self-incrimination (see privileges)
severance and joinder, 32.11, 32.28
Speedy Trial Act, 31.2, 32.11n, 32.22, 33.14
stipulations, 32.21, 32.33
subpoena, 32.24
transcripts, 32.33
transfer of civil case, 31.2
trial, 32.3–32.34
verdict, 32.33
voluntary disclosure, 32.24
witnesses, 32.24, 32.31, 32.33

CROSS CLAIMS/COUNTERCLAIMS,
31.133, 33.22, 33.32, 41.3

DAMAGES
antitrust litigation, 33.11, 33.14n
bifurcation of liability, state laws
precluding, 33.28n
class actions
assessed on class-wide basis, 33.54n
individual damages, 30.47
prerequisite for appeal under Rule 54(b),
25.11n

punitive damages, 33.262n
recision versus damages, 33.33
damage-sharing agreements, 23.23, 41.3
discovery of, 21.41, 21.61, 33.11, 33.27
facilitating settlement, 33.11
interrogatories regarding extent, 33.27
mass tort litigation, 21.61n, 21.631, 33.28
partial settlements, 23.21
proof, individualized, 21.61, 30.47, 33.11
punitive
class actions, 33.262n
mass tort litigation, 33.2
separate class for, 33.262n
state laws governing, 33.2
referral to special master, 21.52
standing to maintain claim for, 33.11
state laws precluding bifurcation, 33.28n
summary judgment, 21.633
theory of, 33.11

DATA
compilation (see SUMMARIES,
COMPILATION(S))
computerized (see COMPUTERIZED
DATA)
databases, 21.442, 21.446, 30.231, 33.12,
33.261, 33.29, 33.53, 33.73, 41.52
economic, 33.12
hearsay rule, 21.446n
incomplete entry, as source of mistake,
21.446
projected effect of errors, 21.446
sample, 21.446 (see also SAMPLING
TECHNIQUES)
underlying, 21.48, 21.492

DEADLINES (see SCHEDULE(S))

DEPOSITIONS
admissibility, 21.423n, 21.455, 41.38
attendance by counsel, 20.223, 21.423,
21.451–21.453, 41.38
"commission" method for foreign, 21.485
concurrent, 21.451, 21.454
conference-type, 21.423, 21.452
confidentiality orders, 41.36, 41.38
coordinated—related litigation, 21.423,
21.455
cost, 21.45, 41.38

settlement, 23.14, 30.41, 33.36

DESIGNATED COUNSEL
  appointment, 20.224
  committees of counsel, 20.221, 33.24,
    41.31 ¶ 3
  communication with other counsel, 20.222
  compensation, 20.223, 20.225, 41.51n (see
    also ATTORNEYS' FEES)
    as factor in selection, 20.224
  consensus, 20.222
  coordinating committee, 20.221, 41.31 ¶ 3
  court's independent assessment of, 20.224
  deferral of selection, 20.224
  deposition, role at, 20.222
  discovery committee, 20.221
  documentation of responsibilities, 20.222
  executive committee, 20.221
  factors in selection, 20.224
  joint appointment, 20.225, 31.14, 41.51 ¶ 1
  lead (see LEAD COUNSEL)
  liaison (see LIAISON COUNSEL)
  limitations
    authority, 20.222
    unnecessary participation, 20.223, 22.22
  MCL 3d, use of, 41.2 ¶ 3(a)
  number of, 20.22, 20.224
  order prescribing responsibilities, 20.222,
    20.224, 41.31
  organization, 20.221, 20.224
  powers, 20.222
  related cases, 20.225, 41.51 ¶ 1
  responsibilities, 20.222, 41.31
  selection, 20.22, 20.221, 20.224
  settlement negotiations, 20.222, 41.31 ¶
    1(c)
  steering committee, 20.221, 41.31 ¶ 3
  trial, 20.221, 22.22

DISCLOSURE
  criminal cases, 32.24
  experts, 21.446n, 21.48, 33.53n
  generally, 21.11, 21.211, 21.421, 21.431
  preclusion/waiver/sanctions for failure,
    20.154, 21.13n, 21.431n, 21.446n, 21.48n,
    21.642n, 21.67n
  prediscovery under Fed. R. Civ. P. 26(a)(1),
    21.12, 21.13, 21.212, 21.33, 21.423,
    21.461, 33.53, 33.651, 40.2

pretrial, 21.64, 22.13, 33.54n
supplementation, 21.13, 21.212, 21.421n

DISCOVERY (see also DISCOVERY
    DISPUTES, DISCOVERY ORDERS,
    DISCOVERY PLAN/SCHEDULE,
    DISCLOSURE)
  abuse, 21.451, 21.456, 21.494
  certification by counsel, 20.21
  checklist, 40.2
  class actions
    class certification, 21.213, 21.422, 30.12,
      33.33
    class members, 30.12, 30.233, 33.53,
      41.30 ¶ 5(b)
    merits, 21.421, 33.33, 33.52
  combined requests, 21.423
  committee, 20.221
  computerized data, 21.446, 33.53
  confidential information, 21.43, 21.431,
    33.27, 33.52 (see also privileged
    information)
  coordination—related cases, other courts,
    21.422, 21.455, 31.13, 31.31, 33.14, 33.21,
    33.34, 33.63
  court's control, 20.21, 21.41, 21.42, 21.421,
    21.424, 33.11, 33.42, 33.53, 33.62
  criminal cases, 32.24, 33.14
    stay in related civil case, 31.2, 32.24,
      33.14
  damages, 21.41, 33.27n
  disclosure (see DISCLOSURE)
  duplicative/excessive, 21.41, 21.421, 21.423,
    21.45, 31.31, 33.27, 33.34, 33.42, 33.63,
    41.30 ¶¶ 5(d)(4), (e)
  existence of privileged documents, 21.431
  expense reduction, 21.41, 21.42, 21.423,
    33.53
  expert opinions, 21.421n, 21.461 (see also
    DISCOVERY PLAN/SCHEDULE)
  extension of time, 21.13
  extraterritorial (see foreign country)
  foreign country, 21.494, 33.64, 41.30 ¶ 5(b)
  government investigations, 21.491, 33.27
  grand jury materials, 21.423n, 21.491 (see
    also GRAND JURY MATERIALS)
  informal, 21.423, 41.2 ¶ 4(c)
  issues, interrelationship with, 21.31, 21.41,
    21.422, 30.12, 33.62, 33.64

scheduling order, 41.33
sequential, 21.211, 21.41, 21.421, 33.27, 33.64, 41.33n
stay
  pending initial conference, 21.12, 41.2 ¶ 4(c)
  related civil case, 31.2, 32.24, 33.14
  settlement negotiations, 23.12
time limits, 21.422, 33.27, 33.64, 41.30 ¶ 5(a), 41.33 ¶ 2(a)

DISMISSAL
class actions, 30.212, 30.42
forum non conveniens, 20.123
involuntary, 30.212
multidistrict cases, 31.132
sanction, dismissal as, 20.154
sua sponte, 20.151
voluntary, 20.123

DISQUALIFICATION
affiliated companies, 41.2 ¶ 3(d)
appealability, 20.23n
"Chinese wall," 20.23n
class actions, 20.121, 20.23, 25.21
consent, hardship or waiver, 20.23
counsel, 20.23, 33.13
  duty to award against, 20.23
early inquiry, 20.23, 21.211
effect on attorney work product, 20.23
judge, 20.12, 33.13 (see also RECUSAL)
mandamus, 20.23n
new partners/associates/clients, 20.23
prompt resolution, 20.23
sanctions for spurious motions, 20.15, 20.23
witness, lawyer as, 20.23

DIVISIONS
cases in different, 20.123, 31.11

DOCUMENT DEPOSITORIES, 21.444
access to, 41.35 ¶ 3
admissibility problems, 21.445
agenda item, 21.211
agreement on procedures, 21.444
centralized, 21.444
computer-based, 21.211, 21.444, 21.446
  protocol to protect work product, 21.444

establishment of, 21.442, 21.452, 31.14, 31.31, 33.251, 41.31 ¶¶ 2, 4, 41.35 ¶ 1
expense, 21.444, 41.35 ¶ 1
filing system, 41.35 ¶ 2
joint, 31.14, 41.51 ¶ 2(a)
location, 21.444
  courthouse, 21.444
  site for depositions, 21.454
reasons for use, 21.442, 21.444, 21.452
related cases, 21.444, 31.14, 31.31, 33.251, 41.51 ¶ 2(a)
sample order, 41.35
subsequent filings, notice of, 41.35 ¶ 4

DOCUMENTARY EVIDENCE (see EVIDENCE, EXHIBITS)

DOCUMENTS
access after termination, 21.432, 25.4
best evidence rule, 21.492n
confidential (see CONFIDENTIALITY)
coordinating requests for, 21.443, 41.30 ¶ 5(d)(4)
copies at depositions, 21.456, 41.38 ¶ 6(c)
criminal cases, 32.21, 32.24
depositories (see DOCUMENT DEPOSITORIES)
destruction after litigation, 21.432, 25.4
discovery
  first wave (see identification, of sources)
  informal, 21.423
distribution by liaison counsel, 20.221, 41.30 ¶ 3, 41.31 ¶¶ 2, 4
evidence (see EVIDENCE, EXHIBITS)
explanation, conference deposition, 21.423
foreign countries, 21.494
grand jury, 21.423n, 21.432n, 21.491
identification
  numbering system, 21.211, 21.441, 41.30 ¶ 5(d)(2)
  of sources, 21.423, 21.461, 33.27, 33.34, 33.53, 41.2 ¶ 4(c)
in camera review, 21.431, 21.48n
joint requests, 21.443
log of documents produced, 21.431, 21.441
numbering system (see identification)
orders (see PRESERVATION OF RECORDS, PROTECTIVE ORDER)
originals (see EXHIBITS)

other cases, 21.423, 21.431, 21.444, 25.4, 31.14, 31.31, 33.251
preservation, 21.211, 21.442, 33.53, 41.34
privileged (see PRIVILEGES)
reduction
    filing, 21.12, 21.211, 21.32, 31.11, 41.30 ¶ 1
    service, 21.12, 21.211, 24.23, 41.30 ¶ 3
subpoenas (see SUBPOENA(S))
summaries, 21.494 (see also SUMMARIES)
third parties, 21.447, 21.456, 32.24
translations, 41.35 ¶ 2
voluminous, 21.444, 21.492, 22.32, 32.24

EMPLOYMENT DISCRIMINATION LITIGATION, 33.5
anecdotal evidence, 33.54
attorneys' fees, 33.54, 33.55
    interim award, 33.54
back pay claims, 33.54
circumstantial evidence, 33.53
class actions, 33.51, 33.52
    certification, 33.51
    class conflicts, 33.52
    modification of class, 33.52
    need for clear definition, 33.52
    res judicata, 33.52
discovery, 33.53
    bifurcation, 33.52
    class members, 33.53, 33.54
    computerized records, 33.53
    confidential information, 33.53
    expert testimony, 33.53
    identification of source material, 33.53
    merits, 33.52
    precertification, 33.52
    putative class members, 33.52, 33.53
    statistical evidence, 33.53
early determination of class, 33.51
EEOC regulations for preserving records, 33.53
expense of notices, 33.52
expert testimony, 33.53
final judgment, 33.52
fund, settlement, 33.55
individual claims, 33.51, 33.52, 33.54
    referral to special master/magistrate judge, 30.47, 33.54, 33.55
injunctions, 33.54

appellate review, 33.54
    monitoring, 33.55
intervention, 33.51
issues, 33.51
    early identification of individual claims, 33.51
    probing behind pleadings, 33.52
joinder, 33.51
notice, 33.52, 33.55
    individual claims identified, 33.51–33.52
opt-out privilege, 33.52
pattern and practice suits, 33.5
preservation of records, 33.53
pretrial proceedings, centralized, 33.5
protective orders, 33.53
referrals to special master/magistrate judge
    individual claims, 30.47, 33.54, 33.55
    monitor injunction, 33.55
related cases, 33.5
reverse discrimination, 33.51, 33.55
right-to-sue letter, 33.51
settlement, 33.55
    after certification, 30.45, 33.55
    explanation to class, 33.55
    hearing, 33.55
    implementation, 33.55
    individual claims, referral to special master, 30.47, 33.55
    meeting in advance with class, 33.55
    notice, 33.55
    precertification settlement, 30.45, 33.55
      court's requirements, 33.55
      negotiations ordinarily deferred, 33.55
      notice to putative class, 33.55
    special master to supervise injunctive features, 21.52, 33.55
    terms, 33.55
      attorneys' fee problems, 33.55
      charges of reverse discrimination, 33.55
statistical evidence, 21.493, 33.53, 33.54
statute of limitations, 33.51n
trial, 33.54
    anecdotal evidence, 33.54
    claims for back pay, 33.54
    class-wide injunctive relief, 33.54
    conducted in stages, 33.53, 33.54
    consolidation, 33.5
    defenses resolved at stage I, 33.54
    discrimination against class, 33.54

individual relief, 33.54
referral to special master, 21.52, 33.5n
special issues, 33.61
union, joinder, or intervention, 33.51

ENVIRONMENTAL LITIGATION (see
CERCLA (Superfund))

ERROR
appeals from findings of magistrate
judge/special master, 21.53n, 21.54
class certification, 30.11
extraordinary writs, 25.151
failure to give limiting instructions, 22.433
preserving claim of error, 22.13, 33.254

ETHICAL CONSIDERATIONS (see also
CONFLICTS OF INTEREST,
FIDUCIARY RESPONSIBILITIES)
attorneys' fees, negotiations for, 23.24,
24.11, 33.55
counsel's obligations to other parties,
20.222, 23.21
failure to submit offers to client, 23.24
settlement agreements, 23.23, 23.24, 30.41,
33.55

EVIDENCE (see also
EXHIBITS/DOCUMENTARY
EVIDENCE)
admissible (see ADMISSIBILITY)
anecdotal, 33.54
automatic reception, 22.13, 41.63 ¶ 17
best evidence rule, 21.482n
circumstantial, 22.432, 33.53
computerized (see COMPUTERIZED
DATA)
court's power to direct order of, 22.13,
22.15, 22.22, 22.23n
depositions
admissibility, 21.453
designation required, 22.332
purging, 22.332, 22.333
reader, 22.333
rulings, how noted, 21.642, 22.332
summaries, 22.331, 22.333, 30.13
tape recordings, 22.333
use at trial, 22.23, 22.33, 41.63 ¶ 3
videotaped, 22.333

disclosure by rule or standing order, 21.423,
21.424
documentary (see
EXHIBITS/DOCUMENTARY
EVIDENCE)
elimination by admissions, 21.641
experts (see EXPERTS)
foreign country, located in, 21.494
foundation for admissibility, 21.641, 21.642
hearings (see RULINGS)
in camera reception, 41.36 ¶ 5
instructions
interim, 22.34, 22.433
limiting, 21.643, 22.433
interrogatory answers, 21.463
limitations/selectivity, 21.643, 41.63 ¶ 3(b)
magistrate judge's findings, 21.53
noninterruption of presentation, 21.64,
41.38 ¶ 12(a)
objections (see OBJECTIONS)
offer of proof, 21.64, 22.15
order of proof (see TRIAL)
partial settlement, 23.21
preclusion (see PRECLUSION)
presented by issues, 22.34
rulings (see RULINGS)
special master's findings, 21.52
statistical, 21.493, 33.53
summaries, 21.492, 21.641, 22.34
summary judgment, 21.34
witnesses (see WITNESSES)

EVIDENTIARY HEARINGS (see
HEARING, RULINGS)

EXCHANGE
court orders, 20.225
discovery materials in criminal case, 32.11,
32.24
experts' reports, 21.48, 33.42
lists of witnesses and documents, 21.641,
22.23, 33.43, 41.33, 41.63 ¶ 4

EXHIBITS/DOCUMENTARY EVIDENCE
(see also EVIDENCE)
access by other parties, 21.492
admissible (see ADMISSIBILITY)
aids to understand other evidence, 22.31

FACTUAL ISSUES (see also ISSUES)
attorney fee hearings, 24.2
comments by judge to jury, 22.432
delineation of, 21.31, 21.33, 21.34, 21.4
narrowed by rulings on summary
judgment, 21.3
referral, 21.5
separate trial under Rule 42(b), 21.33, 22.3
statements (see JOINT STATEMENT OF
FACTS)

FIDUCIARY RESPONSIBILITIES (see also
CONFLICTS OF INTEREST, ETHICAL
CONSIDERATIONS)
class counsel, 23.24, 30, 30.43, 30.45
class representatives, 23.24, 30, 30.44, 30.45
counsel regarding settlement, 20.222, 23.21,
23.24

FIFTH AMENDMENT, 21.431, 31.2, 33.14
(see also PRIVILEGES)

FILE, MASTER (see MASTER FILE)

FILING
attorneys' time/expense records, 20.223,
21.211, 24.212
confidential documents, 21.432, 41.36 ¶ 7
eliminating/reducing, 21.12, 21.432, 21.452,
41.30 ¶ 1(c)
under seal—confidential portions of
depositions, 41.36 ¶ 4(b)

FINAL JUDGMENT, 25.3
appeals, 25.1, 25.3
attorneys' fees, motion for, 25.3n
class described with specificity, 25.3
form for entry by clerk, 22.453, 25.3n
post-judgment motions, 25.3
separate document, 25.3

FINAL PRETRIAL STATEMENTS, 41.61n
(see also JOINT STATEMENT OF
FACTS)

FINDINGS AND CONCLUSIONS, 22.52,
30.13, 33.43
by special master/magistrate judge, 21.52,
21.53, 41.37 ¶ 3
oral dictation, 22.52

proposed findings prepared by parties,
21.33, 22.52

FOREIGN COUNTRY (see DISCOVERY)

FORUM NON CONVENIENS, 20.123

FREEDOM OF INFORMATION ACT,
21.447, 21.491

GLOSSARY, 22.31, 33.61

GOVERNMENT
INVESTIGATIONS/REPORTS, 21.491

GRAND JURY MATERIALS
access to, 21.432, 21.491
restrictions, 21.423n
copies held by private parties, 21.491
disclosure order, 21.491
other courts, 31.2
testimony, 31.2n
use immunity, 21.491n

GRAPHS (see SUMMARIES)

HAZARDOUS WASTE CLEANUP (see
CERCLA (Superfund))

HEARING (see also MOTIONS,
OBJECTIONS, RULINGS)
attorneys' fees, 24.2
class action
certification, 21.213, 30.13
motions, 30.11
settlement, 30.44
designated counsel, appointment of, 20.224
expert witness, 21.48
joint, 31.14, 31.31, 32.11, 41.51
magistrate judges, 21.53
pretrial hearing on admissibility, 21.33,
21.34, 21.491, 21.642
special motions, 21.32
takeover litigation, 33.41

IDENTIFICATION
class counsel/representatives, 30.211
complex cases, 20.11
confidential materials, 21.432n
exhibits/documents for trial, 21.441, 22.13,
41.30 ¶ 6

narrowing issues, 21.461
objections, 21.463
  made promptly, 21.464
preliminary to other discovery, 21.461
procedures to reduce burden, 21.464, 41.30
  ¶ 5(e)
related cases
  single set, 21.423, 33.27, 33.34, 41.30
  ¶ 5(e)
requests for admission, as complement to,
  21.461
securities litigation, 33.34
successive responses, 21.464
supplementing responses, 21.463, 21.47
time for answering extended, 21.464
use
  against other parties, 21.461
  in other litigation, 21.464
  summary judgment, 21.461
written (see WRITTEN
  INTERROGATORIES)

INTERVENTION
  as class representative, 30.11, 30.15, 33.33
  class members, 30.15, 30.16, 30.213
  employees/union in discrimination cases,
    33.51
  intervenors in takeover litigation, 33.41
  judicial, 21.424, 22.35, 30.24
  new representative, 30.16
  other parties, 30.41, 33.51, 33.55
  pursuing class claims, 33.55

ISSUES (see also FACTUAL ISSUES, ISSUES
  OF LAW)
  abandonment of claims/defenses, 21.33
  amendments, time for, 21.32, 41.33 ¶ 2(e)
  bifurcation of liability and damages, 33.11n,
    33.28
  broadening, 21.41
  cause of action, listing elements of, 21.33
  class for special issues, 30.17
  counsel's early views, 33.41, 41.2 ¶ 3(c)
  defining, 21.31, 21.33, 21.34, 21.41, 33.11,
    33.32
  discovery, interrelated with, 21.31, 21.41,
    21.422
  early determination, 21.211, 21.31, 21.41,
    33.32

evidence presented by issues, 22.34
joint trial, 33.254, 33.26
judge's comments to jury, 22.432
jurisdictional/venue problems, 31.131,
  31.32, 33.41
jury and nonjury, 21.62, 22.53, 21.631,
  21.632
mass tort litigation, 33.21, 33.254
narrowing, 21.211, 21.33, 21.34, 21.41,
  21.64, 21.642, 33.11, 33.32
  government studies, 21.491
of fact (see FACTUAL ISSUES)
of law (see ISSUES OF LAW)
pleadings
  amendments, deadlines for, 21.32, 41.30
    ¶ 4(b), 41.33 ¶ 2(e)
  consolidated, 33.32
preliminary, discussion at first conference,
  21.211, 33.41
resolution under Rule 12 or 56, 21.34, 33.32
revision, 21.31
schedule for narrowing, 21.34, 33.41
separate trial under Rule 42(b), 21.33,
  21.632, 22.34, 33.28n
severance, 21.62, 21.631, 21.632, 22.34,
  33.11, 33.28, 41.62 ¶ 3
summary judgment, 21.34, 41.30 ¶ 4(c)
threshold issues, 33.41

ISSUES OF LAW (see also ISSUES)
  appellate resolution, 21.33, 25.11
  defined after denying summary judgment,
    21.34
  early consideration, 21.31
  identifying, 21.211, 21.31, 21.33
  interrelated with discovery, 21.31
  patent litigation, 33.62, 33.651
  pleadings, 21.31, 21.32
  rulings, 21.32
  state law, 31.31
  summary judgments, 21.33–21.34

JOINDER
  additional parties, 21.12, 21.32, 21.453,
    33.251, 33.51
    limitations, 21.211, 41.30 ¶ 4(b), 41.33
      ¶ 12(e)
  criminal cases, 32.28
  refusing to permit, 21.211, 41.33 ¶ 2(e)

JOINT CONFERENCE
cases in different courts, 20.123, 31.14,
31.31, 33.23
consent, when necessary, 31.14n

JOINT DISCOVERY REQUESTS, 20.221,
21.423, 21.443, 31.14, 31.31, 33.24, 33.27,
41.30 ¶¶ 5(d), (e), 41.51 ¶ 2

JOINT ORDERS BY SEVERAL COURTS,
20.123, 20.225, 31.14, 31.31, 41.51

JOINT STATEMENT OF FACTS, 21.47,
21.641, 30.13, 33.43, 41.61
annotations to evidence, 21.641, 41.61 ¶ 3
objections to admissibility, 21.47, 41.61
¶ 2(c)
sample order, 41.61
sanctions, 21.47

JOINT TRIAL (see CONSOLIDATION)

JUDGE(S) (see also COURT, JUDICIAL
SUPERVISION)
appellate courts, 25.1, 25.2
assignment (see ASSIGNMENTS OF
JUDGES)
availability during depositions, 21.456,
41.38 ¶ 12
certifying orders for appeal
28 U.S.C. § 1292(b), 25.11
Rule 54(b), 25.11
state certification procedures, 33.254
cooperation in related cases, 20.225, 31.14,
31.31, 33.41
coordination of counsel, 20.22
depositions
foreign depositions, 21.494
judge in deposition district, 21.424,
21.456
judge in forum district, 21.424
designated in transferee district, 31.131
disqualification (see
DISQUALIFICATION)
duty to control discovery, 21.451, 21.456
exchange of orders, 20.225
findings and conclusions, 21.33, 22.52,
33.43

informal communication regarding
protective orders, 21.432
instructions to jury (see JURY
INSTRUCTIONS)
interlocutory appeals, 25.1
joint/parallel orders in related cases, 20.123,
20.225, 31.14, 31.31
other judges, 20.122, 21.211
partisanship, 22.24
powers in multidistrict proceedings, 31.13
pretrial rulings (see RULINGS)
questioning witnesses, 22.42
recusal, 20.121, 21.211 (see also
DISQUALIFICATION)
relief from other assignments, 20.12
selection of designated counsel, 20.224
settlement role, 23.11–23.14, 30.4 (see also
SETTLEMENT)
structuring trial, 21.631
suspension of local rules, 21.12
techniques to narrow issues, 21.33
transferee judge
exclusive jurisdiction, 31.131
intra- or intercircuit assignments, 31.131,
31.133
powers, 31.131, 31.132
pretrial order, 31.133
suggesting remand, 31.133
tag-along actions, 31.132
terminating action, 31.132
transferor judge, 31.131, 31.133

JUDGMENTS (see also FINAL
JUDGMENT, SUMMARY JUDGMENT)
as sanction, 20.154

JUDICIAL CONTROL (see JUDICIAL
SUPERVISION)

JUDICIAL NOTICE, 21.47

JUDICIAL PANEL ON MULTIDISTRICT
LITIGATION, 31.13 (see also
MULTIDISTRICT TRANSFER)
antitrust cases, 31.13, 33.14
authority over transferee judge, 31.131,
31.132
criminal cases, 31.2
denial of transfer, 33.63
patent cases, 33.63

voluntary agreements among parties, 21.424

MAGISTRATE JUDGES (see also REFERRALS, SPECIAL MASTER)
admissibility, determination of, 21.53
attendance at conferences, 21.23
conducting *in camera* inspections, 21.431, 33.62n
discovery, 20.14, 21.423, 21.53
evidentiary hearings, 21.53
findings, 21.53
privilege, claims of, 20.14, 21.432, 21.53
referral under, 28 U.S.C. § 636, 21.53
selection of designated counsel, 20.224
settlement
 administration, 41.44n
 negotiations, 20.14, 23.12
specialized factual issues, 21.5, 21.53
special master, acting as, 21.52
supervision of pretrial, 20.14, 21.53

MANDAMUS (see also INTERLOCUTORY APPEALS)
disqualification orders, 20.23n

MARY CARTER AGREEMENTS, 23.23

MASS TORTS, 33.2, 41.52
aircraft crashes, 33.2, 33.25n
case-management orders, 33.22
centralized management, 33.21, 33.22, 41.52
certification of state law questions, 25.1, 33.23
choice-of-law rules, 33.2, 33.254
claim/issue preclusion, 33.254
class actions, 33.26
conference, joint, 33.21, 33.23
consolidation, 33.2, 33.261
counsel, organization of, 33.24
damages, 33.2, 33.21, 33.25, 33.26, 33.261, 33.27, 33.28
"deemed" pleadings, 33.252
defined, 33.2
discovery, 33.21–33.25, 33.27
document depositories, 33.23, 33.251, 33.27
experts, 33.2, 33.22, 33.23, 33.261, 33.27
government investigations, 33.27
insurance coverage, 33.2, 33.21, 33.254

interlocutory review, 33.254
issue identification, 33.22, 33.254
joinder additional parties, 33.2, 33.251
joint pretrial conference, 33.23
later filed cases, 33.21, 33.252, 33.27, 41.52 ¶¶ 1–5
master docket, 21.12, 21.211, 33.22, 33.252
multidistrict proceedings, 33.21, 33.22, 33.23, 33.261, 33.27
parties, 33.251
product liability cases, 33.2, 33.22, 33.25, 33.26
related litigation, 33.2, 33.21, 33.22, 33.25, 33.27, 41.51, 41.52
schedules, 33.22, 33.25, 33.27
settlement, 23.12, 33.25, 33.28–33.29, 41.52 ¶ 10
special master, 33.22, 33.23, 33.261, 33.27, 33.28, 33.29
state/federal cases, 33.22, 33.23
statute of limitations, 33.2, 33.22, 33.25
third-party complaints, 33.251, 33.252
transfer, 33.21, 33.22, 33.252
trial, 33.28
 bellwether, 33.27, 33.28, 33.29
 joint trial
  liability, 33.25
  other issues, 22.22, 33.25, 33.28
 separate trials, 33.2, 33.21, 33.25, 33.28
 special verdict, 33.261

MASTER (see SPECIAL MASTER)

MASTER FILE, 21.12, 21.211, 31.11, 33.22, 33.252, 41.30 ¶ 1(a)

MEDIATION (see SETTLEMENT)

MONITORING
discovery plan, 21.42
schedules, 20.13

MOTIONS
bill of particulars, 32.24
captions, 41.30 ¶ 1(b)
challenging jurisdiction or venue, 21.61
class actions, timing of, 30.11
compelling discovery, sanctions, 20.15
deemed filed in related cases, 21.32, 41.30 ¶ 1(a), 41.52 ¶ 6(d)

NOTICE
  class actions (see CLASS ACTION
    COMMUNICATIONS)
  deposition subpoenas served on third
    parties, 21.447n
  initial conference, 21.11, 33.41
  method of taking foreign depositions,
    21.494
  sanctions, 20.154

OBJECTIONS
  admissibility (see ADMISSIBILITY)
  class members at settlement hearing, 30.41,
    33.55
  continuing, 22.22
  deemed made by similar parties, 22.22
  depositions, 21.642
  documentary evidence, 21.642
  evidence, 21.641, 21.642, 22.13
  grounds, specifying additional, 22.22
  pretrial rulings, 21.642, 22.13
  rulings (see RULINGS)
  waived, 21.642

OPENING STATEMENTS, 22.21 (see also
  TRIAL)
  multiparty cases, 41.63 ¶ 14

OPT OUT (see CLASS ACTIONS)

ORDER(S) (see also DISCOVERY ORDERS,
  PRESERVATION OF RECORDS,
  PROTECTIVE ORDER)
  appointing counsel, sample order, 41.30
    ¶ 2, 41.31
  attachments to orders, 41.1n
  attorneys' fees, sample order, 41.32
  captions, 41.1n, 41.30 ¶ 1(b)
  case management, sample order, 41.30
  certification, 30.18
  certifying orders for appeal, 25.11
    28 U.S.C. § 1292(b), 25.11
    Rule 54(b), 25.11
    state certification procedures, 25.11
  class action (see CLASS ACTION)
    sample orders, 41.41–41.44
  class certification, 30.18
    modification, 33.52n
  collateral, 25.11

confidentiality, 21.211, 21.423n, 21.43n,
  21.431
  sample order, 41.36
converting interviews into deposition,
  21.452n
coordinating multiple litigation, 41.51,
  41.52
"deemed" orders, applicable to new cases,
  21.32, 33.252
deferred supplemental deposition, 21.453
deposition guidelines, sample, 41.38
document depositories, sample, 41.35
drafted by counsel, 21.22
exchange of orders, 20.225
ex parte, 33.41
extraterritorial discovery, 21.494, 41.30
  ¶ 5(b)
failure to obey, 20.153, 20.154
final pretrial, sample order, 41.63
incorporation by reference, 41.1n
initial pretrial
  after, sample order, 41.30
  setting, sample order, 41.2
injunctions, appealability, 25.11, 25.12
joint/parallel by several courts, 20.123,
  20.225, 31.131, 31.31
management of case, 41.3
multiple litigation, sample format, 41.1
  numbering, 41.1n
preclusionary orders, 20.154
preservation of records, 21.12, 21.442,
  33.53, 41.34
referral, 20.14
  sample order, 41.37
related cases, 41.30 ¶ 1, 41.51, 41.53
resulting from initial conference, 21.211,
  33.41, 41.30
sanctions, 20.15
scheduling, 21.11, 21.212, 21.421n, 33.23,
  33.41, 41.33
standing order for disclosure, 21.421
statement of uncontested/contested facts,
  sample, 41.61
sua sponte orders, 21.12
takeover litigation, 33.41
to show cause, 30.18
unnecessary filings, 21.32

settlement, 21.211, 23.11, 23.12
suspension of local rules, 21.12, 21.211
telephonic, 21.22, 33.41
time of, 21.11, 21.212, 33.41
trial, 21.211, 41.30 ¶ 6

PRIVILEGES, 21.43, 21.431
assessment by parties, 21.463
attorney–client, 20.222n, 21.463, 33.34,
    33.62, 33.64
    abrogation resulting from fraud, 33.62
claims, 21.43, 21.431
deposition, 21.451
disputes, 20.14, 21.431, 21.432, 33.64, 41.37
documents, 21.431, 21.432, 41.38 ¶ 5(c)
    protected from copying, 21.432n, 41.36
      ¶ 9
    specifically identified, 21.432, 41.37 ¶ 2
effect on discovery, 21.43, 21.431, 21.432,
    33.34, 33.62, 33.64
grand jury, 21.422n (see also GRAND JURY
    MATERIALS)
in camera review, 21.431, 41.37
nonwaiver orders/agreements, 21.431
referral
    fees and expenses, 41.37 ¶ 4
    findings and conclusions, 41.37 ¶ 3
    magistrate judge/special master, 20.14,
      21.431, 33.64, 41.37
    sample order, 41.37
self-incrimination, 21.431, 21.491, 31.2,
    33.14, 33.84
trade secrets, 21.43, 21.446, 33.12
"Vaughn" index, 21.431n
work-product, 21.43, 21.43n, 21.431,
    21.446, 33.64

PROTECTIVE ORDER, 21.423n, 21.43n,
    21.432, 33.34, 33.42, 33.53, 33.64, 41.36
antitrust cases, 33.12
civil investigation demands, 21.432n
computers, 21.446
copying protected documents, 21.432n,
    41.36 ¶ 9
depositions, 41.36 ¶ 4, 41.38 ¶ 7
disclosure to associates/experts/others,
    21.431, 21.432
exemption from filing, 33.64
modification, 21.432, 31.14n

related cases, 21.432
reserving authority to modify, 21.432
sample order, 41.36
standard provisions, 21.432
trade secrets, 21.43, 21.446, 23.22, 33.73

QUESTIONNAIRES
to prospective jurors, 22.41, 32.32, 41.7

REASSIGNMENT, 20.121, 31 (see also
    ASSIGNMENTS OF JUDGES)

RECUSAL, 20.121, 21.211, 23.11, 33.13 (see
    also DISQUALIFICATION)
agenda topic, 21.211
interest in class member, 20.121
reassignment, 20.121

REDUCTION
multiple service, 21.12, 21.211, 31.131
scope of discovery, 21.34, 33.53
time period for discovery, 33.53
unnecessary filings, 21.12, 21.211, 31.11,
    31.131

REFERENCES (see REFERRALS)

REFERRALS, 20.14, 21.5–21.54, 41.37 (see
    also SPECIAL MASTER, MAGISTRATE
    JUDGES)
agenda topic, initial conference, 21.211
claims of privilege, 20.14, 21.431, 41.37
conference, attendance by special master,
    21.52
description of matters referred, 20.14, 21.5
designated counsel, selection of, 20.224
discovery disputes, 20.14, 21.424, 21.431
ex parte communications, 21.51
factual disputes, 21.51
    to expert, 21.51, 21.54
    to special master/magistrate judge, 20.14,
      21.52–21.53, 33.35
in camera reviews, 21.431
joint referrals in related cases, 31.14, 41.51
    ¶ 3
nonjury cases, 21.52
not appropriate, 33.41
order, 20.14, 41.37
other judges, 20.122, 21.211, 23.13, 33.29

privilege disputes, 20.14, 21.431, 33.64, 41.37
protective orders, 20.14, 21.446n
sample order, 41.37
selection of designated counsel, 20.224
settlement
    administration, 21.52, 30.47, 33.35, 33.55, 41.44 ¶ 3(d)
    employment cases, 33.55
    negotiations, 23.13, 33.29, 33.35
special referrals, 21.5, 21.54
status reports, 20.14
supervision of pretrial, 20.14
takeover litigation, avoidance, 33.41
team of experts, 21.54
Title VII cases, 33.51n

RELATED CASES, 20.123, 20.225, 31.11, 31.32, 41.30 ¶ 1, 41.51 (see also MULTIDISTRICT TRANSFER)
admissions, 21.47n
antitrust litigation, 33.14
assignment, 20.123, 31.11, 32.11, 33.21, 33.31, 33.5
attendance at conferences, 21.23, 33.41
centralized management, 33.14, 33.21, 33.31
class actions and other cases, 30.3
comity, 31.32
communication between judges, 20.225, 21.432, 31.31, 41.51n
consolidation (see CONSOLIDATION)
coordination, 20.123, 21.211, 30.3, 31.11, 31.13, 31.31, 33.14, 33.21, 33.31, 33.41, 33.5, 41.30 ¶ 1(d), 41.51
criminal and civil, 20.123, 21.431n, 31.2, 32.24, 33.14 (see also CRIMINAL CASES)
discovery (see JOINT DISCOVERY REQUESTS)
duplicative discovery, 21.41, 21.423, 21.432, 21.442, 21.455, 21.464, 31.131, 31.14, 41.53 ¶ 17
employment discrimination litigation, 33.5
individual and class actions, 33.14
injunctions against state actions, 30.3, 31.32, 33.14n
interdivisional transfer, 31.11
joint appointments, 31.14, 31.31, 41.51 ¶ 3

joint conference, 31.14, 31.31
joint document depositories, 21.444, 21.452, 31.14, 31.31, 33.23, 41.30 ¶ 5, 41.31 ¶¶ 2, 4, 41.35, 41.51 ¶ 2(a)
joint orders, 20.123, 20.225, 31.14, 31.31, 41.51
later filed cases, 41.2 ¶ 5, 41.52
mass torts, 33.2, 33.26, 41.52
master file, 21.12, 21.211, 31.11, 33.252, 41.1n, 41.30 ¶ 1(a)
orders
    coordinating cases in separate courts, 41.51
    exchange of, 20.225
other courts, 20.123, 20.225, 31.131, 31.31, 33.41n, 33.63
pendent jurisdiction, 31.32
remand, 31.32
rulings, 20.123, 33.252, 41.51 ¶ 3
same court, 20.123, 21.455, 30.3, 31.11, 33.31, 41.30 ¶ 1, 41.52
service list, 41.2 ¶ 1(b), 41.31 ¶ 2(a)
state and federal, 31.3, 31.32, 33.14, 33.2, 33.22, 33.23, 41.51
takeover litigation, 33.41
transfer
    28 U.S.C. § 1404 or 1406, 20.123, 33.41
    from other courts, 20.123, 31.13, 31.31, 33.14, 33.41
    from other divisions, 20.123, 31.11
    pretrial, 31.11

RES JUDICATA, 30.11n, 30.14n, 31.32, 33.14n, 33.52, 33.82 (see also COLLATERAL ESTOPPEL)

RESPONSIBILITIES (see also FIDUCIARY RESPONSIBILITIES)
class representatives, 30.43, 30.44, 30.45
counsel, 20.21, 41.31
    class, 23.24, 30.45
    committee of, 20.221, 41.31 ¶ 3
    lead, 20.221, 41.31 ¶ 1
    liaison, 20.221, 41.31 ¶¶ 2, 4
    multidistrict transfer, 31.13

ROUTINE CASES
MCL 3d, use of, 10.1–10.2

written warning, 20.154

SCHEDULE(S)
class certification, 21.211, 21.213, 30.11, 33.33
completing pretrial phases, 21.211
conflicts, 20.221
criminal cases, 32.22
deadline for new claims, defenses, parties, 21.32, 33.32, 41.30 ¶ 4(b), 41.33 ¶ 2(e)
depositions, 21.454
derivative action determination, 33.33
establishment at initial conference, 21.11, 33.251, 33.32, 33.41
expert opinions, 21.48, 33.27, 33.34, 33.65
initial conference, 21.11
initial responses, 21.12, 21.32, 33.32, 41.30 ¶ 4(b)
modification, 20.13, 33.41
monitoring, by court, 20.13
narrowing issues, 33.41
need, 20.13
next conference, 33.41
orders (see SCHEDULING ORDER)
pleadings, 21.32, 33.32, 33.41, 41.30 ¶ 4(b), 41.33 ¶ 2(e)
refinement, 20.13
settlement discussions, effect on, 20.222
stay of pretrial proceedings, 31.14
takeover litigation, 33.41

SCHEDULING ORDER, 21.212, 21.421, 21.424, 31.131, 40.1 ¶ 3, 41.33
sample order, 41.33

SEALING (see CONFIDENTIALITY)

SECURITIES LITIGATION
brokers and brokerage houses, 30.211, 30.47, 33.32, 33.33
business judgment rule, 33.32
centralized management, 33.31
class actions
class definition, 30.14, 30.16n, 33.33
conflict of interest in class, 30.16n, 33.33
determination, 33.31–33.33
discovery, 33.33, 33.34
multiple classes, 33.33
notice, 33.33
consolidated complaint, 33.31, 33.32

coordination, 33.31
court-appointed experts and special masters, 33.35
derivative actions, 33.33
discovery, 33.34
experts, 33.34–33.35
"fraud on the market", 33.32–33.33
joint trial, 33.32, 33.36
lead case, 33.31
multidistrict transfer, 33.31
narrowing issues, 33.32
nominees, 30.211
pleadings, 33.32
privileges, claim of, 33.34
proxy statements, 33.31n, 33.33
referral, 33.35
related cases, 33.31–33.33, 33.36
settlement, 30.47, 33.32–33.36
street names, 30.211, 33.33
takeover (see TAKEOVER LITIGATION)
trial, 33.36

SELECTION
class representative, 30.14, 30.15, 30.16
designated counsel, 20.224, 41.31

SERVICE
documents, 41.30 ¶ 3
liaison counsel, 20.221, 41.30 ¶ 3
reduction of parties upon whom service made, 21.12
rulings before class certification, 30.11
service list, 41.2 ¶ l(b), 41.31 ¶¶ 2, 4

SETTLEMENT, 23–23.24, 33.29 (see also NEGOTIATION)
agenda item at conferences, 21.211, 21.6, 23.11, 23.12
alternative dispute resolution, 23.15
another judge, 23.151
antitrust governmental actions, 23.14
approval (see judicial review)
arbitration, 23.151, 41.52 ¶ 10
attorneys' fees (see ATTORNEYS' FEES)
class action (see CLASS ACTION SETTLEMENT)
clients, participation by, 21.23, 23.11, 23.12, 23.24
conflicts of interest, 20.222

privilege claims, 33.64, 41.37, 41.51 ¶ 3
related cases, 31.14, 33.23, 41.51 ¶ 3
settlement
   administration, 21.52, 30.41, 30.43,
      30.47, 33.55, 41.44 ¶ 3(d)
   negotiations, 20.14, 21.52, 23.13, 33.261,
      33.29, 33.73, 41.52 ¶4
supervisory responsibilities, 20.14, 21.424,
   21.456, 41.51 ¶ 3
status reports, 20.14

SPECIAL VERDICT, 21.33, 21.633, 22.451
complex tort cases, 33.261
copies given to jury, 22.434
general verdict with interrogatories, 21.633,
   22.45
jury instructions, 22.434, 33.73
nonjury findings after special verdict, 22.45
patent cases, 33.67
proposals by counsel, 21.633
Rule 49, 21.633n, 22.451

STANDING
agenda topic for first conference, 33.41
antitrust cases, 33.11
settlements, 23.14

STATE COURT LITIGATION
injunction against, 30.3, 31.32, 33.14n
MCL 3d, use of 10.2
related cases in state court (see RELATED
   CASES)
removal, 31.32

STATEMENT
of contentions, 41.61
of facts, 21.641 (see JOINT STATEMENT
   OF FACTS)

STATISTICAL EVIDENCE (see also
   COMPUTERIZED DATA, SUMMARIES)
employment discrimination, 33.53

STATISTICAL METHODS, 21.493
polls and surveys, 21.493
   admissibility, 21.493
   expert opinions, 21.493
   hearsay exception, 21.493
probability of error, 21.446, 21.446n
   disclosure to jury, 21.493n

stipulations as to, 21.446
reliability, 21.493
sampling techniques, 21.422
standards, 21.493

STATUTE OF LIMITATIONS
antitrust cases, 33.11
case selected for class action certification,
   30.11
effect of reduction in class, 30.45
employment discrimination, 33.51
interlocutory review, 33.254
notice to class, 30.211
order anticipating problems, 33.32n
resolution under Rule 12 or 56, 33.11, 33.32
state statutes, 33.2, 33.51n
tolling, 23.23, 33.22, 33.29
variations in state law, 33.2

STEERING COMMITTEE (see
   DESIGNATED COUNSEL)

STIPULATIONS, 21.47
admissibility
   authentication, 21.47
   foreign depositions, 21.494
class certification, use in, 30.13
client participation, 21.47
court reporter, 21.452
court's role promoting, 21.47
depositions, 21.423, 21.452
discovery, facilitating, 21.423
effect of findings by master, 21.52
facts established, 21.47, 30.13
foreign litigant's reluctance to enter, 21.494
foundation for other evidence, 21.47
juries
   nonunanimous verdict, 21.633, 22.41,
      22.44
   reduction in size, 22.44
   waiver if no verdict, 21.633, 22.44
limited purposes, 21.47
projected range of error, 21.446
sanctions for refusal to stipulate, 21.47
special master or magistrate judge, use of,
   21.47, 21.52
telephonic depositions, 21.494n
withdrawal based on new evidence, 21.47

STREET NAMES, 30.211, 33.33

SUBPOENA(S), 21.447, 21.494, 22.23
confidential documents, 41.36 ¶ 6
documents at deposition, 41.38 ¶ 6(a)
grand jury, 21.491
hearings before special master, 21.52n
witness having no knowledge of facts, 41.38
¶ 7

SUMMARIES, 21.48, 21.492, 33.12, 41.33 ¶ 1
(see also COMPUTERIZED DATA,
EXHIBITS)
accuracy, 21.492, 21.493, 33.12
admissibility, 21.492, 21.493
aids in understanding other evidence,
21.492, 22.32
attorneys' time/expense records, 24.211
best evidence rule exception, 21.492n
computerized evidence, 21.446, 33.12
depositions, 22.331, 30.13, 33.43
disclosure to opposing parties, 21.492
discovery, 21.492, 33.34, 41.33 ¶ 1
disputes as to weight and significance, 21.47
experts, 21.48, 33.12, 33.53
methodology, 33.12
nonjury cases, 21.492
tabulations, charts, graphs, extracts, 21.492,
33.12
testimony provided before hearing, 33.43
trial use, 21.492, 22.32, 33.12, 33.34, 33.53
underlying data as evidence, 21.492, 22.32,
33.12
verification prior to trial, 21.492, 33.12
voluminous data, 21.492, 33.12, 33.53

SUMMARY JUDGMENT, 21.32, 21.34,
21.66, 33.11
affidavits, 21.34, 41.30 ¶ 4(c)
antitrust cases, 33.11
discovery, 21.34
evidentiary hearing, 21.34
frivolous motions, 21.34
identification of issues for early, 21.34,
41.30 ¶ 4(c)
issues narrowed at hearings, 21.34
multidistrict cases, 31.132
notice of hearing, 21.32, 21.34
partial, 21.34

precertification, 30.11, 30.11n

SUPERVISION, JUDICIAL (see JUDICIAL
SUPERVISION)

SURVEYS (see SAMPLING TECHNIQUES,
STATISTICAL METHODS)

SUSPENSION
attorneys, as sanction, 20.154
discovery
pending initial conference, 21.12, 21.13,
41.2 ¶ 4(c)
related civil cases, 31.2
local rules, 21.12, 41.2 ¶ 4
pending motion for transfer, 31.131
pleading, 21.32, 33.32

TABULATIONS (see COMPUTERIZED
DATA, SUMMARIES)

TAKEOVER LITIGATION, 33.4
briefs, 33.43
conferences, 33.41, 33.43
control, 33.4
counsel
attending conference, 33.41
meetings of, 33.43
critical dates, 33.41
depositions, 33.41, 33.42, 33.43
discovery, 33.42
documents, 33.41, 33.42
emergency matters, 33.41
evidence under seal, 33.41
exchange lists of documents/witnesses,
33.43
ex parte orders, 33.41
findings and conclusions, 33.43
government agencies, 33.41
hearing, 33.4, 33.41, 33.43
in camera proceedings, 33.41
initial conference, 33.41
issues, 33.41
media, 33.4
multidistrict transfer, 33.41
objections, 33.43
orders, timing, 33.41
preliminary injunction, 33.41
protective orders, 21.432, 33.42
reassignment, 33.41

referral, 33.41
related cases, 33.41, 33.42
ruling from bench, 33.43
sanctions, 33.41
schedules shortened, 33.41
telephone conference, 33.41
testimony, form of, 33.41, 33.42, 33.43
timing of rulings, 33.4, 33.41
transfer to single district, 33.41
trial preparation, 33.43

TECHNOLOGY (see COURTROOM
   TECHNOLOGY)

TELEPHONE
conferences, 31.14, 33.41
depositions, 21.423, 21.452, 21.494, 41.38
   ¶¶ 9–11
   resolution of disputes, 21.424
exercise of judicial powers in another
   district, 31.132
joint conference of district judges, 31.14
pretrial conference, 21.22, 33.41
resolution of discovery disputes, 20.14,
   21.424, 21.494
takeover litigation, 33.41

TEST CASE (see BELLWETHER TRIAL,
   LEAD CASE)

THIRD PARTIES
access to documents, 21.432
CERCLA, 33.72, 33.73, 41.53 ¶ 3
complaint, 21.32, 33.2, 33.251, 33.252,
   33.32
credibility of, affecting interrogatories,
   21.461
discovery from, 21.447, 21.451
   confidential materials, 41.36 ¶ 2
motions for remand, 31.133
motions to compel, 21.447
notice of deposition subpoenas, 21.447
Rule 31 depositions, 21.451
subpoena for production of documents,
   32.24

TIME LIMITS (see SCHEDULE(S))

TIME RECORDS (see also ATTORNEYS'
   FEES)
document fee requests, 20.223, 24.21, 41.32
sample order, 41.32

TRADE SECRETS (see
   CONFIDENTIALITY, PROTECTIVE
   ORDERS)

TRANSCRIPTS
computer-aided, 34.38
conferences, 21.22, 41.1n
confidential information, 41.36 ¶¶ 1, 4
deposition, 21.423, 21.424, 21.452, 21.453,
   21.456, 22.333, 41.36 ¶ 1, 41.38
   videotaped, 41.38 ¶ 8(b)
discovery, 21.424
evidence, 32.25
expedited, 32.33
for non-English speakers, 34.39
jury instructions , 22.435
trial, 22.14, 32.33

TRANSFER (see also MULTIDISTRICT
   TRANSFER, RELATED CASES)
adversary proceedings in bankruptcy,
   20.123
initial conference, agenda topic, 21.211
potential transfer under 28 U.S.C. § 1404 or
   1406, 20.123, 21.61

TRIAL, 22 (see also separate headings such
   as EVIDENCE, EXHIBITS, VERDICT(S))
arguments
   closing, 22.34, 22.434
   interim, 22.34
   opening, 22.21
   sequenced by issues, 22.34
arrangement of courtroom, 22.12, 32.31
bellwether (see BELLWETHER TRIAL)
closing arguments, 22.34, 22.434
conferences during trial, 22.15
confidential information, 41.36 ¶ 5
conspiracy, 22.22, 22.432
continuance, 21.61, 23.21, 32.22
continuing objection, 22.22
counsel

bias, 23.23
character, 21.643
class certification hearing, 41.30 ¶ 4(d)
class members, 33.54
court-appointed expert, 21.51
credibility, 21.47, 22.35, 22.432, 22.51,
   23.23, 30.13
cross examination, 21.461, 21.53, 21.643,
   22.11, 22.334, 22.51, 22.6, 24.223, 32.33,
   41.63 ¶ 15
distant, deposed by telephone, 21.452
examination
   by judge, 22.24, 22.35
   by jury, 22.42
   estimate of time, 21.643
   local customs as to conduct, 22.24
   redundant, 22.35, 32.33
expert (see EXPERTS)
identification, 21.461, 33.27, 33.34, 33.43,
   41.2 ¶ 4(c), 41.61 ¶ 3
impeachment, 21.452n, 21.455, 21.67,
   22.333, 41.61 ¶ 4(b)
informal interview, 21.423, 21.452
interpreter, 22.51
joint examination, 22.35
limitations on number, 21.643, 30.13, 33.54
lists, 22.23, 41.61 ¶ 3
   precluding witnesses not listed, 41.61 ¶ 3
order of calling, 22.23, 22.34
related cases, 21.455
subpoenas, 22.23 (see also SUBPOENA(S))
testimony, 22.334, 22.34, 22.51, 33.43
   form, 33.43
   in person, 21.51, 33.41, 33.43
   presented by deposition, 22.23, 33.41,
     33.43, 41.61 ¶ 3
   summaries, 21.64, 30.13, 33.43
written statement, 22.51, 30.13, 33.41, 33.43

WORK PRODUCT, 20.222, 20.23n, 21.43n,
   21.446, 21.48n, 24.212, 25.11, 32.12, 33.64,
   33.73, 41.53 ¶¶ 18, 19

WRITTEN INTERROGATORIES (see also
   INTERROGATORIES)
 depositions on, 21.452, 33.25
 with general verdict, 21.633, 22.34, 22.451,
   33.86

WRITTEN STATEMENTS
 adopted as direct testimony, 22.51, 30.13,
   33.41, 33.43
 attorneys' preliminary views, 21.11, 21.33,
   41.2 ¶ 3(c)

KF 8900
.M35
1985
c. 2